DATE DUE

Terrorism and
Personal Protection

Terrorism and Personal Protection

Edited by
Brian M. Jenkins

BUTTERWORTH PUBLISHERS

Boston • London

Sydney • Wellington • Durban • Toronto

*All references in this book to personnel of male gender are used for
convenience only and shall be regarded as including both males and
females.*

Library of Congress Cataloging in Publication Data
Main entry under title:

Terrorism and personal protection.

Includes index.
  1. Kidnapping—Addresses, essays, lectures.
2. Terrorists—Addresses, essays, lectures.
3. Terrorism—Prevention—Addresses, essays, lectures.
4. Ransom—Addresses, essays, lectures.   5. Executives—
Crimes against—Addresses, essays, lectures.
6. Extortion—Addresses, essays, lectures.   7. Hostage
negotiations—Addresses, essays, lectures.
I. Jenkins, Brian Michael.
HV6595.T47   1984   364.1′54   84–14245
ISBN 0–409–95126–9

Butterworth Publishers
80 Montvale Avenue
Stoneham, MA 02180

10 9 8 7 6 5 4 3 2 1

Printed in the United States of America

Contents

PART I. THE THREAT

PART II. MANAGEMENT ISSUES

The Contributors

E. C. "Mike" Ackerman

A principal of Ackerman & Palumbo Inc., an independent consulting firm offering a full range of services in executive protection and other aspects of counterterrorism including hostage negotiations, Mr. Ackerman graduated magna cum laude from Dartmouth and holds an M.A. from Columbia. Prior to entering the consulting field, he served for eleven years in the CIA's Clandestine Services and is the author of *Street Man,* a reasoned defense of the CIA. He is an acknowledged authority in counterterrorism with particular expertise in the recovery of hostages.

Arthur J. Alexander

An economist with degrees from M.I.T., the London School of Economics, and Johns Hopkins University, Dr. Alexander joined the staff of the Economics Department of The Rand Corporation in 1968 and is presently associate head of the department. He has taught economics at the University of California and at the Rand Graduate Institute of Policy Analysis, where he is also a member of the Advisory Board. He is a member of the U.S. Army Science Board and the author of a large number of books and studies on economics, technology, sociology, and Soviet weapons acquisition and military research and development.

David W. Barkey

Mr. Barkey is an M.A. candidate in sociology at Colorado State University while serving as a chaplain at the Penitentiary of New Mexico in Santa Fe. During the decade of the 1970s, a period when Argentina was the battleground of both right- and left-wing terrorist groups, he served as a missionary in the rural and underdeveloped provinces of Northwest Argentina.

Carol Edler Baumann

Dr. Baumann graduated from the University of Wisconsin-Madison and received her Ph.D. from the London School of Economics and Political Science, University of London, which she attended as a Marshall Scholar. She is a professor in the Political Science Department of the University of Wisconsin-Milwaukee, where she also serves as Director of the Institute of World Affairs and Director of International Studies and Programs. Dr. Baumann is the author of *Western Europe: What Path to Integration?* and *The Diplomatic Kidnappings.* From 1979 to 1982 she served in the United States Department of State as Deputy Assistant Secretary for Assessments and Research in the Bureau of Intelligence and Research.

Gerardo Capotorto

Mr. Capotorto is a retired high-ranking

officer of Italy's *Carabinieri,* in which he had twenty years of specific experience in the security sector. For the past ten years he has dedicated himself to the security problems of one of Italy's largest corporations, as well as to directing and coordinating research activities and to the planning of integrated security systems for industrial, military, and civil facilities in Italy. He is a member of technical-advisory interministerial commissions on integrated security for infrastructures of national interest and of the Board of Directors for ARSI (Association Responsible for Industrial Security).

Richard Clutterbuck

Formerly a British army major-general, Dr. Clutterbuck now teaches International Relations & Political Conflict at the University of Exeter, England. He is also a director of Control Risks Ltd., a company providing professional advice on preventive security against terrorist risks on crisis management, kidnapping, ransom, and other forms of extortion. For the past ten years he has had a research grant to study political violence and has written nine books, among them *Living with Terrorism, Guerrillas and Terrorists, The Media and Political Violence,* and *Kidnap and Ransom,* which is accepted as the standard work on the subject of kidnapping worldwide.

H. H. A. Cooper

An international authority on terrorism, executive protection, and corporate security assessments, Dr. Cooper has published extensively in these fields and serves as a consultant on these issues to both corporations and government agencies. He is a professor of law

and has a distinguished record with Her Majesty's Civil Service. Dr. Cooper is president of the Neuvevidas International Consulting Corporation in Dallas, Texas, and a senior associate of Richard W. Kobetz & Associates, Ltd., North Mountain Pines Training Center in Winchester, Virginia.

D. Stanley Eitzen

A professor of sociology at Colorado State University, Dr. Eitzen received his Ph.D. from the University of Kansas. He has served as editor of *The Social Science Journal* since 1978 and has written some sixty articles for scholarly journals in the areas of political sociology, social stratification, and social problems. His books include *In Conflict and Order* (1982) and *Social Problems* (1983).

Mary Helen Gallagher

Mary Helen Gallagher was educated at the University of Pennsylvania and graduated magna cum laude from Georgetown Law School in 1980. She has been employed by Covington & Burling since 1980.

Richard J. Gallagher

Mr. Gallagher was awarded Bachelor of Laws and Juris Doctor degrees from Harvard Law School and a Master of Laws degree from George Washington University Law Center. He is a member of the bar in New York and Rhode Island and has been admitted to practice in many federal courts including the U.S. Supreme Court. He served as assistant director in the Office of Planning and Evaluation of the FBI and retired in 1977 as assistant director in charge of the Criminal Investigative Division. Since his retirement Mr. Gallagher has been a consultant to multinational corporations on crisis management, hostage survival, aircraft security, and white collar crime.

Richard J. Healy

Internationally known as a writer, consultant, and administrator in the security field, Mr. Healy was president of Professional Protection Enterprises, Inc., Long Beach, California. He formerly was with the Aerospace Corporation in Los Angeles, where he was Director of Security and Safety for more than twenty years. Mr. Healy was certified as a protection professional (CPP) by the American Society for Industrial Security and listed in the current issues of *Who's Who in the West and Who's Who in Finance and Industry*. He authored *Design for Security* (1968) and *Emergency and Disaster Planning* (1969), both published by John Wiley and Sons, New York. Mr. Healy died in December 1983.

James R. Jarrett

Mr. Jarrett, a specialist in political terrorism, counterterrorist operations, executive protection methods, and weapons and tactics training, graduated with highest distinction from Phoenix College in 1978. He spent nine years as a Green Beret and was selected for Project Delta, where he served as a Long Range Reconnaissance Patrol and Special Action Team leader. After leaving the military, he spent five years in law enforcement in a variety of agencies. Mr. Jarrett is currently the director of Phoenix Firearms Training Center, a division of Security Industries, which provides a complete spectrum of security services to clients in the United States and Free World. Phoenix Firearms Training Center pro-

vides some of the most advanced, state-of-the-art tactical training available.

Brian M. Jenkins

Mr. Jenkins is one of the world's leading authorities on international terrorism. One of the first analysts to conduct research on this topic, he currently directs The Rand Corporation's research program on subnational conflict and political violence. He has also served as a consultant to a number of U.S. government agencies and to major corporations. Before coming to Rand, Mr. Jenkins served in the Dominican Republic during the American intervention and later in Vietnam, where he was decorated on several occasions for valor in combat. He later returned to Vietnam as a member of General Creighton Abrams' Long Range Planning Task Group. His work with this group earned him the Department of the Army's highest award for civilian service. He is the author of *International Terrorism: A New Mode of Conflict* (1975) and a coauthor of *The Fall of South Vietnam* (1980); he is also the editor of *Terrorism and Beyond* (1982). In addition to these books, Mr. Jenkins has authored chapters in more than a dozen books on political violence and has written numerous articles on the subject.

Richard W. Kobetz

Dr. Kobetz is the director of Richard W. Kobetz & Associates, Ltd., North Mountain Pines Training Center, Winchester, Virginia. He is an acknowledged authority on issues of security and executive protection and serves as the executive secretary of the Nine Lives Associates, a fraternity of professional personal protection specialists.

His training program on "Providing Protective Services" is the original and acclaimed offering in executive protection. Dr. Kobetz is a former assistant director of the I.A.C.P., a retired command officer of the Chicago Police Department, and has served as an appointed member of the U.S. Task Force on Disorders and Terrorism.

William F. Niehous

Mr. Niehous is vice president of the Plastic Products Division and general manager of multipak operations for Owens-Illinois, Inc. In 1974 he was appointed vice president of Owens-Illinois de Venezuela. He was kidnapped from his suburban home in Caracas in February 1976 and held for ransom. Negotiations never developed. Mr. Niehous was rescued in 1979 when Venezuelan security forces came upon the hideout where he was being held.

Vittorfranco S. Pisano

Dr. Pisano is an attorney-at-law and specialist in Italian and comparative security matters. He holds a Master of Comparative Law from Georgetown University and a Doctorate in Juridical Science from the University of Rome. A former Senior Foreign Law Specialist in the European Law Division, Library of Congress, and a Professorial Lecturer in the Department of Government, Georgetown University, he has authored numerous monographs, papers, and articles on terrorism and intelligence. Dr. Pisano, a major in the Military Police Corps of the U.S. Army Reserve, served in command positions with divisional military police units in Germany and as a commander of the U.S. Army Garrison in Verona, Italy.

He is a recipient of the Order of Merit of the Republic of Italy.

Susanna W. Purnell

Ms. Purnell received a B.A. in Political Science from Allegheny College and an M.A. degree in American Studies from the University of Maryland. She is an associate researcher with The Rand Corporation, working on issues related to terrorism and national defense. In addition to classified case studies of selected diplomatic kidnappings, her Rand publications include: *The Problems of U.S. Businesses Operating Abroad in Terrorist Environments, Long Range Development Planning in the Air Force,* and *Review of Federal Programs to Alleviate Rural Deprivation.*

Leon D. Richardson

Mr. Richardson is Chairman of Directors and Founder of the Magna Group of Companies which are comprised of several international corporations dealing with welding alloys, lubricants, and metalworking aids in Australia, Canada, the United States, and other countries. After studying engineering, his interest in welding led to his special assignment to the Oak Ridge Project in Tennessee in 1942, where he was appointed chief welding engineer. The Oak Ridge Project developed the first atom bomb, and Mr. Richardson was cited by President Roosevelt's Secretary of War, The Honorable Henry Stimson, for his contribution to the project. Since then, he has performed consulting services for more than 100 universities as well as the military, Atomic Energy Commission, and their contractors. An internationally known lecturer and author, Mr. Richardson has presented over 3,000 lectures throughout the world and written over 1,000 published papers.

Charles Ruff

Mr. Ruff graduated from Swarthmore College and received his law degree from Columbia University Law School in 1963. His former positions include Trial Attorney, Criminal Division, Department of Justice from 1967 to 1972, Special Prosecutor and Director, Watergate Special Prosecution Force, 1975 to 1977. He served as Principal Associate Deputy Attorney General, Department of Justice, in 1979. He is presently at Covington & Burling, a law firm in Washington, DC.

Charles A. Russell

Dr. Russell has a J.D. degree from Georgetown University and a Ph.D. from American University. He is a member of the bar of the U.S. Court of Appeals and U.S. Court of Military Appeals. For years he was the director of the U.S. Air Force Office of Special Investigations program on terrorism. He has lectured extensively on the subject of terrorism and has appeared as a witness before Senate and Congressional committees examining terrorist operations. Dr. Russell is now the senior analyst for Risks International, Alexandria, Virginia. This corporation maintains a current computerized data base of terrorist incidents dating from 1970 and also provides monthly and quarterly reports used by business and government agencies to make political and economic risk assessments.

William F. Sater

Mr. Sater is a Professor of History at California State University, Long Beach. A graduate of Stanford and the University of California, Los Angeles, Mr. Sater specializes in South American history. In addition to this essay, the author has also written case studies of the Puerto Rican separatists and several other Latin American guerrilla organizations as well as a joint study on the mind sets of dynamite terrorists. He has also authored various monographs.

William Lee Saunders, Jr.

William Lee Saunders graduated from the University of North Carolina in 1976 and Harvard Law School in 1980. He has been at Covington & Burling from 1981 to the present.

David T. Schiller

A citizen of both the Federal Republic of Germany and Israel, Dr. Schiller holds a doctoral degree in social sciences and economics from the Free University of Berlin. He has worked extensively on various aspects of terrorism and high-intensity crime. With an army background in counterinsurgency tactics, weapons, and demolitions, he has acted as a consultant to various law enforcement agencies in Europe and the United States and has taught SWAT techniques in the German police force.

Anthony J. Scotti

An engineer and a race car driver, Mr. Scotti is president of the Scotti School of Defensive Driving (SSDD), Somerville, Massachusetts. SSDD has trained more than 800 students from around the world in defensive, pursuit, and antiterrorist driving techniques. His teaching methods are internationally known and his school has traveled to Europe, South America, Canada, and the Middle East to conduct various driving/security programs for clients. Mr. Scotti has written four books and is a member of both the International Association of Chiefs of Police and the American Society for Industrial Security.

Kevin Sinclair

Mr. Sinclair assisted Leon Richardson in bringing the story of his captivity to the public. See Kevin Sinclair, *Kidnap: A Victim's Story,* Hong Kong: Ted Thomas Limited, 1982.

Eleanor S. Wainstein

A graduate of Canal Zone Junior College and Mount Holyoke College, Ms. Wainstein received an M.A. degree in Economics from Stanford University. She has been associated with The Rand Corporation for the past twenty-five years and has contributed to studies in the field of Soviet economy, the net assessment of U.S.-U.S.S.R., international terrorism, and a variety of defense-related issues. Her many publications include *The Problems of U.S. Businesses Operating Abroad in Terrorist Environments,* Rand, R-2842, 1981; *The Cross and Laporte Kidnappings, Montreal, October 1970,* Rand, R-1986, February 1977; and *Effectiveness of Phase II Price Controls,* Rand, R-1989, 1976.

Don E. Wurth

Mr. Wurth is a former Army paratrooper, a Los Angeles policeman, and a Special Agent with the U.S. Secret Service. For the past several years he has worked in the private sector as a consultant and executive protection specialist. Mr. Wurth has done security work in fourteen countries while in private service, including an assignment in West Germany for an important industrialist during the height of the Baader-Meinhof era in the late 1970s. A former employee of Fluor Corporation in California, he also served as a consultant to the American Society of Travel Agents during two of their annual international conventions.

Dr. Zeta (nom de plume)

Dr. Zeta is the nom de plume of a prominent Latin American businessman who has personally negotiated with kidnappers in eighteen cases.

Preface

This book is about personal security in an age of terrorism—about the threat that terrorists and ordinary criminals pose to the security of individuals who by reason of office, prominence in the public eye, personal wealth, or corporate or family connections may be considered targets of kidnapping, assassination, or extortion. The focus is the problem of kidnapping, which does not imply that assassination merits less attention, but that security against kidnapping tends to provide a degree of security against assassination. Moreover, if security fails and an assassination occurs, the deed is done; whereas if security fails in the case of a kidnapping, the episode has just begun—for the government, the corporation, the family, and the hostage.

The book is aimed at several audiences: (a) those with management responsibilities in government or corporations who must make crucial decisions during negotiations; (b) those with direct security responsibilities who must assess the threat, heighten awareness among potential targets, design and manage security programs, hire security personnel, identify consultants, conduct exercises, operate training programs, advise management during crises, conduct negotiations, and supervise recovery efforts; and (c) potential targets and their families, who by their own personal comportment may increase or decrease their own vulnerability and who, if security fails, could face the ordeal of captivity. The three audiences overlap: Depending upon the size and structure of the corporate organization, those in management may have direct security responsibilities; they are also possible targets.

Twenty-eight authors contributed to this volume. They reflect the diverse aspects of the problems of terrorism and security and are a diverse group: Ten are currently involved in some aspect of the security profession, ten are members of the academic or research communities (four are staff members of The Rand Corporation), four are practicing lawyers, three are corporate managers. In that group are historians, political scientists, sociologists, economists, and lawyers. Five have law-enforcement backgrounds, five have military backgrounds, three have intelligence backgrounds. They have served in the U.S. Army, the British Army, the *Bundeswehr,* the *Carabinieri,* the FBI, the CIA, the U.S. Secret Service, the U.S. State Department, and various local police departments in the United States. Six nationalities are included, and the book was originally written in four languages.

Any enterprise of this type is bound to be uneven. The authors represent different cultures, different philosophies, and different personal experiences; not surprisingly, they hold quite different and often controversial notions about terrorism and kidnapping and about how to deal most effectively with these problems.

This volume is not intended to be read from front to back. Rather it is intended to be used as a reference volume in assessing threat, designing and managing security programs, determining obligations, setting policy, entering negotiations, preparing awareness programs, briefing potential targets, and handling returning hostages.

Brian M. Jenkins

Introduction

It has become a grimly familiar triptych in our time: The first photograph we see is usually a formal portrait, the kind that comes from the public affairs office. The subject smiles the dignified smile of a corporate executive or high-level government official. The headline announces that he has been kidnapped.

The second photograph is delivered by the kidnappers. The subject stares forlornly into the camera, coatless, unshaven, uncombed hair brushed back with fingers, obviously compelled to pose but somehow faintly startled as if interrupted from the solitary task of survival. He grips a placard bearing the ponderous slogans of his captors; the wall behind him bears the symbol and initials of their cause. It is the picture of a man who no longer controls his appearance, who no longer gives orders, whose remaining days depend on others.

The contents of the third photograph depend on the outcome of the episode. We may see a bearded, gaunt, but grinning ghost looking out on a swarm of police and press. A tearful, smiling woman stands beside him, not yet aware of how much the experience has changed the man she knows so well. The strains of fatigue show in his eyes, but he has survived. The haunting alternative shows a gray day, a parked car, the trunk open. With impassive faces, men accustomed to death stare down at a crumpled corpse.

The subjects of these photographs—Geoffrey Jackson, the Born brothers, Tiede Herrema, Françoise Claustre, Hans Martin Schleyer, Aldo Moro, William Niehous, James Dozier—are all the victims of terrorist kidnappings, the footnotes of a new industry built on fear. Members of an exclusive but growing club, former hostages include an ex-premier of Italy, a former president of Argentina, the brother of a president, the sister of a president, the daughter of a president, cabinet ministers, ambassadors, and other diplomats from a score of nations. The targets of kidnappers have included a king, a prince, and the Pope. The club remains dominated, though, by business executives representing many of the world's largest corporations.

THE GROWTH OF TERRORISM

Terrorism, although not a new phenomenon, has grown enormously since the late 1960s. Despite the success of a number of governments in combating terrorists, for the last 16 years the total volume of such violence has continued a ragged course upward. Statistics vary according to collection criteria and procedures, but the long-range trend is indisputable. Terrorism in our era has become an increasingly sophisticated—and for many, an increasingly accepted—political instrument.

Political and religious extremists regularly resort to terrorist tactics. A small but increasing number of governments are also using terrorist tactics, employing terrorist groups, or exploiting terrorist incidents as a mode of surrogate warfare against their opponents. Diplomats have come to accept terrorism as a part of diplomatic life. Corporations accept the terrorist threat as a price of doing business in certain areas of the world. The public is beginning to accept terrorism as part of the normal news diet; indeed, except for the spectacular episode, terrorist acts no longer make headlines.

How quickly this acceptance has come about! In the mid-1960s, no one had heard of kneecappings, car bombs, or people's prisons. Private sector body-guards, defensive driving courses, body armor, kidnap insurance, ransom negotiations, hostage recovery consultants, and many other concepts and services discussed in this book did not exist. Passengers boarded airplanes without passing through metal detectors or being frisked in the presence of armed guards, concrete barriers did not surround government buildings, embassies had not yet become fortresses. Dawson Field, Lod, Munich, Khartoum, Maalot, Entebbe, Mogadishu, Desert One, and Beirut were simply the names of places—exotic places, obscure places, but just places, not battlefields in the hundred wars of terrorism.

Terrorism also has become bloodier. In part, this change reflects the crossing of a major threshold: Terrorists are now more willing to attack persons instead of property. The increased security around facilities has also encouraged them to attack a soft target—people.

Incidents involving hostages, such as kidnappings, hijackings, and takeovers of buildings with hostages, comprise about 17 percent of all incidents of international terrorism. Kidnappings account for between 6 and 8 percent of the total. For all incidents of local as well as international terrorism, the percentage of kidnappings is lower, reflecting the greater number of little bombings carried out by less sophisticated organizations that operate only at the local level.

Terrorists seize hostages in order to create human dramas by putting lives in the balance, thereby guaranteeing intense interest in the event and heavy news coverage. They seize hostages to increase their leverage over governments reluctant to see life sacrificed. Terrorists kidnap businessmen—the most frequent targets—to demonstrate their opposition to the capitalist system and to protest economic exploitation by foreign firms, but above all, to finance their operations.

A MAJOR INNOVATION

Kidnapping corporate executives to finance terrorist operations must be seen as one of the major terrorist innovations of our era—an ingenious scheme in which the targets of terrorism are compelled to finance a war directed against themselves. The first terrorist group to carry out a major operation of this type had some reservations. Until that time, most terrorists got their money the old-fashioned way: They robbed banks. Ransom kidnappings by bandits from Sardinia to Shanghai provided numerous but unappealing precedents to high-minded revolutionaries for whom kidnappings were purely political affairs. Indeed, in the early 1970s, Cuban officials were quietly advising guerrilla groups in Latin America not to engage in ransom kidnappings until their reputations as something other than common criminals were well established.

Once the line was crossed, however, the tactic quickly spread throughout Latin America and the rest of the world. Ransom kidnappings gave terrorists access to huge sums of money; multimillion dollar ransoms, which soon became common, provided terrorists with far more funds than they could get by robbing banks. Guerrilla and terrorist groups in Argentina, Colombia, El Salvador, Spain, and Italy began to obtain a large share of their operational funds from these kidnappings.

In large measure, the proliferation of ransom kidnappings by guerrilla and terrorist groups in the 1970s reflected changes in guerrilla strategy and in the world's economic environment. In the late 1960s and early 1970s, guerrilla groups had shifted their theater of operations from the countryside to the cities, the hubs of commercial activity. There the presence of large foreign business communities provided suitable targets. In this sense, the growth of terrorist kidnappings reflected the spread of multinational corporations. As a price of doing business, these corporations had to be—and were—willing to pay large ransoms.

Having tapped such a good source for funds, the terrorists needed access to arms traders who would sell them weapons. In this respect, terrorist kidnappings have been encouraged by the growth of the international arms market, where government credentials or ideological affinity are not issues in the making of a deal. One former diplomat who dealt with Nicaragua's Sandinistas before they came to power recalls a guerrilla commander paying arms traders with wads of bills taken from a shopping bag sitting at the side of his desk. Much of this money came from ransoms collected by Marxist guerrillas in El Salvador, which incidentally later obliged the Sandinistas to assist these groups in their own struggle. Many observers lament the support given terrorists by the Soviet Union and its Communist allies. While these countries certainly do provide certain kinds of valuable support, the use of ransom kidnappings by terrorists to buy arms actually represents a triumph of free trade. It seems likely that future guerrilla groups who lack state backers will continue to finance their struggles, at least in the initial stages, through kidnappings.

We seldom hear of ransom kidnappings by right-wing terrorists. Often less structured than their counterparts on the left, right-wing terrorist groups are popularly believed to receive secret financial support from wealthy figures in the local political establishment, draw their weapons from sympathizers in the army or police, or make withdrawals from hidden caches of Nazi gold, but they too rely on crime—bank robberies and extortion—to obtain their funds.

THE CRIMINAL CONNECTION

Terrorist kidnappings represent only a small portion of the total number of ransom kidnappings. Ordinary criminals carry out the vast majority, though sometimes the two categories overlap. Members of terrorist groups have occasionally carried out kidnappings for purely personal profit, or in some cases have collected the ransom paid to the terrorist group and run off on their own. Ordinary criminal kidnappers sometimes pretend to be terrorist groups, hoping thereby to collect a higher ransom and throw authorities off their trail. In other instances, terrorists and ordinary criminals have cooperated in kidnappings or in ransom negotiations.

The Cirillo kidnapping in Italy in 1981 provides a splendid example of cooperation between terrorist kidnappers and criminals. Italian authorities paid several million dollars in ransom for the return of Ciro Cirillo, a prominent Naples politician who had been kidnapped by the Red Brigades. A million and a half went to the Red Brigades, while $3 million went to a Naples crime syndicate whose imprisoned leader had negotiated the settlement.

While sometimes difficult to distinguish, a group's identity can be crucial in ransom negotiations. In Argentina, for example, a high level of political kidnappings inspired numerous criminal imitators. These criminal gangs were smaller and not as well organized as the terrorist groups. They did not have the hideouts or logistical support to hold a hostage for a lengthy period of time and therefore were under pressure to settle quickly. According to one corporate official, determining whether the kidnappers were genuine terrorists or criminals posing as terrorists meant the difference between a million-dollar and a hundred-thousand-dollar ransom. This distinction, however, does not apply to well-organized criminal gangs, such as those operating in Italy.

Ransom kidnappings have become a large and well-ordered business. Kidnappers launder huge ransoms through legitimate banks and sometimes even invest in the stock market to provide themselves with a steady cash flow. They have become increasingly sophisticated in their abductions and in their negotiations: They have developed an arsenal of techniques to intensify the psychological pressure on their targets. This success, ironically, is making the payment of multimillion-dollar ransoms less frequent. Because large corporations have increased the security surrounding their executives, kidnappers have been forced to go after less-protected executives of local firms who are less able to pay huge ransoms.

The decline in ransom size is also due to the employment of professional negotiators and hostage recovery consultants, people whose considerable experience with kidnappers' methods has given them a reputation of getting captives back alive at the lowest possible price. Increasingly, ransoms are paid by insurance policies that cover ransom, the salary of abducted executives, and other kinds of related losses. Despite this institutionalization of kidnapping as a business with its own peculiar support industry, the act itself remains a commerce in human life.

The next stage in the industry could be the gradual elimination of physical abduction, with extortion based on the threat of kidnapping or assassination becoming an effective substitute. Although figures are not available—extortion is a notoriously unreported crime—in numerous instances corporations have quietly paid protection money to avoid kidnappings. Argentina's terrorist groups seemed to be moving in this direction before they were destroyed in the mid-1970s.

Extortion offers advantages to both sides. For the kidnappers, it eliminates the risks incurred during an actual kidnapping as well as the dangers and costs of keeping a hostage for a lengthy period. Corporations are attracted by the reduction of risk to personnel, who are in great danger both at the moment of capture and if the kidnappers' hideout is discovered and assaulted by the authorities. Giving in to extortion reduces the losses they would sustain from the lengthy absence of a hostage. For potential victims, of course, extortion reduces their chances of suffering the dangers and discomfort of capture and captivity.

Extortion without credibility, however, is an empty threat. Kidnappers have a live hostage whom they can kill if their demands are not met. Extortionists must persuade the target of their demands that they can and will take someone's life. Psychological factors may enter in here as well. A corporation is under considerable pressure to yield in the case of a kidnapping. The threat in an extortion is more remote, more diffuse, easier to resist. An extortionist solution might be to demonstrate capability by an actual murder. An economist's solution might be for the extortionists to lower their demands—in effect, offering a discount for corporate uncertainty.

HOW MANY? HOW MUCH?

How big is the kidnapping problem? Risks International, a private research organization that has maintained statistics on terrorist activity worldwide since 1970, lists nearly a thousand terrorist kidnappings from 1970 to the end of 1983. This figure excludes the greater number of ransom kidnappings carried out by ordinary criminals and, of course, does not include the numerous unreported kidnappings by political or criminal elements. On the basis of my own conversations with government security officials in various parts of the world, I suspect that the Risks International total comprises something like one-tenth of the real total of all kidnappings, political and criminal. As mentioned later in this book, Vittorfranco Pisano reports that between 1970 and 1982, political terrorism in Italy carried out 25 kidnappings, while during the same period criminal gangs carried out 487. This is a better than 15-to-1 ratio, but Italy is a country with a well-developed kidnapping industry. A recent report by Geoffrey Williams concludes that about 200 major ransom kidnappings occur every year. Other experts have estimated that several kidnappings occur every day, which would mean that more than 1,000 kidnappings take place each year. Altogether, we are looking at perhaps 10,000 terrorist and criminal kidnappings during the last 12 to 15 years.

How much money have kidnappers collected since the tactic became fashionable in the 1970s? Precise figures are hard to come by. While ransom demands are often reported in the press, the amounts paid are usually closely guarded secrets. It has been estimated that, during the 1970s, corporations paid between $150 and $250 million dollars in ransom to terrorists. In his 1982 study of ransom kidnappings, which probably recorded the best-known cases with the largest ransom payments, Geoffrey Williams estimated that corporations paid out $500 million in ransom to terrorists and criminals between 1972 and 1978. Adding six years and the other, unreported cases could put the total ransoms at close to a billion dollars.

To a terrorist, a billion dollars would represent a million submachine guns plus ammunition. The Red Brigades at their peak, with over a hundred full-time members and several hundred part-time terrorists, operated with an annual budget estimated by intelligence authorities to be between $3 and $5 million, $8 to $10 million at the very outside. A billion dollars would have kept them going for several centuries. From the sketchy information available about the cash flow of terrorist organizations, you could assume that a billion dollars would fund just about all the major terrorist groups of Western Europe for 30 years and would also pay for the annual renewal of a $9.5 million subsidy reportedly given in 1982 by Colonel Qadaffi to the four most militant Palestinian terrorist organizations in return for their promise to continue the armed struggle. Or it could also support several thousand full-time terrorists for a decade.

TERRORISM AND SECURITY

The Threat

The book is organized into five parts. Part I focuses on the threat. It does not attempt to provide a current assessment of the kidnapping threat around the world. Such an assessment would be quickly out of date. Rather, it provides an overview of the kidnapping problem as it has affected various countries in order to illustrate the nature of the threat and its effects.

The section begins with a look at kidnapping from the terrorists' point of view. Written by Gerardo Capotorto, a former intelligence officer in Italy's *Carabinieri,* and based on captured documents and informants' accounts, Chapter 1 examines how terrorists select their target and plan their operation.

Nearly half of all terrorist kidnappings are directed against the business community and its large resources. In Chapter 2 Charles Russell, a senior analyst at Risks International, provides a statistical review of 298 kidnappings of businessmen in the 1970s and early 1980s. At the international level, terrorists concentrate their attacks on the diplomatic community. Carol Edler Baumann, a former deputy assistant secretary of state in the State Department's Bureau of Intelligence and Research, examines the patterns established in 130 kidnappings of diplomats in Chapter 3.

The next five chapters focus on kidnappings in Western Europe and Latin America. David Schiller, a German scholar, reviews the major terrorist and criminal kidnappings in Germany, France, and Austria in Chapter 4. Chapter 5 was written by Vittorfranco Pisano, an Italian lawyer, who reviews the kidnappings carried out by Italy's Red Brigades and looks at the record of 487 criminal kidnappings in a country where kidnapping is a major industry.

Most ransom kidnappings have occurred in Latin America. In Chapter 6,

Susanna Purnell, a researcher at The Rand Corporation, looks at Argentina, where the tactic was invented and developed to its highest form. The multimillion-dollar ransoms collected by Argentina's terrorists did not prevent them from making strategic errors, nor did their success prevent their brutal destruction by government authorities in the late 1970s. At nearly the same time, the threat shifted to Central America, as leftist guerrillas in that part of the world filled their war chests. In Chapter 7, Eleanor Wainstein, an economist at The Rand Corporation, examines the kidnapping problem as it affected El Salvador in the 1970s, and in Chapter 8, William Sater, a professor of history specializing in Latin America, examines the continuing problem of kidnapping in Colombia, where in 1983 terrorists kidnapped the brother of the president of that country.

In the 1920s and 1930s, ransom kidnappings occurred frequently in the United States. Criminal gangs crossed state lines more easily than local police, thus evading apprehension. This situation changed dramatically in subsequent years. Today, ransom kidnappings are a comparatively rare crime in the United States, owing to the very high rate of apprehension and conviction. Many observers credit this change to the development of the federal kidnapping statute following the shocking Lindbergh kidnapping in 1932 and to the expanding role of the FBI. In Chapter 9, Richard Gallagher, a former assistant director of the FBI, examines kidnapping in the United States and traces the development of the federal statutes.

Management Issues

Part II examines the issues that management faces in dealing with kidnappings. Chapter 10 begins the section with an examination of the direct costs associated with preventing and handling terrorist attacks, as well as the less obvious effects on business firms' organization and operations.

When faced with a terrorist threat, most corporations increase the security around their exposed executives, pay their insurance premiums, pay ransom when necessary, and continue to make money. They may withdraw their executives, but rarely do they pull out altogether. In extreme circumstances, however, corporations may have to evacuate their personnel. The problems of getting them out are discussed in Chapter 11 by H. H. A. Cooper, an experienced security professional.

A number of corporations have responded to the threat of terrorism with efforts to improve their image through corporate philanthropy. In Chapter 12, two American scholars, on the basis of their examination of the experience in Argentina, conclude that corporate philanthropy must (and should) be its own reward: It does not buy protection against terrorist kidnappings.

Corporate executives who are skilled at making profits often appear to be naive consumers when it comes to decisions about security expenditures. In Chapter 13, Arthur Alexander, the associate head of The Rand Corporation's Department of Economics, provides an economic analysis of security, recovery, and compensation in terrorist kidnapping, thereby reducing the imponderables of the problem to straightforward economic terms that businessmen will find more familiar.

What are the obligations of a corporation to its employees facing a terrorist threat? Although there have been several lawsuits, case law does not provide a certain guide. In Chapter 14, Charles Ruff, with the assistance of Mary Helen Gallagher and William Lee Saunders, Jr., of Covington & Burling, provide the first comprehensive guide to the legal aspects of corporate responsibility.

Whether or not to pay ransom and how much to pay are two of the biggest questions facing management in dealing with either terrorist or criminal kidnappings. In Chapter 15, I explore the arguments for and against the payment of ransom and the many factors that influence the amounts ultimately paid. The section concludes with a review of the complex issues involved in managing a kidnapping episode by Richard Clutterbuck, a world-renowned British expert on terrorism.

Negotiations

Part III addresses the problem of negotiations by offering several perspectives. The section begins with another chapter by Richard Clutterbuck, who draws on the vast experience of London-based Control Risks, of which he is a director, to review the structure and tasks of the negotiating team and the utility and role of the professional negotiating consultant.

Chapter 18 offers a detailed case study of the negotiations in the case of Monica Gómez, a fictitious name but a real case. The chapter was prepared by a Latin American businessman writting under a nom de plume—or one might say nom de guerre—who has successfully negotiated in 18 kidnapping cases.

Chapter 19 provides another case study. In 1981, Leon Richardson, a highly successful Australian businessman, was kidnapped in Guatemala and held for 100 days while a member of his corporation, assisted by professional consultants, negotiated his release. Both similarities and differences can be found in the negotiating strategies followed in the Gómez case and those employed in the Richardson episode. In the latter case, a low initial offer was held for a considerable time until the kidnappers softened and entered a familiar pattern of bargaining with the company's negotiators. In the Gómez case, the initial offer was just high enough to dissuade the kidnappers from killing their captive; the negotiator then waited for them to weaken. At the critical moment, he seized the initiative, made a single offer, and refused to bargain further.

In Chapter 20, Gerardo Capotorto offers some further thoughts on negotiations, focusing on the tasks of the corporation's "security committee" in managing a kidnapping. Mike Ackerman, in Chapter 21, draws on the experiences of Ackerman and Palumbo, a firm that has handled a number of kidnapping cases around the world, to describe the role of the hostage recovery consultant. In the final chapter of this section, I discuss the many problems of communication in a kidnapping episode.

Security Issues

Part IV considers the technical issues of security, the principal domain of the security officer. Chapter 23, by Don Wurth, a former U.S. Secret Service agent, deals with the proper function and use of the private sector bodyguard; it is a useful guide to hiring, managing, and employing private bodyguards. Chapter 24, by Richard Healy, focuses on the requirements of security at the potential target's office. Most kidnappings occur while the individual is in his automobile on his way to or from work. In Chapter 25, Anthony Scotti, who operates a defensive driving school, describes the questions involved in acquiring an armored car and developing security procedures that will make a person a more difficult target. The first and last line of defense is often the individual himself. How can he prepare himself to meet the threat? Should he resist? Should he be armed? These are largely matters of personal choice. James Jarrett, who teaches survival at his own school in Arizona, examines these choices in Chapter 26 and describes the kind of survival training, some of it admittedly controversial, that might be considered.

The Person

Part V focuses on the person. Chapter 27, written by Richard Kobetz and H. A. A. Cooper, Kobetz, discusses the issues involved in personal security. In Chapter 28 Gerardo Capotorto outlines personal measures to avoid capture, and how to survive captivity, if they fail. The next two chapters are written by two remarkable men who have been there: Leon Richardson, the subject of the negotiations described in Chapter 19, describes in Chapter 29 how he survived 100 days totally isolated in an underground cell in Guatemala. William Niehous, an executive of Owens-Illinois and the author of Chapter 30 on surviving captivity, was himself held captive by terrorists in Venezuela for more than three years before he was rescued. Chapter 31 concludes with a discussion of the difficulties faced by the returning hostage.

I

The Threat

How Terrorists Look at Kidnappings

Gerardo Capotorto

Most kidnapped persons never imagined that they would become the target of such a crime. Today's civilization exposes us to the continuous impact of frightening possibilities, against which individuals unconsciously defend themselves by retreating to psychological bunkers and rejecting the reality of such threats. News of a kidnapping concerns us only for a moment; after a fleeting thought of sympathy for the victim, we are distracted by the activities of our own lives.

What crime provokes more devastating effects than political kidnapping? How much does it cost our organized society to heal the wounds opened by this crime? And what is the price that we will have to pay for the contribution of this crime to the destabilization of democracy—the system of which it is the child? Whether kidnapping flourishes with terrorism is a recurring issue. In my opinion, terrorism and kidnapping are born and proliferate in industrialized societies with democratic systems whose evolution has reduced the power of those who govern. These democracies generate forms of liberty often misunderstood as license.

The same phenomenon occurs in states in which a dictatorial regime has exhausted its capacity to control individual liberties, and greater tolerance or permissiveness appears. Kidnapping is almost unknown where the rule of law and coercion of the individual are absolute. But permissive societies, comprising both positive and negative factors, worthwhile innovations and deep injustices, economic well-being and economic deprivation, permit the radicalization of attitudes and conditions favorable to the growth of both terrorism and kidnapping.

THE CHOICE OF THE KIDNAPPING VICTIM

At first glance, choosing kidnap victims seems easy, but actually it entails a lot of patient research and analysis. Whether the crime is economically or politically motivated, the amount of preparation is impressive for every terrorist kidnapping. Furthermore, the criminal organizations who perpetrate this crime are usually formed by people already sought by the police, fugitives who are forced to live in a clandestine manner and consequently have a great amount of free time on their hands. They have all the time they need to make plans in minute detail.

One often hears of successful police operations that discover clandestine hideouts where documents, card catalogues, and complete plans for kidnapping operations are hidden. Analysis of these personal files, labeled with the names of potential victims, is one way to discover what mechanisms or preparatory processes cause a person to become a target of this type of crime. Another factor to examine is the typical lifestyle of the members of criminal organizations and, more specifically, terrorist groups. Members of such organizations must, for security motives, limit the time they spend outside the hideout. Their lives must be organized around the small space of the hideout, where, not infrequently, members of the opposite sex stay together.

Hideouts offer few outlets for recreation: Erotic games soon exhaust themselves, card games become monotonous, other hobbies usually prove unsatisfactory. Reading and political debate become the greatest commitment. Many daily papers are read and commented upon; the events referred to in the papers are placed under a magnifying glass; and everything is analyzed and discussed. For each potential kidnapping victim, members cut out articles that constitute a news base for the personal file. Some annotations, written by the "planners," are used to indicate whether the potential target is already known. Thousands of such files, some containing only a single news item, have been found.

At this point it is well to ask, Which news items interest kidnappers? The answer is simple enough for criminal organizations with financial motives. What they save usually contains details of the economic means of the potential target or of his profession, mundane news about his organizing or attending glamorous parties, publicity, and finally, information that helps them imagine how the potential victim could be captured. Much of the documentation that has been seized is part of the detailed planning of kidnappings that are researched by single criminals or small groups who are not able to undertake the kidnapping themselves. Instead they sell the plan and their own participation for compensation or a percentage of the ransom money.

Terrorist groups are attracted by a much wider spectrum of news items because their interests and targets are more numerous. A strong motive is their need to obtain financing for their often costly activities. Terrorist groups may undertake a kidnapping to satisfy social demands or to elicit agreement from sympathizers who might become new recruits. They usually choose crimes that may be seen as a punishment for wrongs suffered by humble and defenseless people.

A potential "target" is someone whose actions are much discussed and thought unpopular—the corrupt politician, the highly visible manager who may be held responsible for deeds that have moved public opinion, the individual thought to be of dubious morality, and the employer who because of his excessive strictness toward employees is seen as the enemy of the people. Actual victims include judges, policemen, doctors, managers, and businessmen. Suitable targets include individuals whose kidnapping guarantees the achievement of not only the economic, but also the social and propagandistic purposes of the terrorists. Terrorists want to control public opinion and cause traumatization through terror. They undertake kidnappings that can definitely foster political destabilization.

A potential target still is not in much danger after a news item has appeared and a file has been opened if nothing more appears in the media. But if a second news item appears, it will be added to the first, and so on, in chronological order. At this point, even though numerous news items may be in the file, the person has usually not yet become a target. The continuing interest of the press or information media, however, may provoke the composition of a note, in which all the information that has been collected is described in depth. In other cases, confederates inside a corporation may provide photocopies of personnel office cards that contain complete information on the career and related salary information of the individuals involved.

No person is actually marked as a target until a catalyst news item appears that allows the terrorists to judge the feasibility and possible rewards of his kidnapping. As soon as the terrorists can predict a successful action against a remunerative target, that person is placed on the kidnap list. At this point, a summary of the estimated outcomes of the proposed kidnapping will be added to the file.

Obviously, not all terrorist groups use the same methods, and not all arrive at the same conclusions; indeed, the same news items, reviewed in the hideouts of different terrorist groups, have produced diverse and often opposite conclusions. What does remain the same, however, is the means for acquiring information. Whatever differences can be found in conclusions are due more to the operative possibilities of an individual case than to any general orientation. Thus, although someone may become a "kidnappable person," he will not be chosen until an assessment has been made regarding the feasibility of the operation. Unfortunately, many persons on these lists have in fact been assassinated or injured in the name of a justice that terrorism arbitrarily arrogates to itself.

THE FEASIBILITY OF THE KIDNAPPING

The second phase in a kidnapping operation is without doubt correlated with the preceding phase and is provoked by it, but there is a notable difference between them. The first is an analytical phase, in which a multiplicity of possible situations are examined; the second is an operative phase, conducted by persons who usually act in full freedom because they have not been identified by the police. Some of these people have even infiltrated the world in which the victim functions. The description of this phase is based largely on my own professional experiences, with priority given to cases that actually happened and to analyses of the copious material recovered from terrorist hideouts.

The terrorists begin by investigating the life of the potential victim: his family, his habits, the world in which he habitually moves—anything that could facilitate a kidnapping. Modern life imposes pressures on people to enlarge their spheres of action, to broaden their opportunities, and to use time better in order to produce more. For that reason, they move about frequently, which makes the car an indispensable part of life. Not by chance, a very high percentage of kidnappings occur while the victims are in cars.

I do not agree with the theory that a good percentage of our work time is passed in a car and that the exposure to risk is great because so many hours are passed moving from place to place. Instead, I think that kidnappings frequently occur when the victims are in cars because normal means of transportation are the most difficult to protect, the situations in which they are involved are the most disparate, isolation is often total, the probability of receiving help at hours of reduced traffic is all but nonexistent, and finally, it is impossible not to be caught by surprise when one is attacked.

This second phase is almost always concluded with the drawing up of reports with scrupulous annotations of every circumstance considered favorable for further developments. Observations often concern the type of the prospective victim's vehicle, the make and color, and any details on security devices, types of armor plating, and the brand and characteristics of the tires. Every part of the car is analyzed. As uncovered documentation reveals, the terrorists' knowledge of anything they observe increases with the number of observations made. For example, after simply ascertaining the presence of radio equipment, a terrorist could pass in subsequent observations to a detailed description of the visible devices on a vehicle. Such thoroughness may also emerge from their study of how to neutralize such devices during an attack.

In one case, the inexplicable presence of additional antennae mounted on a vehicle led to the abandonment of an action: The terrorists were not able to predict what defensive systems would have been activated by the apparatus, whose characteristics and possibilities for use they knew nothing about.

The presence of escorts of any type is attentively evaluated; terrorist documents describe how often the service is used, its effectiveness, the number and weapons on each of the guards, and the type of vehicle employed. Attack plans must deal with a number of contingencies—whether escorts would intervene with gunfire or use anti-projectile clothing, how they would communicate with the targeted individual, whether police form part of the escort, and any other item of interest.

After deciding that the risk of attacks or kidnappings had risen, one industrial company had its own managers transported in three separate company vehicles, escorted by one vehicle of the security service. This arrangement was noted many times by the terrorists, but they made an error of evaluation. They thought that one car was used for the transport of the managers and the other four were used as escort. Seized documentation indicated that the target was the director of the company; but from the results of the observation, the terrorists gauged the operation to be dangerous and too risky to succeed. These meticulous observations were made in the five working days of a week; only rarely are notations and reports dated Saturday or Sunday.

Observations are usually repeated for several weeks to reliably establish the day on which movements regularly occur. Very often annotations cover the entire route completed by the car, so it must be presumed that full-scale espionage is conducted. In other cases, detailed and precise observations are made only in the immediate neighborhood of the dwelling.

Vans equipped with polarized glass or with special fissures are often used for observation. It is astonishing that such vehicles are not discovered, since these crude and obvious contrivances should make anyone suspicious. In fact, however, in the cases for which documentation was found, no one among the many people who passed through the areas had noticed any irregularity, nor had the person who was kidnapped or his bodyguard noticed an unusual vehicle reappearing for many weeks.

Unfortunately, it is the principle of surprise that often allows the attacker to have a decisive advantage over the target. The victim frequently overlooks routine security measures, and after some time, pays little attention to security. His habitual presence at restaurants and other public places is often attentively followed and analyzed. Evidently, terrorists seek to establish which movements are foreseeable in environments and circumstances that are the least risky for their operations.

Observations include characteristics of any routes that the victim frequently uses. It has been proven that terrorists sometimes foresee a problem in the route and introduce concurrent operations in anticipation of the principal operation. These support operations may include the temporary obstructing of an area, the neutralization, or overpowering, of those who normally are present in the place selected for the attack, the screening off of telephones in that sector, or the obstruction of traffic by deliberately creating accidents.

If the operation is very important and the risks connected with it are great, the entire life of the person in question may be observed, including his emotional ties, his dwelling, his friendships, his use of free time, and any other elements of interest. For example, one successful police operation led to the discovery of a voluminous file on the activities of a highly placed industrial manager. The file included vast photographic documentation, carried out in many circumstances and over a long period of time. Evidently, pictures of the target were of particular importance to the terrorists, because the first photos were those carried in the newspapers; subsequent photographs showed television accounts of meetings relating to an assembly of industrialists, and others had been taken during espionage and observation activities. Very often, photographic documentation is obtained exclusively by reproducing television images.

In this particular case, the first pages of the file related to activities carried out by the manager and focused on a circumstance that had occurred five years earlier; subsequent news related to the manager's interventions in national and international problems. An appointment to public office increased the interest in this person, and the documentation about him was enriched by items relating to activities of his youth and to his industrial career. A newspaper item concerning the good progress of his company and a communication relating to a drastic reduction of its work force immediately made him a top-priority target whose kidnapping could be highly remunerative.

The file revealed continual observation using a car and a motorcycle. Long-winded annotations appeared on numerous sheets, some concerning investigations of details that were initially considered of secondary importance. The terrorists studied the personnel of an automotive workshop that repaired the car of the target's wife, as well as the personnel of the laundry that served the family and of a food store they habitually patronized. All the manager's habits were noted, including his presence in public locales and his regular presence at religious functions. The documentation covered characteristics of the building in which he lived, the heating and air-conditioning devices, and the details of the main entrance and the service entrance. His wife's habits and the friendships of the children were also part of the file.

Finally a scrupulous observation was made of the methods of defense, the men comprising the escort, their personal cars, the security systems they employed. No reference was found in the documentation to operative methods for the possible kidnapping, nor were indications found of the management of the case. These omissions supported an early hypothesis that the file was an exercise undertaken for training of new recruits.

A subsequent police operation led to the arrest of four persons, two of whom collaborated with the police. One of the arrestees clarified the entire case in all its disquieting reality. Each observation listed in the file had been finalized by research on the group's capability to plant a network of supporters around the target who would be ready to assist in the kidnapping. The investigations also led to the arrest of an employee of the food store, previously held under observation, who would have allowed the kidnappers to go inside the apartment during the delivery of foodstuffs.

Further police work resulted in the arrest of a woman terrorist, previously unknown to the police, who had been hired by a publishing house for the house-to-house sale of books and who had already succeeded in winning the trust of the future victims. (As was later discovered, the terrorist group had scrutinized the organization and sales operations of the publishing house.) Without the successful police operation, the kidnapping would have occurred. The family members and the target were to have been anesthetized and the manager transported away in a suitcase. This technique has been used successfully in Europe, in particular in Germany, France, and Italy, where it was used most recently in the kidnapping of General James Dozier.

Another interesting case is that of a young man from an excellent family who became engaged to the daughter of a police officer. The young man constantly visited the home of the officer. After some time, he was arrested, and it was discovered that he had been given the responsibility of helping to attack or kidnap the officer.

So many diverse situations are generated by our mode of living that the dangers to which we are exposed are always increasing. To attempt a complete analysis of them is impossible; however, it is certain that the more eminent and successful a person becomes in entrepreneurial, social, economic, or political areas, the greater is his level of exposure to risk.

2

Kidnapping as a Terrorist Tactic

Charles Russell

THE PRIMARY TARGET

In contrast to other terrorist tactics, all of which are deployed against a variety of political, governmental, diplomatic, military, and commercial targets, kidnapping primarily involves a single entity—the corporate executive. Of the 781 terrorist abductions recorded during the twelve and a quarter years extending from January 1, 1970 through March 31, 1982, 48 percent targeted wealthy businessmen. The remaining 52 percent involved, in descending order of importance, government officials, politicians, diplomats, media personnel, and police/military officers. None of these target categories, by itself, accounted for more than 15 percent of all terrorist kidnappings. The 48 percent affecting businessmen are of very real importance to many terrorist groups, as business firms have paid an estimated $200 million in ransoms since 1970. It is these ransom payments that have played a crucial role in financing many of the terrorist organizations active today.

All statistics, percentages, and other numerical materials used in this chapter were obtained from the computer data base of 14,000 terrorist incidents maintained by Risks International, Alexandria, Virginia. Materials in the data base relate only to significant actions carried out by terrorist groups operating in the United States and abroad. Actions by purely criminal elements are not recorded.

Incidents included in the data base are categorized by type of activity: kidnapping, hijacking, assassination, attacks against facilities, maiming, and bombing. Only selected bombings are included where the damage in human or material terms is substantial.

Data recorded on each kidnapping action includes the following: date of incident; country and city in which the action took place; number of persons abducted; names of persons abducted; nationality of those abducted; position in corporation, government agency, etc.; name of company, agency, etc.; ransoms demanded and paid; date victim(s) were released, killed, rescued, etc.; group conducting the operation; number in group; demands made other than ransom; and background on incident. Information is derived from foreign and U.S. government publications, police reports, and the foreign/English language press.

Developed and tested by Latin American terrorists during the early 1970s, the idea of abducting businessmen for ransom spread quickly to Western Europe, the Middle East, and even Asia. In these areas, as well as in Latin America, the tactic has been exploited primarily by terrorist groups active within a limited geographic area or a single nation. While these intranational organizations may be capable of mounting transnational actions, which cross national boundaries, they rarely do so. The groups active on a transnational level—most of whom are Palestinian in origin and tied to Middle Eastern bases—have not favored corporate abductions. In fact, over 96 percent of *all* business kidnappings since 1970 have been conducted by intranational versus transnational terrorist organizations. This same trend is evident in abductions involving such nonbusiness targets as governmental, diplomatic, political, police, or even media personnel. For these groups, slightly more than 98 percent of the 405 kidnappings affecting them since 1970 have been carried out by intranational terrorist organizations.

There are obvious reasons for transnational groups rejecting corporate abductions (or for that matter any type of kidnapping) and for the importance accorded this tactic among intranational terrorist entities. For the transnationals, a primary consideration in any type of operation is the leverage they can gain against a target country. Quite obviously, the hijacking of an aircraft filled with passengers has greater impact on any target country than the abduction of one or even a dozen businessmen, no matter what their positions might be. In addition, many transnational groups active today receive substantial financial assistance from patron states or sympathetic Arab nations and thus rarely lack funds. This is not the case for intranational organizations, which must depend almost entirely upon their own skills to obtain needed operational funds. One of the easiest routes to such funds is through the abduction for ransom of corporate personnel. Substantially less risky than bank robberies, these actions also promise a greater reward.

The financial importance of corporate abductions as a means of replenishing depleted terrorist coffers or obtaining funds to initiate new operations was illustrated clearly in the 1981 case of Spanish businessman Luis Suñer Sanchis and a series of earlier 1978 actions in El Salvador. In the latter operations, a total of five executives with Dutch, Swedish, Japanese, and British firms were kidnapped for ransom between August 14 and December 8, 1978.[1] Taken by the radical Marxist group Armed Forces of National Resistance (FARN), these men were abducted solely to obtain funds for an expansion of terrorist efforts in El Salvador. Known ransoms paid for the five executives totalled $18 million. These funds did much to improve the shaky finances of the FARN and associate groups. They also provided a monetary basis for a subsequent expansion of the guerrilla effort.

As with these kidnappings, the January 18, 1981, abduction of Luis Suñer Sanchis also was prompted by purely financial considerations. The Basque Fatherland and Liberty Movement (ETA), a Marxist-influenced separatist group active in Spain for 19 years, had seen its influence undercut steadily by government actions granting limited autonomy to the five Spanish Basque Departments— a goal ETA had espoused for over two decades. Because of these actions and the resultant declining support for its terrorist activities, contributions to ETA had dropped substantially, as had payments of its "revolutionary tax"[2]—an assessment levied upon most wealthy Basque businessmen. Nonpayment of the tax often resulted in assassination of the offending executive or destruction of his business.

As a result of its financial difficulties, ETA decided upon a single abduction to solve these problems. The target selected was 71-year-old Luis Suñer Sanchis, Spain's wealthiest businessman and president of Avidesa, a firm involved in the production of candy, ice cream, and food products. Known popularly as the "ice cream and chicken king" of Spain, Suñer Sanchis was taken from his Avidesa office at 8:45 P.M. by a five-member kidnap team armed with submachine guns. The team was led by a woman. Held for 90 days, Suñer was released following the payment of a ransom estimated by the former Spanish Minister of the Interior Juan Jose Rosen at between 4.5 and 5.6 million dollars. Payments were arranged by family attorney Pedro Ruiz Balerdi and made into ETA accounts in France. Spain has no legal agreements with that nation to recover these funds.[3]

In addition to its importance as a source of funds, the abduction of corporate executives also has an ideological significance. Of those terrorist groups operational today, slightly over 80 percent describe themselves as "radical Marxist" in political outlook. More strongly influenced by the simplified Marxism of Regis Debray, Abraham Guillen, Carlos Marighella, and Herbert Marcuse than the more orthodox works of Lenin, many modern terrorist groups see "North American imperialistic capitalism," directed by U.S.-based multinational corporations, as their primary target.

Summed up succinctly by the Italian Red Brigades, ". . . multinational imperialism thus emerges as a system of global domination in which various national capitalisms are merely its organic fingers and toes."[4] Since these national capitalisms are ". . . at once an instrument for domestic repression and a national interpretation of the dominant imperialism headed by the U.S.A. . . . ,"[5] they can be eliminated by attacking their foundations—domestic and foreign business firms. Terrorist theoretician Abraham Guillen points out, ". . . By making these firms the object of permanent harassment, the foundations of the national economic system and the state itself can be destroyed."[6] As most terrorists have learned, a particularly effective means of harassment is the kidnapping of corporate personnel. Thus, ideology and financial gain coalesce in a single act. The state is weakened and terrorist coffers are filled.

TRENDS IN CORPORATE KIDNAPPING

Although businessmen remain the largest single target category for abduction by terrorists, the total number of these operations have steadily declined over the last 12 or so years. As is evident from the data set out in Table 2.1, this decline has been substantially greater than any overall drop in the use of kidnapping as a terrorist tactic.

As indicated in Table 3.1, total terrorist kidnappings declined from 132 in 1979 to 95 during 1981—a drop of 28 percent over the three-year period. Within the same time phase, however, business abductions fell at a substantially greater rate, dropping from 66 in 1979 to 33 for 1981, a reduction of 50 percent. While

Table 2.1 Terrorist Kidnappings Worldwide, 1970–1982

	1970–78	1979	1980	1981	1982 (1st Qtr)	Total
Total Incidents	404	132	124	95	26	781
Incidents Against						
Business	208	66	57	33	12	376
Domestic business	143	54	47	28	10	282
Foreign business	20	8	3	4	2	37
U.S. business	45	4	7	1	0	57
Total vs U.S. Targets	73	7	7	6	0	93
Total Killed	50	34	54	32	4	174

these changes were taking place, business kidnappings as a percentage of all terrorist abductions also were dropping. In 1979 these operations accounted for 51 percent of all kidnaps; by 1981, however, the comparable figure was only 33 percent.

The decline in business kidnapping is probably due to a combination of factors. Particularly significant are the improved security procedures adopted over the past four to five years by many large firms. The 1977 kidnap-murder of Daimler-Benz Chairman of the Board Dr. Hanns-Martin Schleyer, the 1977 death of German banker Juergen Ponto, and the 1978 abductions of foreign businessmen in Latin America seem to have made a lasting impression upon many corporations operating overseas. High-risk executives no longer followed the same routes to work nor used identical modes of travel each day. Cars were changed frequently, as were travel times. Chauffeur-driven vehicles gave way to small locally manufactured cars. Closed circuit television, cipher locks, motion detectors, and personal communication/warning systems as well as protective security details became commonplace in countries where terrorists were active.

Recognizing that terrorists invariably turn to softer and more vulnerable targets when faced with tight security, a substantial number of U.S. and foreign companies have simply upgraded their overall security posture, thereby cutting the risk of a corporate kidnapping. These actions, coupled with improved police capabilities in some areas (particularly Western Europe), have reduced company losses and turned terrorists toward the abduction of personnel affiliated with domestic firms (those companies indigenous to a particular country rather than U.S. or other foreign corporations operating there). Underestimating the threat to their personnel and frequently unwilling to channel substantial funds into better security programs, these domestic firms are now the preferred targets for corporate kidnappings.

The data set out in Table 2.2 illustrate this trend toward the increased abduction of personnel affiliated with domestic firms. They also show the decline in operations targeting U.S. and foreign executives. As indicated in the table, 69 percent of all corporate kidnappings during the 1970–78 time span involved persons affiliated with domestic companies, compared to 31 percent for U.S. and other foreign-based firms. By 1979, however, these percentages had changed substantially.

Table 2.2   Corporate Abductions, 1970–1982

	1970–78	1979	1980	1981	1982 (1st Qtr)
Total Kidnap Incidents	404	132	124	95	26
Total vs Business	208	66	57	33	12
Nr. vs Domestic Firms	143 (69%)	54 (82%)	47 (83%)	28 (85%)	10 (84%)
Nr. vs U.S. and Foreign Firms	65 (31%)	12 (18%)	10 (17%)	5 (15%)	2 (16%)

Thus, corporate abductions of personnel affiliated with domestic firms increased from 69 percent over the 1970–78 time period to 85 percent in 1981, while the kidnapping of businessmen with U.S. and other foreign companies declined from 31 percent (1970–78) to 15 percent in 1981. This drop is even sharper when only U.S. firms are counted. Within the 1980–78 time frame, 21 percent of all corporate abductions involved U.S. business personnel. By 1979 this figure had fallen to 6 percent, by 1981 to 3 percent, and by the first quarter of 1982 to zero. These changes in targeting patterns, as noted earlier, appear to be primarily a reflection of the improved security accorded most U.S. and other foreign corporate personnel operating in high-risk areas.

Closely linked with the decline in U.S. and foreign corporate abductions (and the percentage increase in those affecting domestic firms) has been a steady drop in ransoms demanded and paid. Demands declined from $69,083,500 in 1979 to $5,804,000 during 1981, and estimated payments fell from $34.5 million (1979) to less than $5 million for 1981.[7] These reductions are seemingly a direct result of the type of target hit. Since many domestic firms do not carry kidnap and ransom insurance on their personnel, pay offs usually come from funds raised by a victim's family. The net result for any abductor is a smaller ransom. This decline in revenue available from corporate kidnappings also may provide a partial explanation for its decreased use as a terrorist tactic.

In looking back over those developments that have taken place in corporate kidnappings since 1970, several trends seem clear.

- There has been an overall decline in the use of kidnapping as a terrorist tactic, 1970–82.
- There has been a gradual drop in the number of business abductions, as a percentage of all kidnappings, 1970–82.
- There has been a decided shift in the type of businessman abducted. Personnel associated with domestic corporations, rather than U.S.- or other foreign-based firms, are now the preferred targets.
- The increasing abduction of domestic business executives, as well as a decline in the kidnapping of U.S. and other foreign corporate personnel, has reduced the amount of money available to terrorist groups from executive abductions.

NONBUSINESS TARGETS

In contrast to victims of those business abductions discussed above, nonbusiness targets are rarely kidnapped for ransom. Instead, the usual terrorist objective is to force a national government into (a) modifying or changing established social, economic, or political programs; (b) releasing imprisoned terrorists; or (c) publicizing terrorist goals and operations.

For the achievement of these objectives, the stature and reputation of those abducted are absolutely critical. In order to force a national government to act, a victim must be a person with close political or other ties to the regime in power. Ideally, the individual should also be a person well known throughout the country, if not internationally. Aldo Moro, a former Italian premier, and Antonio Maria de Oriol y Urquijo, personal advisor to Spanish monarch Juan Carlos, typify the ideal type of victim. In the absence of such a target, the abduction of a foreign diplomat can generate the same or greater pressure on a national government. Accordingly, it is not surprising to find that the primary nonbusiness targets are politicians; high-level government officials; foreign diplomats; ranking military or police officers; and, more recently, media personnel. Together these target categories account for 66 percent of all 405 nonbusiness abductions since 1970. The remaining 34 percent include a wide variety of victims ranging from religious personnel and missionaries to teachers, school administrators, students, personnel assigned to international and regional organizations, musicians, laborers, and peasants.

Although politicians, high-level government officials, diplomats, police/military officers, and media personnel remained the major nonbusiness targets throughout the 1970–82 time span, the relative importance of each category did vary during these years. Between 1970 and 1978, for example, diplomats accounted for 13 percent of all nonbusiness kidnappings, compared to 6.6 percent for the years 1979–82. Similar changes were noted for governmental employees (9 percent between 1970 and 1978 and 27 percent for 1979–82) and military/police officers (5 percent for the 1970–78 time span and 10 percent between 1979–82).

The substantial increase in the last two categories seems largely attributable to expanded terrorist/guerrilla activity in El Salvador and Guatemala. In both countries governmental and police/military personnel have been taken with increasing frequency. Together, these two nations accounted for 66 percent of all government and police/military abductions during 1980–81. In Guatemala alone, victims included the Minister of Public Health, Supreme and Criminal Court Justices, ranking National Police officers, and several congressmen. Guatemala and El Salvador, in the last two years, also accounted for 46 percent of all the politicians who were abducted worldwide.

Among the major nonbusiness target categories, one of the most interesting changes noted during the 1970–82 time span concerned media personnel. Whereas these individuals accounted for less than 2 percent of those nonbusiness kidnappings reported between 1970 and the close of 1978, their percentage jumped to 11.6 percent for the 1979–82 time period. Concentrated primarily in Colombia, Guatemala, and Peru, such abductions—as of now—seem to be a totally Latin American phenomenon. Most cases parallel the May 22, 1982, kidnapping of Gloria Arguelles, Arturo Donaldo, and Rafael Arrieta, reporters for the Bogotá, Colombia daily newspapers *El Espectador* and *El Heraldo*. Taken in a downtown Barranquilla park where they had gone for an interview with members of the 19th of April Movement (M-19) terrorist group, the reporters were held for a total of 15 hours, lectured on M-19 goals, and then freed.[8] The purpose behind this and similar operations in the past was to ensure favorable publicity for M-19. Media victims are well treated and the result is often a highly favorable article concerning the group.

U.S. TARGETS

As is obvious from a review of Table 3.1, U.S. nationals have been infrequent kidnap targets. During the years 1978–82, only 93 operations targeted U.S. personnel—11.9 percent of all 781 kidnappings reported for that period. Of these 93 actions, 57 involved members of U.S. business firms.

Latin America has been the focal point for both business and nonbusiness incidents affecting U.S. nationals. Over the period 1970–82, 91.4 percent of the 93 kidnapping operations involving Americans worldwide took place in Latin America, as did 50 of the 57 abductions affecting U.S. firms. Within this region, most U.S. kidnappings occurred in Argentina, El Salvador, Guatemala, Honduras, and Colombia. Nonbusiness targets have included diplomats, missionaries, journalists, government personnel, teachers, and students. Among the most frequent U.S. business abductions have been those of bankers, geologists, petroleum engineers, and corporate executives, including local managers of American firms. Other areas recording kidnap actions against U.S. targets between January 1970 and the end of March 1982 were Asia, the United States itself, and the Middle East.

TARGETING BY GEOGRAPHIC AREA

Latin America and Europe

Since 1970, the vast majority of terrorist kidnappings have taken place in just two world regions: Latin America and Europe. Together they account for 86.2 percent of all 781 abductions reported during the 1970–82 time span. Of the two areas, Latin America is the clear leader, with 65.1 percent of the world total, followed at a substantial distance by Europe with 21.1 percent. Table 2.3 lists kidnap totals and percentages by world region for the period 1970–82.

The substantial difference between the number of terrorist abductions recorded in Latin America and other areas of the world—particularly second place Europe—probably results from a number of factors. Two of these seem rather obvious: The first is the level of terrorist activity within each region and the second is the relative strength of the police/military.

Table 2.3 Kidnappings by Geographic Area, 1970–1982

World Region	No. of Incidents	% of World Total
Latin America	508	65.1
Europe	165	21.1
Middle East–North Africa	58	7.5
Asia	33	4.2
Sub-Saharan Africa	12	1.5
North America (United States)	5	0.6

Since the early 1970s, more terrorist groups have been operational in Latin America than in any other area. A total of 53 such organizations have functioned in 16 nations of that region, compared to the 30 groups found in nine European countries and the substantially smaller numbers in other parts of the world. In brief, Central and South America simply have been much more active areas for guerrilla and terrorist groups—a development that in turn has generated a larger number of abduction operations.

At the same time the level of terrorist activity in Latin America has been increasing, police counter-terrorist capabilities have remained essentially the same. By contrast, many European nations substantially improved their police and military counter-terrorist skills following the 1972 massacre of the Israeli athletes at the Munich Olympics. Additionally, the upgrading of security by government facilities and private firms has taken place more rapidly in Europe than in Latin America.

One element that may help explain the slower reaction to terrorist activity in Latin America than in Europe is the almost integral part that guerrilla operations have had in Latin American life for many years. In Colombia, for example, the "roots" of the present-day Revolutionary Armed Forces of Colombia (FARC) extend back into the late 1930s and the "liberated zones" established by the Communist Party near Viota, Sumapaz, and Marquetalia in Tolima and Cundinamarca Departments. Many of these enclaves were not entered by government forces until the late 1960s. Operations of the FARC itself began in 1966. Similar patterns are evident in Venezuela, Guatemala, Peru, Argentina, and Chile. Terrorist actions in all these nations have been a continuing problem for national governments since the early 1960s.

In contrast to an almost fatalistic acceptance of terrorist operations (including kidnapping) as a part of daily life in many areas of Latin America, this activity is a new development in Europe (except for Spain). Growing out of the student disenchantment of the 1960s, the subsequent organization of active terrorist groups was a surprise to most national governments. With more and better trained police personnel, these governments tended to react rapidly and decisively, in contrast to their Latin American counterparts. This speed may also help to account for the great disparity in abduction figures between the two areas.

While Latin America and Europe are poles apart in regard to the total number of terrorist kidnappings recorded in each area, some significant targeting similarities can still be found between the regions. In both, business personnel are abducted more frequently than any other target group. For Latin America, 50.3 percent of all 508 total kidnappings since 1970 involved businessmen. In Europe the comparable percentage was 55.1 percent. Additionally, both regions recorded almost half of all terrorist abductions since 1970 within the last three and one quarter years. In Latin America, 49.4 percent of all kidnappings occurred during this time span, contrasted to an almost identical 49.7 percent for Europe. Further, all abductions in the two areas were by intranational rather than transnational terrorist groups. Finally, nonbusiness kidnap victims had similar occupations in both areas. Within each region governmental personnel were favored; politicians were second in Latin America, while diplomats were the second choice in Europe.

The similarities between the two areas did not extend to victim survival. In general, this rate has been quite high, particularly among abducted businessmen. On a worldwide basis in the period 1970–82, only 9 percent of those persons taken by terrorist groups were killed. The bulk of these died in police rescue operations rather than at the hands of their abductors. During the 1979–82 time span, Europe accounted for only 10 percent of all persons killed in terrorist abductions. By comparison, 85.5 percent of all kidnap deaths (77 of 90 worldwide fatalities) occurred in Latin America.

Within Latin America, the most active nations for terrorist kidnappings were Argentina, Colombia, and Mexico (during the years 1970–78) and more recently Guatemala, Colombia, and El Salvador (1979–82). In the last three and one-quarter years, the latter nations accounted for 82.1 percent of the 251 total terrorist abductions in the region. Among these states, Guatemala led with 86 kidnappings, followed by Colombia (67) and El Salvador (53). In Guatemala and El Salvador a majority of the abduction actions took place in major urban centers, while in Colombia a number involved wealthy ranchers and farmers taken from their rural estates. Within all these nations, as noted earlier, the prime targets were business personnel, governmental officials, and politicians.

In Europe, terrorist abductions also were concentrated in a few countries. Between 1970 and the end of the first quarter in 1982, Italy and Spain led all other nations. Within the last three and one-quarter years, these two states accounted for 85.4 percent of the 82 kidnappings reported in Europe. Italy had a total of 36 incidents and Spain 34. The bulk of the Italian operations took place in 1979 (29 actions), while those in Spain were rather evenly spread over the entire period.

In both Spain and Italy, business, political, and governmental officials were primary victims. Both nations also experienced actions involving extremely high-level personages. In Italy victims have included Aldo Moro, a former premier and leader of the Christian Democratic Party, Assistant Attorney General Mario Sossi, the personnel chiefs of Fiat and Sit-Siemens, and high-level leaders in the Italian labor movement.

Within Spain, similar level abductions have involved Javier Ibarra y Berge, Chairman of the Board of the Iberduero Corporation, the nation's largest electrical supplier; Antonio Maria de Oriol y Urquijo,[11] a former Minister of the Interior and past personal advisor to King Juan Carlos; General Emilio Villaescusa, former

President of the Supreme Council of Military Justice; and deputies of the nation's major political parties.

Other Areas

Outside Europe and Latin America, terrorist kidnappings have been minimal. All other world areas account for only 108 of the 781 total abductions in the period 1970–82.

As noted earlier, the most active region outside Europe and Latin America has been the Middle East–North Africa. There, Lebanon has been dominant, accounting for more than three quarters of the 58 total incidents reported for the entire region over the last twelve and one-quarter years. Most victims have been politicians or business personnel—the latter held for ransom to fatten the pockets of the various warring factions active in that country.

In Asia, abductions have been limited almost entirely to the Philippines. There the Moro National Liberation Front and the Communist New People's Army have carried out all 33 actions reported between 1970 and the first quarter of 1982. Businessmen, including personnel employed by U.S. firms, have been the major targets. For Sub-Saharan Africa, the 12 actions there are scattered throughout the continent. Political figures were the main victims. Finally, within the continental United States there were five abductions recorded between January 1970 and the close of March 1982. Persons taken included businessmen, police, and local government figures.

THE KIDNAP TEAM

Since data on the organization and structure of abduction teams were initially analyzed during 1978, there has been remarkably little change in either the typical team or its methods of operation. The only three areas in which variations of significance have been noted are (a) a slight increase in team size during recent years; (b) the expanded use of women in these actions; and (c) the increased use of automatic weapons in abduction operations.

Overall kidnap team size remained constant during the early 1970s at 4.1 persons. By 1978, however, this figure had grown to 5.2 and today it stands at 5.8 persons. Female participation during the 1970–76 time span was documented in less than 6 percent of all abductions. In 1978 this figure jumped to 18 percent and currently is close to 25 percent. Within Colombia and some other Latin American nations, as well as Spain, this percentage is even higher.

Coupled with a growth in kidnap team size and female participation was an expansion in the use of automatic weapons (submachine guns). Early in the 1970s, such weapons were used in only 15 percent of all recorded kidnaps. By 1978, however, this figure had doubled to 30 percent, where it now remains.

Looking at these changes, all appear directly related to improved target security. Quite simply, only a larger and better armed group could counter the well-trained security details now assigned to almost all governmental figures and ranking corporate executives. In order to abduct a target, these security elements must be neutralized. Terrorist groups appear to have concluded that the best way to accomplish this goal is by upgrading their weaponry and expanding the abduction team.

Heightened female participation also seems to be security related. Despite the steadily growing proportion of females carrying out active terrorist functions, most males (particularly police officers and security personnel) continue to view women as minimal risks. Working as members of an abduction team, females can use this male viewpoint to their advantage. As noted earlier in this chapter, the Basque Fatherland and Liberty Movement group that abducted wealthy Spanish businessmen Luis Suñer Sanchis on January 13, 1981, was led by a woman. As it turned out, she was the person who was able to by-pass security personnel and reach the intended victim.

While some changes have taken place over the last 12 years in the "typical" terrorist kidnap team, the location of most abduction actions is still the same. Almost 95 percent of all incidents involve a single victim taken while at home, at work, or riding in a vehicle between these two points. With few exceptions, the typical victim continues to be a male. Those few females taken are usually the spouses of an intended victim. Generally, they are abducted only when the primary target is not available for one reason or another. Within a few countries of Latin America, primarily Guatemala and El Salvador, a number of terrorist kidnappings (or attempts) have targeted the children or close relatives of leading governmental figures. The objective in all these actions was to exert maximum political pressure on the target personage, usually through threats to his children or young relatives. In these operations, all targets were heads of state or other very high ranking government officers.

A December 1981 variation on the "proxy" abductions just described involved Spanish surgeon Dr. Julio Iglesias Puga. The father of well-known vocalist Julio Iglesias, the doctor was kidnapped by ETA in downtown Madrid not far from his office. His abduction was designed to extort a $2 million ransom payment from Julio Iglesias, who then resided in Miami, Florida, far from ETA's reach. Since Julio himself could not be abducted, his father was taken as a proxy. Fortunately, Spain's highly capable Special Operations Group of the National Police (trained by the German GSG-9 and very similar in function to that organization) tracked the doctor to an ETA safehouse in the small northern village of Trasmoz. Dr. Puga was taken there in the trunk of a car after being injected with a tranquilizer following his Madrid abduction. The safehouse in which he was held had been used earlier to house Spanish millionaire Luis Suñer Sanchis during his 90-day kidnap ordeal. Assaulting the house during the early morning hours, the Special Operations Group freed Dr. Puga without injury.[11]

As is obvious from this incident, as well as from kidnap statistics that show a 93 percent success rate for the 781 abductions recorded between January 1970 and the close of March 1982, terrorists involved in this type of action are highly skilled. They normally include the most effective members of any terrorist organization. As a result, the Iglesias Puga incident notwithstanding, the probability of rescue is quite low. In too many cases where such rescues are attempted by inept police personnel, as in the August 13, 1981, effort by Guatemalan police to free Goodyear executive Clifford Bevens, the abduction victim dies.

COUNTERMEASURES

Since kidnapping remains an important terrorist tactic despite a recent decline in its use, an obvious question is, Can a potential victim reduce his (or her) chances of abduction by a significant margin? The answer is an unqualified yes. An analysis of the 781 kidnap operations since January 1970 shows clearly that in the vast majority of all cases victims failed to exercise even elementary security practices. Had such practices been followed, the number of abductions probably would have been cut by 50 to 70 percent.

Most of the cases mentioned in this chapter occurred because the targets failed to exercise basic security. Aldo Moro and Daimler-Benz executive Schleyer *invariably* followed the same routes to and from work. Suñer Sanchis *always* worked late despite the fact that his security detail had been reduced. The Dutch, British, Swedish, and Japanese executives discussed earlier were all highly predictable in their daily movements. Dr. Puga maintained the same work schedule day in and day out. Oriol y Urquijo *always* worked on Saturdays, the day he was abducted. Invariably he had a reduced security detail on that day, and he frequently permitted them to play cards in a room down the hall from his office. On the day of his abduction, Oriol y Urquijo literally was taken from the building under the noses of his guards. In case after case this same pattern emerges: an almost total disregard for even the most common sense elements of security.

The recent abduction of U.S. Army Brigadier General James Dozier is another graphic case in point. Although aware the Red Brigades intended to kidnap a senior U.S. officer, the general did not consider himself a target. He continued to follow the same daily routine. No security detail was requested. No residential security practices were implemented. Callers were not screened and his apartment door was opened to almost anyone. The result of these actions is a matter of record.

Interestingly enough, an examination of Italian reporting on this case indicates Dozier probably was not the primary target. Another officer had been selected; however, by accident or design, this individual followed an erratic schedule that made it literally impossible for the Brigades to set up an appropriate abduction site. Without missing a beat, the terrorists turned from this hard target to a "softer" one: the predictable General Dozier.

To enhance unpredictability, a potential target should change his (or her) routes to work daily, on a random basis. Vehicles used in this travel must be exchanged frequently, daily if possible. Locally manufactured cars should be used in preference to the more obvious American or European executive limosines.

If drivers are hired, they must be trained in "offensive" driving tactics and screened for reliability. Professional chauffeurs, whose primary concern is preventing vehicular damage, should be avoided at all costs. In the abduction of Daimler-Benz chief Dr. Schleyer, just such a chauffeur's *predictable* reaction to a crisis situation made the entire operation possible.

Approaching an intersection about 200 meters from Schleyer's home, the driver faced the following situation. Blocking a portion of the intersection was a yellow Mercedes. Moving from left to right across the street was a woman pushing a baby buggy. At this point, the chauffeur had three options: (a) crash through the blocking Mercedes; (b) strike the woman with the buggy; (c) stop. Although aware Schleyer had been threatened by terrorists a number of times and that he had a police escort behind him in another car, the chauffeur reacted predictably: He stopped. Within less than two minutes he had died along with those in the escort vehicle, and Schleyer had been abducted successfully.

Avoiding established patterns of activity is equally important in other areas of personal security—such as at work, at home, or while traveling. By eliminating predictability in all such areas, the potential victim exploits a terrorist group's weakest link: manpower. With a very limited manpower pool, terrorists cannot devote unlimited resources to any single action. Even at the height of European terrorist activity during the period 1976–79, reliable police statistics indicate that the total number of active terrorists in all European groups was only 970–1,000 members.[12]

In the Schleyer case, only 15 persons were involved, which included the six-member assault team. With these limited manpower resources, had Schleyer taken police advice and varied his route as well as travel times each day, it is highly unlikely there would have been enough personnel to even survey the various routes. The net result might well have been his survival. Again, unpredictability is the best single countermeasure against a terrorist abduction.

FUTURE TRENDS IN KIDNAPPING OPERATIONS

Although kidnapping operations have declined somewhat since 1979, they still remain an important terrorist tactic, particularly for the generation of operational funds. As a result, looking toward the immediate future, businessmen probably will remain the primary abduction targets—especially in Europe and Latin America. Even though revenues from such actions have dropped, a single successful action on the scale of the Suñer Sanchis incident will solve a group's financial problems for years to come.

Aside from business personnel, other important abduction targets include government figures, politicians, and quite possibly more U.S. military personnel. In regard to this latter group, the abduction of General James Dozier should be studied carefully. It may well be a harbinger of things to come.

Although technically a failure, the Dozier kidnapping met many of the objectives sought by any terrorist group. First, it seriously embarrassed the Italian government by demonstrating its inability to counter an operation of this type—much less to protect important Allied personnel. Police confusion and a continued failure to apprehend the abductors were shown "live" to a worldwide audience day by day. Second, the action was a propaganda bonanza for the Brigades and clearly demonstrated their operational expertise in comparison to that of the police. Finally, the incident reflected Italian terrorist solidarity with other European revolutionary groups and urged them to emulate the operation. Viewed from these perspectives, the action was by no means a failure. It would not be surprising to see an attempted replay of the scenario in another nation within the not too distant future.

The possibility of such a replay is enhanced by the current tough line taken by the U.S. government against terrorist activity. An integral part of this position is assistance to the military and police forces of those nations attempting to curb terrorism. In such assistance programs, the U.S. military invariably plays an important role. For the terrorists, then, members of the U.S. military establishment become logical targets, even though they may not be directly involved in counterterrorist training or assistance. This fact, along with an increasingly visible and expanding U.S. military presence in many areas of the world, greatly increases the possibility of another Dozier-type abduction.

NOTES

1. The executives taken were Kjell Bjork of Telefonico L. M. Ericson (Swedish); Fritz Schuitema, Phillips Corp. (Dutch); Michael Chatterton and Ian Massie, Bank of London and South America (British); and Takakuzu Suzuki, Insinca Corp. (Japanese). Details on the incident may be found in *Regional Risk Assessment–Latin America, April 1979* (Alexandria, VA: Risks International), p. 60.

2. For more information on the "revolutionary tax" see "Desafía Industrial del País Vasco a la Organización ETA," *Agency France Press,* San Sebastian, Spain, report dated April 30, 1981.

3. The Suñer Sanchis incident is well summarized in the following press reports: "Se Encuentra Secuestrado el Ciudadano que Declaró más Ingresos a la Hacienda Española" *EFE* (Spanish News Agency), Valencia, Spain, report dated January 15, 1981; "Pide ETA 2 Milliones y Medio para Librar al Millionario Industrial Luis Suñer Sanchis," *UPI,* Alicante, Spain, report dated January 17, 1981; "Secuestran a uno de los más Ricos Industriales," *UPI,* Alcira, Spain, report dated January 14, 1981; "Lanza la Policía Centenares de Refuerzos en la Búsqueda del Industrial Secuestrado," *UPI,* Alicante, Spain, report dated January 17, 1981; "Prominente Abogado Vasco Sirvio como Intermediario en el Secuestro de Suñer Sanchis," *UPI,* Madrid, Spain, report dated April 20, 1981; "Intrigada España por el Rescate de Luis Suñer Sanchis," *EFE,* Madrid, Spain, report dated April 18, 1981; and "Costo $4 Milliones Rescatar a Luis Suñer," *EFE,* Valencia, Spain, report dated April 16, 1981.

4. *Brigate Rosse: Rizoluzione della Direzione Strategica,* February 1978, p. 2.

5. *Ibid.,* p. 41.

6. Abraham Guillen, *The Philosophy of the Urban Guerrilla: The Revolutionary Writings of Abraham Guillen,* trans. Donald C. Hodges (New York: Morrow, 1977), p. 295.

7. These figures represent estimates based on known ransom payments in 32 percent of the 781 abductions, for the period 1970–82.

8. See "Secuestra el M-19 a 3 Periodistas," *Agency France Press,* Barranquilla, Colombia, report dated May 24, 1982.

9.   The best and by far the most accurate work on Italian terrorism has been done by Vittorfranco S. Pisano of the Law Library, Library of Congress. See his excellent *Contemporary Italian Terrorism: Analysis and Countermeasures* (Washington: Library of Congress, Law Library, 1979).

10.   Additional detail on this act is found in *Operación Cromo: Informe Oficial de los GRAPO,* Madrid, 1977.

11.   The Iglesias Puga case is summarized in the following press reports: "Se Anota Importante Exito la Policía Española al Liberar Sano y Salvo al Doctor Iglesias," *EFE,* Madrid, Spain, report dated January 18, 1982; "Historia del Secuestro," *EFE,* Miami, Florida, report dated January 21, 1982.

12.   *Regional Risk Assessment, Europe, February 1979* (Alexandria, VA: Risks International, 1979), p. 2.

3

Diplomatic Kidnappings

Carol Edler Baumann

THE TACTIC OF "DIPLONAPPING"

The technique of kidnapping diplomats and holding them for ransom—or "diplonapping"[1]—shares the same rationale as international terrorism in general, though it embodies certain unique attributes that add to its special appeal for terrorists. As one type of political violence, terrorism is used by terrorists as a psychological weapon that magnifies its impact far beyond its immediate victim onto a larger stage and for a larger audience, including governments both directly and indirectly involved. Diplonappings are particularly qualified as terrorist acts because they automatically affect both the government of the host state in which the act was committed and the government of the kidnapped diplomat. The act itself may be aimed against either—or both.

Kidnapping diplomats was specifically recommended by Carlos Marighella, one of the early theorists and advocates of terrorism as a tool of revolutionary violence. In his *Minimanual of the Urban Guerrilla,* the Brazilian terrorist emphasized the aggressive, offensive nature of urban terrorism, the need to attack and retreat in quick and efficient operations, and the aim of distracting and demoralizing "the enemy." Marighella's "action models" included the liberation of prisoners, executions, kidnappings, sabotage, terrorism, armed propaganda, and a constant war of nerves against the government in power. Though Marighella wrote that the "liberation of prisoners is an armed operation designed to free the jailed urban guerrilla,"[2] the difficulty and relative lack of success in accomplishing that task by direct raids and assaults led to the increased use of diplonapping as an alternative tactic—bartering the kidnapped diplomat in exchange for the release of jailed prisoners.

In his *Minimanual* Marighella recommended the capturing and secret holding of a police agent, "North American Spy," political personality, or "notorious enemy of the revolutionary movement" as a technique "to exchange or liberate imprisoned revolutionary comrades, or to force the suspension of torture in the jail cells."[3] Acting on his own advice, Marighella participated in the successful 1969 kidnapping of then U.S. Ambassador to Brazil, C. Burke Elbrick, which resulted in the release of 15 designated "political prisoners" and in the publication of the entire text of the terrorists' manifesto. The Elbrick case, representative of several in Latin America,

23

clearly illustrated the double value to terrorists of diplonapping as a way both to liberate jailed prisoners and to secure worldwide publicity for their cause.

Extensive publicity in itself has frequently been sought by terrorists as a major aim of their struggle; again, the kidnapping of diplomats has been particularly suited to serve that purpose. Diplonappings derive their effectiveness as weapons of political leverage, propaganda, and publicity primarily because they so blatantly violate the principle of diplomatic inviolability and thus automatically concern not only the governments of the kidnapped diplomats and the host governments that bear responsibility for special protection, but also the entire diplomatic community as well. Because of the media attention captured by the drama of a high-level kidnapping, diplonapping is able to give what might be in reality a relatively small and impotent group of terrorists an image of being a well-organized, strong, and determined political force.

Terrorism, in fact, has generally served as a weapon of the weak, not the strong. It is resorted to when the political and military organization of an insurgent group has not developed sufficiently for full-scale revolution or even for guerrilla warfare. Because the struggle therefore may be a long and protracted one, the violence of terrorism must also be continued and/or its impact magnified. The latter can be done most effectively by the media. It is a truism that "the media are the terrorist's best friend. The terrorist's act by itself is nothing; publicity is all."[4] The publicity naturally attendant upon the kidnapping of a foreign diplomat and further extended by press and TV coverage is thus manipulated by the kidnappers in an attempt to gain the attention of a broad and significant audience, to propagandize their goals and so legitimize their *raison d'être,* to instill fear in the diplomatic community and in the populace at large, and to discredit and demoralize the government in its reputation abroad and in its effectiveness at home.

Diplomats have thus emerged as the prominent targets of terrorist kidnappers both because of their utility as ransom trades for the release of imprisoned terrorists and because of their symbolic value as representatives of foreign governments. Kidnappings of diplomats provoke immediate and dramatic responses, not just by families or corporations, as in the case of international business targets, but by governments themselves—and usually at high levels. Seeking to influence governments to act or not to act regarding specific terrorist goals as well as to gain media exposure and publicity for their own political programs, diplomatic kidnappers use their victims as tools for those purposes, regardless of whether the specific victim is associated in any way with the actual area of conflict.

> Although some may argue that attacks against diplomats are senseless, in the mind of the terrorist it is a calculated act with deliberate goals and objectives. . . . It is the symbolism of the individual terrorist act, and not necessarily the act itself, which gives it significance. The terrorist uses the act to make a political statement to the target (which is not the victim) and to the world at large.[5]

To assess the tactic of diplonapping more comprehensively requires taking a closer look at the statistics on the nationalities of the victims involved and on the regions and countries in which kidnappings or kidnapping attempts took place. It is also necessary to examine a sampling of the kinds of demands made and the outcomes that followed in response to them. At this point, however, a few numbers may suffice to provide a brief summary of those cases in which diplomats have been kidnapped and held hostage for specific political and/or monetary ransom demands. According to a 1981 statistical overview of international terrorist attacks against diplomatic personnel and facilities, published by the U.S. Department of State, at least 130 diplomatic kidnapping incidents have taken place in the period surveyed (January 1968–July 1981).[6] Diplomats from 54 different countries have been taken hostage, and diplomatic kidnappings have occurred in 57 countries, almost half of which are in Latin America.[7]

The actions of terrorist groups that have engaged specifically in diplonappings are representative of the broader categories of terrorist attacks directed against the diplomatic community in general. For example, Brian Jenkins of The Rand Corporation has identified five principal types of terrorist activities directed against diplomats: (a) those associated with guerrilla warfare, insurgency, or ongoing terrorist activity, (b) those by ethnic, emigré, or exile groups against a particular nation or regime, (c) worldwide attacks by terrorists abroad as part of a larger campaign against a specific government, (d) those by indigenous groups to protest the actions of a foreign government, and (e) government use of terrorist tactics or groups in surrogate warfare against a foreign foe. Diplomatic kidnappings have been employed in all five of these categories, although most of them have taken place in conjunction with categories one, three, and four.

Alternatively, if one categorizes terrorist attacks against diplomats by *motivation,* three principal groups may be identified for purposes of analysis and policy formulation: (a) the ideologically motivated, (b) ethnic/religious/linguistic separatists, and (c) revolutionary insurgents. Here again, the terrorists who have engaged in diplonappings are represented in all three categories, although a larger number of them have been motivated by ideology or by revolutionary goals than by separatism, which has more frequently led to assassination or bombing than to kidnapping.

A final distinction may be useful for the purpose of this overview of the diplonapping tactic. The next section points out that although the number of cases of kidnapping and holding diplomats hostage to specified ransom demands has not increased in tandem with terrorist attacks on diplomats in general, the number of "barricade-hostage" incidents or seizures of diplomatic facilities has multiplied significantly. Whereas the kidnappings of diplomats that took place in the late 1960s and early 1970s exemplified a serious, but relatively low-level trend of small-scale violence, in recent years a noticeable and disturbing increase in mob violence has occurred. Between 1970 and 1980 there were over 70 forcible incursions into diplomatic premises; more than 50 percent of these took place after the seizure of the U.S. Embassy in Tehran.[8] The implications inherent in this statistic will be examined in those sections dealing with policy issues and future trends, but at the least they include the problems of embassy security and the contention that "the success achieved in that incident created a model for other terrorist groups to emulate."[9]

DIMENSIONS OF THE PROBLEM

The problem of diplomatic kidnappings and terrorist attacks against diplomats in general represents a significant dimension of the overall problem of international terrorism and personal security within the politically turbulent and frequently violent world of the end of the twentieth century. The total number of international terrorist incidents directed against diplomats and/or foreign embassies and consulates has increased exponentially since 1968 (a fivefold increase in 13 years) and represents 25 percent of all international terrorist incidents. Although specific cases of "traditional" diplomatic kidnappings in which the diplomats were held hostage to specified ransom demands have not increased correspondingly, the number of terrorist seizures of diplomatic facilities, including the diplomatic personnel within ("barricade-hostage" incidents), has paralleled the overall growth in terrorist attacks against diplomats.

According to the State Department's statistical overview of international terrorist attacks against diplomatic personnel and facilities,[10] international terrorist incidents aimed at diplomats increased from 80 in 1968 to 409 in 1980 (excluding "threats," which grew from 69 to 312). During the same period, barricade-hostage incidents involving diplomatic personnel increased from 1 in 1968 to a total of 25 in 1980. Specific incidents of diplomatic kidnappings, however, ranged from a low of 1 in 1968 to a high of 30 in 1970 down to 4 in 1980. Not only have these terrorist attacks against diplomats increased in absolute numbers, but they also have resulted in more casualties and have involved diplomats from a growing number of countries.[11]

The dimensions of the problem of international terrorist attacks against diplomats extend far beyond the recitation of mere numbers, significant and dramatic though they are. Diplomats have been singled out for such attacks specifically because of the positions they hold and the functions they perform. International relations between sovereign states have traditionally been conducted under the international legal rules of "diplomacy" and through regularized contacts between "diplomats." Despite the burgeoning of summit conferences between heads of state and the frenzied dispatching of ad hoc troubleshooters around the world on special assignments, the day-to-day conduct of diplomacy has continued to be the domain of the resident diplomats. To ensure the continuity of those contacts, states have sought to protect the personal inviolability and security of their diplomatic agents through the concept of diplomatic privileges and immunities, which developed historically in tandem with the growth of diplomacy itself.

Diplomatic privileges and immunities thus developed both in customary and in codified international law as adjuncts to the legal principle of the personal inviolability of diplomats. That inviolability in turn arises from necessity itself—the recognition that international diplomacy is vitally dependent upon the personal security of those diplomatic agents who conduct it. These precepts have been codified in the Vienna Convention on Diplomatic Relations,[12] the Vienna Convention on Consular Relations,[13] and the Convention on the Privileges and Immunities of the United Nations.[14] The diplomatic kidnappings, therefore, not only challenge the general principles and established customs of international law, but also transgress against widely accepted international treaties and codified conventions.

A third dimension of the problem involves state responsibility for the protection and security of diplomats. Under international law, all states are obligated to provide special protection to diplomats precisely because of their diplomatic inviolability. Any injurious acts, attacks, or insults against a state's diplomatic agents may be considered as injuries against the state itself, and a claim for redress may be brought by that state on its own behalf. Diplomatic inviolability may be infringed either by the direct action of the state itself or by private individuals who were not prevented from engaging in such acts by adequate state protection. Although the degree of due diligence a state must exercise to prevent such injury or the extent of special protection that is required may vary according to circumstances, both require extra effort to prevent anticipated injuries (particularly if the threat or danger is notorious or recurrent), as well as prosecution and punishment, apology and redress for those injuries that the state is unable to prevent.

Formalistic as they may sound, these obligations are not merely theoretical abstractions or legal niceties. One of the principal aims of terrorist attacks against diplomats is to demonstrate the weakness, incapacity, or unwillingness of a host government to carry out its legal obligations and security responsibilities. It is precisely because of the personal inviolability that surrounds diplomats and the special protection that states owe to them, that international terrorists have singled them out as their favorite targets. The kidnapping of an American diplomat in Brazil, for example, presents not only an affront to the dignity of the United States, but, equally, a challenge to the domestic tranquillity and international stature of the government of Brazil.

A final and related aspect of the problems created by terrorist attacks against and successful kidnappings of foreign diplomats is the policy issue of asylum versus extradition or prosecution. Since many diplomatic kidnappings have been conducted to secure a trade of designated "political prisoners" in exchange for the kidnapped diplomat, a temporary asylum for any freed prisoners in some foreign embassy has frequently been presented as part of the demand. Such "extra-territorial" asylum is neither sanctioned by international law nor generally granted in practice, except in Latin America where it exists as a regional exception. In that region, those prisoners who have been traded for the release of various diplomatic hostages were on several occasions accorded temporary asylum within designated foreign embassies.

More relevant to the problem of terrorism in general, however, are the legal and customary rules regarding the granting of territorial asylum to the terrorists themselves. All states possess the right to grant or to deny asylum to those accused of political offenses; likewise, extradition to the state in which the alleged crime took place may be granted or denied on the basis of whether or not the state of potential asylum regards the refugee as a political offender.

Political offenses have usually been defined more by excluding certain acts from that category than by specifying those acts included in it. In domestic criminal codes and statutes, however, such acts as treason, rebellion, sedition, insurrection, sabotage, and espionage are usually classified as political offenses and therefore may be exempt from extradition procedures. Recent international treaties and conventions have clearly designated both terrorism and the kidnapping of diplomats *not* as political offenses, but as common crimes subject to extradition or prosecution.

Thus, the 1971 Organization of American States (OAS) Convention[15] to prevent and punish acts of terrorism specifies kidnapping and other assaults on specially protected persons as common crimes, subject to extradition or prosecution. Similarly, the 1973 U.N. Convention on the Prevention and Punishment of Crimes Against Internationally Protected Persons, Including Diplomatic Agents[16] obliges signatory states to make punishable the acts of murder, kidnapping, or other attacks against internationally protected persons, and requires states in whose territory the alleged offender is present to extradite or to prosecute the offender. Finally, in 1979 the U.N. General Assembly adopted the Convention Against the Taking of Hostages,[17] which specifically defines an offender as:

> Any person who seizes or detains and threatens to kill, to injure or to continue to detain another person (hereinafter referred to as the "hostage") in order to compel a third party, namely, a State, an international intergovernmental organization, a natural or a juridical person, or a group of persons, to do or abstain from doing any act as an explicit or implicit condition for the release of the hostage, commits the offence of hostage-taking within the meaning of this Convention. (Article I)

In summary, then, terrorist attacks against diplomats have increased dramatically in recent years, inhibiting if not preventing the normal conduct of international diplomacy. Such attacks have infringed upon the legal precepts of diplomatic privileges and immunities and have placed into such serious question the practical significance of diplomatic inviolability that a recent scholarly paper on the subject went so far as to assert: "There is no longer any such thing as a local war. There are no bystanders. There is no diplomatic immunity. Terrorists have defined diplomats as 'legitimate' targets."[18]

The ability of states to carry out their obligations of special protection for diplomatic personnel has been severely stymied, if not vitally impaired. The only ray of light that slightly penetrates this gloomy assessment of the dimension of the problem is the limited progress made in defining terrorism in general and attacks against diplomats specifically as common crimes, subject to prosecution or extradition.

THE SETTING: VICTIMS AND LOCATIONS

The following statistical charts provide a comprehensive overview of the extent to which diplomatic kidnappings have been attempted or carried out by terrorists on a global scale. All three tables are based on an open-source computer search of all reported diplomatic kidnappings, unsuccessful kidnapping attempts, and kidnapping plans or threats (as identified by the CIA's Terrorism Analysis Unit) between

January 1968, and January 1982. Table 3.1 classifies all of these kidnappings, attempts, and threats on the basis of the nationality of the victim. Table 3.2 classifies them on the basis of the region and country location of the event itself; it is also broken down into the number of incidents involving U.S. diplomats and those involving all other diplomats. Table 3.3 depicts all incidents involving U.S. diplomats only, and distinguishes between actual kidnappings, unsuccessful attempts, and uncovered plots or reported threats.

It may be of interest to compare and contrast the Table 4.1 statistics on specific incidents of diplomatic kidnappings, attempts, or threats with those on all terrorist attacks directed against diplomats, including kidnappings.[19] Whereas North American diplomats have the dubious honor of being the most frequent targets of all diplonapping attempts as well as the most frequent victims of terrorist attacks in general, the runners up diverge. Diplomats from the countries of Western Europe are the next favorite targets of would-be diplonappers, but Middle Eastern diplomats stand second in line as victims of all terrorist attacks. On a country-by-country basis the line-up also differs: For all terrorist attacks against diplomats, the most frequently targeted victims, in order, are from the United States, Israel, the Soviet Union, the United Kingdom, Cuba, and Turkey; for diplomatic kidnappings the ranking is the United States, West Germany, France, the United Kingdom, and Iran.

Table 3.2, which classifies diplomatic kidnappings by the region and country of occurrence, also presents some interesting contrasts when compared with the statistics on which regions and countries are the favorite locales for *all* types of terrorist activities directed against diplomats. Whereas over 28 percent of *all* terrorist attacks on diplomats took place in Western Europe and over 26 percent of such attacks occurred in Latin America, Latin America emerged as the favorite region, by far, for specific incidents of diplomatic kidnappings or kidnapping attempts. Out of a total of 150 such incidents (between 1968 and 1982) 76, or over half, took place in Latin America, and 29, or about one-fifth, occurred in Western Europe.

Whereas over 12 percent of all terrorist attacks on diplomats took place in the United States (more than in any other single country), the United States was the locale of only three kidnappings or kidnapping attempts. Most of the incidents in the United States have been symbolic bombings. Those countries in which most kidnappings, attempts, or threats have taken place are Mexico (11), Colombia and Guatemala (9 each), and Brazil, El Salvador, and Lebanon (8 each). In contrast, the country ranking for all types of terrorist incidents involving diplomats is the United States, France, the Netherlands, West Germany, Greece, and Argentina. It also is of interest to note that although the statistics show that Soviet and East European (East German) diplomats were among the victims of kidnapping attempts, no such attempts or threats occurred either in the Soviet Union or in Eastern Europe, at least according to the public record.

Finally, Table 3.3 also illustrates the predominance of Latin America as the favorite locale of successful diplonappings and kidnapping attempts directed against *U.S.* diplomatic targets. Of a total of 53 kidnappings, kidnapping attempts, or plots and threats thereof that were aimed at U.S. diplomats, some 28 or over

Table 3.1 Classification of Kidnapping Incidents by Nationality of Victim, 1968–82

Region and Country*	No. of Incidents	Regional Totals
Africa		1
South Africa	1	
East Asia		5
Indonesia	2	
Japan	2	
Philippines	1	
Latin America		20
Bolivia	2	
Brazil	1	
Chile	1	
Costa Rica	1	
Cuba	2	
Dominican Republic	1	
Ecuador	1	
Guatemala	1	
Mexico	1	
Nicaragua	2	
Panama	3	
Paraguay	1	
Uruguay	2	
Venezuela	1	
Near East and South Asia		18
Egypt	3	
India	2	
Iran	5	
Israel	3	
Jordan	1	
Lebanon	1	
Saudi Arabia	1	
Tunisia	1	
Turkey	1	
North America		54
Canada	1	
United States	53	
Western Europe		44
Austria	2	
Belgium	4	
Denmark	1	
Federal Republic of Germany (West Germany)	10	
Finland	1	
France	8	
Italy	1	
Netherlands	2	
Norway	1	

Table 3.1   (continued)

Spain	2	
Sweden	1	
Switzerland	4	
United Kingdom	6	
Yugoslavia	1	
USSR and Eastern Europe		2
German Democratic Republic		
(East Germany)	1	
USSR	1	
International Organizations and		
Nongovernmental Organizations†		6
N.A.		6
GLOBAL TOTAL		150

* The regions listed and the countries included therein correspond generally to those used by the Department of State, except that Canada has been included here in a North American region and Europe has been divided between Western Europe and the USSR and Eastern Europe.

† Included here are incidents and threats against international civil servants, employees of non-governmental organizations, and generalized threats against the diplomats of several countries.

Table 3.2   Classification of Kidnapping Incidents by Location of Event, 1968–82

Region and Country	U.S. Diplomats	Others	Regional Totals by Nationality of Victim U.S.	Others
Africa			6	6
Burundi	1	—		
Ethiopia	3	2		
Lesotho	—	1		
Sierra Leone	1	—		
Somalia	—	1		
South Africa	—	1		
Sudan	1	—		
Uganda	—	1		
East Asia			2	3
Bangladesh	—	1		
Malaysia	—	1		
Philippines	2	—		
Thailand	—	1		
Latin America			29	47
Argentina	2	4		
Boliva	3	—		
Brazil	4	4		
Columbia	3	6		
Cuba	—	2		

Table 3.2   (*continued*)

Region and Country	U.S. Diplomats	Others	Regional Totals by Nationality of Victim U.S.	Others
Dominican Republic	3	1		
Ecuador	1	—		
El Salvador	—	8		
Guatemala	3	6		
Haiti	1	—		
Honduras	—	3		
Mexico	3	8		
Nicaragua	2	—		
Puerto Rico	—	1		
Uruguay	3	2		
Venezuela	1	2		
Near East and South Asia			11	11
Afghanistan	1	—		
Algeria	—	1		
Iran	3	1		
Iraq	—	2		
Israel	—	1		
Jordan	3	—		
Kuwait	—	1		
Lebanon	4	4		
Tunisia	—	1		
North America			1	5
Canada	1	2		
United States	—	3		
Western Europe			4	25
Austria	—	1		
Belgium	—	1		
Federal Republic of Germany (West Germany)	1	—		
France	—	4		
Greece	1	—		
Italy	—	2		
Netherlands	—	4		
Norway	—	1		
Spain	—	3		
Sweden	—	4		
Turkey	2	2		
United Kingdom	—	2		
United Kingdom (Northern Ireland)	—	1		
			U.S.	Others
TOTALS			53	97

Table 3.3 Kidnapping Incidents Involving Only U.S. Diplomats, 1968–82

Region and Country	"Successful" Kidnappings	Unsuccessful Attempts	Uncovered Plots/ Reported Threats
Africa	3	—	3
Burundi	—	—	1
Ethiopia	2	—	1
Sierra Leone	—	—	1
Sudan	1	—	—
East Asia	—	—	2
Philippines	—	—	2
Latin America	17	6	6
Argentina	2	—	—
Bolivia	—	2	1
Brazil	1	2	1
Colombia	3	—	—
Dominican Republic	2	—	1
Ecuador	—	—	1
Guatemala	3	—	—
Haiti	1	—	—
Mexico	2	—	1
Nicaragua	—	1	1
Uruguay	3	—	—
Venezuela	—	1	—
Near East and South Asia	8	3	—
Afghanistan	1	—	—
Iran	2	1	—
Jordan	2	1	—
Lebanon	3	1	—
North America	—	—	1
Canada	—	—	1
Western Europe	—	—	4
Federal Republic of Germany (West Germany)	—	—	1
Greece	—	—	1
Turkey	—	—	2
TOTALS	28	9	16

half were "successful" in the sense that the targeted diplomat was actually captured and held by the terrorists for a specified period of time. (They were *not* all successful in actually getting demands met.) Of those 28 successful cases, 17 took place in Latin America; of the total number of 53 incidents directed against U.S. diplomats, 29 or almost three fifths occurred in Latin America. This figure compares with only 6 such incidents in Africa, 11 in the Near East and South Asia, and only 4 in Western Europe.

The conclusions that might be drawn from all three charts are apt to read like an insurance company's risk calculations: The premiums for any coverage against diplomatic kidnappings would be highest for U.S. diplomats (followed by those from Western Europe) assigned to Latin American posts. If the insurance were to include protection against terrorist activities in general, Western Europe would vie with Latin America as a high-risk locale, and diplomats from the Middle East would be included in the high-premium category. Unfortunately, the policy calculations demanded by the imperatives of international diplomacy and national interest are far more complex than those derived from an insurance chart. The next section delineates these principal policy issues and explores relevant strategic alternatives directed toward their solution.

POLICY ISSUES

Strategies

The policy issues raised by diplomatic kidnappings may be divided into questions of strategy (how best to deal with them in terms of prevention and control) and questions of tactics (how to handle actual kidnapping cases when they occur). They also may be analyzed theoretically and generically (what theoretical approaches might produce which desired responses) or in very practical and specific terms (what policy was followed and what action was taken by which government in any particular situation). For the purpose of an overall summary, this section first sets forth various strategic approaches in general terms, illustrating them with specific governmental policies; it then briefly examines some of the tactical options presented by actual diplonapping cases and the actions taken by the states involved.

Most policy recommendations of a strategic nature have been based on the concepts of prevention and control. But there are assumptions implicit in such concepts that are not entirely self-evident. The argument has been developed,[20] for example, that the concept of prevention

> . . . assumes, first of all, that deterrence is possible; that if adequate security and other preventive policies are adopted, the diplonappers can, in fact, be deterred. This in turn assumes that the kidnappers are rational, can draw the proper conclusions from previous governmental statements and actions, and will weigh the actual risks involved against the potential rewards in any actions they undertake. Secondly, the concept of prevention assumes that the problem of diplonapping has escalated to a level where it can no longer be tolerated as a mere fact of international life and that the governments most concerned must and can act jointly to institute preventive measures. Finally, prevention implies the adoption of policies which will both "maximize the risks" and "minimize the rewards" which can reasonably be expected by those contemplating a diplonapping attempt. This means both increased security measures in order to make any kidnapping attempt as difficult and dangerous as possible, and a firm position on no ransom and no asylum if such security measures do not immediately succeed. The latter policy of minimizing the rewards by refusing to accede to ransom demands is, of course, the most difficult to deal with—both politically and morally.

The concept of control, on the other hand, recognizes that not all potential kidnappers *will* be deterred by the risks of injury or death, of capture or imprisonment, and that the rewards of freed compatriots may not be all they seek. For example, maximizing the risks will do little to deter the determined nihilist who plots the *Götterdämmerung* of all existing political and economic institutions with neither plan nor program to substitute in their place; nor will it deter the dedicated revolutionary who wants nothing more than to be remembered as a true martyr to his political cause. Likewise, minimizing the rewards of ransom will do little to deter those terrorists who are motivated less by the prospects of securing the release of political prisoners, than by the excitement engendered by the terrorist act itself and by the worldwide attention and publicity it evokes.

Recognizing that absolute deterrence is not possible, the concept of control attempts to augment that of prevention by an increased emphasis upon intelligence, security, and punishment. Intelligence operations for this purpose are generally designed to penetrate terrorist groups, to gain advance knowledge of their plans and targets, and to foil or limit the damage of those exploits that deterrence alone has failed to prevent. Improved security measures are also advocated, not only to *deter* by threat or risk of death or imprisonment, but to implement that threat if deterrence fails, to protect the intended victims and their premises, and to limit the extent of damage. Finally, the concept of control emphasizes the prosecution and punishment of convicted terrorists, again not only to deter other would-be kidnappers, but to eliminate further terrorist activities by those already captured. Control is thus aimed at limiting the effectiveness of terrorist groups, the degree of damage that they wreak, and the injuries or deaths that they otherwise might cause.

A strategy based on concepts of prevention and control involves the adoption and consistent implementation of the following parallel and mutually reinforcing policies:

- (a) expanded security measures for all diplomatic personnel and their premises (including intelligence collection and analysis on terrorist groups) both to deter potential diplonappers by maximizing risks and by minimizing rewards, and to limit the extent of damage and the number of injuries and deaths by protecting the intended victims and targets;
- (b) no ransom of either money or released prisoners in exchange for kidnapped diplomats and no asylum for the alleged kidnappers of diplomats, who would be prosecuted or extradited as common criminals;
- (c) advocacy and support for national legislation and for regional and international cooperation to implement the above, as well as for worldwide agreement on the definition, prevention, and punishment of crimes against diplomats (universal ratification of the 1973 New York Convention regarding internationally protected persons and of the 1979 U.N. Convention Against the Taking of Hostages); and
- (d) renewed emphasis upon the dual obligation of all states both to protect diplomatic personnel and to refrain from any acts of acquiescence or complic-

ity in terrorist activities; such a policy would aim directly at the problems created by state-supported or state-sponsored terrorism.

In practice, many of these policies have been adopted and pursued by several states, including the United States and countries of Western Europe. Enhanced security procedures that have been followed by these governments and others include such measures as the employment of more bodyguards and armored cars, a reduction in the size of embassy and consulate staffs, curtailment of travel and increased secrecy regarding travel plans, switched and staggered work hours, the use of nonofficial license plates and nondescript vehicles, and improved protection of embassy/consulate premises. The United States, for example, has attempted to reduce the vulnerability of its overseas diplomatic missions ". . . by constructing perimeter defenses, building secure safehavens to which staff can retreat in the event of an attack, improving access controls, and installing nonlethal entry denial systems."[21] In addition, all State Department personnel are required to attend a seminar on coping with violence abroad, which alerts them to the dimensions of on-going security problems and educates them on how to reduce their own vulnerability to terrorist attacks.

But these security measures, necessary though they may be, have not been introduced without costs—both functional and monetary. In functional terms, for example, two of the traditional tasks of U.S. embassy and consular staff have been to represent the goals and policies of the United States to the governments and to the people of other countries and, in turn, to gain an understanding of the official policies of those governments and of the attitudes and opinions of their people and to report back on them to Washington. Such representational and reporting functions can only be severely hampered by the use of bodyguards, reductions in travel, and curtailed communications with the local citizenry. In addition, the U.S. Department of State now spends approximately 14 percent of its entire budget (about $140 million annually) on security measures and protection devices.[22] Moreover, other governments have been estimated to be devoting an annual 3,000 man-years solely to the protection of U.S. diplomats abroad (a total cost of $200 million annually).[23]

The other policies mandated by a strategy of prevention and control have been implemented on a less consistent basis than those of increased security. On the no-ransom issue, the United States has made it abundantly clear that

The U.S. Government will make no concessions to terrorists. We will not negotiate the payment of ransom nor the release of prisoners. We will work to ensure that the perpetrators of terrorist acts are brought to justice. . . . Concessions, whenever they are made, only encourage further attacks and put additional people at risk.[24]

It is highly conceivable, however, that certain situations could arise in which an absolutely adamant no-ransom, no-concessions policy would be sorely strained by the pressures of political realism. Moreover, other nations, particularly some in Latin America, have been less enamored of a tightly structured no-concessions policy and have frequently engaged in ransom trades.

Although the policy of no asylum for captured kidnappers or other terrorists has also met with mixed adherence historically, the adoption of three major regional and U.N. conventions that call for the prosecution or extradition of alleged violators of diplomatic immunity may gradually lead to more uniform practice. The OAS Convention of 1971 that specifies kidnapping as a common crime, the 1973 New York Convention on the prevention and punishment of crimes against diplomats, and the 1979 U.N. Convention against the taking of hostages have already been mentioned in this regard. However, the efficacy of these international agreements has been sadly impaired by the fact that there are only six parties to the OAS Convention, and the 1973 and 1979 U.N. conventions had been ratified by only 53 and 17 states respectively as of June 1982. Without a universal agreement, even a modest increase in the number of states that have ratified these agreements would be a helpful step toward developing the broad consensus required for an *internationally* effective strategy.

Finally, in reviewing the practice of states with regard to a policy requiring both positive commitment to diplomatic protection and negative restraint from any act of acquiescence or complicity in terrorist activities, a mixed record again emerges. Although most states ascribe at least implicitly to the Vienna Convention on Diplomatic Relations[25] (which requires receiving states to take all appropriate steps to prevent any attack on the "person, freedom or dignity" of diplomatic agents), their conduct toward state-sponsored or state-supported acts of terrorism directed at or involving diplomatic personnel or facilities has been less unanimous. The failure of the government of Iran to prevent the takeover of the American Embassy in Tehran and its ultimate complicity in hostage detention and ransom demands for their release, the culpability of the Libyan government in targeting the diplomats of other countries for assassination, and the acquiescence by the government of South Yemen in the use of its territory for terrorist training camps are all too well known and documented to require more than a mention in passing.

Widespread international agreement that such actions are clear violations of international law has not led to unified international action to prevent or limit them. It has been logically argued that since all governments send diplomatic representatives abroad and there is basic consensus that they should be protected, then a reasonable assumption is that "a stringent convention reasserting diplomatic immunity and calling for the isolation of those nations that are negligent in providing security for diplomats . . . should have a good chance of widespread acceptance."[26] Likewise, it has been posited that the general condemnation of state-supported or state-sponsored terrorism in principle could become the basis for a new agreement calling for collective sanctions against an offending state, on the order of the Bonn Agreement on hijacking.[27] However, the same study also emphasizes the limits to international cooperation and to uniform enforcement of international agreements, in that "for economic reasons, for domestic political reasons, for reasons of foreign policy, not all nations may be able or willing to take active measures against violators in every instance."[28]

Tactics

Turning now to the tactical questions that must be considered by governments when actually dealing with diplonapping cases, some options (e.g., releasing prisoners) may be ruled out in advance by the adoption of a clear no-ransom policy. Others, however, arise as matters for ad hoc decision making: negotiations with the terrorists on such nonransom matters as safe transit for themselves or the health and welfare of the kidnapped diplomat; communications with the terrorists, the host government, the home government, and the publics involved; coordination of activities and crisis management; and pros and cons of proposed rescue attempts or assault operations.

A no-concessions or no-ransom policy does not necessarily imply a no-negotiation stance. Some governments, for example, may adamantly refuse to release any imprisoned terrorists in a ransom trade, but they may be willing to negotiate with the diplonappers regarding their own safe transit to another country of asylum if they release their hostage unharmed. Or they may negotiate the terms for specified media exposure or for the supply of food and medicine in exchange for assurances regarding the health or welfare of the kidnapped diplomat. On the other hand, some governments regard negotiations themselves as "concessions," arguing that they provide the very media exposure sought by the kidnappers and/or give the terrorists stature equal to that of the government itself.

Communications, as opposed to negotiations, present their own unique set of problems. "Holding a hostage guarantees that the kidnappers will be heard. On the other side, the government not only is concerned with obtaining the safe release of the hostage or hostages; it also wants to communicate its position in the contest with the terrorists. When the hostage belongs to another government, that government also must communicate its concerns about the safety of one or more of its citizens, its policy with regard to political kidnappings, and its attitude toward the local government."[29] The media in turn play dual roles as neutral conduits for the messages of others and as active participants with the option of publicizing or not publicizing the demands or goals of the kidnappers and the policy statements of the host government, as well as those of the state whose diplomat has been abducted. Hostages themselves have sometimes become part of the communications process, as have intermediaries.

Communications do not exist in a vacuum, however; they are aimed at a specific audience or frequently at a number of different audiences. The kidnappers' specific audiences may include "their perceived constituents, the local population in general, the American public, a world audience, other potential targets whom they might attack in the future, and other terrorists. A different message is aimed at each audience."[30] The host government must communicate directly or indirectly with the terrorists, its own public, the government of the hostage in question, and world opinion. The government of the kidnapped diplomat, in turn, may communicate with the terrorists, the local government, its own public, and perhaps world opinion as well. To complicate things further, as one analyst has noted, because most messages are public, "everyone reads everyone else's mail. Since each actor's objectives differ with regard to different audiences, the total traffic may be confusing and conflicting."[31]

To minimize the confusion and possibility of conflicting messages, some suggested communications guidelines[32] for government officials include the coordination of all communications (both within and between involved governments); the careful identification of various audiences and the realization that all messages will be heard by each of them; low-keyed public responses to terrorist demands; blunt, simple, and direct messages to the kidnappers themselves; and policy recognition of the differences between concessions, negotiations, and communications. In addition to communications coordination, the necessity for overall coordination of all activities and responses and for an in-place organizational structure for crisis management has also been aptly demonstrated by diplonapping cases.

The U.S. government has designated the Department of State as its lead agency for organizing and directing the U.S. response to those international terrorist incidents, including diplomatic kidnappings, that take place outside the United States. Domestic incidents, on the other hand, are usually handled by the Department of Justice. The Department of Defense provides specialized military support for both foreign and domestic antiterrorist operations. In foreign terrorism incidents, the Department of State has responsibility for developing operational guidelines and, through its Office for Combatting Terrorism, provides the leadership and core personnel for the formation of a crisis management task force. Such a task force, drawn from departmental and other experts, operates on a 24-hour, round-the-clock basis until the case is resolved or brought under control.

A final tactical question that relates to all of the above—negotiations, communications, coordination, and crisis management—is the question of whether or when to attempt to rescue a kidnapped diplomat or to initiate an assault operation on an identified terrorist hideout. Any decision to mount a rescue operation requires

- (a) political determination that negotiations should not be undertaken or, if underway, have not proven effective and that further communications will be useless or counterproductive;
- (b) prior agreement and close coordination between the crisis management efforts of the local police and/or military forces of the host government and the parallel crisis management operations of the other government(s) involved; and
- (c) careful consideration of the possible dangers to the life or person of the hostage that are inherent in any rescue attempt. Assault operations that do not involve a rescue are far simpler to mount, in both political and police/military terms.

The policy issues involved in dealing with diplomatic kidnappings, as with international terrorism in general, are manifold, complex, and frequently interrelated. As outlined above, they include both questions of strategy and of tactics, and no widespread international consensus exists on either. Although a strategy of prevention and control would contribute to deterrence and damage limitation, it requires broad international support to be more than marginally effective—and that support has been agonizingly slow in emerging. Nonetheless, some governments, both alone and in concert, have begun to devise some fairly consistent policies based on that strategy and some even more effective tactics for managing terrorist incidents when they occur. What this development portends for future trends and prospects is examined in the latter part of this chapter.

TRENDS

One trend is certain: International terrorism will continue to be used—by revolutionaries and ideologues, by nihilists and separatists, by left-wing radicals and right-wing extremists, by individuals, groups, and governments—and terrorist attacks against diplomats will continue to be employed as a favorite tactic of that terrorism. It has been mentioned that there has been a dramatic increase in the total number of terrorist incidents involving diplomats and diplomatic facilities during the late 1970s and early 1980s;[33] the number of injuries and deaths resulting from those incidents has also increased, as has the number of governments involved, both those of the diplomats and those of the states in which the terrorist attacks took place. Although "traditional" diplomatic kidnappings have declined somewhat since the heydays of 1970–71, the number of barricade-hostage incidents involving the seizure of diplomatic premises and their occupants has increased.

A summary here of some of the major findings set forth in the recently published State Department statistical overview[34] of international terrorist attacks against diplomatic personnel and facilities may provide some insights into recent trends and future prospects. Most of the international terrorist attacks on diplomats have occurred in the industrialized democracies of Western Europe and the United States. In the time frame from January 1968, through June 1981, 28.6 percent of such attacks took place in Western Europe and 12.3 percent in the United States; Latin America placed as a close runner up to Europe with 26.4 percent of all such incidents. Since 1968, diplomats from 108 countries have been the victims of terrorist incidents, 20 ambassadors from 12 countries were assassinated, diplomats from 39 states were kidnapped, and the embassies of 38 countries were seized.[35]

The geographic spread of international terrorist acts directed against the diplomatic community is in itself dramatically illustrated by the statistics. Although diplomats from over 100 different countries have been the targets of terrorist attacks, the most frequent victims have been North American diplomats, followed by those from the Middle East. The individual states whose diplomats have been most frequently targeted are the United States, Israel, the Soviet Union, the United Kingdom, Cuba, and Turkey. Incidents of international terrorism directed against diplomats have been recorded in 125 countries, but more than 70 percent of the attacks have occurred in only 20 of them. Most took place in the United States, France, the Netherlands, West Germany, Greece, and Argentina. Interesting, perhaps, for purposes of greater future control is the fact that in most of these incidents the attacks were perpetrated by foreign-based terrorists, rather than by those indigenous to the countries in which they took place.

Although almost all kinds of terrorist violence have erupted in all regions of the world, certain specific types of terrorist attacks against diplomats have been employed more frequently in some regions than in others. The State Department study points out, for example, that diplomatic kidnappings and barricade-hostage incidents involving diplomatic premises occur most frequently in Latin America, whereas bombings and assassinations are employed more often in Western Europe and the Middle East. In the past, terrorists have tended to prefer bombings that involve less risk of capture, but handgun assassinations with their built-in benefits of media attention have come to account for a growing proportion of the attacks against diplomats.

An even more chilling portent of potential future prospects is the fact that the *level* of violence directed against diplomats is also on the rise. Not only has the number of terrorist groups in general increased significantly, but "many of the new groups that appeared during the last few years have tended to single out diplomats for attack and to use more deadly violence, perhaps because they calculate that increasingly higher levels of violence are required to obtain the international publicity they seek."[36] According to Robert M. Sayre, Director of the State Department's Office for Combatting Terrorism, the most recent Department figures show that a total of 455 diplomats around the world were victims of terrorism in 1983. This figure represents an increase of 42 over 1982. It also reflects the fact that diplomats represented the group with the highest number of victims. Military personnel held the dubious honor of second place and business people third place. Of the 898 total terrorist incidents recorded in 1983, 311 occurred in Western Europe, 207 in Latin America, and 193 in the Middle East and North Africa. Ambassador Sayre stated, "More American diplomats and military personnel lost their lives to terrorist acts in 1983 than in all the previous years combined."[37]

Finally, turning specifically to the tactic of kidnapping diplomats and holding them hostage to ransom demands (both in traditional diplonapping cases and in incidents of embassy seizures), the State Department overview summarizes the statistics as follows:

> Since 1968, there have been at least 130 attacks in which diplomats were taken hostage to satisfy political or monetary demands by international terrorists. Diplomats from 54 countries have been taken hostage, most often from the United States, West Germany, France, and the United Kingdom. The taking of diplomatic hostages has occurred in 57 countries, but almost half of these incidents took place in Latin America, especially in Mexico, Brazil, and Colombia. Over 1,000 persons have been taken hostage in attacks on diplomats.[38]

With regard to demands made and concessions given, it is not entirely irrelevant to point out that in some of the more highly publicized cases, the ransom demands were met, at least partially. For example, in the September 1974 Japanese Red Army attack on the French Embassy in The Hague, an imprisoned JRA terrorist was released, $300,000 in ransom was paid, and the terrorists themselves were provided safe passage to Syria. Similarly, in the notorious 1980 Colombian April 19 Movement (M-19) seizure of the Dominican Republic's Embassy in Colombia, $2 million in ransom was ultimately paid and the terrorists were granted safe passage to Cuba.

Such "success," it has been argued, can only lead to further emulation in the future. In fact, although the number of simple diplonappings has leveled off, the incidents of embassy seizures have multiplied significantly throughout the 1970s, with more than half of the total takeovers occurring in the 1979–82 time frame. However, according to a 1981 Rand Corporation study[39] of 48 embassy takeovers that took place from 1971 to 1980, ". . . terrorist demands were fully met in less than 17 percent of the embassy seizures. Terrorists were arrested, captured, or killed in 48 percent of the cases where they made demands. One-third of the terrorists who participated in embassy seizures were killed or captured, although the remainder escaped punishment."[40] This less-than-impressive record (from the terrorists' point of view) has not discredited the tactic, which even in relative failure has produced widespread publicity and, as noted above, some occasionally spectacular gains.

FUTURE PROSPECTS

What generalizations about future prospects might be drawn from these recent and current trends? If one accepts the fairly safe conclusion set forth at the beginning of this section—that international terrorism in general and international terrorist attacks against diplomats in particular are likely to continue—what can be postulated about any increase or decrease in the number of such attacks in the future? If the patterns of terrorist activities persist into the 1980s with similar trends to those of the past decade, there is likely to be a steady increase in the number of barricade-hostage incidents involving the seizure or attempted takeover of embassies or other diplomatic premises. In contrast, traditional diplomatic kidnappings[41] are more likely to follow a "steady state" pattern of between 5 to 12 diplonappings or kidnapping attempts per year.

The distinction between barricade-hostage situations and so-called traditional kidnappings may be clarified as follows:

> There are two basic types of hostage situations. In traditional kidnappings the hostage is taken to a secret underground hideout and kept during the ransom negotiation. The kidnappers communicate by note or telephone, at their own initiative, and they may break off communications at will. They can be talked to only during phone calls; otherwise they might be reached indirectly by broadcasts or press publications.
>
> The second type is commonly called a barricade and hostage situation. The kidnappers seize one or more hostages but make no attempt to reach a hideout, or are prevented from doing so. They are, or allow themselves to be, surrounded in a public place. In effect, they are also hostages. They usually barricade themselves in a building or a plane, and immediately warn that any attempt to kill or capture them will imperil

their hostages. The terrorists then include their own escape as part of any subsequent bargain.*

One principal variable that could impinge on and therefore modify the continuation of those patterns is the effect of the stringent security measures which only recently have been introduced and/or enhanced by several governments to protect diplomatic personnel and premises against terrorist attacks and takeovers. As these become more effective in deterring attacks on embassies by raising the potential risks and costs in bodily harm, death, or imprisonment, would-be terrorists might return to the more traditional diplonappings of the early and mid-1970s. As has been pointed out elsewhere,[42] although both types have their advantages and disadvantages, one advantage of traditional kidnappings is that they entail only a relatively short period of exposure to danger during the initial phases. Barricade-hostage incidents, on the other hand, possess the advantage of involving a larger number of hostages and therefore have the possibility of receiving greater attention and publicity.

Another variable that could disrupt the trend continuation projected above is the potential impact of more universally applied policies of no ransom. Although it may well be true that terrorist demands were only *fully* met in less than 17 percent of the embassy seizures which took place in the 1970s and that the risks of capture and death were extremely high, yet even the partial satisfaction of some demands was hardly negligible ($300,000 granted to the JRA in 1974 instead of the $1 million demanded, or $2 million paid to the M-19 in 1980 instead of the $50 million originally asked for). Moreover, in virtually all cases extensive publicity was accorded both to the incidents and to the terrorists' goals and grievances. If no-ransom or no-concessions policies were more uniformly applied without major exceptions, the chances of dramatically curtailing even the barricade and hostage incidents rise greatly.

Any more detailed prognosis for future prospects is likely to be unproductive or highly speculative, but a few further generalizations might usefully be mentioned in conclusion. Many experts in the field have given credence to the idea that terrorists in the future may well escalate the level of their violence and perpetrate large-scale incidents, for example, chemical, biological, or nuclear threats to major cities. It is not overly pessimistic to postulate the possibility of large-scale "mass hostage" situations[45] involving not just diplomats, but the governments they represent. Another reasonable conclusion is that, in the absence of any panacea to the continuing threat of terrorism, governments will be forced to devote sizable and increasing resources of attention, personnel, and money to the protection and security of their key domestic facilities (e.g., energy systems, communications networks, nuclear plants) and other vulnerable targets as well as their overseas missions. Finally, although the logic of greater international cooperation may not be persuasive enough to lead to more comprehensive and stringent international agreements,

* In Jenkins, Brian; Johnson, Janera; and Ronfeldt, David, "Numbered Lives: Some Statistical Observations from 77 International Hostage Episodes," p. 9. Rand Paper Series, P-5905. (July 1977).

the strategic imperatives created by international terrorism will eventually compel governments to develop their own policies of prevention and control and their own systems of crisis management, if only on a national level.

NOTES

1.   Coined by Carol Edler Baumann, *The Diplomatic Kidnappings* (The Hague: Martinus Nijhoff, 1973).

2.   Carlos Marighella, *Minimanual of the Urban Guerrilla* (Havana, Cuba: Tricontinental, 1970), p. 43.

3.   *Ibid.,* p. 44.

4.   Walter Laqueur, cited by Yonah Alexander, "Terrorism, The Media and the Police," in Alan D. Buckley and Daniel D. Olson (eds.), *International Terrorism* (Wayne, NJ: Avery Publishing Group, 1980), p. 90.

5.   Frank H. Perez, "Terrorist Target: The Diplomat" (June 10, 1982) (Washington, DC: U.S. Department of State, Bureau of Public Affairs), unpublished address.

6.   "Terrorist Attacks Against Diplomats" (Washington, DC: U.S. Department of State, Office for Combatting Terrorism, December 1981), p. 8. This is a statistical overview of international terrorist attacks on diplomatic personnel and facilities from January 1968 to June 1981.

7.   Due to the use of slightly different databases and time frames, these numbers differ somewhat from those used in the third section of this chapter, The Setting, which were based on the CIA's open source computer search.

8.   Perez, p. 2.

9.   *Ibid.*

10.   "Terrorist Attacks Against Diplomats" (Washington, DC: U.S. Department of State, Office for Combatting Terrorism, December 1981), p. 8.

11.   In 1980, 409 incidents involved diplomats from 60 different countries.

12.   Adopted by the U.N. Conference on Diplomatic Intercourse and Immunities in April 1961.

13.   Adopted in April 1963.

14.   *The American Journal of International Law: Official Documents,* 43(suppl), 1949.

15.   *Convention to Prevent and Punish the Acts of Terrorist Taking the Form of Crimes Against Person and Related Extortion That Are of International Significance.* In OAS/Official Records/Ser.P/English. Third Special Session, General Assembly, AG/doc. 88 rev. lcorr. 1,2. February 1971. Original: Spanish.

16.   23 UST 3227; TIAS 7502; 500 UNTS 95.

17.   International Legal Materials, vol. XVIII, no. 6, Nov. 1979, pp. 1457–1463; Senate Exec. N, 96th Congress, Second Session (1980).

18.   Brian M. Jenkins, "Diplomats on the Front Line," P-6749 (Santa Monica, CA: The Rand Corporation, 1982), p. 3.

19.   See the last sections of this chapter, Trends and Future Prospects.

20.   Baumann, pp. 129–130.

21.   Perez, p. 3.

22.   *Ibid.*

23.   Jenkins, pp. 7–8.

24. Ambassador Walter Stoessel (Under Secretary of State for Political Affairs), Testimony before House Committee on Foreign Affairs, September, 1980.

25. Entered into force April 24, 1964, with 40 governments party to it. U.N. Doc A/CONF. 20/13, April 16, 1961.

26. Brian M. Jenkins, "Combatting Terrorism: Some Policy Implications," P-6666 (Santa Monica, CA: The Rand Corporation, 1981), p. 5.

27. *Ibid.*

28. *Ibid.,* pp. 5–6.

29. Brian M. Jenkins, "Talking to Terrorists," P-6750 (Santa Monica, CA: The Rand Corporation, 1982), p. 1.

30. *Ibid.,* pp. 4–5.

31. *Ibid.,* p. 6.

32. *Ibid.,* pp. 14–15.

33. "In 1975, 30 percent of all international terrorist attacks were directed against diplomats; in 1980 the number increased to 54 percent of the total." Jenkins, "Terrorist Attacks," p. 2.

34. *Ibid.,* pp. 2–9.

35. *Ibid.,* p. 4.

36. *Ibid.*

37. *State* (The Newsletter) (Washington, DC: U.S. Department of State, March 1984) p. 5.

38. Jenkins, "Terrorist Attacks," p. 8.

39. Brian M. Jenkins, "Embassies Under Siege: A Review of 48 Embassy Takeovers, 1971–1980," R-2651-RC (Santa Monica, CA: The Rand Corporation, 1981).

40. Jenkins, "Diplomats," pp. 3–4.

41. Brian M. Jenkins, Janera Johnson, and David Ronfeldt: "Numbered Lives: Some Statistical Observations from 77 International Hostage Episodes," P-5905 (Santa Monica, CA: The Rand Corporation, 1977), p. 9.

42. *Ibid.,* pp. 10–13.

4

The European Experience

David T. Schiller

THE ORIGINS OF KIDNAPPING

The increase in kidnappings in the 1970s should not have come as a surprise to victims, the police, or the public. Europe has a long history of hostage taking for political and/or profit-making reasons. As in Sicily or Italy, where kidnapping had been a century-long source of income for criminal organizations like the Mafia, similar activities in countries such as Germany, Austria, and France date back to the Middle Ages, when robber-barons raided caravans and held merchants for ransom in the dark dungeons of their hilltop castles.

Such endeavors, embellished by legends and fairy tales and romanticized in the late nineteenth century, are part of the folklore of most parts of Middle and Northern Europe, where nearly every dark forest or ruined castle has its own version of noble-minded robbers like Robin Hood or "Schinderhannes." This nineteenth-century figure emerged during the French occupation of the Rhineland, fighting French and German authorities alike. Best classified by the Hobsbawn of "social bandit," he was arrested in 1802 and executed together with 19 followers in November 1803.

On the national level, political kidnapping can be dated back to the twelfth century, when the Archduke of Austria and the German Emperor for years held the English king Richard I hostage in a Rhine castle, finally releasing him for a "king's ransom" and a pledge of alliance. Similarly, Lindbergh-type precedents can be dated back in British history to the seventeenth century, when a proliferation of infant stealing for ransom shook the rich classes and the nobility alike. During that period children were often taken to be sold as slaves or farmhands in the colonies—the expression, "kid-napping," originated then.

THE BEGINNINGS OF MODERN GERMAN KIDNAPPING

The modern spree of kidnappings in the original sense of the word—the abduction of a small infant or a child—emerged in post–World War II Europe with the taking and eventual killing of the Peugeot grandchild in France and the Goehner child in Germany in the late 1950s. Since then, kidnapping incidents have become a common occurrence in countries like Germany. Until 1971 ten cases had been registered by the German police, in four of which the victims were killed. Ten years later, the chances of survival for ransom-held infants appeared similarly bleak: Of 18 abducted children, 9 were killed by their captors, often shortly after their abduction; the criminals were unable to hide the child effectively, feared recognition, or "just wanted to be on the safe side."

Though the police have been quite successful in more than three quarters of all known cases of kidnapping and the perpetrators caught and convicted, the number of incidents per year has not decreased and intervals between episodes are shorter than ever. It appears that kidnapping and hostage taking have become the new criminal fashion in which professionals and amateurs similarly indulge, often copying their mode of operation from highly publicized events such as the terroristic abduction of the Berlin politician Peter Lorenz. With the beginning of the 1970s a distinctive change in these criminal exploits could be detected, which seemed to be a direct outcome of widely publicized Latin American incidents of hostage taking.

- In August 1971 three masked men forced 71-year-old clubowner Bernhard Keese and his fiancee to drive them out of town in Keese's Mercedes. Demanding 1 million German marks at a remote forest location, the trio agreed in the end to the sum of 100,000 marks, a reduction accomplished by the bargaining techniques of the experienced businessman Keese. As soon as the banks opened, the kidnappers permitted Keese's fiancee to leave the car and get the requested ransom from the victim's bank account.
- Also in 1971 a financial lawyer and a convicted safebreaker cooperated in the abduction of the owner of a supermarket chain, Theo Albrecht, who was released after 17 days when the 7-million-mark demand was paid. A high-ranking clergyman was the go-between. Albrecht was held the whole time in the closed law office of his abductor. Both men were arrested later through registered banknotes from the ransom, though more than half of the haul never reappeared.
- Two years later, in November 1973 the daughter of the worldwide restaurant chain–owner Friedrich Jahn ("Wienerwald") was kidnapped by three amateurs, who committed a number of mistakes that made their arrest quite easy. Among other oversights, the car used for the pick-up of the 3-million-mark ransom was registered in the name of one of the abductors. Nonetheless, police waited until the Jahn daughter was safely released before arresting the perpetrators.

In all three cases adults, not children, were selected as victims and for the first time in post-war West German criminal history, the ransom demands exceeded the six-digit requests previously encountered in the more traditional cases of kidnapping. This trend was escalating at the time Peter Lorenz was taken hostage—an act that demonstrated the effectiveness of kidnapping. The abduction of Lorenz was not the first such attempt undertaken by German terrorists. Earlier incidents could have prepared the West German security officials and led them to anticipate that type of event.

POLITICAL TERRORIST ACTIONS

The Drenkmann Case

In April 1970 a petrol bombing took place against the Office of the West Berlin judge Gunther von Drenkmann. It was undertaken by the local terrorist group, the 2nd of June Movement, whose activities until then had consisted of minor bombings and bank robberies. However, when German terrorist Holger Meins died in the course of his hunger strike in prison, members of the group decided to switch to more "direct action."

On the evening of November 10, 1974, the sixty-fourth birthday of Chief Justice von Drenkmann, three young people rang the bell at the door of Drenkmann's apartment, carrying flowers. Two more members of the group were stationed on the stairs, securing the approach and escape route. The plan was to kidnap the judge and press for the release of arrested gang members; but as Drenkmann put up a violent and unexpected resistance, he was shot at point-blank range, suffering mortal wounds from large-caliber hollow-point projectiles. The group escaped in two vehicles that had been parked in front of the victim's house. Less than five months later the group carried out a better planned kidnapping.

The Lorenz Kidnapping

At approximately 9:00 in the morning of February 27, 1975, the Mercedes of Peter Lorenz, lawyer and chairman of the West Berlin branch of Germany's conservative Christian Democratic Union (CDU), came to a violent halt in a Berlin residential suburb. Masked men jumped out of a car that had pulled up in front of Lorenz' limousine, clubbed his driver into unconsciousness, and pulled the struggling 52-year-old party politician into their car. With the remark that further resistance would only bring on him the fate of Chief Justice von Drenkmann, the terrorists gagged, tied, and blindfolded the subdued Lorenz. He was then carted off to a cellar room in a downtown building, which had been prepared as a cell: The room, 10×7 feet with bars, had a bed, chair, and washbowl, and was situated underneath a second-hand furniture store that had long been used as a safehouse by the group.

The choice of this front showed how well-organized the underground operation had become. The business of the second-hand shop masked the frequent visits by a number of people who might otherwise have aroused the suspicion of neighbors. Large boxes or a back-up van, in which a potential hostage could be transported or guns stored, would not seem out of place in connection with a retail furniture store. While police raided hundreds of apartments and living communes in search of the Lorenz kidnappers, this safehouse went undetected. Business went on "as usual" and, in order to prevent the revenue office from nosing around, all sales were carefully registered according to trade and tax regulations.

The cellar in which Lorenz was held until the late night hours of March 4 would have also served as a "people's prison" for Drenkmann, if that abduction had succeeded. Later evidence suggested that the group had checked out a number of highly placed individuals in the administrative ranks of the city of Berlin, among others, the mayor, judges, and members of the city parliament. They chose Peter Lorenz as a "soft target": He usually went to work unaccompanied (save for his unarmed driver) and his position as the chairman of the opposition party gave extra political leverage to the kidnapping. On March 2 elections were scheduled for the city council and any uncompromising move on behalf of the Berlin city government would have cast a negative shadow on the integrity of the governing party, the Social Democrats.

Additional leverage was provided by the terrorists' threat to deal with Lorenz as they had with Drenkmann. Via a letter to the authorities, the group demanded the freeing of convicted or suspected terrorists from German prisons with 20,000 German marks for each as "compensation" for their prison time; the televised reading of political announcements; and a plane to fly the released individuals to a country of their choice, accompanied by a public figure as a guarantee for their safe passage. The threat was underlined with a Polaroid photo of Lorenz in his cell, a placard on his chest reading "Peter Lorenz—a prisoner of the Movement of June 2nd."

The German government complied. Horst Mahler refused to be released, but six other imprisoned terrorists were flown to Aden, given passports and 120,000 marks, and accompanied by a former Berlin secretary of interior. On their arrival in Aden, a special password was released by the freed terrorists and announced via German radio and television broadcasts. Lorenz was set free the same night, March 4, in a public downtown park. He was unable to give any hints about the identity of his captors, who had been careful to be always masked and gloved in his presence. Only months later his prison was discovered by pure chance.

The Stockholm Embassy

The Lorenz incident showed clearly that the German government (the "System" in the nomenclature of leftist extremists) was willing to give in to extortion when confronted by a no-win situation. Two months later a second attempt was made by German terrorists to pressure the Bonn government into releasing captured gang members. This time Chancellor Schmidt decided not to give in to the demands: On April 24, 1975, the German embassy in Stockholm was assaulted by six members of the Baader-Meinhof gang and its staff held hostage. An explosion occurred when negotiations stalled and two attackers as well as two hostages died. Swedish police stormed the burning building, freed the victims, and arrested the terrorists, who were later turned over to the German police.

Obviously as an act of vengeance, a Sweden-based branch of the German terrorist group headed by Norbert Kroecher planned to abduct Sweden's former minister of interior, Mrs. Anna-Grete Leijon.* The operation called for two cars to roadlock the street Mrs. Leijon would be travelling on from her home in a Stockholm suburb, as well as possibly using a kidnapper dressed in a policeman's uniform to approach Mrs. Leijon's car. A wooden box was to be used to transport the victim and an intricate plan for escape was prepared, which involved a change of cars and the use of a speedboat to evade possible police roadblocks. The plan came to nothing when Kroecher was arrested in Stockholm before it could be put into effect.[1]

The intricacy of the plan nonetheless showed that German terrorists, in conjunction with other foreign nationals residing in Stockholm, were prepared to undertake the risks and necessary research for kidnappings and that a high level of organization was already in existence. Some of these terrorists also participated in the OPEC hostage incident in December 1975, which was headed by the Venezuelan I. R. Sanchez, known as "Carlos." Half a year later two German terrorists headed the team that hijacked an Air France jet and redirected it to the Ugandan airport of Entebbe.

POLITICAL TERRORIST ACTS

The Buback Murder

In April 1977 two men on a rented motorbike used a red light at an intersection to overtake the car of the West German Chief Prosecutor Siegfried Buback on his way to work. The passenger on the bike drew an automatic assault rifle out of a suitcase and sprayed the car with 22-caliber fire: Buback and his driver died instantly; his bodyguard, sitting in the back of the vehicle, was mortally wounded and died five days later. After making sure that their victims had been hit, the men on the bike—who wore helmets, making identification difficult—sped away. They later changed to a car, which they also abandoned.

For a short while it appeared that the German extremist groups had abandoned their earlier mode of operation and switched from kidnapping to assassinating their targets. A number of security measures to protect government and administration officials were set into motion by German security organizations. A "hardening" of potential targets took place, with known politicians and judges supplied with bodyguards and 24-hour protection in their homes and offices and on their way to and from work. The terrorists, however, had meanwhile switched to a different category of targets.

The Murder of Jurgen Ponto

On July 7, 1977, three persons, one man and two women, entered the villa of Jurgen Ponto, head of a large West German bank. Though the place was well

---

* A full account of the planned kidnapping of Mrs. Leijon can be found in Jacob Sundberg, "Operation Leo: Description and Analysis of a European Terrorist Operation," in Brian Jenkins (ed.) *Terrorism and Beyond*, R-2714-DOE/DOJ/DOS/RC (Santa Monica, CA: The Rand Corporation, 1982), pp. 174–202.

equipped with the usual alarms, the three young people gained easy entrance to the building. One of them, Susanne Albrecht, was well known to the family of the banker, being the daughter of an old friend. With the words, "here is Susanne," she announced herself over the intercom at the door and introduced the two strangers in her company as "friends." She was carrying a bouquet of red roses and was invited to have a cup of coffee on the veranda. When the banker's wife absented herself from the group in order to make a telephone call, the three made their move. Producing large-caliber handguns, they demanded that Jurgen Ponto follow them.

According to his wife, the banker stayed calm, answered the command with, "You must be absolutely crazy," and struggled with the male attacker for the control of his handgun. At that moment the attacker fired a shot. The second woman from the group then came forward and fired more shots at Ponto, who was already on the ground. The three then fled. Obviously, as in the case of the Drenkmann murder, the terrorists decided to use deadly force the moment they encountered resistance by the intended kidnap victim.

Five weeks later another attempt to kidnap a well-known public figure succeeded. Though the terrorists could reasonably expect security measures around public figures associated with politics and commerce to be stringent, they were under pressure to achieve the release of their imprisoned comrades. Their plans took all possible resistance, including armed, into account, while information on possible target personalities was gathered in libraries and from newspaper clippings.

The Kidnapping of Hanns-Martin Schleyer

Instead of well-guarded politicians, "capitalist figures" soon became a new category of kidnap victim, and as such, fitted very well into the hodge-podge leftist ideology of the Baader-Meinhof followers. Hanns-Martin Schleyer was the president of the West German Industrial Employers Federation, a well-known man with a longstanding membership in the "exploiter" class and one, who, in his university days, had belonged to a Nazi organization. Schleyer had been classified a "Category III endangered person" since 1975, which meant an attack on him could be likely. In the beginning of August 1977 he was upgraded to Category I ("highly endangered, an attack is considered possible"). His two homes were guarded by two police officers on a 24-hour basis and all his movements to and from work were shadowed by three guards, who followed his vehicle in an unmarked police car. Apparently, Schleyer's movements and the routine of his guard detail had been studied by the terrorists for a long time prior to the attack.

On *September 5, 1977,* shortly after 5:00 in the afternoon, Schleyer left his office in Cologne to drive home. His chauffeured Mercedes was closely followed by three police officers in a second car of the same make. Close to Schleyer's home, the two cars encountered a fatal ambush in a narrow sidestreet. At approximately 5:28 P.M., the lead limousine (with Schleyer in the backseat) stopped abruptly. From the opposite side of the street a yellow Mercedes suddenly swerved to the right curb, effectively blocking the path of the oncoming cars. At the same moment a blue pram was rolled into the middle of the street, and Schleyer's driver, the 41-year-old Heinz Marcisz, was forced to brake. The second Mercedes of the entourage, following too closely, crashed into the rear of Schleyer's vehicle.

Five people appeared on the left side of the street and poured a hail of fire into the police escort. Using two H&K .223 assault rifles (the same type of weapon used in the Buback assassination), one Polish submachine gun, and two riot-type shotguns with large-caliber slugs, plus various handguns, they concentrated their fire on the second Mercedes. The three police officers never stood a chance, though one was able to squeeze off eight rounds from his submachine gun and the driver returned fire with his pistol. Schleyer's driver was killed at point-blank range, his murderer making sure that the intended kidnap victim was not hit by his line of fire.

Schleyer was then pulled from the Mercedes and pushed into a white Volkswagen van, which the Schleyer entourage had overtaken unknowingly on its way to the ambush site. The police arrived at the scene less than nine minutes after the initial onslaught, but they were unable to follow the terrorists' tracks or determine their escape route. Less than 30 minutes later the German Federal Bureau's special division for investigations on terrorism (called "Bundeskriminalamt/Abt. TE") in Bonn and the German Chancellor Helmut Schmidt were informed.

At 7:47 P.M. the white van used in the kidnapping was found near what was identified as the safe house that the terrorists had obviously used for the planning stage of their operation. In the van was found the first message from the kidnappers, addressed to the federal government and threatening the execution of Schleyer in case of police searches. The typed message was signed "RAF" for Rote Armee Fraktion, the German terrorist group better known as Baader-Meinhof for their (already imprisoned and convicted) founders, Ulrike Meinhof and Andreas Baader.

The whole Schleyer abduction—the month-long negotiations, the procedures of the terrorists as well as of the government institutions—can be seen as the prototype of a kidnapping with a political motivation, exceeding in intensity and length as well as decision level anything that up to then had ever been encountered in Europe. As became evident later, the Schleyer case was used as a model in the Aldo Moro event—to such a degree, in fact, that there still remains an unproven but persistent suspicion that German terrorists were involved at least on the planning level if not in the execution stage. The proceedings in the Schleyer case therefore deserve close examination as a source of inspiration for both police and criminals.

Though it was obvious from the beginning that the real target of the kidnappers was not the Schleyer family but the German Federal government, the terrorists did not deal directly with the decision-making political level. The first of a number of intermediaries was a Protestant clergyman in Wiesbaden, a town more than 200 km from Cologne, who was to relay the message to the government. This first letter, stated the following demands: release of 11 imprisoned terrorists by Wednesday, 8:00 A.M.; 100,000 German marks for each of them; use of a plane at the Frankfurt airport to fly them to a country of their choice; televised broadcasts of the released gangmembers; and the placement of two known left-wing liberals on the flight as a safeguard. A short telephone call to the priest made sure that he had received the letter. The demands and release procedures closely followed those used in the Lorenz abduction.

While the receipt of the message was acknowledged by the government via a brief message broadcast on the same evening during the 8:00 news, the kidnappers' demands were not met at the given deadline. At 10:00 A.M. on Wednesday, September 7, a second radio broadcast requested the kidnappers to give an unmistakable sign that Schleyer was still alive. Further instructions were to be released via radio on the same afternoon.

The authorities were stalling for time by letting the first deadline pass, thus gaining more time for police operations—an obvious procedure that was clearly recognized by the kidnappers. They refused to respond to personal questions about Schleyer posed by the government, which only Schleyer, if alive, could have answered. Another Protestant clergyman, this time in the city of Mainz, was instructed by telephone call that a message to the government can be found in his letter box. On Wednesday at 5:25 P.M. a package with two handwritten messages, a video-tape, and a message of the terrorists was thus relayed, giving clear evidence that Schleyer is alive. Three hours later another clergyman in the same town found a tape in his letterbox, on which Schleyer gave the answers demanded by the police. The authorities refused to televise the video-tape via national television, and the terrorists responded by a telephone call to the German DPA Press Agency in Dusseldorf, threatening "consequences" for Schleyer if this demand was not fulfilled.

By this time, the earlier government decision to curtail all incoming information on the case had affected the terrorists, for whom newspaper coverage was an important goal of their attacks. In a number of messages to news agencies and a Frankfurt newspaper, as well as to a close friend and colleague of Schleyer, the kidnappers attempted to slip by this news embargo and get their announcements into the headlines. In a rare compliance with government wishes, all agencies and newspapers contacted were silent on the case. On Saturday, September 10, five days after the initial abduction, the kidnappers complied with a police request to use a go-between for negotiations: The Geneva-based lawyer, Denis Payot, a known left-wing liberal and representative of a Swiss Human Rights League who was named in an earlier letter of the abductors, was contacted by the gang. There were indications that he had had earlier contacts with terrorist circles in Germany. Payot was a problematic mediator whose often-emphasized neutrality let him assume a stand-offish attitude toward the German government. He proved unwilling, for example, to supply hints on the possible whereabouts of the terrorists or the sources of messages.

For 43 days—until the murder of the victim on October 18—Payot remained the main relay station between the abductors and the authorities. Various attempts to use different channels and to increase pressure for compliance with their demands were used by the terrorists:

- In a number of instances, press agencies and/or newspapers were contacted, sometimes by telephone, in other cases with letters and enclosed Polaroid shots of Schleyer holding placards.
- Numerous messages were sent to Eberhard von Brauchitsch, a close friend of the victim and his family. As in other cases, messages were handwritten or taped recordings. These messages were directed to Brauchitsch personally; to Schleyer's family; or to a friend of the victim, Helmut Kohl, a leading politician of the German opposition party, the Christian Democrats.
- On the eighth day, direct contact was established for the first time with Schleyer's family, first with a telephone call, then with a relayed letter from the victim to his eldest son. These contacts continued parallel to the negotiating process with the government authorities and were at a later date referred through Payot's Geneva office. Around October 15, these contacts generated an abortive attempt by Schleyer's son to deliver $15 million as a ransom, but the kidnappers failed to pick up the money.

Beginning October 13, 1977, at 2:38 P.M. the tension increased with the hijacking of a Lufthansa airliner by four Palestinian terrorists who declared their action to be in solidarity with the German terrorist demands. In the following days the kidnappers' messages sent to the government took on a new turn, as they matched their requests with those of the hijackers. The hijacking ended with the assault of the plane at the Somalian airport of Mogadishu, undertaken by the German special force GSG 9, which freed the hostages. The very same night, October 18, four leading figures of the German terrorist scene attempted suicide in the high-security prison of Stammheim; three were successful. Their deaths spelled the end for Schleyer. In their twenty-fifth message, the kidnappers announced the "execution" of Hanns-Martin Schleyer on October 18 and described the place where his body could be found. A few hours later the body of Schleyer, who was killed by three 9 mm rounds to the head, was found in the baggage compartment of a private car parked in the French border town of Mulhouse, confirming long-held suspicions that Schleyer had been held captive near the French border.

Negotiations in the Schleyer kidnapping had a number of interesting similarities with those in hostage/barricade cases. Though the exchange of demands, answers, and delaying methods was complicated through the use of intermediaries, letter-drop systems, and announcements, an up-and-down anxiety curve similar to that in hostage/barricade contacts could be read into the terrorist messages. The chief psychologist in the Schleyer case, Wolfgang Salewski, felt that the amount and intensity of contacts between the negotiating parties had been appropriate and effective. Six terrorist-imposed deadlines passed without drastic actions by the kidnappers. By delaying the abductors, the techniques of the German government and their crisis team (of which Salewski was an advisor) were successful. To reduce the chances for an immoderate response by the terrorists, the crisis staff yielded to certain small demands whenever it felt that anxiety among the captors had reached a high point.

In this context, curtailing information to the press was effective. Very shortly after the first contact between the kidnappers and the government, the public televis-ing and broadcasting of terrorist messages became a bargaining point. Official confirmations of the reception of letters or tapes became "stepping points," which could be used in the bargaining process to reduce tension. Similarly government requests for signals from or about Schleyer became a tool for keeping the terrorists busy and their minds off the fact that the crisis staff in Bonn was not caving in under the pressures of deadlines.

The overall tactic of the government team was dictated by their strategy of not giving in to requests for release of the gang. Their primary goal, which followed from this stance, was to stall for time so that police search teams could try to locate Schleyer's "prison." Extra time, they hoped, might also result in a psychologi-cal bond between captors and captive, which could prevent Schleyer's being killed. These hopes were confounded by the large number of people involved on the terrorist side. More than five participated in the actual hit, and a total of at least 12 to 15 people were later suspected of having had a part in the whole operation. The growth of special relations between the victim and his guards must have been hampered by the sheer number of persons who probably took turns guarding him.

An analysis of various terrorist messages showed another complicating factor for the government, one that could cause a sudden change of tactics on the terrorists' side. Apparently, there were two groups of hostage takers with conflicting opinions on the best steps to take: One opted for a continuation of the bargaining process, on the assumption that Schleyer was a very valuable pawn; the other group tended toward a drastic end of the affair as an example for future kidnappings, which were obviously being planned.

The varying intensity of messages sent out by the terrorists could be used to separate them into three stages, or groups. In police experience, kidnappers used quieter stages to perfect their supply and safehouse system and, as later investigations showed, this observation held true in the Schleyer kidnapping. Schleyer was moved from his first prison, an apartment in a high-rise in a Cologne suburb where he was held inside a padded wardrobe, in one of these quieter phases.

As a hostage Schleyer was a prime example of strength. A careful analysis of tapes and letters shows that his psychological condition was much stronger than indicated by the texts his captors forced him to write and read. For a man of 62 years, he held up amazingly well under the strains of captivity, though losing an estimated 20 kg in weight. He may have used at least one recording to give hints about his location, but if so, criminologists were unable to understand them. Schleyer had understood his chances of becoming a target for terrorist attacks before he was kidnapped and had always appeared to regard such a threat as a personal challenge to his strength and character (similarly, Ponto had decided beforehand that he would resist any kidnapping attempt—and told his wife so). In his 43-day-long ordeal the stubborn endurance for which he was known in industrial circles and which had helped him through many a marathon conference helped him to remain sane and calm in the face of lasting uncertainty.

Considering the circumstances, it is amazing that Schleyer's messages and letters always hinted that he understood well the dilemma that the government had to face. Though the overall content of the handwritten notes was obviously dictated by the abductors, the wording chosen by the captive—especially his repeated endings that "the decision [for exchange] was not his to make" and that "he would always submit to the government's conclusion of the affair"—conveyed his own will to resist the terrorist blackmail. In one letter, which was a sure sign of Schleyer's loss of nerve while pressing for a fast decision by the government one week after the kidnapping, he included the sentence "I have never whimpered for staying alive!"

Throughout the six weeks of uncertainty Schleyer's bearing proved to be an enormous help in the decision-making process of the government as well as to his own family, which more or less submitted to the path chosen by Chancellor Schmidt. For a long time the family abstained from putting further pressure on the government. Schleyer's oldest son, addressed in a message by his father in the course of negotiations, coordinated his own actions with those of the government. Being a lawyer himself, he and a colleague attempted to obtain a court order from the Federal Constitutional Court for a release of the imprisoned terrorists, which was turned down. Nonetheless, it was a worthwhile attempt to find a face-saving solution that would permit the government to fulfill the kidnappers' demands without actually giving in to their pressure. As a third party, the highest legislative authority would have pressed for an exchange in order to save Schleyer's life.

Though tensions inside the family naturally increased the longer the ordeal lasted, the family, supported by friends and especially by the strong decisive stand of the oldest son Eberhard, held together. Apparently, the second son of the victim wanted to use public announcements by the family to press for a government release of the requested terrorists. Except for a few statements by the family, published in daily newspapers, no such action was undertaken. Any such publicity, according to Eberhard's assessment, would only have conflicted with the state's response and given the terrorists further leverage, while offering only a slim chance for success.

The Palmers Case

While the Schleyer abduction had a clear political motive and was meant to blackmail the Bonn government into releasing imprisoned members of the Red Army Faction, a similar kidnapping undertaken by the 2nd of June Movement in Austria had a different motive. It was intended to replenish the depleted war coffers of this West German– and Berlin-based terrorist group. In the summer of 1977 (at the same time that intense police searches were carried out in neighboring Germany for the murderers of Ponto and Buback), two female members of the 2nd of June Movement, Inge Viett and Gabriele Rollnik, contacted Austrian extremists at the Vienna university by accosting them quite openly on campus. At that time Austrian society harbored the unfounded view that their country was spared from terrorism. Cooperation between German and Austrian authorities was poor, and Austrian police were not diligent in supporting West German searches for political criminals. The Austrian government was also working hard to establish good relations with Palestinian organizations, who were known to harbor German and other international terrorists.

The two women were looking for local helpers in the abduction of an Austrian businessman. A target was selected by simply leafing through the pages of a book entitled *The Rich and Super-Rich in Austria,* in which the intended victim was described as often moving large sums and preferring cash payments. He was Walter Michael Palmers, 74 years old and of Jewish descent, the senior owner of a large textile corporation in Austria. While the Austrian recruits supplied the German terrorists with on-the-spot information and falsified documents plus other logistical help, the female 2nd of June members rented safehouses and cars, planned the operation, and observed the victim's daily routine. On November 9, four people waited next to the garage door of Palmer's residence, rushing the home-coming businessman in the dark and escaping in a Peugeot 504, which they later switched for a Volkswagen van with curtained and padded interior.

Contact with the victim's family was quickly established by telephone. No clues were given that this kidnapping was the act of a terrorist group. For a long time (until ransom money was found on arrested 2nd of June members) the authorities were led to believe that they were dealing with "simple" criminals. Amazingly enough, while the largest man-hunt ever conducted in post-war Germany was under way for the murderers of Ponto, Buback, and Schleyer, this group was able to pull off smoothly yet another abduction in neighboring Austria. The Palmers family, never totally committed to cooperating with the authorities, came to a fast agreement with the kidnappers. A sum of 31 million Schilling (some $2 million) was the agreed ransom; and while two family members led police and journalists on a false trail, the victim's son slipped unnoticed out of the residence and carried the ransom (34 kg of small banknotes in a Samsonite suitcase) to the kidnappers. The handover occurred finally—after the courier was guided on a criss-cross paper-chase all over Vienna to shake off possible police observation—in a taxi-cab, which happened to be the Peugeot used in the abduction. A few hours later, a week after Palmers was kidnapped, he was set free.

A similar method was used a few weeks later in another kidnapping in Vienna, in which the wife of another textile magnate, Lotte Bohm, was freed on December 19, 1977, for a ransom of 20 million Shilling. As the pattern of abduction and ransom demands was nearly identical to that in the Palmers case, the same circle of terrorists was assumed to have perpetrated both acts. Later investigation showed that the kidnappers were in fact common criminals who had based their abduction plans as closely as possible on the Palmers incident.

PROFIT-MAKING KIDNAPPINGS—THE CRIMINAL ENDEAVOR

The Schleyer and Palmers kidnappings occurred at a time when criminal abductions were at a peak in Western Europe. Probably encouraged by the successful blackmailing of the state in the Lorenz kidnapping, a series of abductions started in autumn 1976. It can be safely assumed that the initial success of each kidnapping prompted other imitations. Without going into too much detail, certain salient characteristics and differences can be pointed out.

Germany
- On October 8, 1976, three men grabbed 32-year-old Wolfgang Gutberlet, partner in two large supermarket chains, at a secluded spot, hid him in a wooden box, and released him after a week on the payment of 2 million German marks. Police later apprehended the three kidnappers, who were not professional criminals. The trio consisted of a butcher, a housepainter, and a parquet flooring maker, related to each other as in-laws and as middle-class craftsmen "who wanted to strike it rich" with a one-shot trick. They lured the businessman with a telephone call to a meeting place, overwhelmed him, bound and blindfolded him, before holding him in a crate at their home. Gutberlet was able to give the police a number of helpful clues about his abductors and the route they took from the scene to the hiding place. He had had the banknotes that he carried to the meeting place registered, as the phone call had raised his suspicions. Two hours after the abduction Gutberlet's wife had alerted the police, which then coordinated all the efforts of the family to rescue the hostage.
- As in the case of the Gutberlet abduction, the two kidnappers who took the brewery owner, Gernot Egolf, hostage chose a victim from their immediate vicinity. On October 19, 1976, they lured their victim by a telephone call to a meeting place, blindfolded him, and kept him in an old bomb-proof cellar. Both perpetrators, later caught, were young workers, 21 and 22 years old, with no prior criminal experience. Egolf's family initially doubted the sincerity of the threat, and police even hinted that the victim and his kidnappers were cooperating in extorting money from Egolf's father. Negotiations went on for 52 days with an abortive attempt to deliver 50,000 German marks as ransom.
  The police failed to coordinate all their moves with the family, who was unwilling to pay the demanded 2 million marks and with the mediators, who were later introduced into the bargaining process. The tactic to stall for time backfired in the Egolf case. Four weeks after the abductors were arrested, the victim's body was found buried in a forest. During the 52 days of negotiating, he had lost 15 kg of weight. Finally he had died of exhaustion and hunger in his cold, dungeon-like hiding place. His abductors had fed him only every three or four days and probably panicked when their initial plan did not work out.

- Hendrik Snoek, 28, a well-known Olympic horseman and junior partner in a supermarket consortium, would have probably died in his "prison-cell," too, if it were not for his own initiative and the alertness of a passerby. The two abductors had grabbed their victim in his own apartment and forced him to accompany them in a stolen car to a large highway bridge in the country. There Snoek was chained inside a windowless enclosure (the blasting chamber) inside the bridge support. He was left with an air mattress, a sleeping bag, candles, writing paper, some food, and toilet paper. A 5-million-mark ransom was demanded from the parents, who from the start hesitated to cooperate with the police. Snoek's father never permitted the police to listen in on the telephone conversations he had with the kidnappers. No follow-up device was used to trace calls, while the only recordings of the kidnappers' calls, made by the family, were technically inferior. Similarly, the family refused to allow the police to follow the car in which the ransom was delivered to the pick-up point.

Snoek was not freed after the kidnappers received the 5 million marks. However, he was able to attract the attention of a passerby to his prison cell by dropping paper shreds and clothes from an airhole, which the kidnappers evidently overlooked when they selected the hide-out. Without such ingenuity, Snoek probably would have died in his prison. The kidnappers were later traced through registered banknotes from the ransom, which was only partially recovered. Again, the perpetrators were nonprofessionals and came from a working-class background. Neither had a significant criminal past.

- On December 14, 1976 the scion of one of Germany's largest businesses was kidnapped after leaving a university building in a small Bavarian town. Richard Oetker, 25, was kept in a small wooden crate measuring $60 \times 70 \times 120$ cm. Inside the crate, in which he had to assume an unnaturally bent and cramped position, the victim was connected to an electrical device. The electrodes ensured Oetker's death should he attempt to free himself or the blackmail fail. Two days later the family delivered the ransom, a staggering 21 million marks in 1,000-DM bills. A few hours later Oetker was found in a forest on the fringe of Munich, crippled for life. Electrical shocks had cracked two breastbones and both thighbones, his heart rhythm was irregular, and a lung had collapsed from the effort of shallow, cramped breathing for 47 hours. Two years later an out-of-work, mechanically inclined economist was convicted of the abduction because a banknote from the ransom was traced to him. Most of the ransom remains lost without a trace, as do any possible accomplices.

France
- In January 1978, the French industrial magnate Baron Edouard-Jean Empain, 40, was kidnapped outside his home on Avenue de Foch on his way to work. The crime looked like a terrorist action at the beginning. The Schleyer kidnapping was still well remembered and one of the attackers, who dragged the baron from his car, spoke German—or so it was believed by the only witness, Empain's driver, who admitted not knowing very much about foreign languages. It later became apparent that the Empain abduction was the work of criminals. A number of messages were in fact received by French newspapers

and agencies that claimed left-wing extremists as the perpetrators: The French NAPAP ("Armed Nuclei for the People's Autonomy"), which was believed to be connected with the German Baader-Meinhof gang; and a Belgian separatist movement voiced certain demands but later disclaimed any connection with the kidnapping.

The classical massive police action, including Paris-wide checkpoints, house and area searches, did not come up with any clues. Meanwhile the kidnappers established contact with the Empain family, requested a ransom in excess of 40 million francs (some $25 million), and entered into a negotiating process on the delivery procedures. As police stalling for time became evident to the hostage takers, they used a cruel method of intimidation: They hacked off one of Empain's fingers and mailed it to the family, which at that point gave in to the demands. A ransom was delivered by two members of the French Anti-Crime Brigade and shortly thereafter Empain surfaced in a Paris suburb, alive, astonishingly well in body and mind after more than six weeks of captivity and an infection in his amputated finger joint. Family and authorities remained tight-lipped on details of the captivity and ransom delivery.

Spain

- In several cases in the years 1977 and 1978, criminal and terrorist blackmail methods overlap. Repeatedly using the same technique, terrorist groups as well as local criminals taped an explosive device to the body of a victim. Typically the individual was freed and watched while he attempted to arrange for the ransom. In two cases, in March 1977 and January 1976, the victims died when the bombs exploded prematurely or were tampered with. In June 1978 local criminals in the city of Orense disappeared after receiving the Spanish equivalent of 100,000 marks and giving their victim information on how to defuse the bomb.

SOME OBSERVATIONS

The foregoing examples clearly show that kidnapping as a crime, which can be accompanied by a number of possible results, is not dependent on the type of criminal—professional or amateur, political or profit-oriented—that undertake it. Kidnapping has become in Europe a criminal fashion, the knowledge and techniques for which are quickly disseminated by the news media, creating new imitators with every new crime. In this field total amateurs and hard-core professionals use the same methods: no predictions on outcome can safely be drawn from the use of an apparently typical technique. Too often terrorist groups copy the methods of criminals and/or try to give their operation this type of "lower profile" (as was the case in the Palmers abduction). Increasingly common criminals jump on the terrorism backwagon because they expect additional leverage in the bargaining with authorities. Therefore, the following generalizations should not be regarded as absolute guidelines, but as findings drawn from the German and West European experiences:

1.   Amateurs—and there are a large number trying their hand at kidnappings—have a tendency to panic and kill their victims (or let them die) when negotiations run aground in the first phase. They tend to view a live captive as a very dangerous factor and have problems in assessing their own risks correctly. For example, most unprofessional abductors have been caught after the end of the kidnapping, when their defenses were down and they have distributed the ransom money without further precautions. On the other hand, their security precautions are normally as careful and intricately schemed as those of true professionals, as could be seen, for example, in the ransom-delivery methods demanded in various cases—often carbon copies of similar terrorist tactics.

2.   Professional gangsters, in comparison, display much more reasonable risk-assessment capabilities and tend to let their victim stay alive, if demands are met. In case of apprehension, they hope this tactic will win a more lenient sentence. Stalling tactics tend to have a lesser effect on these kidnappers than on amateurs, who may suddenly see their dream of quick riches shatter and abort an operation, killing the victim to cover their tracks. On the other hand, professionals might resort to such drastic blackmail methods as those experienced in the Empain case. Finger chopping has become a traditional technique for this "classical" type of blackmail artist.

3.   Terrorist groups have shown a tendency "to be true to their word," that is, to release their victims when their demands are met or to kill them when faced by a flat denial. This reliability is mainly due to an ingrained characteristic of all terrorist actions: wanting to be recognized as an opponent in the struggle for power, a "partner in the game." Again, their risk and security assessments are within reasonable bounds, and they view their victim more as a tool in the war against the authorities than as a figure in his own right. Certain considerations shown to the victim (in the case of Lorenz, for example, giving him his medications) stem from these circumstances. The German terrorists who held Schleyer struck an amazingly soft-spoken tone in their messages to the Schleyer family. All the usual cynicism and propaganda tirades were absent, once more underlining the fact that the real addressee of the abduction was not the family but the state and its "system."

Having invested a great deal of time and money in kidnapping a certain person, terrorists will hold onto their victims for as long as he (or she) appears useful to the group's aims—often longer than criminally oriented perpetrators will accept. The headlines and constant news coverage of the bargaining process give the terrorists a chance to convey their importance to the public. The society at large is the main target of the terrorist act, and *any* type of publicity is an important side-effect of the undertaking. With this in mind, the many messages in the Schleyer case sent to the authorities, family, news media, and public figures can be understood. It was here that the information embargo, ordered by the government, became an effective countermeasure in the fight against terrorism and served as an additional bargaining chip.

A similar news curfew was used by the German police in other kidnapping cases, though no general rules can be drawn from the results. In at least one case, that of Gernot Egolf, the curfew lasted 52 days but probably only resulted in information being withheld from the public and hinderance of police searches. In other cases since then—for example, in the kidnapping of a 4-year-old in autumn 1977—the blackout was an asset in securing the safe release of the child. It remains debatable how long such a total blackout should be maintained in a kidnapping case and when the public should be asked for help. The latter course involves such administrative problems as crazy calls, unusable calls, and false alarms. In the Schleyer case the most important bit of information, that on the safehouse in which the victim was held for the longest period, was lost in the overbureaucratic mass of investigation teams from national and federal levels.

4. Safety precautions appear inadequate: They probably frighten off only the less resolute type of kidnapper. As the Schleyer case showed, terrorists will not shrink from a major gunbattle when they are after a worthwhile target. Large-scale safety precautions, such as those taken in the "hardening" of political target figures, are extremely costly and beyond the resources of any except the biggest corporations. Today the protection of one of the sixty highest politicians in the Federal Republic of Germany costs close to 500,000 marks ($200,000) which includes armored limousines (price of each: 280,000 marks) and guard details.

On the other hand the abundant number of unprotected targets allows potential criminal kidnappers to take their pick. All the abovementioned cases of criminal kidnappings were attacks on unprotected and unguarded individuals. Since that abduction spree West European industrialists (who up to then looked with a slightly malicious grin at the precautions of their Italian counterparts) have upgraded their personal security programs considerably. Among other things, bodyguards and ransom insurance have come into vogue, though the efficacy of both is debatable. According to recent information, most potential victims do fear an attempt on themselves less than one on a member of their family.

Recent incidents have shown a new tendency, creating renewed anxieties. Abductions of small children have occurred again at an alarming rate. On December 18, 1981, 8-year-old Nina von Gallwitz, daughter of a rich banker, was grabbed on her way to school from her home in an upper class suburb of Cologne. Three attempts at delivery of the 1.2-million-mark ransom have gone astray. The last sign of life appeared at the end of January, and it is questionable how much hope remains for the life of the girl. It is the second such abduction from the same suburb in 12 months; obviously the arrest of the kidnappers in the earlier case did nothing to deter the second kidnapping.

5. A new mode of hostage taking has occurred in Germany in the last two years, alarming potential victims and authorities alike. With banks now a hard target because of video-cameras, bulletproof glass, and alarm systems, criminals have turned on the families of employees, often holding these hostages in their

own homes until the employee (normally a branch director, or somebody holding the keys) enters the bank, takes the requested amount out of the safe, and delivers it to the kidnappers. This type of kidnapping holds little risk for the perpetrators, who sometimes send one of their number along with the employee to make sure that the police are not notified. The duration of these attacks is very short, seldom longer than 10 or 12 hours, making accidental detection and exposure time to the victims a minimal risk. No countermeasures outside of passive defenses, such as silent alarms in the homes and offices of bankers, have proven effective against this type of short-duration kidnapping, which has surfaced especially in smaller towns in the countryside. Abduction has become a very mobile scourge and does not limit itself anymore to the large cities and population centers.

By all indications, kidnapping will persist, remaining a very real threat to executives, their families, and lifestyles in Western Europe. The Federal Republic of Germany is especially vulnerable, with its highly industrialized regions, its abundance of possible targets, and its extremist groups who present additional problems outside the sphere of the common criminal. Certain security precautions have become part of the habits of concerned politicians and businessmen; more needs to be done in this direction, especially in terms of consultations with police and government authorities on the guidelines of future negotiations and cooperation. Active police protection and speedy apprehension of kidnappers should go a long way toward limiting the damage, though neither tactic can be expected to become a strong deterrent.

6.   More experience is needed in the use of psychological advice to decision-level officials and in regard to press coverage and the overall aspects of publicity in these cases. The role of the media and the effect of publicity on imitators are only barely understood and should be researched in depth. In regard to the safety and sanity of the victim and the family involved, consideration should be directed toward shortening the negotiating and bargaining process to relieve the severe pressure they experience. The traditional tactic of stalling for time and drawing out communication with the abductors for weeks may be losing its effectiveness, in the light of a recent experience in which this tactic failed.

More than anything, specific lines of cooperation and coordination between all concerned (authorities, police on local and federal level, corporations, and families) should be developed and set in motion immediately when an emergency occurs. In this way, reaction time can be limited to a minimum, friction between the various decision and action levels reduced, and a maximum in response (negotiation process, information gathering, and search activities) be achieved.

5

The Italian Experience*

Vittorfranco S. Pisano

Since the early 1970s, Italy has experienced an unprecedented escalation in the number of kidnappings perpetrated by common criminals, politically motivated individuals, and occasional groupings of both elements. Governmental and parliamentary efforts to combat this disquieting phenomenon have produced—notably during the period 1977–1980—legislative enactments that render the provisions of the Criminal Code of 1930 and of the Code of Criminal Procedure of 1935 stricter and more effective, respectively.

The Criminal Code defines kidnapping as "the deprivation of someone's personal liberty" and makes it punishable by six months to eight years of imprisonment.[1] However, if the offense is committed "for purposes of extortion," the current applicable penalty ranges from 25 to 30 years of imprisonment.[2] Moreover, the same penalty is applicable to the newly specified crime of "kidnapping for purposes of terrorism and subversion."[3]

Similarly, the pertinent Rules of Criminal Procedure have been amended to vest with territorial jurisdiction on kidnapping cases the court of the place where the abduction is carried out, rather than the court of the place where the victim is ultimately returned to liberty, as previously established.[4] The new rules unquestionably simplify and speed up investigations.

Yet, a number of overriding factors somewhat frustrate the laudable intent of this recent legislation. To the political terrorist, whatever his ideology, a successful abduction affords more intensive and prolonged media coverage than the "mere" wounding or murder of an adversary. At the same time, a kidnap situation enables the political terrorist to seize the initiative and to impose, regardless of the outcome, some form of a dialogue as a co-equal with the institutions he is attempting to subvert. To the common criminal, a kidnapping for ransom represents a close-to-certain high profit, accompanied by a comparatively smaller risk than is present in other highly lucrative criminal ventures. In either instance the benefit potentially outweighs the risk. Given these premises, what the Italian media have labeled the "kidnap industry" can be expected to remain a booming business in the foreseeable future.

---

* Several events have taken place since the preparation of this chapter and are not included herein.

THE TERRORIST SCENE

Insofar as political crime is not nearly as pervasive as common criminality, ideologically motivated abductions are considerably fewer but almost always draw far more attention. They are regarded as a substantive threat not only to Italy's democratic institutions—painfully reacquired and further developed amid difficulties in the years that followed the fall of Fascism at the conclusion of World War II—but also to the orderly functioning of Italian society, which continues to be torn by social conflicts fed by highly discordant political and ideological platforms.[5]

The incidence of terrorism, a basic appreciation of which is indispensable in analyzing and planning against political kidnappings and analogous forms of violence, is clearly reflected by the statistics furnished by the minister of the interior to the Parliament in March of 1982 and subsequently updated at the beginning of July of the same year. Since 1969, Italian terrorist groups of various persuasions have carried out 13,000 criminal actions, the most violent of which resulted in 315 murders and 1,075 woundings. Terrorist elements confined to Italian prisons include 1,477 extremists of the left and 451 of the right.[6] Besides these two ideologies, Italian terrorism is kept alive by anarchists and separatists.

Of the four, the leftist or Marxist-Leninist component has consistently been the largest in terms of both overall members and number of terrorist formations present within that component. In fact, over 100 groups have been identified. Three in particular, the Red Brigades (Brigate Rosse, BR), the Armed Proletarian Nuclei (Nuclei Armati Proletari, NAP), and Front Line (Prima Linea, PL), have achieved highly menacing records, although the militant activities of the latter two now largely take place in the court rooms and in the prisons, following operational setbacks at the hands of the law enforcement agencies. Their surviving assets outside of captivity have generally been absorbed by the BR, the most resilient formation of the entire terrorist spectrum.

Besides enjoying the greatest numerical strength, the leftist component is also the most sophisticated with respect to structure and dynamics. Moreover, its choice of targets is more selective and its ideological commitment is clear-cut and comparatively more firm. On the whole, the leftist component is responsible for the most damage.

The BR and kindred terrorist organizations of the left draw their origin and much of their inspiration from the student, labor, and prison unrest of the late 1960s and early 1970s. In fact, the universities, the factories, and the prisons were and continue to be primary sources of terrorist recruitment, as well as of sociopolitical issues over which such groups conduct their campaigns in the name of a Communist revolution to end capitalist "exploitment." The avowed objective of the BR in particular is "to strike at the heart of the imperialist state of the multinationals," a campaign relentlessly conducted over a period of 12 years.

In the 1970s, five patterns ostensibly characterized the terrorist left. The first, principally associated with the BR, entailed practically full-time clandestine activity on the part of the militants and systematic pursuit of selective violence, which was progressively aimed at an increasingly broad range of targets. From the initial targeting of rightist activists and executive employees in the industrial sector, the BR extended their selection to executive employees in other economic and financial sectors, to judges, prosecutors, attorneys, professors and journalists allegedly aligned with the establishment, and—not least of all—to political figures associated with the relative-majority Christian Democratic Party. At the same time, the geographical area of operations gradually expanded from Milan to the industrial triangle of the north, comprising Milan-Turin-Genoa, to Rome, and ultimately to the rest of the peninsula. Less visible has been the BR presence in the islands of Sicily and Sardinia.

The second pattern, attributed to PL and its various satellite groups, reflected a flexible organization for the conduct of political action and propaganda, on one hand, and "armed struggle," on the other. Consequently, most users of this pattern led a double life as political activists with a clean police record and a regular job and as part-time terrorists. Their method of target selection did not differ from those of the BR or other groups using the first pattern.

The third pattern involved sporadic and spontaneous terrorist acts carried out by minor groups that would frequently disappear from the scene after an attack or two—which were usually negligible, against property rather than persons. This pattern, however, has also been used by the more solidly established groups for purposes of cover and psychological warfare (for example, training and testing of recruits, initial expansion into new geographic areas, and disinformation as to the breadth of the revolutionary movement).

The fourth pattern consisted of actions planned and/or executed jointly by two or more terrorist organizations maintaining permanent or occasional liaison.

The fifth and final pattern—auxiliary support—included logistical and, less frequently, operational aspects. The more systematically established organizations would draw varying types and degrees of support (e.g., cover, intelligence, medical and legal assistance, recruitment, communications) from sizable elements of the extra-parliamentary left that sympathized with the terrorist philosophy but did not necessarily share clandestine operational styles or permanent commitment to violence.

With the start of the 1980s, however, modifications in patterns began to emerge and new insights were acquired into terrorist structures and dynamics. This latter development was largely the result of the "great spring offensive of 1980," as well as of other successful law enforcement operations against the terrorist left. Significantly, by the summer of 1980 the BR had totally or largely absorbed a number of no longer viable formations, including the October XXII Circle (Circolo XXII Ottobre), the Partisan Action Groups (Gruppi di Azione Partigiana, GAP), the NAP, PL, and less notorious groups. The BR's absorption of these residues caused adoption of some of their specific aims and led to a partial imitation—whether willful or unwitting—of their patterns and techniques. Consequently, the BR no longer appears to be totally underground: Influenced by the PL, they are believed to have adopted a structure that now includes full-time "regulars" and part-time "irregulars." This change indicates a balanced merger of the original first two patterns.

The third and fourth patterns, on the other hand, have either been largely discontinued or are being held in abeyance. With respect to the third pattern in particular, the last semi-annual public intelligence report available in print notes the remarkably diminished role of the once proliferating minor groups.[7] The fifth pattern, in contrast, remains unaltered, but the BR have been apparently relying more on their own irregulars for services and logistics. The trial of forefront elements of the extra-parliamentary "Autonomy," set for this fall, may reveal more details regarding this pattern.

It is extremely important to monitor and record all such patterns and their relative variations because the terrorist phenomenon, particularly that of the left, displays enormous flexibility in coping with changing conditions. Both evolution and involution can be expected in the structure and dynamics of viable groups and of those that might attempt to resurface.

The rightist or neo-Fascist component, has been in existence since the mid-1960s. Its menace takes second place only to the left, yet, its potential is considerably inferior. First, the ideology of the rightist formations is extremely hazy and contradictory. In some instances, as in the case of Third Position (Terza Posizione), they combine rightist and leftist ideologies. Moreover, the few existing rightist groups, whose numerical strength is also small, are generally remnants of earlier groups, reinforced by new recruits, under a different name. For example, New Order (Ordine Nuovo) re-emerged as Black Order (Ordine Nero), which, in turn, gave life to two "new" formations: Revolutionary Armed Nuclei (Nuclei Armati Rivoluzionari, NAR) and Popular Revolutionary Movement (Movimento Popolare Rivoluzionario, MPR).

In the late 1960s and early 1970s, the terrorist right pursued "blind" violent tactics, that is, it would indiscriminately target public places with explosive devices. Toward the end of the 1970s, it began to pattern its techniques after the selective terrorist actions of the left. At this point, individuals—primarily law enforcement officials and former fellow militants regarded as traitors to the cause—were selected for gunning attacks, while landmarks were chosen for bombings on the basis of the institutions they represented. The bombing of the Bologna railroad station on August 2, 1980, which caused an unprecedented 85 deaths and 200 injuries, could be an isolated return to the blind tactics of earlier years—if indeed it was an action by the right. They have been blamed, but no conclusive evidence has yet emerged.

The anarchist component, which is also small, has mostly operated in conjunction with extremists of the right and of the left, establishing a minority presence in such groups. The most notorious formation of this component is Revolutionary Action (Azione Rivoluzionaria, AR), whose ideology is anarchist/Communist and whose activities were most prominent in the period of 1977–80. Its ranks have included a number of foreign elements (Chileans, Germans, and Englishmen) arrested in Italy. The targeting techniques of the anarchist component are reminiscent of both the left and right.

The separatist component, present in German-speaking South Tyrol and in Sardinia, is basically concerned with obtaining independence from Italy. Some evidence suggests an initial cooperation in Sardinia between left-oriented separatists and the GAP in the early 1970s and again with the BR in the latter part of the same decade. Both separatist groups, small but potentially dangerous, generally target property rather than persons. Police and military installations, as well as power lines, are favored objectives. Explosives are the most frequent device.

In addition to the four domestic components discussed above—all of which maintain some form of contact and/or cooperation with foreign kindred groups—the Italian landscape is also marred, from time to time, by transnational terrorist elements whose objectives are, as a rule, non-Italian targets. Such elements include Libyans, Armenians, and sundry nationals from the Middle East. To date, the Libyans have singled out for attack primarily expatriates who refuse to live under Qaddafi's regime; the Armenians have targeted Turkish diplomats and airline offices of several nationalities; and the various Middle Easterners have extended feuds peculiar to that area of the world by attacking pertinent representatives and their offices on Italian soil. In the process, however, Italian and other foreign bystanders have occasionally been hurt by explosives or firearms. Italy's geographic position at the center of the Mediterranean, which links three continents, will inevitably continue to encourage transnational operations or use as a staging area.

POLITICAL KIDNAPPINGS

Of the four terrorist components—five, if the transnational one is included—only the left and right are known to have carried out abductions since the outburst of contemporary political violence: The left was successful with 23, the right with 2. While rightist kidnappings are not especially noteworthy, the same encouraging assessment cannot be made regarding leftist actions, particularly those perpetrated by the BR. From one perspective, they account for only a minimal percentage of the total statistics cited by the minister of the interior in his 1982 report. When considered as "military operations" in a program of "political objectives" to exploit social, economic, and political situations, however, these kidnappings not only acquire a great deal of significance, but also reflect the development of terrorist strategies.

Before examining individual kidnappings perpetrated by the terrorist right and left, it should be stressed that planning and execution for these operations do not substantially differ from those for other terrorist ventures, such as murders and woundings. Target selection is based on both the importance (or symbolic representativeness) of the victim and operational feasibility. The potential victim's habits are closely surveyed through personal observation and acquisition of information from open sources and, where possible, informants or "plants." Once the decision is made to target a specific individual, the attacking group, which is usually disguised but rarely masked, relies on the element of surprise.

While as few as two to four persons are usually employed in wound or kill missions, a larger number is common for projected kidnappings, especially if the potential victim moves by car under armed escort. More careful reconnoitering of the avenues of escape is necessary, as well as considerably more preparation for the phases that follow the snatching of the victim. Additional personnel and logistical assets are particularly important if the captors intend to "try" the victim, issue "communiques," and bargain for his release.

Two Rightist Operations

Two early rightist kidnappings were conducted exclusively for revenue purposes. On November 22, 1973, at 7 P.m., four members of the Revolutionary Action Movement (Movimento di Azione Rivoluzionaria MAR, a neo-Fascist group that operated primarily in northern Italy and ran paramilitary camps) abducted Aldo Cannavale, a 28-year-old industrialist and race car driver, in front of his Milan residence. The so-called gentleman driver was released in the same city on December 4th, at 2 A.M., after payment of a ransom amounting to L. 350 million. Subsequent investigations into rightist extremism eventually uncovered the identity of the group responsible for the abduction.

The second rightist kidnapping, that of Luigi Mariano, 39 years of age, owner of extensive real estate holdings and former president of the Banca Agricola Salentina, occurred in front of his home in Gallipoli (Lecce) on July 23, 1975, at 7:50 A.M. The initial ransom demand reportedly amounted to L. 2 billion, but the kidnappers settled for L. 280 million and the victim was released on September 9th in Palagiano (Taranto). The police investigation and trial determined that the abduction was executed by hired common criminals, whereas the principals were associated with rightist organizations headed or coordinated by convicted extremist Pierluigi Concutelli.

Apart from the politico-financial nature of these kidnappings, their only noteworthy aspect lies in the failure of the groups involved to claim responsibility.

Early Leftist Kidnappings

The very first leftist kidnapping was carried out by the now defunct October XXII Circle, founded in 1969 on its name date by former members of the Italian Communist Party no longer satisfied with the party's "inadequate revolutionary stance." The group soon attracted younger elements of heterogeneous social and political extraction. On October 5, 1970, at 11:30 P.M., three masked members of the group kidnapped 19-year-old Sergio Gadolla, a student and member of a wealthy Genoa family, as he was opening the garage door to park his car. After payment of L. 200 million, which was used for paramilitary training, young Gadolla was dropped off, tied and blindfolded, along a country road. He finally disentangled himself and walked to the Carabinieri station in Rezoaglio. On October 11th, at 2 A.M., he was finally back home. The reconstruction of his captivity indicates that he was held in a tent in a mountain area. The Circle did not claim responsibility for the kidnapping, which was only established following a number of arrests for other crimes intended to provide financing.

The NAP, whose autonomous operations spanned the period 1974–78, were responsible for three kidnappings. Although patterned after the BR, the foremost objective of the NAP was the organization of an armed struggle inside the prisons through external revolutionary links. They initially embarked upon a self-financing program that included two abductions in Naples a few months apart. On July 25, 1974, at 2:30 P.M., they kidnapped student Antonio Gargiulo, son of a prestigious local physician, in front of his residence. He was released on the same day at 11 P.M. in exchange for L. 70 million (as opposed to the L. 100 million originally demanded) paid by the family. The victim apparently never left the abduction vehicle. On December 18th, shortly after 6:30 A.M., the NAP kidnapped Giuseppe Moccia, a Naples liquor producer, by forcing him at gun point out of his car after he had stopped along the road because of a fake road sign. He was released on the 22nd, at 7:45 P.M., following the payment of L. 1 billion in ransom money. Neither kidnapping was claimed by the NAP. The proceeds from the first one were used to strengthen the Naples units, whereas those from the second enabled the NAP to expand their presence and operations to Rome and other areas.

Interestingly enough, the only action that brought the NAP national notoriety was the abduction, under uncertain circumstances, of Giuseppe Di Gennaro, a Supreme Court judge detailed to the Ministry of Justice. The action occurred in Rome in the afternoon of May 6, 1975. The NAP did claim responsibility for this action and attributed their gesture to the fact that Di Gennaro, by virtue of his assignment to prisoner rehabilitation programs, was being instrumental in masquerading the "ongoing repression." While in captivity, the judge was interrogated on the internal functioning of the penitentiaries. As noted below, the methods used by the NAP during the Di Gennaro affair were borrowed from the BR. The judge was released in Rome on the 11th at 10:30 P.M. in exchange for the transfer of three rebellious NAP inmates from the Viterbo prison to penitentiaries of their choice.

Kidnappings by the Red Brigades

Within Italy's contemporary terrorist scene, political kidnappings have been initiated, developed, and refined by the BR. Altogether, the BR has carried out 15 demonstrative/political abductions and two known kidnappings for self-financing. Contrary to the other groups of the left and right, which initially embarked upon kidnap ventures for revenue purposes, the BR has used kidnappings from the very start as political tools. During the period 1972–74, as they expanded from Milan— their geographic cradle—to the industrial triangle of the north, the BR perpetrated six political kidnappings. These can be analyzed as a technically, politically, and strategically interrelated cluster.

Of this cluster, the first two abductions lasted only long enough for the BR to propagandize against capitalism and Fascism. Both victims were released in a matter of minutes. Idalgo Macchiarini, 43 years old, personnel manager of Sit-Siemens in Milan, was kidnapped in that city on March 3, 1972, at 7:30 P.M., a few minutes walk away from the plant, where he had parked his car in the morning on the way to work. Three young men overpowered him, forced him into a van, tied him, briefly gagged him, took him for a 30-minute ride, photographed him with a BR poster around the neck, and ultimately abandoned him inside the van, which turned out to be stolen. He was hit with a fist three times on the face: twice when initially overpowered and a third time when he tried to resist inside the van. The BR left a leaflet in the van as a claim for this demonstrative action.

The second victim, Bartolomeo Di Mino, 44 years of age, a blue-collar worker and deputy secretary of the Cesano Boscone (Milan) section of the rightist Italian Social Movement (MSI, a party with parliamentary standing, but frequently termed neo-Fascist) was seized late in the evening of March 13th—ten days after the Macchiarini abduction—inside the MSI section offices, where he had lingered, all alone, after a meeting. The four attackers, including one woman, hit him on the head with the grip of a pistol, tied him and gagged him, and then photographed him. They also spray-painted "Red Brigades" on the walls, searched the premises, and took off with several files. The next day responsibility for this action was confirmed with a leaflet.

The third and fourth kidnappings lasted longer and displayed more sophistication. Bruno Labate, 29 years old, a Fiat clerical employee and provincial secretary of the CISNAL metal workers (a rightist labor union connected to the MSI), was kidnapped in Turin on September 12, 1973, at 9:30 A.M., as he was walking from his residence to work. He was seized by two men, who hit him with their fists on the head and on the mouth to dissuade him from resisting. He was quickly pushed into a van, where two more men were waiting. A witness, attracted by Labate's shouts, noticed that two kidnappers were wearing workers' overalls, a "uniform" often used by the BR for actions of this nature. The victim was then driven to a small garage, the hair on his head was shaven off, and a photograph was taken. An unprecedented addition to this treatment was his subjection to an interrogation by two of his captors, who probed into Fiat hiring practices and the numerical strength of CISNAL in the area. Four hours later, he was dropped off in front of Gate 2 of the Fiat Mirafiori plant with a poster around his neck indicating his identity. The BR also issued a leaflet claiming responsibility. Shortly after Labate's release, they also circulated a transcript of the interrogation.

The fourth victim, Michele Mincuzzi, a 56-year-old executive employee of Alfa Romeo, was abducted in Milan on November 28, 1973, at 7 P.M., in front of his home as he was about to park his car. In trying to hold off his aggressors, who moved in from behind, he suffered a broken nose. He was forced into a van, taken to what he later described as a "hall," and subjected to a "proletarian trial" that turned out, according to the victim, to be a rather subdued ideological discussion. He was released at 11:45 P.M. in Arese (Milan) with a poster around his neck depicting the red star of the BR. A batch of leaflets left with the victim explained the reason behind this action. These writings described Mincuzzi as one of many executive employees who "try to shift the cost of the crisis on the blue-collar workers by using such instruments as extortion, high cost of living, terrorism, provocation; that is to say, antiproletarian violence."

The fifth and sixth abductions of this cluster are indicative of the BR's achieved mastery over the craft of political kidnapping. The sixth also reflects the extension of terrorist operations from the private to the public sector.

Ettore Amerio, 56 years old, Fiat's personnel manager, was kidnapped in Turin on December 10, 1973, at 7:20 A.M., as he was walking toward the garage where he habitually parked his car at night. He was literally lifted into a van and then transferred into a sedan that took him to a hideout, the site of a "people's trial." Amerio's captivity, the longest carried out by the BR at that time, lasted eight days. Significantly, his abduction coincided with the negotiations for the renewal of the national collective bargaining agreements. Also for the first time, the BR scientifically exploited the publicity derivable from prolonged media coverage. A number of communiques were issued reporting on the "trial," which included further probings into the Fiat hiring practices that had been already disclosed in part by Labate. Amerio's captors released him in Turin on December 18th at 6 A.M. after photographing him. The victim indicated that he had been interrogated approximately three hours per day by a well-educated individual. The rest of the time he had been allowed to read or listen to music. Amerio said that he was "treated with kindness" and believed that "this too is an experience in life and, like all other experiences, it causes us to mature and to reflect more profoundly."

The sixth and last target of this cluster was Genoa Assistant State Attorney Mario Sossi, 43 years of age, who had prosecuted some members of the October XXII Circle. He was seized on his way home from the court house on April 18, 1974, at 9 P.M., thrown into a van, and taken to a hideout. This abduction symbolized the BR's first direct challenge to the authority of the state. Not only was Sossi "tried" by a people's court, but the release of eight convicted terrorists of the October XXII Circle was demanded in exchange for his freedom. During the 35 days of captivity, eight communiques were issued by the BR. The court of appeals with jurisdiction decided to grant a provisional release to these terrorists, but the chief prosecutor there appealed to the Supreme Court, which prevented the release. The BR, however, in the belief that the authority of the state had been sufficiently shaken, did release Sossi. (The chief prosecutor himself, Francesco Coco, was murdered together with his escort in Genoa two years later by the BR.) On May 23rd, at 11 P.M., Sossi was left in a park on the outskirts of Milan.

The purpose of this choice of locale was to complicate the investigation since, under the procedural rules still in effect at the time, territorial jurisdiction would thus be acquired by the Milan court and taken from the Genoa court that had already begun the investigation. Sossi foiled the BR by immediately taking a train to Genoa. He also demonstrated great courage in actively assisting the investigators. Although he lost five kg while in captivity and suffered a broken rib when forced into the van, he acknowledged that during his detention he received humane treatment. Throughout the interrogations in the "people's prison," Sossi never strayed from his moderately conservative convictions.

The four abductions that followed this initial cluster are not as significant. Two of them were revenue ventures, while the remaining two were basically demonstrative but devoid of deeper political meaning. Their comparatively modest caliber may be attributable to the need for self-financing and to the then ongoing changes in BR's human resources. The original membership, or "historic nucleus," of the BR was being replaced by a second generation that lacked the intellectual sophistication and, at first, the operational experience of their predecessors, who were being rounded up by the Carabinieri and the national police.

On June 4, 1975, at 5:30 P.M., wine producer Vittorio Vallarino Gancia was abducted in Canelli (Asti) while driving away from his villa. A man disguised as a road maintenance worker stopped him by waving a danger flag; a van moved behind Gancia's car; another man forced him out of the car at gun point and ordered him into the van. At noon of the following day, even before the ransom demand could be issued, Gancia was freed at Arzello di Melazzo (Alessandria) by a Carabinieri reconnaissance patrol that accidentally engaged in a fire fight with Gancia's captors near their hideout in the country.

This successful abduction, but abortive revenue venture, was followed by two demonstrative kidnappings one day apart in different cities. Enrico Boffa, 41 years old, manager of the Singer plant at Leinì, had just returned to his home in Rivoli (Turin) on October 21, 1975, when, as he was about to lock the garage door, three armed men suddenly appeared, forced him to kneel, hung a BR poster around his neck, and photographed him. As they were apparently leaving, two pistol shots were fired, one of which hit Boffa's right leg. The following day, Vincenzo Casabona, 47 years old, personnel manager of Ansaldo Nucleare, was seized in front of his residence in Arenzano (Genoa), as he was coming back from work. After being forced into a van, he was held there for one hour, beaten, subjected to a haircut, interrogated on corporate matters, and finally dropped off in Recco (Genoa). In claiming responsibility for this action with a leaflet one day later, the BR alluded to their previous threat on a similar occasion: "Today Amerio, tomorrow Casabona."

The last of this series was the abduction of shipowner Piero Costa, 49 years old, in Genoa on January 12, 1977, at 7:45 P.M., in front of his villa. Armed men forced him into a Fiat 132. He was released 81 days later, on April 3rd, at 8 A.M., after payment of a L. 1.5 billion ransom. Costa was insured against kidnappings with Lloyds of London. After the release, the BR finally claimed responsibility for this action and justified it as "taxation of a multinational." The revenue from this "tax" was partially used to finance the abduction of Aldo Moro the following year.

The Moro Kidnapping

The kidnapping of Aldo Moro, former premier and incumbent president of the Christian Democratic Party, constitutes the most astounding BR operation and marks the highest organizational peak achieved to date by that terrorist formation. Unquestionably, at that point in time, the remaining elements of the historic nucleus and the second generation of the BR had not only established a formidable terrorist machine, but had refined the political kidnap techniques displayed over the previous six years.

The elder statesman combined two highly desirable targeting characteristics: importance and vulnerability. In addition to his formal political credentials, he was the *de Jacto* most influential public figure in Italy. At the same time, his habits were quite methodical, including attendance at Mass each morning at the same church near his apartment before proceeding to work. Moreover, although Moro was accompanied by a five-man armed escort and a back-up vehicle, his own car, a blue Fiat 130, was not armored.

On March 16, 1978, at 9:10 A.M., as Aldo Moro was following his habitual route from his residence, a BR commando squad, comprising eight men and one woman, went into action. At the corner between Via Fani and Via Stresa, a stolen white Fiat 128 with diplomatic corps license plates backed up into Moro's vehicle, whose driver was unable to take evasive action, thus boxing the vehicle in between the Fiat 128 and the escort car. Two men from the Fiat 128 fired their pistols at Moro's driver and at the escort commander, who was also sitting in Moro's sedan. Another BR fire team, disguised as airline personnel, stepped out from behind a bar's decorative shrubbery, pulled out automatic weapons from leather handbags, and fired on the three policemen in the back-up car. Moro was snatched from his car and pulled into a strategically placed blue Fiat 128, from which he was later transferred to a van that took him to the so-called people's prison. Other members of the squad used guns to keep traffic away from the escape route.

Beside the five dead escort members lay 92 ammunition casings. Two of those rounds were fired by the sole guard who managed to step out of his vehicle—the back-up car—and draw his pistol. He managed to slightly wound one member of the commando squad. The assault and snatch operation lasted no more than three minutes. The precision and attention to detail with which it was conducted even included sabotaging the telephone lines in the immediate vicinity in advance. Moreover, the night before, a florist's pick-up truck—usually parked during the day time by the intersection where the abduction took place—had all four tires slashed in another part of town: This encumbrance to the abduction was thus effectively eliminated. In all, nine vehicles, including one or two vans, were used by the BR for this operation.

Notwithstanding the most massive manhunt ever mounted by the police forces, augmented by military units, Moro was held in captivity for 54 days—perhaps in more than one hideout—and was finally "executed" on May 9th, following the government's refusal to release 13 leftist terrorists who were standing trial. During Moro's captivity the BR used all the techniques already tested during previous political kidnappings. Not only did they "try" Moro, but in the course of the captivity they issued nine communiques (an additional one was repudiated by them), and on two separate occasions they provided a photograph of the victim. Furthermore, the BR allowed the prisoner to write to a number of political figures, friends, and family members. Altogether he wrote 37 letters, at least 22 of which were delivered by the BR. BR telephone operators were also in touch with newspapers, the Moro family, and the statesman's closest friends. The victim was the prime mover in attempting to negotiate his own release with the government. Although the hard no-deal line prevailed, Italy's political spectrum was divided between those who were for negotiating and those who were not. This disagreement in itself was a form of psychological success for the BR.

Moro was never abused beyond being deprived of his freedom. Even the interrogation methods were "humane." He was not informed of the decision to kill him, although he was given the opportunity to draft a will. After being led into the trunk of a stolen red Renault, he was shot with a submachine gun and a pistol. The BR abandoned the car with the body, covered by a blanket, on the Via Caetani, half way between the headquarters of the Christian Democratic Party and those of the Italian Communist Party (PCI). Interestingly enough, Moro had been abducted on the day of the parliamentary vote of confidence for the newly formed Christian Democratic government, which for the first time under the Constitution of 1948 drew the support of the PCI. However, since the decision to kidnap the senior Christian Democrat had been made by the strategic directorate of the BR several months before that event could have been foreseen, the symbolism of the date may well be casual. Less casual is the location where the body was deposited.

The Rome "column" of the BR, augmented with elements from columns operating in northern Italy, was given the task of carrying out the Moro operation. Despite the expenditure of resources required to manage the Moro affair, the BR was able to carry out a number of complementary activities during his captivity. The most significant of these were two murders and six shootings in the leg.

At this writing, the Rome Court of Assizes is trying 23 members of the BR indicted for the Moro affair. The same court is also trying a total of 63 defendants for all the crimes perpetrated by the Rome column of the BR during the period December 1976–May 1980. Much of the prosecution's evidence has been turned in by "repentant" terrorists who either were not present at or performed a marginal role in the Moro abduction and murder. Recent legislation on such informers,[8] which has led to many arrests, allows those who cooperate a considerable degree of clemency. While the results have unquestionably been beneficial to law enforcement efforts in terms of arrests, the credibility of the testimony so obtained in terms of specific facts is open to debate. Such "confessions" can also be powerful disinformation tools. The outcome of the BR trial, therefore, may prove disappointing as an explanation of the entire Moro operation, as well as of the BR structure and leadership.

The D'Urso Kidnapping

One year and a half after the conclusion of the Moro operation, the BR chose another kidnapping target representative of the state: Supreme Court Judge Giovanni D'Urso, 47 years old, detailed to the ministry of justice as head of the Third Division of the General Directorate for Penitentiaries. Just as in the targeting of Aldo Moro, in whom the BR had symbolically merged their attack against a plurality of institutions—the national executive, the Parliament, and the Christian Democratic

Party—the abduction of D'Urso was a simultaneous attack against the judiciary and the prison system.

D'Urso was abducted in Rome on December 12, 1980, at 8:30 P.M., on his way home from the ministry. Because of parking difficulties, he had to leave his car some distance from his apartment and slowly proceeded on foot in the darkness. He was suddenly seized by four men, who moved in from different directions and, notwithstanding his resistance, forced him into a van. To the victim's recollection, the trip lasted two hours. He ultimately found himself in a tent, presumably pitched inside some sort of a brick structure since he never heard any noises. Nor did he ever see the faces of his captors, who either were hooded or blindfolded the judge during periods of contact, including the interrogation conducted by two of the three men whose presence he was aware of during captivity.

The D'Urso affair lasted 33 days and reflected the refinement of past BR procedures. In all, ten communiques were issued by the BR. While the BR in general advised different newspapers or press agencies by telephone of the places where the communiques were dropped, in this case they displayed a preference for *Il Messaggero* of Rome. As usual, the same typewriter was used to assure authenticity. In the very first message, the BR demanded "the end of differentiation between inmates" and the shutting down of the maximum security prison in Asinara (Sardinia).

On December 26th, the government announced its decision to close that prison, underscoring that this determination had been reached well before the D'Urso abduction. The BR replied that they did not trust the promises of the government. On December 28th, the terrorists held in the maximum security prison in Trani (Bari) broke out in revolt, taking hostages in the process. The next day the previously unpublicized Special Intervention Groups (GIS) of the Carabinieri swiftly and bloodlessly quelled the uprising. (The BR retaliated on New Year's Eve by murdering Carabinieri Brigadier General Enrico Galvaligi, deputy director for the coordination of prison security, in front of his Rome apartment.) On January 4, 1982, "Communique no. 8" stated that D'Urso had been "sentenced to death," but that the ultimate decision would be left to the "comrades" in the maximum security prisons. Their decision would have to be published by the Italian press and aired on television.

At this point, part of the press opted for a news black-out, at least with respect to the BR's communiques, while other dailies and periodicals decided to apply selective criteria. This difference in media attitudes paralleled the conflict among the political forces, which, as in the Moro case, were divided between the hard line and the soft line. Meanwhile, as the BR continued to insist on publicity, some papers did publish the communiques; and one weekly, *L'Espresso* of Rome, published not only the BR's "interrogatory" of Judge D'Urso, but also an interview with an emissary of the BR.[9] Moreover, a private television channel aired an appeal from D'Urso's daughter, who publicly read a communique in which her father was defined as an executioner.

In consonance with the "decision" of the inmates of the maximum security prisons in Palmi (Reggio Calabria) and Trani (Bari), the BR finally released D'Urso on January 15th in Rome. The judge recollects a return ride of approximately one hour and 45 minutes, which included two car changes en route. Throughout the trip he had on a blindfold and stereo earphones. In captivity he was never tied or chained; in fact, he was kept abreast of developments and fed well-prepared foods. Although he did write a letter to his superiors supporting the BR's demand for the closing of the Asinara prison, he did not become involved in attempting to manage his own release, as had his more illustrious but less fortunate predecessor.

The Cirillo Kidnapping

In 1981, the BR outdid themselves by perpetrating four political abductions during an overlapping period of time. These four kidnappings, carried out in widely separated areas and aimed at different objectives, should still be regarded as a cluster: In many respects they represent coordinated campaigns over several fronts.

The abduction of Ciro Cirillo, 60 years old, former president of the Campania Region and incumbent Christian Democratic councilman for regional urban planning and economic affairs, had two objectives. On one hand, it deepened the BR's operational penetration in the south. On the other, it was calculated to exploit at the revolutionary level the deficiencies of the central and regional governments in providing assistance and reconstruction following the earthquake of the previous year. In that disaster a number of municipalities in the region, including Naples, its capital, had been badly damaged or destroyed.

Cirillo was abducted in Torre del Greco (Naples) on April 27, 1981, at 9:30 P.M. The councilman, accompanied by his secretary and two escort members, was putting his armored car into the garage of his building. The escort commander, who was in charge of opening the garage door, carelessly left his car door unlocked when he got out of the car. Equally inattentive, the driver did not wait for the garage door to be closed before opening his door after parking. At this point, three members of a BR commando squad, already in place, rapidly moved in. One fired a submachine gun at the escort commander by the garage door and another fired a pistol at the driver: Both were killed. The secretary was shot in the legs with a pistol by the third terrorist. Cirillo was pulled out of the car and loaded into a van, which, in the interim, had pulled up to the entrance of the garage, thus totally blocking it. Two more BR cars were parked in the vicinity, one serving as a lookout and the other as an escort vehicle. The squad, in preparation for the attack, had tampered with the local telephone line. It is estimated that the entire commando squad, which operated unmasked, comprised 15 members. Responsibility for this action was claimed the following day with "communique no. 1" of a series of 12. Cirillo was held for 88 days.

During Cirillo's captivity, the BR made three well-publicized demands: the requisitioning of empty dwellings for victims of the earthquake, subsidies to the local unemployed, and publication of the record of Cirillo's "trial." Notwithstanding the usual split between proponents of the hard and soft line, these demands were substantially met. The BR forced Cirillo to write some 20 letters to his family and political figures in which he concurred with the BR's demands. In one municipality they also broadcast a taped "address" by Cirillo to the victims of the earthquake and provided both a Naples and a Rome private television station with a videocassette of the trial. The BR's communiques were indicative of thorough familiarity with local affairs, including data pertaining to NATO installations in the area.

Cirillo was released on July 24th at 6:20 A.M. in an area of Naples particularly damaged by the earthquake. After releasing him, the BR announced that a ransom in the amount of L. 1 billion 450 million had been paid by Cirillo's family and the Christian Democratic Party. The party consistently denied any such payment on its part; however, Cirillo finally acknowledged that the ransom was in fact paid solely by his family.

Throughout his captivity, Cirillo was kept in a 2 × 2 m soundproof wooden structure and spent his entire time either sitting or lying on a cot. Ventilation was artificially induced from the outside at regular intervals. At noon he was fed a full meal, while in the evening he was served tea and biscuits. Before the beginning of the interrogations, he was given doctrinal materials to read so that the questioning would be "fruitful." It has been determined that his prison was actually mounted inside a cooperative physician's office in the municipality of Cercola near Naples.

The Cirillo case remains a national political issue, not only with respect to the actual payer or payers of the ransom, but also with regard to alleged illegal involvement on the part of the intelligence services in trying to obtain Cirillo's freedom. Supposedly the services used jailed elements of Neapolitan organized crime as intermediaries. Although the government has excluded any unlawful activity on the part of the intelligence establishment, attacks and insinuations of wrongdoing are still being made. To date only one facet of the debate has been settled. A document published by L'Unità, the official daily of the Italian Communist Party, "proving" that illicit acts were undertaken by Christian Democratic members of the government and by officials of the intelligence community, has been shown to be a forgery carelessly or negligently reprinted in that party's press.

The Red Brigades Offensive Continues

Less than one month after Cirillo's successful kidnapping, the Veneto column of the BR abducted Giuseppe Taliercio, 53 years of age, manager of the Montedison petrochemical plant in Marghera (Venice). On May 20, 1981, at 1:30 P.M., five BR members, one disguised as a finance guard, gained access to the engineer's apartment in Mestre (Venice) and overpowered him together with his wife and two children. The commando squad chained Taliercio's relatives, searched the premises, and after 45 minutes departed through a secondary door with Taliercio. He was held in captivity for 46 days, during which time no demand was made in exchange for his release. "Communique no. 5," issued on June 26th, reported that a sentence to death had been "decreed" and stated: "In 30 years of antiproletarian activity, he personified the role and the functions of the imperialist personnel that plan and carry out the restructuring at the service of the multinationals." The BR were again focusing on capitalism as their adversary. Taliercio was executed on July 6th. According to the findings of the autopsy, seventeen 7.65 caliber rounds were fired into his body with two different pistols, after he was stunned with a blow on the head. He had lost ten kg of weight, his hair had grayed, and one tooth was missing. After a telephone call by the BR to the news agency ANSA on the same day as the murder, his body was found at 1:30 P.M., in a stolen car whose speedometer had been broken to conceal the mileage after the theft. The car was parked a short distance away from Taliercio's plant.

On June 3, 1981, at 7:30 A.M., the Milan column of the BR conducted a parallel operation with the abduction of Renzo Sandrucci, 53 years of age, an executive employee of Alfa Romeo at Arese (Milan). His specific duties entailed production and labor organization at the plant. He was kidnapped a few hundred meters from his home as he was driving to work. His car—an Alfetta 2000—while travelling on his habitual route, was boxed in by a Fiat 124 and an Opel Ascona. A number of terrorists got out of a van parked near there, ordered some bystanders into a bar at gun point, overpowered Sandrucci's corporate bodyguard, who was sitting next to him in the car, and pulled Sandrucci into the Fiat 124. It is estimated that the commando squad had seven to nine members, some of whom were wearing workers' overalls.

Sandrucci was held for 51 days, during which time eight communiques were issued by the BR and several letters written by Sandrucci were delivered. In one of them, he tendered his resignation from Alfa Romeo. In their communiques, the BR demanded the withdrawal of disciplinary measures vis-a-vis certain employees of the Arese plant and the publication of some "documents." Sandrucci was released on July 23rd, at 6:10 P.M. A BR telephone call to a private radio station indicated, as usual, where he could be found. He had been left tied in a stolen Alfa Romeo Giulia Super near the Ercole Marelli plant in Crescenzago (Milan).

After his release, the victim indicated that he had been kept in a tent set up inside an apartment. As in Cirillo's case, prior to being interrogated, he was given doctrinal material to read. According to Sandrucci, he received humane treatment and felt that the "forced experience" was a "positive one at the personal level." On the whole, he has been reluctant to enter into details.

Roberto Peci, younger brother of the most famous "repentant" BR member, Patrizio, was kidnapped in San Benedetto del Tronto (Ascoli Piceno) on June 10, 1981. He was last seen in the afternoon getting into his car with two men. With this action the BR established a precedent: until they killed Taliercio, they held four captives at one time for nearly one month. Peci was himself a former extremist who had abandoned political militancy, but the true purpose of the abduction was to intimidate talkative terrorists. Throughout his captivity, which lasted 54 days (as many as Moro's), the BR issued the usual communiques and forced Roberto to write polemical letters to his brother Patrizio, thus their purpose was to contradict his brother's confessions. Roberto Peci was murdered on April 3rd with 20 pistol shots fired at close range by a 7.65 caliber automatic pistol and a .38 caliber revolver, both with silencers. The victim was tied and his eyes, ears, and mouth were held shut with cotton and tape. The body was left wrapped in a

BR flag inside some ruins along a road perpendicular to Rome's Appian Way, an area that is a kind of impromptu garbage dump. A poster on one of the ruin's walls read: "Death to traitors."

The Dozier Kidnapping

This cluster was followed, also in 1981, by the BR's final political abduction in that period, that of U.S. Army Brigadier General James Lee Dozier, Deputy Chief of Staff for Logistics and Administration of NATO's Southern European Land Forces Command in Verona. The action against Dozier injected an element of novelty in BR targeting, but not in their ideology or strategic goals.

Prior to this action, the BR had consistently expressed in resolutions and even in communiques their solidarity with "proletarian internationalism"; they also linked "reactionary exploitation" to the "imperialist centers" of the United States, the Federal Republic of Germany, and Japan. Another subject of condemnation was the presence of "the American party in Italy." In a strategic resolution of February 1978, the BR termed the Italian government "an instrument of the interests of imperialism headed by the US and the FRG." That document further defined NATO as "the political-military organism to which imperialism entrusts the guiding role in relation to both the defense against the 'external enemy' and the annihilation of the 'internal enemy.' " Analogous language appeared in other writings, including a communique issued just before the summit of the most industrialized Western nations, which was hosted by the Italian government in 1980. That statement labelled the participating nations as "the world's principal oppressors who will meet in June in an occupied Venice."

Even though the Dozier kidnapping is the BR's only known action against a foreign national on Italian territory, the BR had materially stepped into the international arena well before the abduction of General Dozier. From the early 1970s, they had developed logistical channels with the German Red Army Faction (RAF), their traditional mentor in the practice of urban terrorism. But even more significant are the operational links between the BR and the French Direct Action (AD). The arrest of three BR members in Toulon in March of 1980, together with their French counterparts, revealed the existence of BR safehouses on the Côte d'Azur, BR training of French terrorists, and most important, joint BR–AD "proletarian expropriations" on French territory.

On December 17, 1981, at approximately 5 P.M., two BR members, disguised as plumbers, gained access to General Dozier's apartment in Verona. Although the general was driven to and from his NATO headquarters by an armed driver who took various precautions along the routes, no other security measures had been adopted. The attackers overpowered both the general, who offered unarmed resistance, and his wife, also present in the apartment. They were subsequently joined by two more men, who assisted in placing the general in a trunk, searching the premises for documentation and tying and gagging Mrs. Dozier. They took along the only papers they could find: the general's personal records. The alarm was given approximately four hours later when the neighbors finally heard Mrs. Dozier's noisy efforts to free herself.

The general was held captive for 42 days, during which time the BR followed their established patterns. They "tried" the general, issued five communiques, the third of which included a transcript of the general's interrogation, and stated that through Dozier they were trying American "imperialism." In the communiques they reiterated the view that the "imperialist state of the multinationals" is viable in Italy insofar as it is nurtured by the NATO structures imposed by the United States on that country and on Western Europe. In these writings, the BR further condemned the modernization of the NATO Theater Nuclear Force (TNF) in Europe and the deployment of the neutron bomb in the United States.

On January 28, 1982, at 11:30 A.M., ten members of the Central Operative Nucleus for Security (NOCS) of the state police broke into a safe house in Padua, where General Dozier was being held by five BR members, three men and two women. No blood was shed and the general was recovered unharmed and wearing a long beard. The raiding party's maneuverability was ensured by two concentric circles of nonuniformed and uniformed policemen, who discreetly isolated the area.

The Dozier case has been reconstructed in some detail because of the capture of the jailers, the "repentance" of some of them, and the general's testimony at the trial.

Dozier's abduction was decided some months in advance by the strategic directorate and entrusted to the Veneto column. L. 18 million were budgeted for the operation and eight terrorists participated in the actual kidnapping. The general was loaded aboard a Fiat 238 van, moved en route to a Fiat Ritmo, and taken to an apartment in Padua, where a tent with a cot had been set up. Although allowed enough space and movement for minimal exercise, Dozier was handcuffed to the cot and earphones put over his ears. He was regularly fed and given the opportunity to bathe. His captors wore ski masks inside the safehouse. (He was aware of three men and one woman.) The general was interrogated seven times at long intervals by the same male inquisitor, always in Italian but with the aid of a dictionary. At no time was any forceful effort used to make him disclose classified matters, nor did the inquisitor display an in depth knowledge of military affairs. Since the general was given reading materials and cards to play solitaire, he kept a secret calendar of his captivity. Except for some ear damage resulting from the loud music played through the ear phones, he suffered no physical injuries. Throughout his captivity, he wore a sweatsuit similar to the ones worn by his captors. Apparently the intent of his abduction, though never publicized, was to negotiate his release in exchange for jailed BR members.

The liberation itself reportedly came about as the result of some arrests made within Verona drug circles, which, in turn, led to political extremists and finally to the driver of the van, who cooperated by taking the investigators to the safe house. At the trial, concluded on March 25th, 16 convictions were handed down.

Two terrorists involved in the Dozier abduction claim to have been tortured. Five members of the state police, including three of the NOCS, have since been arrested amid extensive public protest. Whatever the outcome of the investigation and judicial proceedings, it is interesting that no similar accusations had previously been made by jailed terrorists, including those of the historic nucleus of the BR. One theory suggests that this is a new BR tactic to discredit the institutions they are trying to subvert. Some analogies can be drawn to the aftermath of the Cirillo case.

Another aspect of the Dozier case that still remains unclear relates to possible Bulgarian involvement. Elements of the BR had reportedly used an international relations specialist of the Italian Union of Labor (UIL) to establish contact with the Bulgarian government for the purpose of buying weapons. The "liaison man," Luigi Scricciolo, had been an activist of the Proletarian Democracy Party (DP) until 1979, the year he joined UIL. During his DP militancy, Scricciolo had allegedly received Bulgarian funding for his party and had subsequently remained in touch with Bulgarian "diplomats." According to this reconstruction, the Bulgarians indicated their willingness to assist the BR in exchange for the management of the Dozier affair. Scricciolo and his wife have been indicted for participation in an armed band as well as for political and military espionage.

Besides the October XXII Circle, the NAP, and the BR, the only other terrorist group of the left that has resorted to political abduction is the Communist Combat Units (Unità Combattenti Comuniste, UCC),[10] which will be discussed below in connection with the links between terrorism and common crime. The UCC represents somewhat of an imaginative anomaly in the Italian kidnap craft. On June 14, 1976, at 5:30 A.M., they abducted meat dealer Giuseppe Ambrosio, 53 years old, in Rome and demanded for his release the distribution of 710 quintals of meat (one quintal equals 100 kg at below-market prices in the less prosperous areas of Rome. Ambrosio was rescued the next day by the Carabinieri before the distribution could take place.

The cases described above constitute all the ideologically motivated abductions of major consequence recorded since the outburst of contemporary political violence in Italy. For the sake of legal precision, however, it should be remembered that the Criminal Code qualifies as kidnappings any "deprivation of someone's personal liberty." Consequently, a few other instances in which terrorists have momentarily chained in place and photographed their victims can technically be categorized as kidnappings under Italian law.

COMMON CRIMINAL KIDNAPPINGS: A COMPARATIVE PERSPECTIVE

The escalation of kidnappings for ransom perpetrated by common criminal elements is a sociological phenomenon that parallels the outburst of political terrorism in contemporary Italy. Briefly, terrorism in that country is the end product of three predominant conditions: social inadequacies, political contradictions, and governmental weakness. The massive migrations from the agricultural south to the industrialized north and from rural areas to urban centers produced highly congested cities unable to care for the new demographic needs of housing, schools, hospitals, and general services, thus breeding widespread discontent.

At the same time, the lack of homogeneous governmental composition, largely due to the absence of an absolute majority party, made discordant multiparty coalitions necessary. This forced relationship ultimately resulted in governmental programs predicated on political contradictions, unworkable compromises, and macroscopic inefficiency. In the absence of governmental solidity, permissive legislation and policies were passed, which, in addition to displaying the weakness of the state, downgraded the viability of existing institutions, from the school system to labor relations to law enforcement.

Common criminal kidnappings, as well as all organized criminality, drew much of their impetus from the same conditions that brought about contemporary Italian terrorism. Among the millions of workers and unemployed citizens who migrated north and to the cities were elements that eventually enlarged the ranks of crime in the more prosperous areas. In this area kidnappings—heretofore a long-established but occasional occurrence in Calabria and Sicily—could and in fact did become an "industry." Moreover, Sardinian bandits, the oldest practitioners of the craft in Italy, introduced their expertise in the north. In a number of instances, convicted common criminals from the south were legally forced to take up residence in the north, with the ironic result that they joined forces with local crime and spread their own methodologies. These factors led to the establishment of organized criminal networks throughout the national territory. The situation was obviously aggravated by the reduced efficiency of the law enforcement agencies. Corrective measures indeed came, but too late.

As opposed to the 25 ideologically motivated kidnappings discussed above, 487 common criminal kidnappings for ransom were recorded between 1970 and June of 1982. Their yearly breakdown, together with estimated aggregate ransoms, follows:

Year	Number	Aggregate Ransom Payments (Millions of L)
1970	10	635,000,000
1971	13	1,735,000,000
1972	8	1,447,600,000
1973	14	3,108,000,000
1974	37	15,122,000,000
1975	62	19,866,450,000
1976	48	11,435,000,000
1977	75	17,976,400,000
1978	44	11,677,000,000
1979	70	9,968,000,000
1980	42	10,803,000,000
1981	43	17,580,000,000
1982	21	3,615,000,000

To date the largest concentration of this type of crime is discernible in the regions of Lombardy, Sardinia, Latium, Calabria, Piedmont, and Tuscany. Typical victims are wealthy industrialists, land owners, and professional men who do not adopt security measures. Political terrorists seek symbolic targets and publicity for their cause and are therefore willing to engage an armed escort in a fire fight or even settle for a demonstrative wounding or assassination in the event of an abortive attempt. Common criminals, in contrast, are interested in seizing victims alive and unharmed without exposing themselves to inordinate risks. Moreover, while the average age of a terrorist ranges from the early 20s to the mid-30s, common criminal kidnappers are frequently older.

On the average an estimated 10 to 15 operators are involved in each common criminal kidnap venture. If this task force is highly professional or part of broader organized crime, it is usually compartmentalized for security purposes. Its members are assigned specific functions by a coordinator. Thus criminals acting as surveillers, snatchers, jailers, telephone operators, mailmen, or collectors are not likely to know one another. The coordinator reports to the planner(s), while the various participants receive either a flat fee or a percentage of the ransom.

The victim is most frequently seized on the street in the proximity of his residence or near another place he habitually frequents. Hours of limited visibility are usually preferred and the attackers are masked. As a rule, the victim is not mistreated beyond the burden of captivity itself, which can be most uncomfortable if the victim is carried to open country or mountainous areas open to the elements or if the hideout is small and lacks hygienic facilities. Periods of captivity vary from a few days to several months. At times the kidnappers exercise pressures on the victim, as well as on the family, that include threats of future harm, such as to other family members. As opposed to political kidnap cases, where to date the victim has always been a male of legal age, common criminals also abduct women and children.

In the vast majority of cases, the abductee is released after the payment of the ransom. Sometimes however, a supplementary ransom has been demanded or, even worse, the victim has been killed after the ransom payment. From 1970 to June 1982, 28 victims were found dead and the fate of 42 more remains uncertain. (Investigators believe that organized criminal operators are less likely to kill victims after their demands have been met than are impromptu groupings of abductors. The latter are in fact considered more dangerous because of their lack of mastery over the craft.) Frequently, the victim is released in a locality far away from the municipality or province of the abduction.

The payer of a ransom can expect to take a long trip with several intermediate stops at check points before being allowed to make the delivery. Postponements in making contact with the collector or drop zone do also happen if the kidnappers fear a trap.

It is estimated that 80 to 90 percent of the laundering of ransom money takes place in Italy, although recent cases indicate that the transporting of funds to Switzerland and even Venezuela is on the rise. If the services of a "specialist" are required, his fee reportedly amounts to 30 percent of the ransom. The usual forms of laundering include use of compliant banks, financial firms, and casinos. Other possibilities are deposits in several different accounts with different banks or use of bearer passbooks, cashier's checks to the order of real or fictitious individuals, and postal money orders. Recent legislation has complicated laundering procedures by requiring depositor identification for sums in excess of L. 20 million.[11]

A final aspect of kidnappings for ransom relates to the links between political terrorists and common crime. The Rome Court of Assizes is currently trying 25 indicted members of the UCC, which carried out the political abduction of meat dealer Ambrosio. Their ranks include both political extremists and common criminals who have carried out a variety of offenses. One of the aims of the UCC was to conduct nonideologically motivated kidnappings. Some of the defendants have admitted to abortive kidnapping attempts, and in one of their hideouts in Vescovio (Rieti) elaborate facilities to hold kidnap victims have been uncovered by the Carabinieri. Although the UCC's case is the most notorious, it indicates the combined criminal potential.

COUNTERMEASURES AND CONCLUDING OBSERVATIONS

An argument can be made that the changes in the Italian lifestyle are more the result of inflation than of fear of criminality in its political and common manifestations. Yet the proliferation of security measures, even at the private level, is indicative of a preoccupation with the ugliest forms of criminality, including kidnappings.

Although no Italian automobile manufacturer produces armored cars off the assembly line, a number of firms specialize in armoring vehicles. The cost ranges from L. 20 million to over 120 million. Of the Italian-manufactured automobiles, two are considered most suited for this purpose: Alfa Romeo's Alfetta 2000 and Fiat's 132 model. And even though only a small minority of the Italian population has reason to resort to this kind of protection, the production of steel doors and home and office alarm systems has become a lucrative enterprise.

Body armor is available in Italy, but it is imported. No security courses—other than martial arts schools and target practice organizations—are conducted in Italy for private citizens. Obviously the police forces have their own, as do private protection agencies for their personnel, which are frequently made up of former policemen and former police officials. Individuals who wish to learn defensive driving techniques and other protective skills generally enroll in courses available in Switzerland.

Over 400 private protection agencies have come into existence. They provide various services, including guards, which banks need pursuant to the terms and conditions of insurance policies. Selection of a specific agency should be based on specific corporate or private needs: No single private protection agency is recommended by the law enforcement community to provide the full range of services.

A number of centers have been set up to train dogs as bodyguards. Some of them also breed dogs for this purpose. The purchase price ranges from approximately L. 300 thousand to as much as 5 million. The cost of training ranges from L. 500 thousand to 1 million. The courses themselves last from two to three months. Reportedly, some 20 thousand such trained animals can be found in Italy.

Applications for gun permits are also on the rise. In order to obtain one, three basic requirements must be met and the waiting period is usually long: need, clean police record, and knowledge of firearm operation. Italian law does not allow private citizens to possess what it terms *war weapons*. Consequently, the only semi-automatic pistols allowed are the 7.65 caliber and smaller ones. Instead, revolvers of all calibers are authorized. No fully automatic weapons are permitted. Apart from permits to carry, police clearance is also required for the simple purchase of firearms for keeping in one's residence.

Directives from the Ministry of Industry bar Italian insurance companies from issuing antikidnapping policies. This obstacle has reportedly been surmounted in hundreds of cases by policies from foreign underwriters, primarily Lloyd's of London. Observers argue, however, that kidnappers have advance knowledge of insurance coverage and capitalize on that precaution.

In some instances, notably in the late 1970s, magistrates froze the assets of kidnap victims and their families to prevent payment of the ransom and to deter the recurrence of abductions. Although in specific instances these measures were beneficial in either reducing the ransom demand or in freeing the victim, the so-called hard line can be circumvented. Given the financial soundness of kidnap victims, their credit ratings are high. (Speculators, however, have asked interest rates of 30 percent.) Moreover, even though the debate between the hard and soft lines continues, a committee appointed by the Superior Council of the Magistrature (in Italy, both judges and prosecutors are part of the magistrature) prepared a report holding, *inter alia,* that the former is not appropriate.

Foreigners in Italy should be encouraged by the fact that kidnappings of nonItalians are to date an extremely rare occurrence. (Two notable exceptions are the cases of Paul Getty, Jr. and General Dozier.) Yet, given the magnitude of the common criminal kidnap industry and the resiliency of terrorism in the country, precautions cannot be overemphasized. In this respect, the Italian law enforcement agencies are very receptive to providing guidance to potential victims. Ultimately, the best protection is an in-depth knowledge of conditions pertinent to the specific area(s) in which the potential victim expects to operate.

NOTES

1. Criminal Code, Art. 605.
2. Criminal Code, Art. 630, as amended.
3. Criminal Code, Art. 289 bis, as amended.
4. Code of Criminal Procedure, Art. 39, as amended.
5. The Italian system of government is a parliamentary one. Electoral laws call for proportional representation. The major parties represented in Parliament in order of numerical importance include: Christian Democratic Party (DC), Italian Communist Party

(PCI), Italian Socialist Party (PSI), Italian Social Movement (MSI), Italian Social Democratic Party (PSDI), Radical Party (PR), Italian Republican Party (PRI), Italian Liberal Party (PLI), and Democratic Proletarian Unity Party (PDUP). Since 1948, when the Republican Constitution of 1947 went into effect, 37 governments supported by varying parliamentary coalitions have succeeded one another.

6. *Il Tempo* (Rome), March 23, 1982, p. 17 and July 7, 1982, p. 16.

7. Atti Parlamentari, Camera dei Deputati, *Relazione sulla Politica Informativa e della Sicurezza,* semestre 23 maggio-22 novembre 1981, presentata alla Presidenza il 7 dicembre 1981, p. 6.

8. Law No. 15 of February 6, 1980 and Law No. 304 of May 29, 1982.

9. *L'Espresso* (Rome), January 11, 1981.

10. Technically, there is one more ideologically motivated abduction perpetrated by the extreme left, but not by a terrorist group as such. Carlo Saronio, an engineer, was kidnapped in Milan on April 14, 1974, by elements connected to leftist extremist Carlo Fioroni. Although the engineer died in captivity as the result of improper gagging, the kidnappers continued the ransom negotiations with the victim's unsuspecting family and obtained Lit. 470 million. Fioroni's objective was to finance subversive organizations.

11. Law Decree No. 625 of December 15, 1979, Art. 13.

6

Business and Terrorism in Argentina, 1969-1978

Susanna W. Purnell

The roots of current terrorist organizations and techniques can be traced to groups active in Latin America in the late 1960s and early 1970s. In particular, the urban guerrillas have their genesis in the Brazil and Uruguay of the 1960s. Such groups generally attacked government, diplomatic, and military targets; however, it was the Argentine terrorists who discovered the efficacy of attacking the business community.

This review of the Argentine experience from 1969 through 1978 serves several purposes. First, it helps explain why terrorists find business such an attractive target. Second, it demonstrates the business community's employment of some basic strategies still used to operate in a high-risk terrorist environment. And finally, the Argentine experience illustrates the consequences for business of both the attacks and the response.

This account is oriented toward the perceptions and response of U.S. businesses in Argentina. Terrorists found foreign businesses particularly attractive targets, although they also attacked local businesses. The author has had access and insight into the U.S. business experience in Argentina, and the conclusions reflect the particular problems foreign businesses have in such environments.

ARGENTINA IN TURMOIL

The activity of leftist, Peronist, and rightest terrorist groups during the period 1969–78 contributed to an overall mosaic of political, economic, and social instability in Argentina. The frequent changes in government leadership during the decade illustrate this political instability. From 1966 until the presidential elections held in 1973, the ruling military junta installed three presidents, each of whom failed to resolve Argentina's deep-seated economic problems or establish the needed political support for the government. In desperation, the junta allowed the return of the exiled Juan Perón, the charismatic leader whose Peronist movement continued to flourish 18 years after his ouster from the country. In September 1973, the

Argentines elected Perón their president and Perón's wife, Isabel, vice president.

During the four years prior to Perón's return, the major terrorist groups organized and began operations. The two most significant groups in Argentina were the People's Revolutionary Army (ERP) and the Montoneros. Established in 1970 under the auspices of the Trotskyite Revolutionary Workers' Party, the ERP advocated civil war against the government and "imperialists" as a means of establishing a Communist regime. With an international outlook, the group subsequently formed a common front with compatible groups in Chile, Uruguay, and Bolivia. Although the ERP began as a rural guerrilla group, the leaders quickly reorganized it into an active urban group with networks in the major cities.

In contrast to the international outlook of the ERP, the Montoneros, who took their name from the romantic rebel gauchos of the past, operated under a highly nationalistic philosophy. Drawn from the Peronist Youth and reorganized in 1970, the Montoneros believed that foreign companies and imperialist interests should be expelled to pave the way for Peronism. In 1971 the group advocated civil war, citing the exiled Perón's call for armed resistance against the military regime.

In addition to the Montoneros and ERP, three other terrorist groups were active through the early 1970s. The Revolutionary Armed Forces (FAR) was a Marxist group when created in 1966 but by 1973 was able to merge with the Montoneros. The FAR has been credited with attacks on army convoys and assassination plots against government leaders as well as with bombings, bank robberies, and kidnappings.

The Peronist Armed Forces (FAP) were active only during the first part of the decade. This extreme group conducted a number of operations against members of the United States Air Force stationed in Argentina. Finally, the Armed Forces of Liberation (FAL), a Marxist-Leninst group active until 1973 when most members joined the ERP, advocated the removal of all foreign businesses. The FAL operations included robberies and the kidnapping of several business executives.

One indicator of the level of violence during this time is a report that in mid-1971 there was a monthly average of 80 terrorist attacks in Argentina. The number had jumped to 170 attacks per week by November 1972 and 225 attacks per week in February 1973.[1]

Juan Perón's return to the presidency provided only a brief respite, as political and economic conditions continued to deteriorate amid increasing violence. Politically, Perón's comeback was based on a diverse Peronist movement ranging from conservative traditionalists, seeking to regain the power they held under the previous Perón regime, to the younger revolutionaries, such as the Montoneros who advocated redistribution of wealth. Perón's return to active leadership only accentuated the lack of concensus within his political base. As Perón increasingly aligned himself with the right wing of the Peronist movement, the coalition began to break up, a process accelerated by Perón's death in 1974 and the accession of his wife to the presidency.

The Peróns had even less success with their economic policies. By freezing prices and increasing wages as a means of promoting political support among labor, the government gave little incentive to businesses to invest. (This trend was aggravated by the enactment of policies inimical to any foreign investment.) The resultant decrease in production created serious shortages of consumer goods and a healthy black market. Moreover, the maintenance of unrealistically high exchange rates precipitated a balance-of-payments crisis as inflation soared, reaching the rate of 335 percent in 1975.

Promoters of Perón's return to power had argued that he would be able to end the violence he had promoted in exile. While the Peronist-based terrorist groups declared a truce upon Perón's election, the other leftist groups, most notably the ERP, continued their campaigns. With Juan Perón's death, the Montoneros announced their return to terrorist strategies.

In 1976, with the country on the verge of economic collapse and wracked by increasing violence, the military arrested Isabel Peron and again took over the leadership of the country. The new junta under the leadership of General Jorge Rafael Videla increased government operations against the terrorists and continued to permit the activities of a right-wing terrorist group, the Argentine Anticommunist Alliance (AAA), that was founded during the presidency of Isabel Perón The AAA consisted of a number of police and military right-wing death squads operating against terrorists and their sympathizers. Although under the unofficial guidance of government officials, little was done to check the growing excesses of its members, who began to indiscriminately target a number of groups. Many leftist politicians, artists, and intellectuals fled the country. According to 1979 estimates, 7,000 to 15,000 Argentines have disappeared as a result of the AAA attacks.

The government succeeded in removing the major terrorist threats of ERP and the Montoneros when police killed most of the former's leaders in a 1976 shoot-out at the terrorists' Buenos Aires hideout and when the surviving leadership of the Montoneros fled the country in 1977 to set up a number of foreign offices in Western Europe and Mexico.

ARGENTINE TERRORISTS TARGET BUSINESS

From 1969 through 1978, then, Argentine terrorism was part of a greater national struggle. While these guerrilla groups ultimately wanted to change the political structure, many of their actions were staged against the country's business establishment. At times the ERP and the Montoneros waged campaigns against selected corporations, trying to intimidate management with threats and assassinations while agitating for support within a company's labor force. During the decade these groups bombed, hijacked, robbed, kidnapped, murdered, and threatened company employees and property. An examination of these attacks reveals that the terrorists derived a number of benefits from targeting businesses.

First, and most important, these groups staged attacks to obtain funding. All terrorists require financing to create a viable organization. The need for money goes beyond the purchase of weaponry and equipment, although groups that attacked military installations, effected jail breaks, and took over towns had heavy expenses in these two categories. The predominantly urban guerrilla groups also required safe houses, transport, and living expenses.

It is not surprising then that the earliest instances of terrorist activity in Argentina during this period were bank and train robberies. In 1972 they began kidnapping and extorting businessmen for ransom. The Montoneros kidnapped a Dutch industrialist and demanded $500,000 in ransom in September of that year. By April 1973 FAL kidnapped a Kodak executive and reportedly demanded $1.5 million for his release. Six months later kidnappers demanded $3.5 million from Amoco Oil Company to obtain the release of the president of their Argentine subsidiary.

Both ERP and the Montoneros collected record ransoms. The ERP received $14.2 million from Exxon for the release of a general manager kidnapped from the oil refinery at Campora in December 1973. The ERP designated part of this ransom, which was the largest paid by an American firm, for the use of a "revolutionary coordinating board" that was composed of terrorist groups from Bolivia, Uruguay, Chile, and Argentina.

In 1975 the Montoneros collected the world record sum of $60 million in cash and supplies after kidnapping Juan and Jorge Born, directors of a Latin American international trading conglomerate. The Argentine government, which opposed the payment, noted that the sum equaled one third of the country's national defense budget. The Montoneros actually invested $12 to $20 million of that sum with a local Argentine financier, David Graivers. Graivers put the money in some of the very kinds of organizations the Montoneros often attacked, such as U.S. banks. The terrorists netted $145,000 to $175,000 in monthly dividends.[2]

So successful was this method of raising money that criminals began imitating the terrorists' methods. In fact, many corporate negotiators involved in these kidnappings believe their ransom was collected by common criminals taking advantage of the credibility achieved by terrorists, who consistently released hostages after payment of ransom.

A second benefit, besides funds for operations, for Argentine terrorists was the way attacks on business complemented the groups' ideological aims. Both the Communist and the Peronist groups felt comfortable justifying their actions as attacks on the "imperialist"—i.e., the multinational—firms. The terrorists often demanded corporate admissions of guilt. To gain the release of their refinery manager, Exxon not only had to pay a ransom to the ERP but also publish a communique stating that the ransom was an indemnity "for superprofits that Esso obtained in the country, thanks to the exploitation of its workers.[3]

Third, the terrorists used businesses as popular targets to increase support for their goals and operations. Attacking foreign corporations, for example, reflected the almost xenophobic fear among Argentines that foreign investors were trying to take over the country. U.S. executives living in Argentina at the time felt that terrorist operations against Yankee interests enjoyed widespread popularity.

The ERP was particularly adept at choosing actions that had a direct impact on the workers whose support the terrorists desired. In 1971, ERP hijacked a number of milk and meat trucks and distributed the contents in the slums. The same year the group bombed the local telephone company in support of striking workers and kidnapped a meat-packing plant executive. In the latter instance the ERP demanded and obtained the rehiring of 4,000 workers with compensation for lost wages.

The Montoneros also increased efforts to win influence within the unions by murdering and harassing executives affiliated with companies having labor problems. In October 1975, for example, the group kidnapped the production manager of a Mercedes-Benz truck factory. The workers at that plant had been on strike, and among the terrorists' demands for release of their hostage was the reinstatement of 119 workers who had been dismissed and a company promise that there would be no further reprisals.

Fourth, Argentine terrorists staged attacks on business because they were very convenient targets. Protection for key government and diplomatic figures had been increased in response to the increase in terrorism. The more vulnerable business world, on the other hand, presented a large range and number of targets. For example, at that time there were approximately 400 U.S. firms, and many more U.S. executives, in Argentina. Moreover, businesses were usually readily accessible to the public. Terrorists bombed and strafed such easy targets as car dealers' showrooms and banks. These operations publicized the groups at little cost or danger to the terrorists themselves.

Finally, terrorists were more likely to gain concessions from businesses than from other targets. A good illustration is the contrasting outcomes between the two earliest terrorist kidnappings in Argentina. In March 1970, the FAL kidnapped a Paraguayan consul and threatened to kill him unless the government released two imprisoned terrorists. The Argentine government, with the support of the Paraguayan president, refused the demands. The FAL eventually released their hostage for "humanitarian" reasons.

In May 1971, the ERP kidnapped an honorary British consul who was also the manager of a Swift del la Plata packing plant. This time the terrorists made their demands on the company instead of the government. To gain the manager's release, Swift agreed to distribute $50,000 in food to the poor, rehire fired workers with compensation, and improve working conditions. The terrorists had discovered that governments may ask their diplomats and their officials to sacrifice, like soldiers, their well-being for their country. Businesses, on the other hand, are unlikely to expect or receive a similar sacrifice from their employees.

THE BUSINESS RESPONSE

Despite the serious threats posed by the terrorists, companies developed a number of strategies to deal with the situation, including changes in organization, personnel, and security measures. Probably the most important aspect of the Argentine experience was the way businesses acted almost entirely on their own, rather than relying on government authorities for protection from and response to terrorist attacks. The necessity for such an approach reflected businessmen's perceptions of the government, the terrorists, and even other businesses.

First, businessmen perceived that they had different priorities from the government. When an employee was kidnapped, the company's first interest was to gain the hostage's safe release. Government authorities often put a premium on capturing the terrorists or at least preventing their gaining concessions. For example, in March 1972, the ERP kidnapped the general manager of Fiat-Concord, and made demands on the government and company in exchange for the hostage's release. Argentine President Lanusse rejected the demands on the government and forbade Fiat from meeting the demands on the company. Three weeks after his abduction, the hostage was killed by his captors when government patrols discovered the kidnappers' hideout. After this incident, companies were reluctant to report kidnappings to the authorities. In fact, when an executive was reported kidnapped, company officials often denied the truth claiming the executive was on a business or vacation trip.

Even when the government changed from the hard-line approach of the junta to the more lenient attitudes of the Peronists, companies continued to handle terrorist threats on their own. The Peronists immediately declared a general amnesty for all guerrillas, thereby releasing up to 500 terrorists, including the murderers of the Fiat-Concord manager. Moreover, Juan Perón found it politically inexpedient to pursue terrorists who attacked foreign firms.

The experiences of the Ford Motor Company illustrate the problem. In May 1973, the ERP extorted $1 million in goods from the corporation's Argentine subsidiary after the terrorists killed one executive and wounded another. Five months later, terrorists murdered another Ford executive and his three bodyguards. Ford immediately evacuated 22 executives and their families from the country. The Argentine government did not even condemn the attacks. In a meeting with Juan Perón, Ford officials had to threaten to close their Argentine operation in order to get government help. As a result, Perón agreed to supply Argentine troops as guards for a threatened Ford plant.

Companies had other reasons for staying away from local authorities, especially when a kidnapping occurred. During the early 1970s, businessmen felt that the relevant authorities were incompetent or that they had been infiltrated by the terrorists. Kidnappings usually occurred in the suburbs as an executive was driving to work. Corporate officials believed the suburban police were more adept at directing traffic than stopping terrorists. Even if the kidnappers were caught, Argentine law provided mild penalties if the victim survived.

Foreign firms found their home governments could do little to assist them. When the Fiat-Concord manager was kidnapped, the Argentine government reportedly rejected pleas from the president of Italy to allow the firm to negotiate with the kidnappers. The U.S. government told its companies that it was the obligation of the Argentine government to protect U.S. citizens in that country. As a result U.S. firms rarely reported threats or terrorist acts to the U.S. embassy since all the diplomats could do was forward the information to the local government.

Businessmen's perceptions of the terrorists' capabilities for infiltration and retribution also inhibited firms from going to local authorities for help. Terrorists often added credibility to their threats by imparting some information known by only a few members of the firm. In one instance, the terrorists phoned a closely held corporate unlisted number. The ERP appears to have been particularly adept at infiltrating not only companies but the Argentine security forces. At one point they recruited the assistant commissioner of the federal police.

Businessmen therefore took seriously the terrorist threats of retribution that warned against informing local authorities. Ransomed executives of foreign firms immediately left the country before local authorities found out about their release to avoid testifying against their captors. Company officials felt this tactic was necessary to protect the managers who remained in Argentina.

Some cooperation existed within the business community itself. Executives report attending group seminars on such topics as the terrorist threat and hostage survival. Moreover, certain banks and airlines assembled the currency required for ransom payments and aided in the quick departure of released kidnap victims. However, even within the business world, individual companies were, to some extent, on their own. Firms were reluctant to share much information about their security arrangements or reveal the extent of their ransom payments. Company officials viewed the release of such information as potentially harmful to their interests. For business reasons they were not anxious to publish the extent of their financial losses. Nor did they want to encourage further terrorist or criminal activity by revealing the amount of a ransom or existence of an extortion payment. In addition, firms wanted to have a more formidable security system than other firms so they would be less likely to be attacked. All of these factors inhibited a complete exchange of relevant information within the business community itself.

Perceptions, therefore, of the government, the terrorists, and the rest of the business community encouraged firms to formulate their own response to the problem. While these responses varied (and some firms did not respond at all), a number of now classic strategies were enacted to cope with the problem. For the most part, these concerned three aspects of the business: its organization, security provisions, and personnel policies.

Organization

Many corporations reacted to the terrorist threat by creating the necessary organizational mechanisms to deal with the situation. These included the establishment of a corporate security officer, a crisis management committee, and contingency plans. Corporate security officers provided in-house expertise and overall protection planning. By making this a top-level position in the organization, companies gave the security officer the necessary power to enact needed procedures.

The existence of an in-house crisis committee with the authority to determine the extent of corporate responsibility and follow through with the necessary action speeded reaction to terrorist threats. In multinational firms, for example, local Argentine officials could not authorize ransom payments, whereas the crisis committee at the home office could.

Contingency plans proved exceptionally useful for firms at risk. One U.S. company that had been attacked once by Argentine terrorists used contingency planning to get its most vulnerable executives out of the country within 24 hours of a second attack. In another instance, an American executive kidnapped by ERP was able to tell his kidnappers who to contact in his company's home office when negotiations broke down. The hostage was able to speed his release because he had been privy to the contingency plans formulated by his corporation to deal with kidnappings in Argentina.

Security Measures

Most firms upgraded security for both employees and company property. Key personnel who were considered most vulnerable were often provided with additional protection. In some cases this meant visible protection—such as bodyguards and follow-cars—to discourage attack. In other cases, corporations encouraged executives to maintain a low profile.

There was an effort especially among foreign companies to promote the anonymity of key personnel. Coca-Cola, having been threatened by ERP, removed many of its most vulnerable executives and did not publicly announce their replacements. The 1977 American Chamber of Commerce membership directory did not contain the name of a single executive. Indeed, most executives refused to give out their telephone numbers or home addresses. Some executives moved from their more visible residence in the well-to-do suburbs to the anonymity of the city. Other new security measures for offices and plants included increased physical protection, such as hiring moonlighting police as guards, or establishing standard operating procedures for such contingencies as bomb threats.

Threatened executives were encouraged not to keep an established routine so that terrorists would have difficulty planning an attack. As the danger increased, many companies moved their foreign executives to neighboring Uruguay or Brazil. Executives would then commute several days a week to Argentina to work at their office. In extreme situations, as in the killing of the Ford Company executives, corporations transferred all or most of their vulnerable foreign managers out of the country.

Personnel Policies

Finally, some firms altered hiring and placement requirements due to the terrorist threats. Foreign firms, for example, often tried to reduce the number of expatriate personnel assigned to Argentina and replace them with less vulnerable Argentine nationals. While this policy did not guarantee that the Argentine managers would not be kidnapped or threatened, they were less conspicuous than foreigners. Estimates of the number of U.S. businessmen living in Argentina dropped from 1,270 in 1972 to 100 in 1975.

Firms enacted other new placement policies for less vulnerable employees.

For example, according to one account, some American companies tended to assign bachelors, divorced persons, or childless couples to Argentina, on the theory that they had more mobility.[4] Another report indicates some firms hired only applicants who were over 30 as a means of preventing the youthful terrorists from infiltrating the company.[5]

CONSEQUENCES OF TERRORISM AND THE BUSINESS RESPONSE

Terrorist acts and the business response had a number of consequences. First, the fact that business had at times acceded to terrorist demands for money and publicity is often criticized as contributing to the problem rather than solving it. Certainly, some terrorist groups did obtain financing for their ventures in this way. However, because the local governments were unable to stop the terrorists or provide protection to most businesses, they were handed a dilemma in which their own interests dictated paying for the safety of their employees.

Many firms did try to limit the payoffs to the terrorists. All of them tried to reduce the ransom demands and at least one U.S. company refused to pay money to terrorists, instead insisting on distributing any "ransom" in the form of goods to the poor. Most firms also tried to get an agreement from the terrorists not to attack their company again. With so many terrorist organizations, splinter groups and criminal gangs, however, such an agreement was unlikely to have much impact.

One consequence of negotiations with the terrorists was that it put the firms at odds with the government. Fiat's desire to negotiate for its manager in 1972 is one example. The aftermath of the Born brothers' kidnapping is another, when the Argentine government opposed the payment of the $60 million ransom. In fact, when four employees of the Borns' company tried to smuggle some of the ransom money into the country from Switzerland, they were arrested. After the ransom was paid and the hostages released, the Argentine government announced a planned investigation into the practices of the Borns' trading company.

The security measures employed by businesses also had consequences. Strategies designed to keep the executive safe—such as keeping irregular schedules or even commuting to work from Montevideo—also had the effect of keeping managers away from their office or plant. Travel restrictions due to the danger made it difficult to maintain quality control on products. Some managers who remained in the country felt they had an advantage over the firms who moved their executives to Uruguay and Brazil. At least one U.S. firm which kept its executives in the country actually improved its market position during the time of highest risk.[6]

The policy of replacing the more highly visible expatriate managers with less conspicuous locals had a number of consequences for multinational firms. Corporations which changed personnel suddenly without time for needed training had difficulty. The hiring of Argentine managers in the mid-1970s was hampered by the fact that many qualified locals had moved to Brazil where there were more opportunities and by the continued terrorism against both local and foreign executives. In some cases adjustments were made. After an Italian manager of an ITT subsidiary was kidnapped, the corporation replaced the manager with a local. However, the job description had to be changed, giving the new manager less responsibility.[7]

The multinationals also benefited from these personnel changes. Their employment of Argentines in high-level posts helped the corporation's popular image during times of intense nationalism. Moreover, locals had a better understanding of the situation. Miguel de los Santos, an Argentine promoted to the presidency of Pfizer Corporation's subsidiary in 1973, commented that one advantage of the appointment was "that a local man can be more adaptable and able to foresee developments in a climate which is unstable politically or economically."[8]

A long-term consequence of the terrorism is that Argentines now fill many more of the top executive slots in Argentine subsidiaries. While this is primarily to the advantage of the multinationals, sometimes local interests and those of the firm conflict. During the recent war between Great Britain and Argentina over the Falkland Islands, a number of U.S. subsidiaries in Argentina made donations to the Argentine war effort, even though the parent firm may have had substantial investments in Britain also. (Ford Motor Argentina, for example, contributed 60 trucks.) These donations were, in part, one way American companies tried to maintain local business in the face of a threatened boycott by Argentines angry over U.S. support of Britain. However, the fact that so many U.S. company executives are Argentines who supported their nation's actions, was also a factor.[9]

While there were positive and negative aspects to the changes in personnel policies, the effects of terrorism on the employees themselves was at times devastating. The need to restrict information and prevent terrorist infiltration created an atmosphere of suspicion and low morale at the workplace. Threatened managers found both themselves and their homes under attack as terrorists phoned threats to their wives, sent package bombs, and strafed their residences with machine-gun fire. Families also had to cope with the stresses of these threats. The wife of one American executive recalled that she was scared whenever her husband or children were ten minutes late from the office or school, and that she herself was held by gunpoint when terrorists blew up the local tennis clubhouse.[10] Under such conditions, many executives asked for transfers; some resigned.

Ironically, for large corporations, the monetary costs of dealing with terrorism may have been of shorter duration than the other consequences, even though costs were substantial. Expensive security measures and high ransoms outstripped the annual profits of some multinational subsidiaries. However, almost all U.S.-based firms continued to do business through and beyond the period of high risk. In 1974 Exxon paid over $14 million in ransom; in 1978 the company was a major explorer for Argentine oil. Corporations which have since pulled out of Argentina did so primarily because the economic market incentives were insufficient to justify continuance of the operation. However most firms continue to do business in Argentina.

NOTES

1.   Robert F. Lamber, "The Peronist Legacy: Terror in Argentina," *Swiss Review of World Affairs* (July 1978), pp. 9–10.

2.   Lester A. Sobel (ed.), *Political Terrorism, 1974–1978,* 2 Vol. (New York: Facts on File, Inc., 1978), p. 112.

3.   Lester A. Sobel (ed.), *Argentina and Peron, 1970–1975* (New York: Facts on File, Inc., 1975), pp. 108–109.

4.   "Despite Kidnapping and Murder, Americans Are Returning to Argentina," *U.S. News & World Report,* Vol. LXXXIII, No. 21, November 21, 1977, p. 26.

5.   *The New York Times,* October 29, 1977, p. 6.

6.   Susanna W. Purnell and Eleanor S. Wainstein, *The Problems of U.S. Businesses Operating Abroad in Terrorist Environments,* R-2842-DOC (Santa Monica, CA: The Rand Corporation 1981) p. 48; and the Harvard Business School and Yale School of Business and Management, "Assessment of Terrorism as It Impacts on the Business Community," joint student research project, August 1980.

7.   "Argentina: Homegrown managers get their chance," *Business Week* February 9, 1974, p. 38.

8.   *Ibid,* p. 38.

9.   Margot Hornblower, "Subsidiaries of U.S. Firms Aid Argentina," *The Washington Post,* June 1, 1982, pp. A-1, A-12.

10.   *The Times* (London), November 25, 1977, p. 8.

7

El Salvador—Attack on the Private Sector

Eleanor S. Wainstein

With few exceptions, Central American revolutions of this century have overturned the political structure of the country involved but have left the economic sector undisturbed. Once the revolution is over, incumbents have traditionally depended upon private enterprise—including the foreign business community—to keep the economy functioning and the work force employed. Despite their Marxism, the Sandinista revolutionaries in Nicaragua followed this pattern until recently. In El Salvador, however, the terrorists and revolutionaries announced their intention of undermining the economy, and in working to accomplish that goal they have repeatedly attacked the nation's businesses and businessmen.

Starting slowly in 1972, dissidents have run through the catalog of violence: bombings, demonstrations, kidnapping and killing of businessmen and public officials, strikes, lockouts, and protest sit-ins. In the 1980s the organized guerrilla groups have concentrated on destruction of the country's infrastructure. By targeting transportation networks—roads, bridges, buses, airports—utility installations, and the distribution of basic products they are hoping thereby to bring the economy to a halt. The terrorists can claim a good measure of success in achieving their goal, as the national product, employment, investment, and other economic indicators have declined significantly.

Foreign businesses operating in El Salvador have suffered serious disruptions. Most foreign managers have left the country, either turning over their duties to local nationals or running their enterprises from neighboring countries. Even more serious, multinational firms have pulled out their investments, and foreign as well as local entrepreneurs have withheld investment in new ventures. Existing firms have had to delay both replacement of obsolescent plant and equipment and modernization of production methods, with the result that Salvadoran businesses are losing their competitive edge in world markets. Such conditions will have a long-term negative effect on the country's economy.

What caused the terrorists to assault the private sector? What is the nature of that assault? How has business reacted? To answer these questions, it is necessary to look first at the politics and social structure of the country and to review its recent history. Following that is an examination of the environment of violence as it has affected the business community.

BACKGROUND OF VIOLENCE

El Salvador, the smallest and most densely populated of the Central American republics, has about 4.5 million people in an area approximately the size of the state of Massachusetts. An aristocracy of wealthy families has traditionally held the reins of power in the country; and the economic structure, until the present struggle, remained essentially static and inequitable. As of 1977, the lowest 20 percent of income recipients received 4.3 percent of the national income. Agriculture dominated the economy, with coffee, cotton, and sugar the chief crops and exports. In this sector the top 10 percent of the economic ladder held over three quarters of the land, and the lowest 10 percent less than half of a percent.[1]

El Salvador's annual population growth of over 3 percent gradually caused strains on the small country. With an economy dependent on crops that require large landholdings, excess population migrated from the countryside to urban areas, adding to the poverty and overcrowding already serious there. For years an escape valve of migration to nearby Honduras mitigated population pressures, but the 1969 so-called Soccer War between El Salvador and Honduras resulted in the forcible return of some 300,000 Salvadorans to their homeland. Thus, severe pressures built up in competition for the limited land and for employment opportunities in both urban and rural areas.

Principally because it had a reservoir of employable manpower in urban areas, El Salvador attracted considerable foreign investment in the 1960s and 1970s. The work force quickly gained a reputation as motivated and adaptable industrial workers. In addition, El Salvador offered the necessary developing infrastructure and the hydroelectric power potential for industry. To encourage foreign investment and industrialization, Salvadoran government representatives and entrepreneurs went abroad seeking foreign capital and offering inducements to investors, such as a free-trade zone near the capital city and tariff advantages. In response, foreign electronics and clothing manufacturers invested heavily in "transformation" industries, by which they sent raw materials or parts to El Salvador, performed the manufacturing or assembling process in Salvadoran factories, and exported the final product for marketing elsewhere. This type of operation allowed foreign firms to take advantage of El Salvador's relatively low cost surplus labor. In most cases the firms could ship the finished items back to their country and pay duty only on the value added to the product overseas.

As foreign investment grew during the 1970s, El Salvador could count among its investors large and small companies from Japan, Germany, United Kingdom, Sweden, United States, and others. The United States continued to be their principal trading partner, with direct investments up to $120 million by 1979. Along with this growth and industrial development, however, came the social and political unrest that has culminated in the present violence. Even though growing industry brought employment opportunities to an increasing number, many Salvadoran workers remained unemployed or underemployed. Restive elements among them saw little hope of improvement through existing channels, so they began to work for change outside the system. In effect, the inducements to foreign capital—a large and willing work force and low wages—were the seeds of the present insurgency that seeks to oust foreign investors from the country.

El Salvador's political leaders made little headway in addressing the nation's basic economic and social problems. From the early 1930s until 1979 the presidency was in the hands of army officers, even though elections were held regularly. In 1972, however, the events surrounding the presidential election alienated many. The conservative Party of National Conciliation (PCN) ran their military candidate as usual, while the moderate, left-of-center Christian Democratic Party (PCD) ran the popular mayor of San Salvador, Jose Napoleon Duarte. The PCN claimed victory. The PCD then claimed widespread election fraud and staged a coup to seat their candidate Duarte—a coup that did not succeed. Party leaders were arrested and sent into exile. Again in 1977 the PCD contested the election and again lost to the PCN, further alienating liberal elements of the Catholic clergy and further polarizing Salvadoran society.

In the early 1970s radicalized leftist elements, having observed the Cuban experience, began to organize in guerrilla groups to overthrow the established government. The first of these, the Faribundi Marti Popular Liberation Forces (FPL), took the name of the leader of a 1932 peasant movement that was crushed by the government. The FPL drew members mainly from Communists and Marxist reformers and operated both in the cities and in the countryside.

In 1972 Marxists and radical Christian Democrats formed the People's Revolutionary Army (ERP). They began by bombing government buildings and taking over radio stations to popularize their cause and later turned to assassinations of government officials and businessmen. The ERP has the strongest military force among the guerrilla groups.

When a split occurred in the ERP in 1975 a third guerrilla group, the Armed Forces of National Resistance (FARN), emerged. FARN has advocated drastic economic pressure on the government, including strikes, lockouts, and kidnapping of both domestic and foreign businessmen. Their proclamations have urged that "if foreign businessmen want to avoid capture by FARN they must promote an economic boycott against all products in El Salvador. . . ."[2] FARN was responsible for most of the kidnappings of foreign businessmen in 1979 and 1980 and is said to have built up a considerable war chest from ransoms, which they have used for arms.

Little is known of a fourth guerrilla group, the Revolutionary Party of Central American Workers. They kidnapped two American businessmen in 1979 and exacted an undisclosed ransom and worldwide publicity for their cause.[3] In January 1982 police in San Jose, Costa Rica, killed terrorists who were attempting to kidnap wealthy Salvadoran industrialist Roberto Palomo Salazar. They identified the terrorists as members of this group.

In the late 1970s each of the three main guerrilla groups formed a large popular organization for the purpose of expressing their cause in the political arena. While the hard-core guerrillas continued their revolutionary activities, their larger political arm operated publicly. The FPL, for example, organized the Popular Revolutionary Bloc (BPR), a broad coalition of nonviolent urban and rural groups. The BPR conducted the many occupations of the cathedral in 1979 and sit-ins of government buildings and embassies. The ERP spawned the 28th of February Popular League (LP-28), and the FARN organized the United Popular Action Front (FAPU).

At the same time, liberal elements in the Catholic church, including one of San Salvador's archbishops, began voicing dissatisfaction with the status quo and with the unresponsiveness of those in authority. When in early 1980 the leftists resigned from the governing junta installed in October 1979 because change was too slow, reformist and leftist groups united with dissident Catholic groups, the three popular organizations, and the Communist Party to form the Revolutionary Democratic Front (FDR). This organization now speaks for the Salvadoran left both at home and abroad. Its leader, Guillermo Ungo, the 1972 vice presidential candidate on a ticket headed by Christian Democrat Jose Napoleon Duarte, is a moderate voice among the revolutionary leaders. The three guerrilla groups also formed a single command structure.

On the right the Nationalist Democratic Organization (ORDEN), the government's paramilitary organization with thousands of peasant members, has operated against leftists principally in villages and rural areas. The present junta outlawed ORDEN, but it still receives credit for incidents directed at the left. The most extreme rightist group, the White Warriors' Union, operated in small groups and claimed credit for attacks on leftists, including members of the Jesuit clergy. Members of El Salvador's armed forces have formed the backbone of the right and are credited with most of the violence against leftists and suspected leftists.

PROGRESSION OF TERRORISM

When the Salvadoran guerrilla organizations began their confrontations with the establishment in the early 1970s, they targeted businesses and businessmen only sporadically. At that time their counterparts in Argentina and Uruguay were making frequent attacks on the private sector and enjoying lucrative returns from kidnapping foreign executives for ransom. In 1972 some local and foreign enterprises were targets of terrorist bombs—a Pan American Airways ticket office and an international trade fair. Local disruptions and pronouncements also served to bring the guerrilla groups into the public consciousness. That year the Salvadoran elite had thrust upon them the seriousness of leftist violence when Ernesto Regalado, a member of a wealthy local family, was kidnapped and killed.[4]

The introduction of kidnapping as a terrorist weapon escalated the violence and had long-term effects. First, it touched off other kidnappings directed at wealthy families and businessmen, garnering substantial funds for the perpetrators.[5] Second, it initiated first a trickle and then a steady exodus of funds and people to safer havens abroad. This continuing flow of capital and manpower was a depressing indicator to the economy. Finally, kidnappings gave notice that the terrorist groups were sufficiently organized to be a serious threat. Bombings and demonstrations are hit-and-run activities requiring a minimum of planning and participants, but a kidnapping requires planning, intelligence, manpower, automobiles, and safe houses. When the terrorist groups demonstrated repeatedly that they had such a capability, the government and society at large took notice.

During the next few years Salvadorans witnessed increasing attacks on businesses and government installations in both the cities and rural areas. In 1975 a significant organizational change occurred within the guerrilla groups. Roque Dalton Garcia, the leader of the ERP, poet, essayist, and historian, was killed by a militarist faction within the ERP because he disapproved of their excessively militarist approach. This split the ERP, and the breakaway faction formed FARN. Also in 1975 the ERP kidnapped Francisco Sola, a wealthy industrialist, and demanded ransom. When $2 million was paid, the ERP released Sola and labeled the ransom a "war tax for the Salvadoran revolution."

The year 1977 saw a marked escalation in violence on all fronts, with two kidnappings occurring in January. The first victim, Dr. Mariano Castro Mangano, was abducted by FARN, held for two days, and released after payment of a $200,000 ransom. On the 27th the ERP abducted Roberto Poma, president of the National Tourist Institute, killing three of Poma's bodyguards who tried to prevent the abduction. Poma's family paid between $1 and $2 million for the ransom, not knowing that Poma had died of wounds inflicted at the time of the kidnapping. Authorities found his body in late February in a shallow grave.

During the election campaign and its aftermath in February and March, terrorism claimed victims on both the right and the left. Estimates went as high as 50 killed in popular demonstrations after the elections that put General Carlos Humberto Romero into the presidency. Taking note, a committee of the U.S. Congress shortly thereafter held hearings on charges of human rights abuses during the Salvadoran elections. Also in March a Jesuit priest was shot to death in the town of Aguilares by right-wing terrorists.

The world began to take note of El Salvador's insurgency when on April 19, 1977, the FPL kidnapped the foreign minister, Mauricio Borgonovo Pohl. The FPL announced that if the government would not free 37 alleged political prisoners and fly them to a neighboring country by April 27, they would kill the hostage. The government refused to negotiate, responding that they had only three of the individuals named in custody, and these three would have to be tried before being released. When the guerrillas let their April 27th deadline for Borgonovo's execution pass, the government still refused to negotiate. San Salvador's archbishop offered to mediate, and both the Pope and the United Nation's Secretary General appealed for concessions on both sides. Replying to Secretary General Waldheim, the FPL asked why he sought freedom for a government official but not for the imprisoned workers and peasants. Borgonovo was found shot to death beside a road near San Salvador on May 11. The FPL credited his death to a "revolutionary war to establish socialism."[6]

Liberal members of the clergy, especially members of the Jesuit order, became known for their advocacy of land reform and other measures to improve the lot of the peasantry. The extreme right saw them as a threat. In June 1977 the role of the Jesuits came to a climax when the White Warriors' Union accused the Jesuits of subversion and threatened to kill all Jesuit priests in El Salvador if they did not leave the country within a month. The government reacted strongly, denying any connection with the rightist group, and putting a heavy security guard around Jesuit facilities. Catholic laymen in El Salvador and abroad and the U.S. Department of State voiced concern to the government. Archbishop Oscar Romero expressed his outrage at the threat and continued to speak out in strong opposition to violence on the part of both the government and the left. Although members of the order were picked off sporadically by rightist activists, the threat to all Jesuits was not carried out.

In July 85-year-old former president Osmin Aguirre Salinas was murdered outside his home in San Salvador. Members of the FPL claimed credit, giving as their reason Aguirre's role in crushing a 1932 land reform movement when he was chief of police. In September FARN members kidnapped the wife of an American businessman after a shoot-out with bodyguards outside her husband's office. Shortly thereafter the FPL shot and killed Carlos Alfaro Castillo, member of a wealthy coffee-producing family and rector of the university. He had had repeated trouble with leftist students. In November industrialist Raul Molina Canas was killed while resisting kidnapping by a group thought to be criminal extortionists.

About this time two new tactics appeared, which were to recur repeatedly: first, occupations of foreign embassies and public buildings by activists and peasant mobs; and second, factory protest sit-ins. In November armed BPR members with a following of peasants, including women and children, occupied the ministry of labor demanding higher wages for coffee workers. For two days they held the minister and 100 employees hostage. Similarly, in February the BPR held members of the United Nations Information Center staff hostage while they demanded release of political prisoners and denounced El Salvador's disregard for human rights. The second tactic became a favorite of militant labor groups. Activists occupied a U.S.-owned plant, the Eagle Glove Company factory, for a day, making demands for the plant's labor force. The American manager and 450 workers were held in the plant and denied access to hygienic facilities, food, and water.

In March 1978 a serious confrontation occurred in the small town of San Pedro Perulapan between demonstrating BPR members and ORDEN. Shooting erupted, and casualties were variously cited between 30 and 300. The security forces took many prisoners. Three weeks later in San Salvador the BPR responded by occupying the embassies of Venezuela, Panama, Costa Rica, and Switzerland. Their demands were that the government retire troops from San Pedro and release prisoners held there. When the government conceded, they vacated.

During this time businessmen also continued to be targeted. In the first four months of 1978 at least five Salvadoran businessmen or members of prominent families were kidnapped. Foreigners, however, remained immune. Then in May San Salvador's foreign community received the shock it had long feared when

FARN guerrillas kidnapped Japanese businessman Fujio Matsumoto. Matsumoto's firm tried repeatedly to negotiate FARN demands for the release of 33 political prisoners and $4 million in ransom, not knowing that the hostage had died shortly after being abducted. Whether his death was accidental or by intent is unknown; his body was found five months after the kidnapping.

Matsumoto's kidnapping served to alert foreign businessmen that they too were caught up in the country's troubles. The months that followed were eventful ones for expatriate businessmen as FARN picked off executives of various nationalities. In response, establishments that could function as well outside El Salvador (such as, for example, Esso Latin American regional headquarters), were removed to safer environments abroad. Some corporate managers of foreign firms began turning over the reins of local operations to Salvadoran nationals. Others sent families home, and all who remained began to adopt strict security precautions that soon became a way of life 24 hours a day.

Of the three principal terrorist groups, FARN was the most skillful as kidnappers of businessmen. They followed the pattern laid down by Argentine and Uruguayan terrorist groups. Their success, particularly throughout 1978 and 1979, was attributable to their discipline and planning. They obtained intelligence on the target, maintained strict security in their cellular structure, had strong logistic support apparatus of safe houses, and trained their men to care for hostages. Such planning paid off when they turned to other revolutionary activities, as they could use the accumulated ransoms to buy arms.

In June the manager of Eagle Glove Company received a kidnapping threat. In the same month, two Salvadoran employees of IBM were kidnapped and held for $200,000 ransom for a month before being released. Two Salvadoran employees of McCann Erickson, a U.S. firm, were abducted, questioned at length about details of the company's operations, and later released.

In August 1978 FARN struck the foreign community again, kidnapping Swedish businessmen Kjell Bjork, the manager of L.M. Erickson. His company paid $1 million and published the guerrillas' manifesto in foreign newspapers to obtain his release. On November 24 the same group seized the Dutch executive Fritz Schuitema, director of Philips Corporation. Philips paid between $1 and $5 million and ran advertisements proclaiming the evils of the Salvadoran government in 32 newspapers worldwide. Such publication alone reportedly cost the company over $1 million. Schuitema was released on December 30. Meanwhile, on November 30 two British bankers with the Bank of London and South America were taken by FARN and held until June of the following year.

FARN struck at the Japanese again on December 17, abducting Takahasu Suzuki, sales manager of a textile firm. Because of varied demands for prisoner release—ransom money in the millions and publication of manifestos—both the British and Japanese hostages were held for a long period while their firms and their respective governments maneuvered to effect their release. In both cases when the hostages were released (Suzuki in April 1979 and the two British bankers in June, with ransoms reportedly over $5 million paid in each case) their governments' diplomatic representatives left El Salvador. In May the Japanese withdrew diplomatic personnel, and most of their nationals also departed. On release of the two British hostages, their diplomats withdrew temporarily without notice, reportedly because of terrorist threats, leaving the British business community irate. Public opinion in the United Kingdom criticized both the diplomatic reaction to the threat and the ransom payments by business, since government policy had steadfastly opposed concessions to terrorism.

During this period the leftists increasingly directed attacks at diplomatic installations and diplomats. In late 1977 U.S. Ambassador Frank Devine received intelligence of FPL surveillance of his movements and their detailed plans for his abduction. Increased security and constant awareness of the problem precluded such an occurrence, but in September 1978 a FPL team directed machine-gun fire at the embassy during the early morning hours before employees were on duty, making a sufficient number of direct hits to cause concern. In January 1979 militants occupied the Mexican embassy, holding 156 people hostage while demanding release of prisoners and publication of a manifesto. The matter was resolved by flight of the terrorists to asylum in Mexico.

The same day Ernesto Liebes, the honorary consul general of Israel and executive of a coffee export firm, was kidnapped by FARN. His body was found in March. In May the BPR took over the Venezuelan embassy, holding it until June 1 when the guerrillas were flown out to Mexico. Meanwhile, the ambassador and some of his staff escaped during a period of confusion when food was being delivered. The following day BPR and police tangled during a demonstration, leaving 14 people dead and many more wounded. The next day terrorists retaliated by killing the minister of education. That month also saw the ambush and death of the Swiss chargé d'affaires. When his car was blocked in a kidnapping attempt, he tried to escape by ramming the terrorists' vehicles. A gunman shot him in the head. The ambassador of South Africa also met death at the hands of terrorists. He was kidnapped in November and negotiations went on for months with the FPL before his death was reported.

In October 1979, just two weeks after the coup that overthrew President Romero, about 200 members of LP-28 demonstrated at the American embassy. After a noisy demonstration they dropped their banners to reveal ladders and started to climb over the wall. When the Marine guards countered with tear gas, LP-28 members opened fire, wounding two Marines and receiving some fire in return. They retreated before any deaths occurred.

The attacks on diplomatic facilities and personnel inevitably caused foreign countries to reduce representation in El Salvador. As did corporations, governments transferred functions to neighboring countries, reduced staff, or closed down completely. Such moves deprived expatriate businessmen of their government's advice and counsel and further eroded their confidence in the local government's ability to deal with the problem of terrorism.[7]

The year 1979 witnessed increased targeting of both foreign and domestic business in El Salvador. Occupation of factories and business establishments by militant labor instigators frequently held both the workers and managers hostage while terms of new labor contracts were negotiated. In January as two labor unions struggled for jurisdiction, activists occupied a plant owned by a U.S. firm, Taller Industries, holding workers and two American managers hostage for five days. In February businessman Jose Ernesto Romero was killed by FPL. The guerrilla group gave as a reason the fact that Romero had been personnel chief for Central American Nylon Industries when that firm had dissolved the labor union. During March the principal bottling plants and a brewery were taken over by labor agitators.

At this same time terrorists started the first serious action directed at utilities by instigating strikes that closed down generating plants and resulted in closings of businesses and schools. In July labor radicals timed an operation at a U.S.-owned glove factory to coincide with the visit of its American executive. They held the executive and his local manager hostage in the plant for seven days, propagandizing them, depriving them of information from the outside, sanitary conveniences, and minimum comforts. After seven days they signed a labor agreement, the conditions of which would have meant operating at a loss. Shortly thereafter the corporation pulled out its investment and closed the plant.

During the summer strikes at three other U.S.-owned plants kept workers off the job for weeks at a time. In August strikers at the Apex Clothing Company held workers and American manager William Boorstein hostage. After ten days Boorstein escaped from the plant and quickly made his way out of the country. Soon thereafter employees of an American-owned hotel took over the hotel and held tourists hostage while making demands on management. In October during labor disputes four U.S. subsidiary companies had their machinery destroyed by fire.

Violence took the form also of bombings of business establishments. In January a FARN unit stole between 500 and 1,000 sticks of dynamite from a sandstone quarry warehouse, and results were felt throughout the country.

By this time the kidnapping tactic had been refined by guerrilla groups, and the threat caused increasing consternation to businessmen, even though most lived very cautious lives and heeded the advice of their security advisers. FARN, as mentioned above, abducted Ernesto Liebes, industrialist and Israeli consul general, and presented a deadline for ransom payment. When the deadline was not met they killed him. In February 1979 they abducted wealthy coffee merchant Jorge Alvarez in Santa Ana. In June terrorists kidnapped William Rocha, manager of National Cash Register office and a Nicaraguan, and demanded $3 million ransom. After negotiations between kidnappers and representatives of the parent corporation, NCR reportedly paid $400,000 for Rocha's release. In August a Spanish businessman was kidnapped and held for 15 days.

The last kidnapping incident to involve American businessmen occurred in September. Two employees of Beckman Instruments, Dennis MacDonald and Fausto Bucheli, were abducted and their driver killed while traveling between their plant and San Salvador. The Revolutionary Party of Central American Workers made demands for ransom of $10 million and publication of their manifesto in foreign newspapers. After six weeks of bargaining, Beckman complied with the publication demand, paid an undisclosed ransom, and obtained the release of their men. Because of this experience and the increasing risks associated with doing business in El Salvador, the corporation made the decision to cut back operations in El Salvador and repatriate their American managers. Local Salvadoran employees wanted to continue on the job, however, so the plant now operates at a fraction of former capacity under local management.

THE TERRORIST ENVIRONMENT AFTER THE COUP

In October 1979 a coup by reform-minded military officers ousted President Romero and installed a five-man junta of moderate civilian and military men, with one member from the business community. Optimism that El Salvador's problems would be solved were short-lived, as violence in the streets continued unabated. Much of the violence was directed at business establishments. Within two weeks of the coup, for example, fires destroyed machinery in four U.S. subsidiaries, a deputy manager of the First National City Bank was shot to death, the Bank of America was bombed, and an armed crowd of LP-28 members attacked the U.S. embassy, as noted above.

The first junta held together two and a half months. After the next junta invited participation by members of the Christian Democratic Party, Jose Napoleon Duarte was appointed to the presidency. His government was committed to instigate reforms in landholding and other areas of the economy and to hold elections in 1982. Promptly in March 1980 the government took over the largest landholdings, involving about 25 percent of the cultivated land, with the intention of turning them over to peasant cooperatives. At the same time the government nationalized banking and export marketing of principal crops.

The centrist junta satisfied neither the left nor the right, however, so violence continued from both sides. Already in January the combined leftist groups issued an appeal for insurrection and a people's war. On January 22 a massive rally of 100,000 protesting against the government erupted in gunfire, leaving at least twenty dead. Terrorism continued to disrupt the cities. In January 1980 the world count of terrorist incidents gave El Salvador first place—a place retained throughout 1980. During that year 231 of the 816 incidents reported in El Salvador, or 28 percent, were directed at business targets.[8]

From the left the drive to disrupt trade and production continued. From the right hit men and security forces took their toll of suspected leftists. Businessmen, while continuing to be targets of the left, were also contributors to the terrorism through financing anti-leftist activities.[9]

The junta was not popular among Salvadoran businessmen—both those in the country and the exiles in Guatemala or Miami—largely because of the agricultural and banking reforms. They responded most effectively by closing down businesses and taking their capital out of the country.

The nature of the struggle changed in 1980 and with it its impact on business. The newly united leftist organizations began to engage in larger operations and, although they still took aim at private enterprises, they increasingly chose military and government targets. In February and March militants attacked police stations and a National Guard installation in the San Salvador area. In two separate incidents in the countryside bands of guerrillas occupied plantations and engaged in shoot-outs with military patrols.

During the summer the combined leftist groups tried a new protest tactic of calling a general strike to bring the economy to a halt. On three occasions a month apart they called on workers to shut down the country. The June strike succeeded in halting most commercial activity, but those called for July and August attracted fewer adherents. Militants placed bombs in factories and began their attack on the transportation system by stopping buses carrying workers, burning the buses, and shooting drivers. This practice was to proliferate during the 1982 election campaign. By resisting the call to strike, the workers demonstrated that they wanted jobs more than they wanted revolution.

After the strikes foundered, the conflict gradually shifted from urban centers to the countryside where guerrillas could raid small towns or rural settlements, take over the area, and then melt into the countryside when security forces appeared. At the same time rightist security forces stepped up their killing of suspected leftists, making for further polarization.

Attacks against business targets continued, however, although the number of kidnappings declined and have continued to do so. The reasons for this are varied. First, business executives became educated in security measures. They cut a low profile, varied their schedules, kept their social and family life quiet, and lived behind guards and electronic guard systems. When their intelligence warned of a threat, they left the country, often anonymously, until advised that the threat had passed. As one corporate security adviser put it, it was more economical to spend lavishly on security protection than to pay a million or more in ransom.

Second, many prominent business executives had been replaced by lesser known managers. By the end of 1980, American executives of all the large corporate subsidiaries in El Salvador had left, with one exception. The one remaining still lives and works in San Salvador under conditions of maximum security. Local citizens who replaced the departing foreigners are less obvious targets of kidnappers. And third, Salvador security forces raided the formerly sacrosanct National University grounds in June 1980 and found access to a network of safe areas where hostages and arms could be hidden. This action robbed guerrillas of urban hideouts and very likely slowed hostage taking in the capital.

Nevertheless, bombings, strikes, and facility attacks against businesses continued. In April militants disrupted work at the Texas Instrument plant, closing the factory temporarily. To deny the government and business their export earnings, coffee and sugar stores were burned. The year ended with an acceleration of violence from both sides. On November 27 rightist gunmen raided a meeting of leaders of the National Democratic Front, killing six of them. In December three American nuns and one lay worker were murdered, allegedly by members of security forces. Presidents of the National Coffee Institute and National Sugar Institute were taken hostage. Many businesses were burned and three banks bombed, among them a branch of the Bank of America.

The new year saw no relaxation of tensions. On January 3, 1981, two American labor lawyers and a Salvadoran agrarian reform official working on land reform were shot and killed as they sat in a lounge of a San Salvador hotel. In February a section of a U.S.-owned Esso Standard Oil compound was firebombed, leaving two persons dead and some damage to the buildings, and a bomb destroyed offices of Citibank in San Salvador. In March offices of ITT suffered bomb damage estimated at $100,000. The American embassy was the target of machine-gun or rocket attacks on at least seven occasions in March and April.

In January the combined guerrilla groups launched their major effort to take over the country. Their efforts to meet government forces in open combat and take control of territory failed, however, when the people did not turn out to support them. After January support for the leftists diminished among some former sympathizers such as church leaders, for example, because of their sabotage of the economy. Labor unions eased up somewhat, and mass street demonstrations in the capital stopped. Guerrilla targeting shifted to the country's infrastructure with stepped-up attacks on utility installations, roads, bridges and buses. On October 15, the second anniversary of the overthrow of President Romero, guerrillas blew up the Golden Bridge over the Lempa River, the most important span in the country, linking San Salvador with the eastern third of the country. Frequent attacks on utility installations and power lines kept power transmission and communications uncertain. Indeed, observers report that at any time during the past year one-third of the country has been without electric power.

CURRENT BUSINESS ENVIRONMENT

Under President Duarte the government continued to battle both sides of the political spectrum. Land redistribution has been a political success but not yet an economic one. The leftists disapprove because it deprives them of a valuable revolutionary issue, and the rightists fight it because of the loss of land from private ownership. In July 1981 President Duarte struck out at businessmen on the right, calling them his greatest threat because of their efforts to undo his reforms. At the same time his government made a concession to the business community when it extended a wage freeze and controls on rent and selected prices.[10]

Despite the fact that the economy is embattled from all sides, that many businesses have closed and their owners gone to safer areas, and that no new private investment is coming into the country, many businessmen have optimistically faced the challenge of keeping viable enterprises operating. One reporter described the hazards:

> Warehouses and factories are favorite targets of guerrillas firebombings, trucks are regularly hijacked, stores are looted and workers are intimidated into not showing up for the job. Extortion payments known as "war taxes" can be demanded on both sides, a curfew limits double-shift production, public utilities are erratic, credit and insurance no longer exist, suppliers demand cash in advance and owners and managers are subject to kidnapping, assassination or simply the unnerving threat of both.[11]

Businessmen know that El Salvador has the potential to be an economic success and feel optimistic that they can succeed once the shooting stops. As one businessman said, "The people who are still here are the ones who are serious about it, the self-made men, the stubborn people or those who don't have the money to go to Guatemala or Miami."[12] Another likened doing business to the Flying Wallendas. "To survive in El Salvador, you have to be like them and do an acrobatic act."[13]

Many entrepreneurs find it necessary to get along with both sides by paying protection money to the security forces and cooperating with leftist labor leaders. One manager of a San Salvador plant told this interviewer of his dealings with a leftist labor organization that threatened a strike at his plant. He used neutral ground of the clergy and the press to express his point of view and succeeded in heading off the strike. Many businessmen pay their labor force above-scale wages and give them extra benefits to keep them loyal. During periods of violence on the streets managers will allow employees to stay overnight at the plants behind security guards. All reports from businessmen on the scene stress gaining and keeping the loyalty of the work force as the key to staying in business.

Small businessmen from San Salvador who visited Washington, D.C., in the spring of 1982 voiced optimism. They complained that the media create an impression that the whole country is at war, whereas the conflict is largely in the countryside. Life and business go on in San Salvador with less fear of threat then in 1980. Although guerrillas may still make lightening raids in the city and threaten lives, the threat of kidnapping has receded. Many businessmen who moved elsewhere during the past few years are now making trips back from exile to test the business climate. If violence abates and political control is stabilized, businessmen no doubt will be the first to return.

NOTES

1. M. J. R. Martz, "El Salvador: U.S. Interests and Policy Options," Congressional Research Service Issues Brief IB80064, October 31, 1980, pp. 1–2.

2. Foreign Broadcast Information Service, *Daily Report, Latin America,* March 30, 1979, p. 6.

3. *New York Times,* March 23, 1982, p. A12.

4. Frank J. Devine, *El Salvador, Embassy Under Attack* (New York: Vantage Press, 1981), p. 221.

5. Observers report that because terrorists often insisted on secrecy when negotiating for a hostage's release, many more kidnappings took place than were documented in press and government reports. Therefore, the present account understates the number of kidnappings of Salvadoran nationals.

6. Lester A. Sobel (ed.), *Political Terrorism, 1974–1978,* Vol. 2 (New York: Facts on File, Inc., 1978), pp. 144–145.

7. U.S. Ambassador Devine in his *El Salvador, Embassy Under Attack* details embassy seizures and attacks. During his tenure (October 1977–February 1980) 20 of the 28 embassies in El Salvador were directly affected by terrorist actions.

8. Risks International, Inc., *Quarterly Risk Assessment,* January-March 1981, pp. 45–46.

9. U.S. Ambassador Robert White, in a speech to the Chamber of Commerce, accused the business community of financing terrorism. *Wall Street Journal,* April 1, 1980, p. 16.

10. *New York Times,* July 2, 1981, p. 18.

11. *New York Times,* May 25, 1981, IV, p. 1.

12. *Ibid.,* p. 2.

13. *Wall Street Journal,* May 7, 1981, p. 1.

8

Terrorist Kidnappings in Colombia

William F. Sater

Colombia is a nation divided by geography and conflicting political ideologies. For much of its history the country's two political parties, the Liberals and the Conservatives, appeared incapable of curing the social and economic problems afflicting the country. Indeed, rather than confront the issues of maldistribution of wealth and economic development, the Conservative and Liberal parties, instead devoted most of their efforts to destroying each other. Eventually this political rivalry degenerated into a civil war, appropriately called "La Violencia," which lasted from 1948 well into the early 1960s. Approximately 250,000 men, women, and children died in the ensuing bloodshed; populations fled to the comparative safety of the cities, and significant portions of the nation fell under the authority of guerrilla bands, which created "independent republics."

Eventually the Liberals and Conservatives recognized the futility of perpetuating such a situation and ended the bloodshed by agreeing to share power through alternate control of the presidency. This practice continued until the late 1970s; since then the two parties have fielded candidates for the post of chief executive. Although domestic order had been restored, Colombia still remained saddled with a political system that seemed incapable of resolving the country's socioeconomic problems. In the early 1960s, a former dictator, General Gustavo Rojar Pinilla, founded a new political party, The National Popular Alliance (ANAPO). Although ideologically vague, ANAPO called for nationalizing the economy and ending the traditional elite control over the political and economic system. After an initial spurt of activity, which included an unsuccessful 1970 attempt to win the presidency, Rojar Pinilla's popularity began to wane and, following his death, the party he founded ceased to be a viable political force.

Although Colombia has emerged as one of South America's few democracies, serious problems still remain. Most of the nation's citizens, conditioned by years of martial law, appear unenthusiastic about the country's political institutions or parties. Others describe Colombia as a corrupt oligarchy and consequently they repudiate traditional methods, seeking instead to alter the nature of society through violence.

THE GUERRILLAS

The Fuerzas Aramadas Revolucionarias (FARC) is one of the oldest and most active guerrilla organizations in Colombia. Unlike its contemporaries, FARC traces its origin to "la violencia." By 1950, guerrilla bands controlled large portions of rural Colombia. Some of the groups were politically motivated; others were simply bandits who took advantage of the vacuum created when the government's officials abandoned various areas. Bogotá, through a combination of amnesties and a counter-insurgency program, reasserted its control over most of the nation; but the pockets of guerrillas survived and continued to operate freely. Recognizing their potential value, Colombia's Communist Party sought to win control of these outlaw bands, officially endorsing guerrilla war as a vehicle for achieving power. In 1956, the party's central committee called for the "self-defense" of the masses, and, in 1964, it created the Southern Guerrilla Bloc. Two years later this organization became FARC, which quickly opened guerrilla foci in Colombia's western and central regions.

Fuerzas Aramadas Revolutionaries (FARC)

Since FARC is the Communist Party's military arm, the guerrillas essentially propound a set of Marxist-Leninist principles modified to reflect the party's perception of Colombia's reality. Following the Cuban example, the guerrillas consider themselves a vanguard of rural revolutionaies who, it is hoped, will develop a constituency in the nation's cities. Once both the urban and rural foci are in place, the guerrillas plan to coordinate their activities in order to depose the regime. While FARC, and eventually its urban counterpart, violently seek to undermine the Bogotá government, the Communist Party, which is legal, would work within the traditional political system toward the same goal.

In 1963, FARC went on the offensive, unleashing a series of raids against military installations. Initially confined to four areas—Caqueta and Putumayo, Huila, Tolima, and Meta—FARC subsequently opened new fronts in Boyaca, Santander, Antioquia, and Cundinamarca. The terrorists have since created additional foci in Cauca and Valle (the Sixth Front), Meta (the Seventh), and in Boyaca and Arauca (the Eighth). As of 1983, there were at least fourteen fronts functioning in various areas of Colombia.

Although it operates throughout the nation, FARC maintains a central headquarters in Sumasaz, where the various front leaders coordinate their activities. Each front has a leader, an executive officer, and one or more squads of 20 to 25 members each. Above the fronts are the Military Staff and a Central Committee of Chiefs (COMMIL), which operates supply lines to urban centers. The chain of command is well maintained and discipline is rigorously imposed. Disobedience is punished by a summary court martial, with execution the usual penalty.

FARC carefully screens potential candidates. Once found suitable, applicants are sent to camps for training and political indoctrination. Most of these bases are located in the interior of Colombia, although certain individuals have attended advanced courses in Cuba, Czechoslovakia, and the Soviet Union. In addition to their military duties, members of FARC often farm in order to keep the units self-sufficient. Participation is a full-time vocation for which each guerrilla receives a very small stipend. Individuals cannot resign and defectors are often executed. This, however, has not prevented some members from accepting the government's amnesties. Little is known about either the leaders or rank and file of FARC. The organization's commander is Manuel Marulenda Velez, "Tirofijo—Sure Shot," a former truckdriver who is now more than 50 years old.

FARC initiated its guerrilla campaign by attacking isolated units of the police and the military. Beginning in 1968, it began to assault military installations and it has since become more ambitious and audacious. The group, for example, has demonstrated that it can defend itself against the military's helicopters, and the organization is capable of attacking and holding towns for brief periods of time. The guerrillas, moreover, have continued to open new fronts despite government attempts to eradicate them. In June, 1981, FARC went on the offensive, forcing the government to respond by launching its own counter-insurgency operation. Later, FARC's leaders proclaimed a unilateral truce for the duration of the 1982 presidential campaign in order, they claimed, to deny giving the government an excuse to intervene in the electoral process. Despite this supposed temporary halt in its military activity, however, FARC continued its operations, and the number of kidnappings, for example, increased. Similarly, although it has continued to evince an interest in reaching some agreement with the Bogotá government, the guerrillas have not reduced their operations.

It is extremely difficult to assess the impact of FARC's activities because it often operates in areas where neither the authorities nor the news media dare to venture. Hence, many of the organization's actions escape public attention. Certain trends still emerge: Attacks on the military and police have increased, as have kidnappings and assassinations. Assaults on towns have also become more common. During the period July 1980–July 1981, FARC committed 40 percent of Colombia's kidnappings, 42 percent of the assaults on towns, and 80 percent of the reported assassinations of civilians. Unlike some of its guerillas and terrorist colleagues, FARC eschews flamboyant activities, such as hijackings or embassy seizures; it does not seek to enlist the support of the press; nor does it, like the M-19, interrupt television programs to broadcast its programs.

FARC appears quite eclectic in its selection of targets. It has assassinated members of the military, government officials, and bureaucrats, as well as peasants who are either accused of being informers or of violating FARC's directives. Although FARC's favorite target is wealthy ranchers, the guerrillas have also seized rural industrialists, emerald dealers, and merchants whom they hold for ransom. Generally FARC confines itself to domestic targets, although it has abducted the honorary Dutch consul, Eric Leupin; Richard Starr, a biologist working for the Peace Corps; and a Venezuelan rancher whom the guerrillas apparently abducted in Venezuela.

Ransoms finance FARC's activities. The guerrillas have also robbed banks to obtain funds and have taken over towns whose shops they loot for food, medicines, and supplies. It appears that at least some elements of FARC have become involved in the extremely lucrative drug traffic in order to obtain additional funds, which are used to purchase equipment and weapons.

19th of April Movement (M-19)

M-19, unlike FARC, did not originate as a rural guerrilla group but as an offshoot of ANAPO. Following the 1970 presidential election, Rojas Pinilla's followers became extremely angry, claiming that the traditional political parties had cheated their candidate of victory. Believing therefore that the peaceful road to power was not open, some dissidents, under the leadership of Carlos Toledo, a medical doctor and former ANAPO deputy in the national legislature, concluded that only armed rebellion could bring social justice to Colombia.

Although willing to imitate the actions of foreign terrorists, the M-19 insists on describing itself as an indigenous reform movement rooted exclusively in Colombia's social reality. While it explictly repudiates the international aspects of Marxism, it nonetheless supports objectives that appear similar to those of FARC: the creation of a democratic and economically independent state, the destruction of monopolies, and the reduction of the power of multinational corporations that, it claims have historically stunted Colombia's economic development.

Although the movement rejects Colombia's political system as corrupt, some of its leaders tried to participate in the 1982 presidential election. The M-19 claims that its use of terrorist violence is only a response to similar activities initiated by the "terrorist regime" of Bogotá. M-19 sees Colombia as a nation ruled by a corrupt oligarchy that has betrayed the country culturally and economically to the national bourgeoise and the multinational corporations. Consequently, the terrorists must use violence to overthrow this oppressive system in order to replace it with a democratic state that will bring its citizens a new social and economic order.

The terrorist program has struck a responsive cord among some Colombians. M-19 has won some support in the universities and among intellectuals. Prominent members of Colombian society, including actors, government officials, military personnel, and even a sports figure, have been implicated as members or supporters of the M-19. The organization also enjoys the support of Fidel Castro, who has provided equipment, training facilities, and possibly financial assistance.

M-19 is organized into cells of approximately five members (aspirants), each under the command of an "officer." The latter belongs to a base command, again composed of between three to five participants, whose leader reports to an intermediate command that, in turn, is responsible to a director of columns. The columns are grouped under the authority of a regional director, who is responsible to a high command. Supervising the entire organization is the general directorate. Although organized by cells, the various groups are also specialized by function—medical, logistics, communications, and finance; some units are exclusively military in purpose. Although concentrating on military activities, M-19 leadership insists that its members devote substantial efforts to political endeavors.

Because it is neither the handmaiden of the Communist Party nor isolated in the countryside, M-19 appears to enjoy close relations with foreign terrorist groups. Various foreign nationals—Chileans, Panamanians, Costa Ricans, and Uruguayans—have participated in various M-19 operations. Some claim that Tupamaros have provided technical assistance to the Colombian terrorists. While difficult to prove, the kidnapping and assassination of Chester Bitterman, discussed subsequently, closely resembled the Tupamaro *modus operandi*. In addition to its ties with the Tupamaros, M-19 also has relations with FAR and Nicaragua's Sandinistas; it claims to have established ties with the Puerto Rican FALN as well as a terrorist group operating in the Dominican Republic. M-19 members, some of whom received training in Cuba and Russia, have participated in various military operations in Central America. M-19 also belonged to the Junta Coordinaria Revolucionaria, an umbrella organization created in the 1970s and presumably financed by the Cuban intelligence service. It was composed of representatives from Argentina's ERP (The Revolutionary Army of the People), Bolivia's ELN (The Army of National Liberation), and Chile's MIR (The Movement of the Revolutionary Left).

There is a substantial amount of information available about M-19's commander, who, unlike FARC's leadership, appears more publicity conscious. M-19's leaders are generally between 30 and 40 and are university educated, with a high number possessing degrees in medicine and the social sciences. Although it is difficult to generalize about the rank and file, a profile of M-19's members in Bogotá indicates that they are younger—generally between 20 and 25—and that only approximately half have completed a high school education. The original leaders of M-19 appear to have been born either in Bogotá or a large provincial city; the lower ranks originally tended to come from a rural environment, although they might now reside either in the capital or other urban area.

Discipline appears to be a little less rigorous than that of FARC. M-19's leadership, for example, tolerates criticism, providing that it is forwarded through proper channels. While orders are subject to some adjustments, once a command is given obedience is expected unless tactical considerations dictate modification. Thus, although centralized, the leadership accepts that field commanders might alter directives. It might be difficult to enforce rigorous discipline because the differences in age and education could produce schisms within M-19. Disputes have already arisen over the issues of tactics and amnesty. One dissident element created the "Heroes of 3 June 1979," which denounced M-19 as being too conservative. It is likely that more schisms will surface if generational differences become more pronounced or as elements either tire of guerrilla life or reject the program that M-19 hopes to implement. Some individuals have defected, although not in substantial numbers.

M-19 launched its career flamboyantly by stealing the sword of Simon Bolivar, Colombia's principal national hero. This clearly publicity-conscious act was followed by other incidents designed to ensure that M-19 occupied the world spotlight.

On February 27, 1980, 17 members of M-19 captured the Dominican embassy in Bogotá. The group, under the leadership of Rosemberg Pabon Pabon—named, albeit incorrectly, in memory of Julius and Ethel Rosenberg—seized approximately 75 people, including 13 ambassadors and the papal nuncio. During the course of the occupation, which lasted two months, M-19 released the nondiplomatic staff and one ambassador, while another managed to escape. Initially the terrorists demanded the release of over 300 jailed terrorists plus a ransom of $50 million. The Colombian government refused to negotiate either demand. Eventually, after protracted negotiations, M-19 members and their diplomatic captives were flown to Havana, where the hostages were released. Apparently the terrorists also received approximately $2.5 million, an amount that was raised privately and did not come from the Bogotá government.

M-19 has hijacked shipments of food, candy, and toys, which it distributed among the poor of Bogotá. It seized a busload of foreign athletes whom it lectured on political topics. In a similar fashion, M-19 members have taken over a church and, on occasion, schools, where they harangued the parishioners and the students. The group also has become quite skillful in interrupting scheduled television shows, either by taking over a station or by electronic means, in order to broadcast its message. Similarly, it has kidnapped important journalists to act as messengers and even has had a hostage photographer take pictures of M-19 guerillas executing two members of the Colombian military who had unsuccessfully tried to infiltrate the organization.

M-19 has become increasingly violent. In 1976, it assassinated Jose Raquel Mercado, a local labor union leader. More recently, a faction of M-19 seized Chester Allen Bitterman, an American working for the Summer Institute of Linguistics, a church-based organization that translates religious material into Indian languages. Claiming that the Institute was a CIA front, M-19 demanded that it leave Colombia. When it did not, the kidnappers murdered Bitterman. In addition to this incident, M-19 has stepped up its attacks on individuals, as well as attacking police stations and military outposts and attempting to occupy towns. Perhaps because it lacks rural support, M-19 tends to concentrate on urban targets, particularly bombings.

The group deviated from its policy of avoiding military confrontations when it launched a spring offensive in 1981. An assault group composed of 300 men and women, who had just completed a training course in Cuba, landed in two separate groups on the coast near the Ecuadorian border. Once ashore, the units united and launched an offensive to capture a provincial capital. The government responded by sending its counter-insurgency troops, which not only successfully repulsed the attack but killed various leaders while capturing both Rosemberg Pabon and Dr. Carlos Toledo.

Initially M-19 appeared severely handicapped by the loss of many of its members, particularly its leaders, but the struggle continued under the leadership of Jaime Bateman, one of the organization's important figures who had escaped. And with the release of members captured in 1981 as part of a broad amnesty program, the organization has essentially recouped its losses.

Like FARC, M-19 finances its activities through kidnappings. During the period

July 1980–July 1981, ransoms produced some 540,000,000 Colombian pesos (approximately $7 million). Another target is banks, while some financial support apparently comes from Cuba. The closing of the Cuban embassy following the abortive M-19 offensive has perhaps curtailed the guerillas' access to Havana's facilities, including the use of its embassy and diplomatic pouch.

Other Groups

FARC and M-19 are only the two most active guerrilla groups operating in Colombia. Many of other elements—MARC (Armed Revolutionary Movement of Colombia), FRAG (Popular Forces of Guerrilla Action), CAOS-14 Septiembre (Command of Armed Worker Self Defense–14 September), FUPAG (United Forces for Guerrilla Action), FPL (Patriotic Front of Liberation), GR (Red Guard), TR (Red Tribune), and MAO (Workers Self Defense)—appear either to have existed for only a short time or to have lost any vigor they once might have possessed. Other organizations, some of which antedate FARC, still function, albeit on a reduced scale. One of these elements is the Popular Army of National Liberation (EPL), a pro-Peking Marxist group, founded in 1967. Although initially a rural-based organization, it operated mainly in northeastern and northern Colombia and later formed an urban contingent. Losses in the countryside made the EPL shift its activities to Bogotá as well as to other provincial cities.

One of the most famous Colombian guerrilla groups is the Army of National Liberation (ELN). Organized in 1964, it was a pro-Cuban organization that operated mainly in the departments of Santander, Antioquia, and Bolívar. Although not one of the most active organizations, it became famous because one of its members was the former priest Camilo Torres, who was killed in 1966 and whose place was taken by another cleric, Father Domingo Laín, a Spaniard who also died in combat in 1974.

A recent newcomer is the People's Revolutionary Organization (ORP), which surfaced in 1982. While little is known about this apparently Bogotá-based organization, the group attracted attention when it kidnapped Gloria Lara, a woman active in social welfare activities in Colombia. The wife of a prominent politician and the daughter of a wealthy family, Mrs. Lara de Echeverri was taken from her car while she was en route to work. The reasons for the kidnapping remain unclear, as do the nature of the ransom demands. In December, after six months in captivity, the authorities found Señora Lara, dead and four months pregnant, wrapped in an ORP flag. The method of execution, which strongly resembled those techniques employed by M-19, suggests that the ORP might be composed of dissident M-19 members. Regardless of its origins, however, ORP had clearly established its credentials as a terrorist organization.

Not all terrorism originates on the left. Indeed, right-wing elements, like the Death Squad and the American Anticommunist Association, have long indulged in violence. The newest addition is MAS (Death to the Kidnappers), which appeared in 1982. Apparently composed of former members of either the police or the military who were forced to retire from active duty because they were psychologically unfit, MAS launched a series of assassinations and kidnappings of individuals believed to belong to M-19. Others have claimed, however, that drug dealers created MAS in order to protect members of their families against M-19's kidnappings. Financed by a war chest of approximately 450,000,000 pesos, MAS hired the services of specialists who were skilled in dealing with this problem. MAS delivered to the police a member of M-19 implicated in the kidnapping of the daughter of a drug dealer. More recently MAS started to devote some of its energies to less laudable activities: recent reports indicate that MAS members are extorting money from businessmen and that, for reasons as yet unclear, they murdered some labor union leaders, a newspaper reporter, and a professor. Indeed, they are accused of killing over 200 people, most of them uninvolved in any political activity. It appears that the right-wing terrorists will simply compete with their left-wing colleagues for a piece of the terrorist action.

GUERRILLA TACTICS

Colombia's terrorists have indulged in two types of activity: actions to finance their operations and actions designed to hurt their enemy. Certain patterns have emerged: FARC, operating essentially in a rural environment, tends to occupy a town, take whatever supplies or medicines it requires, dispense revolutionary justice—generally resulting in an execution—and then withdraw into the hinterland. FARC, of all the groups, is a state within a state. Just in the area of Huila, the guerrillas control an area of 3,000 square kilometers known as El Pato, which the government admits that it has not ruled for over 14 years. The peasants of El Pato live under the rules of FARC, whose word is law. Recently, for example, the guerrillas killed two common criminals who, they learned, had threatened to kidnap local landowners. The group also recently executed over 100 peasants when they refused to cooperate with FARC directives.

Most of the guerrilla organizations finance their needs through bank robberies and kidnappings. It is sometimes difficult to separate terrorists from criminals since both bank robberies and particularly kidnappings have become extremely common and popular. On the whole, however, Colombian guerrillas do not seem to use kidnapping as a political statement, as did the Tupamaros, but more as a purely financial resource.

All of the terrorist organizations have demonstrated a great deal of skill, ambushing military personnel, the police, assaulting military installations, and assassinating government officials. The most audacious event was MAO's 1981 attempted assassination, by a remote control bomb, of Colombia's President Julio Turbay and American Vice President George Bush when the latter's plane was to land at Bogotá's El Dorado airport. M-19 has, moreover, twice attacked the president's palace, once with a car bomb and the other time with a mortar.

Certain guerrilla groups have focused their attacks on oil companies. The ELN, for example, not only destroyed portions of an oil pipeline belong to ECOPE

TROL, the Colombian national oil company, it also attacked drilling crews. M-19, perhaps reflecting a strong nationalist bent, has targeted U.S. oil companies, hijacking one company's helicopter, along with 60 kilos of dynamite; it also assaulted a drilling crew and murdered a Colombian geologist. Some organizations, like the ELN, have destroyed power transformers, blackening out portions of Bogotá. Others tried to intimidate the population by bombing movie theatres and buses, as well as occupying buildings in order to extort their temporary captives to become more radical.

Predictably foreign capitalists and multinational corporations have suffered their share of terrorist violence. American businessmen and ranchers have experienced terrorist assaults. The corporate offices or factories of General Electric, Gillette, Burroughs, and IBM have been bombed. Insurgents robbed a Chrysler outlet of radio equipment. M-19 threatened to maim Coca-Cola executives when the company became involved in a labor dispute. A Texaco distributing plant was robbed of 2,000,000 pesos. The EPL also threatened to kill both American and other foreign businessmen, accusing them of persecuting their workers. American diplomats and consulate have been the targets of attempted bombings as well as kidnappings and telephone threats.

Kidnapping as a Terrorist Operation

Kidnapping has become a major industry in Colombia. Kidnappers have abducted businessmen, ranchers, merchants, and industrialists. The families of the wealthy have also suffered: Children have been taken en route to schools; youngsters have been abducted from their homes. Aware of the economic potential of this crime, terrorists quickly learned the necessary techniques and, due to the combined activities of common criminals and terrorists, Colombia led the world with 34.3 percent of 102 kidnappings in 1982.

One of the most brutal examples occurred in 1976, when a female member of M-19 enticed Jose Raquel Mercado, a prominent labor union leader, to meet her for a sexual liaison. When he arrived, he was seized and held for 64 days. M-19 demanded that the press make public a proclamation denouncing Mercado as a traitor to the labor movement; that the government change certain laws in order to allow the rehiring of civil service employees who had been dismissed; and that Bogotá declare an amnesty for striking workers and pay a ransom of $800,000. After two deadlines had passed with the demands unsatisfied, the kidnappers shot Mercado.

Like their criminal counterparts, terrorists have seized members of wealthy or prominent Colombian families. In one case, M-19 entered the campus of the University of Antioquia and abducted a student, Señora Marta Nieves Ochoa de Yepes. Initially held in a house, the victim was later moved to the country. After 96 days, M-19 drove her to a nearby small town and released her. The family claimed that they had not paid any ransom nor had the government given anything in exchange. MAS, however, had threatened to take reprisals against the families

Table 8.1 Terrorist Kidnappings in Colombia by Month, 1980–1982

Month	1980	1981	1982
January	4	2	8
February	3	2	5
March	0	0	2
April	2	0	0
May	1	0	3
June	4	0	2
July	0	1	3
August	5	1	11
September	0	0	0
October	1	3	5
November	0	5	0
December	0	1	1

Source: Risks International, Inc., (Alexandria, Virginia) *Quarterly Risk Assessment & Executive Risk Assessments,* (1980–1982).

of members of M-19 if Mrs. Yepes was not released. The fact that the MAS had recently claimed that it had engineered the assassination, in the maximum security section of a local jail, of two men held for the kidnap and murder of a young man may have influenced the terrorists to free their victim.

The Threat to Americans

Increasingly, kidnapping has emerged as a potential danger for American executives working in Colombia or for nationals employed by U.S. multinational corporations. The first incident occurred in August 1975, when five men and one woman of

Table 8.2 Significant Kidnappings Involving Prominent Foreigners and Colombians

Date		Victim	Abductor	End Result
February	1975	Eric Leupin	FARC	Freed
August	1975	Kenneth Cooper	ELN	Freed
February	1976	Jose Mercado	M-19	Murdered
September	1976	Gustavo Curtis	Unknown	Freed
February	1977	Richard Starr	FARC	Freed
May	1978	Nicolas Escobar	M-19	Murdered
August	1980	Ira Hubbard	FARC	Freed
January	1981	Chester Bitterman	M-19	Murdered
November	1981	Marta Nieves Ochoa	M-19	Freed
November	1982	Gloria Lara	ORP	Murdered
March	1983	Kenneth Bishop	ORP	Freed
November	1983	Jaime Betáncur	ELN	Released

the ELN kidnapped Kenneth Cooper, a high-ranking executive of Sears Roebuck Company, from his home. The U.S. government proclaimed that it would not support negotiations with the abductors, although it stated that Sears could decide what course of action to follow. Cooper, after three months in captivity, eventually won his freedom after his family presumably paid a large ransom.

Less than a year after Cooper's kidnapping, on September 28, 1976, unknown assailants abducted Gustavo Curtis, the American manager of a company belonging to Beatrice Foods. Taken from his car, Curtis remained in the hands of his kidnappers for approximately eight months. As later discussed, the negotiations leading to Curtis's release were prolonged and complicated. Finally, Beatrice Foods, working through a security consultant, obtained his freedom after paying a reported ransom of $500,000.

The next case involved an employee of the American government, Richard Starr, a Peace Corps biologist who was working in a Colombian national park when FARC seized him in February 1977. This was not the first time that terrorists had kidnapped an individual with ties to a foreign government. In February 1975, members of FARC captured Eric Leupin, the honorary Dutch consul to Cali, when he visited his lumber mill. The Leupin case was complicated because the guerrillas initially seemed unsure whether to seek a ransom or demand the release of one of the group's jailed members. Because Leupin was an honorary consul, the situation became more complex. The Dutch government refused to become involved, although Leupin had earlier played host to Crown Prince Bernhard when he visited Colombia, while the Colombian government opposed negotiations and apparently tried to prevent the payment of the ransom demands. Because of these problems, Leupin remained in the custody of FARC for approximately 20 months and was released on October 3, 1976, when members of his family paid a substantial ransom.

Although Starr was an employee of the U.S. government, in accord with its stated no-ransom policy, the State Department did not respond to the kidnappers' demands or move to comfort Starr's family. Indeed, instead of assisting Starr's mother, government officials tried to prevent her from traveling to Colombia where she hoped to establish contact with the terrorists. Not until seven months after his abduction did it become clear that Starr was even alive.

Approximately one year after his capture, FARC finally announced that it would release Starr in exchange for Jaime Guaracas, a terrorist incarcerated on a penal island. Since neither Bogotá nor Washington would agree to an exchange, however, the plight of the Starr family appeared hopeless. When Guaracas subsequently obtained his freedom, through a legal technicality, FARC changed its demands, stating in May 1978 that it would kill Starr unless it received a payment of $250,000. American officials were to demonstrate their acceptance of these terms by taking out an ad in a Bogotá newspaper. Even before this announcement became public, Starr's relatives had begun negotiating with the kidnappers, tentatively settling on a payment of $50,000. Members of the American embassy, fearing that the kidnappers might kill Starr, indicated that they would negotiate with FARC. This act not only contravened Washington's official policy, it effectively ended the ongoing discussions between Starr's family and the terrorists, who obviously preferred to hold out for a higher ransom. FARC, therefore, broke off negotiations with the Starr family.

When Washington again refused to negotiate, the terrorists spirited Starr into the jungle, where he remained isolated although embassy officials managed to use local contacts with the left wing to send him letters and food. Starr only won his freedom after his family, working with their congressman, contacted the noted newspaper columnist, Jack Anderson, who took charge of raising the $250,000. Finally, in 1980, Starr was exchanged for the ransom and flown out of Colombia.

While Starr remained in captivity, M-19 kidnapped Nicolas Escobar Soto, the head of Texaco's Colombian subsidiary, in May 1978. Soto, who was aware that he might be in danger, was dragged from his car when he tried to park it in downtown Bogotá. Although he had a radio transmitter, he could not obtain help before the terrorists broke the car window and dragged him from the automobile. Negotiations were presumably under way when a group of soldiers, searching for some weapons, accidently stumbled upon the place where he was being held. Rather than permit Soto to escape, one of the group of six men and two women kidnappers fatally shot him.

On August 17, 1980, FARC kidnapped Ira Chase Hubbard, Jr., an agricultural businessman. Hubbard was abducted while visiting a banana-growing region. He was subsequently released, after the payment of $2 million on October 28, 1980.

On January 19, 1981, M-19 carried out a political kidnapping, taking Chester Allen Bitterman from his office at the Summer Institute of Linguistics, a religious organization that translated the Bible into Indian languages. Presumably part of a hard-line faction of M-19, the abductors demanded the publication of a communique denouncing Bogotá as South America's most ruthless dictatorship and condemning its presumed mistreatment of the local Indian tribes. In addition, the kidnappers, denouncing the Language Institute as a front for the CIA, demanded that it leave Colombia by February 19th or they would kill Bitterman. The government responded that it could do little besides increase its attempts to rescue the American. Although M-19 extended its original deadline, the Institute's directors refused to leave the country. True to their word, the kidnappers executed Bitterman by shooting him in the head, leaving his body wrapped in the red and black M-19 flag, to be discovered in Bogotá on March 7, 1981.

A recent example of kidnapping activity directed against foreigners was the seizure of Kenneth Bishop on March 7, 1983. Bishop, married to a Colombian and himself a long-time resident of the nation where he worked for Texaco, was seized when three men and a woman, all belonging to the ORP, used a stolen Mercedes Benz car to force his Datsun sedan off the road. After killing his driver and bodyguard, the terrorists removed Bishop from his car. Typical of standard kidnapping practices, the authorities received a picture of Bishop and a warning that he would be killed if the kidnappers' demands were not met by March 29th. After the Lara episode, the authorities could not dismiss ORP's demands, although Bogotá still opposed payment of a ransom, as did Texaco. Neither one, however, prevented members of Bishop's family from responding on their own. After an extension of the original deadline, the family managed to raise the funds to pay ORP. It is still not clear if Bishop's relatives in fact paid the ransom or if they merely acted as a conduit for Texaco. Regardless of the money's origin, it bought Bishop his freedom after 38 days in captivity. Bogotá refuses to acknowledge that a ransom had been paid.

Another recent kidnapping involved an American gem dealer who was abducted while traveling in San Marta. Happily for him, the police, solely by good luck, managed to secure his release. More recently, in April 1983, FARC seized Catherine Woods Kirby, a 62-year-old American woman who owns a ranch in an area east of Bogotá. At present, her fate is unknown.

Characteristics of Kidnapping in Colombia

Site.   Certain similar characteristics have emerged from these kidnappings. FARC generally confines its activities to rural areas where it can easily seize a farm or provincial businessman and spirit away its victims. Urban activities tend to require more planning, particularly now when most executives are aware that they might be kidnapped. Although Cooper was abducted from his home, most businessmen appear to be the most vulnerable when traveling en route to their places of work or residence. Bishop and Escobar Soto, for example, were taken from their cars. The work place also constitutes a second potential danger spot, particularly when located in a rural area.

Techniques Used.   Colombia's kidnappers employ a variety of ruses. Members of M-19, for example, once dressed as a group of nuns and priests in order to abduct Nicaragua's ambassador from his office. FARC often uses Colombian Army uniforms to win the confidence of potential victims, thus gaining access to their ranches or persuading them to pull over to the side of the road. The ELN, on the other hand, gains entry to homes by claiming to be members of the police either serving a warrant or investigating a crime.

Negotiations.   The payment of ransoms or negotiations with the kidnappers can prove extremely complicated, particularly for Americans who are unused to bargaining. Kidnappers generally begin by demanding huge sums and then often lower their sights. Bishop's abductors apparently demanded $50 million and settled for much less.

In addition to the delicacy of ransom bargaining, problems with the government may also develop. Bogotá has opposed the payment of ransoms, arguing that these will merely encourage other operations, although this has not been enforced. Consequently, an adversary relationship has developed between victims' families, who will do anything to assure a victim's safe return, and the authorities, who may oppose the payment of a ransom. Perhaps for this reason, large corporations like Sears and more recently Texaco have officially stated that they will not pay ransoms. It is unclear if this represents official company policy or merely constitutes a public gesture to appease the Bogotá government while the company continues indirect negotiations in secret.

This conflict between the authorities and the victims' families has sometimes produced tragic results. The police often keep families under surveillance in hopes of catching the kidnappers. While sometimes this covert activity has succeeded, it also has failed. The police, for example, intercepted the transfer of funds to secure the release of 17-year-old Isabel Cristina Zuniga Jimenez. By interfering, the police aborted the payment and the infuriated terrorists—in this case the ELN—murdered the girl after first raping her. It should be noted, however, that the payment of ransom does not always guarantee the victim's safe return. FARC, for example, has killed ranchers even after receiving payments, and recently members of M-19 and ELN decided to murder their captive when they began to argue over the division of the ransom. As the Escobar Soto kidnapping demonstrated, abductors murder their victims rather than surrender them, even when resistance is futile.

Resistance.   It is difficult to discover how vigorously a potential kidnap victim should resist. Recently an industrialist was first beaten and then shot for refusing to cooperate with his captors. Similarly, attempting to flee may produce the same result. FARC shot a young man when he tried to escape. Yet, on January 20, 1980, M-19 tried to kidnap a U.S. corporate executive as he drove to work. The executive's bodyguard and a passing policeman managed to repel the kidnappers. Clearly this armed resistance thwarted the kidnapping.

Treatment.   Victims are usually treated roughly at the beginning. Treatment generally improves following the first hours of the kidnapping. As the Lara and Zuniga cases have revealed, sexual abuse may occur. Bishop also indicated that he suffered ill treatment while he remained in ORP's hands.

Duration.   The amount of time in captivity seems to vary. Because it operates in a rural setting, FARC can hold a kidnap victim for lengthy periods. Richard Starr, for example, remained a prisoner for three years. Terrorists operating in an urban area have not kept their prisoners in custody for similar periods of time. M-19, for example, only imprisoned a Colombian industrialist in a "people's jail" for five months—far less than what Starr endured—before releasing him.

The Future of Terrorism

Bogotá has tried a variety of tactics to counter guerrilla activities. The authorities have created the Administrative Department of Security (DAS), formed in 1953, which was entrusted with the authority to deal with terrorists. Certain police units are also trained to deal with urban guerrillas. In addition, the authorities have created special rural antikidnapping groups, often volunteer militias either under the control of civil defense or military authorities. After it became clear that the police alone could not control terrorists, the government founded special counter-insurgency military units—the Hunter, Colombia, Vargas, Juanambu battalions—and deployed airborne brigades. A special antikidnapping unit was placed under the authority of the commander of the Brigada de Institutos Militares (BIM).

Special legislation has been formulated to deal with terrorists, particularly kidnappers, who are often confined on a penal colony located on an island. Periodically the authorities have stationed large numbers of troops and armored vehicles in big cities and have ordered army patrols into the streets in hopes of curtailing terrorist violence. These acts sometimes work: The massive police sweeps that followed the 1978 seizure of Nicaragua's ambassador are believed to have convinced the terrorists to release their captive. Civil libertarians and international organizations, however, claim that the counter-insurgency organizations have used torture to extract information and that they have mistreated innocent civilians.

Another governmental response has been to try to minimize the importance of the terrorists. In 1981, for example, the administration requested that television and radio stations not report on guerrilla activity. Similarly, it has limited press coverage. Recently an American journalist was arrested when he tried to leave Colombia carrying taped interviews with members of the EPL.

Bogotá has also tried the carrot approach. In July 1980, President Turbay offered an amnesty for terrorists who had not committed any act accompanied by a "savagery or cruelty." Terrorists had three months to accept the clemency, but few chose to surrender to the authorities. Turbay subsequently constituted a peace commission, headed by a former president of Colombia, which was to find a way to initiate negotiations. This effort failed because the commission offered concessions that Turbay considered too generous. Just prior to the end of his term, however, Turbay lifted the state of siege that had been in effect for most of his administration and that has ruled the nation for most of the past 34 years.

In 1982, Belisario Betancur began his administration by releasing all political prisoners, including those convicted of terrorism. That meant the leaders of M-19 captured after their abortive offensive were once again free. In addition, the president also offered another amnesty, claiming that he did not want "another drop of blood shed by Colombians, be they peasants, soldiers, or guerrillas." Betancur sought to integrate former terrorists into Colombian society by allocating funds to provide them with job training, housing, medical care, jobs, and farms.

The responses of the insurgent organizations have varied. The smaller groups, the ELN and EPL, violently oppose the amnesty program; the larger M-19 and FARC debated what posture to adopt. In April 1984, FARC announced that it would accept a truce for a year. During that period the guerrillas, who have certain demands they wished met—institution of social programs, restoration of civil rights, and extensive plans for economic development—will negotiate with Bogotá. It is unclear whether the truce will hold—past efforts have failed—and given the long history of disappointment it is questionable if this effort to obtain a settlement will succeed. M-19 appears equally intransigent. In 1983, prior to death in an airplane accident, Jaime Bateman called for a six-month truce during which the government would negotiate with representatives of various professional, economic, political, and social groups, but also representatives of the terrorist organizations. The Betancur government has initiated discussions with various terrorists but, as of mid-1983, nothing concrete had transpired. In the meantime, individuals were assassinated; businessmen and ranchers were kidnapped; and the military continued to fight skirmishes.

The private response to terrorism has varied. Citizens have hired bodyguards, generally retired military personnel; they have fortified their houses; many have chosen to leave Colombia for protracted periods of time. Individuals have sold their suburban houses or ranches, moving into urban houses or apartment complexes that have been reinforced to become fortresses. Companies have hired security experts, who themselves have become the objects of terrorist violence; they have also purchased bulletproof cars. As the kidnap statistics indicate, however, such measures have failed to accomplish their principal purpose. The terrorists, if confronted with too much security, have kidnapped the children of wealthy executives. It appears unlikely that businessmen can easily avoid future abductions.

Terrorism does not appear to be decreasing in Colombia. In part the insurgents seem ideologically incapable of accepting a compromise with a bourgeois government. Criminal elements, moreover, have discovered that terrorism is a lucrative profession. Finally there is a long tradition of violence in Colombia and guerrilla groups have become almost institutionalized. Regrettably, the government's options seem limited. As Belisario Betancur demonstrated, good will and a desire to integrate the insurgents is not enough. Although individual terrorists may be willing to return to ordinary life, the vast majority, either for ideological, psychological, or economic reasons, prefer to remain. Colombia, its citizens, and its foreign business community appear to be fated to endure continued violence.

9

Kidnapping in the United States and the Development of the Federal Kidnapping Statute

Richard J. Gallagher

Every age and every civilization has experienced kidnappings. Kidnapping has long been regarded as a heinous crime; in many instances the life of the victim is in jeopardy and its effect on the victim's family, relatives, and associates is traumatic. Courts have realized the seriousness of the crime and have dealt harshly with persons convicted of kidnapping.

Kidnappings have occurred throughout our national history but received little publicity. In the 1930s, due to improved communications the public became more aware of these crimes. The area around St. Louis, Missouri experienced many kidnappings in which the handicap of a state boundary hindered or defeated the efforts of the St. Louis police officers to apprehend the perpetrators. The improvement of the automobile and a better highway system made it easy for kidnappers using high-powered automobiles to cross a state line, terminating the jurisdiction and power of arrest of the police authorities at the site of the offense. It was apparent that a federal presence was necessary to ensure continuity of jurisdiction.

In 1931 St. Louis officials formed a committee to convince Congress of the need for federal legislation. Their efforts were greatly assisted by public sentiment aroused by the kidnapping on March 2, 1932 of the son of Charles A. Lindbergh. Congress acted and a federal kidnapping law was enacted on June 22, 1932.

Throughout the years there have been several amendments to this law. The federal kidnapping statute now provides:

(a) Whoever unlawfully seizes, confines, inveigles, decoys, kidnaps, abducts, or carries away and holds for ransom or reward or otherwise any person, except in the case of a minor by the parent thereof when:

(1) the person is willfully transported in interstate or foreign commerce;

(2) any such act against the person is done within the special maritime and territorial jurisdiction of the United States;

(3) any such act against the person is done within the special aircraft jurisdiction of the United States as defined in section 101(36) of the Federal Aviation Act of 1958, as amended (49 U.S.C. 1301(36)); or

(4) the person is a foreign official, an internationally protected person, or an official guest as those terms are defined in section 1116(b) of this title, shall be punished by imprisonment for any term of years or for life.

(b) With respect to subsection (a)(1), above, the failure to release the victim within twenty-four hours after he shall have been unlawfully siezed, confined, inveigled, decoyed, kidnaped, abducted, or carried away shall create a rebuttable presumption that such person has been transported in interstate or foreign commerce.

(c) If two or more persons conspire to violate this section and one or more of such persons do any overt act to effect the object of the conspiracy, each shall be punished by imprisonment for any term of years or for life.

(d) Whoever attempts to violate subsection (a)(4) shall be punished by imprisonment for not more than twenty years.

(e) If the victim of an offense under subsection (a) is an internationally protected person, the United States may exercise jurisdiction over the offense if the alleged offender is present within the United States, irrespective of the place where the offense was committed, or the nationality of the victim or the alleged offender. As used in this subsection, the United States includes all areas under the jurisdiction of the United States including any of the places within the provisions of sections 5 and 7 of this title and section 101(38) of the Federal Aviation Act of 1958, as amended (49 U.S.C. 1301(38)).

(f) In the course of enforcement of subsection (a)(4) and any other sections prohibiting a conspiracy or attempt to violate subsection (a)(4), the Attorney General may request assistance from any Federal, State, or local agency, including the Army, Navy, and Air Force, any statute, rule, or regulation to the contrary notwithstanding.[1]

EARLY HISTORY OF KIDNAPPING

Kidnapping goes far back in history. In the Bible the crime is defined and the punishment fixed. "He that shall steal man and sell him, being convicted of the guilt, shall be put to death."[2]

In Rome, kidnapping was known and practiced from the days of the Republic down to the time of Justinian, the 6th century after Christ. Indeed, in the time of Constantine (315 A.D.), a law was enacted that seems to indicate crime had assumed the proportions of modern time: in writing to his vicar in Africa, the Emperor assails the inhumanity of its perpetrators, and after expressing his sympathy for the misery and suffering inflicted on the parents of a victim, specifies that slaves convicted of kidnapping be exposed to wild beasts and free men, no matter what their rank, perish by the sword. Kidnapping for ransom does not seem to be one of the crimes Justinian spoke of; at that time, victims were usually sold into slavery by their captors.[3]

At common law kidnapping was considered by England and the U.S. Courts to be an aggravated form of false imprisonment. The aggravating element consisted in sending a detained person into another country, thereby depriving him of the protection of the laws and established means of regaining his liberty. In the United States, such a crime was committed by sending detained persons out of state. Any other unlawful detention was false imprisonment.[4]

In this country hundreds of kidnapping probably occurred long before its development as a highly specialized criminal activity; however, the cases were isolated. In most instances, the motive was other than ransom. Its occurrence was so rare, the country so sparsely settled, and the facilities of communication so primitive that little or no attention was paid to these actions outside of the particular locality or community in which one occurred.[5]

The two following incidents are good examples of early American kidnappings. In July 1874 Charles Brewster Ross, the 4-year-old son of Christian K. Ross, a well-known citizen, was abducted in Philadelphia, Pennsylvania. No trace was ever found of Charles Ross, although his parents received 23 notes, over a several-month period, which demanded a $20,000 ransom. On December 18, 1900, Edward Cudahy, son of the meat packer, was taken from his Omaha, Nebraska, home and $25,000 ransom was demanded. Young Cudahy was released the same day.

Not until after World War I did kidnapping become big business. This change was due in part to the development of the automobile and other rapid means of transportation. Such increased mobility caused conflicts in jurisdiction and a lack of coordination among enforcement authorities. Kidnappers became aware of the monetary possibilities and, as a consequence, began to carry out these operations in rapid succession.[6]

At first, few victims were transported across state lines. For example, on May 21, 1924, Robert Franks, son of wealthy Chicago parents, was seized and murdered by Nathan Leopold and Richard Loeb, who demanded $10,000 for the safe return of the boy. On December 5, 1927, Marion Parker, 12-year-old daughter of a Los Angeles banker, was seized and murdered. $1,500 was demanded for her safe return. The murderer was sentenced to San Quentin.

By 1931 the public began to be aware that kidnappings were becoming more numerous and that the hit-or-miss methods of the lone criminal had given way to the carefully planned activity of professionals. Kidnappings became the business of organized criminal groups who took advantage of the inadequacies of the law and the apparent indifference of the public to their activities.[7]

One city that was especially hard hit by kidnappings was St. Louis. In 1931 the officers of the St. Louis Chamber of Commerce, the mayor, chief of police, and others of that city organized a committee for the purpose of trying to secure federal legislation on the subject.[8] As a result, Senator Patterson of Missouri, on December 10, 1931, introduced a kidnapping bill in the Senate.[9] Four days later, on December 14, 1931, Congressman Cochran, also of Missouri, introduced a similar bill in the House of Representatives.[10]

Reports from chiefs of police of 501 cities, aired at a hearing before the House Judiciary Committee on Representative Cochran's bill, showed that 279 kidnappings had taken place in 1931, with unreported cases estimated at three times that number. Forty-four of the victims, of whom 13 were later killed, had been transported across state lines. Only 69 persons had been convicted, although over 2,000 persons were estimated to have been involved and ransoms running as high as $125,000 in a single case had been demanded and often paid. Families of victims preferred to pay rather than risk the life of a captive by either refusing or reporting the matter to the police.

THE LINDBERGH KIDNAPPING AND CONGRESSIONAL REACTION

The kidnapping of the Lindbergh baby on March 1, 1932, aroused the public: There was an instant demand that Congress take action. The Senate, spurred on by public clamor, passed its bill, which did not include a death penalty. Instead, it was left to the discretion of the trial judge to give as many years of imprisonment as he saw fit.[11] The House Judiciary Committee reported out a bill that imposed the death penalty; however, it also provided that the jury might recommend mercy or life imprisonment.[12]

Opposition to the passage of the kidnapping bill took two forms: One faction favored the bill but opposed the death penalty; the more formidable opposition claimed it would be the opening wedge for the federal government to encroach on the powers of the states in law enforcement. The latter group also argued that the bill would saddle further expenses on an already overburdened federal government and that states, given their recognized tendency to shift the burden of cases under federal jurisdiction to that government, would avoid their enforcement duties. At the time, all the states had antikidnapping statutes, six of which in 1931 provided for the death penalty.[13]

Congressman Cochran, speaking for his bill, declared,

> My bill does not seek to supersede the responsibility of the local authorities, but all I ask is that the Federal government assist in apprehending the violator when the victim is taken across the boundary of the state where the victim was seized. The Commerce clause in the Constitution prevents the states from extending their police power to an adjoining state, and at the same time gives the Congress the Constitutional authority to enact such legislation as I suggest.[14]

When it became apparent late in the session that insistence on the wishes of the House would cause further delay and possibly defeat for the legislation, Congressman Cochran recommended the passage of the bill already passed by the Senate. The suggestion was favorably received: The Senate bill was passed by the House and signed by President Herbert Hoover on June 22, 1932. Interstate kidnapping had become a crime against the laws of the United States.[15]

THE LINDBERGH LAW

The original Federal Kidnapping Statute, popularly known as the Lindbergh Law (18 U.S.C. Ann. § 408a) provided:

> Whoever shall knowingly transport or cause to be transported, or aid or abet in transporting, in interstate or foreign commerce, any person who shall have been unlawfully seized, confined, inveigled, decoyed, kidnapped, abducted, or carried away by any means whatsoever and held for ransom or reward shall, upon conviction, be punished by imprisonment in the penitentiary for such term of years as the court in its discretion,

shall determine: Provided, That the term "interstate or foreign commerce" shall include transportation from one State, Territory, or the District of Columbia to another State, Territory, or the District of Columbia, or to a foreign country; or from a foreign country to any State, Territory, of the District of Columbia: Provided further, That if two or more persons enter into an agreement, confederation, or conspiracy to violate the provisions of the foregoing Act and do any overt act toward carrying out such unlawful agreement, confederation, or conspiracy such person or persons shall be punished in like manner as hereinbefore provided by this Act.

Between June 22, 1932, the date of the passage of the Federal Kidnapping Statute, and its subsequent amendment on May 18, 1934, some 26 cases involving interstate kidnapping were investigated. Twenty-four of these cases resulted in prosecutions. Dr. Raymond Moley in his report to the president, May 18, 1934, said

The high ratio of results evidenced by the above figures has done much to restore the prestige of Federal justice after the miserable failure registered by the prohibition division during the past 15 years.

These achievements are attributable to the coordinated efforts of State and Federal offices. Local authorities have the advantage of better information concerning local people and local geography. They can more easily pick up probable suspects and will be of more aid in pursuing a kidnapping just after abduction. At the same time the Federal government has made available resources not otherwise at the command of State or county authorities.[16]

Amendments to the Lindbergh Law

On January 11, 1934, Senator Copeland of New York, speaking for a subcommittee of the Committee on Commerce that had been appointed to investigate the subjects of kidnapping, racketeering, and other forms of crime, introduced an amendment to the Federal Kidnapping Statute. This amendment added a three-day presumptive clause. In speaking for the legislation, Senator Copeland stated that

a person disappears and the question is, has he been kidnapped? Many times it is ultimately determined that the victim was actually kidnapped and taken across the state line. . . . It happens then that the Division of Investigation [now the Federal Bureau of Investigation] is called when the clues are cold and there is no opportunity to study the case firsthand. The committee has seen fit to recommend an amendment to the so-called Lindbergh Law providing that in the absence of the return of the person or persons so unlawfully seized . . . for or during a period of three days it shall be presumed that such person or persons have been transported in interstate or foreign commerce.

That gives an opportunity for the Federal government to go in early, not to interfere with local authorities, but to get all the evidence at firsthand as early as possible on the presumption that if a missing person has been gone three days he has been transported in interstate commerce.[17] On March 24, 1934, the Senate Committee on the Judiciary favorably reported on this bill, which had been designated Senate Bill 2252.[18]

On May 3, 1934, the House Judiciary Committee, after considering Senate Bill 2252, reported

> This bill as amended proposed three changes in the act known as "Federal Kidnapping Act." First it proposed to add the words, or otherwise except in the case of a minor or by the parent thereof. This will extend Federal jurisdiction under the act to persons who have been kidnapped and held not only for ransom but for any other reason except that of a kidnapping by a parent of his child as specifically exempted.
>
> Secondly, a provision is added to the effect that the failure to release the kidnapped person within seven days after such kidnapping shall create a presumption that the person has been transported in interstate or foreign commerce. Such presumption is not conclusive, however.
>
> The purpose of this provision is to clear up borderline cases justifying Federal investigation in most of such cases and assuring the validity of Federal prosecutions in numerous instances in which such prosecution would be questionable under the present form of this act. The legality of such presumption would seem to be fairly within the rule established by the Supreme Court in *Railroad Company* v *Turnipseed,* 219 U.S. 35, 1910.
>
> That a legislative presumption of one fact from evidence of another may not constitute a denial of due process or a denial of equal protection of the law, it is only essential that there shall be some rational connection between the fact proved and fact presumed, and that the inference of one fact from proof of another shall not be so unreasonable as to be a purely arbitrary mandate.
>
> The third addition to this act is to permit the jury to designate a death penalty for the kidnapper. However, this penalty is not to be imposed by the court if the kidnapped person has been liberated unharmed, prior to the imposition by the court of the sentence.[19]

The House Committee reinstituted the death penalty, which it dropped from its original proposal in 1932. It recommended a seven-day presumptive clause rather than a three-day one, as had been the recommendation of the Senate. The committee added the death penalty and the "or otherwise" clause. On May 14, 1934, both the Senate and the House agreed to these changes proposed by the House to Senate Bill 2255.[20]

President Roosevelt made the bill a law by his signature May 18, 1934. The Federal Kidnapping Statute now provided:

> Whoever shall knowingly transport or cause to be transported, or aid or abet in transporting, in interstate or foreign commerce, any person who shall have been unlawfully seized, confined, inveigled, decoyed, kidnapped, abducted, or carried away by any means whatsoever and held for ransom or reward *or otherwise,* except in the case of a minor, by a parent thereof, shall, upon conviction, be punished (1) *by death* if the verdict of the jury shall so recommend, provided that the sentence of death shall not be imposed by the court if, prior to its imposition the kidnapped person has been liberated unharmed, or (2) if the death penalty shall not apply nor be imposed, the convicted person shall be punished by imprisonment in the penitentiary for such term of years as the court in its discretion shall determine: Provided, that the failure to release such person *within seven days* after he shall have been unlawfully seized,

confined, inveigled, decoyed, kidnapped, abducted, or carried away *shall create a presumption* that such person had been transported in interstate or foreign commerce, but such presumption shall not be conclusive.

Sec. 2. The term "interstate or foreign commerce" as used herein, shall include transportation from one State, Territory, or the District of Columbia to another State, Territory, or the District of Columbia.

Sec. 3. If two or more persons enter into an agreement, confederation, or conspiracy to violate the provisions of the foregoing Act and do any overt act toward carrying out such unlawful agreement, confederation, or conspiracy, such person or persons shall be punished in like manner as hereinbefore provided by this act.[21]

The next change in the statute occurred when Senator Ashurst of Arizona, in order to plug up a loophole in the law, introduced Senate Bill 242 on March 28, 1935. This bill was reported without amendment by the House Committee on August 7, 1935. On January 20, 1936, this Bill passed the House.[22] It read:

Be it enacted, etc. that the act entitled "an act forbidding the transportation of any person in interstate or foreign commerce, kidnapped or otherwise unlawfully detained and making such act a felony as amended (48 Stat. 781, U.S.C. Tit. 18, §§ 408a, 408b, 408c) be and it is hereby amended by the addition of the following section.

Sec. 4, whoever receives, possesses or disposes any money or other property or any portion thereof which has at any time been delivered as ransom or reward in connection with a violation of Section 1 of this Act knowing the same to be money or property which has been at any time delivered as such ransom or reward, shall be punished by fine of not more than $10,000 or imprisoned in a penitentiary for more than 10 years or both.

This so-called Money Changers Statute was signed by the President on January 24, 1936.[23]

During the late 1930s kidnappings for ransom decreased. They were practically unheard of in the 1940s and in the early 1950s. Kidnapping ceased to be of concern to the public and to Congress. On September 28, 1953, an event occurred that jarred the public from its complacency. Robert Cosgrove Greenlease, 6-year-old son of a wealthy Kansas City automobile dealer, was lured from his school. His body was located a few days later; and as he had been transported in interstate commerce, his kidnappers, Carl Austin Hall and Bonnie Brown Heady, were prosecuted by the federal government.

Hall and Heady entered guilty pleas in federal court at Kansas City to a charge of kidnapping for ransom. A jury then heard the evidence and on November 19, 1953, recommended death. Judge Albert L. Reeves, who presided, said, "I think the verdict fits the evidence. It is the most cold-blooded murder I have ever tried." The killers of the Greenlease boy were executed on December 18, 1953.[24]

An aroused public demanded action, and several bills were introduced to amend the Kidnapping Statute. Most were aimed at reducing the time element under the presumptive clause. Congressman Hosmer of California introduced a bill into the 83rd Congress—HR 6897, introduced on January 6, 1954[25]—that provided for an immediate presumption of interstate transporting. On the following day Senator Kefauver of Tennessee introduced S 2614, which reduced the time of the presumption from seven days to 24 hours.[26] These bills were not enacted into law.

On January 5, 1955, Congressman Keating of New York introduced HR 800 at the first session of the 84th Congress.[27] This bill was identical with Senator Kefauver's. Congressman Keating's amendment lay dormant until another tragic event occurred on July 4, 1956. On this date 33-day-old Peter Weinberger was stolen from his carriage at Westbury, Long Island, New York. The local police conducted an immediate investigation, and seven days after the kidnapping the FBI entered the case under the Lindbergh Kidnapping Law. As a result, Angelo John LaMarca was arrested on August 23, 1956. The body of Peter Weinberger was found the following day, and the FBI withdrew from the case once it was established that the child had not been carried across the state line.[28] For his crime LaMarca was executed by the New York State authorities on August 7, 1958, after a year and a half of appeals reaching to the United States Supreme Court.[29]

Once again the public demanded action and Congressman Keating's bill that had been lying inactive in the Committee on the Judiciary was favorably reported out of committee on July 18, 1956. The committee in its report stated:

Since the enactment of the act of May 18, 1934 the record of the Federal Bureau of Investigation in the apprehension and conviction of persons violating Section 1201 of Title 18 of the United States Code has been outstanding. The Committee on the Judiciary is well acquainted with the remarkable and efficient technique developed by the Federal Bureau of Investigation in the detection, apprehension and the conviction of perpetrators of the heinous crime of kidnapping. The Committee feels that it is not necessary to dwell upon the ability of the FBI along these lines, since the record is so well known and speaks for itself.

There appears to be no valid reason why the FBI should be compelled to stand by for 7 days after the date of the occurrence of the crime before initiating an official investigation. Here it should be noted that when subsection (b) of the present statute was enacted into law the Senate version of the act provided that the FBI should initiate its investigation within a period of 3 days after the kidnapping. The report which accompanied the bill as it was reported by the House does not explain why the change was made from 3 to 7 days. It can only be surmised that the 7 day period was a compromise.[30]

Congressman Keating, in speaking on behalf of his bill, stated that it had been introduced in the wake of a tragic kidnapping (Robert Cosgrove Greenlease) and that, regrettably, only another terrible crime could give it the necessary impetus to get out of committee. Since seven days had to elapse before the FBI could enter such cases, vital clues might be lost. Keating stated that even interstate cooperation between police officials might not be sufficient. Only the FBI, according to Keating, with its tremendous record in all criminal matters and its interstate jurisdiction could curb the menace of kidnapping. He also pointed out that these crimes lend themselves to interstate action.

This bill moved rapidly through Congress. It was passed by the House July 23, 1956 and referred to the Senate committee on July 24, 1956. Reported favorably by the Senate Judiciary Committee on July 27, 1956, it passed the Senate on the same day. The president was given the bill for approval on July 31, 1956 and signed it August 6, 1956.[31] In this way the waiting period under the presumptive clause was reduced to 24 hours.

Congress, in adding the presumptive clause to the amendment of 1934, stated that its purpose was to clear up borderline cases justifying federal investigation in most of such cases and assuring the validity of Federal prosecutions in numerous instances in which such prosecution would be questionable under the Act as it was at that date.[32] By enacting this clause, Congress gave the FBI jurisdiction to conduct investigations in those cases where the victim was kidnapped but there was no evidence of interstate transportation, which was a necessary element in the original kidnapping statute.

As a practical matter, this clause has been primarily used to give the FBI jurisdiction to enter many cases. If the investigation discloses that the victim of a kidnapping has not been transported from one state to another or from a state to a foreign country, the kidnapper is turned over to local authorities for prosecution. This separation of duties was clearly enumerated by the Court of Appeals of New York in considering one of Angelo John LaMarca's appeals. The court stated: "Thereafter the FBI, having determined it was without jurisdiction of crime because no state boundaries had been crossed by the kidnapper, surrendered the defendant to the Nassau County police authorities [for prosecution]."[33] Throughout the years there have been several highly publicized kidnappings in which the FBI entered the case under the presumptive clause, conducted extensive investigations, and— when it was determined there had not been interstate transportation of the victim— turned over the results of the investigation to the local prosecutor.

Cases Investigated under the Presumptive Clause

On February 9, 1960 Adolph Coors, chairman of the board of the Coors Brewing Company, was kidnapped while en route to Golden, Colorado, from his home near Morrison, Colorado. A $500,000 ransom demand letter was received by the Coors family. This letter was not followed up by the kidnapper. The remains of Adolph Coors were found by a hiker near Sedalia, Colorado. A coast-to-coast search was conducted by the FBI for suspect Joseph Corbett, Jr., an escapee from a California prison where he was serving a sentence for second-degree murder. Corbett was arrested in Vancouver, British Columbia. Again, as there was no interstate transportion, Corbett was tried in state court. After a guilty verdict, he received a mandatory life sentence.

On December 17, 1968, Barbara Mackle, 20-year-old daughter of a Florida real estate millionaire, was abducted from a motel near Emory University in Atlanta,

Georgia. She was entombed in a coffin-like box for 83 hours. A ransom of $500,000 was paid for her release. As no interstate travel was involved, her abductors were tried and convicted in Georgia State Court.

On August 8, 1975, Samuel Bronfman, son of the president of Seagrams, was kidnapped in Purchase, New York. A $2.3 million ransom was paid for his release. The FBI entered the investigation under the presumptive clause. FBI agents and New York City police officers rescued a bound and blindfolded Bronfman in Brooklyn, New York, on August 17, 1975. The kidnappers were prosecuted by the Westchester County, N.Y. District Attorney's office. The jury returned a verdict of guilty of extortion and acquitted the accused of kidnapping.

Just six days before Christmas, 1972, Amanda Dealey was abducted outside her apartment in University Park, a suburb of Dallas, Texas. The 22-year-old daughter-in-law of the president of the *Dallas Morning News* was held for two and a half days, handcuffed and blindfolded in an unheated, abandoned house. The abductors demanded $250,000. The FBI entered the case under the presumptive clause, coordinating their investigation with the efforts of several local Texas law enforcement agencies. Dealey was released, after the payment of the ransom, just south of the Dallas-Highland Park city limits. She had been wrapped in a sheet like a mummy. FBI agents and local police officers recovered the ransom money and arrested the perpetrators. Also recovered was a list of the names, addresses, telephone numbers, and children of prominent Dallas residents. Again, the abductors were tried and found guilty in local court.

The "Or Otherwise" Clause

The second addition in the amendment of May 18, 1934, contained the "or otherwise" clause. The Senate Judiciary Committee, in approving the amendment, stated that "the object of the addition of the words 'or otherwise' is to extend the jurisdiction of this act to persons who have kidnapped and held not only for reward, but for any other reason."[34] The original kidnapping law provided that the victim who had been kidnapped must be held for ransom or reward. Congress, by adding the "or otherwise clause" greatly expanded the law by making it a violation to hold the victim not only for ransom or reward, but also for many other purposes such as robbery, rape, for transportation, etc. The House Committee on the Judiciary approved the amendment with the following comment: "First it is proposed to add the words 'or otherwise' except in the case of a minor (kidnapped) by a parent." The intention was to extend federal jurisdiction under the act to persons who had been kidnapped for any reason except that of a child by his or her parent.[35]

A leading case exemplifying the use of this clause is *Gooch* v. *United States*.[36] In this case the defendant had been indicted on the charge that he and someone else, to prevent arrest in Texas, kidnapped two police officers in Texas and transported them to Oklahoma. The defendant contended that the words *ransom or reward* imported some pecuniary consideration or the payment of something of value; that the words *or otherwise* should be strictly constructed and limited to the implications of these words, not be used to enlarge them. The court rejected this contention, citing the House and Senate Committee reports mentioned above. "Evidently," the court continued, "Congress intended to prevent transportation in the interstate commerce of persons who were unlawfully restrained in order that the captor could secure some benefit to himself. And this is adequately expressed by the words of the enactment." The court also added, "The words 'except in the case of a minor by a parent thereof' emphasize the intended result of the enactment."

Throughout the years the courts have given an extremely broad interpretation to the "or otherwise" clause. Convictions have been upheld in many types of cases, such as

- *Sanford* v. *United States,*[37] where robbery was the intent.
- *Poindexter* v. *United States,*[38] where the purpose was to rape the victim.
- *United States* v. *Parker,*[39] where the defendant kidnapped the victim to obtain a confession of a crime and so enhance the defendant's reputation as a detective.
- *Wheatley* v. *United States,*[40] where the purpose was to secure transportation in the victim's automobile.
- *Langston* v. *United States,*[41] where the purpose was to rob the victim and prevent him from reporting a crime.
- *United States* v. *Bassell,*[42] where the purpose was to place the victim in a house of prostitution.
- *Brooks* v. *United States,*[43] where the defendants, who were members of the Ku Klux Klan, kidnapped a man and a woman. They transported them to another state, where they flogged the victims, told them to stop living together and making liquor, and to go to church.
- *United States* v. *Isaac,*[44] where the defendant posed as a representative of a milk company to obtain a 2-week-old baby.
- *Loux* v. *United States,*[45] where the defendants escaped from the Washington State Penitentiary and forced the victim to accompany them to Oregon in order to assist in the defendants' escape.
- *Bearden* v. *United States,*[46] where the defendants hijacked an airplane in an effort to secure passage to Cuba. In this case Leon Bearden and his son boarded a Continental Airline at Phoenix on August 3, 1961. At gun point they ordered the crew to fly them to Monterey, Mexico. The plane landed at El Paso for refueling, where it was disabled and the Beardens arrested. At that time there was no crime-aboard-aircraft statute that covered an aircraft hijacking. The Beardens were charged with kidnapping under the "or otherwise" clause. As a result of this case, Congress amended the Federal Aviation Act of 1958 and included the Crime Aboard Aircraft Statute (September 5, 1961).

Cases in Which the Death Penalty was Invoked

The third clause added to the Federal Kidnapping Statute in 1934 provided for punishment by death if the kidnapped person had not been liberated unharmed and if the jury so recommended.[47] Although there have been cases investigated by the FBI that have resulted in the death penalty in state courts—such as the execution of Angelo John LaMarca in 1958 for the kidnapping of Peter Weinberger[48] and the execution of Demetrius Gula and Joseph Sacoda in 1940 for the brutal kidnapping of Arthur Fried, a White Plains, New York contractor cremated by his assassins[49]—there have been only six persons executed under the death penalty clause of the Federal Kidnapping Statute since its enactment.

One of those six was Arthur Gooch, who was executed on June 19, 1936. He had entered a guilty plea to an indictment charging that he and a companion (who was killed in a gun battle) commandeered an automobile occupied by police officers and forced them to accompany them to Oklahoma for the purpose of avoiding arrest. Serious bodily harm was inflicted on one of the officers, and he was suffering from his injuries at the time he was liberated in Oklahoma. After Gooch's guilty plea, the facts were presented to a jury, which recommended the death penalty.

Gooch appealed his conviction all the way to the U.S. Supreme Court. The question before the Supreme Court was the applicability of the "or otherwise" clause. The constitutionality of the death penalty clause was not considered by the Court.[50]

On March 19, 1938, John Henry Seadlund was executed for the kidnapping and murder of Charles B. Ross. Seadlund entered a guilty plea to a federal kidnapping charge involving the abduction of Charles Ross on September 25, 1937, in Franklin Park, Cook County, Illinois, and the subsequent transportation of Ross to Minnesota. In this case a $50,000 ransom was demanded and paid. After his guilty plea, a jury heard the evidence and recommended the death penalty.[51]

In 1953 Carl Austin Hall and Bonnie Heady entered guilty pleas to federal charges involving the abduction of Robert Cosgrove Greenlease in Kansas City, Missouri, and his subsequent transportation to Kansas where he was murdered. The kidnappers had demanded $600,000 ransom, which was paid. After the guilty pleas a jury heard the evidence and recommended the death penalty. Heady and Hall were executed December 18, 1953.[52]

Arthur Ross Brown in December 1955 pleaded guilty to an indictment charging him with the kidnapping of Wilma Frances Allen in Kansas City, Missouri, and her subsequent transportation to Kansas where she was murdered. The purpose of the abduction was robbery and sexual gratification. After hearing the evidence, the jury recommended the death penalty and Brown was executed on February 24, 1956.[53]

The last case in which a kidnapper was executed followed the kidnapping of Dr. Edward Roy Bartels, a Dubuque, Iowa, physician on July 11, 1960. On that date Victor Henry Feguer inveigled Bartels with the story that his wife was ailing and needed attention. The doctor's body was located in a small wooded ravine near East Dubuque, Illinois. Robbery was the apparent motive. Feguer was tried before a jury in the U.S. District Court, Northern District of Iowa. The jury returned a guilty verdict and recommended the death penalty. On March 15, 1963, Feguer was executed.[54]

Feguer was the only one of the six who were executed who stood trial: The other five entered guilty pleas. Three of the executed kidnappers had demanded ransom, while three were convicted under the "or otherwise" clause. In all cases except that of Gooch, the kidnapped person had been brutally murdered.

DEATH PENALTY CLAUSE RULED UNCONSTITUTIONAL

In September 1966 Charles Jackson and two other men kidnapped the driver of a truck containing $150,000 worth of Schick Eversharp products. The abduction took place in Milford, Connecticut. The driver and the truck were transported to Alpine, New Jersey, where the driver was left tied to a tree and not seriously hurt. The U.S. District Court in Connecticut, in dismissing the kidnapping count in the indictment, held the Federal Kidnapping Act was unconstitutional because it made "the risk of death" the price for asserting the right to jury trial and thereby "impairs . . . free exercise" of a constitutional right.[55]

The Supreme Court agreed with the District Court that the death penalty provision of the Federal Kidnapping Act imposed an impermissible burden on the exercise of a constitutional right. It felt, however, that the provision was severable from the remainder of the statute. The Court held that there was no reason to invalidate the law in its entirety simply because its capital punishment clause violated the Constitution. The Supreme Court ruled that The District Court, it ruled, had erred in dismissing the kidnapping count in the indictment.[56] The case was remanded and on July 3, 1968, a jury in the U.S. District Court for Connecticut found Jackson guilty on the kidnapping count.[57]

The Supreme Court in discussing the death penalty clause stated,

One fact at least is obvious from the face of the statute itself: In an interstate kidnapping case where the victim has not been liberated unharmed, the defendant's assertion of the right to jury trial may cost him his life, for the federal statute authorizes the jury—and only the jury—to return a verdict of death. . . . Under the Federal Kidnapping Act therefore the defendant who abandons the right to contest his guilt before a jury is assured that he cannot be executed; the defendant ingenuous enough to seek a jury acquittal stands forewarned that, if the jury find him guilty and does not wish to spare his life, he will die. Our problem is to decide whether the Constitution permits the establishment of such a death penalty, applicable only to those defendants who assert the right to contest their guilt before a jury. The inevitable effect of any such provision is, of course, to discourage assertion of the Fifth Amendment right not to plead guilty and to deter exercise of the Sixth Amendment right to demand a jury trial.[58]

The Court disagreed with the government's argument that the Federal Kidnapping Act gives the trial judge discretion to set aside a jury recommendation of death:

> So far as we are aware, not once in the entire 34 year history of the Act has a jury's recommendation of death been discarded by a trial judge. The Government would apparently have us assume either that trial judges have always agreed with jury recommendations of capital punishment under the statute—an unrealistic assumption at best—or that they have abdicated their statutory duty to exercise independent judgment on the issue of penalty. In fact, the explanation is a far simpler one. The statute unequivocally states that, "if the verdict of the jury shall so recommend," the defendant "shall be punished . . . by death. . . ." The word is"shall," not "may." In acceding without exception to jury recommendations of death, trial judges have simply carried out the mandate of the statute.[60]

The Court's decision affected other federal laws. The Federal Bank Robbery Statute contained similar language concerning the death penalty, and as a result of the decision in the Jackson case, The Supreme Court on June 17, 1968 vacated the sentence of Duane Earl Pope, who had been convicted by a jury of robbing a bank in Nebraska of $1,500 on June 4, 1965. He killed three bank employees during that robbery.[61] The jury had recommended the death sentence pursuant to the provisions of the Federal Bank Robbery Statute, which provides the accused "shall be imprisoned not less than ten years or punished by death if the verdict of the jury shall so direct."

THE 1972 STATUTES

The kidnapping of Charles Lindbergh in 1932 was the catalyst that led to the passage of the Federal Kidnapping Law. The kidnapping of Peter Weinberger in 1956 moved Congress to amend the presumptive clause and another incident, the killing of the Israeli athletes at the 1972 Olympic Games in Munich, Germany, led to further amendments. As a result of the Munich tragedy, the U.S. Congress stated that acts of physical violence against members of the diplomatic corps, other foreign officials, and official guests in the United States are alarming and could pose a real threat to the free intercourse between the United States and the nations of the world.

Between January and October 1971, 79 major documented incidents against members of the diplomatic corps and other foreign officials and guests had taken place.[62] In considering amendments for the Federal Kidnapping Statute, Congress proposed to make the kidnapping of a foreign official, a member of his family, an official guest, or a conspiracy to kidnap such individual, a felony, if committed anywhere in the United States, thus eliminating the necessity for travel in interstate or foreign commerce. The thrust of the offense would be the kidnapping itself rather than the interstate transportation of the kidnapped person. This switched emphasis would assure that a kidnapping that occurred in a hijacked situation would be an extraditable offense from a country that does not recognize an offense keyed to interstate transportation.

While amending the Federal Kidnapping Statute in 1972 (§1201, Tit. 18, U.S.C.), Congress passed or amended other federal statutes aimed at protecting foreign officials and official guests of the United States:

- Sections 1116 and 1117, Tit. 18, U.S. Code—Murder or Manslaughter of Foreign Officials, Official Guests or International Protected Persons and Conspiracy to Murder
- Section 112, Tit. 18, U.S. Code—Protection of Foreign Officials and Official Guests and Internationally Protected Persons
- Section 970, Tit. 18, U.S. Code—Protection of Property Occupied by Foreign Governments
- Section 878, Tit. 18, U.S. Code—Threats and Extortion Against Foreign Officials, Official Guests and Internationally Protected Persons

Another federal law that is sometimes used to prosecute a kidnapper is the Hobbs Act.[65] This act basically prohibits extortions induced by violence or fear of financial loss when interstate commerce is affected. It may be applied to several different types of violations, such as payoffs demanded by labor union representatives or extremists, connected with organized crime rackets, extorted from banks or other forms of business enterprises, and obtained by state or local authorities for the benefit of such contractors or businesses. The Hobbs Act is often used to prosecute where a member of a banker's family is kidnapped or held hostage and a payoff is demanded of the bank.

The vast majority of the kidnapping incidents in the United States have been criminal in nature. The February 4, 1974 kidnapping of Patricia Hearst by the Symbionese Liberation Army was an exception: that was a political kidnapping. The kidnappers of Reginald Murphy called themselves The Revolutionary Army, but in fact no such group existed.

Events throughout the years have resulted in amendments to the kidnapping statute expanding federal jurisdiction. In the years to come, undoubtedly there will be additional changes. At the present time the kidnapping of a minor by a parent is not a violation of the Federal Kidnapping Statute. In the last several years there have been efforts by some members of Congress to do away with the exception and to make it a federal violation when one parent kidnaps his child.

Kidnapping is an effective tool in the hands of the terrorist, the criminal, and the psychopath to achieve a goal. The Federal Kidnapping Statute has been an effective weapon for law enforcement authorities at all levels.

NOTES

1.   Title 18 U.S.C. §1201 (October 24, 1972, October 8, 1976, October 9, 1978, October 24, 1978).

2. H. A. Fisher and M. F. McGuire, 12 N.Y. University Law Quarterly Review. (1935) 646.

3. Fisher and McGuire, p. 647.

4. 29 Cornell L.Q. 207 (1943, 1944).

5. Fisher and McGuire, p. 649.

6. *Ibid.*

7. Fisher and McGuire, p. 652.

8. H. L. Bomar, Jr., The Lindbergh Law, 1 L & Contemp Probs 435 (1933).

9. S. 1525, 75 Cong. Rec. 275, 72nd Cong. 1st Session (1932).

10. H.R. 5657, 75 Cong. Rec. 491, 72nd Cong. 1st Session (1932).

11. Fisher and McGuire, p. 655.

12. Robert C. Finley, The Lindbergh Law, 28 Georgetown L. Q. 911 (1940).

13. 75 Cong. Rec. 13,2845–13,2876, 72nd Cong. 1st Session (1932).

14. 75 Cong. Rec. 6,240, 72nd Cong. 1st Session (1932).

15. Finley, p. 912.

16. H. L. Bomar, Jr., The Lindbergh Law, 1 L & Contemp Probs 438, 439 (1933).

17. 78 Cong. Rec. 448, 453 73rd Cong. 2nd Session (1934).

18. S. Rep. No. 534, 73rd Cong., 1st & 2nd Sess. (1934)

19. H.R. Rep. 1,457, 73rd Cong., 2nd Sess. (1934)

20. 78 Cong. Rec. 8,767, 73rd Cong., 2nd Sess. (1934).

21. Fisher and McGuire, pp. 655, 656 (18 U.S.C.A. §408a).

22. 80 Cong. Rec. 742, 74th Cong. 2nd Session (1936).

23. 80 Cong. Rec. 1,191, 74th Cong. 2nd Session (1936) (49 Stat. 1099).

24. Don Whitehead, *FBI Story* (N.Y.: Random House, 1956), pp. 243–248.

25. 100 Cong. Rec. 20, 83rd Cong. 2nd Session (1954).

26. 100 Cong. Rec. 55, 83rd Cong. 2nd Session (1954).

27. 101 Cong. Rec. 47, 84th Cong. 1st Session (1955).

28. Don Whitehead, *FBI Story* (New York: Random House, 1956), pp. 323–325.

29. 355 U.S. 920 (1958).

30. H.R. Rep. 2,763, 84th Cong., 2nd Sess. (1956).

31. 102 Cong. Rec. 14,022, 14,167, 14,933, 15,041, 15,300, 15,303, 84th Cong. 2nd Session (1956).

32. 1 S. Rep. 534, 73rd Cong., 1st & 2nd Sess. (1934).

33. 144 N.E. 2d 423.

34. S. Rep. 534, 73rd Cong. (1934).

35. H. R. Rep. 1,457, 73rd Cong., 2nd Sess. (1934).

36. 297 U.S. 124 (1936).

37. 169 F.2d 71 (1948).

38. 139 F.2d 158 (1943).

39. 103 F.2d 857 (1939).

40. 159 F.2d 599 (1946).

41. 153 F.2d 840 (1946).

42. 187 F.2d 878 (1951).

43. 199 F.2d 336 (1952).

44. 389 F.2d 60 (1968).

45. 389 F.2d 911 (1968).

46. 304 F.2d 532 (1962), cert. den., 372 U.S. 252 (1963).

47. 18 U.S.C.A. §408a (1934).

48. *People* v. *LaMarca,* 165 N.Y.S. 2d, cert. den., 355 U.S. 920 (1958).

49. New York Journal American, January 12, 1940.
50. *Gooch* v. *United States,* 297 U.S. 124 (1936).
51. *Seadlund* v. *United States,* 97 F.2d 742 (1938).
52. Don Whitehead, *FBI Story* (New York: Random House, 1956), pp. 243–248.
53. *Kansas City Times,* February 24, 1956, p. 1.
54. *Feguer* v. *United States,* 192 Fed. Supp. 377 (1961), cert. den., 371 U.S. 872 (1962).
55. 262 Fed. Supp. 716, 718 (1967).
56. *U.S.* v. *Charles Jackson* 390 U.S. 570 (1968).
57. New Haven, CT *Journal-Courier,* November 30, 1968, p. 32.
58. 390 U.S. 570 (572), 1968.
59. 390 U.S. 570 (574–575) 1968.
60. 392 U.S. 651 1968.
61. S. Rep. 92–1105, 92nd Cong. (1972).
62. H.R. Rep. 92–1268, accompanying H.R. Rep. 15,883, July 31, 1972.
63. S. Rep. 92–1105 Supra.
64. 18 U.S.C. §1951 (1946).

II

Management Issues

10

The Effects of Terrorism on Business

Brian M. Jenkins
Susanna W. Purnell
Eleanor S. Wainstein

Before the 1970s terrorism was not a problem that concerned American corporate management: Terrorist targeting of businessmen or business facilities was negligible. Since the early 1970s, however, terrorists have turned to private enterprise as a relatively vulnerable and lucrative objective. In response, businesses have devoted considerable resources to the problem and developed strategies to deal with it. These efforts have had an impact not only in the cost of doing business but also in the areas of management, personnel, and operations.

This chapter examines the direct costs associated with preventing and handling terrorist attacks, as well as the less obvious effects on business firms' organization and operations, particularly the impact of the terrorist threat on employees and their ability to work efficiently in a high-risk environment. We show the potential repercussions of a corporation's response to terrorist attacks on its relations with the local government, and finally, we address the long-range consequences of terrorism on business operations.

DIRECT COSTS

The most obvious costs of terrorism are those directly derived from a terrorist incident or campaign—the loss of human lives, casualties, property damage, robberies, ransom or other extortion payments to terrorist groups. Worldwide reported losses from terrorist bombings and attacks on facilities totaled about $88 million in 1982 and over $100 million in 1981.[1] Since not all losses are reported, these figures probably underestimate the actual costs of these two forms of attack. They do not include the costs of ransom or extortion payments, or those of unreported crimes, which can result in multimillion-dollar payoffs. Total losses, therefore, could easily run several hundred million dollars a year.

Sometimes the cost of dealing with the terrorist threat is more expensive than that of dealing with an actual terrorist act. Bomb threats, for example, may force a costly shutdown or disruption of operations. The resultant start-up costs and loss of production may be substantial. In addition, terrorists keep finding new areas of corporate vulnerability. One particular concern is the security of company computer records and systems, targets that have been attacked by terrorists in several countries. It has been estimated that banks would have difficulty staying in business more than 2 days if their computer systems failed completely; distribution companies, 3.3 days; manufacturing companies, 4.8 days; and insurance companies, 5.6 days.[2]

Terrorists and guerrillas have increasingly waged economic warfare, mounting concerted campaigns against particular companies or sectors of the economy, especially utilities. Successful attacks on power lines, pylons, and transformers can cause blackouts that shut down production for hours and sometimes days. The cumulative economic losses can be substantial.

The tactic of attacking utilities has been used by leftist groups in Peru, Spain, and Italy. In El Salvador, guerrillas have concentrated on attacking the economic infrastructure. Of the 210 acts of sabotage reported in that country during January and February 1983, 33 percent were directed at electrical plants, 30 percent at transportation, and 10 percent at the agricultural sector. The fishing industry was compelled to dump millions of pounds of spoiled seafood after power failures cut off refrigeration. Bus cooperatives are nearly bankrupt because they must still repay loans on buses the guerrillas destroyed. And it is reported that some farming cooperatives pay the guerrillas as much as $1,300 a week in protection money to save their crops from destruction.[3]

Terrorists have rarely managed to shut down operations, but they did succeed in doing so in Spain. A concerted effort by Basque terrorists has prevented the completion of a large nuclear power plant at Lemoniz and has imposed enormous costs on the utility company, Iberduero. The Basque separatists began small-scale attacks on Iberduero facilities in 1967. They carried out their first significant operations against the Lemoniz nuclear power plant in 1977. These attacks began with bombings at the construction site, corporate offices, and warehouses, and at the power plants providing electricity to Lemoniz. In 1978, a bomb planted by the terrorists at the construction site killed two workers and caused $700,000 in damage. A year later, another bomb killed a third worker.

As the terrorist campaign against Lemoniz continued, physical security at the site was increased. In response, the terrorists focused their threats and attacks on company personnel. They threatened to assassinate the president of Iberduero, warned Japanese investors against participating in the project, and kidnapped a Ministry of Industry official. In 1981, they kidnapped the chief engineer at Iberduero and threatened to kill him if two thirds of the plant were not dismantled within a week. Iberduero took no action, saying only that it would accept whatever decision the regional Basque government took concerning the future of the plant. The blindfolded body of the engineer was discovered a week later. Other key officials were threatened with death if they returned to the site. Giving in to the terrorist pressure,

Iberduero suspended construction for a year. In May 1982, the company decided to resume activity. A week later, Basque terrorists shot and killed the manager of the plant. Operations at the site were again suspended.

As of late 1983, five company employees had been killed, and damages suffered by Iberduero as a result of terrorist attacks between 1977 and 1981 were estimated at two billion pesetas (approximately $20 million). In addition, the company must pay 100 million pesetas per day (approximately $1 million) in interest for a plant that has become, in the words of one Spanish official, "a three billion dollar mausoleum."[4]

INDIRECT COSTS

Indirect costs include security program costs, increased premiums on ordinary insurance, special insurance policies to cover ransom and extortion payments, and the costs of lawsuits resulting from terrorist incidents. A major consequence of the increase in terrorism against business is businesses' acceptance of the responsibility to protect their personnel. This has resulted in a growing security burden on the private sector. On the whole, corporate officials feel a moral commitment to their employees who have to face risks to their lives for the sake of working for the firm. Also, on the practical side, companies would have recruiting problems in their high-risk posts if they did not provide adequate security for their employees there. Moreover, a negative public image resulting from neglect of employee and facility security might have an adverse impact on business.

From a legal standpoint, U.S. courts have, to a degree, made U.S. firms accountable for their employees overseas. Although the legal guidelines for a firm's responsibility are not clear-cut (see the discussion in Chapter 15), corporations generally have assumed responsibility for handling the kidnapping of executives or corporate officers, whether employed by the parent firm or by distant subsidiaries. The degree of involvement diminishes, however, as the relationship between the victim and the parent firm becomes more remote, such as in the case of employees of local franchises or distributors.

The acceptance of responsibility for the safety of employees and operations may necessitate organizational changes. Most large corporations have created corporate security officers to implement and oversee the provision of protection. In some large corporations, security experts serve the entire organization through lieutenants at country, regional, and headquarters level. In others, subsidiaries take responsibility for their own protection. Common to all is a responsibility to advise employees on matters of personal protection against the local terrorist threat and on guidelines for conduct if they are targeted. Corporate security advisers also assure the safety of the workplace.

For most companies, protection against terrorism means buying hardware and employing the services of a growing corporate protection industry. The increased demands for services of U.S. private security firms since 1976 are reflected in an estimated 12 percent annual growth rate and $12.5 billion market.[5] Corporations may invest in electronic warning devices and barriers, surveillance systems, and armored vehicles; they may also hire facility and residential guards, as well as bodyguards for key personnel. Armoring a car with plates, bulletproof glass, and other devices may run from $20,000 to $60,000—and this does not include the cost of the car itself. Bulletproof tires alone cost $2,000. Bombproof cars cost over $100,000. Round-the-clock bodyguard protection in the United States may involve hiring as many as ten operatives at a cost of $5,000 per week. Prices in foreign countries may run much higher, depending on the risk. The costs of closed-circuit television surveillance systems start at about $10,000.[6]

Security against terrorist attacks is particularly difficult because terrorists can attack anything. Corporate headquarters, manufacturing plants, warehouses, pay-rolls, power supplies, corporate aircraft, company executives at the office or at home may all be potential targets.

Another factor that drives up costs is the philosophy that corporate security is a relative achievement. Corporations do not attempt to combat the terrorists themselves but rather to affect the terrorists' selection of targets. By putting a better security wall around its corporate assets, the company hopes to displace the terrorist threat to easier or "softer" targets in another company. Therefore, to discourage attack, the security of any corporation in a high-risk area must be compa-rable or superior to that of other potential targets. As one firm increases the quantity or quality of its protection, others are forced to follow suit.

Not all companies can or want to invest in extensive protection. Some camou-flage their multinational corporate connections and encourage employees to keep a low profile. According to this philosophy of corporate security, highly visible security measures attract attention, and therefore, terrorist threats.

Insurance premiums constitute another element in the security budget. Re-duced uncertainties and increased competition have lowered the premiums for ransom insurance since the early 1970s, when such policies first made their appear-ance, but coverage in some countries can still constitute a sizable budget item. In addition to ransom payments, insurance policies may cover "in transit" insurance on the delivery of ransoms, fees for hiring independent negotiators, interest on bank loans for ransom, and court expenses for lawsuits related to the handling of a kidnapping. The prospect of terrorist attacks may also increase ordinary insur-ance rates. In some cases, high insurance rates alone have discouraged prospective investors from risking their capital in terrorist-prone countries.

Lawsuits and out-of-court settlements constitute still another indirect cost of terrorism. In some cases, corporations have given kidnapped employees, or their survivors, promotions and cash settlements to forestall a court suit. A judge dismissed a suit for $185 million in the only instance in which a former hostage took the parent corporation to court. Since the decision hinged in part on whether the hostage, an executive in an overseas joint venture, was legally an employee of the parent firm, the whole area of a corporation's legal responsibilities and liabilities is still unresolved.

EFFECTS OF TERRORISM ON CORPORATE OPERATIONS

The most publicized and most easily identifiable costs of terrorism are direct casualties and losses and indirect expenditures for security and insurance. However, the greatest costs are often the effects that terrorist threats have on corporate operations. Some of these effects are obvious, some less so.[7]

Effects on Personnel Policies

Employee morale may become a serious problem in corporations threatened by terrorists. This is especially true where a terrorist group is believed to have infiltrated the company or to have sympathizers within the labor force, and where the terrorists seek more than simple extortion or ransom for a kidnapped executive. On the plant floor, workers who cooperate too enthusiastically with programs to increase productivity may be threatened. The terrorists' campaign may involve assaults on security guards, accusations of foremen for being in league with management, spreading suspicion that workers are informers, or competition with union officials for control over the workers. Whether the terrorists attempt to gain constituents among workers or to destroy the economic viability of the corporation, they ultimately reduce productivity.

At the executive level, corporate officials who are threatened by terrorists or who believe themselves to be threatened by terrorists may be rendered ineffective as a result of fear. They may demand security measures considered excessive by others. They may require counseling. They may take lengthy business trips abroad or request long vacations, transfers, or even retirement. In some corporations, the way an executive performs in a high-risk environment has become a factor in recruiting and promotion. The costs of providing heavy security, the possibility of long absences, and possible loss of performance are considered by some companies to be the costs of the man, along with his salary. Other corporations consider the possible loss of an executive as a factor in assignment. Executives who are highly valued may not be sent to a post where there is a high risk of assassination or kidnapping. The corollary of this is that executives who otherwise might not warrant a high-level position abroad might get one because of the personal danger involved. The higher salaries that they would not otherwise attain in the corporation represent a form of compensation for the risk.

For the most part, however, executives who willingly continue to work in a high-risk environment have a high commitment to the success of the operation. Such an individual takes great pride in the business he has helped to build, has strong loyalties to his employees, and is willing to deal with any terrorist threats in order to continue to work for the operation. Companies sometimes literally have to order such highly motivated executives out of harm's way, such is the extent of their commitment to the local operation.

Terrorists often infiltrate companies to obtain information that they can use for planning an attack on the firm. Knowing that terrorists have access to "inside" information generates distrust between management and labor as well as among employees. Fear of infiltration can also influence hiring practices. For example, it was reported that some American firms in Argentina hired only applicants over the age of 30 in order to screen out youthful terrorist sympathizers.[8]

Effects on Labor Relations

Terrorists have been successful in undermining the loyalty of workers, especially in manufacturing industries. During the 1970s many foreign-owned Argentine firms, most notably in the auto industry, suffered from terrorist tactics. When small organized groups of employees established shadow labor union hierarchies and attempted to gain the support of workers in the plants, violence often resulted. On one occasion terrorists killed a labor union delegate in a Mercedes-Benz truck plant who had questioned the activities of such a shadow union.[9]

Terrorists also try to extend their popular support by demanding better wages and working conditions for labor. In Argentina and Italy, terrorist kidnappers demanded that the companies whose executives they held halt terminations, rehire workers who had been laid off, provide general salary increases, and make other concessions to the work force. In El Salvador, leftist terrorists instigated lock-ins, in which radical labor groups held management and workers hostage in the plant until the company agreed to increase the wages and benefits of the work force. In other cases, extremist elements within the labor force have joined with the terrorists to carry out acts of physical sabotage. Although workers may benefit in the short run from concessions extorted by terrorists, company efforts to reduce production costs are sabotaged, profit margins and the ability to compete are reduced, and ultimately, plants may be closed and jobs lost.

One unexpectedly positive consequence of the threat of terrorism is that a firm may be forced to take stock of relationships inside the company. Such a review may actually bring about improvements in relations between management and labor—a long-run result quite the opposite of that intended by the terrorists. Establishing better channels of communication between workers and managers so that problems can be detected in their early stages, for example, may improve morale and operations. Companies may also foster a sense of participation on the part of the workers and in that way may give them an awareness of their stake in the survival of the company.

Effects on Management

Kidnappings and other terrorist crises divert top management for often lengthy periods of time. Although routine security matters may be dealt with by corporate security officials on a day-to-day basis, a kidnapping requires decisions on major issues such as the payment of ransom or other concessions that only top management can make. The almost total distraction and near paralysis of government during the terrorist kidnappings of Hanns-Martin Schleyer and Aldo Moro and during the holding of American hostages in Iran provide some idea of what the kidnapping of an executive can do to a corporation.

In countries where terrorists have carried out sustained campaigns against certain corporations, kidnapping or killing executives, demanding concessions from the labor force, threatening lower-level employees, carrying out bombings and acts of sabotage, or coercing and intimidating the management and workers to the extent that plans to expand or increase productivity are ineffective, the issue has become one of who actually runs the company: corporate management or the terrorists. "Frontline managers"—an Italian term—have at times found it inexpedient to implement directives from corporate headquarters, because doing so would risk lives. When such a schism develops between local managers and corporate head-quarters, adverse effects are felt throughout the entire corporation. Such problems can discourage potential investors.

At local branches of foreign corporations, terrorists may try to reduce the ability of the parent company to manage the local operation effectively. Through kidnappings, killings, and continued threats, terrorists in Argentina drove top execu-tives out of the country, usually to Uruguay or Brazil. This in itself imposed a cost, as local replacements were not always fully prepared and had to learn on the job. The terrorists also sought to prevent effective remote management by threatening the indigenous managers who had been left behind to run the firms. One local executive of a large American firm who took on greater management responsibilities when top officials retreated to Uruguay was warned by terrorists, who obviously received information from inside corporate headquarters, that he was not paid to make such decisions. The terrorists instructed him to stick to his old job or risk becoming their next target.

Effects on Production

In a high-risk situation, the parent firm or even the Department of State may embargo travel by U.S. nationals. If technical experts cannot visit foreign plants to repair machinery, install updated production lines, and train the labor force, the plants become relatively inefficient. Machines may sit idle or operate inefficiently for long periods of time. A breakdown formerly requiring a matter of days to repair may require weeks. Producers become reluctant to risk sending in new ma-chinery to update production lines in high-risk areas, causing operations to lag behind those of competitors and making production facilities less able to compete.

Travel restrictions also hinder the ability of company representatives to visit local plants or make quality control checks on the product sold by local distributors. Corporations may suffer a declining market for their products if quality erodes in the face of competition.

A foreign subsidiary may be only one part of a large and intricate corporate system, all of which is managed to some degree by the home office. Production lines, costs, and marketing factors for plants located around the world are formulated into the overall corporate goals. If production lines in a subsidiary become obsolescent due to a high-risk environment, as has happened in some plants in El Salvador, it becomes more difficult to integrate that subsidiary into overall corporate production goals. If the situation persists, the corporation may establish the needed line in another country and phase out the obsolescent plant.

EFFECTS OF TERRORISM ON EMPLOYEES

Terrorism can affect the lifestyle and job performance of the employee, as well as the operations of a firm. Under extreme risk, employees may alter behavior at work and at home, a necessity that almost inevitably affects morale and strains relations within the firm.

Among the employees, managers are the most popular target for attack. Terrorists perceive a number of benefits in threatening executives because they, like a nation's ambassadors, are representatives of the corporation. Moreover, threats against one executive may intimidate the others into making corporate concessions. Well-informed terrorists may attack unpopular managers as a means of garnering support among the work force. Terrorists also kidnap expatriate managers of a foreign subsidiary and publicize their act as punishment for the firm's crime of "exploitation."

Consequently, corporations increasingly provide for the safety of key personnel in high-risk areas. Businessmen are encouraged to adopt behavior patterns that make them less conspicuous and their daily activities less predictable. By making them a more difficult target such changes reduce the probability that executives will be attacked. Such changes also may entail a different life-style for the corporate executive, a consequence that may have a negative impact on him and his family and cause serious dissatisfaction with the position. Keeping a low profile may eliminate many of the rewards of an executive position for some. If the security adviser insists upon restrictions that run contrary to the life-style enjoyed by the executive and his family, friction could develop between them.

When the executive is forced to make himself less visible and employ stringent protective services, he finds it more difficult to perform his job. For example, in order to be less predictable, the businessman must vary his established routine and keep erratic hours at the office. As a consequence, his co-workers receive limited information as to his movements, and scheduling of appointments and meetings becomes more difficult. The need for secrecy may promote feelings of distrust between the executive and his employees.

As the executive protects himself under high-risk conditions, he gradually removes himself from his workplace and runs the operation from a distance. Such work patterns can penalize the operation of the firm. If the situation becomes so critical that the executive has to leave the country, he may manage the firm's business from abroad by telephone, or he may make unannounced trips back to the office. In Argentina terrorist kidnappings, killings, and threats drove many top executives out of the country to conduct their business from Uruguay or Brazil.

At that time the number of American businessmen living in Argentina declined from approximately 1,270 to 100.[10] These moves imposed a cost, as local replacements were not always trained to take over the responsibilities and had to learn on the job. If the executive remains in the risky environment, security often becomes a round-the-clock concern, one that hampers his ability to concentrate on his work.

The executive's family and home life also suffer. Wives and children worry about his safety and sometimes have to adjust their routine for security purposes. Families have had to move from affluent suburbs to the anonymity of the city or to a more secure dwelling with limited public access and an array of security devices. As public places become unsafe, the family is obliged to curtail its social life. As the danger grows, expatriate businessmen usually send their families back home, and if it persists, they also leave.

LOCAL GOVERNMENT RELATIONS

In handling terrorist attacks, a corporation prefers to work with the government. However, sometimes the company and government necessarily pursue divergent goals, especially when the government can or will not protect business operations, a situation that can affect the relations between the two during and sometimes beyond a crisis. The firm exists to make profit and therefore must maintain a viable business operation and protect its employees. On the other hand, the local government puts its highest priority on local security, which means rooting out terrorism. From the government point of view, acceding to terrorist demands by paying ransom or extortion and publishing their manifestos only provides the means for the terrorists to continue their campaign against the government.

Many governments have made the payment of ransom and negotiation with terrorists illegal on the grounds that they foster further terrorist activity. Since businesses must protect their employees, they will usually negotiate with terrorists to ransom a kidnapped executive. Consequently, the corporate negotiators may either circumvent local authorities or use their influence to keep local security forces at a distance.

In Argentina, where laws prohibited payment of ransom, corporations experiencing kidnappings in the early 1970s went to great lengths to keep their negotiations secret for fear that police intervention would cause harm to the hostages. Colombia also makes ransom payments illegal. When an American oil company executive was kidnapped there early this year, the corporation announced that it refused to negotiate and disclosed no details of the demands or of the conditions of the executive's release. The press, however, reported that company negotiators were sent to Colombia and that the family of the kidnapped manager reported a ransom payment of several hundred thousand dollars.[11]

The Spanish government, which has been combating Basque Fatherland and Liberty Movement (ETA), a Basque terrorist group, has a history of granting no concessions to terrorists. The ETA finances its operations through kidnap ransom payments and the collection of "revolutionary taxes" from businesses in the Basque

region. Early in 1983, the director general of state security announced the government would be taking stronger measures to prevent such transfers of funds to
the terrorists. He warned that people who act as intermediaries would be prosecuted,
and legal steps would be taken to prevent the transfer of funds. The latter raised
the possibility that the government might freeze the bank accounts of those involved
to prevent payments of ransom. In January 1983, when ETA kidnapped the son
of a wealthy industrialist, the family circumvented the authorities by paying the
reported million-dollar ransom outside the country. In the aftermath of the incident,
during which the kidnapped son became the object of much public sympathy,
the government announced it was not against "humanitarian means" to gain a
hostage's release. However, future clashes with the government policy are possible
as the government continues to oppose the payment of ransoms.[12]

A private company may also want to circumvent local authorities and negotiate
on its own with terrorists because the local security forces are not trained to handle
the crisis situation. In El Salvador, for example, where the security services lack
the competence in such matters, the firms and victims' families have exerted great
efforts to prevent their involvement.

A conflict between a foreign corporation and the local government over the
handling of terrorist crises can have significant consequences for the firm. In 1976,
an Owens-Illinois executive was kidnapped by Venezuelan terrorists. In defiance
of government policy, the company, complying with the terrorists' demands, published the terrorists' criticisms of the Venezuelan government in the foreign press.
In response, the Venezuelan government declared that as a matter of domestic
policy, the government and not the company should handle the kidnapping. The
government further initiated proceedings to take over Owens-Illinois's Venezuelan
holdings, although the expropriations were never carried out.

If the local government perceives that the terrorists are threatening the country's stability, it may take measures that are inimical to a company's welfare, such
as imposing currency restrictions to keep businessmen from moving their assets
out of the country. In such cases, firms may find it more difficult to conduct everyday
business, as suppliers and customers adjust to the situation by altering either their
credit practices or the manner in which they transfer money and credit. Should
the terrorism result in a serious challenge to the government, businesses may choose
to distance themselves from local authorities to negotiate better relations with a
new government.

LONG-RANGE CONSEQUENCES

For the most part, corporations continue to operate in terrorist environments, accepting the additional costs as part of the price of doing business. Although some
companies are better able to sustain losses than others, management usually takes
a long-range view in which the episodes of terrorism are balanced against the
longer-term viability of the company. As a result, businesses rarely shut down an
operation solely because of terrorism.

Operating at a loss for a while may be acceptable if the corporate management views the problem as temporary or if the costs of withdrawing—closing down plants, selling off property—are considered greater than the costs of staying on. Some manufacturers in highly competitive industries feel that the viability of their business depends on the economics of Third World labor and resources; therefore, wherever they locate, they risk some problem like terrorism, and they tend to "live with it," while configuring their investment to minimize the risk. They rent rather than buy equipment or space, take out insurance, postpone expansion plans or new projects, and set up alternate operations. Top executives temporarily operate from a distance or turn their jobs over to others.

Some firms may actually find opportunities in situations where their competitors are preoccupied with the risky environment. There are indications that some companies that kept their management in Argentina during the mid-1970s actually increased their market share at the expense of those who managed their businesses from outside the country.[13] Even in extreme cases where political violence escalates to war, such as during the invasion of Lebanon or the Iran-Iraq war, many businesses continue to operate in some form.

Terrorism thus does have some long-range consequences for corporations. Among the multinationals, it appears to speed up the process of using local personnel to manage overseas operations. In addition, terrorist attacks over the last decade, combined with recent revolutions in the Middle East and a general perception of increasing political instability, have made firms more cautious. Before investing, they carefully investigate the political risks involved. Firms are more likely to hedge against such risks with insurance, alternative sites, and increased monitoring of daily political events. The taking of precautions thus appears to be the major legacy of terrorism against business during the past decade.

NOTES

1.   Risks International, Inc., *Quarterly Risk Assessment,* 1981–1982, pp. 225–233.
2.   Andrew Pollack, "Computer Disaster: Business Seeks Antidote," *The New York Times,* August 24, 1983, p. 1.
3.   Lydia Chavez, "Rising Costs on Salvador's Second Front—The Economy," *The New York Times,* April 17, 1983, p. E3.
4.   Private discussions with Spanish officials.
5.   Christopher Dobson and Ronald Payne, "Private Enterprise Takes on Terrorism," *Across the Board,* January 1983, p. 36.
6.   Dobson and Payne, p. 37; Warren Hoge, "New Growth Business—Arming Cars," *The New York Times,* June 9, 1981, p. D1; "Rise in World Terrorism A Boon for Bodyguards," *Journal of Commerce,* June 3, 1982, p. 3-B; Dorothy J. Gaiter, "More Stores Seek Camera Monitors," *The New York Times,* October 20, 1982, p. A23.
7.   For further discussion, see Susanna W. Purnell and Eleanor S. Wainstein, "The Problems of U.S. Businesses Operating Abroad in Terrorist Environments," R-2842-DOC, The Rand Corporation, Santa Monica, CA, November 1981.
8.   *The New York Times,* October 29, 1977, p. 6.

9.   "Businessmen Under the Gun in Argentina," *The New York Times,* February 22, 1976.

10.   A description of how businessmen lived during this time in Argentina can be found in Ernest McCrary, "Letter from Buenos Aires: Coping with Terrorism in Argentina," *Business Week,* March 9, 1974, pp. 40–41.

11.   *The Washington Post,* April 15, 1983, p. 27.

12.   *The New York Times,* January 20, 1983, p. 2.

13.   "Assessment of Terrorism as It Impacts on the Business Community," Harvard Business School and Yale School of Business and Management, joint student research project, August 1980.

11

Getting Out: The Evacuation of Business Personnel

H. H. A. Cooper

"Yea, from the clutching hands, the wanton crowd, I sped across the waves. . . ."
—Aeschylus[1]

We live in troubled, uncertain times. Worldwide, industry, agriculture, and commerce, activities in which human beings invest so much of themselves and their resources, are taking place against this unpromising backdrop. The optimistic, expansionist spirit with which these activities were undertaken at the beginning of the century has been replaced by caution and retrenchment as it draws towards its close. The years have seen a revulsion against "colonialism" and a constant clamor against the exploitive nature of what has come to be called Big Business. But the national "liberation" consequent upon these movements in different parts of the world has done little to incorporate a new genus of producers into the ranks of Big Business, or to add many new consumers to those who would enjoy substantial benefits from its undertakings.

After two disastrous world wars; countless revolutions, major and minor; massive decolonization; changing attitudes and burgeoning technology; the disparities between the rich and poor nations are as great as ever. As we approach the year 2000, deepening economic gloom at home and abroad seems to belie the optimistic belief that government and business can solve the world's problems and produce a happier more bountiful life for all. Yet adventurous souls remain, and the businessman, ever eager to turn a profit, has cast his nets farther and farther afield. The growing expense of manufacture at home has forced more and more American businesses to transfer some of their processes overseas where labor is cheap and governments, at least, relatively grateful for this boost to their native economies. But this gratitude, such as it is, has no guarantee of permanence. Business has, perforce, left itself at the mercy of events such as those which, but a short while ago, engulfed American interests in Iran.

TRADE FOLLOWS THE FLAG

It is a time-honored mercantile precept that trade follows the flag. The merchants of old followed warriors into distant lands, benefiting from their conquests and rejoicing in the protection that pacification and colonization conferred on their endeavors. Colonial powers maintained permanent garrisons and their armies and navies policed the trade routes as well as the investments of those who exploited the riches of the subjugated lands. Only minor acts of brigandry and the ever-present threat of war among the great powers served to disturb the even tenor of the new world markets opened up by these intrepid adventurers. Now, with the collapse and discrediting of the old colonial system and the uneasy division of the world into two major camps and a host of nonaligned nations, the problem of business security has to be faced anew. To whom can the businessman look, with confidence, for protection? How safe is his investment in this age of uncertainty? In recent times, the winds of change have blown chill indeed for the foreign business-man in areas where once he might have operated safely at considerable profit.

The rising tide of nationalism has seen expropriations and exclusions that have been costly and painful. Generations of patient endeavor have gone up in smoke in a single afternoon before howling mobs, urged on to reclaim what they consider to be their own patrimony. The rightness—or the futility—of such claims is neither an issue nor the subject of commentary here. What all this political "energizing" *has* done is to make some parts of the world very unsafe for business of all kinds and for American businesses in particular. Yet the fundamental profitabil-ity of such undertakings remains. The extraction of energy resources, mineral wealth of all kinds, the entry into the highly profitable manufacturing field all depend, in the main, on foreign capital, foreign know-how and technology. Rarely are the primary possessors of raw resources able to exploit or market them unaided.

In the nature of things, American business interests have played, and continue to play, a leading, if not always welcome, role in developing and supplying the needs of world markets. American know-how, manifested in thousands of skilled personnel, has been sent overseas to promote, encourage, and consolidate business opportunities of all kinds. Many have come to live in foreign parts for extended periods. Some have had to face the ugly problems of being suddenly, forcibly uprooted from their homes and possessions through a change in the political climate.

These upheavals are never pleasant and often traumatic. Sometimes they are transitory episodes, a response to some international storm that, however intense, soon passes and allows life to go on very much as before. Other events have more enduring consequences. Those touched by them are never quite the same again, and what is left of their lives is played out in some different arena altogether. All business activities involve risk taking. Profit and loss depend on judgments concerning the degree of risk involved in any particular enterprise. The businessman learns to evaluate the risks in what he is doing so as to know when to invest and when to withdraw; business and military skills are not as dissimilar on this point. Business and war are both games of strategy.[2] In the present connection, there are striking parallels.

QUITTING THE GAME

Withdrawal, or "quitting the game," is always a hard decision to have to take. No one likes to pull out while there still seems to be a chance of profit in the game. Here, the gambler in us is always prone to take over. Many mixed emotions tend to influence the critical decisions that have to be taken. Where the game has been pleasant on the whole and the disturbing episode out of character, there is a tendency toward staying put on the grounds that it will all blow over. Sometimes, such a gamble pays off. The disinclination to pull out is generally proportionate to the size of the stake; where a business investment is large and of long standing, there is no readiness to abandon it in a hurry. Most successful businessmen are risk takers, but few have an all-or-nothing attitude toward their assets. Strong nerves and a certain amount of machismo are useful attributes in a crisis, but there is really no substitute for sound judgment in these matters. And sound judgment is based upon good operational intelligence.[3]

The decision maker must not only have the facts; he must know what they mean in relation to the matter at hand. Political risk assessment is a must for the businessman with substantial interests in foreign countries. If he does not have the requisite skills himself, he must purchase them elsewhere. The decision to stay in the game or to leave it should at least be an informed one.

Here we are dealing with but one part—though a part of the highest importance—of the overall problem: When does a business withdraw its expatriate personnel, and how does it accomplish this? Both questions are extremely complex and no definitive answers can be offered here. The subject is not one that has been studied anywhere in depth and the record shows that evacuation of business personnel, when it has taken place, regardless of the setting or nationalities of those involved, has generally been somewhat chaotic. There is a noticeable absence of advance planning. Those who have evacuated smoothly and efficiently did so by getting out early. This may well have its drawbacks from a business perspective, but it gives a generous measure of comfort and safety to those most closely concerned. Nothing is worse than the hurried exodus, with its accompanying fears and tensions and the inevitable abandonment of treasured personal possessions. If matters must be left until the last moment, than there must be adequate preparation for the move.

The evacuation of business personnel is something like a military operation. Both call for a high degree of organization and leadership. Both require a great deal of advance preparation and discipline. The heart of the matter lies in the communications aspects of the operation.[4] Does everybody know what to do and how and when to do it? Who will give the "word of command?" How will it be transmitted? These things are difficult enough when highly trained troops are involved. But when we speak of the evacuation of business personnel, we mean harried civilians and their families and dependents. We cannot expect military reactions and we must make allowances in our planning and preparation. These are undertakings in which the operation of the well-known Murphy's Law is likely to be influential, which should be built into all calculations.

In circumstances of extreme and unexpected danger, the U.S. government might be expected to intervene to secure the evacuation of its citizens from an area that has become unsafe. But the occasions on which it can be expected to act are few indeed, and it will almost never act alone or directly with its own armed forces to arrange the physical removal of those in danger. Government efforts will almost always be indirect, cooperative, designed at facilitating rather than effecting the move. There are sound practical as well as diplomatic reasons for such a posture. A generous measure of self-help is called for in these matters. Short of a situation resembling the outbreak of World War III, it is as well not to rely too much on government in any aspect touching on the evacuation of business personnel. Nevertheless, the government and its positions, official and unofficial, are of the highest importance to those doing business in foreign countries and must be taken into prudent consideration by those planning for the type of contingencies examined here. The U.S. government has valuable sources of information and agencies engaged constantly in the analysis of relevant data. Ideally, it should have its finger firmly, if diplomatically, on the pulse of the countries to which its representatives are accredited so as to be able to make a fair prediction on the state of affairs relevant to business and other matters.

Unfortunately, for a variety of reasons, some relevant to policy, others to resource management, the United States is (like many other countries, friendly and otherwise) sometimes taken by surprise, or overtaken by events, so that those who look to it for guidance are, in turn, surprised and disappointed. Official information, suggestions, or guidance should never be disregarded or held in low esteem. It should always be prudently evaluated against a reliable yardstick of privately developed information, however, and where there is a wide divergence in the two, careful inquiry must be made. The decision maker must use his own judgment on the results. Sound information is a necessary prerequisite to effective planning and preparation for the evacuation of business personnel. It is simply unwise to rely on government—any government—to give that information and even more unwise to expect government to give the word when evacuation ought to take place.[5] History is replete with unhappy experiences of those who have proven unwise in this regard.

The U.S. government may, at any time, declare that some part of the world can no longer be considered safe for its citizens, at least for the time being, and that they should be withdrawn while unfavorable conditions persist. Every private entity doing business in a foreign country, even the most stable, should develop a realistic, up-to-date plan for the evacuation of those for whom it is responsible. Every contingency plan of this kind should be comprehensive and detailed, and it should be developed by those having a thorough, intimate knowledge of the affairs and policies of the business entity concerned.

Expert, specialist advice should be sought, where appropriate, but the plan should be developed in-house and all managers should be familiar with the overall plan and thoroughly acquainted with those aspects of it that have particular relevance to their own departments. The plan should be coordinated with such official contingency plans and policies as may be in effect for the area in question and should,

whenever possible, take into consideration the plans of other foreign business entities. Cooperation with these may be possible and desirable, but, in any event,
knowing what they propose to do under crisis conditions lessens the possibilities
of confusion and conflict. The plan should be written in simple, uncomplicated
language and its contents should be communicated to all those likely to be affected
by its implementation. Nothing is worse, in these situations, than uncertainty as
to the arrangements made to cope with a need for evacuation. If everyone knows
what to expect, anxieties are lessened and all can set about playing their assigned
parts so that the operation goes as smoothly as possible. Essential aspects of a
plan for the evacuation of business personnel are outlined below.

Assignment of Responsibility for Ordering Evacuation

While policy on when, and whom, to evacuate can and should be developed at
the highest level, the decision to order implementation of the evacuation plan is
most conveniently vested in the highest on-the-spot authority. He may consult, as
appropriate, but he will have the best feeling for when the decision to move should
be taken. The plan should provide for others to act in his place if, for any reason,
he cannot discharge this function.

The plan should provide, in detail, how the orders for evacuation are to be
transmitted, and particular attention should be paid to communication with personnel in remote areas. It may be advisable to develop a code, for speed and security.

Operational Phases of the Evacuation Proceedings

The plan should identify the following phases and what is to be accomplished
during each of them:

1. *Alert.* During this phase, personnel will be advised of the possibility of evacua-
    tion within a given period. They should begin advanced preparation for a
    possible move and hold themselves in readiness to receive further instructions.
    This is a precautionary position from which they may proceed to other phases
    of the evacuation procedure or from which they may stand down if the emer-
    gency is deemed to have passed.
2. *Readiness.* During this phase, personnel should be prepared to move the
    moment they are instructed to do so. Packing of possessions to be moved
    should be complete and all personal affairs should be in order. This represents
    the final stage before the evacuation proper is initiated.
3. *Movement.* During this phase, personnel and other dependents will be moved
    from the places they normally occupy to staging areas and then onward to
    sea and airports or land exits. Staging areas should be selected with care
    and clear instructions given on how to reach them. Arrangements for reception
    and care as well as transportation should be spelled out.

4.   *Transit.* This is an intermediate phase, involving much upheaval and a certain amount of discomfort. The primary concern will be to remove personnel from the danger area as quickly as possible and arrangements have to be made for transportation, care and shelter, and reception at designated places outside the evacuated area.

5.   *Resettlement.* This stage generally means repatriation, although in some cases employees may simply be moved to another, safer area where business may be continued. Arrangements for housing the relocated personnel and their integration into the business organization elsewhere, as well as compensation and other adjustments, will need to be considered during this phase.

Liaison with the Authorities

Unless there has been a complete breakdown of government, an orderly evacuation can *only* proceed if certain necessary formalities are observed. Customs and other fiscal clearances will be required and movements may, for many reasons, be restricted or subject to official scheduling. An evacuation can only go smoothly if these matters are competently attended to by persons familiar with official routines and requirements.

Personnel Remaining in Post

Circumstances may suggest the desirability of a partial evacuation—of dependents and nonessential personnel, for example. In this case, the plan should make special provisions for the safety of those remaining in place and may include special living arrangements, travel and other restrictions, and enhanced security.

Time, and timing, are crucial in evacuation operations. A major objective is securing as much time as possible for the accomplishment of each of the tasks assigned to the various operational phases. In practice, everything seems to take much more time than has been allowed for it. Racing against the clock heightens anxieties and, in the worst of cases, induces panic. Time is especially important in the alert and readiness phases. The more time available, the more orderly the process and the less obtrusive is the sense of loss and separation following the forced abandonment of personal property and entry on the strange discomforts of the transit phase.

It is important, too, that time, when it is available, not be wasted. Careful scheduling and close operational supervision of all phases of the evacuation are necessary to ensure the right degree of urgency. Too much time can be as great a bane as too little. The right amount of time is that which will allow the job to be done thoroughly without undue tension being placed upon those concerned. Remember that government does not necessarily work more quickly in a crisis: Allow the appropriate amount of time for obtaining clearances, exit permits, and the like. Timing—knowing when to make certain decisions and initiate certain actions—is no less important. Some actions cannot be easily recalled once they are set in train. Being neither too early nor too late is a difficult art to master.

Above all, the human aspects of the evacuation of business personnel should receive constant sympathetic attention. There must be real sensitivity to the implications of a move for those affected. These people's business and personal lives have been grossly disrupted by events over which they have no control. For many, this turbulence may strike with all the swiftness of a natural disaster.[6] After the "heroic" phase, in which everybody is trying to cope with the problems at hand, there comes a period of adjustment and reflection. An evacuation is capable of generating strong emotions and deep resentments. It can inspire an abiding loss of faith, lasting suspicion, and lawsuits. There may be real loss, calling for prompt relief and compensation. Often overlooked is the psychological damage suffered even by those who have made it safely out of the danger area. Counselling and other help may be needed and ought to be generously provided by any business truly interested in the welfare of its personnel. Much can be done to relieve the severe emotional stress induced by an evacuation. Continued, useful service by affected personnel may well depend on appropriate measures being taken in a timely fashion.

NOTES

1. *The Suppliants.*

2. On this, see Myamoto Musashi, *A Book of Five Rings,* (Woodstock, N.Y.: The Overlook Press, 1982), a work that has acquired an almost cult-like following in the business world.

3. ". . . You might have better judgment concerning a situation than me but given that our judgments are equally powerful, I'm in a better position than you if I have more information." Kenneth M. Colby, *Artificial Paranoia,* An NIMH Program Report (Washington, DC: U.S. Government Printing Office, 1976), p. 22.

4. Even the best information is reduced in value if it cannot be or is not adequately communicated. "We forget that communication is a two-way street. We have to pay attention to what others are saying and relate to their message. . . . We believe that there is a direct relationship between the volume of communication and the amount of information conveyed." "Why We Fail as Communicators," in *Communication Briefings,* vol. 1, no. 1., 1982.

5. U.S. government policy in relation to Iran during 1977–79 is particularly instructive and deserving of close study by the business community. More recently, the anti-Lybian policy pursued by the current administration has led to business evacuations that would not otherwise have taken place.

6. See, on this, the very useful "Human Problems in Disasters: A Pamphlet for Government Emergency Disaster Services Personnel," Publication (ADM) no. 78–539 (Washington, DC: U.S. Department of Health, Education and Welfare, 1978).

12

Terrorist Targeting and Corporate Philanthropy: The Argentine Case[*]

D. Stanley Eitzen
David W. Barkey

The decade of the 1970s was an era of unprecedented terrorist attacks against representatives of affluent countries, primarily in the Middle East, Western Europe, and Latin America. According to Central Intelligence Agency data, of the 2,072 recorded international terrorist attacks on U.S. citizens and property from 1970 to 1980, 32 percent were aimed at business facilities or executives.[1]

Among Latin American countries, one of the most notorious for terrorist activity has been Argentina. One analysis has recorded 182 incidents of terrorist attacks from 1969 to 1978.[2] The junior author of this paper was a resident in Argentina during most of this period and it is his judgment that many more incidents were perpetrated than were recorded, especially kidnappings, as the families of many victims negotiated directly with the kidnappers rather than notified the authorities.

The purpose of this study is to examine the posture of the business community in a hostile environment. How does the executive cope with the treatment of terrorist attack on his person, company personnel, or facilities? How does he perceive the motives and ambitions of the terrorist? Is there a role that the multinational corporation (MNC) can play in the prevention of terrorist activity? Will MNCs engage in philanthropic activities and expend resources for the alleviation of social needs in order to escape the tactics of terrorist blackmailers?

U.S. BUSINESS IN ARGENTINA

More than 200 U.S. corporations have subsidiaries, branches, or offices in Argentina. As has been the case wherever U.S. business has penetrated, their presence and

---

[*] This article is an extensive revision of David W. Barkey and D. Stanley Eitzen, "Toward an Assessment of Multinational Corporate Social Expenditures in Relation to Political Stability and Terrorist Activity: The Argentine Case," *Inter-American Economic Affairs* 34 (Spring 1981), pp. 77–90.

influence have been regarded with mixed appreciation and suspicion. Argentines do not make a distinction between a U.S. enterprise and the United States itself. The presence of a subsidiary connotes the presence of the parent company and even the U.S. government as well. Since the MNC is not accountable to any public authority that matches it in geographical reach and since it represents the aggregate interests of all the countries affected, continual destructive, political tension and agitation have plagued many U.S. enterprises. MNCs have often been the most reliable issues in domestic political struggles as they provide the politician with an opportunity to display his nationalism. The foreign oil companies in Argentina, which have been central issues in presidential election campaigns, are a good example. They were nationalized by the civilian government but regained their independent status under military rule, only to lose it again when Perón returned. At present, again under military rule, they are independent though controlled.

The presence of MNCs has brought about cleavages within the national elite: Some are bolstered by MNC ties and others are weakened. Intellectuals outside the establishment have regarded the policies favoring foreign investment as a move to strengthen the position of the establishment and weaken the status and influence of others. This cleavage has tended to paralyze economic progress in various sectors. A case in point observed by the junior author was the University of Tucuman's opposition to the terms of a government contract giving international mining interests the opportunity to exploit mines in Catamarca province. Prolonged litigation deprived hundreds of miners of several months of income.

The behavior of MNCs in Argentina and elsewhere in the Third World has been scarred by questionable actions. Government officials have been bribed to gain favorable treatment or to obtain government contracts. The companies have often failed to train local nationals for upper management positions, while using "creative bookkeeping" to rob the country of revenue. Diplomatic support has often been used to give leverage in government disputes: the promise of U.S. government aid or credit can be a factor in maneuvering favorable policies.

On the positive side, MNCs in Argentina, as well as in other countries, often represent profound progress in the effort of peoples to cope with their aspirations in a world of limited resources. These companies have made contributions to the international exchange of knowledge and understanding, opened schools for children of employees, sponsored literacy campaigns, donated funds for the construction and support of local schools, hospitals, and community centers, opened plants for work-experience programs for students enrolled in local universities, and provided technicians and instructors for community projects. The junior author has observed that laborers usually prefer employment in a foreign enterprise because its prestige, coupled with the wages, working conditions, benefits, and possible advancement it offers, is greater than in most national companies.

STRUCTURAL AND HISTORICAL CONDITIONS
PROMOTING ARGENTINE TERRORISM

The roots of revolutionary activity in Argentina are both political and social. As is true in other parts of Latin America, Argentina has provided fertile soil for the seeds of rebellion. Since 1955, most of its governments have lacked legitimacy, which has forced the opposition underground or into exile. Land is inequitably distributed, with a few powerful families controlling most of it. The result is an inefficient use of agriculture and other resources, especially in the Argentine interior. Landowners operate with unskilled labor and invest a minimal amount of capital in technological advances.

Rural and urban migrations involve 8 percent of the population per year over all of Latin America. The burgeoning cities cannot provide sufficient employment for the inflow of unskilled laborers, as more than half the population competes for a livelihood there.[3] Unemployment is high, which benefits the landowners, who can easily avoid demands for better conditions by hiring a readily available and desperate labor force. Hunger, poverty, illness, and ignorance result.

The major political antecedent for violence in Argentina was the exile of Juan Domingo Perón in 1955 after a military take-over ended his ten-year dominance of the country. Peronist groups carried out sporadic attacks on the government. From Madrid, Perón gave his support to their activities, stating on one occasion that if he were younger he would be among their ranks.

In mid-1969, one of the Peronist groups, Fuerzas Armadas Revolucionarias (FAR) bombed 14 Minimax supermarkets in protest of the arrival of Nelson Rockefeller. This was the first attack on U.S. business by a terrorist group. In 1971, three Peronist groups combined forces against the military government. President Lanusse opened conversations with the Peronists for the establishment of a civilian government in 1971. In spite of this concession, the guerrillas continued their activity. The People's Revolutionary Army (ERP), the most powerful of the Peronist groups, opposed the elections and moved to force a break between the government and the military.

Though Perón was proscribed from the ballot due to a technicality, his hand picked candidate, Hector Campora, won 51 percent of the vote in a field of several candidates. His first act as president was to grant amnesty to all political prisoners, which vacated most of the country's prisons. After a few weeks in office, Campora declared new elections, paving the way for a Perón landslide victory. Surprisingly, subversive activity increased with a surge in assassinations and kidnappings.

On the day of Perón's arrival, a huge delegation was to receive him as he came from the airport. Rival unions and terrorist groups clashed over the seating arrangements on the podium. A wild shoot-out ensued, leaving hundreds dead. Perón condemned the actions of his militant followers and vowed to repress them until they were eliminated. The result was a war between left- and right-wing terrorists that lasted through the presidency of Perón's widow, Isabel, and was finally stopped by military repression under the present regime. The extent of terrorist activity can be seen in the fact that in 1973 alone the ERP received $20 million in ransoms. Right-wing terror under the leadership of Isabel's welfare minister accounted for 200 deaths in a ten-month period. In 1974 there were 250 major assassinations. Six hundred people were killed in six months of 1976.

The main targets of the Peronist groups were North American MNCs. The United States was regarded as the root of all capitalist evil. One of the revolutionaries referred to a "holy alliance of repression whose strategic epicenter is the Pentagon and whose economic resonance box is Wall Street."[4] The kidnapping of executives and giving of ransom to the poor were applauded by the public. However, the assassination of kidnap victims or cold-blooded sniping caused a decline in public support.[5]

Highly visible companies with U.S. ties seem to have been most attractive targets to the terrorists. The chronological record of terrorist attacks on U.S. business property and personnel indicates that companies having obvious American identities are the most prominent victims.[6]

The aim of the terrorists apparently was harassment and not destruction. Kidnapping became the favorite tactic: It permits the manipulation of powerful individuals and their parent companies. Guerrillas concerned with public image tend to favor the more sophisticated operation that kidnapping requires. More media coverage is commanded by the abduction and subsequent ransom and release of a victim than is usually given to explosive attacks or bombing incidents. Kidnapping also provided an easy source of funds with little risk. Ransoms far exceeded the amounts heisted from banks and kidnappers operated at a 94.3 percent success rate. The terrorists also appreciated the fact that kidnappings were a very effective means of embarrassing the government.

The philosophy of the terrorists has been summed up in the words of one of their spokesmen, Abraham Guillen:

> Society consists of the contradition between the haves and the have nots. The human mass is ruled by the tyranny of private capital which concentrates and accumulates the direct product of thousands of craftsmen, laborers, etc. To make a social revolution it is necessary to overthrow by violence the old ruling class, to dissolve the old social relations between the exploited and exploiting classes and to create a new mode of production (socialism).[7]

The strategy for obtaining this objective is "to demoralize the militarists, the military dictatorship and its repressive forces and also to attack and destroy the wealth and property of North America, foreign managers and . . . the upper class."[8]

THE RELATIONSHIP BETWEEN CORPORATE PHILANTHROPY AND TERRORISM

The possible link between corporate social expenditures and harrassment by terrorist groups is explored here by addressing four key issues.

Social Expenditures and Terrorist Harassment

The first question addresses the issue of corporate responsiveness in a volatile social environment: Will MNCs increase their social expenditures when they perceive that they are vulnerable to terrorist harassment? Will they attempt to avoid the blackmail of "Robin Hood" terrorist tactics by making significant contributions to social agencies for the alleviation of the health, economic, and educational needs of the poor?

Very little in the literature on the subject of terrorism and business encourages corporate executives to attempt to avoid harassment by enhancing the corporation's community image. Most of the strategy proposed regards improved security and precautionary measures. Brooks McClure has indicated that community relations are a factor in corporate vulnerability.[9] Terrorists will probably seek to exploit exiting grievances. However, they may target a company with a good community image in order to intimidate the population as a whole. Since eleventh-hour social expenditures would be of little value in altering a poor image, such a tactic is not likely to be considered by executives who regard their company to be highly vulnerable to attack.

The response of MNCs to terrorist threats is determined by the decision makers' assessment of the cultural, psychological, and political motivations of the protagonists. If, as in the case in Argentina, the objective of the guerrillas is to bring down the government, corporate executives will perceive their responses as inconsequential and probably will not expend funds for philanthropic projects, at least not for the avoidance of terrorist blackmail.

Social Expenditures and Political Instability

A second question is derived from the thesis of Frances Piven and Richard Cloward, who state that corporate social expenditures are related to fluctuations in political stability.[10] Will corporate social expenditures increase in epochs of political instability and decrease in time of stability? These authors have indicated that, in the United States, public relief arrangements are initiated or expanded by the government during the occasional outbreaks of civil disorder produced by mass unemployment and are then abolished or contracted when political stability is restored. In this manner government elites manipulate relief programs to regulate the labor force by quelling outbreaks of violence with increased benefits.

The question then is, Do MNCs attempt to control their publics by making contributions to the social, physical, and educational needs of their community? The analysis of this question is complicated: An MNC cannot have a clear, unambiguous will. Among its decision makers will be found a coalition of interests, each with a unique sense of the corporation's common objectives that will precipitate a conflict of priorities. Among its managers may be some who take a conventional approach to the issue, regarding the link between the business and the context of operation as purely a market transaction. Their position has been expressed by Milton Friedman: "The social responsibility of business is to increase its profits."[11]

A study by Robert Green has indicated that there is no relationship between political instability and the overall allocation of U.S. investment.[12] He found that though executives indicated that political instability was an important factor in determining allocations, the data showed that there are several other overriding factors, such as the potential for high profits, that minimize the instability factor. We suspect that if labor, social unrest, and civic disorder are of minimal import in corporate investment decision making, such conditions will not provoke social expenditures either.

The answer to the question of MNC public manipulation also depends on the status of the organization and its philosophy of operation. James Post has elaborated three models that companies may follow in determining their relationship to their environment.[13] The *adaptive* model is one in which management assesses and evaluates change and moves the organization toward a preferable available state. The *proactive* model posits an aggressive management that endeavors to change the environment to achieve a state of external conditions that are most favorable for the organization's operations. The *interactive* model recognizes that the organization and the environment are changing but not at the same rate. A company's ability to choose a model will depend on its status (i.e., importance to the local economy, size of employment, position in an industry, and importance to the society).

Social Expenditures and Terrorist Attacks

A third question focuses on the nature of corporate social expenditures in relation to the possibility of terrorist attack. Will corporations make philanthropic contributions in a highly visible manner when terrorist attack seems to be eminent? Will corporate contributions be distributed in the form of material goods that meet immediate physical needs in order to avoid terrorist harassment?

To answer these related questions, we must understand the context of cultural expectations and environmental circumstances. In the event of natural disasters, epidemics and other calamities, MNCs as well as other entities have responded with donations of medications, food, and clothing that have been widely publicized through the media. The Latin concept of patronage also demands material amenities to be given to employees and their families. Prakesh Sethi stresses the importance of the cultural and temporal framework in the evaluation of corporate social performance.[14] MNCs are faced with a variety of challenges that each social system may come to consider appropriate for them to tackle.

We must go beyond the financial outlay to indicate exactly what was given, the circumstances involved, the means used to make the contribution, and the way it was publicized. The Robin Hood style of terrorism that has characterized some incidents may have established a precedent that corporations on their own would resist. An attack on the Ford Motor Company subsidiary brought about a terrorist demand for 154 ambulances, $200,000 to be sent to a children's hospital, another $200,000 for a children's home, and $200,000 worth of powdered milk for children in the slums. Ford negotiated with the terrorists and ended up giving $1 million in the forms requested. Further research is needed to establish a relationship between such Robin Hood tactics and voluntary social contributions in kind.

Excessive visibility of social actions may be counter-productive, creating suspicion of corporate behavior. Studies by the Council on Economic Priorities, for example, show that companies with the worst pollution records are the largest advertisers of achievements in pollution control.[15] Terrorists and the public at large may perceive widely publicized good deeds as a disguise for an exploitative, unresponsive company.

The maxim that guides Philip Morris, Inc., "Our business activities must make social sense, and our social activities must make business sense,"[15] is typical of an MNC's stance on social responsibility. In all likelihood, they will not undertake social contributions that meet human needs without any promise of increased sales and profits. Contributions in kind can be expected only under duress from government or social forces (other than terrorist activities).

Social Expenditures and Vulnerability

The final issue concerns the vulnerability of businesses to terrorist harassment. Are businesses having a poor social image (in other words, low wages, a large number of expatriate executives, and a proportionately small amount of social contributions) more vulnerable to harassment by terrorist groups than will businesses that are known for social responsiveness? What criteria are used by the extremists to determine which businesses are to be targeted?

The terrorist objective, as previously noted, is typically aimed at provoking antigovernment feeling. To accomplish this goal a terrorist organization must maximize the propagandizing and psychological effects of their actions. An attack on a little-known company or the kidnapping of an executive of a small operation is of little value to guerrillas. A well-known company is more susceptible to public scrutiny of its wage and price levels. For the same reasons, the large, well-known company will be more vulnerable to terrorist attack.

Good community relations are no guarantee against terrorist activity: Labor disputes, layoffs, contamination of the environment, expatriate management, and social callousness may be exploited, but their replacement by good deeds and responsible citizenship will not assure immunity to attack.[16] The Coca Cola Company, for example, manufactures syrups that it sells to independent bottlers and canners. It has very few employees overseas. That one of its Argentine executives was kidnapped twice and the company harrassed on at least four other occasions over the past ten years has more to do with the popularity of its product than with a negative social image.

Crisis management capability cannot be minimized. Easy capitulation to terrorist demands simply invites more harrassment with higher stakes. Members of one terrorist group told one of their kidnap victims, "All they [the Phillips Corporation] had to do was go around to the Bank of Orlando and draw out the money and give it to us, the next day almost. It was too easy!"[17] The Otis Elevator Company received a threat almost identical to that which Ford received demanding $1 million in goods. Otis refused and, evidently, was not bothered anymore.[18]

These examples show that, in spite of terrorist idealism, corporate targets are selected on the basis of their visibility and symbolic representation of U.S. interests. A corporation's negative social image is only of value to the terrorists as a lever for popular support. Since their objective is the destruction of their country's social and economic system, these groups will not be easily swayed from their path by companies with a responsible social conscience.

CONCLUSION

Having reviewed the relatively meager research on philanthropy by multinational corporations and terrorism, we have come to four tentative conclusions: (1) the perception of terrorist threats by corporate officers does not appear to be related to increased corporate philanthropy, (2) corporate social expenditures are not related to the stability or instability of the political and economic environment of the host country, (3) multinational corporations tend to respond to increased terrorist activities by means other than increased social expenditures, and (4) terrorists select business targets for their propaganda value and not by their social conscience.

These conclusions lead to the pessimistic assertion that corporate social expenditures do *not* buy immunity from terrorist attack. This realization should not discourage multinational corporations from good citizenship within host countries: There are numerous positive business and social benefits from such philanthropy. But, to reiterate, if the goal of corporate generosity is to protect the corporations and their employees from the dangers of terrorism, social largesse is by no means a guarantee of success.

NOTES

1. Central Intelligence Agency, *Patterns of International Terrorist: 1980,* research paper (June 1981, in *Current News,* special ed., no. 738 (Washington, DC: The Department of Defense, 1981).

2. Susanna W. Purnell and Eleanor S. Wainstein, *The Problems of U.S. Businesses Operating Abroad in Terrorist Environments,* R-2842-DOC (Santa Monica, CA: The Rand Corporation, 1981).

3. Ross E. Butler, "Terrorism in Latin America," in Yonah Alexander (ed.), *International Terrorism* (New York: Praeger, 1976), pp. 46–61.

4. Bowman H. Miller and Charles A. Russell, "Terrorism and the Corporate Target," in Yonah Alexander and Robert Kilmarx (eds.), *Political Terrorism in Business: Threat and Response* (New York: Praeger, 1979), pp. 56–65.

5. J. Bowyer Bell, *Transnational Terror* (Washington, DC: American Enterprise Institute for Public Policy Research, 1975).

6. Edward F. Mickolus, "Chronology of Transnational Terrorist Attacks Upon American Business People 1968–78," in Yonah Alexander (ed.), *International Terrorism;* Purnell and Wainstein.

7. Miller and Russell, p. 56.

8. *Ibid.,* p. 57.

9. Brooks McClure, "Corporate Vulnerability—And How to Assess It," in Yonah Alexander, *Political Terrorism and Business* (New York, Praeger, 1979).

10. Frances F. Piven and Richard A. Cloward, *Regulating the Poor* (New York, Random House, 1971).

11. Lee E. Preston (ed.), *Research in Corporate Social Performance and Policy,* vol. 1 (Greenwich, CT: Jai Press, 1978).

12. Robert T. Green, *Political Instability as a Determinant of U.S. Investment* (Austin, TX: University of Texas, 1972).

13. James E. Post, "Research on Patterns of Corporate Response to Social Change," in Preston (ed.), *Corporate Social Performance.*

14. S. Prakesh Sethi, "Corporate Social Audit: An Emerging Trend in Measuring Corporate Social Performance," in Dow Votaw and Prakesh Sethi (eds.), *The Corporate Dilemma* (Englewood Cliffs, NJ: Prentice Hall, 1973), pp. 214–231.

15. *Ibid.*

16. McClure, pp. 84–85.

17. Gerald McKnight, *The Terrorist Mind* (Indianapolis: Bobbs-Merrill, 1974), p. 119.

13

An Economic Analysis of Security, Recovery, and Compensation in Terrorist Kidnapping

Arthur J. Alexander

This chapter lays out an economic analysis, from a business firm's point of view, of resource allocations responsive to possible terrorist kidnapping of its employees for ransom.[1] Specifically, it reviews the tradeoffs among security expenditures, recovery costs, and compensation. In order to review these three policies, they are first set in a framework that establishes their relationships to each other and to the several parties to the transactions. The opening section, then, establishes a context for the analysis.

THE MAIN ACTORS: VICTIMS AND KIDNAPPERS

To begin with, it is important to note that a terrorist kidnapping involves the interactions between two central actors: kidnappers and victims. The victims are usefully separated into a number of players: society as represented by the public control agencies (such as police, courts, and jails); the business community; the targeted firm; and the kidnapped individual. Analysis requires consideration of the nature and characteristics of all participants—the kidnappers and the several players on the victims' side. Thus, an effective corporate strategy depends, for example, on whether terrorists are confined to a small number of tightly organized groups, or are widely drawn from the general population and largely independent of one another; or whether the company's activities are concentrated in one facility or dispersed throughout the country. The important point here is that neither analysis nor strategy can be based on a partial view.

Each of the different actors facing the terrorist threat has its own goals, motivations, and repertoire of behavior. Most often, this behavior is complementary; for example, the police, the firm, and the individual contribute in different ways to the protection of the individual. On other occasions, though, conflict may arise; the police—acting for the general public good—often prefer a no-ransom policy and give priority to the apprehension of terrorists, whereas kidnapped individuals—with different priorities—favor a policy of paying ransom. A firm must account for both the complementary and conflicting goals of the different actors in its own analysis.

TRADEOFFS AMONG POLICIES

Faced with a potential threat, a firm has the task of determining the amount of resources it should allocate to any of several alternatives. The firm can spend its resources on security measures to reduce the risk of danger; it can strengthen its ability to recover a kidnapped employee through measures such as ransom insurance and the establishment of crisis management plans; or it can compensate its risk-taking employees for working in an unusually dangerous environment.

Placing the firm's alternatives into the three broad categories of security, recovery, and compensation makes it possible to identify the relationships among them and to compare the relative costs and benefits of each. These relationships are portrayed in Figure 13.1. Resources spent on security reduce the probability of kidnapping. Should a kidnapping occur, efforts devoted to recovery diminish the probability of death or injury to the kidnapped employee. Since employees fear both the pain and suffering of a kidnapping (even if they are recovered unharmed), as well as the possibility of death or injury, the probabilities of both kidnapping and of death or injury will affect the compensation they require to work in a dangerous situation.

For its part, the firm should attempt to minimize the sum of the expected costs of security, recovery, and compensation. This is where the tradeoffs arise. More effective security would reduce both expected recovery costs and compensation for risk. If the probability of kidnapping could be reduced to zero, for example, both recovery and compensation costs would vanish. But there are decreasing returns to security expenditures, and it is often prohibitively costly to buy absolute protection.

Some hypothetical, but reasonable, numbers make the calculation more con-

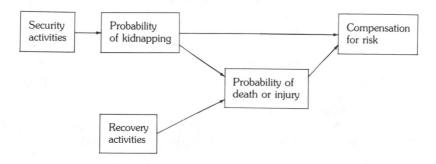

Figure 13.1 Relationships among security, recovery, and compensation.

crete. Suppose it cost an additional $200,000 per year in security to reduce the annual probability of kidnapping from one in a thousand (0.001) to zero; and that the total management compensation package (added up across all relevant executives) for working in the risky situation were $150,000. If an average ransom were $1 million, with crisis management expenses of an additional $100,000, the expected value of recovery costs per year would be $1,100. (The $1,100 figure is derived by adding together the average ransom of $1 million and the crisis management cost of $100,000. This sum of $1,100,000 is then multiplied by the kidnap probability of 0.001 to get $1,100.)

With these assumed figures, reducing the terrorist threat to zero by increasing security expenditures security by $200,000 would not be balanced monetarily by the savings in compensation and recovery. However, if reducing the risk of danger were less expensive, or the required compensation were greater, or ransom demands increased, or the probabilities of being kidnapped were substantially larger (say, a one out of ten chance of kidnapping), it could very well pay to make the additional security expenditures.

ACTIONS SUPPORTING SECURITY, RECOVERY, AND COMPENSATION

The data below show how security, recovery, and compensation can be broken down into narrower categories. The two broad goals of an antiterrorist policy for a business firm are the prevention of terrorist acts—in particular, kidnappings; and the recovery from such acts, should they occur.

I. Prevention
    A. Deterrence
        1. Reduction of probability of terrorist success
            (a) Security (government, corporate, private)
            (b) Recovery by force (government, corporate, private)
        2. Reduction of payoff to terrorists in successful kidnappings
            (a) Corporate and government policy against ransom
            (b) Incapacity to pay
        3. Increased penalty for failure
            (a) Probability of death or injury to terrorists
            (b) Probability of capture
    B. Protection
        1. Security (government, corporate, private)
            (a) Physical security
            (b) Procedures
    C. Threat reduction (capture or incapacitation of terrorists)
    D. Removal of targets
II. Recovery of Hostage
    A. Ransom

    B. Crisis management
    C. Recovery by force (government, corporate, private)
III. Compensation for Risk
    A. Wages
    B. Life insurance
    C. Payment for pain and suffering

Prevention

Prevention can be accomplished in several ways—through deterrence, protection, reduction of the threat, and removal of potential victims. Of course, some policies that enhance one of these programs may do double duty by strengthening another.

Deterrence, generally speaking, reduces the expected payoff to the terrorist of a terrorist act. Deterrence can therefore work through several avenues. The probability of a successful attack can be reduced by increased security (provided by government, business, or the individual). Success can also be reduced by the forceful recovery of the victim or by the capture of the terrorists. Reducing the payoff in a successful abduction will also increase deterrence. Limited ability to pay or seemingly effective policies and laws against ransom payment should lower the expected payoff to a terrorist act. Increasing the risk of death, injury, or capture and increasing the penalty if captured can also increase deterrence.

Protection seeks to foil an attack once the terrorists have decided to launch one. Protection therefore not only deters an attack from occurring, but is also a shield should an attack occur. It is a function of the security provided by all parties: the government, the firm, and the individual. Included here are not only physical security, but also the various procedures that individuals and firms can take—generally at some cost to themselves—to make terrorist attacks more difficult (for example, irregular routines).

Reduction of the threat through incapacitation and incarceration of terrorists can act directly on potential terrorists by diminishing their numbers. (*Incapacitation* is meant to include the death or physical disability imposed on a terrorist by security agents, public and private.) Its effectiveness as a policy depends on the character of the terrorist phenomenon. A small number of self-contained groups can be dealt with in this manner; but a broadly based movement drawing its membership from a large reservoir of people willing to become terrorists will not be sharply affected by incapacitation or capture of some of its members. These two possibilities are illustrated by the example of bank robberies in the United States in the 1920s and the 1970s. In the earlier period, a small number of criminal gangs committed most of the robberies. The work of the FBI led to the death, or arrest and imprisonment, of the leading gangs and reduced the number of bank robberies by more than 80 percent in seven years.[2] By the 1960s and 1970s, however, the number of bank offices had increased by many times and bank robbery became a broader-based activity of individuals acting alone. In this case, arrest has very little impact on the number of participants. Its value now lies mainly in the realm of deterrence.

Similarly, when potential terrorism is endemic, arrest and punishment of active participants will not reduce the numbers of those on the sidelines, but it could very well act to limit their actual involvement in terrorist acts.

Terrorist kidnapping can also be prevented by removing the potential victim from the hostile environment. In the case of business operations, options include moving a facility from a country, closing down a business, moving from one area to another, or sending targeted individuals to safer regions. If the costs of terrorist acts or of measures taken to ameliorate them become too great, reducing the exposure to risk by a variety of techniques, including removal of the individuals or of the firm itself, must be considered.[3]

Recovery

Turning to the subject of recovery shifts attention from prevention of a kidnapping to what happens after a kidnapping takes place. Indeed, many recovery policies become operational only after an attack. Some recovery activities, though, can take place prior to an actual event; they include arrangements for ransom through insurance or other means; the formation of corporate contingency plans, strategies, and assignments of responsibility for dealing with terrorist acts; and the retention of specialized firms with experience in negotiating with terrorists. Recovery can also be obtained through forceful physical means by military, police, or private agents.

Compensation

Prevention and recovery activities are intended to reduce the risk and danger of a job. If not reduced to zero, additional compensation may be required to induce people to accept such positions.[4] Variations in wages that compensate for disagreeable characteristics of jobs, including risk and danger, were described by Adam Smith two hundred years ago.[5] Smith's theory forms the basis for the best recent economic inquiries on the effects of job risk on wages. Additional compensation for risk can be found not only in the present level of monetary income, but also in fringe benefits (such as life insurance), promotion prospects, or in rank and status (i.e., a job title—and salary—greater than normally assigned for a given task).

DIFFERENT ROLES FOR DIFFERENT PLAYERS

The chief players in the different policies suggested above vary across countries and situations and according to custom. Government, through the police, courts, and prisons, is typically responsible for the arrest, penalty, and imprisonment of terrorists. Government is also the likely promulgator of antiransom policies, and the user of armed force in the recovery of victims. Government, business firms, and individuals are thus jointly responsible for security in overlapping and complementary ways. Ransom payments and wage differentials fall under the firm's authority. The nature of a firm's response to terrorist threats depends on the interactions of all these elements. Even though "everything depends on everything else," an attempt to disentangle some of the analytical strands indicates the general features that should be considered in concrete situations.

INDIVIDUAL CHOICE, SCALE ECONOMIES, AND PUBLIC GOODS

The choice of the appropriate parties to carry out the policies outlined in the previous section can be informed by several general principles based on economic efficiency. That is, these policies can be judged on a cost standard, seeking the lowest cost alternatives that will attract and keep key employees.

Individual Choice

The first principle (a central assumption of economic analysis) is that individuals are usually the best judges of their own welfare. This calls for granting as much autonomy and decision-making power to the individual as possible, which is most easily done through the payment of money to the individual, rather than through the provision of income or services in kind. Of course, other factors, some of which are examined below, may vitiate this principle; but if these other factors are absent, a company trying to decide how to allocate its antiterrorism budget would have an easy task. It would not have to decide how much to put into ransom insurance, security, seminars on employee protection, or guard forces. It could simply negotiate a payment with its employees such that they would agree to work for the company and to hold the company blameless for future events that befall them. With this payment, the employees would buy the mix of services that best suited their own preferences. If an employee were primarily concerned with financial security, he would commit himself heavily to insurance; a strong concern for physical security would lead to bodyguards, alarms, locks, and firearms; if he preferred risk and high living, he could spend the payment in a casino. The point is that the individual can be counted on to select a package of services that serves his welfare better than could an external decisionmaker acting on the individual's behalf but without intimate knowledge of the individual's preferences.

A common objection to individual choice involves the technical complexities of decisions, the difficulty of obtaining sufficient information, and the expertise required for efficient choice. Personal security, of course, is not the only area of life with these characteristics: medical care, education, buying a house, or occupational choice are other common examples. In all these cases, expert advice can be purchased. Security is no different. Many firms in the security field can provide information and advice to clients. However, the cost of providing a survey and advice to an individual may be too expensive for a single person. At the given price, it is often more appropriate to provide such services to a larger group, or to the firm as a whole. This is an example of economies of scale.

Economies of Scale

Economies of scale represent one of the important exceptions to the principle of individual choice. The second principle, therefore, is that scale economies can sometimes make it inefficient for an individual to provide a service for himself. Some types of physical security and some forms of insurance can often be produced at lower cost if designed to cover a large number of people. This usually comes about from the large fixed costs of installing physical equipment and systems, or (in the case of insurance) through the consolidation of numerous transactions into a single contract between an insurance company and the insured firm. Similarly, the security department of a large company will often have sufficient information and expertise to provide a service in kind to its executives, or would find it efficient to have a specialized security firm furnish the same range of services. In all of these cases, the inefficiencies of individual purchase of such services could call for the transfer of decisionmaking and the authority over resources from the individual to the firm, and for the subsequent provision of services by the firm to the individual.

Public Goods

Another impediment to efficient individual choice is the "publicness" of an activity. Whereas an individual could choose not to participate in a group insurance scheme, he cannot choose not to accept the increased security provided by a plant guard force. The service generated is such that if it is provided for one person, it is provided for all. Similarly, if an individual purchases his own private security, protection would be provided to others in his immediate vicinity, whether or not they contributed to the cost of the services. This is an example of a public good. Public goods and services are those whose benefits extend beyond a single individual to others who cannot be excluded from the benefits, and at no additional cost to the provider or to the recipients. Common examples include national defense, public health, police protection, and fire protection.[6]

Note that the above-mentioned services are typically provided by government. It is appropriate that public goods be provided collectively by government, or for government to compel universal participation (for example, through immunization or the meeting of fire regulations). A main reason for collectivization and compulsion lies in the incentive for individuals to become free-riders and therefore to benefit from the actions of others without contributing themselves. Without public provision of these services, too little of them would be produced privately. A firm can also produce services that have the characteristics of public goods to those within the firm (and sometimes to others, as well). Plant security (as already mentioned) is one example.

Public goods are not always found in pure form. A private security firm hired to patrol an individual's home will generate added security to an entire neighborhood. Public police can be assigned to protect individuals and specific companies and thus provide a private benefit. Because of this mix and overlap in the private and public nature of security, a wide diversity exists in the means of producing it—from national gendarmeries to private bodyguards. When one level of protection breaks down or becomes inadequate, occasionally another level will step in to take over some of the functions. If public police protection for some reason falls below expectations, firms are more likely to increase their own activities, especially if they can act collectively with other similarly placed firms so that benefits would accrue to the group of participants. Intelligence collection and analysis and joint crisis management plans are examples.

Vigilante-like behavior against terrorism, though, is rare, mainly for the reason that terrorism against a specific firm or its employees is quite random. Even at the peak of terrorist kidnapping activity aimed at business in Argentina in the 1970s, about 85 percent of all the companies affected were involved in only a single incident, and fewer than 100 companies were directly involved. However, since a large proportion of the targets were branches of American multinational corporations, there was some rationale for cooperation among this class of establishments.

What follows from this discussion is the third principle: if a service has the characteristics of a public good, there is a strong argument for producing it collectively—either by a firm, or by a higher-level agency if the benefits spill over the boundaries of the firm.

Differential Tax Rate

An additional factor often makes it more efficient for a firm to provide income in kind. Different tax rates on individual income and corporate profits have such an effect. Or the tax treatment of certain expenditures as a business cost, but not as a deduction from individual income, can generate powerful incentives to transfer the purchase of services from the individual to the firm. In general, employees are worse off when taxes change incentives in this manner unless the benefits accruing to the firm through tax advantages are so large that most employees would prefer a larger income in kind to a smaller income in cash.

Conclusion

When provision of a service involves scale economies, "public goods" characteristics, or certain differential tax rates, it can be more efficient for a firm and its employees if the firm purchases the service and provides it to the employees as income in kind rather than in cash. Companies can continue to support the principle of individual choice by negotiating the remainder of a person's compensation package, with the income in kind specified in advance.

SECURITY

Definition

We can define security broadly and functionally as the set of actions taken by firms or individuals that increases the costs to terrorists of carrying out terrorist activities—in this case, kidnapping. Terrorists faced with these actions are forced to use greater resources to carry out any given act. (This notion should be understood in terms of unit costs rather than total costs; that is, security measures the attack resources required to obtain a specific payoff at a specified probability of success.) These resources include people, equipment, technical knowledge, information, and skills. Note that this definition of security does not include a notion of absolute safety. Rather, it assumes that increasing the cost will reduce the probability of a given act. As described earlier, a smaller likelihood of a successful attack can come about through deterrence or through active protection should an attack occur.

Raising costs reduces the number of terrorist organizations that can plan and manage an attack at a given level of probable success. It does not, however, guarantee immunity. There is some truth in the security specialists' aphorism: "What level of force can be expected in a terrorist attack?" "Enough." That is, because the consequences of failure can be severe, an efficient terrorist organization will determine the security of the target and assemble a sufficient number of resources to carry out the attack. The resources necessary to gather intelligence, organize, and carry out an attack, however, are not independent of a company's level of security. The statement is therefore correct—so far as it goes, which is not far enough. The probability of attack falls as a function of increased costs to the terrorist—because of both deterrence and active protection. If an attack *is* undertaken, though, the probability of terrorist success does not necessarily diminish with increased security.

Probably because of increasing security levels, kidnap team size has grown by about 50 percent in the past ten years (from about four to six people) and the use of automatic weapons has doubled.[7] An estimate of criminal kidnap gang sizes in Italy now places the number at 10 to 15 operators, including intelligence collectors, snatchers, jailers, and negotiators.[8] The cost to the terrorist organization cannot be measured solely in terms of the number of active participants; the "tooth-to-tail" ratio must also be considered. Efforts to support the "shooters" over extensive periods can involve an extensive logistics organization that must, itself, be sustained. Security measures, therefore, that place greater demands on the size of attack teams can place even greater strains on the terrorist organization as a whole. This effect of increased security should help price some groups out of the more complex operations.

Despite the potentially serious consequences of failure and the increased average size and capabilities of kidnap groups, not all kidnap attempts succeed. According to several estimates, approximately 5 to 7 percent have failed.[9] Neither information nor planning can be perfect. Measures taken by firms and individuals that create uncertainty and surprise increase the difficulty of both planning and carrying out an attack, and consequently can help deter or foil a kidnapping, although the greater effect will probably be through deterrence.

Evidence of Security Effectiveness Against Criminals

The evidence related to the assertion that increased costs are related to reduced probability of attack is sparse, but consistent. Since this evidence does not come from analyses of terrorism, but from bank robberies and other criminal activities, it must be applied to terrorist kidnapping with caution. A study of bank robberies in Philadelphia showed that the presence of a guard made a difference of almost one robbery per year for the more robbery-prone banking offices.[10] Interestingly, however, a guard force did not appear to influence the size of the take, once a robbery took place. No other security measure was statistically related to the probability of a robbery.

In another study, interviews with more than 150 bank robbers indicated that in more than 75 percent of the robberies, the robber had determined in advance whether or not the bank was guarded.[11] The presence of guards was the only security measure of which robbers took notice; this finding is consistent with the Hannan study.

Another piece of evidence comes from a corporation whose headquarters building has one section under constant guard with controlled access, and another section with relatively open entry. Over a three-year period, thefts from the controlled-access part of the building were only one-third as many as from the open section.

This evidence consistently demonstrates that guards make a difference; they · reduce the probability of an offence against the company. The research also shows that other physical security devices—such as cameras and alarms—do not seem to be an effective deterrent against initiation of robberies. The claim of security specialists that attacks, on average, will be "large enough" is also confirmed. When a gang recognized that a guard was present and decided to carry out the act anyway, their actions were planned so that the probability of success was about the same as without a guard.

Two other points from the bank robbery studies deserve mention. The first is that the major statistical determinant of a robbery was neither the level of security nor the amount of money the bank normally held, but rather the location of the office. Offices that were hit more often were located in the high-crime areas of central cities, where a larger number of criminals were concentrated. This evidence transfers easily to the analysis of terrorism: the probability of a firm's being the target of a terrorist act depends primarily on the general level of terrorism in a region. This would hold most strongly for regions where terrorism is endemic, rather than for regions where terrorism represents the actions of a few, self-contained groups.

The second point is that the average take in bank robberies was relatively small. In the study on Philadelphia banks, it was less than $3,300.[12] For a nationwide sample, it was less than $4,500.[13] A bank's cost-benefit analysis of guards versus losses would clearly indicate that it does not pay to hire a guard to reduce the probability of robbery by one per year if the average losses are of the cited magnitudes. But this evidence demonstrates something that is more important than the cost-benefit ratios of guards: Losses are reduced more through internal operating procedures than through physical security.

The Importance of Security Procedures

The simple procedure in banks of removing cash from the tellers' areas reduces easy access to money. Decreasing the access to cash—in other words, raising the unit cost of a robbery by reducing the payoff—is effective security as evidenced by the small take in bank holdups. This point is further demonstrated by the ratio of burglaries to holdups. Burglaries usually take place after business hours and involve breaking into a bank's vault. This act requires more people, skill, and equipment. Over the years, despite a substantially higher payoff, the number of burglaries has been only one third to one fifth the number of holdups.

Applying these results to terrorist kidnappings strengthens the point that procedures that increase the costs to terrorists are likely to reduce their probability. Consider, for example, the simple expedient of an executive randomly taking alternative routes to work and leaving his residence at varying times. When compared with regular commuting habits, the variable pattern would require more terrorists to observe the target's behavior and longer periods of observation. It would make planning more difficult and perhaps require several teams operating at different locations. The requirements for communications, and command and control would also be increased. Demands on resources, information, and skills would grow. Other security procedures are covered elsewhere in this book; but their evaluation can be put on a common footing by asking how, and by how much, they raise the costs to terrorists. Of course, it is also essential to consider the cost of security to the firm.

The Cost of Security

Security costs to protect a company's executives can be substantial.[14] Twenty-four-hour protection for one person requires at least four bodyguards, at a total annual cost of at least $150,000.[15] A bulletproof car can cost at least $20,000–$30,000.

Detection and alarm systems, controlled-access entrances to premises, locking devices, and television monitoring systems for a company headquarters run into hundreds of thousands of dollars. There is considerable uncertainty among security specialists about the effectiveness of such measures. Better data and analysis are necessary to fully assess the returns from these types of physical security.

Spillover Effects: One Firm's Security Affects Its Neighbors

The effectiveness of specific security measures can depend on the measures taken by other firms (i.e., by other potential targets). If terrorists know that a specific firm has increased its security, and the pool of potential targets is large relative to the number of terrorist attacks, then the danger to the relatively unprotected firms will rise.[16] On the other hand, if terrorists only know that security in general has increased, but do not know by what means or for which firms, the general cost of terrorism will increase (as the terrorists upgrade their capabilities to meet the higher average security level), and terrorism as a whole should fall. Here we run into the familiar case of homeowners placing a sign on their property noting that they are protected by some service or device. This is a technique for shifting attacks elsewhere through the provision of information.[17]

If we now change the assumptions and allow the number of targets to be much closer to the number of victims the terrorists intend to attack, increasing the security level of a few firms could reduce the overall incidence of terrorism because it would require greater effort to find suitable targets.[18] This would be the case, for example, if intelligence indicated that terrorists were targeting a small number of companies for particular purposes. Increasing security at these few companies would probably lead to an overall reduction in the probability of attack.

One estimate suggests that if elementary security precautions had been taken, 50 to 70 percent of abductions could have been avoided.[19] The chief question for decisionmakers—both private and public—is whether the targeting would have shifted to less well protected individuals. For example, it has been suggested that in the General Dozier kidnapping, Dozier was not the primary target.[20] Another officer, who happened to have been following an erratic schedule, was initially selected. The Red Brigades shifted their attack from this difficult target to an easier one.

Spillover effects are also evident in one other trend noted by Russell: Worldwide, the preponderance of attacks against the business community has shifted to locally owned businesses. United States firms operating abroad have witnessed a two-thirds decline in the proportion of attacks directed against them (from 22 percent in 1970–78 to only 7 percent in 1979–81) and all foreign firms showed a 50 percent fall; whereas the local business share of business-oriented attacks rose from 69 percent to 85 percent. One explanation for these shifts is that the greater resources available for security measures in large, multinational companies, particularly U.S.-based firms, have made smaller, local companies relatively more vulnerable. Similarly, because of the locally owned companies' smaller assets and their decisions not to carry ransom insurance, Russell notes that average ransom payments have fallen sharply—as has the number of incidents.[21] This later effect is a clear example of the effect of deterrence (broadly conceived) on kidnapping.

Policymakers must balance the costs of increased security against the probability of the threat and the reduction in those probabilities brought about by increased security. And they must also consider the precautions taken by their neighbors—one does not want to be the victim of spillover effects. Finally, good intelligence can greatly aid the planning of security operations by gearing security to specific threats.

COMPENSATION

We shall begin this section by showing that compensation for the assumption of risk is widespread in a variety of occupations, and then consider its use by business in terrorist environments.

The Evidence on Compensation for Risk

It is clear that the law allows the assumption of risk in employment and, in fact, casual observation indicates that it is a rather common occurrence. Movie stuntmen, policemen, and soldiers are examples. The hard evidence that extra compensation is paid for such an assumption, however, is more difficult to find. Often the added pay is hidden in the salary structure of an occupation. Sometimes, though, it is explicit, as in the combat pay of a soldier or hazard allowance in a number of other jobs where excessive risk is a common but avoidable attribute of the job. (The bomb squad on a police force, for example, often draws extra hazard pay.)

By statistical analysis of almost a thousand men, one major study has attempted to measure the risk premium associated with 36 unusually risky occupations.[22] The analysis demonstrated a distinct correlation of wages with risk of death in these occupations (while accounting for other influences on wages such as age and education). The extra compensation required for a person to work in an occupation with an increased probability of death of 0.001 was about $200 per year.[23] Therefore, a firm with a thousand employees receiving income similar to that in the cited study and a risk of death of one per thousand would pay about $200,000 per year in added compensation, compared to a perfectly safe company. Obviously, it would pay the firm to reduce the risks to zero—if it could do so for less than the added amount of compensation.

Applying the Evidence: Some Numerical Examples

The above results were obtained for workers with average annual earnings of about $6,600 (a bit less than average earnings among male manufacturing workers in

1967). Economic analysis agrees with common sense perceptions that the compensation for risk should rise with the economic status of an individual. A simple scaling up of the risk premium found in the industrial labor market suggests a figure of around $2,000 per year for someone earning ten times the industrial salary, at a probability of death of 0.001. If risks increased to 0.01, the premium would increase by a factor of ten to $20,000. These calculations are based on the risk of death. Compensation for less severe risks would be lower. Kidnapping, though a severe enough ordeal, does not usually result in death to the victim. In Argentina, from 1969 to 1978, terrorists kidnapped approximately 65 business executives. Of these, six were murdered and the rest were recovered without serious harm done to them.[24] Over this same ten-year period, about 25 other executives were murdered in terrorist attacks, along with a dozen bodyguards and bystanders.

This period of 1969 to 1978 in Argentina represents one of the most intense examples of terrorist kidnapping behavior in the modern, industrial world. Even so, the recorded number of business kidnappings was only about 6.5 per year (approximately three times that figure in the peak years); somewhat less than one out of ten kidnappings resulted in death to the victim. It is difficult to establish an appropriate base figure to calculate the probabilities of an individual business executive being kidnapped, but if there were 6,500 executives in the target pool, the risk of kidnapping would be about 0.001 per year on the average during this period, and the risk of death from kidnapping about one in ten thousand.[25] Risk of death from other terrorist attacks adds another 0.0004 probability of death, for a total of approximately 0.0005 (or 50 deaths per hundred thousand man-years of experience). For employees of U.S. companies in the peak-intensity terrorism years of 1972–74, the probability of being kidnapped was 0.0036 and the probability of death about 0.0004.[26] These probabilities can be compared to the risks in the dangerous occupations cited earlier[27] (Table 13.1). Business executives during that period in Argentina suffered a risk of death from terrorism at around the same rate as U.S. firemen and police in the 1960s.

Examination of the Argentine incidents by industry shows that one class of business—automobile production and sales—absorbed a disproportionate share of attacks. More than one quarter of all terrorist incidents aimed at businesses were directed against automobile companies. But these companies possessed large establishments employing thousands of employees, or they had many dispersed sales offices. In both cases, they presented targets that were larger or more available than an average business. It is not clear, therefore, whether the automobile companies suffered more per employee or per executive than might be expected.

Perceptions of Risk

An important aspect in considering compensation for risk is the perception of risk by those in danger. Interviews with foreign companies operating in terrorist environments disclose a two-phase pattern. Before an incident hits close to home, the view of those on the scene is that "it can't happen to me." They estimate the possibilities of terrorist acts as being remote; they consider themselves capable

Table 13.1 Sample of Dangerous Occupations and Risks (United States, 1955–1964)

Occupation	Risk*	Occupation	Risk*
Linemen and servicemen	2	Cranemen	147
Power plant workers	6	Sailors and deckhands	163
Firemen	44	Miners	176
Business Executives,	44	Marshals, constables,	
Argentina, 1969–78	40–50	sheriffs, and	
Police and detectives	78	bailiffs	181
Railroad brakemen	88	Taxicab drivers	182
Electricians	93	Structural iron workers	204
Truck drivers	98	Lumbermen	256
Longshoremen and stevedores	101	Guards, watchmen	267
Road machine operators	103		
Teamsters	114		

Source: Society of Actuaries, cited on Richard Thaler and Sherwin Rosen, "The Value of Saving a Life: Evidence from the Labor Market," in N. Terleckyj (ed.), *Household Production and Consumption* (New York: National Bureau of Economic Research, 1976). Based on 3.25 million policy years of workers' experience.

* Units of measure are extra deaths per 100,000 policy years. The expected number of deaths based on the age distribution of persons in each occupation was subtracted from the raw data to yield extra deaths attributable to the specific occupation. To convert to the probability of an extra death per year in each occupation, multiply figure by 0.00001.

and in control of the situation; they want their local venture to succeed and do not want excessive central control or withdrawal of support. After an event—usually not to themselves, but to someone with whom they identify—the local perception of risk shoots up well beyond that of outsiders. Now, headquarters cannot provide enough security, or care enough, or really understand the situation—in the view of those on the scene. This pattern of biases has been well described in the experimental literature on the psychology of risk assessment and the behavior of decisionmaking.[28] The implication of biased perceptions to a business firm is this: If independent, objective assessments are needed to make efficient decisions, information must be sought from outside the risky area. As the manager of an American company operating in El Salvador put it, "The local manager cannot make security decisions because he is too close to the problem." He advised hiring an external consulting firm to provide objective analysis.

Employee Mobility as a Factor in Risk Compensation

The notion of compensation for risk needs a slight amendment at this point. People require *extra* compensation for enduring an *increase* in risk. If an individual does not face a safer alternative, then he does not have to be paid to accept danger— regardless of what that level may be. For this reason, managers sent to a more risky environment than they have been accustomed to may require something extra to accept the job; local citizens, however, who live in the area and will continue to remain there do not have to be paid an extra amount. It is for this reason that a conflict sometimes arises between a company's headquarters that wants to withdraw its expatriate managers and shut down an operation and the local employees who fight to maintain the business. What is extra risk for one party is an unfortunate condition of life for the other.

Insurance as a Form of Compensation

One form of compensation to individuals is insurance. Life insurance, medical insurance, or payment for the pain and suffering (mental and physical) of a kidnapping is a substitute for compensation in current income. A number of economic analyses have indicated that with actuarially fair insurance, the extra compensation required does not change as a function of risk (it *will* change as a function of income).[29] In essence, the individual trades off some amount of current income for a large lump sum if the insured event actually transpires. The company faces the choice of whether it should buy the insurance for the individual or compensate the individual in cash and allow the employee to purchase the insurance himself if he so chooses. However, the greater the load or cost of insurance, the greater the amount of compensation to the individual that is required at a given level of risk. Since group insurance generally carries a much lower load than insurance purchased by individuals, there is an incentive for firms to provide insurance—kidnap, ransom, medical, life—to their employees who are at risk. Also, because of the general tendency for individuals to be averse to large risks, they would prefer the relative certainty of insurance to the alternative of regular payments of added income in combination with the small probability of a large, uncompensated loss.

An individual shows that he is risk-averse when he prefers a certainty to a gamble that has a higher expected value of outcome. For example, an individual is risk-averse when he chooses to take $10 rather than a 50-50 coin toss that pays nothing for heads and $21 for tails—an expected value of outcome of $10.50.) An individual who is averse to risk would prefer to buy insurance (whose premiums accurately reflect the underlying probabilities) than to take his chances with nature. With insurance, the premiums are fixed and a large part of the uncertainty of a loss is covered by the insurance. Therefore, anyone who buys insurance that carries a load or cost that makes it inferior to a fair gamble demonstrates aversity to risk.

RECOVERY

Expenditures on the recovery of a kidnap victim involve more than just the ransom to be paid after the event. Usually also included are the hiring of a firm specializing in negotiations, the daily costs of operatives, special operations (such as aircraft to deliver cash from one country to another), the time and attention of top management, and the restoration of the physical and emotional health of the victim. Recovery can also involve the search and forceful seizure of the victim from the terrorists. Although not a typical response—especially from private parties—this kind of behavior has been resorted to on a few occasions when recovery by other means seemed hopeless. In addition to activities taken during or after an incident, security and crisis planning before the event should also be considered an integral element of recovery programs. Despite the importance of all of these activities, we shall not consider them any further: Recovery operations are treated extensively elsewhere in this volume. For present analytical purposes, these activities can be grouped under the heading of general recovery costs.

Ransom Policy—To Pay or Not to Pay

Turning our attention to kidnap ransom, the first issue that a firm must confront is its policy toward payment. When considering this problem, firms will quickly find themselves in a dilemma. If all companies can agree in advance *not* to pay any ransom demands, this agreement should reduce the probability of terrorist kidnapping, especially in regions where kidnapping is intended primarily to raise funds for terrorist groups. If the probability of kidnapping falls because of an antiransom agreement, extra compensation will also decline, as will expected recovery costs.

Suppose, however, that deterrence fails and that an executive is seized by terrorists. Once this action occurs, a deterrence policy for the affected firm (and certainly, for the kidnapped individual) will probably not rank as high as the goal of recovering the seized executive. If the other firms that are party to the no-ransom agreement possess imperfect information on the ransom negotiations, and if their sanctions against violators are weak, the agreement will fall apart. Only if a terrorized firm, either voluntarily or under compulsion, agrees to give up its immediate goals in exchange for a greater common good, will a no-ransom agreement prevail. The fact that we do not observe such no-ransom agreements in force indicates that firms do not see sufficient benefits from collective action, possibly because it is very difficult to police the agreements and sanction offending members.

Four Ransom Policy Possibilities

Considering the problem from the executive's point of view, a dilemma arises again. There are four logically possible cases to analyze: (1) The firm announces that it will *not pay* ransoms, but actually *does;* (2) the firm announces it will *not pay* ransoms, and actually *does not;* (3) the firm announces it will *pay*, and *does;* and (4) the firm announces it will *pay*, but *does not*. For the same compensation under each policy, the individual will clearly find (1) to be the dominant choice and (4) to be the least preferred. His preferences between (2) and (3) will depend on an evaluation of how an announced policy of nonpayment affects the probability of his being kidnapped versus the consequences if a kidnapping actually occurs. That is, policy (3) increases the liklihood of a kidnapping *and* of a safe return should one take place; whereas (2) reduces the probability of both.

Of course, terrorists can also make these calculations and realize that an executive may proclaim a no-ransom policy but desire ransom to be paid if he happens to be the victim. Therefore, an important aspect of this issue is that the potential (and, sometimes, actual) targets are the same people who establish corporate policy. If one of their own becomes a victim, the decisionmakers are likely to identify closely with their unfortunate colleague; their attitudes toward principles of general welfare will tend to be displaced by immediate and personal values. Management should then evaluate the immediate benefits of capitulation against the losses engendered by abandoning their own no-ransom policy or the collapse of a cooperative agreement. Since the firm may have to exist for a long time in an environment with higher levels of terrorism and higher costs to itself, it could be in its best interests to maintain a stand against ransom payments. One of the most important elements of this management problem is the evaluation of how ransom payments influence the probability of kidnapping.[30] Unfortunately, we have little evidence on this central issue.

In light of this reasoning, any external constraints on a firm that reduce the firm's ability to negotiate ransom could help to preserve a no-ransom policy and therefore advance the public good of all firms. Enforced laws against ransom, sanctions by other firms against violators,[31] and good information on negotiations with terrorists (for example, by having representatives of other firms involved in a crisis management group) will all act to reduce the payment of ransom.

A perverse effect, however, may arise if companies are able to maintain no-ransom agreements. Individual executives could find it advantageous to purchase ransom insurance on their own. Personally acquired insurance would vitiate the intended effect of the corporate policy—terrorists would not care whether a ransom passed through the company or the individual on its way to their pockets. Unless the price of insurance to an individual were significantly higher than to the company, a company or industry policy could have little effect.[32]

The Probabilities of Kidnapping

The considerations involved in a firm's buying kidnap ransom insurance coverage for its employees are little different from those faced in other kinds of insurance. More generally, the question falls into the class of "make-or-buy" decisions: Should an activity be performed in-house, or should a specialized firm be given the job? The elements entering the kidnap ransom insurance decision include the probability of kidnap, the range of possible ransom payments (not *demands,* because these are usually reduced through negotiation), the price of insurance, and the internal capacity of the company to self-insure (i.e., the ability of the company to cover possible ransom payments through its own reserves and assets).

Argentina in the years 1972–74 can serve as a benchmark for measuring the probability of terrorist kidnapping of businessmen for ransom. Those years in that country probably witnessed the highest rate of this type of behavior in the industrialized world in the past 30 years. According to the chronologies of events published by the Rand Corporation, approximately 53 kidnappings of businessmen occurred in Argentina in the peak three-year period 1972–74.[33] Of these, 16 were directed against U.S.-owned businesses. According to several estimates, approximately 1,500 U.S. executives resided in Argentina during the early portion of this period.[34] (Somewhat more than 600 companies belonged to the American-Argentine Chamber of Commerce in 1979.)[35] These figures yield a probability of 0.0036 of an executive of a U.S. company being kidnapped.

Turning to the risk of death, we find that in 1972–74 in Argentina, about 6 percent of all kidnapped executives were killed. In Italy, also, in the four-year period 1974–77, 6 to 8 percent of kidnap victims were killed or vanished.[36] For the longer period of 1970–82 in Italy, approximately 6 percent of almost 500 criminal kidnap victims were killed. Over this same 12-year period, of 25 Italian political kidnappings, 13 percent (three victims) lost their lives in the incidents.[37] Russell claims that on a worldwide basis from 1970 to 1982, 9 percent of those persons taken by terrorist groups were killed—most often during police rescue operations.[38] These figures are somewhat larger than the reported worldwide experience of the specialist security firm of Control Risks; of 55 kidnappings on which Control Risks had advised, only two hostages (3.5 percent) failed to return safely.[39]

As should be clear now, these figures represent only the crudest attempts to arrive at a gross level of kidnap and death probabilities, but they do place some bounds on the estimates. The Argentine figures on risks to personnel of U.S.-based firms suggest odds of about three and a half kidnappings per thousand executives per year—in one of the most dangerous situations that American business-men have encountered. Such an estimate may be compared with the subjective assessments of those on the firing line. In a widely quoted article in the *Wall Street Journal*, for example, a U.S. banker in Argentina was reported to have gloomily stated, "If you look at the statistics of kidnappings of executives from major firms, you stand a one-in-10 chance of being caught."[40] If the estimates calculated here bear any resemblance to reality, the banker was almost 30 times too gloomy. The actual figures, however, are bad enough—at least 100 times worse than the risks in the United States. Insurance premiums reflect these differences.

Kidnap-Ransom Insurance Premiums

Over the past ten years or so, both the structure of the industry writing kidnap-ransom insurance and the type of policy have undergone substantial change. In the earlier years, Lloyds dominated the field; experience was limited; information was sparse; premiums were high; and policies were narrowly constructed. As experience accumulated, several other companies entered the field and introduced broader coverage along with lower premiums. For many years, a typical policy covered only a few key executives, with rates that varied with the geographical area in which the executives were located. More recently, policies are being written to cover all employees of a firm with the rates depending on the number of employees, income, and asset value. In the most high-risk areas, however, the older, limited type of policy is still the rule.

The first thing one notices in reviewing kidnap-ransom insurance premiums is the variation in the price. The lack of good data and the inherent inability to estimate solidly based probabilities generate differences in quoted prices that can vary by factors of two or three for the same coverage. With growing competition in the number of insurance companies dealing in this area, an insurance broker can shop for his client to get the lowest bids. Nevertheless, despite the necessarily subjective calculations by which premiums are established, they do vary with the risks, if only in a rough way.

In the mid-1970s, with only narrow coverage available, a large U.S. firm, operating in the United States with only infrequent trips by its executives to relatively safe areas (Great Britain, Northern Europe), would have paid around $0.01–$0.03 per hundred dollars face value of insurance, or about $100–$300 for $1 million maximum coverage for one executive per year. Increasing the number of people covered caused the premiums to rise, but somewhat less than proportionately. If the executives traveled to risky areas, the rate increased by three to ten times (to about $0.05–$0.30 per hundred). For an American executive who was a resident in a risky area, the rate rose to 75–150 times the base rate, or $1–$5 per hundred. Deductibles cut the costs considerably. One expert gave the following example: An Argentine subsidiary of an American multinational buying a policy with $5 million face value would pay about $2 per hundred for a single executive, or the same amount for four executives with $125,000 deductible.[41]

Broad coverage policies, as developed in the 1980s, usually provide protection for all employees and their families. A typical U.S.-based corporation with ordinary foreign activities that has $100 million in sales could probably purchase a $5 million limit policy for $5,000 in annual premiums, and a $10 million limit for $7,500. These premiums are equivalent to $0.10 and $0.075 per hundred.[42] Deductibles are used only in the most troubled areas and often there are no aggregate limits specified. For the dangerous areas of the world, however, the rates specified earlier for the narrow-coverage policies are still applicable.

Ransom Payment Experience

Insurance premiums, at least over the long run, should converge toward the expected level of payouts. This tendency is driven by competition. When competition is not intense, we can expect premiums to diverge from the actually determined levels. Indeed, this trend was observed over the past 10 to 15 years.

Although we do not have complete statistical distributions of ransoms, a few figures are available. In late 1973, newspaper reports implied average ransoms of $750,000 in Argentina for that year.[43] (In the United States, average ransoms paid are considerably smaller—about $36,000 in the mid-1970s; moreover, about 95 percent of these are recovered.)[44] Data reported in the Rand chronologies for Argentina and El Salvador yield the following estimates for average ransoms paid:

- 1972, Argentina, $414,000 (6 observations)
- 1973, Argentina, $2,345,000 (10 observations)
  $1,030,000 (9 observations)[45]
- 1975–79, El Salvador, $2,000,000 (10 observations)

Average ransoms from criminal kidnapping in Italy from 1970 to 1982 varied by a factor of ten over the years, from a high of $1.1 million in 1974 to a low of $114,000 in 1982. (For comparison purposes, the lira figures were converted to constant 1981 U.S. dollars.) For the seven Italian political kidnappings for which ransom figures are known, the average level was about $500,000 (1981 dollars).[46] These figures probably represent an overestimate of average ransoms paid in these countries because only the more spectacular sums would tend to be publicized by the terrorist organizations. In the few instances where both demands and actual payments are available, the latter can be as little as 10 percent of the former (although Russell implies average payout ratios of 50 to 80 percent of the ransom demand). Some care is required, therefore, in using published estimates. The experience in Argentina and El Salvador may be at the extreme upper end of the distribution, especially when compared to the rather low average ransom for the United States. Italy leans somewhat toward the high side in ransom payments, but not as high as the Latin American example.

What all this amounts to is that the average level of ransom payments, as well as their statistical distribution, should affect the cost of an insurance policy. Under certain conditions, therefore, deductibles can yield significant savings. If typical ransoms are less than $150,000 (for example) and a company could absorb such payments, but would find it difficult or impossible to come up with $5 million for a seized top-management official, insurance with a deductible amount may be the best choice—if the insurance companies reflect this experience in their rates. As mentioned in the previous section, for an American multinational in Argentina, inclusion of a $125,000 deductible would have enabled a company to quadruple the number of covered executives at the same premiums and maximum limits as without the deductible. Such a premium structure implies that about three fourths of the expected ransom payments are less than the deductible amount.

The observant reader will have noticed from the various estimates shown above that kidnap ransom insurance appears to have been overpriced. Consider, for example, Argentina in 1973. If kidnap probabilities were 0.01 (three times greater than the figures calculated above), and if average ransoms were $2.5 million (again, a figure on the high side), the average expected payout for a $5 million policy would have been no more than $25,000 (0.01 x $2.5 million). However, premiums for a $5 million policy at the typical rate of $2 per hundred (actual rates were as high as $5–$8 per hundred) would be $100,000. That is, the premiums were at least four times the expected payout. Such calculations are consistent with aggregate estimates of premiums and ransoms.

The average amount of ransom paid per year in the past 10 to 15 years is estimated at about $20–$30 million worldwide, with an increasing trend over this period.[47] Premiums, on the other hand, have been placed at $80–$100 million per year by these same sources. The gap between the figures is no doubt even larger than suggested since not all ransoms are insured. Unless these figures are grossly incorrect, it appears that premiums were running at least twice the average level of payouts. This is perhaps the reason that more companies are entering this business: In recent years, four to six companies have become active in the field. Of course, it is necessary to realize that information has been gradually accumulating over this period. In the early 1970s, little was known about kidnap probabilities or ransoms. Insurance underwriters were working in largely unknown areas. With the growth of information and competition, prices are coming closer to experience-based levels of risk, and the range of insurance options is expanding.

Insurance and Security

Tradeoffs between ransom insurance and security measures have been recognized explicitly by Lloyds in their premium structure. A client that undergoes a Control Risks security survey receives a premium discount of up to 20 percent.[48]

Several of the major insurance carriers provide access to the services of security response teams in the event of a terrorist incident. This is equivalent to bringing a claims adjustor on to the scene to help limit loss while the event is still in progress.

Factors other than security over which executives have some degree of control also affect rates. One of the more important is lifestyle. Lavish and highly visible behavior will drive up rates, as will inattention to simple security precautions, such as varying one's habits. Other factors, however, can not be manipulated by firms— its product line, nationality, and reputation or general knowledge of the corporate name. Some insurance underwriters say that these company variables can influence rates by at least as much as the region or country in which the company operates.

In summary, all of the elements of the security, compensation, and recovery package are tied together—they affect each other; analysis is possible; and information is often available, but it must be searched for. More important than any one piece of data is a notion of what to do with the information you have.

NOTES

1.   In addition to or instead of ransom, terrorists have occasionally demanded other things from firms in exchange for the return of the kidnapped employees. These have included food for the poor, publication of political tracts, hiring of more workers, and a variety of social actions. However, in this chapter, we only consider terrorists' ransom demands. The analysis, therefore, is also applicable to criminal kidnapping.

2.   George M. Camp, "Nothing to Lose: A Study of Bank Robbery in America," Ph.D. diss. (Yale University, 1967), pp. 15–16, 144.

3.   For specific examples of such behavior, see Susanna Purnell and Eleanor Wainstein, "The Problems of U.S. Businesses Operating Abroad in Terrorist Environments," Rand Paper Series No. R–2842–DOC (Santa Monica, CA: The Rand Corporation, 1981), pp. 27–29.

4.   Additional compensation will be required when employees have equivalent job possibilities at lower risk, or higher pay at the same risk. Without such alternatives, market forces do not require compensation for risk.

5.   These compensating variations are rather fully described in the *Wealth of Nations,* particularly in Book 1, Chapter 10, part 1: "Inequalities arising from the nature of the employments themselves." The Modern Library (Random House), New York, 1937; pp. 100–118.

6.   Even if police or fire protection is purchased privately and the service is only provided to the purchasers, others may benefit when, for example, a thief is jailed or a fire, which endangers other structures, is quickly extinguished.

7.   Russell, Chapter 2.

8.   Pisano, Chapter 5.

9.   Russell, Chapter 2; Eitzen and Barkey, Chapter 12.

10.   Timothy H. Hannan, "Bank Robberies and Bank Security Precautions," *Journal of Legal Studies,* 11 (January 1982), pp. 88–89.

11.   Camp, pp. 110–114.

12.   Hannan, p. 91.

13.   Camp, p. 144.

14.   This subject is treated more completely elsewhere in this book.

15.   In addition to salary, it is also necessary to account for fringes, operations (travel, hotels, special equipment, etc.), and overhead (scheduling and planning, secretarial, etc.).

16.   An analogy here is a large herd of cattle from which only a few are selected each year for slaughter. If some cattle could somehow act to reduce the probability of their selection—perhaps by being at the other end of the pasture—their survival probabilities would rise, but those of the other cattle would fall.

17.   Of course, this could lead to bluffing, but we shall not go into that subject here.

18.   The analogy now is closer to hunting game than to slaughtering cattle. In this case, the probability of a kill depends on the number or density of targets. Increasing security reduces the number available. If some of the deer of the forest took precautions by keeping away from roads and trails, hunters would bag fewer number of game for similar efforts than in previous years.

19.   Russell, Chapter 2.

20.   Russell, Chapter 2.

21.   Russell, Chapter 2

22.   Richard Thaler and Sherwin Rosen, "The Value of Saving a Life: Evidence from the Labor Market," in Nestor Terleckyj (ed.), *Household Production and Consumption* (New York: National Bureau of Economic Research, 1976), pp. 265–298.

23.   *Ibid.,* p. 292. This figure is for 1967 dollars and for workers below the average industrial wage.

24.   Purnell and Wainstein, pp. 64–80. The number of unreported incidents is difficult to estimate; one source places the figure at "several times" the reported number (Eitzen and Barkey, Chapter 12). However, in most of these incidents, it was the victim's family rather than employer from whom the kidnappers sought ransom.

25.   If we consider the top five people of a company to be at risk, then our assumed figure of 6,500 people implies a target pool of about 1,300 companies. There were 1,500 members in the Argentina Chamber of Commerce, Industry, and Production.

26.   These calculations are made in the following section on recovery.

27.   Thaler and Rosen, p. 288.

28.   James P. Kahan, "How Psychologists Talk About Risk," Rand Paper Series P–6403 (Santa Monica, CA: The Rand Corporation, 1979), pp. 14–15.

29.   Thaler and Rosen, p. 276; M. W. Jones-Lee, *The Value of Life: An Economic Analysis* (Chicago: University of Chicago Press, 1976), p. 101.

30.   Much of this argument is derived from an unpublished paper by my colleague Steve Salant.

31.   One device aimed at motivating nonpayment of ransom is the payment of a large bond into a pool maintained by some policing agency—either a collective of firms or a government agency. The bond would be forfeited if ransom were payed.

32.   Prices would be higher to an individual if insurance companies provided such policies at bargain rates to protect their other business with large corporate clients, or if they offered the policies as loss leaders, or if the transactions costs of dealing with many small buyers drove up the costs to individuals.

33.   Purnell and Wainstein, pp. 64–80.

34.   *The New York Times,* "Foreigners in Argentina Growing Wary," August 8, 1973, p. 10; *Business Week,* "Coping With Terrorism in Argentina," March 9, 1974, p. 40.

35.   *The New York Times,* "Argentine Policies Please U.S. Business," December 7, 1979, p. 8.

36.   John Savage, "Terrorists v. Bodyguards," *Top Security,* 3 (February 1978), p. 305.

37.   Pisano, Chapter 5.

38.   Russell, Chapter 2.

39.   *The New York Times,* "Where Kidnapping Is Business," December 27, 1979, p. 27.

40.   *Wall Street Journal,* "In Argentina, Business Is Thriving—At Least for All the Kidnappers," June 13, 1973, p. 1.

41.   Roger M. Williams, "Executive Kidnapping—The Rise of a Grim New Business," *Saturday Review,* January 5, 1980, p. 16.

42.   These figures were provided by William L. Pope, senior vice president of John Burnham and Company, insurance brokers. These rates are not directly comparable to the rates cited above for the narrower type of insurance that just covered a few individuals. The rate *per person covered* of the broader policies would be a tiny percentage of the older policies.

43.   *The New York Times,* "Most Foreigners Are Undaunted by Latin Violence," December 2, 1973, p. 24.

44.   *The Washington Post,* "Parade Magazine," January 8, 1978, p. 13.

45.   If one extreme outlier is omitted from the data, the average ransom is cut in half. The omitted observation is the $14.2 million paid for the return of Victor Samuelson, Esso oil refinery general manager.

46.   Pisano, Chapter 5.

47.   See, for example, *The New York Times,* "Business Fights Terrorism on Its Own," November 19, 1979, Section IV, p. 1; *Security World,* "Insurance Against Terrorism a New Defense" (quoting Risks International), October 1981, p. 21.

48.   Williams, p. 18.

14

Terrorism: Legal Aspects of Corporate Responsibility

Charles Ruff
Mary Helen Gallagher
William Lee Saunders, Jr.

The legal issues posed by acts of terrorism against multinational corporations are, as the *Curtis* decision described below reveals, in some respects susceptible to routine analysis but are likely to arise in unfamiliar factual settings. This chapter discusses the extent to which standard legal principles governing employer-employee relationships offer guidance to corporate officials and their counsel. In addition it highlights some of the special problems that may be confronted in litigation arising out of terrorist kidnappings and suggests how the courts may respond, as well as how corporations may protect themselves against liability stemming from such incidents.

EXAMPLE: THE CURTIS KIDNAPPING

On September 28, 1976, Gustavo Curtis was kidnapped on the streets of Bogotá, Colombia, by terrorists who held him hostage for almost eight months before releasing him in exchange for a ransom of over 15 million pesos (about $500,000). These events would probably have gone unnoticed (except by those immediately involved) and would have been recorded only in brief newspaper accounts were it not for the fact that Mr. Curtis, after the payment of the ransom, brought suit against the Beatrice Foods Company, the parent company of his employer. He alleged that it was responsible for his capture and extended confinement. That lawsuit gives us a glimpse of both the background of the kidnapping and the efforts made to secure Mr. Curtis's release; it is also one of the very few reported decisions dealing with the responsibility of corporations for the welfare of their foreign-based executives.

Background

Curtis had gone to Bogotá from Venezuela in 1969 to manage a company by the name of Fabrica de Dulces Gran (Fabrica)—although, so the court found, he and his wife knew that Colombia had a long and current history of violence and that kidnappings for ransom "were virtually day-to-day news." In 1971 Fabrica, which was wholly owned by Beatrice, was consolidated with another company to form Industrias Gran Colombia, S.A. (Industrias), and Curtis became the general manager of that company. Industrias was wholly owned by five companies, which in turn were wholly owned by Beatrice.

In July 1976 Curtis was called to the American embassy, shown a picture of himself that had been found in the possession of an "underworld figure," and told that he might be a kidnap target. Shortly thereafter, the head of Beatrice's Latin America operations visited Bogotá, and Curtis took him to the embassy to see the picture and discuss the danger of a kidnapping. Curtis asked to be transferred but was told that the Beatrice official did not have the necessary authority and would have to talk to his superiors in Chicago. Curtis continued to press his request during the next two months but was told that no other openings were available.

On September 28, 1976, Curtis was being driven home from work when his driver turned off the main road into a narrow street. Their path was blocked by two cars, and Curtis was abducted at gunpoint, taken to an unknown location, and held in a 4 x 8 ft. cell until his release on May 18, 1977. Immediately on being informed of the kidnapping, Beatrice assigned responsibility for the matter to their head of security, a former FBI agent named Klein, and he in turn retained a security consultant, Control Risks, to deal with the situation on the scene.

In a note sent to Industrias's attorney, the kidnappers initially demanded a ransom of $5 million and said that they would negotiate with "the company." Control Risks recommended that Beatrice, which had secured kidnap insurance covering its executives and those of its subsidiaries, counteroffer no more than $100,000 until the terrorists lowered their demand. In almost 40 telephone contacts between Control Risks and the kidnappers from October 1976 to April 1977, the ransom figure was eventually negotiated down to the final amount of around 15 million pesos. Negotiations were hampered by the unfriendly attitude of the Colombian authorities, who were concerned that the amount of any ransom not serve to encourage further kidnappings,[1] and were affected as well by the efforts of Mr. Klein to establish that the kidnapping was actually a hoax designed to extract money for Curtis from Beatrice. Mrs. Curtis was even brought to Beatrice headquarters, where she consented to take, and passed, a lie detector test.

In the months following his release, Curtis and his wife vacationed in the United States while he recuperated from his ordeal. Although physically in reasonable health, he suffered lingering psychological effects. In November 1977, Curtis informed Beatrice for the first time that he was unwilling to return to Colombia, but his superiors told him that they expected him to resume his work there. Negotiations continued into 1978, but eventually Industrias terminated Curtis's employment after paying all salary and other sums due him.

Lawsuit

On March 3, 1978, Curtis filed suit in New York Supreme Court against Beatrice Foods Company.[2] The complaint set forth a variety of claims arising out of the kidnapping and confinement of Curtis, but the principal theme was that Beatrice had negligently violated its duty as Curtis's employer to protect him and had negligently carried out its duty to rescue him once he had been kidnapped. In addition the complaint alleged a breach of contract between Beatrice and Curtis, loss of consortium on behalf of Mrs. Curtis, and willful misconduct giving rise to claims for punitive damages. After considerable pretrial motion activity, these claims were all but abandoned, and the case was actually tried on three entirely different theories: First, that Curtis was entitled to recover under Colombia's labor code—the equivalent of a workmen's compensation statute; second, that he was entitled to recover under the Colombian Civil Code for injuries resulting from Beatrice's refusal to transfer him before the kidnapping; and third, that Beatrice had breached its duty under the civil code to exercise due care in its efforts to rescue him.

The Labor Code Claim

The theory underlying the Labor Code claim was that Curtis, as an employee of Beatrice, was entitled to recover for injuries sustained as a result of what he claimed was a "work accident." Finding that Curtis had entered into a written contract directly with Fabrica; that Industrias operated virtually independently of Beatrice and that Curtis had almost complete authority to manage its affairs; that Curtis's salary was paid directly by Industrias, although he participated in Beatrice's stock option plan; and that Beatrice's power to cause Curtis's discharge was no more than the authority always implicit in the owner of a company's stock, Judge Pollack rejected the essential premise of this claim—that Curtis was employed by Beatrice. He also found that, in any event, the kidnapping did not, under the law of Colombia, have a sufficiently direct and causal relationship to Curtis's employment to be considered a "work accident." Curtis may instead have been targeted because of his and his wife's high visibility in the Bogotá community. Mrs. Curtis, for example, was a "well known . . . personality" on Colombian television.

The Civil Code Claims

Judge Pollack next addressed the claim that Beatrice had caused Curtis's injuries by its "fault" in refusing to transfer him to another position before the kidnapping. First, he concluded that Beatrice had no obligation to effectuate such a transfer, pointing out that Curtis had full authority to take whatever protective measures were required and that Beatrice had never promised to transfer him if he were subjected to a kidnapping threat. Curtis was free to leave Colombia if he thought it necessary; by remaining with notice of the danger, even if he would have lost his job by leaving, he assumed the risk of being kidnapped.

In 1975 Curtis had attended a meeting of managers of Beatrice's international subsidiaries at which a representative of Control Risks had described precautions to be taken to minimize the risk of kidnapping and the audience was advised that Control Risks was available for individual assistance in security matters. Curtis attended a similar lecture at the U.S. embassy in Bogotá in early 1976. Nonetheless, the court found, he had taken no steps to implement any security precautions. The court also pointed out that, under Colombian law, only two forms of damage were recoverable—pecuniary loss and "moral damages." The former had been taken care of by the payment to Curtis, while the latter, limited by statute to 2,000 pesos ($60), covers only "psychic depression" brought on by permanent disfigurement.

With respect to the claim that Beatrice was liable for delaying Curtis's release, Judge Pollack noted that under Colombian law the doctrine of the "officious agent" (the equivalent in some respects of the American "Good Samaritan" doctrine) creates liability only where the agent acts with intent to injure or with "grave fault" or where he prevents another from acting, in which case simple fault is sufficient. The judge found that Beatrice had not prevented Mrs. Curtis from seeking other assistance and also found that Beatrice and Control Risks had conducted the negotiations without any fault, grave or otherwise. He characterized Beatrice's decision to retain a consultant experienced in kidnapping matters as "conscientious" and found that the company "reasonably and fairly accepted and followed the advice of its hired experts." Rejecting the notion that he should "second guess the whole negotiation process," the judge refused to speculate whether the company could have secured Curtis's release at an earlier date by offering more money sooner and concluded by saying, ". . . [I]t would seem that Beatrice did quite well simply to get Mr. Curtis out alive."

KIDNAPPING AND THE COMMON LAW

Before discussing a corporation's responsibility for injuries to its personnel as the result of terrorist activity, it is useful to set out the common law duties generally owed by employers to their employees.[3] Liability principles applicable solely to terrorism and its reverberations have not been developed in the case law. Until such principles are developed (and that time seems far away given the limited number of cases), a court will look to this general body of law for guidance.

The common law has imposed a number of duties on the employer for the protection of the employee: An employer must warn of unsafe conditions in the workplace and take steps to protect the employee; must aid an injured or endangered employee; and, in certain circumstances, must protect the employee from third parties. The extent of these duties in any particular situation is governed by a reasonableness standard, so that, for example, the duty to protect or warn will depend on the type of work to be performed and the dangers it normally entails. Of course, if the employer knows that unusual dangers are present, the degree of care required will be greater. Even if the employer breaches one of these duties, however, it may not be liable if the employee was contributorily negligent or assumed the risk of injury.

Common Law Duties

The Duty to Warn

The principle that an employer must warn the employee of dangers in the workplace is well established.[4] This duty extends to any dangers of which the employer has notice[5] but about which, or the extent of which, the employee neither is nor should be aware.[6] Notice will be imputed to the employer if other employees with a responsibility to report to the employer learn of possible danger.[7] Even if the employee is aware of the danger, the employer will be required to exercise ordinary care to shield the employee from any obvious danger.[8]

The duty to warn, tempered by a reasonableness standard, does not require an employer to warn of remote or improbable dangers, but the duty does encompass potential criminal acts of a third party if the employer knew of the risk but the employee did not.[9]

The Duty to Protect

Paralleling the duty to warn an employee is the duty to protect. In practice there will often be little difference in the two doctrines; to protect an employee in a given situation may involve giving a warning. An employer is required to inspect the workplace and take reasonable precautions against any defects or dangers discovered.[10] This duty includes protection of an employee against criminal acts by third parties if (as with the duty to warn) such acts are foreseeable.[11] In a leading case,[12] a female employee, working at night in an unsafe area, was assaulted when she answered a knock at the door. It was impossible to ascertain the identity of the person at the door without opening it. The Supreme Court held that the employer, who was aware of these facts, was required to take precautions against the danger.[13] Similar reasoning has been applied to other types of criminal conduct such as robbery[14] and violence directed at the employee because of the nature of his job.[15]

Where similar duties exist, similar rules of liability for criminal acts by third parties have been applied.[16] Thus, it has been held that, unless prison officials had notice of extraordinary danger, they owed inmates only the duty of ordinary care,[17] but a bank in a high crime area may be liable if it takes fewer precautions than similarly situated banks and a customer is injured in a robbery.[18]

Again, as with the duty to warn, no duty to protect arises if the employer is justifiably unaware, or has no notice, of the danger.[19] It is, of course, impossible to predict what facts will or will not constitute notice, but years of operation without incident may permit an employer to assume the workplace is safe, even from the criminal acts of third parties.[20]

An important aspect of the common law duty to protect is that it is not limited to the physical workplace but extends to other areas within the employer's control. Hence, an employee may be entitled to protection even though his work day is finished[21] or he is not working when injured.[22] The employee must, however, be within the scope of his employment when injured. Generally, an employee in the workplace or on property under the employer's control will be acting within the scope of his employment; however, some activities such as commuting are *not* within the scope of employment.[23] Once the employee has left the premises for his own purposes, he steps outside the scope of his employment and remains outside until he resumes his duties.[24]

Terrorism and Corporate Liability

Warning the Employee

Much of the previous discussion is applicable to a corporation with operations in a foreign country.[25] If a corporation is considering assigning personnel to a country in which it knows there is danger to business executives from terrorism, it is obligated to warn its employees. If it does not warn them or does so incompletely, it may be liable if an employee is injured by terrorists. Since knowledge of certain of its employees may be imputed to it, the prudent corporation would also assure itself that at least its middle- and upper-level employees have been advised to pass along any information they obtain about possible terrorist activity.

Even if the danger from terrorists were so widely known as to be obvious to everyone, a prudent employer would be wise to apprise his employees of that danger. Although merely learning about potential terrorist activity will not render the employer liable for subsequent acts of violence, the employer must recognize that the reasonableness of his conduct will be determined after the fact by a court weighing the evidence with the benefit of hindsight. Thus, a wise course would be to err on the side of overwarning. Of course, certain information may indeed be so remote or implausible that it can safely be disregarded, but the corporate employer will want to be conservative in making such evaluations.

The precautions required of the employer will be greater as the indices of potential violence increase, but at a minimum, an employer beginning or continuing operations in another country must evaluate thoroughly the terrorist "climate" and decide what, if any, protective steps are necessary. Obtaining such information will not subject the employer to an increased risk of liability. Indeed, under the common law duty to inspect the workplace, failure to investigate could render the corporation liable in negligence. Although an employer is not liable for the unforeseeable, a distinction must be made between unexpected acts and expected but "sudden" acts. If an employer knows that a terrorist attack is likely, the timing of that attack will probably not be significant in determining liability.

Protecting the Employee

If an employer chooses to operate in an area where the risk of terrorist activity is significant, the company must take affirmative steps to protect its employees. Although the reasonableness standard provides no definite answer to the question "What steps must be taken?" as an initial step the employer should consider retaining experts to give advice on security matters. The mere employment of experts will not insulate the employer from liability, but it will serve as evidence of a reasonable response. The fact that Beatrice had provided Curtis with lectures by experts on how to avoid a terrorist kidnapping, for example, was one factor cited by the court in its finding that, even if Beatrice had been Curtis's employer, it had discharged its duty to him.

Under what is sometimes known as the "Good Samaritan" doctrine, if one renders services to another that are necessary for that person's protection, those services may not be rendered negligently.[26] For example, if an employer provides chauffeur-driven "armored" cars to transport important employees to work, and the route taken is so predictable as to facilitate a terrorist attack, a corporation could face liability.[27]

In an emergency, a person only need exercise such judgment as is reasonable under the circumstances, in other words, not judgment of the kind that would be required if reflection were possible.[28] During a terrorist attack, this emergency doctrine would govern, and steps to repel or otherwise deal with the terrorists (as opposed to whatever actions were necessary in *anticipation* of such an attack) would be judged by their reasonableness under these special circumstances.

The passage of time will dilute an emergency. Once the immediacy of the initial attack has passed, a higher standard of conduct will be required. Also, once the assault has ceased, the corporation should evaluate precautions previously taken to see if they were adequate. If any future attacks occur, protective measures will be tested by insights (or notice) that *should* have been gained from the first attack.

Dealing with a Kidnapping

What must the corporation do if an employee has been kidnapped? The Good Samaritan rule renders it liable if it undertakes to rescue the employee, through negotiations or otherwise, and then performs negligently. On the other hand, an employer has a duty to aid an endangered employee, and, in any event, nonlegal corporate concerns will presumably militate in favor of attempting to secure the employee's release.

Although an employer has a duty to rescue an employee injured or endangered in the course of his employment, that duty has never been explicitly extended to the terrorist context. The cases focus on medical aid (including aid for nonwork-related illness); and rescue cases in whatever context (as when a seaman falls overboard), though there may be time for deliberation, typically involve situations where prompt action might succeed. With a terrorist kidnapping, this is not likely to be true. Nevertheless, a court may well hold that an employer, at a minimum, could not ignore the plight of an employee kidnapped in the course of his employment, even through no fault of the employer.

In any case, if a duty did arise, that duty certainly would not require that the corporation go it alone. It has been held in a nonemployment context that, if criminal acts of third parties create unreasonable risks, the person owing the duty may seek police assistance,[29] and this rule would presumably be extended to the employment context. Indeed, any action that would increase the danger to either the rescuer or the victim would appear on its face to be unreasonable.

One of the most difficult questions a corporation faces is whether to seek assistance from police or other authorities. As seems to have been the case with the Curtis kidnapping, it may well be that the police will be more interested in capturing the terrorists or, at least, in limiting the size of the ransom, than in rescuing the victim. It is difficult, but not impossible, to conceive of an American court's finding an employer negligent in having gone to the police, but it may well be more troublesome to convince a court after the fact that a decision *not* to seek official assistance was reasonable.

If the decision is made to try to secure the employee's release, the employer should realize that liability could result from either (a) negligent performance of whatever portion of the task it undertakes, or (b) deliberate interference with, or prevention of, another potential "rescue."[30] Thus, even though there is no absolute obligation to pay ransom, a company could not unilaterally break off negotiations. Likewise, while it may be prudent to dissuade rescue attempts by other interested parties such as family members, the company must not unreasonably obstruct any efforts they may make.

Employee Responsibilities

Even if the corporation was negligent, it may escape liability if the injured employee was either contributorily negligent or assumed the risk of injury. Although the distinction between the two doctrines is not of major practical concern since either may bar or limit liability, they may be distinguished as follows: When the dangers encountered are those typically incident to the job, the doctrine involved is assumption of the risk; when the dangers are not such ordinary ones, an employee's voluntary exposure to them would be contributory negligence. In extreme circumstances, assumption of the risk would itself constitute contributory negligence because no reasonable person would voluntarily subject himself to certain dangers.[31] In considering whether either doctrine applies, the following factors may be evaluated: as between the employer and the employee, relative control of the activities involved, relative knowledge of the danger faced, and relative ability to eliminate the danger; the voluntariness of the employee's conduct; the alternatives available; and the obviousness of the danger.[32]

The general rule is that there is no contributory negligence if the employee has no reasonable alternative but to proceed despite the risk[33] or to take on the risk or be fired ("economic necessity").[34] These principles appear to have been modified somewhat when the risk being assumed is criminal action by third parties. Courts sometimes find that requests for additional security indicate the employee had the requisite knowledge of the danger and that, by not removing himself from it, he was contributorily negligent. In one case,[35] a service station employee who continued to work in a high crime area after his protests were ignored was injured in a hold-up: the court found him contributorily negligent. Compare the *Curtis* decision with this case: Curtis was familiar with the situation in Colombia before taking the job there. A different issue might be posed if an employee were hired by a firm with operations in many countries and then transferred into a country with a high risk of terrorist activity.

Thus it may be that the doctrines of assumption of the risk and contributory negligence are weakening the employer's duty to protect employees from the criminal acts of third parties. Nonetheless, it is unlikely that a court will find that an employee assumed the risk where the employer could have remedied the situation by ordinary caution or where the employee reasonably believed the employer was addressing the danger.[36] Further, in order to avoid the economic necessity defense to an allegation of assumption of the risk, the employer should make clear its willingness to transfer employees who are faced with the risk of terrorist incidents.[37]

ISSUES OF LIABILITY

This section will consider the most significant issues which are likely to arise if a corporation is sued in the United States by an employee, or the employee's family, for injuries arising out of the kidnapping of the employee by terrorists. Because lawsuits arising out of corporate kidnappings have been infrequent, and resolution of many of the issues involved will vary from state to state, this discussion seeks only to identify the questions on which corporate officials should focus and to suggest the answers a court might give.

Theories of Liability

A lawsuit against a corporation, arising out of the kidnapping and death of a corporate employee, will typically involve one or more of three statutory causes of action—wrongful death, survival, or worker's compensation. An action for wrongful death is designed to compel the party at fault to recompense a decedent's beneficiaries for the injuries they have suffered by virtue of the decedent's death. A survival action, on the other hand, is concerned with injuries not to the decedent's beneficiaries but to the decedent; a survival statute allows certain causes of action accruing to a person to "survive" his death and permits them to be brought by his estate. Under a worker's compensation statute, an employee covered by worker's compensation who suffers a personal injury arising out of and in the course of employment will be compensated for medical expenses and lost wages.

Wrongful Death Statutes

As noted, the purpose of a wrongful death statute is to compensate a deceased's family for the loss it suffered from his death; the deceased's own injuries are not at issue.[38] The proper party to bring a wrongful death action is typically "the personal representative" of the decedent's estate, in many jurisdictions a term synonymous with *administrator* or *executor* of an estate. Under wrongful death statutes, recovery typically is vested in designated beneficiaries and does not inure to the estate (and thus is not reachable by the decedent's creditors).[39] One class of beneficiaries, in other words, spouses and children, is generally presumed to have sustained pecuniary loss and is not required to prove dependency on the deceased, while parents and siblings must prove dependency to establish a right of recovery.

The availability of compensatory and punitive damages varies. Punitive damages may be awarded in cases where the defendant's conduct was either intentional or the result of gross negligence; however, some states do not allow any recovery for such damages in wrongful death actions. Depending upon the statutory and case law of a particular state, compensatory damages may be recovered for some or all of the following losses.

- Loss of financial support from the reasonably expected earning capacity of the decedent
- Loss of services of the decedent
- Loss of the society of the decedent, including loss of companionship, consortium, care, assistance and counsel
- Loss of prospective inheritance
- Pain and suffering, including mental anguish, incurred by the beneficiaries

Most states, in one form or another, allow recovery for all of the items listed above except the last one; many states prohibit recovery for the beneficiaries' pain and suffering.

Although the statute sets out the damages recoverable in a wrongful death action, the case law frequently expands or restricts the apparent meaning of the statute. For example, the Washington wrongful death statute provides only that "the jury may give such damages as, under all circumstances of the case, may to them seem just,"[40] but the courts have held that neither punitive damages nor damages for the beneficiaries' pain and suffering are allowed.[41]

When, as would likely be the case with the death of a corporate executive, a family's principal wage earner dies, the main element of damage is loss of support, measured by what the decedent could have been expected to contribute to the support of the statutory beneficiaries had he lived. The wrongful death statutes are generally silent as to how to compute that support, but the Washington cases, for example, have developed a measure of recovery based on the probable current cash worth of the decedent's net earnings had he lived to his normal life expectancy. They suggest that the decedent's personal expenses, including cost of living expenses, gifts, entertainment and medical care, should be deducted from probable future gross income to reach the net.[42]

The computation of punitive damages, if allowed, and of damages for noneconomic injuries such as pain and suffering and loss of consortium is within the discretion of the jury. Against a corporate defendant these damages can be enormous. The Supreme Court of Florida upheld a punitive damages award of $800,000 against a defendant whose net worth was $13,145,000, stating that it was proper for the jury to consider the defendant's net worth and impose punitive damages that would hurt, but not bankrupt.[43]

Survival Statutes

Survival statutes merely preserve, as an asset of a decedent's estate, whatever causes of action he would have had if he had lived. Thus, if a kidnap victim, before he died, suffered loss of income, pain and suffering, or physical injuries as a result of being kidnapped, a survival statute might permit his estate to recover for these injuries. Like the wrongful death action, a survival action is a creature of statute, and the nature of the action can only be determined by reference to a particular state statute and the gloss put on it by the case law.[44]

As in a wrongful death action, the decedent's personal representative is usually the proper plaintiff. The action is brought for the benefit of the deceased's estate, and in a particular case may be used by family members who are the deceased's heirs but who would not qualify as beneficiaries under the wrongful death statute. As with wrongful death actions, punitive damages and a variety of compensatory damages may be available under a survival statute.[45] The compensatory damages recoverable in the type of survival action at issue here, in addition to damages for pain and suffering, usually include the deceased's medical expenses, his burial expenses, and his lost earnings from the time of injury to the time of death. Some states also allow recovery of the probable future earnings of the decedent, had he lived.[46] Plaintiffs in these cases are, of course, entitled to trial by jury, and damage awards area almost wholly within the jury's province, subject to reversal only if the verdict is so excessive that it "shocks the conscience" or is the result of "passion or prejudice".[47]

Worker's Compensation

The kidnapping of a corporate executive by terrorists and any resulting injuries could be covered by a state worker's compensation law. If so, it would be the exclusive remedy available, and the employer would not otherwise be liable for any injury or death arising out of the employment. The amount of money recoverable under a worker's compensation law would be much less than, indeed insignificant compared to, the amount potentially recoverable under a wrongful death or survival action.

A typical worker's compensation act has these features:[48]

1. An employee is automatically entitled to certain benefits whenever he or she suffers a personal injury arising out of and in the course of employment.
2. Fault is irrelevant.
3. Coverage is limited to persons having the status of employee.
4. Benefits to the employee include cash-wage benefits, usually around one half to two thirds of the employee's average weekly wage, and hospital and medical expenses; in death cases benefits for dependents are provided; arbitrary maximum limits are imposed on the amount and duration of benefits.
5. In exchange for these modest but assured benefits, the employees give up their rights to sue the employer for any injury covered by the act.
6. To be covered by the law, an employer must pay insurance premiums into the state's worker's compensation fund.

Thus, the three questions that are critical in determining whether a worker's compensation statute applies to the kidnapping and death of a corporate executive by terrorists are:

1. Was the executive an employee of the United States corporation (as opposed to being the employee of the foreign branch or subsidiary)?
2. Did the kidnapping and death arise out of and in the course of employment?
3. Does the worker's compensation statute cover an injury that occurred in a foreign country?

Whether the U.S. corporation was the "employer" will depend on the applicable state statute's definition of the term and the exact nature of the relationship between the executive and the U.S. corporation.[49] The analysis in the *Curtis* decision[50] is indicative of how the courts may approach this issue.

Although there are no reported cases in which a U.S. worker's compensation statute was applied to a corporate kidnapping, depending on the facts of a particular case, a strong argument can be made that injuries from a kidnapping did "arise out of and in the course of employment." Under the "positional risk" theory, increasingly used by the courts, an injury arises out of the course of employment if it would not have occurred but for the fact that the conditions and obligations of the employment placed the employee in the position where he was injured.[51]

For example, an employee who had been repairing tires in his employer's garage was injured when, as a result of an altercation with one of his customers, the employee fired a shot at his customer, which ricocheted and hit the employee: The injury was held to be within the course of the employee's employment.[52] Similarly when a stray arrow shot by a child in a neighboring yard struck a butcher's helper in the eye as he was on his way to empty trash, the injury was held to be covered by worker's compensation.[53]

In several cases, American courts have applied a state worker's compensation law to an employee's death that occurred in a foreign country. For example, a New York court held that when the employee of a New York firm who was sent to Israel on business was shot by an Arab while on a sightseeing trip there, he was acting "within the scope and course of his employment" at the time of death.[54] The court concluded that there was a "New York employment,"[55] noting that the employer hired the employee in New York; the employer directed the activities of the employee at various places outside New York; the employer's business was done outside New York on instructions that came directly from New York; the employee was paid from New York; the employee was considered to be an employee of the New York office; and the employee was paid expense money when away from New York, including airplane transportation back to New York. The court also found that even though the employee was on a voluntary personal sightseeing trip when he was killed, he was within the scope of his employment. A significant fact in the court's view was that the employer had sent the employee to Israel, knowing it to be a country where there had been warfare for a long time and where an uneasy truce was in effect.[56]

Choice of Law

The question of which jurisdiction's law will be applied is one of the most important facing the court, for, as the previous discussion makes clear, its resolution may well determine the rights of the parties. One principle is clear: the forum will apply its own choice-of-law rule. A state court will apply that state's choice-of-law rule, and a federal court exercising diversity jurisdiction will apply the choice-of-law rule of the state in which it sits. Increasingly, these rules are defined by the "governmental interest analysis," which requires a court:

> (1) to ascertain the underlying policies and interests sought to be regulated and protected by the rules of the relevant jurisdictions and to determine whether on the facts of the case these differing state interests are in conflict; and
> (2) if the interests are in conflict, to determine which jurisdiction has the most substantial interest in the resolution of a particular issue.[57]

In a corporate kidnapping case brought under a wrongful death or survival of action statute, the governmental interest analysis is applied to three main issues:

1. Which jurisdiction's law will be applied to determine the existence of a cause of action and the applicable standard of care.
2. Which jurisdiction's law will be applied to determine the types of injuries compensable and the amount of compensation recoverable.
3. Which jurisdiction's law will be applied to determine the availability of, and standards for awarding, punitive damages.

In deciding whether a cause of action exists and what standard of conduct should be applied, the places where the injury and the conduct causing the injury occurred are usually found to have the strongest interests in regulating the conduct. If these are different jurisdictions, courts usually apply the rule of the place where the conduct occurred, at least if this is a stricter standard than the law of the place of the injury.

For example, in a case brought under the Illinois wrongful death statute for a death occurring in Mexico,[58] plaintiff alleged that the defendant airline had invited the decedent, an Illinois travel agent, to take an expense-paid trip to Acapulco, knowing that the region of Mexico to which it invited the decedent was overrun by armed bands of guerillas and bandits. She alleged that the defendant negligently failed to warn the decedent of this hazardous condition; negligently failed to supervise the decedent, to provide guards, or to alert local authorities of the presence of numerous foreign visitors; and negligently enticed the decedent to visit the state. Defendant, contending that Mexican law governed, moved to dismiss for failure to state a claim.

The court found that Illinois, where the conduct occurred and the decedent and his beneficiaries lived, had the most significant relationship to the parties and the occurrence. It therefore applied Illinois law in deciding that the defendant owed no duty to warn the decedent or protect him against the criminal acts of third parties.

The corporation's duty to warn its employees of the risks of an assignment will probably be governed by the law of the employing entity's principal place of business because that state has the strongest interest in regulating corporate conduct. (That law, is likely to be more favorable to the plaintiff than the law of the foreign country.)

With respect to the corporation's responsibility for rescuing a kidnapped employee, if decisions regarding the rescue operations were made in the United States by a business headquartered there, the state where the business was located would have an interest in regulating its conduct. However, the country in which the rescue was carried out presumably has a strong interest in dealing with acts of, and plans to fund, domestic terrorism. The strength of this interest would depend, in part, on whether the country has a well-established policy of how to deal with terrorists.[59] A similar analysis would govern the choice of law applicable to the corporation's failure to protect its employee after he started work.

The residence or domicile of the victim of a tort has the most important interest in seeing the victim or his beneficiaries adequately compensated, for it will bear the responsibility for their welfare if they are not. Thus, the law of the decedent's domicile will usually be applied to the issue of compensatory damages in a wrongful death or survival action, unless the laws of the defendants' residence or the law of the place of the conduct are more favorable.[60]

Since the purpose of imposing punitive damages is to punish the defendant's wrongdoing, it is the defendant's residence and the place of the wrongful conduct that have the dispositive interest. Many jurisdictions, both foreign and domestic, do not allow punitive damages in order to protect resident defendants from excessive liability. Assuming that the country in which a corporate kidnapping took place did not allow punitive damages but the state of the defendant's principal place of business did, there would be no real conflict in governmental interests. Because the defendant corporation was not a resident of the foreign country, that country would have no interest in shielding it from excessive liability, and thus the law of the corporation's principal place of business would apply.

Because only the administrative agency created by statute can administer claims under a state's worker's compensation law, rights created by the compensation act of one state cannot ordinarily be enforced in another state or in a federal court.[61] The "conflicts" question in a compensation case will not, therefore, be which state compensation statute should be applied but rather whether a state can apply its compensation act to a particular injury.

In that regard it is clear that any state having a legitimate social interest in the injury and its effect on the worker, the employer, or the community can apply its statute.[62] While there are no reported cases discussing the problem in the context of a corporate kidnapping, there are cases which suggest that, as a matter of conflicts of law, a U.S. compensation statute would be applicable to the kidnapping and death in a foreign country of an employee of a U.S. corporation. For example, in a New Jersey case,[63] an electronics engineer working for a Washington, D.C., company died in Bogotá, Colombia. The court held that both New Jersey, where the employee had been a long-time resident and performed a substantial amount of consulting work for the company, and Washington, D.C., where the company was located, as well as Colombia, would have jurisdiction over the claim.

The court considered the following factors in determining which compensation law could constitutionally be applied:

- Place where the injury occurred
- Place of making the contract
- Place where the employment relation exists or is carried out
- Place where the industry is localized
- Place where the employee resides
- Place whose statute the parties expressly adopted by contract[64]

Jurisdiction

In order to subject a defendant who is not present within the territory of the forum to a judgment *in personam,* the court must find that he has "certain minimum contacts with it such that the maintenance of the suit does not offend traditional notions of fair play and substantial justice."[65] Virtually every state has a long-arm statute that permits a court to exercise personal jurisdiction over any corporation "doing business" in that state, and federal courts may exercise their diversity jurisdiction on a similar basis.[66]

The more difficult question, as it was in the *Curtis* case, is whether the U.S. corporation is the proper defendant. If, on the facts of a given case, the foreign subsidiary is the only proper defendant, there may be insufficient contact between the subsidiary and any one of the states to establish personal jurisdiction over the subsidiary.

Federal district courts have jurisdiction of civil matters where the amount in controversy exceeds $10,000 and the action is between "citizens" of different states. In a wrongful death or survival action it is the citizenship of the personal representative, not that of the decedent or beneficiaries, that is looked to in determining diversity.[67] An individual is a citizen of the state in which he is domiciled,[68] while a corporation is a citizen of the state in which it is incorporated and in which it has its principal place of business.[69] Thus, in a corporate kidnapping case, there will be diversity of citizenship so long as the decedent's personal representative is domiciled in a state in which the defendant is not incorporated and which is not its principal place of business.

OTHER CONSIDERATIONS

Apart from the purely legal considerations outlined above, the corporation confronted with a terrorist attack on one of its employees will be constrained in its response by a variety of other concerns. Whether that response will be seen as reasonable and legitimate if it is not motivated entirely by a desire to secure the release of a kidnapped employee is an issue not fully addressed in the limited case law available, but it is important to identify at least some of the questions that may arise.

In the typical employment relationship, the employer is not likely to face choices with either the political or financial implications involved in the rescue of a kidnapped employee. In such a typical relationship policy decisions must be made concerning the investment necessary to meet standards of safety in the work place, as must decisions of how much money should be paid to settle a claim or law suit arising out of a work-related injury; but these are not decisions tied to an ongoing crisis or to the immediacy of a life at stake. Nor will the decision on how to handle the ordinary problem of employee safety have such a potentially dramatic impact on other employees, on the corporation's stockholders, or, for that matter, on the corporation's competitors.

Yet, in the setting of a terrorist kidnapping and ransom negotiation, concern for these collateral effects will weigh importantly in the corporation's policy and operational judgments. For example, the employer may well be caught between two conflicting forces in deciding how readily and much he is willing to pay: Will a willingness to pay a substantial ransom without undue haggling improve the morale of those assigned to overseas positions, but at the same time increase the risk to them by encouraging terrorists to believe that they represent a ready source of funds? Can the company take a hard line in negotiating payment or even announce its refusal to pay any ransom in order to discourage kidnappers without severely damaging morale or even risking retaliatory attacks?

Further, in a country where terrorist activity is a continuing problem, what is the obligation of one employer to the other companies doing business there? Some countries undoubtedly have a recognized "going rate" for kidnap victims, and there is sometimes formal or informal pressure in the business community to hold that line. If maintaining that ceiling is the price of what may be a critical need for cooperation among employers of past, present, and future kidnap victims, can the company weigh that factor in deciding how much it will pay?

The answers to these questions bear not only on corporate planning for emergencies and on tactical and strategic decisions during the course of a kidnapping, but also on the legal issue of whether the corporation has met the standard of reasonableness on which its liability for any injury to its employee hinges. With respect to such decisions as the amount and timing of the ransom payment, it may well be that a court will give considerable weight to the advice of experts on negotiation strategy—for example, a judgment that too ready a willingness to pay the first amount demanded would lead only to an increase in the ransom. But it is less clear how a court would treat a corporate decision to place an artificial limit on the amount it was willing to pay, particularly if that limit were linked to the amount of insurance or to some historically established rate for corporate executives.

The issue of how much a corporation is willing to pay for the release of one of its employees may arise not only through an employee's complaint that too little was paid too late but through a stockholder's complaint that too much was paid too soon. For example, as the result of Exxon's decision to pay $14 million to ransom one of its executives who had been kidnapped by Argentine terrorists in 1973, two stockholders brought a derivative action in the California state courts against the individual members of the board of directors, claiming that the payment was *ultra vires* and was a "gift" of corporate funds.[70]

The suit was dismissed for want of personal jurisdiction over the defendants, and six years later a virtually identical suit was filed in the New York Supreme Court.[71] The Exxon board then established an independent committee on litigation to investigate the handling of the kidnapping and negotiations, and that committee, made up of directors elected to the board at least three years after the events at issue, concluded that the ransom payment was a reasonable exercise of corporate authority. The defendants then moved to dismiss the complaint.

The judge denied the motion, holding that the plaintiffs were entitled to limited discovery to test whether the decision of the committee constituted an exercise of independent business judgment. He noted, however, that, in the absence of a showing that the committee was not disinterested or had acted in bad faith, the court was required to abide by their decision; and with respect to the claim that the payment of ransom was *ultra vires,* he wrote:

> The decision to pay ransom for the release of a corporate employee, albeit a large ransom, cannot reasonably be stated to be against the corporation's best interests. The employee was engaged in corporate business at the time he was kidnapped, and his ransom affected the morale of other corporate employees, whose fear for their own safety would greatly affect the operation of the corporate enterprise.[72]

Although it seems unlikely that payments made to rescue corporate employees will be found to be *ultra vires,* it is clear that the reasonableness of the decision to pay ransom or not to pay and risk liability to the employee for failing to rescue him will be subject to judicial review. It can only be hoped that the courts will judge corporate conduct, whether in suits on behalf of a kidnapped employee or on behalf of disaffected stockholders, against a flexible standard which takes into account both the special circumstances in which the corporation was required to act and the absence of any meaningful body of learning on the steps that a reasonable employer must take to protect or rescue its employees.

NOTES

1.   Indeed, after Curtis's release, those involved in negotiating with the terrorists were held by the Colombian police for two months.

2.   The case was transferred on defendant's motion to the Southern District of New York (Judge Milton Pollack). Judge Pollack's decision is reported at 481 F. Supp. 1275 [S.D.N.Y. 1980, *aff'd,* 633 F.2d 203 (2d Cir. 1980].

3.   For purposes of this discussion, we will treat the common law as if it were a unified whole, although its content varies, of course, from state to state. Statements of universal legal principles are not possible, but the general principles discussed should give guidance and identify areas of concern. (The discussion also assumes that, unlike the decision in *Curtis,* the court will apply American, not foreign law.)

4.   See, e.g., *Stevens* v. *Kasik,* 201 Neb. 338, 267 N.W.2d 533 (1978).

5.   "Notice" includes any danger of which the employer "knew or should have known."

6.   Restatement (Second) of Agency, §471 (1957).

7.   Restatement (Second) of Agency, §496 (1957).

8.   For instance, an employer may be required to place feuding employees on separate shifts. *LaBonte* v. *National Gypsum Co.,* 113 N.H. 678, 313 A.2d 403 (1973).

9.   E.g., *Robinson* v. *United States,* 422 F. Supp. 121 (M.D. Tenn. 1976).

10.   An employer is not, of course, required to provide an absolutely safe work place. See, e.g., *Harrison* v. *Harrison,* 264 Md. 184, 285 A.2d 590 (1972).

11.   Though some states reject such liability on the theory that the employer cannot control the criminal acts of third parties, that position is against the modern trend and courts uphold it with difficulty. See *Fleming* v. *Sedgewick,* 328 F.2d 307 (5th Cir. 1964) (the federal court felt itself bound to apply Georgia law, which did not impose liability, but noted that, if it were not so constrained, it would determine for itself whether the criminal acts had been foreseeable.)

12.   *Lillie* v. *Thompson,* 332 U.S. 459 (1947).

13.   In *Parham* v. *Taylor,* 402 So. 2d 884 (Ala. 1981), the Alabama Supreme Court, basing much of its reasoning on parallel Kentucky law, found that certain occupations, such as bank teller and operator of a 24-hour store, by their very nature pose greater risks for the employee. The court said it would be necessary to show that the employer had greatly increased that risk without taking safety precautions before liability could be imposed. Where the employer had, among other things, provided the employee with instructions as to what to do if a robbery were attempted, the duty to protect had been met.

Presumably, the court reasoned that, because the dangers attendant to the employment were obvious to both employer *and* employee, the employer need exercise only reasonable care in those circumstances. In *Lillie* v. *Thompson,* the danger was also presumably obvious to the employee, and implicit in the Supreme Court's holding there may be a finding, consistent with *Parham,* that reasonable action by the company under the circumstances would have included installation of a mirror or other device by which the employee could have learned the identity of the person at the door.

14.   *Hartel* v. *Long Island R.R.,* 356 F. Supp. 1192 (S.D.N.Y. 1972), *aff'd,* 476 F.2d (2d Cir.), *cert. den.,* 414 U.S. 980 (1973).

15.   *Swanner* v. *United States,* 309 F. Supp. 1183 (M.D. Ala. 1980) (governments paid informant threatened by criminals).

16.   Of course, if there is no duty, there can be no liability. For instance, in *Semmelroth* v. *American Airlines,* 448 F. Supp. 730 (E.D. I. 1978), a travel agent was killed by either guerillas or bandits while visiting, at defendant's invitation, the hotels owned by the defendant in the expectation that he would recommend those hotels to his clients. The defendant knew that the area to be visited was overrun by bandits and guerillas. However, the court bound that there was no special relationship between the parties and, thus, no duty to warn or protect.

17.   *Garza* v. *United States,* 413 F.2d 23 (W.D. Okla. 1975).

18.   *Drake* v. *Sun Bank & Trust Co.,* 400 So. 2d 569 (Fla. Dist. Ct. App. 1981). With regard to the liability of common carriers, see, e.g., *Kenny* v. *Southeastern Pennsylvania Transportation Authority,* 501 F.2d 351 (3rd Cir. 1978), *cert. den.,* 439 U.S. 1073 (1979) (carrier had knowledge crime was on the rise in its system). See, also, *Day* v. *Trans World Airlines, Inc.,* 393 F. Supp. 217 (S.D.N.Y. 1975), *aff'd,* 528 F.2d 31 (2d Cir. 1975), *cert. den.,* 429 U.S. 890 (1976) (through deciding under the Warsaw Convention, court also looked to common law and implied that airline carrier's duty to protect extended to passengers attacked by terrorists while going through preboarding procedures.

19.   E.g., *Herold* v. *Burlington Northern Inc.,* 342 F. Supp. 862 (D. Minn. 1972) (no liability where employee assaulted in employer's parking lot by nonemployee who had ill feelings toward the employee).

20.   E.g., *Inman* v. *Baltimore & O.R.R.,* 361 U.S. 138 (1959) (railroad crossing employee injured by drunken driver).

21.   *W. R. Grimshaw Co.* v. *Martin Wright Electric Co.,* 283 F. Supp. 628 (W.D. Tex. 1968), *rev'd on other grounds,* 419 F.2d 1381 (5th Cir. 1969), *cert. den.,* 392 U.S. 1022 (1970).

22.   *Moore* v. *Chesapeake & O.R.R.,* 649 F.2d 1004 (rth Cir. 1981) (injured in cafeteria on premises).

23.   *Penn Central Corp.* v. *Checker Cab Co.,* 488 F. Supp. 1225, 1228 (E.D. Mich. 1980).

24.   E.g., *Fowler* v. *Seaboard Coastline R.R.,* 638 F.2d 17 (5th Cir. 1981) (employee rode motorcycle off premises, returned to employer's parking lot, and was killed in accident). In dealing with terrorist acts in a country where the danger from terrorist activity is admittedly high, a court is likely to focus on the extent of the general obligation to protect within the country and any assumption of the risk by the employee, rather than on whether the employee was within the scope of his employment.

25.   Our discussion does not assume that the problem of terrorism cannot arise within the United States. Indeed, the legal principles, unencumbered by a debate as to which country's law applies, should be easier to apply. Given historical precedent, however, it seems more likely that these issues will be faced in cases arising in foreign countries.

26.   Restatement (Second) of Torts, §323 (1964). Though generally accepted, some states do not follow the doctrine.

27.   In light of the Good Samaritan rule, if such service is provided as a mere gratuity, i.e., if the duty to protect does not require such action under the circumstances, purely as a legal matter the corporation might consider discontinuing it.

28.   Thus, it may be reasonable to resist a gunman even if, as a consequence, a hostage is wounded. *Johnson* v. *Gallatin County,* 418 F.2d 96 (7th Cir. 1969). Likewise, although a landowner may owe a duty to provide safe premises for business invitees, he may not be under a duty to negoiate with robbers in the course of a robbery (depending on the law of the jurisdiction). See, *Adkins* v. *Ashland Supermarkets, Inc.,* 569 S.W.2d 698 (Ky. App. 1978).

29.   *Rodriquez* v. *New Orleans Public Service, Inc.,* 400 So. 2d 884 (La. 1981) (driver not negligent for failing to intervene when streetcar passenger was assaulted).

30.   See, e.g., *Sneider* v. *Hyatt Corp.,* 390 F. Supp. 976 (N.D. Ga. 1975); and see, *Rappenicker* v. *United States,* 509 F. Supp. 1018 (N.D. Cal. 1981) (action by crewman of ship *Mayaquez*).

31.   See, *Mumma* v. *Reading Co.,* 247 F. Supp. 252 (E.D. Pa. 1965).

32.   See, *Miller* v. *Employers Mutual Liability Insurance Co.,* 349 So. 2d 1353 (La. Ct. App.), *cert. den.,* 352 So. 2d 235 (La. 1977).

33.   E.g., *Parker* v. *Travelers Ins. Co.,* 400 So. 2d 682 (La. Ct. App.) *cert. den.,* 406 So. 2d 590 (La. 1981) (employee knew of oil leak but descended ladder anyway).

34.   E.g., *Independent Nail and Packing Co.* v. *Mitchell,* 343 F.2d 819 (1st Cir. 1965).

35.   *Comer* v. *Texaco, Inc.,* 524 F.2d 1243 (5th Cir. 1975).

36.   See, Restatement (Second) of Agency, §§521, 522 (1957).

37.   In *Curtis,* though the court found no *duty* to transfer, Curtis was hired by a local company for a local job, not by a multinational corporation for its general management program.

38.   While the exact nature of the wrongful death action varies from state to state, the Washington state statute is a typical one. It provides that: "When the death of a person is caused by the wrongful act, neglect or default of another, his personal representative may maintain an action for damages against the person causing the death; and although the death shall have been caused under such circumstances as amount, in law, to a felony." Wash. Rev. Code §4.20.010.

39.   Again, the Washington statute's provision on beneficiaries is typical: "Every such action shall be for the benefit of the wife, husband, child or children of the person whose death shall have been so caused. If there be no wife or husband or child or children, such action may be maintained for the benefit of the parents, sisters or brothers, who may be dependent upon the deceased person for support, and who are resident within the United States at the time of his death." Wash. Rev. Code §4.20.020. Some statutes only allow recovery by spouses or children and still others require proof of dependency before recovery can be had even by spouses or children.

40.   Wash. Rev. Code §4.20.020.

41.   See *Barr* v. *Intervay Citizens Bank of Tampa, Florida,* 635 P.2d 442, 443 (Wash. 1981); *Kramer* v. *Portland-Seattle Auto Freight,* 261 P.2d 692, 696 (Wash. 1953).

42.   See, e.g., *Hinzman* v. *Palmanteer,* 501 P.2d 1228 (Wash. 1972). Other questions to be considered in computing damages for loss of support are how to discount the award to present value, whether income taxes should be deducted from a decedent's gross earnings in arriving at the award (personal injury awards are not subject to federal income tax), and whether the award should include interest, and if so, whether the interest should be computed from date of death or date of judgment.

43.   *Bould* v. *Touchette,* 349 So. 2d 1181 (Fla. 1977). Other cases that have upheld proportionately large punitive damages awards include *Sperry Rand Corp.* v. *A.T.O., Inc.,* 447 F.2d 1387 (4th Cir. 1971) (punitive damages $175,000, net worth $750,000); *Fuchs* v. *Kupper,* 22 Wis. 2d 107, 125 N.W. 2d 360 (1963) (approved punitive damages 12½ percent of net worth).

44.   Again the state of Washington's survival statute is typical: "All causes of action by a person against another person or persons shall survive to the personal representatives of the former and against the personal representatives of the latter, whether such actions arise in contract or otherwise, and whether or not such actions would have survived common law. . . ." Wash. Rev. Code §4.20.046.

45.   For example, Ohio allows recovery for the deceased's pain and suffering as well as punitive damages if the deceased suffered personal injury before he died. See *Rubick* v. *Huffman,* 374 N.E.2d 411 (Ohio 1978). By contrast, under the Washington statute, recovery for "pain and suffering, anxiety, emotional distress, or humiliation personal to and suffered by a deceased" is specifically excluded, Wash. Rev. Code §4.20.046; nor are punitive damages available.

46.   In these states, the possibility is raised of a double recovery of probably future earnings when actions are brought under both the wrongful death and survival statutes. A court in such a state would undoubtedly fashion a remedy that would eliminate that possibility. See, e.g., *Crescuola* v. *Andrews,* 507 P.2d 149, 150 Wash. 1973).

47.   See, e.g., *Kramer* v. *Portland-Seattle Auto Freight,* 261 P.2d 692 (Wash. 2953); *Bould* v. *Touchette,* 349 So. 2d 1181 (Fla. 1977).

48.   See generally, A. Larson, *Workmen's Compensation Laws* §1.10 (1978 ed.) (hereinafter called Larson).

49.   The Ohio worker's compensation statute, which is typical of many, defines an employer as "every person, firm, and private corporation, that . . . has in service one or more workmen or operatives regularly in the same business or in or about the same establishment under any contract of hire, expressed or implied, oral or written. . . ." Ohio Rev. Code Ann. §412.301(B). An employee is defined as "every person in the services of any private corporation" that falls within the above quoted definition of an employer. Ohio Rev. Code Ann. §412.301(A).

50.   Discussed above at p. 202.

51.   See Larson at §6.50.

52.   *General Acc. Fire & Life Assur. Corp.* v. *Industrial Acc. Commn.,* 200 P.2d 419 (Cal. 1921).

53.   "It [the employment] brought him unwittingly into the line of fire of the arrow, where he would not have been except for his employment." *Gargiulo* v. *Gargiulo,* 97 A.2d 593 at 596 (N.J. 2953). The similar "increased risk" theory would apply if an employee works in a neighborhood where the risk of encountering a stray bullet is above average. See Larson §10.13.

54.   *Lewis* v. *Knappen Tippetts Abbott Engineering Co.,* 108 N.E.2d (N.Y. 1952).

55.   This is more a conflicts of law issue than a substantive worker's compensation issue.

56.   108 N.E.2d at 612. See also *Beeny* v. *Teleconsult, Inc.,* 388 A.2d 1269 (N.J. 1978); *Shannon* v. *Communications Satellite Corp.,* 302 A.2d 582 (Md. 1973), *cert. dism.,* 419 U.S. 989 (1974).

57.   See *Schlup* v. *Demaras,* 410 F. Supp. 1190 (D.D.C. 1976). The "interest analysis" is discussed in the Restatement (Second) of Conflict of Laws, §§6, 145, 156, and 157.

58.   *Semmelroth* v. *American Airlines,* 448 F. Supp. 730 (E.D. Ill. 1978).

59.   In *Tramontana* v. *S.A. Empresa De Visca Aerea Rio Grandense,* 350 F.2d 468 (D.C. Cir. 1965), *cert. den. sub nom, Tramontana* v. *Varig Airlines, 383* U.S. 943 (1966), the court applied the Brazilian limitation on recovery to a case involving a plane collision in Brazil that killed a Maryland resident. The court concluded that Brazil had a strong interest in the financial health of its airline industry and had enacted the limitation to protect that industry. The court decided that Maryland's interest in compensating its residents was outweighed by Brazil's interest.

60.   A limit on damages is seen as reflecting a state's interest in protecting resident defendants from excessive liability. When it is the plaintiff's jurisdiction that limits recovery, applying the law of the plaintiff's state would not further this interest. See *Hurtado* v. *Superior Court of Sacramento County,* 114 Cal. Rptr. 106, 522 P.2d 666 (Calif. 1974).

61.   See Larson, at §84.20.

62.   See Larson at §84.30. More than one compensation statute can apply to the same injury so long as a deduction is made for a prior award.

63.   *Beeny* v. *Teleconsult, Inc.,* 388 A.2d 1269 (N.J. 1978).

64.   See also *Shannon* v. *Communications Satellite Corp.,* 302 A.2d 582 (Me. 1973), *cert. dis.,* 419 U.S. 989 (1974).

65.   *International Shoe Co.* v. *Washington.* 326 U.S. 310, 316 (1945).

66.   28 U.S.C. §1391(c).

67.   *Lang* v. *Elm City Construction Co.,* 217 F. Supp. 873, *aff'd.,* 324 F.2d 235 (2d Cir. 1964).

68.   Domicile requires the concurrence of two elements: (a) actual residence within a state, and (b) an intention that it remain one's principal residence for an indefinite period.

69.   28 U.S.C. §1332(a).

70.   *Flick* v. *Exxon Corp.,* 58 Cal. App. 3d 212, 129 Cal. Rptr. 760 (1975), affirming dismissal by Superior Court, Sacramento County.

71.   *Flick* v. *Exxon Corp.,* No. 4443/80, Supreme Court, New York County (filed July 14, 1980).

72.   *Id.,* Memorandum opinion of Cahn, J., July 24, 1981, p. 13.

15

The Payment of Ransom

Brian M. Jenkins

Terrorist groups finance themselves primarily through armed robberies, extortion, and kidnappings for ransom. It is difficult to say with any precision how much ransom terrorists have collected in recent years. Family members and corporate officials are naturally reluctant to discuss the amounts paid for the safe return of relatives or company executives, and many ransom kidnappings are not reported at all. It has been estimated that during the 1970s corporations paid between $150 and $250 million dollars in ransom to terrorists.[1] Since then, kidnappings have increased and ransoms in excess of $1 million are not uncommon. The total amount of ransom paid probably lies in the region of several hundred million U.S. dollars and could be much more.

How did it come about that corporations started routinely paying ransom to terrorists? To answer that question, one must go back to the first terrorist kidnappings of corporate executives in Latin America at the beginning of the 1970s. The Tupamaros in Uruguay carried out a number of abductions in the late 1960s, but these were primarily for propaganda purposes. The terrorists sought to embarrass the government by kidnapping members of the country's business elite and personal friends of the president of Uruguay, then obtaining information from their hostages about corruption involving business and government officials that the terrorists could use to discredit the political and economic system. It is in Argentina that one finds the precedent for the contemporary practice of kidnapping corporate executives to finance terrorist organizations.

The precedent-setting case was the abduction in May 1971 of Stanley Sylvester, the honorary British consul in Rosario, Argentina, and the manager of the Swift Company's meat-packing plant. The kidnappers made no demands on the Argentine or British governments, both of whom by 1971 had adopted no-concessions policies. Instead, they demanded that the Swift Company rehire 300 workers who had been dismissed by the company, reduce work quotas for Swift employees, terminate indiscriminate firing of workers, provide medical attention and reduce cold working conditions in the packing plant, distribute $50,000 worth of food to specified working-class neighborhoods, and publish the kidnappers' communiques in all the public media. The company promptly agreed and Sylvester was released one week after his abduction.

The kidnapping of Sylvester marked the first time in the world that a terrorist organization had forced an international corporation to change working conditions in its plant and distribute goods to the poor. The kidnapping of the executive of a foreign corporation also marked a departure for the terrorist organization, which had until then limited its operations to assaults on police and military installations, and gained its funds from bank robberies—the traditional Bolshevik method of financing revolution.

At the outset, the Sylvester kidnapping apparently caused considerable debate within the terrorists' ranks. The kidnapping was planned and executed by the Rosario group without approval of the terrorist group's national command. The Rosario group hoped to win sympathy among the workers, provoke the government into repressive measures on behalf of the foreign business community, and force the national leadership of the terrorist organization to adopt a new tactical-strategic line of attack. The demand to pay for the distribution of food was something additionally calculated to appeal to the workers. It was not yet seen as a means of financing terrorist operations. Although the kidnapping of Stanley Sylvester fell within the terrorists' broad aims of improving the lot of the workers and eliminating foreign enterprises from Argentina, the group's national leadership considered the kidnapping a departure from orthodox revolutionary tactics and also feared that such an act of terrorism would lead to increased police repression that would imperil the group itself.[2]

Thus, the kidnapping and ransoming of Stanley Sylvester represents an innovation, not one carefully designed, or even imagined by its perpetrators at the time, as a method of financing terrorist operations, but rather something they fell into, and not without internal debate. Had the operation failed, the national leadership's objections would have been justified, and ransom kidnappings might have for a time remained in the domain of ordinary crime. As it turned out, however, the demands were met.

Viewing the outcome of the Sylvester case as a success, Argentine terrorists struck again in March 1972, this time kidnapping Oberdan Sallustro, president of Fiat of Argentina. They demanded that the Argentine government release 50 prisoners, and that Fiat reinstate 250 workers who had been fired in a labor dispute and provide $1 million in the form of school supplies and shoes to children in poor areas of the country. Fiat accepted the ransom demands but the Argentine government refused to release any prisoners and warned that Fiat executives would be prosecuted for "illicit associations" unless they broke off contact with the kidnappers. Police launched an all-out search and discovered where Sallustro was being held. Sallustro was killed when police assaulted the hideout.

The government's strong response in the Sallustro case did not arrest growing terrorism in Argentina or prevent further kidnappings. The kidnappers switched from extracting corporate funds for philanthropic enterprises on behalf of the workers and the poor to demanding direct cash payments. In June 1972, terrorists kidnapped the president of the Buenos Aires branch of the Italian Banco di Napoli. They demanded and received $200,000 in ransom. In September, another terrorist group kidnapped the Dutch head of Philips Argentina and demanded $500,000 ransom. In November, an Italian industrialist was kidnapped in Buenos Aires. He was released after $500,000 was paid.

The ransom demands began to escalate. In December 1972, terrorists in Argentina kidnapped the managing director of a British firm and held him for $1 million ransom. In April 1973, terrorists kidnapped an American executive of the Kodak corporation and held him for $1.5 million. In June, they kidnapped a British executive and demanded $7.5 million in ransom. In October 1973, the kidnappers of a Swissair executive demanded $10 million in ransom. In March 1974, the kidnappers of an Esso plant manager reportedly received $14.2 million in ransom; and in September 1974, the kidnappers of the Born brothers, directors of the Bunge and Born Company, one of the world's largest trading conglomerates, demanded an incredible $60 million ransom. The pattern of corporations paying ransom for kidnapped executives was set.

In the early 1970s, however, this kind of terrorism was a new phenomenon. Political kidnappings were still comparatively rare occurrences targeted almost entirely against government officials and diplomats. The corporations faced with ransom demands in these first cases probably had no notion that they were establishing precedents that would later become customary practice for the corporate community worldwide, ones that would ultimately give rise to a new service industry of kidnap and ransom insurance and hostage recovery consultants.

But if corporations had little notion of establishing precedents for the future, they did have precedents set in the past on which to base their decisions; and the precedents pointed toward paying ransom. Most kidnappings up to that time had been carried out by common criminals who demanded ransom from the family of a victim. Families almost always paid, and the authorities often cooperated in the hope that in taking delivery of the money, the kidnappers would expose themselves to arrest. In countries with effective law enforcement establishments, kidnappers usually were caught. Even in the rare cases in which a family was unable or unwilling to meet the kidnappers' ransom demands, the authorities usually arranged a bogus payment to bring the kidnappers to the surface.

The growing number of airline hijackings that had occurred by the early 1970s provided another kind of precedent. Here again, the practice was to yield to the demands of hijackers. Faced with threats to passengers and crew members and expensive aircraft, airline companies agreed to the demands of hijackers whether they wanted to simply change the destination of the plane or asked for money and parachutes. There was no notion that passengers or employees would be imperiled by refusals to comply with the demands of hijackers.

It should also be recalled—particularly by governments who now wish that corporations would follow their lead and adopt no-ransom policies—that in the early 1970s when the corporations first confronted terrorists demanding ransom, many governments themselves routinely yielded to the demands of terrorists holding hostages. Between 1969 and 1971, the government of Brazil released prisoners on four occasions to save the lives of foreign diplomats kidnapped by terrorists in that country. In July 1970, the Greek government released seven prisoners in exchange for the safe release of passengers held aboard a hijacked Olympic Airways plane. In September 1970, Switzerland, Germany, and the United Kingdom released prisoners to obtain the safe release of airline passengers held hostage by Palestinian hijackers in Jordan. In 1972, West Germany released the terrorists responsible for the Munich incident in return for the release of hostages aboard a hijacked Lufthansa airliner, and in 1975 the German government released German terrorists to obtain the freedom of a kidnapped German official. Between 1970 and 1973, the governments of Guatemala, Haiti, the Dominican Republic, and Mexico all yielded to the demands of terrorists holding government officials or foreign diplomats.

The United States, currently an advocate of a no-concessions policy, also had a different view at the time of the first kidnappings. Because of the presumed influence that the United States exercised over local governments, urban guerrillas abducted American diplomats. While not in sympathy with the kidnappers, the United States realized that in many cases, the local governments were in fact authoritarian regimes whose opponents were subject to arbitrary arrest: The political prisoners whose release was demanded in exchange for the release of an American diplomat might be just that—political prisoners. On March 24, 1970, a U.S. Department of State spokesman announced as a matter of policy—the first such policy pronouncement on the topic—that the United States favored the release of political prisoners if it were the only way to free kidnapped American diplomats. This policy did not begin to change until 1971, and a firm no-ransom policy did not really emerge until 1973. Even then it was debated within the government.

Argentina was the first country to pronounce a no-concessions policy in March 1970, although it occasionally departed from this policy in subsequent incidents. Guatemala and Uruguay followed later that year. No-concessions policies, however, were not widely adopted until the middle of the 1970s, and many countries continued to yield to terrorists holding hostages. As late as 1977, the government of Japan paid $5 million dollars to Japanese Red Army terrorists who had hijacked a Japan Airlines plane. In 1978, the government of Nicaragua paid $500,000 to Sandinistas holding hostages in the national assembly building. The government of Italy in 1981 found a way of negotiating a $1.5-million ransom paid to the terrorist kidnappers of an Italian politician in Naples, despite a no-concessions policy that had been declared and adhered to during the Moro kidnapping.

With so many governments publicly yielding to terrorist demands, in many cases releasing convicted felons, it was not likely that corporations were going to adopt a contrary position and refuse to pay ransom for sequestered executives. Once the precedent was established in the corporate community, it became increasingly difficult in subsequent cases to take a position out of line with widespread corporate practice.

The nature of the terrorists' demands in the first kidnappings of corporate executives also made it hard to refuse. The terrorists demanded not cash for themselves but financial backing of various philanthropic efforts, such as the deliveries of food to the poor demanded by the kidnappers of Stanley Sylvester. Large foreign corporations could not easily refuse to provide such charity even under duress. (At the same time, as discussed in Chapter 13, corporate philanthropy itself provides no immunity against terrorist kidnappings.) Later, terrorist kidnappers switched from philanthropy to cash payments paid directly to the terrorists.

If, in the early 1970s, the corporations had foreseen a long struggle with terrorism in which the companies were to be the unwilling financiers and principal targets of terrorists, they might have thought differently, but no one saw this coming. For one thing, companies did not take a collective view when faced with kidnappings; although as the problem persisted, particularly in Argentina, the corporations did begin to share information and take a more united stand in demanding government action. But in each kidnapping, the corporation was very much on its own and saw its problem as an isolated event. There was a presumption that once it got through *its* kidnapping, paid *its* ransom, obtained the release of *its* executive, it would not again be attacked. In Argentina this perception was mostly correct. Companies were seldom targeted again in subsequent kidnappings, at least, not by the same group. In Italy, it was a different story. There, the Red Brigades repeatedly attacked the same corporations.

ARGUMENTS FOR THE PAYMENT OF RANSOMS

Few corporations have adopted no-ransom policies, but the debate over the decision to pay or not to pay ransom repeatedly surfaces. There are many obvious arguments in favor of paying ransom, the principal one being humanitarian. Paying ransom is often the only way to save the life of the hostage, and for the corporation, the life of a valuable employee. A willingness to pay ransoms also aids employee morale and recruiting. While some employees might derive comfort from a publicly declared no-ransom policy, figuring that it will make them less of a target to would-be kidnappers, it is more likely that a no-ransom policy would make it more difficult for a company to recruit personnel for areas where kidnapping is a problem. Clearly, the death of an employee resulting from a decision not to pay ransom would have an adverse impact on employee morale. It could also have a disastrous impact on the corporate image, particularly when the corporation is foreign and the hostage a local employee. Refusal to pay ransom, moreover, could result in lawsuits— even though it has never been established in a court of law that a company is obliged to pay ransoms.

A further argument for the payment of ransoms is that delivery of the money may assist the authorities, if they have been notified, in apprehending the kidnappers. This expectation holds in the United States and a few other countries, but not in many Third World countries where the adversaries are sophisticated terrorist organizations.

Paying ransoms is not costly. Although multimillion-dollar ransoms are not uncommon, ransom insurance policies reduce a company's expenditure to the deductible, usually something around several hundred thousand dollars. In the United States at least, this amount is tax deductible.

Paying ransoms is by now a widely accepted corporate practice and for most corporations, it is a one-time affair. A company whose executive is kidnapped is not likely to have to go through the same experience twice in the same country. In some cases, corporations have sought and received assurances from terrorist kidnappers that if they pay the ransom, their employees will not be kidnapped again. No enforcement of such a bargain is possible, of course, and it does not work in countries where several independent groups are active. In cases where a company is subject to repeated kidnappings and other terrorist actions directed against its employees that are financed by the ransoms it pays, the arguments against the payment of ransoms are stronger.

ARGUMENTS AGAINST THE PAYMENT OF RANSOMS

There are also several arguments against the payment of ransoms. Of most merit is the argument that ransom payments merely finance further terrorist activity, which certainly is not in the country's or the corporate community's long-term interest. Put it this way. A million-dollar ransom can support 10 to 20 full-time terrorists for a year, or it can buy an arsenal of weapons. Suppose a terrorist organization with an established record of assassinations and bombings demanded that a corporation deliver 500 machine guns and enough dynamite to make several hundred bombs. The humanitarian argument in favor of saving the life of a single hostage would be outweighed by the obvious violence these weapons would bring. In such a case the corporation probably would refuse.

The willingness of corporations to pay large ransoms has made them a lucrative target. Then, would not a policy of not paying ransom provide a deterrent to terrorist kidnappings? It might, if all the companies agreed and stuck to a no-ransom policy, but the evidence is mixed. A declared no-concessions policy did not reduce terrorist hijackings and other hostage seizures aimed at extracting concessions from the government of Israel, although the record shows that Palestinian terrorists successively reduced their original demands in an unsuccessful attempt to entice Israel into making a compromise. No-concessions policies did not reduce terrorist kidnappings in Uruguay, Argentina, or Italy. Terrorist kidnappings declined when the terrorist groups were destroyed.

A careful examination of government policies on ransom and terrorist kidnapping trends finds little convincing evidence to support the assumption that no-concessions policies are a deterrent. On the other hand, as we have seen already, a no-concessions policy announced by the Argentine government in 1970 may have shifted terrorist sights to the corporate community; and no doubt the willingness of corporations to pay sizable ransoms provided an incentive to further kidnappings of corporate executives. But to whom would the risk be displaced if all the corporations in the world were to magically agree to pay no more ransom? Probably individual families would be faced with the ransom demands, as they already have been in many cases. That trend may save corporations money but would not necessarily solve recruiting and morale problems. Nor can it be automatically considered a positive achievement in a broader definition of the public good, except that families generally have less financial resources than large corporations and are less able to pay large ransoms. Shifting the ransom burden to families would theoretically reduce the volume of funds going to the terrorists.

Two further arguments against the payment of ransom are that the government and corporate stockholders may object. Stockholders have on occasion objected to ransom payments but the single case to reach the courts failed. Governments may express their objection to ransom payments by administrative means—ruling ransom payments not to be deductible, imposing restrictions on currency exchange—or in legislation by outlawing "illicit associations" with terrorists or the payment of ransom itself. Such laws, however, can have unintended adverse effects, as we shall see in a moment.

For governments, the arguments for and against yielding to the demands of kidnappers are different. Here the issue is not simply the payment of cash but a matter of governance: Terrorists seldom seek access to the national treasury. Instead, they demand political concessions, most often, the release of imprisoned terrorists. This constitutes subversion of the judicial system, and if conceded to, represents an abdication of the government's responsibility to uphold the law. The government also must weigh an individual's interest against its responsibility to protect all citizens who may be endangered by releasing imprisoned terrorists or making other concessions that strengthen the terrorists' group. And, finally, a government can demand more of its officials than can a corporation. A person may be asked to risk his life for his country, but seldom can he be asked to die for his company.[3]

SHOULD PAYING RANSOM BE OUTLAWED?

Governments have adopted various approaches toward kidnapping. Some governments, while following no-concessions policies in dealing with any demands that kidnappers may levy on the government, have not tried to interfere with the payment of ransom by private parties. Other countries have outlawed the payment of ransom by making it illegal under any circumstances to give money to terrorist organizations or by making it a crime to act as an intermediary between a hostage and terrorists in a kidnapping.

Such laws are not evenly enforced. Some governments have used laws against ransom simply to keep ransom payments out of the newspapers, which could encourage more kidnappings, but have not tried vigorously to prevent negotiations or prosecute those who pay ransom. In still other cases, laws outlawing the payment of ransom have been used by government authorities to insure that government authorities are brought into the case. Companies whose executives are kidnapped are informed that they may negotiate a ransom but are warned to keep government authorities posted on the negotiations or risk prosecution. Or the law may be used to discourage certain kinds of corporate concessions that are unacceptable to the government. For example, a government may not object to a quietly arranged cash payment but will object to a corporation agreeing to pay for the publication of terrorist manifestos in newspapers around the world. The government will warn the corporation that its executives will face prosecution if they make such a concession. In other countries, the target of a no-ransom law may be aimed at the transfer of funds abroad. To avoid taxes and currency regulations, some families have faked kidnappings and conducted phony negotiations that end in large sums of money being transferred out of the country to family accounts abroad.

Laws against ransom make the target of a ransom a participant in the crime. In addition to the negative aspects of criminalizing victims of crime, a law against ransom, if enforced, can become an obstacle to effective law enforcement. Faced with prosecution, many companies probably—and certainly families—will attempt to negotiate with kidnappers secretly. Argentina went through this experience in the early 1970s when it warned that companies paying ransom could be prosecuted. Cooperation with Argentine police ceased as companies secretly negotiated ransom payments. Argentina subsequently dropped the idea of outlawing ransom payments. Cooperation with the authorities increased somewhat, but the apprehension and conviction record was dismal and the kidnappings continued until the terrorist groups were destroyed.

In the United States, where ransom kidnappings have been carried out by ordinary criminals rather than political terrorists, ransom payments are almost always arranged, with FBI officials present, and the kidnappers are almost invariably apprehended as a result. Owing to the apprehension and conviction record, kidnapping remains a comparatively rare crime in the United States.

It is noteworthy that while some corporations favor laws against ransom as a means of relieving them of making life and death decisions, most corporations oppose such laws.

HOW MUCH RANSOM?

As ransom demands escalated in the 1970s, and before the purchase of ransom insurance policies had become more common and less costly, corporate heads asked, How much ransom should a corporation pay? A ransom of several hundred thousand dollars would not impose a great burden on most corporations, but what if terrorists asked for $50 million or $100 million? It is difficult enough to set a price on human life, although economists, insurance companies, and the courts do so all the time. And it is impossible to say how much ransom is appropriate as a final offer or will suffice in any particular case. Kidnappers demanding $5 million have settled for several hundred thousand. In other cases, terrorists demanding $10 million have refused offers of $5 million.

In a sense, the question is the wrong one. There is no "correct" price for a hostage any more than there is a "correct" price for a Rembrandt. The final amount depends on many things. The rank of the individual is a factor in the company's decision. A million-dollar ransom may not seem unreasonable for an executive who receives an annual salary of a half million—an expression of the value the company places on him.

While not to be used as a formula for calculating ransom, a rough idea of how much an individual is worth to a corporation can be worked out if we set the present value of his future services to the company as the discounted sum of his future earnings. Suppose, for example, a 45-year-old executive draws a current salary of $100,000 a year. If we figure in a 10 percent discount (a standard often used) to reflect the corporation's expected internal rate of return from the employee's 20 remaining years before retirement, his present value would be $850,000.[4] Most corporations do consider at least their senior employees as investments. This approach may not work for easily replaced lower-level employees. However, for reasons relating to its public image, there might be tremendous public pressure on a corporation to pay ransoms for low-ranking employees.

It is difficult historically to find much relationship between the rank of an individual kidnapped and the amount of ransom ultimately paid. Such values are set, of course, when a company purchases a ransom insurance policy. (It is the author's own impression that ransom insurance policies have had a leveling effect on ransom payments by providing teams of skilled negotiators who are able to significantly reduce the initial ransom demands of the kidnappers, and by providing broad policies that cover all employees instead of just a handful of men at the top.)

Another important factor appears to be the "going market rate." In countries where kidnapping is a frequent occurrence, professional negotiators may have a fair idea of how much the kidnappers are likely to accept. This, however, is frequently distorted. Terrorist kidnappers may be especially desperate for a quick settlement to pay for a shipment of guns; or while holding several hostages from several firms, they might be willing to satisfy their short-term cash needs with a quick settlement of one case. Or the terrorists could decide to kill one of their hostages in order to encourage others to settle quickly on their terms.

Terrorists, if they are at all sophisticated, are going to have a pretty good idea of a corporation's financial situation prior to the kidnapping of one of its executives. We know now from arrests and interrogations that in many cases, terrorists had confederates within corporations who had provided the kidnappers with details of its operations. A corporation must take special precautions to ensure that kidnappers are not receiving information from its response or negotiating team even during a kidnapping. Terrorist kidnappers are also going to know how much they or other groups active in the country have ultimately settled for. Unless the corporation has received information from government sources or other companies, or has contracted consultants who are familiar with previous cases in the country, it will operate at an informational disadvantage.

CONCESSIONS OTHER THAN CASH

Paying money is the easiest thing a company can do. Concessions other than cash can cause major problems for corporations. In a number of cases, kidnappers have tried to develop constituencies among workers by demanding that companies rehire workers who have been dismissed or make other concessions to the labor force. Such concessions are sometimes more difficult to resist because they may be popular. Terrorists have been skillful in exploiting labor disputes or situations where workers are exposed to dangerous conditions and accidents have occurred. For the corporation, however, such concessions involve both economic and management issues. Rehiring workers, increasing wages, or other economic concessions directly affect profits—more so than a single ransom payment—complicate relations with labor unions where they exist, and undermine management itself. The question becomes not one of concessions but one of who is going to run the corporation: corporate management or a group of terrorists.

Demands that corporations pay for the publication of terrorist manifestos have caused serious problems between corporations and governments. Understandably governments are opposed to the worldwide publication of manifestos that are calculated to embarrass the government. In the Niehous case (see Chapter 30), the Venezuelan government threatened to nationalize the local assets of Owens-Illinois for agreeing to publish terrorist manifestos.

In all probability, while governments continue to resist terrorist demands, corporations will continue to pay ransom. With continuing kidnappings, the growth of ransom insurance, and the appearance of hostage recovery consultants, kidnapping has become an institutionalized form of extortion.

NOTES

1. The low estimate was made by E. Patrick McGuire, "International Terrorism and Business Security," *The Conference Board Information Bulletin,* no. 65, New York, 1979, p. 6. The higher estimates come from *Terrorism and International Business,* (New York: Business International Corporation, 1979), p. 2.

2. Details of the Stanley Sylvester case are based upon a detailed case study of the episode by Edward Gonzalez of The Rand Corporation.

3. For further discussions of the arguments for and against ransom, see Brian M. Jenkins, "Should Corporations Be Prevented From Paying Ransom?" Series No. P-5291 (Santa Monica, CA: The Rand Corporation, 1974); or an excellent article by Paul Wilkinson, "Kidnap & Ransom—To Pay or Not to Pay?" *International Security Review,* March/April 1983, pp. 32-36.

4. The author is indebted to Arthur J. Alexander for this point.

16

Managing the Episode

Richard Clutterbuck

RISK MANAGEMENT

Risk management of terrorism is like risk management of fire. Every corporate security officer or fire officer is accustomed to facing up to the fire risk, probably assisted by a fire surveyor provided by his insurance company. He first assesses the risk and the possible cost of damage—both of these being very much higher in some parts of his establishment than others. Risks can be ignored, removed, reduced, or transferred. He clearly does not ignore the fire risk, nor can he remove it altogether; he must therefore examine the various methods of reducing it (fire precautions and fire fighting plans) and transferring it (by insurance). He assesses the cost of each of these not only in money, but also in inconvenience, staff morale, loss of efficiency, and thus loss of earnings.

He then tells his management board how much they should authorize, in these terms, to reduce and transfer the risk, because these are management decisions. Given these decisions and the necessary resources and powers, he spends money on protection and fire precautions, devises a plan of action in the event of fire, and trains and practices the staff in implementing it. Then, if a crisis occurs, everyone can pass judgment on how well he carried out his precautions and contingency planning.

The corporate security director should approach the terrorist risk on precisely the same principle, including calling in expert advice, which is the equivalent of a fire surveyor. He must first assess the terrorist (or criminal) threat: bombing, arson, hoax calls, extortion by threat (for example, to bomb, burn, kill, maim or kidnap or to pollute the company's product), hijacking, hostage taking, short-term abduction, long-term kidnap, or murder. In a multinational corporation with overseas subsidiaries, the nature and level of the risks will vary considerably from one country to another.

He should next assess the likeliest targets (e.g., premises; installations; people, including families) the likely scale and intensity of the problem, if this or that target is selected; the possible costs, both commercial (money, disruption of production, sales) and human (including staff morale and possible legal implications); the moral factors (which also affect the corporate image); and considerations of public policy (which may in some countries put at risk the ability of the company to continue trading there).

232

He should then examine and cost the various methods of reducing the risks: by physical protection, procedures, and training. In this step he should work on the principle that if a terrorist or criminal surveillance reveals that these security measures and standards of alertness are noticeably better than those in otherwise similar alternative targets, the would-be attackers are likely to turn away and seek an easier target. Next is an assessment of the price of these various measures, in money, morale, inconvenience, loss of efficiency and thus company profit. These losses must be balanced against the costs of failure to prevent or defeat an attack, just as one balances the possible cost of any loss against the premium needed to insure against it.

The security director will then consider the insurance itself, and whether to transfer at least part of the cost to underwriters (the human and other intangible costs cannot be transferred). He may recommend insurance, not only against arson and bomb damage, but also against extortion, whether by threat of damage, violence, or product pollution, or in the form of kidnap and ransom. His proposals on expenditures for security, security procedures, training and insurance are then passed on, together with his estimate of their costs and alternatives, to his board of management. Having been given a budget and authority for the procedures he needs to introduce, he can then make detailed proposals for contingency planning, staff orientation, and training.

The heart of a contingency plan in a large corporation is a Crises Management Committee (CMC). When distant subsidiaries are involved, they should have their own CMCs or Local Negotiating Teams (LNT), the latter ready to handle extortion demands of all kinds. The roles of CMCs and LNTs are discussed later in this chapter and the next. The purpose of contingency planning is to establish CMCs/ LNTs as living organizations that have developed working relations with others involved (e.g., local government, the police, and the media) and have faced up to and taken as many of the foreseeable policy decisions as possible in advance, to save time, argument, and management diversion when a crisis does occur.

The best way to identify and resolve these policy decisions is by running simulation exercises on various forms of threat or attack. These are most likely to be effective if they are conducted by an outside agency that specializes in the subject. The best choice is one that has experience not only in advising on security precautions but also in handling a number of actual crises: The agency should be able to present scenarios and problems tailored to the environment encountered, which will realistically highlight the policy decisions needed and familiarize the members of the CMC/LNT with handling such a crisis.

Like fire risks, terrorist risks today are too big to be ignored and there can never be 100 percent protection against them. Terrorist risks vary much more from country to country than fire risks. Again as with fire, the possible cost of damage is vastly greater than the cost of reducing and transferring the risk. Easy rationalization, however, is a constant temptation for an executive: "it won't happen to me"; "if they want me they'll get me"; "I can't do my job if I'm hemmed in by security"; or "it's my life anyway. I'd rather take the risk."

The last of these attitudes, common enough in a senior executive who has reached the top by taking risks, is the most pernicious and selfish of them all. It is *not* just his life that is at risk. If, for example, he is kidnapped for ransom, his family and his colleagues may suffer at least as much mental anguish as he does himself; the management of his company will be disrupted; and the cost, if either group has to pay a ransom to save his life, may be enormous.

Two examples of the damaging effects of a kidnap will suffice to illustrate this outflowing of harm. In 1974, the two sons of the head of the biggest firm in Argentina, Bunge and Born, were kidnapped by the Montoneros. Their father eventually had to pay a ransom of $60 million for their release after nine months in captivity. In 1976 William Niehous, vice president of a subsidiary of Owens-Illinois in Venezuela, was kidnapped in Caracas (see Chapter 31). The firm first conceded to a demand to publish a manifesto from the kidnappers and were promptly threatened by the government with nationalization of their assets for breach of Venezuelan law. They also paid a ransom but heard no more until Niehous was rescued—in a chance contact by Venezuelan security forces—after 3 and a half years of incarceration. He survived his ordeal heroically and now admits, "I had never taken seriously the possibility that I might be kidnapped. . . . I didn't listen when people tried to give me some basics on how to reduce the risks of being kidnapped. I should have." He also stresses the ordeal of his family: "I knew where I was, and that I was alive and being fed and cared for reasonably well under the circumstances. They, for long periods of time, did not know whether I was alive or dead."[1]

THREAT ASSESSMENT

The first stage of contingency planning is to assess the threat. A realistic assessment results from an amalgam of in-house and external inputs, both at corporate and subsidiary levels, or in the case of government targets, in government departments and outstations; parent government sources (e.g., diplomatic and intelligence services at the center and on location); local government sources (e.g., foreign, police, and intelligence departments); personal contacts (e.g., trusted and experienced indigenous or expatriate friends and associates); and commercial organizations specializing in political, criminal, and terrorist risk assessments.

The degree of risk will vary enormously and it can change quite sharply due, for example, to changes in the law, the powers of the police, or leadership in a terrorist movement. In Italy, for example, the arrest of men like Renato Curcio in 1974—the so-called historic nucleus of the Red Brigades—led to a more violent faction emerging and a marked increase in terrorism in 1975–78. Argentina between 1974 and 1976 was probably the most dangerous country in the world for businessmen, who ran the risk of both kidnapping and assassination; by 1978 it had become one of the safest in Latin America. The 1976 military coup effected the change, but a underlying instability in the country's political system could rapidly cause a reversal.

In El Salvador, prior to November 1978, the Fuerzas Armadas Revolucionarias

Nacional (FARN) was one of several little-known terrorist groups in that country; within two years FARN had accumulated over $40 million by kidnapping expatriate executives from five multinational corporations (from Japan, the Netherlands, Sweden, United Kingdom, and United States). Since 1980, however, the pattern has changed, and the incidence of kidnapping in El Salvador has fallen from its peak of 21 in 1980 to 6 in 1982. Most of the victims are now indigenous, which may actually be misleading: Very few expatriates now live there.

On the other hand, nationals from many countries, including Austria, Bangladesh, Canada, Denmark, France, Germany, Pakistan, United Kingdom, United States, and Yugoslavia as of 1982 still worked in Kurdistan in northern Iraq, a recent area of high risk. From those trends one can deduce the importance of making fresh assessments of the threat in high-risk countries at frequent intervals and immediately following any major internal change in government, criminal or terrorist groups.

Assessing the threat to a particular company or establishment must be done through the eyes of the terrorist or criminal gangs known to be operating in the area. What are their organizations, methods, and aims? (Ninety percent of kidnaps, worldwide, are for money.) What targets will best advance those aims? What methods of attack are most likely to succeed and to have the desired effect—bombings, repeated hoaxes, product pollution, short-term abduction, kidnap, wounding, assassination, or extortion by threat? What has been the pattern of previous attacks? Size, type, and method of firing of bombs? Size of ransom demands and of settlements? Duration of kidnap? Percentage of kidnap victims released or killed? What impression is given of the determination and sophistication of the various groups, and of their collaboration or rivalry? Do links exist between terrorist and criminal groups that would result in subcontracting of abductions, guarding or laundering of ransom money? Is there evidence of collaboration with political dissidents, student organizations, labour unions, or particular newspapers or journalists?

An important factor to examine is the government and its security and intelligence services. Questions concern their record of efficiency, integrity, popular acceptance, and attitude to expatriates and expatriate organizations. What are the economic and social conditions, political rivalries, likelihood of survival of the incumbent regime, and the nature and potential stability of its possible successors? Is there rivalry or cooperation between the army, police, and intelligence services, and how much support do they enjoy in the community? Are they corrupt or politically motivated? Are their powers adequate, including emergency powers? Are the judiciary and the processes of the law effective? Are judges, juries, or witnesses frequently intimidated?

Against this background, those responsible for contingency planning must consider the likelihood of a company, embassy, or individual being picked as a target, as well as the likeliest form of attack. How well would such an attack advance the aims of the attacker? Will their reconnaissance reveal good security, with a high degree of alertness and awareness by security staff and potential victims? In other words, how high will would-be attackers rate their chances of success for a particular target? If the purpose is extortion or coercion, what opinion do the terrorists probably have about the prospect of the victim's government, company, or family giving way?

Has the company been picked because it was a target of a previous attack (once bitten, twice shy)? What is the target's financial strength? (Or what will the attackers think is its financial strength? Banks and oil companies are often believed to have unlimited resources.) Have there been labour problems? (If so, the chances of in-house betrayal or availability of inside knowledge from ex-employees will be much higher.) What is the local public image of the organization and of its parent country? What would be the public reaction to an attack on it? What would be the publicity impact—for example, of a big fire or of the involvement of a well-known figure?

In assessing the likelihood of being picked, and therefore in looking through terrorist or criminal eyes, it is wise to remember that they almost always have one or more of three aims: political blackmail (release of prisoners or inducement of pressure on a government); publicity; and, most commonly of all, money.

FORMS OF TERRORIST ATTACK AND CRIMINAL EXTORTION

Little need be said about bombing and arson, for which protection is broadly the same as for breaking and entering. Statistically, bombing is by far the most likely form of politically motivated terrorist attack. The response involves well-planned briefing of telephone operators (preferably with a pro forma beside each telephone) and an efficient search, evacuation, and damage control system.

Hoax calls can be more difficult to handle. At a peak period of IRA violence in Belfast, there were up to 40 hoax bomb warnings per day; and one particular firm received an average of three per week. Fortunately many of these were from self-evident crackpots or busybodies. Political terrorists are also well aware that if, due to disbelief, the threatened premises are not evacuated, they will lose much sympathy from the heavy casualties that will result. They therefore often agree to a secret codeword with the police to prove the authenticity of their warning.

Extortion by product pollution may take many forms. In one typical case, the extortioners placed poisoned samples on the shelves of three branches of a supermarket chain and delivered a message on the following lines:

> In your branches at X, Y, and Z you will find amongst the barbecue sauce three jars, each marked with red labels on the base. Analyze these and you will find that they contain a lethal dose of poison. Place an advertisement in the Courier on Monday to read "Joan. See you at the barbecue. Jack," to indicate your readiness to have $500,000 available for payment by Wednesday. You will then receive instructions for payment.
> You may react to this warning in three ways:

1. You can comply with the instructions and that will be the end of the matter.
2. You could pretend to comply with the instructions, but play for time and inform the police. In that event we will at once inform the Press.
3. You could refuse to pay, in which case we would flood all your branches with a wide variety of unidentified poisoned products.

It is encouraging to record that, in this case, skilled responsible action by the firm, the police, and the media resulted in the criminals being caught and convicted. Such threats always need cool and careful handling.

Extortion by short-term abduction is usually aimed at banks or similar cash-holding institutions. Typically, a bank manager may be interviewing an apparently bona fide client when his telephone rings. His wife says that two armed men have her and their children at gunpoint in the house and will either kill them or take them to a secret hideout unless they receive a return telephone call from the "client" within 5 minutes confirming that he has received $10,000 in cash from the safe.

Kidnap implies a longer-term incarceration in a secret hideout (though it can arise from a short-term abduction), coupled with a demand by telephone, letter, or newspaper advertisement for a considerably larger ransom. Being the most difficult and prolonged type of incident to manage, kidnapping will be the primary basis of the contingency planning and crises management techniques discussed below. Personal attack, to kill or wound, requires the same kind of protection as protection against kidnap: It will be regarded as part of the same problem and not given a separate examination.

THE COST OF FAILING TO PREVENT A CRIMINAL OR TERRORIST ATTACK

A parallel was drawn earlier with the cost of failing to prevent a fire. The cost of being the victim of bomb or arson attack is of a similar nature, while the costs of extortion are more complex and may be much larger. If the extortion is by threat to release polluted food or drink products, management has to consider four types of cost: management diversion, commercial, moral, and legal. Management diversion may be similar in kind, though on a smaller scale, to that in a kidnap extortion, which is discussed below.

Commercial costs can be horrific. A mere rumour that some of the foods in a large supermarket chain are polluted has caused sales losses running into millions of dollars within a week or two. Extortioners will therefore almost always threaten to tell the press. Substantial losses may also result from a moral obligation to destroy the entire stock of suspect items, which may, in itself, result in panic. On the other hand, failure to remove the stock or to warn the customers could in the end be even more expensive. Moreover, management would have to justify the morality of its response in the event of customers being poisoned. This quandary, in turn, could lead to heavy legal liabilities if no warning had been given of a known risk. Public policy also enters here: If a firm gives way and pays a large ransom to keep the matter quiet, the government or other firms may complain it is encouraging repetition of the crime.

Extortion by short-term abduction probably will involve immediate and relatively small costs—or nothing at all if there is a really efficient alarm system and good liaison with the police, coupled with an astute playing for time. Well-educated staff and sensible physical measures, such as time delay locks, can also give management an edge.

Much larger costs are likely to result from a long-term kidnap. The size of some of the ransoms paid has already been mentioned, the largest being $60 million. Ransoms over $1 million are by no means unusual in Italy and Latin America. Consequential costs, some of which are not at first apparent, must also be anticipated. These costs include the diversion of management time and effort from running the business and the salaries of senior executives taken away from their normal jobs. Coupled with these factors are the trading losses resulting from commercial disruption. These costs can be greatly reduced with good contingency planning and simulation exercises—which help create an efficient crisis management organization that can move smoothly into operation with minimal disruption of management and many decisions already made.

Since many kidnaps occur in subsidiaries of multinational corporations, there may often be communication costs, plus travel and accommodation for senior executives, which can mount considerably during prolonged crises. Other costs may arise from the engagement of consultants and advisors; legal costs and potential liabilities; and expenditures on public relations and the welfare of the victim's family. Human costs, are, of course, incalculable, which underlines the importance of preventing incidents from happening at all—and, if they do, of resolving them with expeditious and effective crisis management.

For any corporation or government operating in a country with even a medium risk of terrorist attack, the potential costs of a single incident, as described above, are so enormous that it is folly not to guard against them and to have contingency plans to deal with them. As an illustration, an analysis of the five kidnaps of multinational executives in El Salvador in 1979 revealed an average cost to each of the corporations concerned (including the ransoms eventually paid) of $100,000 for each day that its executive was held as a hostage. In at least one case where the corporation called in a professional advisor from an experienced consulting firm to advise on crisis management, the cost was less than half that average.

The analysis of contingency planning included in this chapter concentrates on the worst case: the prolonged kidnap of a senior executive of a subsidiary operating in a high-risk area geographically remote from the corporate headquarters. The participants involved in such a kidnap include the victim and his family, the kidnap gang, the police, the corporation or establishment where he works, and whoever is appointed as negotiator. Other players include the local government and its security forces; perhaps the parent government of a foreign subsidiary, or other corporations, joint venture partners, and stockholders; lawyers—perhaps several, representing the victim, the corporation, and others; and professional consultants on security and crisis management along with medical and psychiatric advisors.

It is against this background that the Crises Management Committee and, where applicable, the Local Negotiating Team must be designed. The CMC will be at the corporate headquarters (where ultimate decisions, human and financial, must be made) or, in the case of an embassy or mission, at the foreign ministry of the parent government.

THE CRISIS MANAGEMENT COMMITTEE

The composition, terms of reference, and functions of the CMC are examined here in what is probably one of the commonest and the worst of cases—that of a multinational corporate headquarters handling a crisis arising from the kidnap for ransom of a senior executive in an overseas subsidiary many thousands of miles away. The LNT's handling of the subsidiary, including negotiation, is examined in the next chapter—as will be the differences between this case, where the corporation is the target for extortion, and cases in which the extortion is from the victim's family, or in which a government is the target either for extortion or political coercion, or in which the primary aim is publicity for an extreme political movement.

The corporate CMC, during the contingency planning stage, will have already formulated a strategy on major policy issues and passed it through the board of directors, many of whom will in any event also be members of the CMC. The issues include what circumstances, if any, justify immediate concession to an extraordinary demand; whether to reject any payment of ransom from the outset or negotiate to pay a lower ransom, thereby playing for time and, if possible, enabling the police to effect a rescue without paying a ransom at all; what are the limits of ransom the corporation is prepared to pay and what consideration, if any, varies these limits; what risks the corporation is prepared to take—human, legal, or commercial—or what damage to the corporate image or staff morale. The terms of reference considered at this point regard cooperation with other participants during negotiation, such as the police, the media, the victim's family, joint venture partners, or other companies (e.g., if they have suffered a simultaneous kidnap); the extent of delegation of authority, if necessary with financial limits, to the subsidiary conducting the negotiation; and under what circumstances the feasibility of continuing to trade in the country concerned might itself be called into question.

The chairman of the CMC is almost certainly the chief executive of the corporation or his nominee. He needs an able deputy chairman, fully versed in the planning, both to relieve him of some of the load and also in case he himself is the victim. Another key member is the crisis coordinator, who acts as executive secretary to the CMC; he should be a senior executive whose duties normally keep him at the corporate headquarters. The corporation's legal advisor is an essential member of the CMC. Some of the legal problems he may face will be discussed later in this chapter.

The finance member will be concerned with the decision on levels of ransom to be offered during negotiation and on how the money should be raised in the

light of any controls on local or foreign currency. He should review the special procedures for accounting that will be used so that the knowledge of ransom details is restricted to the smallest possible number of people (clearly including certain bank officials and auditors as well as selected corporate staff). Other considerations in his preparation are the effects and conditions of corporate insurance and whether ransom payments are tax deductible. This officer will have to balance any proposed ransom payment and its effect on the viability of the company against moral considerations, especially the risk to human life, the corporate image, and staff morale.

The personnel member is involved at almost every stage in planning and crisis management. Should a victim be replaced? Or would this action have too damaging an effect on his family or on staff morale? Family evacuation will have to be discussed with the LNT, as well as the effect of the whole incident on the staff's perception of the company's concern and commitment—or conversely of their callousness. It could have a crucial effect on subsequent labour relations and on the willingness of expatriate and local staff to work with that company in high-risk areas.

One member of the CMC needs to be actively responsible for public relations. The media can have a benevolent or a damaging effect on negotiations and on the prospect of a victim's survival. The image of the corporation at home and of the subsidiary on the spot will need to be safeguarded by careful planning and foresight. Well-synchronized press releases and the securing of positive cooperation on humanitarian grounds by selected editors and journalists can play a decisive part in negotiation.

> The power of the media can best be illustrated by an example. When Mr. Rolf Schild and his wife and daughter were kidnapped in Sardinia in 1979, some newspapers were at first grossly irresponsible, publishing false and damaging conjectures about his wealth, which induced the kidnappers both to increase their ransom demand enormously and to hold out for it for far longer than they would normally have done. After 16 days they released Schild with instructions to raise an impossible ransom if he wished to see his wife and daughter again. After a further four and a half months of negotiation (contrasting with a normal maximum of about six weeks with Sardinian bandits), they released his wife for ransom allegedly less than 5 percent of the demand they had made when they first saw the newspapers. They still held his daughter.
>
> The news of Mrs. Schild's release was briefly kept from the media; when it did leak out, they behaved with commendable restraint in response to a plea by the Schilds and the police. A media blackout of Mrs. Schild's release was maintained for ten weeks. At that point the Pope agreed to break the silence with a dramatic personal appeal to the kidnappers, made publicly in front of the press and television cameras. The media then co-operated positively, giving maximum publicity to the Pope's appeal and convincing the kidnappers of the fate that would await them at the hands of the judiciary and of a now thoroughly aroused local community, some of whom knew their identity, if the girl were to be harmed. She was released five days after the Pope's appeal, after a total of 214 days in captivity. Thirteen of the gang were later arrested and convicted.

Another good example of positive cooperation with the media occurred in London in November 1975. An 18-year-old Cypriot girl, Alio Kaloghirou, was kidnapped and a ransom demanded from her family with the usual warning not to tell the police. They did tell the police at Scotland Yard but wisely told no one else. The police decided to take the media into their confidence, since one of their reporters was almost sure to run across something before the case was finished. They therefore invited the editors of 20 London papers and of all radio and television news departments to Scotland Yard; told them the story; and said that, provided the kidnappers did not find out that the police were involved, there was every chance of a successful rescue. They promised to brief the media representatives every day and to tell them, all together, as soon as it was safe to release the story. During the next nine days they managed to locate the hideout and put it under discreet surveillance. They instructed the family to negotiate and pay a ransom. The girl was then released and, three hours later, the police arrested the entire gang, who were all convicted, and recovered the money.

A similar case in London in January 1983 gave further confirmation that, if editors can be convinced that lives are at risk, they will respect a police request for a news blackout—provided they are confident that their rivals will also respect it. On January 4th Emmanual Xuereb and his wife arrived home, to be met by three masked men who took them to a hideout. Xuereb's father, a diamond merchant, received a telephone demand for £2 million ransom, later followed by other calls, photographs, and tapes containing vicious threats—for example, that they would cut off and send him one of his son's fingers for each day of delay in paying the ransom, and his severed head would be the final message. Despite the usual warnings, he had informed Scotland Yard who, as in the Kaloghirou case, at once informed the media and requested a total blackout, which was, once again, respected.

In full co-operation with the police Xuereb's father negotiated and the ransom demand was lowered. At the same time he gathered money to meet it and prepared to pay. On the fourth day, unexpectedly, his daughter-in-law was released with a written demand for £525,000. Police surveillance meanwhile located the hideout: They raided it early on the morning of January 9th, rescuing Xuereb and arresting three men. The triangular co-operation—family, police, media—had been perfect. The father described the police as "really terrific" and Assistant Commissioner Kelland of Scotland Yard thanked the media, describing their relationship as one of "complete mutual trust."

These experiences all underline the message that it does pay for those concerned—family, CMC, or LNT—to inform trusted police officers and to take a positive attitude toward the media. Once a case has become public (which may, of course, be from the start) co-ordinated press releases and access to the various participants must be strictly controlled. Within a corporation and its subsidiaries and especially with a victim's family, there will be a pressing need for reassurance and for as much information as can safely be released. It is desirable, however, to prevent independent and potentially damaging press interviews.

The corporate security director is obviously a member of the CMC and may well be its crisis coordinator. Security of a victim's family during negotiations, and of the negotiator and his family, is particularly important; so is that of any other potential "second victim" who might be kidnapped to apply extra pressure during negotiations. Vigilance is needed to guard against any accessories of the kidnappers within the staff. Security of meetings, documents, information, and communications must be strict.

The crisis coordinator will normally be the only member of the CMC involved in full-time management of the negotiation. He will be responsible for continuity and the liaison between the headquarters and the subsidiary. He arranges meetings of the CMC, briefs them, presents the agenda for decisions, and promulgates these decisions. Also, not least because of possible later legal implications, he should supervise the full and accurate recording both of CMC meetings and of the communications and progress in the incident itself.

Depending on the circumstances and on the structure of the corporation, it may be desirable to have an international vice president or director as a member of the CMC. Someone with intimate knowledge of the country where the incident is occurring may be essential if a proper account is to be taken of the effects of corporate negotiating policy. Local implications could affect the short-term or long-term viability of the company's trading in the country. There may also be questions of temporary or permanent evacuation of individuals or their families.

If the corporation has engaged specialist consultants to give advice on crisis management and negotiation, or if consultants have been offered as part of the services of their insurance company, this advice will mainly be given to the negotiating team at the subsidiary level (unless the negotiation is being conducted with the headquarters itself). The role of such advisors is discussed in the next chapter. The corporation will also, however, normally ask a representative of the consulting firm to join some meetings at the CMC level to advise on policy or techniques: This is in practice where some of the most useful advice can be given.

The LNT is headed by the senior executive of a subsidiary company but, as the likeliest kidnap victim, he may appoint a deputy during contingency planning. Other possible participants are a visiting representative from corporate headquarters, a legal advisor, or possibly a professional consultant. The group should also consult with police or security forces. Members of the family affected are not normally included on the LNT, but effective liaison with them should be maintained. The LNT must not become too large: Other disciplines, such as public relations, personnel, and security, are usually handled by regular LNT members. The key member of the LNT remains the negotiator. His particular qualities and his role, and the roles of other LNT members, are further examined in the next chapter.

The first necessity is good and secure communications between corporate headquarters and the subsidiary. Negotiations are handled by the LNT on location. The CMC at corporate headquarters has to endorse important decisions, especially those involving money (e.g., the offer of an increased ransom). Emotional involvement at the subsidiary may limit objectivity: misunderstandings, delays, or loss of confidence resulting from poor communications could put not only money but also morale and lives at risk. The corporate attitude towards its responsibility for the lives of its staff on duty in dangerous places is crucially important. The need for secrecy in delicate negotiations has to be balanced against the need to keep a worried staff informed of developments—a particularly important balance for arranging the care for any victim's family.

One job of the contingency planning stage is building up a good working relationship with local government departments and police. While the media is not directly involved in contingency planning, good relations with a number of journalists in the course of normal commercial contacts will clearly pay dividends. If a crisis does occur, it will be an enormous asset to know not only the names of people who cannot be trusted but also which officials, police officers, and members of the media *can* be trusted and treated as friends. A policy for dealing with the media in this event should be established in advance. As has already been demonstrated, reports, interviews, and conjecture in the press, radio, and television can be either constructive or dangerous.

Every staff member at risk should be asked to provide data for a confidential personal file on himself and his family, to be kept locked up until an emergency arises. This should contain full details of names; ages; addresses; schools; telephone numbers; descriptions of identifying marks (e.g., scars, dental information); serial numbers of identity cards, passports, and credit cards for every member of the family; and medical data, including blood group and any special drugs or treatment required for heart or other ailments. An efficient police force can make good use of photographs, handwriting samples, voiceprints, and fingerprints, but tact and diplomacy may be needed in recording these. Addresses, such as of clubs, can be useful; so can details of any regular activities of children to indicate where they might be found on a particular evening; other pertinent data are the names and addresses of family doctors, lawyers, trusted neighbours, and friends.

Each file should include enough data for immediate proof of a group's claim of holding a victim, though more intimate data may be needed for that purpose in the later stages of negotiations. Staff members can be invited to provide, if they wish, an envelope, with a seal to be broken only in stated emergencies, that contains intimate data for disclosure to only those who need to know. At least one distinguished kidnap victim had a mistress at an address of which his family was quite unaware—but the police did know, and acted on the information.

TAKING ACCOUNT OF THE LAW IN CONTINGENCY PLANNING

During contingency planning, CMCs will certainly consider the level of insurance against fire and bomb damage; they may also consider insurance against extortion, by product pollution, by threat, or by kidnap and ransom. Such insurance can provide indemnity against a wide range of consequences, as well for extortion, including management diversion, commercial disruption, and consequential costs. Lloyd's of London is so confident of their reputation that they will insure against virtually any risk in the world.

Some governments attempt to ban insurance against extortion or kidnap and ransom on the grounds that it could encourage kidnappers to select an insured victim, which would result in the payment of a higher ransom. This is a fallacy. A large proportion of the Fortune 500 biggest firms do insure their staffs and families against these contingencies, and in most cases the staff concerned are unaware that they are covered. A condition of Lloyd's policies is that their existence must be kept secret, known only by a select list of those who need to know. Kidnappers select their targets on the basis of their wealth and of a perceived security weakness. The existence of insurance is irrelevant in this context.

Responsibly managed insurance in practice makes kidnap less likely because Lloyd's underwriters retain experienced consultants who advise companies on improved security. Just as the advice of the underwriters' fire surveyors reduces the risk of fire, so the equivalent security advice reduces the risk of kidnap or terrorist attack. If this advice is taken—again as with fire insurance—the premiums for antiterrorist kidnap and ransom insurance is also normally reduced. It is therefore rare for insured clients to be kidnap victims: The would-be kidnappers' surveillance would reveal that their security and awareness of risk will make them more difficult targets. Of the 247 victims kidnapped in Italy in 1978–82, only three were insured.

Lloyd's underwriters have clear priorities when an insured client is kidnapped. The first and overriding priority is the safety of the victim: obviously, any other policy, moral considerations aside, would be commercially suicidal. Their second priority is to cooperate with the police. As with any other insurance, the premium covers a specified maximum indemnity. Lloyd's will not provide cover in excess of the client's assets; and it is from these assets that the ransom is paid, not by the underwriters, who later reimburse after normal loss adjustment procedures.

If an insured client is kidnapped, Lloyd's sends consultants to give advice on handling the crisis and negotiation. Their instructions follow the same priorities as described above, the overriding priority being the safe release of the client, which has almost always been achieved. A client's insurance cover is a factor to be borne in mind, but only insofar as he (or those negotiating for his release) so wish. The client is under no obligation to accept the consultants' advice on any matter. They are paid by the underwriters, but their relationship is directly with the client.

Lloyd's make it a condition of their policies that the police must be informed, which enhances both the handling of negotiations and the prospects of successful police action against the kidnappers. Some governments, such as the U.S. government, have a rule that no ransom or other concession will be given for any kidnapped government employee. This is an admirable policy and has resulted in the number of diplomats kidnapped being greatly reduced since the early 1970s, simply because they are now known not to be paying targets. The policy is therefore almost universally approved by diplomats themselves, though there is some flexibility in its implementation.

In an ideal world, the same standard would be applied by private individuals and corporations. This, however, is a policy that could never be enforced: Unlike diplomats, who accept risk like front-line soldiers, neither corporations nor families regard hostages in this light. Nor do they have the resources on which governments can call for protection of officials in dangerous places. If corporations abandoned kidnapped executives to their fate, they would pay heavily in staff morale. In the long run it might be cheaper as well as morally more defensible to pay a ransom. And the father of a family will certainly pay a ransom to save a kidnapped child.

Some governments have attempted to enforce a no-ransom policy by legislation, but these laws are unenforceable, as are laws to ban communication with proscribed terrorist gangs or criminals (some Latin American governments have tried to enforce this rule). While some governments, such as in El Salvador in 1979–80 give freedom to negotiate ransoms up to an agreed maximum provided that no political concessions are made, other governments are attempting to take full control of negotiations themselves or to at least control communication. Such a policy is hard to enforce: it is the kidnappers who decide when and to whom to telephone their demands.

The Italian government along with others has tried to ban insurance, prevent the company or family of a kidnap victim from obtaining currency to pay ransoms, and frozen assets, although the legality of these measures has been challenged. It is not against the law, as written, to negotiate with kidnappers or to pay a ransom. The argument is that such bans strengthen the hand of the firm or family by enabling them to plead with the kidnappers that they have no way of producing the money.

All such laws are both impractical and counterproductive. The firm or family of a hostage will give overriding priority to getting the victim released alive. If they are inhibited by the law, they will find a way around it. They may even take illegal pre-emptive action, such as many rich Italian and Latin American families have done by smuggling undeclared contingency funds into foreign banks. Worse still, if they fear that the law will inhibit them, they may keep the kidnap and the negotiation secret from the police. This response is not only likely to result in their rewarding the kidnappers with a larger ransom more quickly; it also means that the police receive no information at all (since the only source of information is from clandestine calls from the kidnappers to the negotiators): there is no chance of arrests or conviction, and therefore every encouragement to the kidnappers to repeat the crime.

In Italy, for example, during the peak kidnapping period 1975–79, when there were on average more than 70 kidnaps per year, the police detection rate was between 5 and 10 percent. By contrast, the FBI reported in 1974 that there had been in the previous 40 years 647 recorded cases of kidnapping in the United States, of which all but three had been solved and over 90 percent of the kidnappers captured.[2] The FBI give full support and freedom of action to firms or families, making it clear that their overriding priority was to recover a hostage alive, with a lesser priority given to the arrest and conviction of the kidnappers. As a result the FBI got full cooperation and were privy to all available information and access from the negotiators. In practice they achieved a far higher detection arrest and conviction rate by giving top priority to the safety of the victim. Other governments and police forces would do well to take these lessons to heart.

Another aspect of the law to be borne in mind in contingency planning is that of legal liability. This has already been mentioned in the context of extortion by product pollution. In cases of kidnapping of business executives, there have been examples of corporations being sued by the victim or by his family for failure to protect him or secure his release; or by stockholders for allegedly unauthorized payment of too big a ransom.

In a recent lawsuit in New York by a released kidnap hostage against his former employees, Judge Pollack defined the legal position of the corporation as follows: "The corporation must show that it was not at fault, that it did act reasonably, fairly and diligently in the unfortunate situation into which the parties were plunged by terrorist action for which neither were responsible." The case was dismissed with prejudice so the corporation was exonerated with a full award of costs. They were well served by taking expert legal advice both in planning for and conducting negotiations.

On the other hand, the Goodyear Tire Company was sued in 1982 by the widow of one of their executives, Clifford Bevens, who had been kidnapped in Guatemala in December 1980 and shot by one of the kidnappers (who then shot himself) when the Guatemalan police attacked the hideout in August 1981. After the hearing of Mrs. Bevens's suit, the *Wall Street Journal* reported that she had been awarded $1,250,000 in a wrongful-death settlement. Both Goodyear and Mrs. Bevens asked the court to seal the record, but the judge decided that it should be open. The *Wall Street Journal* quoted Goodyear's opinion as follows: "It was, and remains, Goodyear's opinion that making the settlement public would serve to encourage terrorists by leaving an impression that refusal to meet their demands would only result in demands in US courts by survivors. Further publicizing a settlement, whether large or small, would establish a price on our employees."

Multinational subsidiaries often have trading or joint venture agreements with local companies and the decision as to how far to consult with them in a kidnap situation may be a difficult one. Depending on the nationality of the victim, they may see things differently: Care must be taken over legal liability for any decisions taken.

To guard against being successfully sued by stockholders, it is important that the board of directors give (and record) their authority to their crisis management committee and local negotiating teams to negotiate and, if necessary, to pay a ransom up to a resolved maximum. Such suits, whether successful or not, can be costly in time and stress for senior executives. It may well happen that an individual plaintiff may go bankrupt without paying the costs awarded against him. All of these legal liabilities should be foreseen and considered in contingency planning to ensure that they do not add unexpected problems to the crisis.

EVACUATION PLANNING

Another aspect of contingency planning in particularly high risk areas (such as Iran and El Salvador in recent years) is to be prepared for evacuation of expatriate personnel, their families, and any local employees who might be victimized for their loyalty to the institution concerned, be it a corporation or an embassy. The plan must obviously be handled with great discretion, both to safeguard staff and family morale and to avoid, in a delicate situation, any impression that the institution is looking over its shoulder.

A great deal of useful preparation can be publicly justified, should that be necessary, as a precaution against more general and self-evident contingencies, such as a collapse of law and order, an outbreak of large scale guerrilla or civil war, or an external invasion. A checklist of preparatory actions should be drawn up, preferably with advice from an organization that has already experienced such an evacuation or, more probably, from a consulting firm with experience in detailed evacuation plans.

Precautions on a personal level by expatriates and trusted local employees at risk need to be extended by them (with some discretion) to their families, who may well be evacuated first. Some of the things to be considered are currency and credit cards likely to be acceptable internationally (including a good supply of ready cash to avoid delays in airports and customs); suitable clothing, food, and water for withstanding siege or travelling; passports, visas and other documentation; vaccination records, medical packs, radios and flashlights with spare batteries. Households, too, should be prepared for siege, allowing for a collapse of public services: Cars should be kept in order with spare fuel and nonessentials packed ready for transport or storage.

An embassy or company should appoint an evacuation committee, under a senior executive, that includes transport, communications, and medical experts and, if possible, at least one trusted local executive. This committee should make appropriate plans for safeguarding premises, assets, and confidential documents, if necessary to withstand siege or riot. It should establish a liaison with local authorities and police. An important duty is a phased evacuation plan, first of families, secondly nonessential personnel and important records or valuable and moveable assets, and finally of all remaining personnel at risk in the event of a collapse of order, a concerted attack on the institution, or threats against all expatriates.

TRAINING AND SIMULATION EXERCISES

Wherever there is a risk either of individual terrorist or criminal attack, or of a collapse of order, executives and staff must be trained to reduce the risk or, should the need arise, to participate in the response. Again, advice by a team of consultants experienced in such matters, who can assist a security director in preparing a program and providing instructions, is probably the best answer. Some discretion may be needed, both to avoid damaging staff morale and to avoid arousing trade union opposition or demands for danger money. The best approach is to convince the staff that the better and more evident the standard of security, alertness, and awareness, the smaller is the likelihood of being picked as a target. "There is always another mug."

The crisis management committee, local negotiating teams, and evacuation committee can best be trained by simulation exercises. One of the best techniques available is termed a *hypothetical*—which was developed by Harvard Law School and promoted by the Ford Foundation. Everyone in responsible positions, seated round a horseshoe of tables facing inwards, handles an ongoing hypothetical situation, which is presented and developed by a skilled moderator. Problems are thrown at the executives or officials concerned and the story is carried forward in the light of their responses.

An alternative is the paper chase, much used by the British Police College and military staff colleges, in which a series of preplanned situations on paper are handed to the committee, which discusses them and moves through a series of crises to a denouement. Normally carried out as a one-day exercise, the CMC is presented with, say, six or eight situations in turn, with an imaginary gap of several days or weeks between them. An alternative is to spread the exercise over several weeks, assembling the CMC for a two- or three-hour session each week to face an ongoing series of decisions. This arrangement provides more realism and gives greater opportunities for role playing; but it also involves more time and expense.

It is noteworthy that a highly successful hypothetical was run jointly by the BBC and the Ford Foundation late in 1979, uncannily predicting the situation that occurred when terrorists seized the Iranian embassy in London in April 1980. Participants included the senior police officer from Scotland Yard, who was destined to handle the actual event when it occurred, army officers, lawyers, and journalists—as well as the BBC television reporter who was on duty when the rescue attack went in and the editor of BBC Television News, who played a crucial role in the operation itself. Though it took many weeks of preparation, the hypothetical simulation took three hours. A large number of the actual problems-to-be were tackled and resolved—often with considerable heat—by those who were later to face them, again with each other, in a few months time. Without doubt this preparation played an important part in the success of the containment, negotiation, and eventual rescue of the hostages.

NOTES

1.   William F. Niehous, "How to Survive as a Hostage," in Martin F. Herz (ed.), *Diplomats and Terrorists: What Works, What Doesn't* (Washington, DC: Institute for the Study of Diplomacy, Georgetown University, 1982), p. 35.

2.   Brian M. Jenkins, "Should Corporations Be Prevented from Paying Ransom?" Series No. P-52 (Santa Monica, CA: The Rand Corporation, 1974).

3.   *Wall Street Journal,* August 17, 1982, p. 31.

Negotiations

17

Negotiations I: Negotiations with Kidnappers

Richard Clutterbuck

THE LOCAL NEGOTIATING TEAM (LNT)

The possible members for a Local Negotiation Team (LNT) were listed in the previous chapter; here its terms of reference and roles are examined. As with the CMC, the worst and commonest case will be studied: that of a kidnap in a multinational subsidiary trading in a high-risk country. Adaption of the study to an embassy or a family is discussed at the end of the chapter.

The LNT should not be too large. Its main functions are first, to secure safe release of the victim; and second, to enable the subsidiary to continue trading, both during and after the crisis. It has to select a negotiator (unless already done), brief him, and decide on negotiating tactics; do its utmost to gain and maintain contact with the kidnappers; and conduct negotiations in the light of a changing situation. It keeps the CMC informed, seeking financial and other authority as appropriate, and maintains liaison with the police, government, press, and any other companies involved. Another responsibility is keeping the victim's family (if still in the country) and its own staff informed of events as far as is possible. The group also maintains security, including that of the family and of any other potential second victims, and takes care of the welfare of the family.

If the payment of a ransom is eventually agreed on, either the CMC or the LNT has to organize it. This involves raising the necessary currency; recording banknote numbers; securing it until delivery; selecting volunteers (preferably two) to deliver it, taking account of any necessary medical or legal problems that could arise; and arranging for the recovery, care, and subsequent evacuation of the victim after his release. Sometimes a CMC has to arrange for cash to be imported, bearing in mind the influence of exchange controls. On the other hand, an LNT may have to carry out most of the functions already described for the CMC, plus a great many more, and usually under considerably more immediate pressure and emotional strain.

This strain is likely to be increased if the LNT includes a member of the family or of the police force. There are examples of both having been included, but their presence may well inhibit frank discussion of tactical options—the family because they are emotionally involved and the police because the LNT may be concerned about infringing on the law. Both family and police should be consulted and kept informed—and may well be invited to specific discussions—but normally they are not regular members of the LNT. In the United States, however, the FBI are frequently welcomed as members in view of their outstanding record in securing the safe release of kidnap victims.

Most of the strain inevitably falls on the senior executive of the subsidiary (or, if he is himself the victim, his deputy). He may be supported by a representative from corporate headquarters and a local legal counsel, and some of the others described in the previous chapter, but generally he will prefer to handle the crisis itself with a small inner cabinet of three or four members. If a specialist consulting firm has been engaged, it will normally provide consultants on a full-time basis, if necessary, two working turn and turn about. This consultant may be able to carry a very large part of the day-to-day load. Though the consultant can only advise, or act within instructions given by the LNT, he may enable the senior executive to largely detach himself in order to continue the company's trading. Otherwise, the company may lose more money than the ransom and other costs put together. In a number of cases, once negotiation is under way, the only people continually involved have been the consultant and the negotiator.

The selection of the negotiator is probably the most important single decision of the LNT. He should be locally born and thus familiar with the nuances, phraseology, idioms, and geography of local streets and villages. He should also, where possible, have been a member of the LNT (or at least regularly consulted by it) during contingency planning. He must be experienced in negotiation and therefore the company's lawyer or industrial relations manager may often be a good choice—provided that he has the other personal qualities needed as well.

Above all, the negotiator must be willing to do the job, which is exhausting and may place him at risk. He must be totally reliable and have the determination and the nerve to handle what are often aggressive and very brief telephone calls. He must be capable of detached judgment and should therefore not be a member of the victim's family nor emotionally too close to him. He must have intelligence, at least matching that of the kidnappers, patience so as not to provoke them, and the initiative to spot, seize, and exploit any opportunity, however small. He should not, however, have too cold a personality: A sense of humor may help him develop a rapport with the kidnappers' negotiator, which can greatly facilitate negotiations and may save the victim's life.

The negotiator must never be the person responsible for making policy decisions (such as the senior executive himself). He must always be in a position to say, "I have no power to agree to that. I will put it to the company and, if you telephone again at the same time tomorrow, I will give you their reaction. I am doing my best, but you must understand my position." He needs precise instructions from the LNT after every communication from the kidnappers. The timing and location of each contact should, if possible, be agreed on with the kidnappers so that the negotiator can take it in a secure environment and at a time that will not unacceptably disrupt his daily routine. This, again, is where any degree of rapport with his adversary will be especially valuable.

NEGOTIATING TACTICS

The first notice of a kidnap may be a written or taped message; more commonly, it is a terse telephone call to the company or to the victim's family, stating that he is a hostage. The kidnappers may demand that a ransom of a certain size be ready by a certain date; or that a terrorist manifesto be published, or that prisoners should be released; or that the company should give certain employment concessions, such as reinstatement of dismissed workers or a pay raise; or that there should be a distribution of food and welfare goods to the poor. In each case, the company will be told to await detailed instructions and warned that, if the police are informed, the hostage will at once be killed. The response to this first message may decisively affect the subsequent negotiations.

There are many different people who may receive such a call, including telephone operators and secretaries, and the caller may refuse to wait for it to be transferred. All of these people should therefore have written instructions beside the telephone, preferably on a prepared form. They should record as much information as possible about the caller, such as a description of voice, accent, sex, whether agitated or calm, young or old, and of any background noise. It would, of course, be ideal if such a call could be taped. An attempt should be made if possible, to establish whether the caller really does hold the victim and is pulling a hoax. The call should be handled in such a way that the caller will call again and, if possible, agree on a time and telephone number for him to call.

The pro forma should also give precise instructions as to whom (with alternatives) the recipient should inform. In most countries the police are not the first choice: contingency planning will have established a confidential arrangement whereby such matters will be reported only by named executives to named and trusted police officers. The instructions should indicate who on a short list of named executives (e.g., managing director or security director) should be informed. This executive will need to use discretion in the timing and extent of a call to the police; but, wherever possible, a trusted police officer should be informed as early as possible.

In assessing the threat and getting clues on the identity of the criminal or political group, it is useful if all those who may receive a kidnap message are aware of the likely organization of such a group. The victim will probably have been selected by a reconnaissance and surveillance cell. A second cell will have abducted him, a third may receive and guard him, and a fourth will conduct negotiations—the last one possible including the leader himself, though he may not personally make the calls. There may be a fifth group organized to collect a ransom and a sixth to launder and dispose of the money. The more that can be pieced together of this organization from the first and subsequent calls, the more likely the police can take effective action.

Before any further calls, certain urgent management decisions have to be made, and some of these may need to be discussed with the CMC. Should the media, or at least selected journalists, be briefed in order to secure their cooperation before they hear of the kidnap themselves? Should the victim's family be moved to a secure place? Or evacuated? Should other possible "second victims" also be guarded? Should joint arrangements be made with the police? Telephones likely to be used for negotiation should be fitted for taping. The police may, of course, also arrange for the line to be tapped. A log should at once be opened to record every event and every call.

At this stage the negotiator is established and briefed in readiness for the next contact and, if the company has engaged an experienced consultant, he will be at the negotiator's side. The next contact may come by the telephone earlier agreed on, or by another telephone, such as an intimidating call to the victim's family if they are still in their home; other choices are by letter, tape, newspaper, message given to a radio or TV station, or through an intermediary (though this is rare except in certain countries like Iraq).

The kidnappers may use a variety of techniques to intimidate or demoralize the victim's family and the firm: The negotiator must be ready for them. They may threaten death or mutilation of the victim or report that his health is deteriorating, possibly sending photographs or distressed letters from the victim. They may try to hustle the negotiator or leave him in suspense with long periods of silence. They may try to apply pressure indirectly by, for example, getting a message to the victim's wife indicating that the company is being uncooperative or parsimonious without regard for her husband's life. Other coercive techniques include the use of audio- and video-tapes, which can be sent to the family or the media.

The treatment of the family is especially important, not only for humanitarian reasons, but also to maintain their cooperation during negotiations. An early blunder, such as tactless, clumsy, or unfeeling behavior towards the family, can quickly cause embitterment. A wife at the end of her tether can make a public outburst or criticism of the company's tactics in the hope of goading it into more urgent action. If the kidnappers hear of this event, it can do immense damage to delicate negotiations. One Latin American terrorist group, according to what they told one of their hostages, specifically urged their target selection teams to select a victim with an emotional and strong-minded wife, who would put pressure on the company.

The question of family relocation will also arise. Generally it is safest for all concerned to relocate them as quickly as possible: They will be prime targets for supplementary threats if the kidnappers feel the need to apply extra pressure. If relocated, however, they should be kept informed and encouraged to cooperate.

Throughout all these pressures, the negotiator will have to keep his nerve. He can remind himself that it is very rare for kidnappers to kill their victim. As the only card in their hand, they lose his value once he is known to be dead. The negotiator should regularly demand proof of life. This can best be achieved by obtaining from the victim's family a question that only he can answer (e.g., "What was the name of the dog we had in 1960?"). Another way is to ask the kidnappers to send a photograph of the victim holding a copy of the current edition of a newspaper with the day's headline visible. Another alternative is a letter in the victim's handwriting or a recording of his voice, again containing a clear reference to a piece of news that could not have been known before the day in question.

Each contact will, in addition, give the negotiator a chance to assess the physical and mental condition both of the hostage and of the kidnappers. It may be worthwhile for the LNT to consult specialists such as physicians, psychiatrists, voiceprint analysts, and graphologists. The kidnappers may send letters or tapes in which the hostage pleads for his life in order to put pressure on his company or his family: These too can be useful in assessing his situation.

The LNT should maintain a continuous assessment of the risk, modified each time there is another message from the kidnappers. Here again, the best guide is the experience of previous negotiations. A good consultant should be able to help the LNT assess the significance of each message, together with other developments, and decide on the tactics for the next call before it comes. It is wise to rehearse each response because the kidnappers, fearful of the call being traced, are likely to make their call very brusque and to hang up after one or two minutes.

Negotiations often follow a pattern. Initially the kidnappers dominate and attempt to bully the negotiator into a quick settlement for a lot more than they really expect to get. When they realize that this is not going to work, but that the negotiator is prepared to talk, a phase of dialogue will begin, punctuated by periods of silence. This phase may last for days, weeks, or months, but all the time the pressure on the kidnappers is increasing. They begin to fear that the police may close in on them and that they will get nothing. To kill the victim would write off their chances of having their threats taken seriously, and they may be reluctant to go through the whole dangerous process of kidnapping again. The negotiator may then begin to detect a note of urgency and anxiety. In the final phase, he will increasingly dominate the negotiation of a ransom and of its means of delivery. If this phase is well handled, and the police have been given time to build up evidence, there will be a better chance of the kidnappers' being arrested and the ransom recovered.

If it does become necessary to pay a ransom, the LNT must bear in mind that assembling the currency may take a long time (since it is usually demanded in used notes of low denomination, not with consecutive numbers), especially if there are government controls, as there usually are. The cooperation of the police and of a bank are essential. It must also be remembered that the ransom may be heavy and bulky. Half a million dollars in $10 bills weighs over 100 lbs.

The police will probably press for details of the arrangements to enable them to monitor the ransom drop, which is sometimes successful. When a ransom was paid for Baron Empain in France in 1978, the police successfully ambushed the drop and arrested the leader of the gang, who was then persuaded to cooperate in getting the baron released and later in making further arrests. Similarly in Australia in 1982, the police managed to secrete a constable with a radio in the trunk of the car delivering a ransom, thereby facilitating an ambush in which the criminal collecting the ransom spotted the police, opened fire at them, and was shot dead.

More often, however, a sophisticated kidnap gang will take complicated precautions to prevent surveillance. The car will be required to go to a series of check points (usually in bars or telephone boxes) at which the next point will be identified by some untraceable means. At one of these points, they may search the car, and it will be required to move along routes where it will be easy to spot any police surveillance. Each case must be treated on its merits but, when there is a risk that police surveillance may be spotted, the safety of the hostage must be the paramount consideration.

THE ROLE OF THE CONSULTANT

Though there have been a number of exceptions, it is rare for a family or corporation to be picked twice as a target for extortion by kidnap. This is largely because, if they have experienced it once, they take such positive precautions thereafter that kidnappers usually turn away and look for a softer target. The corollary of this, however, is that when they do face such a crisis, they are usually facing it for the first time. As a result, they may have little idea what to do, and react in a state of shock. This response can have a disastrous effect, increasing the risk to the victim's life, the duration of his ordeal, and the prospect of having to pay a very large ransom.

There has been a dramatic growth in kidnapping in the 1970s and 1980s. Some families and firms have paid out enormous sums in ransom accompanied by a damaging diversion of management time and effort and sometimes a catastrophic effect on trading. The demand for specialist advice, both for preventative security and crisis management, has grown. A number of security companies were formed to meet this demand, and some of these have now built up a large fund of experience, both in prevention and its crisis management and negotiations. They are able to put this experience at the disposal of a client who has never previously handled such a situation. The best comparison is with an accountant or doctor who applies his experience both to preempt his client's troubles and to help him to handle them if they occur.

Before seeking advice from a consultant, a client should know what to look for and have a realistic idea of what such companies can and cannot do. The following description of the consultant's role is based on the experience of the company with which the author has been associated since its foundation in 1975. The organizations and techniques used by other companies will vary, but the principles are much the same. The consultants of this company had, up to January 1983, carried out preventative surveys for over 400 clients, and had participated in crisis management and negotiation in 110 extortion-related incidents. These negotiations covered more than 50 countries, the largest proportion of these being in the highest-risk countries of Latin America and in Italy. Consulting firms vary in size and organization, but this company has divisions covering information services, prevention, equipment advice and project management, education and training, and response services.

The information service was originally developed to provide the firm's own consultants with the back-up they needed, based on a network of confidential contacts in the countries where they operated, and supplemented by a team of analysts and translators monitoring daily events at headquarters. This information has since 1980 also been available as a subscription service for corporations, including monthly reports on some 60 countries (based on a client's requests) which give an up-to-date assessment of political and security risks. This subscription service was by early 1983 used by over 200 corporations, including a high proportion of the 50 largest industrial companies in the world. It also provides immediate security assessments and intelligence alert reports, in between monthly reports, to cover urgent developments, such as a change of government, an outbreak of fighting, or emergence of a new terrorist threat. The quarterly reports on some parts of the world that go into more depth and monthly assessments of risks to travellers worldwide. In addition, individual assessments are made of specific situations or countries as requested by clients. It is worth noting that Lloyd's underwriters provide the subscription service for their clients.

The prevention division sends consultants to carry out preventative security surveys; to join with corporate security staffs in making crisis management plans, including, if necessary, contingency plans for temporary or permanent evacuation; and to provide security advisors for VIP visits, conferences, and trade fairs. Security surveys are usually done in two phases. The first phase concerns senior management at corporate headquarters, normally taking two or three days. The aim is to produce a corporate crisis management plan in conjunction with the corporation's security staff and tailored to its needs. In the second phase, the surveys are detailed investigations and security plans for specific locations, including recommendations to cover physical and procedural aspects of security at the office and the residence and for local travel of the individuals concerned and their families. Local crisis management procedures can be included if required. Each of the surveys is confirmed in a detailed written report.

The equipment and project management services are designed to obviate the need for a client to involve himself or his resources in areas in which he may not be familiar, including security of premises, residences, and information, covering if required, a project planning and on-site project management service. The service includes an independent appraisal of equipment available and of the manufacturer's efficiency in installation and post-installation services, with advice on which equipment will best integrate with the client's operations and security plans.

Education and training are provided in the form of seminars and simulation exercises for top and middle management, covering kidnap and other forms of extortion, contingency planning, crisis management, hostage survival, evacuation planning, and travel security. Training courses are also run for management and other staff taking up appointments overseas; for security, office, and domestic staff; and for bodyguards and drivers. All the above can be carried out in London or, most commonly, on the client's own premises.

The response service is provided to give advice to clients in crisis management and negotiation when a kidnap has occurred or some other form of extortion is being applied. For corporations or individuals insured with the Lloyd's syndicate, which covers the majority of such insurance, this service is provided at the underwriters' expense until the incident is resolved. Alternatively, the client can subscribe to a security agreement under which an annual subscription guarantees the fees (but does not insure against ransom) for a priority service by the consultants. For other clients, consultants are provided as available on a normal daily fee basis. Should the incident or negotiation be prolonged, the consultant will be relieved at intervals. He will have at his disposal both his own personal experience of similar incidents and the consolidated experience of the other negotiations in which he or his colleagues have been involved. The consultant is normally used as a member of the LNT, assessing each contact or message and advising the negotiator. The client, whether insured or not, is under no obligation to accept his advice. In most cases, however, a degree of trust has been established that enables the crisis to be handled almost entirely by the negotiator and the consultant, leaving other executives free to concentrate their time and effort on their normal task of continuing trading.

As in any new field expanding fast in response to an upsurge in demand, quality varies. There are a number of sharks in this field, as well as some companies of very high quality. Selection from the field is particularly hazardous in that, especially in response to a crisis, it may have to be made with great urgency. The best guide to choice is to consult other corporations or individuals who have had occasion to use professional consultants in a similar situation. There is nothing to compare with personal recommendation from a trusted source. Other considerations are (a) be wary of consultants who have links with equipment manufacturers, since their advice may not be wholly objective; (b) find out the number of cases handled by the consulting firm under consideration and in particular the number handled in the country concerned, or in similar or neighboring countries; and (c) find out as much as possible about the professional background of those engaged as consultants.

All of these considerations underline the desirability of making such a selection in advance. This person could be part of a contingency list of people to be called on in an emergency (along with, for example, fire services, medical services, lawyers, and trusted police officers) Preferably, however, the selection should be a part of specific security planning. The potential cost of a kidnap or extortion crisis is so high that it is wise not to leave it to chance.

CRISIS MANAGEMENT BY A FAMILY

When a ransom is demanded from a victim's family rather than from a corporation, the principles remain the same, but there are some important differences in procedure. The family will be more limited in resources and money, and will probably have no office to support the negotiator unless the victim is a senior executive's wife or child, or one of the victim's close relations is himself a business executive. Geographical separation is also less of a factor, though the family of the victim might be evacuated from an outstation to their home, leaving someone else to handle the case for them.

Generally, therefore, the CMC and the LNT will be combined. A member of the family can choose to chair the CMC but may prefer to let someone else do so. The latter choice may be preferable if there is anyone suitable in whom the family has complete trust. The negotiator himself, however, should not be chosen from the close relations of the victim: They are too emotionally involved to negotiate with sufficient coolness and detachment.

A family CMC/LNT is smaller than a corporate CMC. If it is headed by the victim's husband or wife as the ultimate decision maker, it is advisable to have a deputy to reduce the load. A lawyer is an essential member, as is a suitable negotiator: These two could be the same person. Apart from these differences, the processes of crisis management and negotiation are similar to those described for a corporation.

CRISIS MANAGEMENT BY A GOVERNMENT

When a government official is kidnapped in his own country, most governments make active the shadow crisis management organization they use to control such incidents, be they hijacks, kidnaps, hostage seizures, bomb threats, or natural disasters. Such an organization is normally headed by the minister of the interior or his equivalent, with a senior permanent official as deputy. It includes representatives of other relevant departments, including the police and intelligence services and probably the army in case a rescue is planned. Most governments have established policies for responding to terrorist demands; generally these include a well-publicized policy that no ransoms will be paid, nor other concessions granted (e.g., release of prisoners) in the face of terrorist demands. Most government employees accept the necessity for such a policy, realizing that it reduces the chances of them being kidnapped at all.

This does not mean, however, that there will be no negotiation. Due to the recent increase in hostage-siege situations, many governments now have a pool of trained police negotiators. Though the handling of a hostage siege is totally different from that of a kidnap, the actual negotiating skills have much in common. In a kidnap extortion aimed at a government, these officers may be used by their governments as negotiators.

Sometimes, despite a no-negotiation policy, governments show some flexibility. When Hanns-Martin Schleyer was kidnapped in West Germany in 1977, for example, the Federal government announced at once that it would not submit to the demand to release the Red Army Faction prisoners or make any other concession, but it did permit the victim's family to attempt to negotiate a ransom. It also sent a number of ministers or senior officials to some of the Middle Eastern capitals to which the world might expect prisoners to be released: This was duly reported by the press. Whether or not they were genuinely there on other business, these visits did arouse speculation that the government were considering a concession despite their demands. This may have contributed to the fact that Schleyer was kept alive for many weeks, during which time the police got very close to rescuing him twice.

When ambassadors are kidnapped overseas, most parent governments also have a policy of no concessions to terrorist demands. Because of this policy, the kidnapping of ambassadors, at a peak in 1970–71, has greatly declined, though seizure and barricading of hostages (often including ambassadors) in embassy sieges has increased. In the now comparatively rare cases in which ambassadors (or other expatriate government representatives) are kidnapped and taken to a secret hideout, the parent government will generally announce that it intends to give the local government every support but to exert no pressure on it. The local government will therefore negotiate (or refuse to do so) exactly as if one of its own nationals were a hostage. The function of the parent embassy will be to maintain a liaison with the local government and its negotiator, and to provide any help that it can.

Government crisis management organizations have handled many embassy seizures (i.e., hostage sieges) successfully, both of foreign embassies in their own countries and of their own embassies overseas, but their success has been more mixed in dealing with cases of hostages kidnapped to secret hideouts.

An uncompromising hard line can work, provided that both the hostage and his family support it. The classic case was the kidnapping of the British Ambassador to Uruguay Sir Geoffrey Jackson by the Tupamaros in 1971. There were a lot of diplomatic kidnappings at that time and Jackson spotted that he was under surveillance by the terrorists; he was also skeptical about the ability of the local police to prevent his being kidnapped. He therefore flew to London, with his wife, to discuss the matter with the Foreign Office. There it was agreed that, should he be kidnapped, he would at once tell his kidnappers "no deals"; that his wife would confirm to the Uruguayan government that this was his wish; and that the British government would also publicly confirm this policy and declare that they would put no pressure on the Uruguayan government.

The ambassador was held for eight months under appalling conditions and stalwartly refused to make or plead for any departure from this uncompromising line.[1] His heroism attracted immense world sympathy and the Tupamaros realized that it would be disastrous for their image if they were to kill him. They eventually got off the hook after a mass escape by Tupamaros prisoners, after which they released him with the explanation that the purpose for which they had kidnapped him had been fulfilled by other means. The aftermath was a massive swing against the left in the Uruguayan general election that followed and the rapid collapse of the Tupamaros. No government, however, can be sure of such a degree of resistance by their ambassadors (or by their wives) as was displayed in this case.

A more complicated case occurred when Richard Starr, a U.S. Peace Corps volunteer, was kidnapped by a Colombian terrorist group, FARC, in 1977. The Peace Corps stoutly preserves its independence from the State Department as a matter of policy, so Starr could not be regarded as a Foreign Service official, and possibly not even as a government employee. Since the Peace Corps had neither the experience nor the resources to conduct negotiations, a joint task force (including the Peace Corps) was set up under the leadership of the Director of the State Department's Office for Combatting Terrorism, Ambassador Anthony Quainton. The task force announced from the start that the U.S. government would pay no ransom and never varied from this stance, though they said that they were prepared to pass messages to and from Starr's family, and they offered (through the Peace Corps Country Team in Bogotá) a channel for passing food, letters, and books to him and receiving letters back.

Negotiations were sporadic and protracted. One of the problems raised in this case was that of dealing with the victim's family by a government department that had a firm policy of making no concessions. Richard Starr had a very determined mother, Mrs. Charlotte Jensen. She, supported by the media and members of Congress, kept up constant pressure on the State Department. Whether justly or not, the bureaucracy was bitterly criticized for a callous, unfeeling attitude towards the family.

After one and a half years, the U.S. embassy in Bogotá received a message from FARC demanding $250,000 for Starr's release, and saying that the State Department should signify agreement by placing a specified want advertisement in a Bogotá newspaper by a stated deadline. Fearing that Starr might be killed if the deadline passed, an advertisement was put in, but the State Department publicly reiterated that no ransom would be paid. The family were highly critical, claiming that the government had spiked some otherwise promising negotiations over payment of a private ransom. Eventually Starr was released on payment of a ransom of $250,000, raised privately (with State Department approval) by newspaper columnist Jack Anderson. Starr had been held for three years.

In retrospect, Ambassador Quainton drew two lessons from this experience:[2] first, that greater effort could have been made to support and assist family members who were under great emotional stress; second, that greater and earlier involvement of appropriate congressional staffs at the State Department's initiative might have reduced the tensions and relieved the pressure on the officers handling the case. He concluded, however, that the basic policy that the U.S. government does not make concessions to terrorists and does not pay ransom had to be, and was, maintained.

The U.S. government (and the victim) again stood firm when a U.S. Army officer serving with NATO, Brigadier General James Dozier, was kidnapped by the Red Brigades in Italy on December 17, 1981. He was taken from his apartment in Verona and held in a tent inside a room on the floor above a supermarket in Padua. He was shackled and subjected to loud music, presumably to prevent him from overhearing the voices of the kidnappers. No demands were issued by the kidnappers and, after 43 days in captivity, he was rescued in a successful raid by the Italian police.

Two important lessons emerge from the Dozier case. First, there was good intelligence that such a kidnap was imminent and Dozier was warned but, to use his own words, "Quite frankly I was so busy in the last months before the kidnapping that I paid no attention to those threats. I accept full responsibility for not heeding the warnings."[3]

The second lesson is that, for expatriates in a high-risk country, the best protection lies in efficient local police and intelligence services, backed by sensible laws; and for these to be backed by the support and cooperation of the victim's own government. The Italian police and intelligence, hamstrung by restrictive action in 1976, were revitalized after the Moro kidnapping in 1978, and an effective package of antiterrorist laws and police powers introduced. The result has been a sharp fall in the number of kidnaps and the arrest of many Red Brigade terrorists, culminating in the rescue of Brigadier General Dozier and the capture of his kidnappers.

NOTES

1. See Geoffrey Jackson, *Surviving The Long Night* (New York: Vanguard, 1974).
2. Anthony C. E. Quainton, "The Starr Case: A Bureaucracy Under Stress," in *Diplomats and Terrorists: What Works, What Doesn't* (Washington, DC: Institute for the Study of Diplomacy, Georgetown University, 1982), pp. 41–44. See also Richard C. Starr, "Callousness and Ineptitude in the State Department" (pp.37 41) and Jack Mitchell, "Botched Relations with Relatives" (pp. 44–47) in the same publication.
3. *Daily Telegraph,* February 3, 1982.

18

Negotiations II: A Negotiator's Experience in a Latin American Kidnapping Case

Dr. Zeta*

Monica Gómez was kidnapped in August 1982. She was abducted in broad daylight in the parking lot of a local university. A group of five men carried out the operation in about 50 seconds. They produced their automatic weapons for the parking lot attendants to see and at the moment that Monica arrived they took her away in her own car without any of the other students in the parking lot even noticing. Fifty meters from the parking lot was a security post, which likewise did not notice the abduction.

A half hour later the university was in turmoil. The authorities arrived. Professors and students were interrogated as well as people who had been in the lot at the time of the kidnapping. Nothing was noted about the criminals except for the fact that they were young. None of those watching could give a description because of the speed with which the action was carried out.

A cell of one of the principal revolutionary groups of the country was believed to exist in the university. The students belonging to this group were well known and immediate suspicion fell on them. There was no positive identification of the kidnappers, however, and these suspicions could not be borne out by the police investigation.

Monica's family sought my help as intermediary and negotiator for her release. Eight years earlier, by one of those strange accidents of fate, I had become involved in my first negotiation of a kidnapping. I had been visiting the home of some close friends to express my condolences following the kidnapping of one of the members of their family. The phone rang, I picked it up because I was next to it, and I found myself negotiating with the kidnappers. Having been successful in that negotiation, I gained the reputation of being a tough but fair intermediary. Acting more impartial than the family and more calm than the kidnappers enabled me to gain the confidence of both parties while at the same time protecting the

---

* Dr. Zeta is the *nom de plume* of a Latin American businessman who has successfully negotiated 18 kidnapping cases.

kidnapped person's life and the financial interests of the family as far as limits allowed.

MY RELUCTANCE TO ENTER THE CASE

In the many subsequent cases I have been involved in I have never accepted any payment. Such negotiations are not my profession. I make a living as an executive of a private local company and I have always considered my involvement in kidnapping cases as an act of friendship to the victims' families as well as a humanitarian act.

I initially opposed accepting the role as negotiator for Monica's kidnapping. I did not know the family personally and what I had heard about them was not good. It was a strange family, reputedly stingy, quarrelsome, and difficult to trust. Nevertheless, two days after the kidnapping, Monica's family showed up at my office along with some personal friends of mine. They told me what had happened and said that they had not yet received any news from the kidnappers. The family was terribly worried because the kidnappers had also taken Monica's car and not brought it back. I tried to calm them, telling them that a kidnapping was not staged for the purpose of stealing a car, and that the kidnappers would not have delayed in calling with the location of the car if that's all they wanted. From the manner in which the kidnapping had occurred, I told them that it seemed to have been carried out by professionals and that they would have to wait until the kidnappers made the first contact.

While at my office, Monica's mother asked to use the phone to call home. When she called the house she was told that someone had called to say that the car could be found in a certain location. They immediately asked me what to do and I told them they had better call the authorities and ask them to check the car for fingerprints and carry out other police procedures. I explained that it would be best to let the police handle it since they were already involved anyway.

When Monica's family asked me to help negotiate I told them that I was very busy. I needed to travel all the time for my work and felt I could not help them with this matter. About 15 days passed during which there was absolute silence on the part of the kidnappers. The girl's mother kept visiting me to beg for help. They could not understand why all this time was passing without any demands being made. The family then received a call telling them to retrieve a message with the ransom demands, which had been left in the northern part of the city. Eight people went to find the message but the note was nowhere to be found. They were frantic thinking someone had taken it.

I kept telling them they had to be patient: Some organizations made demands immediately, only to cut short negotiations from then on with the intention of putting pressure on the family. In other cases, however, the kidnappers keep silent at first and make the first contact only after some time had passed. In this second case I explained the simple strategy that the kidnappers used of maintaining silence for a while in order to weaken the family and obtain the best possible advantage when they began negotiations. I kept telling them that when the kidnappers were ready to negotiate, the message with the demands would appear.

About one month after the kidnapping, the family, with the support of their friends, resorted to a priest to help them beg for my services. Since so much time had passed without hearing from the kidnappers, the family wanted me to help them find a way to contact the kidnappers. This moral pressure got to me and I could not say no. I had to accept the role as negotiator even though I knew neither the victim nor her family—a confusing situation in which I was not sure if they were telling me the truth or lying to me.

THE FIRST MESSAGE

Monica's mother received the first call 28 days after the kidnapping. She came to tell me that the kidnappers told her to expect a call in the next few days when they would give the details of the ransom required to get their daughter back alive. I reminded her that the system of these professional organizations after the initial request is to remain quiet another 20 to 30 days. In this case I suspected that they would opt for the latter period—another wait. Exactly 30 days after the abduction, the kidnappers called with their ransom demands, making believe that this message had been sent earlier, but that they were sending a copy of the demand.

The message was left near the family's residence. After receiving the information by phone on the whereabouts of the message, Monica's mother went with her chauffeur to get it. It took them a long time to find the note since it was left inside a plant in the plastic paper inside of a cigarette pack. The note contained the following message:

> Operation Monica Gómez, 1982: Señora Mother: We have your daughter and will give you the details explaining how you can have your daughter back without any problems as soon as you have strictly complied with the written demands in this letter. First, for the liberation of your daughter we demand the sum of 5 million U.S. dollars. Second, you are not to advise the authorities since whatever false moves you make will result in your daughter's death. The money should be in 100, 50, and 20 dollar bills; not in a series; not new bills; unmarked; without any special ink on them so as to be noticeable. Third, the moment that the money is ready put an ad in the most widely circulated newspaper in the city. Don't put the ad in the paper until the money is ready. We have studied your family's financial situation and your properties; it is a study that we've been making over the past years and we know that the ransom demand we are making is within your capacity to pay.

The family brought me the message, which also contained a letter from their daughter in her own handwriting. From this letter you could tell that she seemed to be in good condition with a normal pulse. Her writing was exactly the same as that in her schoolwork at the university. They had also sent two pictures, which showed that she was in good condition.

I was not surprised by the amount of money that they had demanded: The custom here is to ask for gigantic sums of money, and always in U.S. dollars. My opinion and experience told me that the bigger the ransom, the easier the negotiation because such a huge sum of money leaves a lot of space for negotiating.

The family wanted to try to negotiate as quickly as possible because they wanted their daughter back by any means. But aside from their common desire to have their daughter back, they argued among themselves. They bickered about how much to pay because never before to my knowledge had that much been paid; they bickered because there were more children at home and Monica was a widow (she has a daughter and lived alone).

THE FAMILY'S INDECISION

I calmed the family and asked them the maximum amount that they could pay. I needed this figure to be able to negotiate with the kidnappers. About ten days passed during which none of the family members could agree on anything. All of them wanted to participate in the negotiations without realizing that the game they were playing was with the life of a person. The money was not the issue. It was hard for me to get them to understand that the material value was just fleeting compared to the value of a human life. Money comes and goes, but a life once lost does not return.

Another problem was how and when to respond to the demands of the kidnappers. The only means of communication with them was to be the ad in the newspaper according to their instructions. My feeling was to remain firm, to not place the ad in order to weaken their position. A month had passed and they had put the family up against a psychological wall; the family was completely exhausted and in my opinion the time was not right for the ad. First it was necessary that the family agree on what they would say and what they would offer. It looked like this was a strange family. I kept silent until they could decide just what they could pay.

My idea was to state an amount in the first ad to make the kidnappers believe that there was money, and to create a situation in which the family appeared ready to pay the money. By including an amount in the newspaper we knew that they would take care of Monica and let nothing happen to her. The family was worried that since she was a woman of approximately 30 years of age, they would abuse her; but I assured them that in kidnapping cases, at least in this country, the money was what they wanted. They would respect her physical and personal integrity as long as they were paid.

Unfortunately, this family never could decide on how much to pay. At the same time, I could not indefinitely postpone the negotiations. After reading Monica's letter carefully, I realized that this waiting part could last one month, two months, or even three months; I just did not know how long it might take. I understood that the first month had gone past, the demands had come, and that we had the opportunity in the next 30 days to conduct successful negotiations for the release of the victim. These terms of the kidnappers seemed fixed, and I thought that there was no way to rescue her before this time period was up.

THE FIRST OFFER

Along these lines, I got the ad ready for the first communication with the kidnappers 12 days after having received the letter with their demands. Without knowing how much the family would offer to pay, I wrote it from a humanitarian standpoint, knowing that the first communications pass with little notice. I realized that the kidnappers could not immediately reduce the ransom amount but would instead appear inflexible to keep pressure on the family. Meanwhile, the family thought I should offer $150,000 while they tried to organize and figure out how much they could actually come up with in the negotiations.

The ad that the family put in the paper read: "Farm for sale of a certain amount of hectares. Information at this number." They published it in the section of the newspaper under real estate. Two days later they received their first call. The kidnappers wanted to talk only to the girl's mother. I had advised the family that when they demanded to talk to her, we should not deny them the right initially. After one or two calls to the mother, I would then enter into the negotiations.

My initial recommendation to the family, especially to the mother and daughter, was to leave the country to give us more power in the negotiation. I suggested that they create the impression that they were in bad health and needed to be checked by doctors abroad. The mother and daughter refused this recommendation, saying they would rather die first. The mother could not abandon her daughter, and she never did understand that her departure was a tactic that we could utilize in order to pressure the kidnappers into a faster solution to the negotiations.

The first, second, and third calls were received by the mother. The kidnappers threatened her several times. They told her all sorts of things to convince her the family should give them the full amount without negotiation. She consistently responded that they should speak with me. They asked her who I was and the mother gave them my name and phone number. Only after several calls and continuing frustration did they agree to speak with a negotiator.

THE NEGOTIATIONS BEGIN

My first call from the kidnappers came after a month and 16 days. I moved to my brother's house where the call came at 6:00 P.M. The kidnappers tried to employ more pressure tactics. They told me that we would have marathon negotiations in order to close them by 11:59 P.M. the following day. If no agreement were reached by then, they would kill Monica.

I kept calm, and before initiating the discussion I told them that their demands were absurd. I reminded them that so far they had only been able to secure ten million pesos ($150,000), the amount that the family had put in the ad. They could obtain much more, but there had been no negotiations. We did not know what their real demands were. Since this was the first call, they put us in an absurd and ridiculous situation by giving a final ultimatum so quickly. I further explained to them that I was just a negotiator, but one who could be trusted. Surely they knew of me from other cases. I gave them a guarantee of my word. I told them that if they wanted to negotiate with me, they were assured no authorities were involved in any situation and that they would receive from me the solemn pact of my word of honor.

They told me that they knew with whom they were speaking, that they respected my name, but that they had made a study of the family that showed that it owned a chain of hotels, office buildings, land, and more. The family were multimillionaires. I explained to them that in every negotiation the custom is to thoroughly review the financial statements and the actual businesses that the people have. It seemed that the kidnappers had only looked at assets, but I explained that the family also had a lot of debts to banks and corporations. (Kidnappers usually add but do not subtract.) This hit them hard and they said it was a lie, that the family had a great deal of money outside of the country, up-to-date accounts, hotels, construction and urbanization projects, and moreover that they treated their workers very badly.

I had to destroy this theory, convincing the kidnappers that because of the economic situation debtors had offered the family part ownership in these hotels, that actually the family was lacking totally in liquidity, and that because of this the kidnappers would lose time if they waited to get all the money that they were demanding.

These negotiations went on in a series of phone calls until almost 10:00 P.M., during which time I took the chance to ask them the favor, since they knew me, of removing the deadline. I explained to them that this was a needless source of pressure that would impede our coming to any conclusion. I proposed the following: They forget about their initial demands; Monica's family did not have liquid assets and they were very tough. The family would prefer to see their daughter dead than to pay a price that was not within their reach. If the kidnappers were certain that they could obtain the original amount of their demand, I would retire from the situation because they were absolutely wrong. If they insisted on killing someone I told them to leave the family alone. I said that they would never get the ransom that they wanted. At the end of this I suggested that we forget the absurd amount that they had asked for and fix a price that could be reached and obtained more easily. If they did so, I said I would help the family sell some property, mortgage other property, obtain bank loans—all in order to collect the amount that we established. At first they rejected this offer, but they agreed to postpone the negotiations for two days to see what money the family could come up with.

I was pleased with the outcome of this first call because I had been successful in getting the deadline removed. The family, however, did not understand this success. The two days passed, during which time the family still could not decide on the final amount they would pay. This made the negotiation most difficult for me: here was a family with so many financial resources within their grasp, but it would not decide on a price to pay for their daughter. The biggest difficulty was the danger of lying to kidnappers. If they suspect a doublecross, they can always kill the hostage. After much discussion, the family let me decide the final amount to pay.

In one of the next conversations with the kidnappers, they said that the family was smart to have reached a decision, and for that reason they would discount the price to $4 million. I told them not to waste their time. A ransom of $5, $4, $3, $2, or $1 million was all the same. They would never get those amounts. They kept telling me about all the property the family owned. The kidnappers wanted the amount paid in dollars, since pesos had been devaluated and they needed dollars to purchase arms.

For almost two months, the negotiations continued between $4 million U.S. dollars and 10 million pesos ($150,000), which was the amount that I had indicated at the beginning of the negotiations. I did not add to it since no purpose would be served by doing so. I knew that whatever amount I might have told them upwards of 10 million pesos at this point in the negotiations would be futile. To barter between 10 million pesos and $5 million or $4 million was senseless: We would never reach an agreement.

After two months, I wearied of the situation and told the family that I felt that the negotiations were over. They were over because we had come to the end of our rope. The first month had weakened the family. Now a second month passed full of psychological pressure, during which time the kidnappers threatened to kill the captive. But I knew that the way to reach an agreement was to dangle the promise of more available money without giving a specific amount. The kidnappers kept insisting on trying to determine the most that the family would pay; under no circumstances did I want to raise that amount from the original offer because I knew that sooner or later they would accept the initial formula I had offered them. That is, they would let me determine the amount with which to finally close negotiations.

THE FINAL ROUND OF NEGOTIATION

The end came on a Saturday when the kidnappers called the mother while she was with her daughter and I was at a centrally located hotel. The kidnappers told her: "If we don't have a settlement today you'll never see your daughter again." There were still problems in the family. They did not want to accept the call. I told them to take it. I believed the negotiations had concluded. In my opinion the kidnappers had no more free rein. They had no alternative than to save face and try to pursue a successful final negotiation with me.

The final round of negotiations lasted from 10:00 A.M. until 4:00 P.M., during which time the kidnappers tried every way possible to weaken the family with threats, warning them that they would never see their daughter again, at the same time offering a discount. Listening on an extension phone, I made signals to the family, telling them not to be intimidated. As long as there was a prospect of making any money they would not kill their hostage. The mother and son kept insisting that the kidnappers talk with me. Finally accepting that they were making no progress with the mother, the phone was passed to me.

When I got on the phone, the kidnappers told me that I had been right all along when I told them they would not be able to do any better by going directly to the family. The kidnappers then told me: "The offer of your first call still stands. You find an amount." I told them that they had my word. "If it is possible to find an amount that we can agree upon, I give you my word and promise that I will do everything possible to locate the money." I told them that it would take me a couple of days to get money and convert it from pesos to dollars.

The negotiations were always complicated by the fact that each call only lasted 30, tops 50, seconds because the kidnappers were worried that we could trace the call. They were very cautious throughout the negotiations. After studying all the cases that I have negotiated, I have never seen such perfection, or such determination on the part of the kidnappers, to carry out the negotiations during which, as far as I know, they never made any mistakes.

After another call was made, since there had been many calls of 30 and 50 seconds during many hours, they began to tell me, "Are you ready to set the amount that you promised that you could get and convert it to dollars?" I told them that I was ready. They told me that with $1.5 million the negotiations would be closed and they would give me the terms necessary to deliver this money to them. I told them again they were wasting time; from the beginning I had told them that this was impossible. If the family had been able to come up with that kind of money these negotiations would have been over long ago. I told them that we were right back where we started. The kidnappers said they would call me back. They called me back and said, "Okay, this time it's definite: $1.2 million and the negotiations are closed." I told them that they were still wasting time, that I did not want to fool them, that I did not want to string them along or appear to be the heavy, but to please free me from this whole thing because I was tired of it. I said I had to travel Monday to attend to my own business since I had lost a month during this affair without anything to show for it. Again they told me they would call me back.

Again they called me. The person on the telephone was agitated by my calm manner. He said, "Okay, now the negotiations are closed. One million U.S. dollars and that's final." I told them that it was still the same futile situation. The speaker did not like my attitude and was getting angry. I sensed that this was the moment in which I needed to do something because their desperation and my calm intransigence were not good. I told him to get the organization together again and to make us a "normal" offer with which we could comply. He accepted. Ten minutes later he called me and said: "Because it's you; if this girl lives she'll owe her life to you; because we know that you're an honest person—with $800,000 U.S. we can close this deal. But if you don't agree to this amount forget everything."

A CRITICAL POINT

In that moment I knew that the negotiations had reached a critical point and that there would be no more calls or negotiations along the same lines that we had been pursuing. I decided to seize the initiative and put some pressure on them. I said, "Tell me, sir. Can you assure me that if I name an amount, you can close the deal? Because I know that what I say I will do. But, will you do what you say?" For a moment he did not answer me. Then he said he would call me back in a few minutes. About 50 minutes later they called back with a different negotiator. The person on the telephone was calm and told me, "Well, you say you can assure us of complying with a deal and you ask us if we can do the same. All right, I'm listening."

In that moment I made a quick mental review of the whole situation and I told him, "I will make you a final offer. You can take it or leave it. If you leave it, please leave me alone." He told me, "Let's hear it." I told him, "Take it or leave it, $400,000 U.S. You have to give me the terms of payment and I'll tell you whether or not we can do it. If you agree, I'll help mortgage certain properties, and find loans from sources in order to collect this amount." He told me that he could assure me of this but he would have to call back in five minutes. I told him that was fine.

Five minutes later he called and said, "You tell me that you can come up with this amount in dollars and that you give me your word that this will be the amount?" I said, "Yes, sir. You have my word." So he said, "This closes the deal. How much time do you need to make these arrangements?" I told him that it was Saturday; by Thursday afternoon I could have everything ready.

THE DELIVERY

I also told the kidnapper that during the negotiations I had had faith in them; that I had never asked for proof about the girl's condition because they had demonstrated that they were honest people, but that on Wednesday they needed to have ready for me the answers to some questions that I wanted the girl to answer in her own handwriting. I also wanted some photographs of her. They told me that on Wednesday I would receive it all. They told me, "You have conducted this negotiation exactly as you wanted to. You established the conditions and we have done what you have said. Now we are going to set a condition and you can take it or leave it." I asked what it was, and they said, "That you deliver the money personally. If you don't bring it yourself, you'll never see Monica again." They left me no choice but to accept their condition. I must say that in all of the cases that I had negotiated prior to this one, this was the first case in which I agreed to personally deliver the money.

On Wednesday I got a call telling me where I could find the proof of Monica's condition, the answers to questions in her own writing, and pictures of her with that day's newspaper showing that she was fine.

On Thursday afternoon I received a call asking me if I was ready. I told them that the plane had arrived late. The money was coming in from outside of the country so as to be sure that the American dollars that I bought were not counterfeit. They told me to give them the numbers of the license plates on the cars that I might use to deliver the money. I gave them a list of seven cars and they selected one of the seven. They told me that at 4:00 P.M. that same day, the car should be in the parking lot of a hotel and that nobody should touch the car until the delivery of the ransom. They told me to go to the hotel at 6:00 P.M. with the money and wait for a telephone call. After waiting several hours, I thought that the operation was not going to go through. Finally I received the call at 10:50 P.M. confirming that everything was ready.

Thursday afternoon when the kidnappers asked about the car, I told them, "Before leaving to deliver the ransom, the girl has to answer a number of questions." At first the kidnappers said this was not possible because the girl was outside of Bogotá. I told them, "Your word and mine are the same for the tranquillity of the family. For my conscience and yours, you must answer these two questions before I bring the money. If I don't get answers, there will be no delivery." They took the questions and at 10:50 P.M. they gave the answers. The answers were right. At 10:50 they told me that I had two minutes to get to the parking lot. They advised me to be careful because there were police and military operations going on along the main avenue of the city (for security reasons not directly linked to Monica's kidnapping). I had to be especially careful, they said, in getting the first message because of these operations.

UNDER SURVEILLANCE

It seemed like they had timed everything. I left the hotel and it took no more than two or three minutes to get to the parking lot and in the car. I turned off the lights inside the car according to their instructions. They had told me on the telephone where to go to find the first message. I left the parking lot and noticed another car by the exit in which there were four people with radios in their hands and antennas sticking out of the car windows; it looked as if they were giving orders. These people were really professionals. They knew what they were doing. It was not like the other cases I had been involved in where there is always a car followed by cars and you know the kidnappers are behind you.

During the ride I found myself right in front of one of the police barricades that they had warned me about. I knew that if the money were lost it would be my loss and that this was why I had been warned. Thank God, I did not have any problem passing through the checkpoint. I arrived at the location of the first message, which I had a little trouble locating since I am not exactly an expert at this type of thing. Also I had never left the city in a car without knowing the directions. But they had guaranteed me that they would guide me, and had assured me that it was not far.

When I finally found the first message, I was, therefore, surprised to find that it said I needed to prepare for a three-hour trip outside of the city. The message repeated the warning that this was the only way the family would again see Monica alive. I remained in the car about five minutes reading the message and thinking whether or not I should continue. In that moment a car seemed to come out of nowhere and pulled up next to my window. The young people inside said, "Get going and don't wait." I understood then that they would show me which way to go. I geared myself up and reminded myself that a life was at stake. The least I could do was to go along with the agreement.

I followed the road, according to the instructions in the message. The car that had come next to mine disappeared and I never saw anyone following me, except I was certain that ever since I had left the hotel the kidnappers were communicating by radio and maintaining a close surveillance over all my movements. Since there were long stretches and broad streets, it was impossible to tell if along somewhere to the side or hidden in *fincas* (farmland) were observers that were monitoring my progress.

In their initial instructions, the kidnappers said that I would see a certain gas station, where I should fill up the tank. I was supposed to open all four doors of the car before I filled the tank. This was so that they could make sure that the car was empty. In the gas station I could observe that, although there were no other cars, there was someone in the distance watching me through binoculars. Without a doubt these people had made thorough plans for this operation.

I stayed on the path, moving according to the instructions from one message to another message, until I arrived two hours later outside of the city. Here I picked up a message which indicated that I had to take a short cut up a narrow road. Being unfamiliar with this area, I veered to the right and got lost for about 50 minutes. No one had followed me. I never saw another car. I returned to the place of the last message and I saw that there were three cars parked on all sides indicating with their turn signals the road I was supposed to take. I went up the road. When I looked back, the cars had disappeared. I continued up the narrow road to get the last message, which was placed on a wall of a finca. I got out of the car. It was about 3:30 A.M. I took the message, which said to turn around there and go a certain distance to where I would meet the kidnappers in person. It was hard to turn the car around on such a narrow road but I finally did it, and drove slowly until there were two fincas on both sides of the road and a reflector or flashlight that they aimed at my face from a distance of about five meters. I braked and let the car roll slowly. Ten meters further, they shined two lights in my face. I turned around to look and see what they were trying to do but it was impossible to tell anything. When I looked back to the front, I saw 15 to 17 guerrillas, hooded, wearing gloves. They had taken only five seconds to totally surround my car. I tried to remain calm. I knew that there were guerrillas on the other side too and that there probably were more of them in cars further down that had advised them of my progress. They were armed with automatic weapons. I recognized modern UZIs (Israeli-made submachine guns).

Their leader told me that they had originally planned to invite me somewhere for some wine and to have a chat, but that since it was now near dawn, this regrettably would not be possible. They told me that they were very grateful for my assistance, and that I had been brave to bring the ransom to them myself. Then they told me that for security reasons, Monica could not be delivered for another three days.

THE RELEASE

As it was still their ballgame, I had no choice but to accept. All had gone according to plan. They told me that I could return in peace. They would follow me in the same manner as when I had come, but I would not notice any cars.

Three days later, Monica arrived in excellent condition. She had been treated very well. They had even compelled her to exercise daily. She had been fed well and provided with newspapers, a radio, color television, and everything else she wanted as long as she behaved herself. She was in good shape.

One of the things that most caught her attention was the following: In the moment that she was taken from the university the first night she slept in a house. The second day she was taken from the house by a different group and slept somewhere else. On the third day still another group took her and guarded her for the next two months. She never again saw the first two groups of people. Strangely enough, the third group never wore masks. She asked why they did not hide their faces, and they told her that they did not need to worry; that they did not have any prior arrests and that no one was interested in them. Every 8 or 15 days, men she assumed to be the leaders arrived. They wore hoods and gloves and asked if she was being treated well. She answered yes. Then they would ask if she needed anything and disappear.

On the basis of my experiences as a negotiator in these cases, I can offer a number of suggestions to those who find themselves in a similar situation.

1. Negotiations of this type must be conducted in an atmosphere of calm. If possible, family members who are closest to the victim should be persuaded to leave the city, or better yet, the country. They are too emotional to participate directly in the negotiations, too vulnerable to threats and ultimatums, and make things difficult for the negotiator. At the same time, a representative of the family with the power to make decisions should be available at a moment's notice throughout the episode.

2. It is necessary at the beginning to make sure that the people you are dealing with are really the kidnappers and not extortionists merely exploiting the event. This can be done by convincing the kidnappers that there are others also claiming credit for the kidnapping who have been making calls to the family. In my experience, they have never rejected a demand for proof that they have the hostage and he or she is well. They know that if they show proof, the ransom will be theirs. At the end of the negotiations and before delivery of the ransom, this proof needs to be reconfirmed. They must prove that the kidnapped person is alive and well, and still in their hands.

3.   The successful negotiator must always remain calm and be concerned for the life of the hostage, but at the same time somewhat detached and unemotional. I also owe my own success to the respect I have shown for the word given by both sides in the negotiations. I convince the kidnappers that I will abide by my word—and I never have tried to trick them—and I treat them as men of honor who will abide by their word. Of course, in a Latin American country, there exist certain cultural values. Honor is valued among all classes. Even criminals will keep their word. There has not been a single case in my experience in which an agreement has been reached and the kidnappers have not kept their word. Besides, the "kidnapping industry," as it is called in this country, is a business; 90 percent are for money, 10 percent could be considered political. One pays, the kidnappers return the hostage. One does not pay, the kidnappers do not return the hostage. It would be counterproductive for the kidnappers not to return the hostage once the demands are met. It would ruin future business.

4.   The kidnappers always hold the advantage. They have the hostage; they make the rules. But by being patient, giving explanations in response to each of their demands, by demonstrating concern for their security, by convincing them that there will not be any obstacles from authorities, by maintaining good faith, it is possible to arrive at an agreement satisfactory to both parties.

5.   It is necessary to give the kidnappers the hope that they will receive some money for their hostage; this will encourage them to keep the hostage alive and in good condition. In my view, however, one must not fall into the trap of bargaining over the amount. The kidnappers are always anxious to know when the family will pay. This information must be kept from them until the final moment of negotiations. Make them name the amounts. Do not bargain up. Make them bargain down. To discourage them from breaking off the negotiations and killing the hostage, always give them hope that they will get more than the low amount initially set but without specifying how much more. When they have at last convinced themselves that you will not bargain, the negotiation can be concluded by your naming the amount the family or company can pay.

6.   I have always felt that the larger the kidnapping group, the better chance there is of achieving a successful outcome to the negotiation and securing the safe release of the hostage. Indeed, I prefer negotiating with professional organizations—guerrillas or criminals. When the victim falls into the hands of a few common criminals or amateur kidnappers, the danger increases because they lack the seriousness and competence necessary for the situation, and they usually do not carry out "clean" negotiations. The outcomes of these cases have also been satisfactory, but the risk is greater that the kidnappers will get nervous, break off the negotiations, and kill the hostage. In my negotiations with smaller criminal groups, I have often made recommendations to them regarding their own security, which they have accepted. One has to help them conduct a professional kidnapping in order to get the hostage back.

7.   Should the authorities be notified of the kidnapping? And if they know about it, should they be kept informed of the details of the negotiations? In principle,

the answer is yes, but unfortunately, in many countries we have to conceal the negotiations, since the authorities do not have sufficient experience, skill, or success in dealing with these groups, which seem to become more expert daily.

8.   As one who has negotiated the payment of ransom many times, it may seem strange that I am opposed to the payment of ransom and would favor government action to prevent it, including the arrest of negotiators. However, with strong government measures to prevent the payment of ransom must come equally strong measures to deal with the kidnappers. Unfortunately, this is not now the case here or in many other countries. The government ought to establish a special group to deal with kidnapping that can operate with freedom. The government has to make a point not to pay ransoms and to be strong. It needs to show that it is stronger than the kidnappers, to the point of putting negotiators under arrest. By being firm the citizens will appreciate the government's stand and unite in their strength and eventually refuse to provide payments for kidnappings altogether.

19

Negotiations III: The Richardson Negotiations

Leon D. Richardson

Kevin Sinclair

"You must realize that there will have to be some sort of economic settlement for our services." Considering the circumstances, the man at whom the gun was pointed thought this style of speech oddly high-toned. He recalled later that the kidnappers never referred to him as a kidnap victim, but only as "the merchandise." And during the negotiations for his release, they never used the word ransom, but spoke only of an "economic settlement" for their "services," as though the man they had kidnapped was a client of some sort.

The man they had kidnapped was Leon D. Richardson, a dynamic business-man, a chemical engineer, the founder and president of Magna Industrial Company, Ltd. On February 10, 1981, while on a brief business trip to Guatemala, Richardson was kidnapped by leftist guerrillas, an unusual occurrence since guerrillas and terror-ists ordinarily kidnap only local businessmen or foreign businessmen who are local residents, those they have time to observe. But Richardson was no mere target of opportunity. As he discovered later, one of his own employees in Guatemala was a leftist sympathizer who had cooperated with the kidnappers. To use the common underworld phrase, Richardson had been set up.

He was held for a hundred days in an underground cell seeing only his hooded captors, interrogated, and psychologically harassed to keep him off balance, while his son-in-law attempted to negotiate his release. A man of extraordinary determination and energy, Richardson recognized the games played by his captors and launched his own campaign of psychological warfare. In Chapter 29, he tells his own story; here, the lengthy and frustrating negotiations that led to his release are described. The story is particularly interesting since we have both the victim's and the negotiator's accounts and can observe how the kidnappers attempted to manipulate both their captive, who in this case was the chief executive of a corpora-tion—someone they no doubt believed could order any economic settlement they sought—and their captive's family. We also see how both the captive and his son-in-law negotiator worked to reduce the kidnappers demands.

Although not a problem in this case, the episode raises a broader issue:

---

* Portions of this chapter have appeared in Kevin Sinclair, *Kidnap: A Victim's Story,* Hong Kong: Ted Thomas Limited, 1982.

ransom negotiations when the chief executive officer, a principal partner, or the head of a family is kidnapped and willingly takes the lead in the negotiations for his own release, or is pressured to do so, possibly agreeing to or demanding the payment of amounts his own subordinates or other family members are unable or unwilling to pay. The chief executives of large corporations report to boards of directors and stockholders; and if kidnapped, they would quickly be replaced by others authorized to make decisions. The problem is not so easily solved in a smaller family-owned corporation.

Should the kidnap victim be considered automatically incapacitated by virtue of his captivity? Does his legal authority over corporate or family finances cease at the moment of captivity? This delicate issue also arises in cases in which a head of family or corporation suffers, or is suspected of suffering, impairment of his powers of reasoning for reasons of health. In the case of a kidnapping, however, no possibility exists for conducting first-hand medical examinations or lengthy legal processes. (As we shall see, the problem also may arise when the former hostage returns "a changed man," inattentive to business affairs or determined to make radical and puzzling changes.) The problem of the captive in charge of negotiations can be reduced by discussing it in advance in those cases where it could arise and, if agreeable, preparing legal documents that specify a transfer authority in the case of a kidnapping.

IMMEDIATE CONCERNS

Seated in his underground cell, Richardson was told that he would have to appoint an outside negotiator to act on his behalf. He selected his son-in-law, Tom Dundon, a man in whom he could place his fullest trust. Dundon had worked with Richardson for two decades. He had sound business experience combined with negotiating skills picked up during his career. Richardson knew his daughter's husband would have the best interests of the family at heart. He gave the negotiator Dundon's address in Sydney, Australia.

The kidnappers' representative said Dundon would have to come somewhere closer to Latin America to negotiate the release. Where did Richardson suggest? Why not Guatemala? No, that was impossible, the terrorist said. They would not negotiate inside the country. Nor would the terrorists meet Dundon to negotiate in the United States. Richardson suggested Mexico as neutral ground and this was accepted.

Word that Richardson had been abducted was first received by his office in Sydney, where his office manager Gloria Donaldson was told the grim news. In turn, she telephoned Richardson's son-in-law who was away on a business trip to Melbourne. Dundon had two immediate concerns. The first was that the kidnapped man might need the four different sorts of heart medicines he had to take daily. The second major worry was concern about Richardson's wife.

Dundon flew back to Sydney, arranging to have his wife, Rebecca, meet him in the office of Magna Industries so he could personally tell her of the kidnapping. After the news was broken, they made immediate plans for Rebecca to fly to Hong Kong to be with Mrs. Richardson when she heard about the kidnapping. Meanwhile, Tom Dundon pleaded with the Australian authorities to try to keep it out of the press until Rebecca got to Hong Kong and told her mother.

The story became public on February 13, when a Sydney radio station broadcasting a news bulletin reported that Don Richardson had been kidnapped in Central America. Tom Dundon knew that the Magna offices in Sydney would be inundated by the press. At dawn, scores of reporters surrounded the Magna office in suburban Drummoyne.

One decision made early on by Dundon was that he should strive as far as possible to keep Richardson's image in the press at a low profile, to try to keep him appearing as unimportant as possible so his captors did not overestimate the amount of ransom they could demand. His main aim was to persuade the press that they should not blow up and exaggerate the status or wealth of the victim.

One thing Dundon continually stressed was that Richardson needed his heart medicine and he needed it swiftly or he would die. He hoped the kidnappers in Central America would get the message via the international wire services, that their captive had to have his medicine or his value to his kidnappers would be nil.

And then began the long, dismal, wearying wait. . . . Days passed and no word was received. Dundon and Mrs. Donaldson had gone to the Sydney office of the Australian Ministry of Foreign Affairs and asked for advice. The ministry staff frankly admitted that their experience with kidnappings was extremely limited. Dundon, however, found out about experts in kidnap negotiations, people who specialized in freeing victims of abductions. The foreign ministry supplied him with a list of about 15 names of companies and individuals in the field. The ministry stressed that it could only give a list of known specialists, not provide any suggestions about who should be hired. That night, Dundon began making telephone calls all over the world to the people on the list of kidnap consultants. One man he spoke to particularly impressed him. The man already knew of the Richardson case and mentioned other cases in which his firm had been involved in the past.

He gave Dundon some preliminary advice. If anyone called claiming to be the kidnappers, he should make sure to find out if possible where they were calling from. Also, he was told, he should obtain proof that Richardson was still alive by asking a question that only the missing man could answer, then making firm arrangements for the kidnappers to call back, or, better still, getting a telephone number where he could call them.

Dundon was impressed. He arranged to meet the kidnap consultant's representative in Mexico. Before he left Australia, Dundon telexed Magna officers throughout Latin America to get a full breakdown on all senior staff there who might be needed to help in future negotiations with the kidnappers.

By February 16th, Dundon was in Mexico City for his scheduled meeting with the kidnap consultant. There was a lengthy discussion lasting more than two hours, after which Dundon decided the firm was very experienced and professional

and could help secure Richardson's release. Dundon also got help and encouragement from the Australian embassy in Mexico City, where he was advised to keep
a low profile and not leave his hotel room. The Australians sent a man to Guatemala
City to find out what they could about who might have grabbed Richardson and
what motives they may have had. The Australians again apologized because they
did not have much experience in the field. But they did have some good news:
After radio broadcasts in Guatemala, the Australians learned that Richardson had
received his medicine.

PREPARING FOR THE NEGOTIATIONS

The consultants insisted they could only give advice and the actual decisions would
have to be made by Richardson's family. They said that one person should be
nominated as the family representative to deal with the consulting firm. Under
the circumstances, that person could only be the Tom Dundon, although the consultants said they would have preferred somebody who was not as close to the
kidnapped man. Personal feelings and friendship might get in the way of tough
negotiating techniques. Also, Dundon himself could be considered kidnap-worthy;
he could be snatched to reinforce the kidnappers' demands. This had happened
in previous cases in which one of the two captives had been slain in cold blood
by kidnappers to drive home their demands.

The consultant then began giving Dundon a quick but detailed education
in the tactics of kidnapping and negotiating for the release of those held captive.
The chances were high, the adviser told Dundon, that Richardson had been kidnapped by a political group trying to raise money to promote their political aims.
The chances were also high that Richardson would, like 98 percent of kidnap
victims, eventually be freed. The adviser told the worried Dundon that he should
not be surprised at the preliminary demands that would be made by the kidnappers
when they eventually made contact. They could ask for as much as $40 million
ransom, and he should be prepared this kind of preposterous demand.

The terror tactics could take many forms, the adviser continued. There would
almost certainly be a long delay, aimed at breaking down the strength and the
will of a family frantic over the fate of a loved one. The kidnappers would play
on emotion and despair. Dundon was advised to stay on a psychologically even
keel, not to let himself go to extremes of either pessimism or optimism.

This education was aimed at making Dundon ready to deal with the captors
when they finally made contact and laid down their terms for the release of their
victim. It was a tortuous, precise, and detailed process and one that took several
hours every day. Dundon and two members of the consulting team spent days
going over all possible scenarios. Every possible contingency was discussed and
the men acted out conversations with the captors. The long rehearsals continued
hour after hour, every step outlined, practiced, and rehearsed time and again until
Dundon was prepared for every possible contingency.

Some of the scenarios were chilling. The consultants put Dundon in positions in which they pretended to be the kidnappers and threatened that they would cut off Richardson's fingers or ears unless a ransom was immediately paid. Dundon had to steel himself and practice giving such calm replies as: "We will not pay for damaged goods." Other simulations illustrated methods by which the terrorists might try to panic the family into paying, for example, by smearing a shirt with the blood of a chicken and mailing it to his wife. Such tactics had worked in the past and the consultants wanted to make sure that Dundon was prepared to deal with every eventuality. For endless hours, the rehearsals went on.

The consultants told Dundon to think of the maximum ransom that could be paid to free his father-in-law. The first demand, he was cautioned, would be an enormous amount, far more than the kidnappers thought they would ever get. He was advised to counter this demand with a definite, relatively low, offer. Supposedly, the demands would come down and Dundon would be able to demand concessions in exchange as his offers went up. But a word of caution: the first offer had to be large enough to ensure that the kidnappers did not indignantly kill their prisoner, deciding that he just was not worth keeping alive. The first move had to be a life insurance policy. After consultations with advisers, Dundon settled on making an initial offer of $550,000.

Dundon worried that the kidnappers themselves might not know how to make contact with the Richardson family or business associates. Despite the warnings about the likelihood of himself becoming a target for kidnappers, Dundon thought there was no alternative but for him to go to Guatemala City and attempt to set up lines of communications through which the abductors could easily contact him. Cautiously, he proceeded to the capital of Guatemala. There he found two men whom he considered trustworthy, hired a post office box and a telephone, and placed fake advertisements in code in the newspapers, which were aimed at tempting the kidnappers to contact the family. There was nothing else to do. It was then more than two weeks since Richardson had disappeared and no word had been received from the kidnappers. Dundon could not do anything further in Mexico City, where he believed he was under observation. Reluctantly, he boarded a plane to fly across the Pacific to try to bring what comfort he could to the missing man's wife.

Privately, Dundon feared that hope was receding. The long delay in hearing from the kidnappers raised the specter that the missing man was dead, either killed in the aftermath of the abduction itself or felled by his heart disease.

ENLISTING THE CAPTIVE

While building pressure on the family by maintaining their silence, Richardson's kidnappers tried to enlist him in the negotiations. About a week after his capture, a negotiator appeared in his cell with a current issue of *Time* magazine and a Polaroid camera. They said they wanted to take photographs of him with the magazine to prove to his family that he was alive. Similar incidents later happened with the *New York Times* and the *Miami Herald*. The guards asked Richardson to write letters about the latest news events, once again to prove he was alive at that date. This sequence happened at least six times. To his rage, Richardson was to find out after his release that the first four times he went through this procedure, it was merely a cruel charade: His family had not been contacted, they didn't know if he were alive. The letters and photographs had never been sent.

One day, the man and woman negotiators came to the cell together. They wanted Richardson to write yet another letter to his son-in-law asking for an "economic settlement." The captive asked them what amount of money they were asking for. The woman said: "We've studied your case and we have decided that $10 million would be a reasonable figure." Richardson exploded. "Don't be ridiculous," he shouted at them. "I am NOT going to write any letter. I am NOT going to make a tape. I am NOT going to cooperate for you to take a picture."

"You are wasting my time and you are wasting yours. My company is much too small to pay that kind of money and you can just forget it if that is the ransom."

Richardson argued that his company had few cash reserves and had been losing $1 million a year for the past three years because of the world recession. He also told them the company was mortgaged to the hilt and could not raise cash from banks. He told them he did not own a car and lived in a small rented apartment in Hong Kong. As Richardson reeled off these details of financial disasters, the woman negotiator seemed a little unsure of herself. It was the first time the victim spotted a chink in the guerrilla armor.

He said that if the company was to sell all its inventory, they might be able to raise $750,000 to $1 million. Could this be done quickly, she asked? He assured her it could. She seemed more interested in getting $1 million in a hurry than in waiting and collecting $10 million later. The male negotiator (always referred to by the others as "The Chief") then broke in to say they had already asked Dundon for $10 million and they would await his answer before considering any reduction in the ransom.

They finally told Richardson they would lower the ransom if he cooperated with them in allowing his picture to be taken and wrote letters and made a tape recording. He agreed, but after his release discovered that his captors had once again been lying to him. They were still demanding that Dundon pay a $10 million ransom.

THE FIRST CONTACT

On Friday, March 20th, Dundon was back in Hong Kong with Richardson's wife. There, he received an urgent message to call Sydney, to contact Gloria Donaldson on a private line where he could speak freely. Dundon raced back to his hotel and placed an urgent call to his Sydney office.

Gloria Donaldson is a sensible, mature, level-headed woman who had worked for Magna Industries for 10 years. Both Richardson and Dundon had the utmost faith in her. The news she had was electrifying. She had just received a telephone call from a person claiming to represent the kidnappers who held Richardson. The telephone rang at the Magna office in Sydney and after the international operator failed to connect the caller with Dundon, a woman calling from Mexico agreed to speak to Donaldson.

"We have an important message about L. D. R.," the caller said. "Don is with us and is doing okay. His health is fine. In order to settle this, Dundon must leave immediately for Mexico City. He is to go to a hotel room which has been booked for him at the El Presidente Hotel in Mexico City. He must be there on Sunday, March 22, in the evening. Once there, our party will get in touch with him."

On the same day, a telex arrived at the Magna office in Sydney, signed "Don." But Dundon had exchanged thousands of telex messages with his father-in-law over their years together in business, and he knew from the wording of the telex that Richardson had not written it.

It was 41 days since Richardson had disappeared, and there was no guarantee that the call and the telex had come from the gang that had grabbed him. It could be a cruel hoax or it could have originated from some individual or group pretending to hold Richardson to extort a ransom. After talking with the consultants, it was decided that it was too dangerous for Dundon to go to Mexico City on such a flimsy lead. Another Magna representative and one of the advisers would make the rendezvous instead. The two men were in the hotel room reserved by some unknown person for Dundon on the appointed Sunday evening when the telephone rang.

A woman with an icy voice asked, "Is Mr. Dundon there?" The company official explained that he was not, but that he was authorized to speak for him. "We will speak only to Mr. Dundon. We want to speak to Mr. Dundon. We do not want to speak to you." Then she slammed down the telephone. There was still no indication that the people who had made the telephone calls had Richardson in their custody, let alone that he was alive.

Two days later, another call was made to the Magna office in Sydney and once again Donaldson found herself talking to a woman in Mexico. Australian officials told Richardson after the kidnapping that this call had come from a telephone box in Acapulco.

"We wonder where Mr. Dundon is," the woman asked. Donaldson said she had passed on the original message and that Dundon had asked one of the firm's most reliable staff members to act in his place.

"He is not the person we wish to talk to," the woman snapped angrily. "We wanted Mr. Dundon to come. That's what Mr. Richardson wanted. Is he coming or not?"

Donaldson said she could pass on the message to Dundon. She was told to tell him to return to the El Presidente. Saying she was concerned whether Richardson was alive or dead, Gloria Donaldson then put forward a question to the caller that only he could answer. She asked the woman caller to get an answer to the question from Richardson. The answer was: "No, I don't think so." The woman's answer indicated that she did not have access, or at least immediate access, to the missing man.

The long silence descended again. Dundon made another lengthy, ten-day trip to Hong Kong to try to help Margie Richardson. With no word of whether her husband was alive, there was little he could do to cheer her up. Dundon got back to Sydney on April 13th. The next day, the telephone rang in the Magna office and once again Gloria Donaldson found herself talking to a woman calling from Mexico. The message was ominous.

"L. D. R. could lose the lot. He could lose absolutely everything in this deal. Also remember the time. Time is beginning to run out for L. D. R. It is absolutely necessary that we speak to Tom Dundon so we can know his attitude, whether he is interested or not."

The woman then gave the correct answer to the proof question that Donaldson had asked during the earlier call, which she noted the answer of without indicating whether it was true. Then the woman gave additional information, telling Donaldson that her Christian name was Gloria and her husband's name was Jim, ending with another demand to speak to Dundon. Gloria said he was not available but that she could get a message to him. She gave the woman a direct telephone number and asked her to call back the next day. The gang rang back the same day, once more asking for Dundon. Again Donaldson handled the call with her calm, soothing manner. During both calls, unknown to the terrorists calling from Mexico, Dundon was sitting anxiously at her elbow monitoring the conversation.

After lengthy consultations with his advisers, he had decided it would be pointless at that stage for him to talk directly to the people they now knew definitely were the kidnappers. The aim was to keep the gang on the defensive and for Dundon to remain remote, keeping the upper hand. This was a difficult, heart-rending decision for him. At last, after the long weeks of waiting, there was someone to whom he could talk, someone who knew the whereabouts of his father-in-law. But for tactical reasons the professional negotiators told Dundon to keep the kidnappers at arm's length, not to appear too eager to talk to them. And, they advised emphatically, under no circumstances should Margie Richardson be told of the contact. They were 90 percent sure that Don was alive, but they did not want to build up her hopes, not without some concrete proof that Richardson was alive and there was a chance he could be freed.

The next day, April 15th, the telephone rang again. Once again, Gloria Donaldson took the call, and, once again, the icy woman was on the line demanding to talk to Tom Dundon.

"We're calling about L. D. R.," said the now-familiar voice from Mexico.

Donaldson said she had passed on the earlier messages to Dundon, but that he was not in Sydney. He was, however, anxious to go to Mexico. But he was only going to Latin America if he could arrange his own travelling plans and his own accommodations. She told the terrorists that this was in the interests of Dundon's personal security. The terrorists' spokeswoman said Dundon should stay at the Holiday Inn. The next sentence staggered the listeners in Sydney. The woman said: "Tell Tom Dundon everything will be okay as long as he plays fair." Donaldson, keeping her voice calm with an effort, replied: "Oh, he will play fair."

Setting up the arrangements to the satisfaction of both Dundon and the terrorists was a complicated matter. But the Sydney team had discussed every possible scenario with the kidnap consultants and they had proposals ready. Gloria Donaldson outlined to the terrorists just how far Dundon would go to meet their demands. She told them that Dundon would have an unnamed collaborator at the hotel the terrorists nominated. The terrorists could call the hotel in Mexico City, and the go-between would give them another telephone number where they could reach Tom. Then they could ask any question they liked, any question from Don Richardson that only Tom would know, to ensure that they were speaking to the right person. This arrangement would give mutual security to both sides. The kidnappers accepted these arrangements.

Before the conversation ended, Mrs. Donaldson insisted on giving the kidnappers another proof question that would have to be answered by the kidnappers when they spoke in three days' time to Dundon in Mexico City. If answered correctly, this would prove that Richardson was still alive and able to think and talk. Donaldson stressed to the terrorist that when Dundon got to Mexico he expected to enter into meaningful negotiations. The kidnapper then indignantly said they did not want to "prolong the dilemma." She made an insistent point. "We want to remind you about fair play," she said four times. "What?" said Gloria. "Fair play," said the terrorist. "We want to remind you about fair play."

"Yes," said Gloria. "I hope that is mutual."

Once again, Dundon was sitting in the Magna office as Gloria Donaldson did the talking. This was an important point and one which the kidnap consultants drilled into the pair time and again: In order to maintain psychological dominance, it was vital that Richardson's friends and relatives not appear over-eager, that they should not be willing to immediately do everything demanded of them by the kidnappers.

After the call, Gloria, Tom, and one of the consultants held a lengthy postmortem. They felt that progress was being made. The long hours of rehearsals and practice were beginning to pay dividends. They believed they had, despite their concern for Don Richardson, managed to appear calm, relatively unworried, and matter-of-fact when talking to the terrorists. It was the first glimmer of hope they had had since Richardson had been snatched. With a faint sense of optimism, Tom Dundon packed his bags and once more set off on the long flight across the Pacific.

NEGOTIATIONS IN MEXICO CITY

Tom Dundon arrived in Mexico City on Easter Friday, April 17. Gloria Donaldson had told the gang he would be arriving Sunday, but the advisers told him to get there early, to travel under a false name, and to book into any hotel except the Holiday Inn where the terrorists originally had told him to stay. From the moment of his arrival, Dundon had the feeling he was under observation. This uneasy feeling was strengthened when he noticed a car at the airport, then saw the car following his taxi to the hotel, where it remained parked outside the building.

Over the next two days, he was joined by one of the kidnap consultants and by Carlos Henriques, the employee who had been with Richardson when he was abducted. They felt Henriques, involved from the very beginning of the drama and fluent in Spanish, might be of help during what were sure to be extensive and delicate negotiations.

Because Mexico has a federal law against blackmail and because the kidnappers would be blackmailing Dundon on Mexican territory, the consultant advised Dundon to inform the local authorities of the planned negotiations with the Guatemalan terrorists. The Mexicans were sympathetic, understanding, and helpful.

A round of hurried, urgent, but well-planned moves were made in preparation for the telephone call expected on Easter Sunday night. The first thing to do was to find a safe telephone number where Tom Dundon could receive the kidnappers' call. Business associates in Mexico City were helpful. They directed Dundon, Henriques, and the consultant to a number of addresses. Finally they settled on the office of a lawyer in a suburb about an hour's drive from the center of the city.

With the secret telephone number arranged, the three men began an intensive round of last minute rehearsals. Once again the consultant, aided by Henriques, played the part of the terrorists, shooting hostile questions and threats at Dundon, going through every possible scenario, acting out every contingency.

They decided to throw another imponderable into the works. In her last talk with the woman, Gloria Donaldson had been very insistent that when the terrorists telephoned the Holiday Inn, they would not be talking to Dundon. Now, the consultant said, it would throw the kidnappers off-stride if in fact Dundon answered the very first phone call and demanded their terms. Here was another example of gaining the upper psychological hand.

The move would confuse the gang. It would also give a slight dominance to Dundon. His game plan was to announce that he was on the phone, then give the kidnappers another number, insisting that they write it down. By giving them instructions and having the kidnappers obey, the gang would become accustomed to taking orders from Dundon, whom they would have expected to have under their control.

One scenario that Dundon practiced was the chilling prospect that the kidnappers might put Richardson on the line to negotiate for his own life. This, too, was rehearsed and Dundon was ready to deal with the possibility. If the familiar voice of Don Richardson came on the line, Dundon was ready to ask him about his health, about how he was being treated, and to pass on his wife's love. But if Richardson were forced by the kidnappers to start making financial demands for his safe return, Dundon had steeled himself to refuse to discuss the matter with his father-in-law and to insist that he would only talk to the terrorists. At no point would he discuss ransom with Richardson.

The rehearsals continued most of Easter Sunday. Dundon handled the dozens of practice telephone calls. Each conversation was different, unexpected, with different twists. At noon, Dundon went to the Holiday Inn. Once again he felt strongly that he was being followed. He sat in the hotel room through the afternoon, "psyching" himself to be ready.

At 7 P.M., the telephone rang. Dundon immediately recognized the voice of the woman whose calls to Sydney had been taped and analyzed over and over again. The cold, calculating voice could not be mistaken. She was surprised to be talking to Dundon. It threw her off. He could hear other voices in the background. The woman, completely off balance, hurriedly said she would have to call back, then hung up.

An hour later, she was on the telephone again. Dundon went straight onto the offensive. "What was the answer of the last proof question?" he asked. But the woman was made of tough stuff.

"Before I answer, I want you to answer some questions," she said, trying to establish Dundon's bona fides. She asked two questions that could only have come from Don Richardson. Dundon answered to her satisfaction.

Dundon then moved into the agreed scenario, pressing the woman into getting pen and paper and taking down the secret telephone number and predetermined times when she could contact him there. The woman abruptly said she would call him back at the new number in an hour. It took about that time to drive from the center of the city to the suburban office. Dundon changed clothes as a slight disguise and walked out the main entrance of the Holiday Inn. He was noticeably being followed, one man behind him and another across the street. He suddenly ducked around a corner, ran down the street, jumped into a passing cab and asked for the suburb where the secret office had been placed at his disposal. The cab circled the area as Dundon checked his tail. He was clear. The kidnap consultant, whom he had telephoned as soon as the terrorist hung up, was already there. They again went through imaginary conversations with the kidnappers.

When the telephone rang, the woman had the answer to the proof question given by Gloria Donaldson. Dundon was elated. This meant that Richardson had been alive at least a couple of days earlier.

Then the woman tried to take control by insisting Dundon return to the Holiday Inn to make contact anew. He kept refusing. There was no way that he was going back there. He felt that if he did, he would become a sitting duck as another potential kidnap victim. Dundon then began to lay down the law. The only way the kidnappers could contact him, he told the woman bluntly, was at the secret telephone between 8:30 P.M. and 10:00 P.M. and only on prearranged days. If a call did not come that day, he would return the following night. But if contact was not made then, the only way the kidnappers could raise him again would be through the Sydney office of Magna. This ultimatum was repeated several times until Dundon was sure the woman understood.

Then she demanded he go to a certain restaurant where he would be contacted that night. Dundon told her: "I'm not going now or any other time." The woman protested angrily. He had to go, she said. No, he repeated. No way was he going. There was a loud, angry Spanish conversation in the background as the woman argued with her colleagues. Once again she said Dundon would go to the restaurant and he would be there at 11:30 P.M. that night. The argument continued for several minutes, interrupted by angry clashes in Spanish at the other end of the line. Finally the woman snapped: "You will go the restaurant and you will go now!" Then she angrily crashed down the phone. Dundon and the consultant waited 30 minutes for another call. None came. They went back to their respective hotels.

The next day, April 20th, the interminable rehearsals continued. It was obvious the kidnappers wanted to get a parcel to Dundon. He badly wanted to receive it, but only on his terms. Back at the secret telephone number at 9 P.M. that night, the woman called on schedule. She was pacifying and friendly. She explained that since Dundon had not wanted to go to the restaurant to pick up the parcel, the delivery had been cancelled. Dundon felt that this was merely an attempt by the gang to save face because he had successfully defied them the previous night. Where, she asked, could something be delivered? What about the Australian embassy, Dundon asked. Certainly not, the woman said sharply. That was out of the question. What about the Holiday Inn, the woman asked. What was in the package, Dundon countered. A tape? Yes, the woman said. Dundon agreed to the Holiday Inn pick-up point, but stressed that he would not be there personally when the package was delivered between noon and 2 P.M. the following day. Between them, after lengthy haggling, Dundon and the woman agreed that another contact would be made via the secret telephone number in two days to discuss the contents of the package.

To ensure the Holiday Inn reception desk would accept the parcel, Dundon phoned the hotel and booked a room in his own name. When he arrived at the hotel after the delivery deadline, he was at first disappointed to find no parcel awaiting him at the check-in desk. Then a receptionist told him that a bellboy had taken a parcel to his room. In the room, there was only one item out of the ordinary for a hotel room anywhere in the world—an attractive square wooden vase containing an impressive display of artificial flowers. Around the vase was a ribbon with a card saying: "Welcome to Mexico from Don and Company."

There was also a small, white-wrapped box. The consultant looked at the two offerings with a jaundiced eye. The pair had considered the possibility of the package containing a letter bomb because Dundon had not blindly carried out the orders laid down by the gang. Gently placing the flowers and the box in plastic bags, the men carried them out of the Holiday Inn and, using different routes, went to a prearranged meeting place. Gingerly opening the package, the consultant laid out the contents.

To Dundon's delight, there was a recently written letter from Don Richardson. It told of the conditions in which he was being kept and showed he was alive. There was also a letter from the kidnappers, setting out in detail their demands. And there was a tape recording from Richardson, which Dundon listened to time and again. He came to the conclusion that the tape had been recorded at gunpoint. It was Richardson's voice, there was no mistaking that, and some of the phrases were from his distinctive vocabulary. But Dundon could spot the discrepancies. On the tape Richardson asked Dundon to make securing his release top priority.

The phrasing on the tape was not typical of Richardson. It sounded as though he was reading from a prepared script. What delighted Dundon more than anything else was a rough Polaroid snapshot of a gaunt, bearded figure holding in front of his chest a current issue of *Time* magazine and the front page of the *Miami Herald*. The figure in the photograph was a grimier, thinner person than Dundon knew, but there could be no doubt that it was a photo of Leon Don Richardson.

At last they now knew, definitely, that he was alive. Dundon's first thought was of Richardson's wife, still living in uncertainty in Hong Kong. He was afraid to use the telephone to call her because he thought the Mexican phone system might be insecure. Instead, he sent a telex in code to Gloria Donaldson, asking her to call Mrs. Richardson and tell her that, as of April 18th, Don was alive and reasonably well.

The surveillance on Dundon continued. Every day or so he would sneak out of his hotel and find a room somewhere else. But it seemed that only a few hours after he made a move, discreet eyes were fixed on him in his new hotel. After closely studying the letters, tape, and photograph, Dundon and the consultant returned wearily to rehearsing the next step, a stage in the negotiations with the kidnappers that could be the most crucial of the entire drama. They went through every option. They examined every avenue open to the terrorists. The consultant warned Dundon that it was becoming time for the kidnappers to begin to make threats, to start to issue warnings that physical retribution would be used against their prisoner if Dundon did not give in swiftly to their demands. The rehearsal continued until the kidnappers made their promised call. It came promptly at the agreed time.

The negotiations were now entering their most delicate and dangerous phase. Over the weeks of rehearsals and discussions with consultants, Tom Dundon had covered every possible contingency they could think of. But there was always the possibility the kidnappers could come up with some proposal so bizarre, so outrageous, that it might take Dundon by surprise.

The first question the woman terrorist asked Dundon was whether he had received the packages delivered to him at the Holiday Inn. "Yes," he answered politely. "Thank you for the flowers." Any irony was lost on the woman.

Speaking in her usual mixture of business jargon, she wanted to know what economic settlement was going to be made for the return of the "merchandise." Dundon quickly pointed out that the ransom demanded in the note left for him at the Holiday Inn was totally ridiculous. He made a counter-offer, which the woman rejected as "completely ridiculous and totally unacceptable." Dundon stood firm. He told her he would not make any other offer until the kidnappers reassessed their demand and made a more realistic request. At that stage, he said, he would look at his position again and, perhaps, make a new offer for Richardson's release. The woman blustered and threatened. "We hold the assets," she warned. But Dundon, steeled by the long hours of rehearsals with the consultants, refused to budge.

Dundon and the consultants had already worked out a strict rule of tactics. As the demands of the kidnappers came down, Dundon's counter-offers would increase until, it was hoped, agreement was reached somewhere in the middle ground. Still dissatisfied, the woman ended the call on an uncertain note, agreeing to call back in two days, on Friday, April 24th.

Now, the consultants advised, was the stage when another twist should be introduced into the negotiating scenario. Dundon would be removed suddenly and unexpectedly from the scene. The kidnappers would be told they would have to talk to somebody else. This strategem was designed to throw them into confusion, to leave them uncertain and on shaky ground. It certainly seemed to work.

The next time the woman called the secret telephone number, Dundon broke the news to her suddenly. He told her he had to leave Mexico and that his place would be taken by a business associate who would act as an intermediary. The woman protested angrily but Dundon was insistent. He told her he had to return to Australia because the business could not be run without one of the partners there. Besides, he told her, he had to go to Sydney to raise the ransom money.

Over her protests, Dundon pushed forward the idea of the go-between. There was a lot of argument and angry discussions in Spanish, which could be overheard, between the woman and two men. The call kept being interrupted as the time allowance for pay phone calls was reached. Finally, the terrorists reluctantly accepted the concept of a stand-in, and Dundon put the man on the phone to talk to the woman so she could recognize his voice in future conversations. (The man's identity has been kept secret, but he is a businessman fluent in both English and Spanish.) Like Dundon, he had been exhaustively briefed and prepared for the role he was about to play as an intermediary. He was identified to the terrorists only as "Francisco."

Tom Dundon returned to Sydney the next day. The kidnap consultant had warned him the new game plan might lead to a period of silence from the kidnappers. He was proven correct.

THE SECOND ROUND

Days passed with no word from the gang. Richardson's friends and family became alarmed, frustrated, and upset. Dundon pondered on the last warning he had received from the woman: "You must remember the full responsibility for the safety of the asset lies on your shoulders." Had Richardson been killed? Had the gang been captured? He read newspaper stories of Guatemalan guerrilla gangs being caught and whose last actions had been to kill their prisoners.

The silence dragged on for two weeks. On May 2, he once more returned to Hong Kong to see Mrs. Richardson. He had been there a week when word suddenly arrived that the gang had made contact. The woman had telephoned the Sydney office and demanded that Dundon return to Mexico City immediately to make a final settlement. Dundon contacted the consultants. At first, it was decided that he should not follow the order. Then they decided that perhaps it would be best if he did return to Mexico.

The deadline given by the gang passed without any telephone call being made to the secret office on the outskirts of Mexico City. The next day, there was still silence. Francisco had been awaiting the call, but none came. Then Dundon arrived two days after the deadline and the phone started ringing. This strengthened his conviction that he was under observation whenever he arrived in Mexico.

The woman spoke in what for her was a friendly voice. "Don't worry," she told Dundon. Everything was going to be fine. She then told Dundon that under no circumstances was he to leave Mexico City. He was to wait there and make sure he had his travel documents with him because he might have to go to Guatemala City. In the cold, calculating tone he had come to know and hate, the woman told Dundon: "We know where you are."

Bargaining continued. The gang's demands were dropping and Dundon's offers were rising. But the ransom being sought by the terrorists was still far too high. "You can pay this amount," she said. "We know how much your business is worth."

By May 17th, the distance between the terrorist demand and Dundon's offer had shrunk. Agreement was finally reached. (Dundon, under agreement with his kidnap consultants, will not disclose specifics of the settlement, the amount, or how it was paid.)

The money was paid. The next day, the telephone at the secret office rang. The woman told Dundon: "I'm glad we reached an agreement." She asked him to nominate three drop points in Guatemala City where Don Richardson could be delivered. Dundon, she said, had to go to Guatemala to collect him. But there were still arguments over where Richardson would be dropped. Dundon wanted an embassy. The woman refused. What about hotels? This option was discussed the following night. "Sit tight," the woman said. "Do nothing. We will phone soon and tell you everything is fine."

The following morning, May 20th, Dundon and his kidnap consultant were having breakfast. He had already booked flights to Guatemala City although they did not expect any developments until the anticipated call that night from the woman. At 11 A.M. the phone in Dundon's hotel room rang. It was one of the kidnap consultants and he had momentous news.

Don Richardson had just telephoned Hong Kong and spoken to his wife. "I was stunned," Dundon recalled later. "I didn't believe it. I couldn't believe it." Dundon put through a call to the British embassy in Guatemala and asked officials there to check if the report was true. Dundon sat anxiously by the telephone. An hour later the phone rang. Not only was Don Richardson free, he was there at the British embassy.

"Hullo, old buddy," said a familiar voice on the phone. It was Richardson speaking. The 100-day nightmare was over.

20

Further Thoughts on Negotiations

Gerardo Capotorto

The governments of various nations, increasingly influenced by public opinion, have gradually assumed extremely firm positions against kidnapping. As a result, criminal and terrorist organizations, aware of the great difficulty of acquiring money from kidnappings, have turned their attention toward companies, especially those that can raise huge sums of money in a brief time.

Companies and the managers that represent them have become the number-one target. Each company must therefore have a plan for managing an emergency arising from a terrorist attack or a kidnapping. These highly complex crimes have implications that involve the entire company, so that it is absolutely necessary to create a security committee for emergency management. The committee must be capable of functioning immediately after the incident occurs to avoid serious errors, and it must have the support of the top management. It must investigate and find documentary evidence of phenomena that constitute risk to the company, and it must extend its investigation to international factors that directly or indirectly influence such phenomena.

The members of the committee must be capable of managing emergency situations from a financial standpoint, from a public relations viewpoint, and from a personnel standpoint. They should include competent security experts whose methods are continually updated through such techniques as computer simulation of actual cases.

The committee can use outside experts: sociologists for interpretation of messages, psychologists for the compilation of company messages, experts in legal matters to guarantee that emergency management procedures are correct and to evaluate legal responsibilities assumed by committee members in making decisions related to the negotiation of kidnapping cases.

After a kidnapping has occurred, the committee, in the name of the company, must make provisions to

- Assure the victim's family of the company's intention to help in achieving his safe return.
- Guarantee that the company will take on the economic burdens arising from the emergency.

- Assist the family in choosing a lawyer and assure them that the financial burden for this and for future needs will be assumed by the company.
- Arrange for the regular assistance of a professional expert on security, to whom the task of family-company contacts will be delegated.
- Guarantee that the kidnap victim will have his job back and will receive appropriate compensation when he returns.
- Provide physical security for all members of the family and psychological support for those who need it.
- Gather information on the kidnapping; reconstruct the event in detail in order to be able to give the police any useful leads; maintain systematic reports to assist the family.
- Filter out and channel, in the most profitable manner, the initiatives of friends, colleagues, city government members, committees, etc.
- Direct relations with the mass media, encouraging useful family initiatives.
- Screen out interference of political/administrative authority with the family.
- Ensure the constant communication between the family and top management by the forwarding of news, replies, and suggestions.
- Be prepared to provide information about emergencies and business intentions, according to formulations developed for managers, boards, employees, and city agencies.
- Report any subsequent useful intelligence about any important development of the emergency.
- Stimulate systematic discussions with important employees of the company to learn their opinions or to single out their worries.
- Seek out systematic discussions with city representatives for the exchange of information and to acquire support for the company.
- Provide for the examination of requests made by the kidnappers and for evaluation, with the help of the police, of possible intervention.
- Examine opportunities to circulate official statements of the company through the available mass media.

When the kidnappers have broken relations for a long time, communiques must be aimed at forcing them to come out of doors, in order to establish whether the victim is still alive.

The committee must systematize ties with the investigating bodies to ensure collaboration and reciprocal information, as well as to maintain relations with government authorities. There must also be an exchange of opinions with organizations of other industrialists to establish consensus and to develop a common line to follow in the event of similar crimes.

Wherever such activity has been prepared and programmed in advance, it has brought about satisfactory results not only in terms of favorable outcomes of episodes, but, perhaps more important, in terms of managing more advantageously the varied emergencies that arise during a kidnapping.

21

The Hostage Recovery

E. C. "Mike" Ackerman

You say to yourself, "This can't be happening." You've just thrown a dozen jute sacks into a Land Rover or a couple of suitcases into a helicopter. In them is cash: $100,000 or $1,000,000 or $10,000,000. You've been told to drive to a small soft-drink stand on Highway Four, seven kilometers north of the city, or to fly to a jungle clearing just west of the spot where the railroad trestle crosses White River, and to await further instructions there. Several such stops will be made before the stash can finally be dropped, as the other side tries its best to ensure that you have not brought the police—or aren't being tailed by them without your knowledge.

You cuss the heat and dust and your unfamiliarity with the local roads, or glance over at the helicopter pilot you somehow managed to talk into making this run. He knows the terrain, but will he go through with it? And has he tried to cover himself by tipping off the police? You offer a small prayer that he has not. Their unexpected appearance at the drop site could put you center stage in "Gunfight at the OK Corral."

There are other questions: Will the terrorists decide, for their own reasons or because of some unexpected snafu, to abort the drop—postpone it for another day? Will they try to take you prisoner? And finally, ultimately, will they be true to their word to release the hostage? And what kind of shape will he be in?

To a businessman of another era, the scenario would seem a nightmare, the fiendish plot of a mad, surrealistic novelist. Corporations do not do things like that. Cash is not dispatched in jeeps or helicopters. Large checks drawn against reputable banks are offered at solemn closings presided over by attorneys. To multinationals operating in the final quarter of the twentieth century, however, the ransom delivery has become a fact of life, just as the executive kidnapping has become a fact of life.

It is to the credit of the enterprise system that it has developed a methodology for dealing with the executive kidnapping, for maximizing the possibilities for obtaining the safe return of a hostage. A central aspect of this methodology has been the development of consultants whose specialty it is to facilitate recoveries, a small fraternity to which it is this writer's privilege to belong.

It is not easy to undertake hostage recoveries, but it may even be more difficult to write about them for publication. Nothing must be said that may be useful to kidnappers or potential kidnappers who, it is assumed, will have access to this study. The discussion of some aspects of the recovery process will therefore be severely restricted and some subjects—such as negotiating strategies—passed over entirely. The reader is forewarned that this essay may well raise more questions in his mind than it answers, and his understanding and indulgence on this score are earnestly solicited.

THE CORPORATE DILEMMA

The executive kidnapping is a multipurpose terrorist tactic. It generates publicity for a guerrilla movement and reinforces its mystique, while simultaneously attacking the economic underpinnings of the status quo by breeding fear and uncertainty in the business community. The terrorists' primary motivation, however, in abducting corporate executives is normally financial.

Kidnappers may levy other demands as well—the publication of political manifestos or the execution of a specific political action—but corporate executives are targeted chiefly for their cash value. Local political figures or diplomats are more rewarding hostages from the standpoint of publicity and as a direct challenge to the political system.

As a general rule, terrorist movements kidnap executives in an intermediate stage of their development. Nascent guerrilla organizations tend to key on members of wealthy indigenous families, and gradually work up to abducting multinational managers; while more advanced movements de-emphasize kidnappings in order to concentrate their resources on military action. Executive kidnappings produce the seed money required to generate momentum, an indispensable prerequisite for attracting the financial and material support of the Cubans, Soviets, and other potential guerrilla sponsors. Once this backing is assured, the insurgents go on to bigger and better things.

For the multinational corporation, the executive kidnapping is perhaps the ultimate nightmare. Natural disasters, accidents, even assassinations—most of the noneconomic crises faced by corporations—present them with an accomplished fact, a breach that managers are obliged to repair as best they can. A kidnapping, on the other hand, forces them to react, often over a long period of time, to an ongoing problem; to face a series of difficult and often extremely complex decisions. It obliges corporate decision makers, prepared by training and experience to confront issues of profit and loss, to deal, quite literally, with a matter of life and death.

Corporate managers, before they have been briefed on the recovery process, tend to view it as almost entirely an exercise in financial decision making: to pay or not to pay, and if the decision is to pay, how much? Would that it were so simple. Even if the corporation can bear the ransom payment or has chosen to ensure itself against this prospect, a decision to satisfy an extortion demand must not be considered as simply a matter of course. In fact, a panoply of issues intrude

into the decision-making process—questions of morality, legality, and business prac-
ticality—and beyond them lie an array of mechanical problems.

Even a partial catalog of some of the moral, legal, and business issues is
intimidating:

- Will payment of a ransom endanger other corporate employees, will it make
  them more vulnerable to kidnapping?
- Or will failure to effect a successful recovery lead to morale problems—and
  the refusal of other employees to serve in high-risk areas?
- Is it morally defensible to supply a guerrilla group with a financial windfall?
- Are there legal problems? Does the country in which the abduction has taken
  place view a ransom payment as an act of complicity with the kidnappers?
- And even if there are no legal prohibitions, how will the government in question
  react to the passage of a large sum of money to an insurgent group? Will
  it endanger the company's future business prospects?
- Under what conditions is it feasible to rescue a hostage without a ransom
  payment?
- What are the company's moral obligations to the victim and his family? What
  are its legal obligations? Will failure to effect a rapid recovery result in a
  suit against the company?
- And how about the stockholders? Is it acceptable to use their funds to pay
  a ransom and will such a payment trigger a stockholders' suit?

And then there are the mechanical problems:

- If the kidnapping has not come to public attention, should it be kept under
  wraps? Should the police be notified and, if so, what type of relationship
  should be effected with them?
- What role can embassies play in the recovery?
- What steps can be taken to ensure that communications from the kidnappers
  are received in a competent manner—that telephone transmissions are fully
  documented and written messages reach the decision makers or their representatives?
- What means can the company use to communicate with the kidnappers?
- Should the company attempt to negotiate the kidnappers' demands and, if
  so, what strategies are appropriate?
- If the hostage has a pre-existing medical condition, can the company communicate it to the kidnappers? What other steps can be taken to preserve the
  victim's health?
- Is it possible to verify that the hostage is alive and well prior to payment
  of a ransom?
- How can funds be safely brought to the country in question, and how can
  they be protected while awaiting word from the kidnappers regarding delivery
  arrangements?

- Is it possible to effect a face-to-face exchange of ransom for hostage? If not, is there any other means of ensuring that the kidnappers will comply with their obligation to release the hostage after the money is paid?

ROLE OF THE RECOVERY CONSULTANT

The foregoing recitation of issues and problems would probably lead even the most self-sufficient of corporate managers to conclude that they would require expert assistance to effect a successful recovery. In a very few countries—among them, fortunately, the United States—law enforcement authorities possess sufficient professionalism and experience to render that assistance; but in most parts of the world they do not. Corporations must seek help elsewhere.

Enter the recovery consultant. The consultant does not necessarily render the decision-making process less painful for his corporate client—none but the charlatan pretenders to the craft claim an ability to obtain an "instant recovery"—but he can make it more rational and more orderly; and he should also be able to render a positive contribution in the area of mechanics.

The keystone of the consultant's usefulness to a recovery operation is his prior experience. It is primarily because the veteran recovery consultant has been there before that he can facilitate resolution of the problem at hand. No single corporation can possibly expect to develop on its own a comparable experience base.

The consultant—or consulting group—should be equipped to provide other forms of assistance as well. He should be sufficiently fluent in the kidnappers' language to read and interpret their demands and to assist in preparing a response, or indeed, if appropriate, to undertake to respond—by telephone, radio, or, in the odd instance, in person—on behalf of the corporation. He should possess, or have the capability to compile, a "book" on the *modus operandi* of the kidnappers in question, in order to facilitate the development of a recovery strategy. He should also be possessed of or at least able to develop high-level contacts in the appropriate police services, for use in the event that the police are to play an active role in the recovery effort. And he should certainly be prepared to employ his professionalism and professional resources to their fullest in order to protect the ransom funds in the critical hours prior to a delivery. In some cases it may even be appropriate for him to deliver ransom funds—and this consultant for one has made more such deliveries than he cares to remember.

The one role that any responsible recovery consultant must decline is that of decision maker. It is the consultant's function to facilitate the recovery process in any way he can, and in this connection it is perfectly acceptable for him to place alternative strategies before corporate officials; but it is management's prerogative, and indeed its responsibility, to decide on the appropriate course of action. Senior corporate officials should oversee the recovery effort from their headquarters; and, as some key tactical decisions must of necessity be taken at the scene of the emergency, their senior representative should accompany the recovery consultant to the appropriate location to supervise field operations.

It is perhaps obvious from the above that corporations should identify a recovery consultant well in advance of an emergency, so as not to be faced with the necessity of having to "go it alone" during the first crucial hours of a kidnapping, while they fumble through an effort to identify potential sources of assistance. Ideally, the company will have established a contractual relationship with the consultant, so that his immediate availability is assured.

The optimum, of course, is to bring the consultant into the planning process well in advance of a kidnapping. It has been fashionable in some quarters to use management consultants and other generalists to prepare corporate crisis management plans and to brief crisis teams. This is patent nonsense. Only the veteran recovery consultant can adequately prepare corporate decision makers for the complex questions they will face in an emergency.

THE POLICE CONNECTION

There is nothing as sensitive in a recovery effort as dealings with local police authorities. Terrorists rarely murder executive hostages. When a hostage is killed in the course of a kidnapping, it is usually the result of some action by the police. In the United States and a handful of other countries corporate crisis managers can count on dealing with law enforcement authorities possessed of both high standards of professionalism and a profound humanitarian regard for the survival of the hostage. The corporation and the law enforcement agency share a common goal: the safe return of the victim. The apprehension of the kidnappers is of course also an objective, but a secondary one.

In some other countries police agencies are entirely competent, but guided by a national philosophy—and a very defensible philosophy at that—which places maximum emphasis on the apprehension of terrorist kidnappers and only secondarily considers the safety of the hostage. And in still others the police possess neither acceptable levels of professionalism nor profound concern for the safety of the hostage. Thus, corporations are in many parts of the world faced with the problem of working at cross-purposes with the authorities.

To those whose primary interest is the survival of a hostage, the ideal police posture is a rather passive one. Law enforcement agencies operating in this passive mode may attempt to identify the kidnappers and determine where they are holding their hostage, but they do so discreetly; and, even if they are successful in locating the "people's prison," they do not raid it unless the hostage's life is thought to be in immediate danger. They allow ransom negotiations to run their course and do not move in on the terrorists until the hostage has been liberated.

Unfortunately, most of the world's security services possess neither the professionalism nor the patience that this passive posture demands. The majority, and especially those facing active terrorist movements and under pressure to make inroads into them, are inclined to be activist—and police activism, in a kidnapping situation, almost inevitably prejudices the hostage's safety.

Police normally zero in on kidnappers in one of two ways: either they arrest terrorist suspects and interrogate them, hoping thus to ascertain the kidnappers' identity and the site of the people's prison, or they intervene in the ransom delivery, with the objective of seizing one of the kidnappers and then "sweating" him for the same information. Both methodologies involve risks, and the latter is particularly hazardous, as kidnappers are apt to become extremely nervous when the comrades dispatched to recover a ransom fail to return at the appointed hour.

Then there is the problem of acting on the information that has been gathered. Suppose that the police do pinpoint the people's prison. Watching it is no simple matter, and there is always the chance that the terrorists will slip away—with or without their hostage. Most police services are inclined to raid the suspect premises sooner rather than later, and such raids, unfortunately, always grieviously imperil a hostage's life. The danger is particularly acute if the assault takes place in a country that does not in general respect due process of law, an observation which requires some elaboration.

In January 1982, Brigadier General James L. Dozier was rescued from a Red Brigades' people's prison in Padua in a lightning raid conducted by a specially trained antiterrorist unit of the Italian police. The successful operation appeared to be a vindication of the "assault" option. Indeed it was, but with some important reservations. First of all, Dozier's status as a high-ranking military officer made it virtually impossible to negotiate his release. Political terms certainly could not be satisfied; neither could monetary demands. And given the high probability that the general would ultimately be executed, even a high-risk assault had to be considered a viable option. Second, Italy's status as a due process country significantly increased the chances of a successful raid. Dozier's captors had every reason to believe that if they spared the life of their hostage and surrendered to police they would have their day in court—and the Italian judicial system would reward their compassion. They were correct. Giovanni Ciucci, the terrorist holding a gun on Dozier when the police broke in, received a 12-year sentence and will be eligible for parole in six. His four comrades received sentences ranging from 14 to 27 years, and will also be eligible for parole upon completion of half their sentences.

Unfortunately, terrorist kidnappers in many Central and South American countries have no such incentive to spare the life of a hostage and throw down their arms. They correctly assume that if taken alive they face torture and, ultimately, death; and they thus elect to murder their hostage and "go down fighting." Under these circumstances, police intervention of any sort in the recovery process becomes a paramount concern of crisis managers. Negotiators must be constantly aware that the authorities may at any time identify, or indeed even stumble on, the people's prison in which their hostage is being held; and it is this ever-present possibility more than anything else that lends urgency to the recovery process. In two instances in the last three years executive hostages have been killed in police raids on suspected terrorist safehouses, safehouses that were not revealed to be people's prisons until after the fact.

Due process is in many instances one of the most exasperating aspects of Western judicial systems. Often frontier justice seems much more efficient, but not to those who from time to time deal in the delicate business of recovering hostages.

COMMUNICATIONS

The uninitiated invariably underestimate the difficulty of a hostage recovery. There is no problem as severely underrated as that of communications. The challenge is to carry out a complicated negotiation and then arrive at satisfactory delivery/ release arrangements with a group of kidnappers whose fugitive status severely restricts the opportunity for a dialogue and who in any case have little patience for entertaining the corporation's point of view.

Nothing can be taken for granted, except Murphy's law. Everything that can possibly go wrong invariably does. Notes delivered to a corporate facility are almost always addressed to an executive on extended leave—and placed in his in-box. Telephone calls are missed because a line is down. If a message is to be delivered on a radio frequency, the atmospheric conditions impede reception. This consultant, on one occasion, had to fly to a remote outpost, far enough from the capital city and the interference it generated to permit a clear reading of the kidnappers' instructions for the ransom delivery.

Outgoing messages can be a problem too. The kidnappers may direct the corporation to reply through a classified ad, which the newspaper will invariably print under the wrong heading or on the wrong page. Or it may simply omit a line of type. If the reply is to take the form of a radio announcement, the station will inevitably run it at the wrong time. In one instance a corporation practically had to buy a station to assure that a particular "public service announcement" was run at the correct hour.

Imagine, under these conditions, attempting to convey to kidnappers that they have failed to satisfy the corporate sponsor's wish to verify that the hostage is alive and well, or that it has proven impossible to obtain the ransom funds in the exact denominations requested, or that it would be infinitely more practical to make the ransom delivery in a locale other than the one that has been designated. Often, it is simply impossible to do so—and the corporate sponsors and their consultant are reduced to crossing their fingers and embarking down the least objectionable path.

THE HOSTAGE FAMILY

The path to a recovery tends to be prolonged. The intractability of communications, for one thing, almost invariably lengthens the recovery process. Obviously, time hangs heaviest on the hostage—and his immediate family. The former is normally not in a position to impede the recovery process. The latter, unfortunately, is.

Most hostage families are at the outset rather cooperative. Shocked by the horrible reality of the abduction and not possessed of sufficient resources to deal with the situation on their own, they react with enthusiasm to the corporate sponsor's offer to undertake the recovery. Understandably, however, their patience is not infinite, and if the recovery operation drags on, as most of them do, strains invariably develop between the family and the corporation.

Crisis managers normally feel themselves obliged to brief the immediate family, in general if not in detail, on the progress of the recovery, which is all to the good. There is always one brother-in-law, however, who never really cared for the hostage but now holds it a sacred familial duty to second guess every move to which he is privy; and there are apt to be other friends and relatives as well who feel compelled to add their own unprofessional counsel. Under these circumstances, it is not surprising that over time cooperation often turns to suspicion and suspicion degenerates into downright hostility.

How can families impede the recovery operation? In a number of ways. They can, through advertisements or press leaks, attempt to open their own communications with the terrorists, conveying an attitude that may well be at variance with the negotiating posture selected by the crisis managers. Or they may open a legal or even a press offensive against the corporation, diverting the energies of crisis managers and, through this pressure, possibly causing them to deviate from a valid game plan. Decisions taken from the perspective of a possible lawsuit are not necessarily those that ensure and accelerate the safe recovery of the hostage.

A POSTSCRIPT ON PREVENTION

Somehow recovery operations usually turn out all right. But there has never been a routine recovery, and this writer never expects to be confronted with an easy one.

If the foregoing has conveyed the impression that a hostage recovery is among the least savory activities in which a corporation may become involved, it has fulfilled one of its principal objectives. The terrorists know that they have the multinational at an extreme disadvantage and they are not at all reluctant to squeeze.

Except for those rare instances in which a hostage has been rescued without fulfillment of any terrorist demands, there is in fact no such thing as a truly successful recovery operation. Sure, releases are obtained, but at what cost? Those of us who have participated in a ransom delivery are keenly aware, despite the momentary satisfaction of having assisted in the rescue of a decent human being, that we have not only facilitated the passage of important financial resources to a malevolent cause, but have also, in all probability, set the stage for a new round of abductions.

Anyone who has ever been close to the wrong end of a kidnapping can attest to the fact that there is no substitute for a conscientious effort at prevention. There are of course no guarantees that such an effort will be successful, but a compelling case can be made that multinational corporations can today decrease their kidnap risks substantially by (a) keeping abreast of the status of the kidnapping problem—which, as far as corporations are concerned, is actually limited at present to a half-dozen or so countries; (b) limiting their exposure in those areas through reducing personnel levels to the bare essentials; and (c) upgrading protective measures for those employees who must reside in or visit high-risk areas. These measures are often inconvenient. They can also be somewhat costly. But they are far, far better than the alternative.

22

Talking to Terrorists

Brian M. Jenkins

Previous chapters have focused on negotiations—the policy issues and tactics of bargaining for human life. Negotiations require communications, principally between the perpetrators of the crime and the target of their demands, but other parties also get involved. This chapter examines the problem of communications with kidnappers.

Communications problems vary according to the type of kidnapping. From the standpoint of negotiations and kidnappings, there are two types. The first part of the chapter discusses the communications problems in kidnappings that are primarily *political* in purpose. In these cases, the kidnappers' specific demands— usually the release of imprisoned comrades—are part of a larger set of political goals: Political kidnappers also want publicity, to inspire fear, demonstrate government impotence, and win adherents. Achievement of these other objectives may be of equal or greater importance than the specific demands.

The second part of the chapter looks at the communications problems in *ransom* kidnappings. Strictly ransom kidnappings may be carried out either by terrorists or ordinary criminals. Victims are selected on the basis of their value, measured only in economic terms, and their vulnerability. Ransom kidnappers may also seek other goals, but the paramount objective in ransom kidnappings is the ransom. Political kidnappers usually select government officials as their victims; ransom kidnappers prefer businessmen or members of wealthy families, though not all kidnappings uphold this distinction. German terrorists in 1977 kidnapped Hanns-Martin Schleyer, a prominent and influential German industrialist, for primarily political purposes. In 1981, Italian terrorists released Ciro Cirillo, a Christian Democrat politician in Naples, in return for a ransom of approximately $1.5 million.

With regard to communications, the principal difference between the two types of kidnappings is that in political kidnappings communications take place directly or indirectly between the kidnappers and public authorities. In most ransom kidnappings, communications take place between the kidnappers and a private party, sometimes with a deliberate effort by both to conceal communications from the authorities.

POLITICAL KIDNAPPINGS

Political kidnappings of diplomats or other government officials are employed by terrorists as a means of gaining international attention and exerting leverage over the local government, on whom they usually levy their demands. A political kidnapping is an act of propaganda; inherent within it is a desire to communicate. Holding a hostage guarantees that the kidnappers will be heard. On the other side, the government not only is concerned with obtaining the safe release of a hostage or hostages; it also wants to communicate its position in the contest with the terrorists. When the hostage is an official of another government, that government also must communicate its concerns about the safety of one or more of its citizens, its policy with regard to political kidnappings, and its attitude toward the local government.

For the news media, a political kidnapping is a good story, a genuine drama; human life hangs in the balance. There are disagreements, confrontations, ultimatums, brinksmanship, rumors. The noise level is high.

Political kidnappings create many communications problems. Resolution of these kidnappings requires communication between at least two parties: the terrorist kidnappers and the government. Governments themselves are, of course, complex organizations comprised of separate entities that sometimes act independently of one another, each having its own means of communicating. This diversity magnifies the problem. When opinions are divided on how to handle the kidnapping, the government may be saying several things at once.

When terrorists seize diplomats, two governments are automatically involved, the local government and the government of the hostage. The captive's government in such a situation may comprise two principal entities: a task force assembled in the capital of the captive's country to manage the crisis and the embassy on the scene. If the kidnapping occurs outside a country's capital, a regional government and a local consul are added to the network. Kidnappers in some cases have contacted the hostage's family as a means of increasing pressure; or the family, dissatisfied with the handling of the incident by officials, may try to initiate direct contact with the kidnappers. In a few cases, hostages have been made to participate in meetings with the press or have been permitted to write letters or make appeals, and thus they, too, become part of the communications. In some cases intermediaries are used. Often they have something to say themselves, and they become yet another component in the complex communications net.

The Hard- and Soft-Line Debate

The problem is not simply that a lot of people must somehow communicate with a lot of other people. There are many prohibitions. The local government often does not want to talk to the kidnappers, or at least does not want to be seen doing so. Communications themselves are viewed by many as a concession that gives terrorists equal status with the government. The local government may not want the embassy or the hostage's family to communicate directly with the kidnappers either, or at least not without government supervision. And the local government often will try to prevent the terrorists from communicating with the public. It may go so far as to prohibit publications by the news media of terrorist communiques. In other words, the local government usually wants to cut off the terrorists, bury the crisis, remain in charge, and conduct its business in private.

The prohibition against direct communications with the kidnappers also applies to the captive's government. Since the mid-1970s, a growing number of countries have adopted a no-concessions policy in dealing with political kidnappings. Sometimes such a policy precludes direct communications between that government and the kidnappers. Moreover, most governments regard the host or local government as being responsible for the safety of diplomats assigned to it. Direct communications incur the risk that the terrorists will shift their demands to the captive's government and lift the responsibility from the shoulders of the local government.

The kidnappers may try to get around the local government's and the embassy's unwillingness to communicate by dealing directly with the hostage's family. The kidnappers, the hostage, and the hostage's family often have a community of interests. All would like to see the kidnappers' demands met so the hostage can be released. Kidnappers may try to manipulate the family in order to exert private and public pressure on the government to make concessions. For that same reason, government officials generally try to keep the family from becoming directly involved. The family's single-minded dedication to the safe release of the hostage makes it unconcerned with abstract policies about terrorism. The family may be willing to offer concessions, exert pressure on the government for concessions, or publicly criticize officials for "abandoning" the hostage.

Generally, terrorists kidnap diplomats or other government officials for political reasons. When they want cash, they abduct businessmen, who are more lucrative targets. However, in a few of the episodes involving government officials, the kidnappers have made demands directly on the hostage's family, usually for a cash ransom. This happened in the case of Terrence Leonhardy, the American consul general in Guadalajara, Mexico. In that incident, the kidnappers instructed the family not to inform local authorities.

A Multiple-Message Problem

The different parties involved in a political kidnapping aim their communications at different audiences. The terrorists probably have the most ambitious program in this regard. Their specific audiences include their perceived constituents, the local population in general, the American public, a world audience, other potential targets whom they might attack in the future, and other terrorists. A different message is aimed at each audience. They must inspire their perceived constituents. They must show the local population that the local government is ineffective, incompetent, impotent. To the public in the captor's country they must explain their cause and thereby undermine its support for the local government. The message to the world is the desire for publicity and recognition. They want to instill terror among local and foreign officials. They must demonstrate their superiority over rival terrorist groups.

The local government must communicate with the terrorists, the local population and, to a lesser degree, the world. Again, there are different messages for each, and sometimes the messages are contradictory. The local government publicly tries to persuade the terrorists that it will make no concessions, that they can gain nothing from the kidnapping and must release their hostage. Privately, the government may at the same time indicate its willingness to reach some sort of compromise to save the life of the hostage. The local government tries to convince the local population—its principal audience—that the government remains in charge, that it will not capitulate to terrorists, that it is competent.

The captive's government talks to the terrorists, to the local government, and to its own public. It tries to persuade the terrorists that kidnapping will not pay and that they must release the hostage. At the same time, it may or may not try to persuade the local government to open a dialogue with the terrorists and come to some kind of agreement that will bring about the safe release of the hostage. The captive's government must also address the public at home. This is probably the primary audience before whom the government must appear strong, unyielding to terrorism, and managerially competent.

One serious problem is that most of the messages are public. In a sense, everyone reads everyone else's mail. Since each actor's objectives differ with regard to different audiences, the total traffic may be confusing and conflicting. The terrorists must figure out if the local government is throwing down the gauntlet or signaling its readiness to bargain. The local government may sometimes be confused as to whether the captive's government places greater emphasis on preserving a policy of no-concessions or on securing the safe release of the hostage. In one case involving an American diplomat kidnapped abroad, U.S. policy was communicated publicly and privately in double-edged language which stated that the U.S. government's policy was not to accede to demands of terrorists holding hostages, but the responsibility for the protection of American diplomats abroad lay with the host government. In this case, the host government demanded to know what exactly that sentence meant. Did the United States want the man back or not? In fact, the officials in Washington who drafted the phrase saw it as a means of preserving a previously established no-concessions policy while opening a window for the local government to cut a deal.

There is no easy solution to this problem. It simply must be kept in mind that in addressing one audience, a government may be causing difficulties in its communications with another audience. This argues for coordination of communications, and it suggests that the fine language of diplomacy may not always be applicable to the more practical problem of dealing with terrorist kidnappers in a crisis situation.

Uses and Misuses of the News Media

In most political kidnappings, the kidnappers and the government communicate with each other through the news media. But terrorists have also communicated through above-ground spokesmen, they have left messages for government officials to find, and sometimes they have established direct telephone contact. (Telephone contact is generally characteristic of negotiations for cash ransom.) In all private means of communication, the terrorists have the initiative. Governments devote a great deal of effort to figuring out how to contact the terrorists directly without addressing them publicly through the news media. Who can get in touch with them? Known sympathizers? A certain journalist? The leaders of other governments? Imprisoned comrades? And even if a means is found, the government can seldom be confident that its messages are accurately conveyed to the kidnappers.

In a few of the political kidnappings, an intermediary was used. While such intermediaries are sometimes necessary, they can be dangerous from the government point of view, and must be chosen and handled with care. The intermediary is rarely a neutral communicator. To be acceptable to the kidnappers, he may have to be someone who sympathizes with their cause to some degree. He may exploit his role to publicly blast the government. Even the politically neutral intermediary may begin to see himself not as a passive conveyer but as an active arbitrator in a dispute. He may become increasingly dedicated to arranging a compromise and may become impatient and begin to publicly criticize the government for not making concessions. Entrusting communications to an intermediary almost invariably translates into eventual concessions; and if the government is not prepared to negotiate, there is no need for an intermediary.

Communicating through the news media has both advantages and disadvantages. One disadvantage is the usual unwillingness of the local government or the captive's government to be seen in public communicating with terrorist kidnappers. Another is the desire to send a variety of messages—tough on terrorists, humane with regard to the hostage and his family, unyielding on the matter of concessions but willing to talk about a settlement—that are intended for different audiences but that will be read by everyone. A third disadvantage is the high volume of background noise. A political kidnapping commands the attention of the national and international press. Newsmen seldom wait for official briefings. They dig for news, ask for interviews, call their informants, reach for rumors. And they have two governments to work on. Each government's message must compete with a barrage of public statements by high-level officials, off-the-record comments, tips, and rumors as interpreted by the press. The message to the terrorists, if there is one, may get lost. There is one unseen advantage to using the media rather than direct negotiations for communication. There is no capability for instant reply. In critical moments, one does not want to assume a position without thinking out the consequences and communicating with the other party involved. Each side has time to consider its moves and coordinate its position.

Terrorists naturally want all the attention they can get. They may even make media coverage or publication of their communiques a part of their demands. Sometimes the local government may try to suppress messages sent by the terrorists by prohibiting their publication. In one case, however—the 1976 hijacking of a TWA airliner by Croatian extremists—an FBI official communicated the hijackers' demand that several newspapers print their manifesto on the front page and asked that the newspapers go along with the demand. The U.S. secretary of state was incensed when he heard about the request, as he considered it a violation of the U.S. no-concessions policy. Although the press went along with the request in this case, the news media are generally reluctant to relinquish command of their space to terrorists or governments.

On several occasions, public statements by high-ranking officials have complicated negotiations and narrowed options. Two American examples come to mind. In 1973, Palestinian terrorists, members of Black September, took over the Saudi Arabian embassy in Khartoum. In return for the release of their hostages—who included one Belgium and two American diplomats, the ambassador and the deputy chief of mission—the terrorists demanded, among other things, the release of the imprisoned assassin of Senator Robert Kennedy. For the first two days, the terrorists took no action. Sudanese officials informed them that a high-ranking American official, the under secretary of state, was on his way to Khartoum. Meanwhile, in the course of a routine press conference at the White House, reporters asked President Nixon if the United States was going to release Kennedy's killer. The president replied that the United States would never give in to terrorist blackmail. This comment was broadcast to the Middle East and rebroadcast to Khartoum. The terrorists reportedly heard it on their radio. Shortly after that, they murdered the one Belgian and two American hostages.

It would be irresponsible to blame their deaths on the president's statement. Less than three months before the Khartoum incident, a team of Black September terrorists holding the Israeli embassy in Bangkok had agreed to a compromise and were strongly criticized within the group. Black September was anxious to demonstrate its resolve at Khartoum. The United States could never have agreed to the release of a convicted assassin, so there was little room to negotiate. On the other hand, the terrorists had appeared willing to wait for the arrival of the American under secretary. The president's statement may have inadvertently undercut a stalling tactic.

In another case, the former U.S. attorney general inadvertently revealed in a Washington press conference that an American diplomat had been kidnapped in Mexico. The kidnapping of the American vice consul in Hermosillo occurred five days before the attorney general's conference, but authorities had kept it secret while attempting in vain to deliver the ransom demanded by the kidnappers. Once the secret was out, the news media in both Mexico and the United States made inquiries. The authorities, who were still hopeful of delivering the ransom and saving the hostage, had to make careful replies; they did not want to frighten off the kidnappers. As it turned out, the attorney general's revelation was irrelevant. The kidnapper, a lone criminal who was later apprehended, had already murdered his hostage and fled. Had this not been the case, however, the attorney general's remarks might have caused serious complications.

In neither case were the high-ranking officials to blame for the diplomats' deaths. In one case terrorists, and in the other an ordinary criminal pulled the trigger. They alone are culpable. But the examples are instructive of the difficulties that can be caused by off-the-cuff remarks during a political kidnapping.

Hoax calls and claims will often equal or exceed genuine communications from the kidnappers. We have seen this in the Dozier case. In some cases, groups unconnected with the kidnapping may make demands; publicity seekers, nuts, or pranksters may get into the act; or the kidnappers themselves may send false messages—"The hostage has been condemned and executed, his body may be found. . . ." These are designed to keep public attention focused on the kidnapping and government tensions high. To assure itself that the claimants actually have the hostage and that he is still alive, the government may demand proof. Governments also have exploited the existence of rival claimants to confuse the kidnappers and entice them to provide additional information. Where further dialogue—particularly over the telephone—is likely, the kidnappers or the government may establish a code to ensure that the right calls will get through without delay.

Kidnappings as Governmental Crises

Not all problems derive from the difficulty of communications between governments and terrorists. The kidnapping of a foreign official creates a major crisis for any government. In such a crisis, the local government closes in on itself. Decisions are made by the chief of state and a few close advisors. The minister of foreign affairs, the ambassador's normal point of contact, may not be part of the inner decision-making group and may be sidelined. This is particularly true in Third World countries where the key figures are likely to include the president, the ministers of defense and interior, and chiefs of the armed forces. The foreign minister is often a respected figure but not part of the inner circle. On tough issues like terrorism, political survival takes precedence over foreign relations.

How does an ambassador get to the people who count? Other contacts, the defense attache, the military mission, an intelligence counterpart, or a personal acquaintance may become crucial sources of information and communications. In some cases, these are not enough and it is necessary for the ambassador to talk directly to the chief of state. In the past, this has been accomplished by sending a letter from the head of state to the captive's country to be hand-delivered to the local chief of state.

In one episode, U.S. embassy officials feared that the local president's inattention to the problem after his government agreed to the terrorists' demands but before the deal was consummated might provide an opportunity for elements within the government who opposed the concessions to sabotage the settlement. In this case, they persuaded the chief of state to come back from his weekend retreat to guarantee that the deal would go through.

Communications between the capital of the captive's country and its embassy have sometimes been a problem. The kidnapping of a diplomat inevitably generates a certain amount of debate regarding policy. No-concessions ceases to be an abstract issue. A life is at stake and that changes things. Diplomats are skilled at resolving differences with vague or double-edged language. But compromise language used to bridge differences in the capital may not be understood by embassy officials who were not privy to the original debate and therefore may not see the intent of the words.

Conclusions

There are no general rules for solving these communications problems, just as there are no formulas for dealing with political kidnappings. Each case is unique. At the same time, there do seem to be some general principles that government officials might try to adhere to:

1.   *The less said in public the better.* The volume of communications is enormous. Anything said is likely to be lost in the noise or, worse, misinterpreted with possibly tragic consequences.
2.   *Off-the-cuff remarks by high-ranking officials should be avoided altogether.* They are likely to get attention they do not deserve. They may inadvertently complicate affairs, foreclose options, and further elevate an event that is likely to have a tragic outcome.
3.   *The government must speak with a single voice; all communications should be coordinated.* The off-the-record interview may have greater effect than the official briefing.
4.   *The various audiences should be identified.* Those communicating should think about the message to be sent and the effect it is likely to have on the other parties. It must be remembered that everything will be heard by everyone.
5.   *The government's public responses should be kept as low-key as possible.* The U.S. government is at the margin; its ability to determine the outcome of a political kidnapping in a positive way is limited. The kidnappers may decide to murder an American official, and we cannot stop them. In such circumstances, there is no reason to elevate the confrontation.
6.   *Messages should be blunt and simple.* This admonition is likely to curdle the hearts of diplomats. But a kidnapping is a time of crisis. The volume of noise is high. Subtle messages are seldom received.
7.   *Policy ought not to equate communications with negotiations and concessions.* They are different things.
8.   *Beware of intermediaries.* They are seldom neutral or passive. They will drive the government toward concessions and denounce it for not making them.
9.   *Committee language does not work.* It will not be understood by those not present at the debate.

RANSOM KIDNAPPINGS

The Corporation's Audiences

Corporations face many of the same problems faced by a government communicating with terrorists, as well as some unique problems. Like governments, corporations have to address several different audiences simultaneously. To the kidnappers, the corporation must communicate that it wants to get its man back and know what it will take to do so. This is not always easily accomplished since the corporation cannot contact the kidnappers directly. It must wait for their call or attempt to communicate its willingness to negotiate terms through means of public statements. But these public statements must not undermine the company's efforts to bargain with the kidnappers.

To the family of the hostage, the company must communicate that it is making every reasonable effort to obtain his safe release. This can become extremely difficult during ransom negotiations. In the eyes of family members, if the company's primary objective is the safe release of the hostage, then the company ought not to imperil the hostage by attempting to reduce the amount of ransom it is willing to pay; it ought to promptly pay whatever the kidnappers demand. If it is not willing to do so, then its paramount interest is not the safe release of the hostage.

This conflict raises the question, To what degree should companies inform families of the course of the negotiations? In some cases, company negotiators have chosen not to keep the family informed of progress of the negotiations. This, however, is a perilous course. For one thing, it generates bad feelings that can lead to family members criticizing the company in interviews with the press and making direct appeals to the kidnappers. By keeping the family in the dark, the company also assumes a greater responsibility for the outcome of the event. Ultimately, bitter feelings and the company's assumption of sole responsibility for all decisions can lead to lawsuits. Whatever the legal merits of any legal action, it does a corporation little good to be seen being sued by wives or widows of hostages. Without making family members direct participants in the negotiations, which all experts advise against, the corporation should try as much as possible to keep the family apprised of their progress. This may involve selecting one member of the family, not necessarily the wife, as a point of contact.

To the public, the corporation must communicate that it is not a callous institution that values its profits above human life. On the other hand, some corporations have stated in public that they will not pay ransom for kidnapped employees. Such statements may be intended to deter would-be kidnappers or reduce ransom demands, or are instead meant to assure a local government that the company is complying with laws against the payment of ransom (while perhaps secretly negotiating).

In cases where kidnappers make demands beyond cash ransom, such as concessions to the work force, the corporation must also communicate to workers and workers' representatives. To workers, it must communicate that the kidnappers' demands are unreasonable, and that although they might benefit workers in the short run, the long-run effect will weaken the company and could eventually cost jobs.

Kidnappers' demands for concessions to workers create special problems for both corporate management and labor union leadership. If the corporation goes along with the kidnappers' demands, its own ability to control the company is reduced; it undermines the authority of the union. If the corporation rejects the demands, the workers see themselves losing something they might otherwise have gained. Similarly, if union leaders endorse the kidnappers' demands, their own leadership will be outflanked, and the kidnappers may be seen by workers as the new vanguard in resolving future labor disputes. If the union opposes the demands, it may be seen as acting contrary to the workers' interests.

Rejection of the demands is probably in the interests of both company and union. However, concessions may be necessary to save a life. At a minimum then, corporate management and union labor leadership ought not to appear divided on the issue. Ideally, the two will act in tandem, denouncing terrorism, resisting certain kinds of demands, agreeing as to what concessions might be possible in extraordinary circumstances. That requires coordination, which in turn requires communication. However, communication during negotiations becomes difficult when corporate management suspects that the kidnappers may have confederates within union leadership who might communicate corporate positions and strategies to the kidnappers—which sometimes has been the case—or when corporate management suspects that union leadership is exploiting the kidnapping for its own purposes. Beyond being aware of this problem, there are no general rules to deal with it.

To corporate executives and other professional employees, the corporation must communicate a message of reassurance: that the company is paying close attention and devoting sufficient resources to their physical security, adding that their security also depends greatly on measures they take as individuals, and that the company will do everything reasonable to secure the release of any employee who is kidnapped.

To government authorities, if they know about the kidnapping, the corporation may want to communicate several messages. One may be its concern over the general problem of security and the necessity that the authorities pay close attention to it. A second message may be to dissuade the government from imposing any limitation or taking any precipitate action that will imperil the life of the hostage. A third message may be that the corporation is complying with the law.

Whether to inform authorities of negotiations, if they do not already know about them, is a major decision for the corporation. Where governments prohibit negotiations with kidnappers or the payment of ransom, corporations and families have sometimes tried to keep contacts with kidnappers secret or move the negotiations to another country. This persistence entails many risks for corporations and negotiators, who in some cases have been jailed. Most ransom insurance policies require that local authorities be informed.

Corporations must usually wait for kidnappers to contact them. In the absence of communications, corporate officials have at times in desperation made public statements or inserted ads in newspapers indicating a willingness to discuss terms or proposing specific offers. Corporate officials have also on occasion tried to reach kidnappers indirectly through known figures in the criminal underworld or political underground but usually contacts in this area are the preserve of government.

Terrorist Tactics of Communication

Terrorists use communications as a tool in the negotiations. Their most common tactic is to delay their initial contact or suspend communications during the negotiations to increase pressure on the corporation and family. Silence for days, weeks, or even months has a devastating effect on the family and colleagues of a hostage, softening them for the negotiations. When kidnappers confront hard negotiators on behalf of a corporation or family, they will frequently insist on talking to the family directly. This tactic often follows a long period of silence, making it difficult for the negotiator to maintain control. Another tactic kidnappers use is to involve the hostage in the negotiations directly, permitting him to write letters or tape messages, pleading for the company or family to yield to the kidnappers demands.

Conclusions

Here, as an addition to those cited earlier, are some general principles that corporations should keep in mind when communicating with kidnappers:

1. *Consider the kidnappers' security needs.* It is in the mutual interest of both parties to develop a means of communication that is private and secure. Efforts to compel the kidnappers to communicate in ways that expose them to capture probably will not work and are counterproductive.
2. *Whether to advise local authorities of contact with kidnappers depends on the situation.* Risks are incurred either way. In the majority of cases we know about, the authorities were informed.
3. *Keep the family out of the communications network but informed of progress.*
4. *Agree in advance that the hostage will not be part of the communications.* Negotiators should be willing to talk to the hostage if that opportunity is offered, but should not discuss terms of his release.
5. *Continued negotiations should depend on the kidnappers continually proving that the hostage is alive and well.*
6. *Be prepared for lengthy interruptions in the communications.* They are part of the kidnappers' arsenal of tactics to put pressure on the family and company.

IV

Security Issues

23

The Proper Function and Use
of the Private Sector Bodyguard

Don E. Wurth

INTRODUCTION

This chapter was prepared for an admittedly limited audience—the few in the private sector who employ bodyguards or are considering their use, and the security managers who supervise protection programs in which they are utilized. Only a small number of private individuals can bear the expense of employing bodyguards or, as is most often the case, the threat a person faces is not sufficient to justify such an extreme measure.

The use of bodyguards outside of government service is typically associated with a handful of exceptionally wealthy or prominent persons—entertainment personalities; visiting oil sheiks; deposed rulers of countries with unfamiliar sounding names; or the occasional well-to-do recipient of a serious threat.

In recent years, however, there has been an increased interest on the part of a number of major corporations, particularly the multinationals, in the personal security of their top executives. For some, this concern has resulted in the establishment of executive protection programs that, not infrequently, involve the use of bodyguards on a full- or part-time basis to protect vulnerable or important executives. The proper use of the professional bodyguard in this "corporate" context is the primary concern of this chapter.

In practice, some programs consist of nothing more than hiring an off-duty, or retired, policeman to watch over the "boss" at major functions or to drive his limousine. In a very few instances the programs are quite comprehensive and involve, in addition to trained bodyguards, such measures as

- The acquiring of kidnap and ransom insurance.
- Performance of risk studies in order to estimate the degree of threat facing a particular executive or existing in a given region.
- Formulation of a corporate crisis response committee authorized to deal with any major criminal or terrorist incident.
- Seminars for concerned executives and their families that suggest various protection measures (e.g., removal of names from telephone books and com-

pany directories; careful screening of domestic employees; avoidance of predictable routines).
- The "hardening" of home and office sites by various physical measures such
as alarm systems, locks, dogs, and uniformed guards.

A Misunderstood Profession

The use of bodyguards in a corporate program can certainly be a key, if expensive,
element in any planned effort to protect top executives. The bodyguards in corporate
programs are often referred to by a number of softer terms, such as *executive
protection specialists, personal protection people, administrative assistants,* or *close
escort personnel.* This rather careful terminology is prompted by a desire to disassociate the corporate security men from the "goon" image that is often conjured
up by the use of the term *bodyguard.* More often than not, the frame of reference
for the term is an image of some Runyonesque character named Louie who shoots,
crushes, or otherwise summarily deals with any threat to his employer. This is
certainly not an accurate image, and obviously not an appealing one for the few
security professionals who specialize in protection work or for the business executives
by whom they are often employed.

The shooting of President Reagan in 1981 and the Sadat assassination that
same year provided the public with yet another perception of what the business
of bodyguarding is about. In a play-by-play account on world television, complete
with stop-action, the shooting of President Reagan was analyzed for a terrified
world audience, probably for the first time, in terms of "nuts and bolts" personal
protection tactics. The various films that forever captured the shooting were broadcast repeatedly, often accompanied by comments of newly minted network security
consultants. We were shown how the two government security men closest to the
president shielded him with their bodies while, at the same time, pushing him
into the limousine for evacuation from the danger area. We were informed how
the security man caught between the president and the gunfire positioned himself
so as to shield the president from further harm—an act that resulted in his own
wounding and a subsequent cash award. We were shown how the security men
furthest from the president focused on the direction of fire and eventually subdued
the assailant.

The assassination of President Sadat, on the other hand, supplied the legion
of commentators and experts with filmed documentation of another sort of personal
protection effort. The televised and photographed images of the mortally wounded
Egyptian president sprawled on the reviewing stand in Cairo with no apparent
protection other than the chairs hastily thrown on top of his body will, no doubt,
be used in future years as a classic example of just how not to protect someone.

These real-life examples have, for better or worse, helped to shape another
kind of impression of the nature of the work of bodyguards—one that might be
called the "presidential" model. For most people, their understanding of what a
bodyguard does is largely an imaginative, if inaccurate, mix of images ranging

from the bodyguard of movie history to the media-nourished presidential style of personal protection.

It is not surprising that these hybrid images exist also, in varying degrees, in the minds of many who employ, or are considering employing, bodyguards. The matter is further complicated by the existence of a growing number of executive protection "experts" who themselves have no accurate understanding of the role of a professional bodyguard.

The bodyguard's movie image is less appealing and easier to debunk, but the presidential model is more difficult to evaluate: It can certainly provide useful instruction for those designing a private protection program, but they must be experienced enough to understand the considerable difference between the needs of the private and governmental sectors.

It is also important to understand that the sophisticated, often successful, terrorist and criminal attacks directed against business targets in recent years have stimulated a considerable change in many corporate security programs. Not many years ago corporate security, even in the largest companies, consisted of hiring a retired man or two to keep an eye out for pilfering employees and to make sure that the lights were out and the doors locked at night. For many, the recent trends have forced a re-evaluation that has resulted in significant changes in the nature and quality of their security programs and in the recognition of the need for executive protection measures.

Many potential bodyguard employers are forced to sift through the applications of a legion of dubious "experts" who find that the increased demand for corporate bodyguards provides a perfect opportunity to make a fast dollar or two. There are, of course, qualified protection specialists, but the potential employer will frequently find himself talking to a colorful, if unqualified, mix of retired federal agents of one sort or another; former motorcycle policemen; karate experts; weight-lifters; gun enthusiasts; aspiring, or former, mercenaries; and paratroopers who have made themselves available for the executive protection market. The variety of applicants in Europe tends to be more exotic than in the United States, where the majority of full-time corporate bodyguards are retired or one-time law enforcement officers.

Bodyguard selection is further complicated by the fact that many potential employers assume that because a candidate was once a policeman, government agent, or army commando, he knows everything about being a professional bodyguard. Stumbling between their own misconceptions of what a bodyguard does and the ready pool of unqualified applicants, these decisionmakers may run a selection process something like this:

> The company has decided that we need the services of a bodyguard to protect our boss as part of our new executive protection program. As we know, a bodyguard is a burly man, often wearing sunglasses, who carries a gun and knows how to shoot or otherwise deal with anyone attempting to harm the man he is protecting. We can't advertise for the position because of the sensitive nature of our program, but we have come up with two prospects for the job: Mr. Smith, a retired police detective, who helped us out with a fraud matter some months ago and Mr. Jones, a former

Green Beret, who is available on a contract basis from the security firm that provides our uniformed guards. I understand that both men are good shots and are of presentable appearance, so it is recommended that we make our decision on the basis of cost.

In many, otherwise very sophisticated, corporate circles this kind of thinking prevails during a bodyguard selection process. This chapter should provide the background with which to make a bodyguard selection decision based on a fuller understanding of the true nature of a professional bodyguard's work.

WHY PROTECT?

The increased threat of some form of terrorist or criminal attack against the businessman target, particularly abroad, has provided the impetus for much of the increased attention paid to personal security. Many executives have found themselves "out front" as attractive targets merely because of their presence in certain countries. Businessmen are viewed by many terrorists as handy and easily exploitable means by which to promote their cause. Attacks on foreign businessmen often provide a ready focus for terrorist goals and, as in the case of kidnapping and extortion, some sorely needed cash. In most cases, the actual identity of the chosen victim is of secondary importance to his value as a symbol of foreign political interests. The principal difference between governmental and business targets to date has been that the latter offers a softer and certainly more profitable opportunity.

A businessman cannot, even if his circumstances permit, fully insure his own safety by avoiding countries experiencing the most terrorist activity. The Munich Olympics of 1972 dispelled for most people the notion that modern terrorism would confine itself to "logical" geographic boundaries. More than one businessman has fallen victim to a terrorist action in places such as London or New York— cities far removed from the political origin of the violence.

The threat of a terrorist episode is not the sole *raison d'être* for the use of bodyguards. A more compelling justification can be the threat of attacks from common criminals. It is certainly true that many kidnappings are not politically motivated: One wit has called kidnapping Italy's number-one cottage industry. The robberies, rapes, muggings, and assaults that occur hourly in every large American city have prompted more than one important executive to hire a bodyguard and have probably made others, to their regret, wish that they had. While American cities do not have a corner on street crime, in few countries does the specter of random violence loom quite so large. Merely this threat of criminal violence can provide compelling logic for the use of personal security by those who can afford it.

Every protection professional is aware of a third possible source of danger to a protectee—the mentally unbalanced. Some unstable people are inevitably drawn to persons of power or prominence. Most are of the harmless crackpot variety, but there are a small number, as history has demonstrated, that can represent a real threat. Most top executives have received crank telephone calls or bizarre, perhaps threatening, letters at one time or another. There is today, however, a sharp awareness that potentially dangerous persons "out there" may fix on a visable personality as a target in order to exorcise a personal demon or as a means to settle some imagined, or exaggerated, injustice.

WHO ARE THE PROTECTORS?

Three use patterns characterize the hiring of bodyguards:

1.   Some companies employ a bodyguard on a full-time basis—the preferred choice when the risk to a protectee is known to be substantial and continuous, or when the protectee is so important that every effort must be taken to eliminate even the mere possibility of risk. An advantage of this option is that the cost is likely to be less than that of a contract bodyguard employed on a regular basis. More important, it gives the employer the most consistent level of professional service from a bodyguard fully familiar with his needs and habits.

2.   A number of companies have only intermittent needs for the services of a bodyguard: They usually contract on a daily basis with one of the many private security firms that provide protection services. The difficulty, aside from the normally hefty cost, is in determining which security firm can provide adequately trained people. A number of firms routinely "front" experienced men (such as retired police supervisors, ex-FBI agents) as salesmen or initial representatives. What the prospective client is not told is that his "bodyguard" will be a retired traffic policeman, or a man with even less experience, who is normally posted as a uniformed guard in the local bowling alley. Probably no more than a handful of security firms in the United States can supply competent bodyguards. A long, hard look should always precede contracting for any company's services.

3.   The final possibility is recruiting bodyguards from an existing corporate security staff. It is unlikely, however, that these employees are trained for personal protection work. To reassign them requires removing them from positions for which they were presumably hired in the first place. Some companies have decided that this option is desirable anyway and have engaged security consultants to train selected staff members or have enrolled them in one of the several training programs developed in recent years to train executive protection personnel.

Utmost care, just as in the case of selecting contract bodyguards, should be taken in choosing a bodyguard training program. Many of the executive protection "schools" appear to be nothing more than a sort of paramilitary boot camp where the students pay handsome fees to learn karate kicks, practice combat shooting and master a dozen methods by which to dispatch an adversary with a commando knife. This is all—to be sure—high drama, but hardly the true core of a corporate bodyguard's responsibilities.

WHAT DOES PERSONAL PROTECTION MEAN?

Whenever there are reports of a successful attack against a person protected by bodyguards, it is not uncommon to hear conversations end with, ". . . So if they want to get you, they can get you and nothing can be done about it." In other words, if the presence of bodyguards cannot prevent or foil *all* attacks, their usefulness becomes suspect.

The logic of this argument pivots on the premise that a bodyguard's job is to simply hang around in the company of his employer, poised to repel attacks with leaping karate kicks and dazzling marksmanship. The fact of the matter is that a carefully crafted personal protection program relies primarily on *preventive* measures rather than on quick reactions at the moment of an attack. The principal function of a bodyguard should be to try to reduce substantially the opportunity for attack prior to the moment of immediate threat. That definition implies that the concept of risk reduction is at the heart of every good protection program. The goal of such a program must be to deny, insofar as possible, the opportunity for attack in such a manner that potential attackers are detected in advance or become discouraged and select a softer target. Of course, the success of prevention efforts is difficult to verify: it is characterized by the absence of any incident. Trying to quantify it is rather like trying to determine how many times a bicycle was *not* stolen because it was locked in a garage at night and chained during the day when not in use.

One is reminded of the Reagan shooting and the murder of John Lennon when considering the importance of preventive measures. The principal lesson for the Reagan bodyguards from that incident was not that every bodyguard should be prepared for the heroics of bodily blocking bullets intended for the president— regardless of how successful that tactic proved to be. In analysis after the event, they probably gave the most careful attention to tactics for reducing the president's physical exposure and to questions of how to restructure the access control procedures that allowed an assailant to hide himself in the press area.

Almost without question, if the president were to appear at the same hotel today, the attending security tactics would be different from those on the day of the shooting. The attack must have prompted a review intended to reduce the vulnerability of the president during public appearances—with particular attention paid to those critical areas of movement between one relatively secure site and another. Any changes in presidential security as a result of the incident were probably predicated on efforts to reduce his public exposure. The difficulty, of course, for the security planners is that the reduction of exposure must be accomplished in the context of the limits tolerated by a democratic society in which freely elected leaders are expected to openly make themselves available to the public.

In the example of the John Lennon murder, Lennon made the fateful decision to exit his limousine on the street in front of his New York City apartment in December 1980, rather than have his driver enter the relative safety of a restricted interior courtyard through an available arched driveway entrance. As the world now knows, Lennon's deranged murderer was waiting for him on the sidewalk armed with a revolver.

A protection professional certainly would have recommended that Lennon, given the opportunity, routinely enter and exit his limousine out of public view. This is not to say that a determined attacker would not have sought other opportunities; it simply suggests a tactic that would have denied easy access to Lennon in front of his home.

An interesting question with regard to the murder is the manner by which the killer learned that Lennon lived at the Dakota apartment building in Manhattan. New York City is, after all, a very big place, yet Lennon's murderer was able to locate him, probably through some public account of where he lived. That possibility should serve to remind anyone with even the remotest reason to be concerned for their own safety to be extremely judicious in allowing any details of their personal life to be made public.

Only when all of the carefully planned *preventive* measures for personal protection have been defeated does it become necessary to defend with force. A protectee is, obviously, most vulnerable at the moment of an attack by a heavily armed, superior force. The use of private bodyguards in situations where this sort of an attack is anticipated makes sense only to the extent that they are able to deny target opportunities to the attackers.

SHOULD WE USE BODYGUARDS?

This question has been addressed by a number of companies planning security measures for their top executives. In some instances, the use of bodyguards has been rejected out of hand because, according to the prevailing argument, a protected person still remains vulnerable to an attack by a superior force. This kind of conclusion, as noted above, is based on the view that a bodyguard is simply a man who, if he works alone, will probably be overpowered by two or more armed men. To disparage this concept of a bodyguard is not meant to suggest that an armed man or two will not go a long way in deterring criminal attacks and perhaps in persuading a terrorist group to reconsider and select a softer target. The true value of a bodyguard, however, must be measured in terms of his ability to anticipate risk and guide the protectee in such a manner as to avoid or minimize that risk. The safety of the protectee will be greatly diminished if his bodyguard is, for whatever reason, unable to perform this task.

In this connection, it is probably true that an executive is better off without a bodyguard than to be stuck with an incompetent one. Incompetent bodyguards tend to be extremely conspicuous and are of minimal value even if armed. Very often an inexperienced, poorly trained bodyguard does not know how to properly use the weapon he is carrying. On one occasion in Sardinia, for example, I observed a team of bodyguards employed by an important businessman carrying weapons that they did not know how to load and that were in such bad condition they probably could not have been fired. The bottom line is that even if a bodyguard is a crack shot and a karate expert to boot, his services are of limited value to a corporate program if he is ignorant of the more sophisticated aspects of providing for personal security.

Most of the techniques in risk reduction can be exercised by the protectee himself if he is properly trained and has the time. Attempts to maintain a low public profile or to avoid behavior patterns should be made by every vulnerable executive. Advice of this sort given to an executive of the highest level, however, is largely gratuitous. Most top executives are thrust into high public profiles by virtue of their position. They are clearly not candidates for the "do-it-yourself" suggestions ordinarily given to middle-level managers taking up assignments in high-risk areas. It has been my experience that top executives of major corporations do not have the time or the inclination to concentrate on the kind of minutiae involved in planning risk reduction or maintaining constant vigilance for developing signs of danger.

A number of corporations understand this problem and hire full-time body-guards for their top executives. This decision is made, in part, in much the same manner as the decision to provide any other service to a chief executive who cannot be burdened with unnecessary details. In some cases, the newly hired security man quickly finds out that the intricacies of advance planning for risk reduction cannot be readily undertaken without cooperation from his executive protectee. It is, ironically, in precisely this area of bodyguard-protectee cooperation that the task of personal protection work is made most difficult.

Any experienced bodyguard will quickly tell you that his job is made immeasurably easier if the person he is protecting feels in grave danger. Executives who find themselves accompanied by a bodyguard, merely as the result of some new company policy, are not usually moved to alter the manner in which they conduct their business and personal lives. Recommendations that routes be varied to and from work, standing appointments changed, and limousines traded for standard sedans are likely to be met with an incredulous stare—assuming that the new bodyguard summons up the courage to make them in the first place.

Try to imagine a bodyguard suggesting to an angry board chairman that he wait inside the relative safety of an office building for a tardy limousine if the chairman is determined to curse the offending driver from the vantage point of the front sidewalk. The bodyguard must be experienced and flexible enough to know when to press his case—Peoria, after all, is not Guatamala City.

Many top executives are strong-willed and hardly accustomed to subordinates attempting to change their lives, even for their own protection. This observation does not doom a bodyguard without a fully cooperative protectee to failure: It simply recognizes a common problem that has reduced the function of more than one bodyguard to that of following his employer around. This "watchdog" role is not without some deterrent value; but when the critical function of planned risk reduction is not coordinated with the protectee, the value of a bodyguard is greatly diminished.

The Presidential Style of Bodyguard

A considerable difference has been noted between most governmental and private protection programs. Nevertheless, it is important for private sector counterparts to understand the basic features of a government-style operation. Rather than being a sort of "Agent 007" kind of operation, most government protection programs in fact, consist of fairly routine efforts in three general categories:

1. *Intelligence.* Most government protection forces maintain intelligence sections with responsibility to collect and evaluate information regarding threats to their protectees. These sections develop their own information as well as receive data from other intelligence sources. In a number of cases, the collected information is stored in computers and made instantly available when required. Intelligence is critical: It gives opportunities to identify, in advance, individuals or groups who may pose threats, as well as providing the option to avoid situations presenting unusual risk.

The legal authority to engage in certain activities and the depth of intelligence resources that are available to most governmental bodyguards cannot be duplicated in the private sector. These obvious limitations do not belittle the attempts of private bodyguards, while staying within the bounds available to them, to identify in advance any threat to a protectee. The private bodyguard who makes himself well informed about the nature and extent of any threat to his protectee can tailor his defensive tactics accordingly.

2. *Advance preparations.* Seldom does a government protectee simply jump into a limousine or board an airplane with his security people merely tagging along in tow. Meticulous planning, carefully reviewed in the best bureaucratic fashion, goes into every aspect of most governmental protectees' schedules. The precise level of thoroughness varies from country to country and has a great deal to do with the professional capabilities of a given security staff. Properly conducted, advance surveys provide a bodyguard with an opportunity to critically evaluate a site prior to the arrival of his protectee, as well as the knowledge of characteristics of the site by which to devise deployment and contingency plans.

3. *The "Working" Bodyguard.* Advance surveys allow most of the security preparations to be in place before a governmental protectee ever ventures forth with his bodyguard escort. In the case of very high officials, the full resources of a government's intelligence capabilities are turned to detailed advance planning before even the most ordinary activities.

In these cases, the bodyguard planners have the advantage of virtually unlimited manpower available from the government's bodyguard corps as well as from the country's military and police services. In many countries, it is not uncommon to see hundreds, if not thousands, of security men protecting a head of state on a single public occasion. This number not only includes the protection "soldiers," but dozens of support players such as medical, communications, explosive, and intelligence specialists.

The manner in which most governments' bodyguards are deployed can be described as the *concentric circle method*. As the term implies, the bodyguard planners position their men in such a fashion as to form a series of protective circles around their protectee. The integrity of the circles is maintained by manning fixed posts that are positioned to complement any natural barriers and by fielding roving patrols. This type of deployment is expected to detect any potential danger in the less critical outer perimeters before the highly sensitive inner-circle area closest to the protectee is reached.

As we saw dramatically illustrated by the Reagan shooting, the greatest defensive difficulty occurs when the protectee moves into areas that have not, or cannot, be secured. Even though the general form of the concentric circle deployment technique is used in crowd situations, it is demonstratedly impossible to absolutely defend against a determined attacker in these cases.

In the concentric circle effort, the outer perimeter personnel have the responsibility of screening persons or objects that may present danger to the protectee. The inner circle personnel deal with any immediate threat and have the hands-on responsibility for protective care. This last perimeter must respond to any threat that has eluded the defensive filtering process.

A careful examination of the films of the Reagan shooting show that none of the three government bodyguards closest to the president during the seconds of the attack had their guns drawn. These men were not simply slow to react to events. On the contrary, their assigned responsibility was to shield the president from immediate danger with their own bodies and to move him as quickly as possible from the area. It was the function of the remaining bodyguards to respond to the source of the attack and neutralize it.

In the United States, as in a number of other countries, the inner circle protective responsibilities are assigned to experienced government civil service bodyguards who have demonstrated a willingness and aptitude for the work and who have been carefully trained. In some countries, the criterion for admission into the ranks of the inner circle of bodyguards is based principally on such factors as personal loyalty, family connections, or region of birth. It is not uncommon in these countries that the ability to perform the protection duties in a professional manner takes a distant second place to the other considerations.

Private Sector Counterparts to the Governmental Bodyguard

This government model provides a useful framework from which to fashion a general approach to a private sector protection program, despite the fact that the same depth of resources is not available. Even if it were, few top executives would, for a moment, tolerate the kind of circus atmosphere a full-blown governmental protection operation inflicts on a hapless protectee.

Anyone who has witnessed the comings and goings of a protected government dignitary, or has observed an appearance by the president of the United States, would have to agree that subtlety, with regard to the attending security measures, is not a featured characteristic. There are, nevertheless, private security firms that tout their protection services as mini-versions of governmental operations. Disparity of resources aside, a true protection professional understands that there are substantive differences between the needs of a private and a governmental operation and, further, that most governmental programs would be inappropriate for a private sector protectee. The best private programs are those able to borrow, and refine, helpful governmental methods while developing those suitable to their particular requirements.

Still, the general organization of a private program can be approached within the framework of the government model:

1. *Intelligence.* As in the government example, every effort must be made by the private bodyguard to develop information about existing, or potential, threats to his protectee. The private bodyguard should, in addition, study the available particulars of reported attacks against other business targets. This information could be brought to bear on the security of his protectee or, at the very least, be instructive by suggesting improved protection tactics.

Information of this type can be obtained from a number of sources, including personal research; material from clipping services; interviews with travelers or employees in high-risk areas; contacts with law enforcement, government intelligence, or diplomatic personnel. There are, in addition, a small number of first-rate security consultant firms that specialize in providing their corporate clients with detailed information about terrorist activity throughout the world.

Most corporate security offices are staffed with former law enforcement people who maintain a kind of "old boy" network of contacts they can tap to develop information about possible threats to their top executives. The difficulty is that the contacts still in government service are legally restricted, in many cases, with regard to the information they can provide, even to former colleagues. It is doubtful that law enforcement sources, even with their full cooperation, will always have the kind of information desired by the private sector.

As of this writing, two government sources are helpful in assisting U.S. business interests with information about the level of terrorist threat abroad. The Office of Security, U.S. Department of State, and the Commerce Working Group on Terrorism, U.S. Department of Commerce, can provide information about the degree of terrorist activity in specific overseas locations. It should, of course, be understood that governmental sources cannot release raw intelligence or sensitive material. Furthermore, the governmental employee who renders the information frequently has not been to the location in question and is simply providing information garnered from cable reports and various, often outdated, government studies.

The hard political reality is that what is good for Uncle Sam is not always consistent with the short-term needs of corporate security planners. Nevertheless, governmental sources offer a logical, often useful, starting point from which to tackle the matter of protective intelligence development.

A difficulty inherent in intelligence gathering is the task of deciding precisely what information should be collected and how, once preserved, to make the best use of it. It is of dubious value for a corporation located in New York City to amass a history of all the bombings of business targets in that city if some method is not developed to extract specific applications that result in improved security.

Hard information that reveals a specific threat can be followed by defensive measures designed to thwart the threat. It is the considerably more sophisticated task of analyzing a volume of far less obvious data that requires special skills. The mere collection of information is of limited value, other than as an academic exercise, if the result is not increased safety for a protectee.

2. *Advance preparations.* Ordinarily, most private bodyguards have to be very resourceful in order to complete the advance work required to ensure reduced risk. Few private bodyguards are able to travel overseas, or great distances, ahead of their protectee to perform advance surveys. Some private bodyguard teams are able to free a man to "leapfrog" ahead, sometimes just minutes prior to the arrival of the protectee, in order to evaluate an unfamiliar site. The common restraints of lack of manpower, increased expense, and time limitations often mean that insufficient attention is paid to the important function of advance site surveys. While these considerations usually reduce private sector advance planning to unacceptable levels, the value of the work remains undiminished if maximum personal protection is the principal goal.

Protection planners should understand that even the rather routine task of accompanying a protectee to a gala dinner at a hotel involves, or should involve, careful preparations. For example, discreet inquiries should be made into a number of aspects of the function: Will the dinner be open to the public or by invitation only? How many guests are expected and do any of them represent possible "targets"? Will any security be provided by the dinner hosts or the hotel; if so, what are the details? Will the press be present? Has the event been publicized? Can the purpose of the dinner be considered political or remotely controversial? Does the hotel have labor problems? Is there any history of terrorist incidents or unusual criminal activity associated with the hotel or the nearby area?

The matter of selecting the travel route for the protectee to and from the hotel should be considered, with care taken to avoid passing through areas of unusual risk or congestion. The exact locations of emergency medical facilities along the route, and near the hotel, should be known.

Liaison contacts should be established with the appropriate hotel employees and a physical inspection of the hotel and actual dinner location conducted. This advance inspection will allow the bodyguard to plan how to move his protectee to and from the dinner in the quickest, safest manner as well as acquaint him with any aspect of the physical setting that may expose the protectee to unusual risk. There are also the practical matters of locating telephones and restrooms for use on the night of the dinner as well as the considerably more important task of selecting a "safe" area near the dinner site for use in the event of an incident that precludes immediate evacuation from the hotel.

This abbreviated look at some of a bodyguard's advance responsibilities should provide a measure of insight into the matter of planning for risk reduction. In practice, the limitations that often prevent advance inspections require that a body-guard be experienced enough to perform the evaluations "on the run." The body-guard, in this case, must develop an "eye" that allows him to assess surroundings quickly, in order to anticipate the risk factors present, insofar as possible, at sites he may be seeing for the first time in the company of his protectee.

This seat-of-the-pants method is certainly not the preferred choice and every effort should be made to conduct a proper advance survey. An extra advantage of the advance survey work for the protectee is that it allows him to move more smoothly and quickly through his schedule—a benefit that many busy protectees come to value very highly.

It is not uncommon for private bodyguards who were formerly in a governmental protection service to have difficulty adjusting to the rather unorthodox, by comparison, style routinely demanded by the special circumstances of the private sector. The former government security people are, after all, products of a system where the preparations for a protected official's activities are often done weeks in advance and then submitted, in detail, for seemingly endless review and approval. The governmental bodyguard is also accustomed to a level of support in manpower, equipment, and intelligence resources that is rarely found in the private sector.

An often overlooked, but very important, aspect of advance work is the body-guard's personal style—the manner in which he comes across to others. A bodyguard is a representative of his protectee, and some bodyguards tend to assume an unbecoming air of importance that usually alienates the people they meet when performing their advance work. A governmental bodyguard has the considerable advantage of the authority and prestige of his government to counter any personal shortcomings. His private sector counterpart, on the other hand, often has no leverage other than good will when conducting his business. In either case, it is not uncommon to see negative feelings generated by prior contact with a bodyguard transferred to an unsuspecting protectee. Even if the bodyguard is not antagonistic in his manner, if he is indiscreet or flamboyant in his style, the result will be increased attention drawn to the protectee and, as a consequence, a more difficult job of providing for his protection.

3. The "Working" Private Bodyguard. a number of differences between the governmental and private sector can be found in the business of actually "guarding" a protectee. For example, many people who engage bodyguards want their employees to look capable of "handling" themselves. The threat of a terrorist attack aside, many protectees desire the sense of security, justified or not, they feel when in the company of an armed man whose physical appearance discourages potential assailants. While there is a fairly good chance that a private bodyguard will have to go one-on-one in a physical confrontation, the legion of bodyguards protecting a government dignitary is seldom faced with a drunk, mugger, or other common street hoodlum.

The generous manpower resources available to most governmental personal security operations, combined with traditional civil service organizational procedures, mean that various protection duties are assigned on the basis of rank or seniority. As could be expected, an unofficial ladder of descending levels of prestige determines who fulfills each duty—a probable result of the practice of assigning higher-ranked bodyguards to command and planning functions while others are deployed, often in military guard fashion, in the outer protection perimeters.

A new government bodyguard quickly understands that he must put his time in the "trenches" before being elevated, by promotion or seniority, to a position of greater responsibility that entitles him to supervise, rather than perform, the tasks that are considered the most onerous. Most of the actual "guarding," like most police work, is boring and far from the popular conception of a glamourous job. Many long hours are spent simply standing in hallways or waiting for a protectee to go about the routine business of a normal day. An old military pilot's definition of flying is perhaps relevant: "Hours and hours of boredom punctuated by moments of stark terror."

It should come as no surprise that most of the "hours and hours" of boredom in a governmental operation are borne by the junior people: this poses an interesting problem when selecting a private bodyguard. The nature of most private operations is such that the bodyguard must not only be capable of undertaking the more sophisticated aspects of protection planning, but also disciplined enough to faithfully perform those tasks usually assigned to the junior men in governmental operations. These circumstances require that the private bodyguard be willing, and capable, of being the chief and the Indian at the same time. Men with lengthy governmental experience might not be willing to go back to the trenches and actually perform the tasks they were accustomed to supervising. Conversely, many less experienced men eagerly stand post in front of a hotel door for hours, but do not have the background necessary to take sole responsibility for organizing a protectee's total security.

The single most important attribute for a bodyguard when actually engaged in guarding is self-discipline. Planning and tactics are useless if the hands-on protection people are inattentive and do not have the discipline required to maintain constant vigilance. The numbing routine, combined with many hours of inactivity, tends to "lose" all but the most dedicated bodyguards. The semimilitary structure of most governmental operations provides a rigid system of accountability and supervision that, with rare exceptions, ensures discipline will be maintained and the protectee constantly covered. Often lacking a comparable system to ensure the integrity of a protection effort, the private protectee must rely on the competence and dedication of the individual protecting him.

If those qualities are missing in his bodyguard, the private protectee is in trouble. I have, for example, often seen bodyguards escort their employer to a meeting that is expected to last several hours and then disappear for an hour or so to conduct personal business. Needless to say, the penalty for this lack of self-discipline could ultimately be paid by the protectee.

Some old-school bodyguards may differ with regard to the matter of where to physically position a private bodyguard to best advantage. They subscribe to the belief that a single bodyguard is most effective when he follows the protectee at a discreet distance and intervenes at the first sign of danger. The logic here is that a bodyguard deployed in this fashion has the advantage of surprise by "hiding" and springing to the rescue of his charge. These tactics were not uncommon in the days when drunks, pickpockets, bullies, or street robbers were the principal worries of a bodyguard, but the days of the shadow bodyguard skulking behind a potted palm or pretending to window-shop fifty feet behind his protectee are over.

The surveillance that routinely precedes any organized criminal or terrorist attack will certainly detect any bodyguards, regardless of where they are positioned, and the risk of a random attack is often diminished if the potential victim is in the company of others. Most attacks, of any sort, occur at close range and with such suddenness that any protection man must position himself in such a manner that allows for a speedy and direct reaction. A squad of bodyguards has the option to deploy in concentric circle fashion, with some men stationed to detect approaching threats and the others providing close coverage for the protectee. The bodyguard working alone, however, should never leave his protectee vulnerable to close threat in order to gain the tactical advantage of a broader field of vision. The matter of physical positioning, particularly in operations fielding few men, is absolutely critical.

The fact that a bodyguard must often position himself in extremely close proximity to his protectee requires a large measure of discretion on his part. While some situations force a bodyguard to stand practically in the hip pocket of his protectee, it does not make sense to do so when the compelling risk factors are absent. More than one bodyguard has found himself suddenly unemployed because he failed to exercise discretion in his tactical positioning, or because his overall manner reflected an inappropriate intensity that was unsettling to his employer.

The Starting Point for Guarding

A bodyguard undertaking protection responsibilities for a new protectee should immediately familiarize himself with the routine and personal habits of his employer, as well as with any circumstances or prior events in the protectee's life that bear on the question of his safety. Insights into the personality of the protectee provided by those who know him well, combined with their impression of his feelings regarding personal security, can be most helpful when developing tactics that are compatible with the protectee. Without question, any history of threats or accounts of prior attacks should be studied in detail.

In this initial study, no relevant aspect of a protectee's life should be considered unworthy of examination. Efforts to review all published material concerning the protectee should be made in order to determine whether any information is publicly available that could enhance the success of some form of attack. A bodyguard's life is certainly made more difficult if his protectee receives frequent press attention.

Public reports featuring the wealth of a protectee or his association with a controversial issue have obvious security implications. It is the nature, however, of the times we live in that some very benign coverage can have dangerous consequences as well. For example, in early 1982 a local magazine in Omaha, Nebraska, published an article featuring their selection of the ten most eligible women in that city. In addition to photographs, the article contained biographical sketches of the women. The result was that a former mental patient was subsequently arrested for the rape of two of the women and the attempted rape of a third. In his statement to police after his capture, the rapist said that he wanted to punish the women and that he had intended to work his way through the magazine's list.

It is in these early stages that a decision should probably be made with regard to establishing a kidnap file for the protectee. This file, to be used by security forces in the event of a kidnapping, should include such items as current photographs; a full set of fingerprints; voice samples (tapes); dental charts; handwriting sample; medical history; and identifying automobile information. The file must be kept under strict control but could be of obvious assistance in responding to a kidnapping episode.

The protectee should be briefed at the first opportunity regarding the actual functions of a bodyguard. It should be stressed at that time how important his own cooperation is in any effort to provide for his personal safety. The problem of trying to force a strong-willed protectee change his established behavior patterns has been discussed; but there is the additional, and very common, problem of a protectee's routine use of his bodyguard for tasks unrelated to personal security. I have, for example, seen bodyguards carrying luggage, holding coats, making telephone calls or reservations, fetching ice cream, delivering messages, and getting drinks. The U.S. government deals with this problem by making it clear to a protectee and his staff, prior to assigning bodyguards, that the security men cannot be used in any nonsecurity manner. The private sector, and many other countries, have no such official policy.

There is certainly nothing wrong with helpfulness and many corporate bodyguards must, from necessity, function in an aide capacity; but it should not be forgotten that security is usually compromised when a bodyguard engages in an unrelated task. Some private bodyguards actually volunteer to perform tasks that require leaving their protectee alone, or forget themselves to such an extent in their rush to perform functions such as carrying luggage that they make the tactical mistake of carrying bags in their gun hand. There was an instance in Europe when I observed a bodyguard unable to carry his walkie-talkie into a crowded soccer stadium because his hands were so filled with blankets, coats, and other items he had volunteered to carry for his protectee and guests. The best way to deal with this common problem is by ensuring that the protectee knows that to tolerate or encourage such behavior is to jeopardize his own safety.

The Matter of Guns

It is extremely difficult, often impossible, in many parts of the United States and abroad for a private bodyguard to obtain legal permission to carry a concealed weapon. Most of a professional bodyguard's duties do not require that he be armed and some corporations have unarmed bodyguards travel with their executives in order to ensure that the essential risk reduction services are provided.

If it is felt that circumstances demand a protectee to travel with an armed man, it is possible to contract for an armed guard on a city-by-city basis to supplement the protectee's personal bodyguard. This arrangement ensures that the protectee continues to receive a professional level of service from a man familiar with his needs and preferences, while, at the same time, having the advantage of an armed presence.

Some contract security firms may represent to potential clients that their bodyguards have legal permission to carry weapons in certain locations when, in fact, they do not. It is recommended that gun permits for any contracted security men be inspected in order to avoid legal problems arising from hiring armed men who do not have proper authority to carry weapons.

Other Hardware

Private programs that have their protectees traveling with one or two bodyguards may want to consider the possibility of purchasing a portable alarm system for use when a bodyguard cannot be posted in front of the protectee's hotel door. The systems consist of a receiver unit; a siren, or sounder, of some sort; a portable "panic button" sender; and, if desired, pressure mats that can be wired to the receiver and used to detect entry through selected doorways. The system provides a means by which to alert a bodyguard, in an adjoining room, of an emergency in the protectee's room.

This system would cost approximately five hundred dollars, but care should be taken with regard to the transportation and use of the system in foreign countries: The portable sender uses a radio frequency, something that is often strictly regulated.

Some thought might be given to the purchase of such items as walkie-talkies, bulletproof vests, and portable smoke alarms. The smoke alarms, in particular, are useful because many hotels in the world do not provide them in rooms and hotel fires certainly represent a possible threat to any protectee.

Bombs

In June of 1980, United Airlines President Percy Wood received a package through the mail at his home from an unknown source. When Wood opened the package, he detonated a spring-activated pipe bomb concealed inside a hollowed-out book. Fortunately, he survived the attack even though it was reported that he received heavy lacerations on his legs and chest.

I was present in Manila, Philippines, in the fall of 1980 when a bomb smuggled into an auditorium inside a briefcase exploded, wounding over a dozen people in the presence of President Marcos. Needless to say, the appearance of any briefcase or package in proximity to myself or a protectee has taken on a whole new meaning since that incident.

It should be remembered that a bomb is an often-used, very deadly weapon and a bodyguard should be constantly watching for its use. While it is not reasonable to suggest that every bodyguard become a bomb expert, all of them should at least be familiar with the general characteristics of the various types of devices.

Letter bombs, in particular, have been routinely employed against business targets. The West German Federal Criminal Office reported that letter bombs were sent to nine U.S. companies in West Germany in June of 1982, presumably by terrorists protesting the visit that month of President Reagan. Incredibly, no injuries were reported because all of the devices failed to explode.

It would seem that to caution a bodyguard about the possible use of a bomb would be gratuitous advice, but it has been my experience that even highly trained bodyguards, unless they have been conditioned by working in an environment with frequent bombings, become lax. For example, a common tactical mistake made by small teams of bodyguards is to leave their vehicles unattended. This particularly occurs at dinnertime when there are not enough men to rotate guarding the vehicles and still ensure that everyone has an opportunity to eat. No one, after all, wants to miss a meal.

A few years ago, to illustrate the point, a team of U.S. governmental bodyguards left their vehicle, keys and all, in the care of a parking lot attendant while they went inside a restaurant to dine with their protectee. When the bodyguards finished their meal and returned to their vehicle, they found their submachine gun missing from the trunk of their car. It would have been just as easy to plant an explosive device in the unattended vehicle as steal the weapon.

In some cases, the purchase of scanning and metal detection devices may be justified as a screen for bombs. The devices are expensive, but extremely valuable if individual circumstances justify the cost.

Conduct and Tactics

No attempt is made here to offer a pat bodyguarding-in-ten-easy-steps formula, which would only be misleading. Tactics vary from case to case and their proper application depends on actual field training and experience. The following suggestions, while not intended to be comprehensive, are meant to provide an elementary foundation with which to evaluate or develop a program employing bodyguards.

Conduct and General Tactics

1.   The self-discipline required to be constantly alert and fully focused on his work is absolutely central to the personal qualifications of any bodyguard.

2.   The nature of protection work is such that a bodyguard must always remain with his protectee when on duty. The irresponsible act of leaving a protectee unattended creates possible jeopardy and cannot be tolerated.

3.   Every effort should be made to discourage patterns of routine behavior by the protectee because they increase vulnerability to planned attacks.

4.   The basic rule with regard to essential bodyguard "positioning" is to place one's self between the protectee and the area of greatest possible risk. This requires the experience and good judgment on the part of the bodyguard to identify, and evaluate, possible sources of danger, while not giving offense through unnecessary boldness at inappropriate times. He must also be assertive enough to act unhesitatingly when danger is possible.

5.   The bodyguard must remember that his primary duty is personal protection and this responsibility may be sacrificed if he engages in unrelated tasks. Some bodyguard's jobs are made almost impossible by the demands of protectees who place high importance on their personal needs and little value on their safety. When circumstances permit, a bodyguard should never volunteer to perform tasks that require him to compromise his security function.

6.   Bodyguards should be careful students of any terrorist or criminal episodes that could bear on the security of their own protectees or suggest improvement in protection tactics.

7.   Bodyguards should be mindful that planned attacks are routinely preceded by periods of surveillance and that children, uniformed "officials," women, elderly persons, and hotel employees may be used as part of a surveillance team. This possibility does not suggest that every person encountered by the bodyguard should be treated as a potential enemy. Some security men forget, often to their later regret, that courtesy and good manners are not inconsistent with constant alertness.

8.   Unless necessary, a bodyguard's role should not be revealed by himself or his protectee. Further, any conversation about the nature of a bodyguard's work should be discouraged or kept to a diplomatic minimum. A number of people, including friends of the protectee, have an understandable fascination with the work of a bodyguard and will often ask to see a bodyguard's gun or will want to talk security shop at a clearly inappropriate time. Most of these indiscretions are not intended to cause harm, but sometimes the transgressor seeks to impress others with his intimate knowledge of the private business of a protectee. In other cases, the bodyguard may himself be indiscreet in his remarks in an attempt at self-aggrandizement at the expense of the protectee. In whatever form, these potentially dangerous indiscretions should be guarded against.

9.   Information about the personal activities or business schedule of a protectee should be restricted to those with a need to know. Families, friends, employees, and business associates often unwittingly divulge information that would be useful to anyone planning an attack.

10.   Many inexperienced bodyguards have a tendency to gawk at their protectee rather than being alert for possible threats. Security men, like almost everyone,

are fascinated by the prospect of seeing important people and almost every news photograph of an important protectee will show at least one protection man looking at his protectee rather than in the direction of any potential threat. Even bodyguards who have ceased to be awed by the company of important people may be distracted at spectator events. A single bodyguard accompanying his protectee to a sporting event could not reasonably spend the entire time facing away from the field in order to protect his protectee's rear, but he should guard against losing himself in the activities on the field.

11.   Every reasonable effort should be made to avoid even the possibility of trouble. For example, a bodyguard escorting his protectee down a darkened street who observes a suspicious activity ahead would be well advised to reverse his direction or cross the street. Some bodyguards feel that because they are armed, or do not wish to appear fearful, they should press forward in situations when basic common sense should tell them that there is risk of danger. Some protectees, as well, feel emboldened when in the company of their armed bodyguard. That kind of ego involvement should never prevail over reasonable efforts to avoid trouble. A bodyguard who finds himself employed by a protectee who provokes incidents or acts recklessly will almost always find the results uncomfortable, if not tragic.

12.   A bodyguard's exterior manner should be calm and unhurried despite the fact that he must maintain intense vigilance. A protectee in the company of a bodyguard who is sweating profusely and moving excitedly about with a frenzied manner is a conspicuous sight indeed. Any protectee who must suffer the constant company of a bodyguard will better tolerate that plight if a decorous aura of calm masks what is fundamentally a rather intense activity.

13.   When possible, a bodyguard should ensure that the physical location of his protectee affords limited target opportunity. This means that attention should be paid to such matters as seating locations, drawing the drapes in hotel suites, and discouraging conversations on open sidewalks.

14.   In crowd situations, the bodyguard should always maintain a good defensive body stance with his weight evenly distributed and his hands free. The bodyguard should pay particular attention to the hands of those persons near his protectee. There is an old expression, "Eyes never killed anyone, but you better watch the hands."

15.   The bodyguard may consider working out a predetermined code to signal distress if deprived of a conventional manner to do so.

16.   As a general rule, it is best to remove a protectee immediately from the scene of any disturbance. Some bodyguards, particularly former policemen, are tempted to react to fights or other disruptions and, by doing so, may leave their protectee vulnerable. Some disturbances may be created as a cover to mask an attack against the protectee.

17.   A trained bodyguard team would probably respond to an attack, other than when in a vehicle, in something like the following manner: The bodyguard

first detecting the threat would shout "gun," or whatever is appropriate, and point to the direction of the attacker in order to alert the others who had perhaps not yet seen the danger. The bodyguard closest to the protectee would, in turn, maneuver him to cover or, if necessary, provide cover with his own body. At the earliest opportunity the bodyguard directly attending the protectee would remove him from the area of danger. At the same time, the remaining bodyguards would attempt to neutralize the threat.

18.   The bodyguard should be aware of any serious medical problems of his protectee and be familiar with basic first aid and CPR procedures. Many protectees are understandably reluctant to provide the full details of the state of their health, but, at the very least, the bodyguard should know how to contact the protectee's physician in the event of an emergency.

19.   The bodyguard should discourage walks at unusual hours or in sparsely populated areas.

20.   Perhaps because they are hesitant to intrude on what is for most busy people a welcomed place of sanctuary, some bodyguards are reluctant to enter public restrooms with their protectee. If the restroom has not been secured, the bodyguard should certainly accompany his protectee.

21.   A few bodyguards attempt to deal with the boredom and stress of their work by drinking while on duty. In no case should such use of alcohol be tolerated.

22.   It is customary for a bodyguard to precede his protectee through a door in order to assess what lies ahead or to detect an imminent threat. Some inexperienced bodyguards are reluctant to go first because their normal instinct is one of good manners.

23.   A protectee should be prevented from entering an elevator with anyone suspicious and should exit at the first opportunity if joined by the same en route. In an elevator, the bodyguard should position himself between his protectee and any unknown passengers, while being mindful to discretely shield the protectee with his own body when the elevator doors open and to precede him, when possible, off the elevator. In the event of an incident while the elevator is moving, a useful tactic is to push as many of the buttons to other floors as possible in order to attract attention and to escape the confines of the elevator as soon as possible.

24.   Beware of the type of bodyguard who makes a point to display his gun, handcuffs, or other "tools of the trade" at every opportunity. Often this "cowboy" mentality results in diminished rather than increased security for a protectee.

25.   The bodyguard should always respect the need for privacy of a protectee. The prospect of having a bodyguard in almost constant attendance is unsettling enough without having one who constantly chatters or intrudes needlessly on a busy protectee's rare moments of privacy.

Traveling

1.   The details of travel plans for a protectee should be highly restricted and divulged only to those who have a need to know.

2.   If travel plans have been publicized in any fashion prior to a trip, the extent and nature of the publicity should be known.

3.   Care should be taken not to make hotel, or any other, reservations in the name of the protectee or in a name identifiable with his.

4.   Home addresses should never be given when registering at hotels or on any other occasion.

5.   Ideally, bodyguards should occupy both adjoining rooms to a protectee's hotel room. If this is not possible, an effort should be made to determine who occupies those rooms.

6.   Unless the room has been secured prior to the arrival of a protectee, or during his absence, the bodyguard should precede his protectee into the hotel room and conduct a search for persons or unusual objects. A story comes to mind about an executive with a major American corporation who was robbed at gunpoint in his hotel room in South Carolina by an assailant who had hidden behind the shower curtain in the bathroom.

7.   A protectee should be reminded to keep his hotel door locked when he is inside and to notify the bodyguard in the event that someone knocks on the door when the bodyguard is in his adjoining room. When possible, hotel room service and telephone calls should be directed to the bodyguard's room and every effort made to shield the protectee from contact with hotel employees or guests.

8.   The most common manner of gaining illegal entry into a hotel room is with a key. Many otherwise first-rate hotels have sloppy key control measures and it is possible that the protectee's room may have a number of "missing" keys at any given time. Another common point of entry to hotel rooms is through open windows or balcony doors that permit access from adjoining rooms or from ground level.

9.   It should be remembered that a "wrong number" call to a protectee's room may be a method of determining whether the room is occupied. Great care should be taken not to compromise security by indiscriminate conversation on any telephones.

10.   Ideally, a protectee's hotel room should be secured by a bodyguard at all times, but private operations seldom have the manpower. In areas of high risk, some thought might be given to contracting with a guard service to secure the room when the protectee is absent and at night.

11.   A bodyguard should be leery of approaching his protectee's room when unknown persons are loitering nearby. Particular caution should be exercised when unknown guests exit an elevator on the same floor with the protectee.

12.   Some protectees are fond of using hotel stairways for the exercise. This practice should be discouraged because of the cover the stairwells could provide an attacker.

13.   The bodyguard should know the particulars of a hotel's security program. I can recall one hotel in Italy that assured guests that the hotel was guarded when the security measures, on investigation, consisted of having two elderly, unarmed

men patrolling the grounds between 10 P.M. and 6 A.M. Extreme caution should be exercised when discussing any information regarding the protectee with hotel security staff or other hotel employees.

14.   Particularly abroad, care should be taken to avoid any discussion of local politics or issues of controversy.

15.   When abroad, the bodyguard should always have local coins in his possession and knowledge of how to operate the telephones as well as the appropriate emergency numbers.

16.   Any waiting at public airports should be done, when possible, in the VIP lounge.

17.   Care of the control of a protectee's luggage should be taken when traveling and only those luggage tags used that conceal identifying information from ready view. The protectee's name and home address, or any other information that could specifically identify him, should not be written on his luggage tags.

Automobile Usage

1.   The bodyguard should remember that a sizable percentage of terrorist attacks take place at the moment when a victim is entering or exiting a vehicle or when he is on the road. Obviously, care should be taken to reduce risk to the protectee at these times.

2.   There is a natural tendency to provide important people with grand, conspicuous-looking limousines. If the protectee's ego will allow it, he should travel in regular sedans that are not known to be associated with his use.

3.   Many attacks on a moving vehicle originate from the direction of the driver's side in order to quickly stop the vehicle by immobilizing the driver. A common method of attack involves the use of at least two attack vehicles—one to box, impede, or stop the target vehicle, and the other carrying the actual assailants.

4.   A protectee's vehicle should, ideally, be guarded when not in use or secured in a locked, alarmed garage.

5.   Most protectees hire limousines for their use when traveling. Often the limousine service is simply selected from the telephone book by some employee of the protectee. Care should, however, be taken to use only carefully screened companies employing scrupulous drivers.

6.   Many protectees use the travel time in limousines to discuss controversial subjects, such as pending travel plans or sensitive matters with fellow passengers. They forget that their newly hired driver's trustworthiness or discretion cannot be guaranteed, and that certain information could be useful to anyone planning an attack. As a further precaution, a hired driver should never be given a copy of an itinerary or told of an intended destination prior to the time of departure. Any driver who must "stop to call the office" en route with a protectee should be immediately suspect.

7.   The doors of the protectee's vehicle should be locked and the windows up when he is in the vehicle.

8.   There have been instances of terrorists disguised in official uniforms stopping a victim's car. Extreme caution should be exercised when anyone attempts to stop a protectee's vehicle.

9.   When driving on roads with more than one lane, the driver should be instructed to drive in the inside lane in order to reduce the chance of being forced off the road.

10.   In some parts of the world, bodyguards must be alert for attackers riding bicycles or motorcycles. These vehicles can easily hide in an automobile's "blind spot" at a traffic signal and then speed to an attack when the light turns green.

11.   The bodyguard should position himself in the front passenger seat and be alert for any vehicles following from the rear. In addition, he must be aware of parked vehicles and pedestrians as well as anything that threatens to impede or stop the car's movement. A classic example of this tactic occurred in a West German terrorist attack in 1977, in which a baby carriage was used to stop a victim's vehicle.

12.   The protectee will normally be seated directly to the rear of his bodyguard and should be trained to immediately drop to the floorboard in the event of an attack or on the command of the bodyguard.

13.   Since a bodyguard must remain fully alert during his time in a vehicle, it is recommended that his conversation with others be kept to a minimum and the radio turned off.

14.   When the car is stopped at a traffic light, care should be taken by the driver not to position the protectee's window directly opposite those in other traffic lanes. The driver should also ensure that there is enough room between the protectee's vehicle and the vehicle in front to be able to maneuver away in the event of an incident.

15.   Many busy protectees want to leap out of their vehicle as soon as it grinds to a halt. The proper procedure, from a security point of view, is for the vehicle's driver to remain behind the wheel prepared for a rapid departure while the bodyguard quickly exits and surveys the arrival area. When the bodyguard is satisfied that no obvious threat is present, he should open the protectee's vehicle door in such a manner as to provide cover with his own body at the moment the door is opened. The bodyguard should not simply swing the protectee's door wide open and stand back, in proper doorman fashion, but rather be careful to provide cover at the critical moment of exit.

16.   Since a number of ambushes have involved the initial blocking of a targeted vehicle, some protection forces immediately exit their blocked vehicle to gain the field of vision necessary to counter a possible attack.

17.   The bodyguard should be familiar with the basics of conducting a quick

bomb check of a vehicle. Even experts require several hours to thoroughly check a vehicle for a bomb, but certain checkpoints should not be overlooked: Wires hanging from under the carriage, objects in the tailpipe; objects behind tires or in wheel wells; doors, gas caps, trunks locked, and no evidence of disturbance; and a visual inspection of vehicle interior, including glove box, for objects or wires.

18. Most government operations use at least two vehicles for bodyguards when they are traveling with their protectee. This pattern allows the protectee to travel in convoy fashion with one security vehicle in front and one to the rear. Most private operations cannot field this many vehicles, but some variation of the convoy technique should be considered if resources permit.

Corporate Aircraft

Many protectees travel in private aircraft, which raises important concerns with regard to its security. These center around measures for guarding the aircraft when it is not in use, as well as the control of maintenance, fueling, and loading of the craft. Naturally, any attempt to ensure the security of an aircraft would have to be closely coordinated with the aircraft commander.

CONCLUSION

The world's handful of private protectees should be guarded by men with whom they can entrust their lives. For an employer to hire an unqualified man to provide for his protection is to court disaster and represents sheer folly in view of the cost and the seriousness of the responsibility.

The process of selecting a competent bodyguard, or providing for the training of a novice, is often muddled by misunderstandings of the true nature of a professional bodyguard's work and by the presence of a number of unqualified executive protection "experts" who seek to exploit the growing private sector demand for personal security. The basic orientation provided by this chapter enables the reader to avoid these predictable obstacles and establish an effective protection program employing private bodyguards.

24

Protecting the Office

Richard J. Healy

As the executive vice president of the Fortune 500, high-technology company came to work in the morning and parked his car in the special parking area reserved for the top executives of the company, he could not help but admire the new signs identifying each parking space with the name and title of the user. He was responsible for all administrative functions as the number two executive in the corporation and had recently directed that the old signs with unattractive small letters be discarded and new, more attractive signs with large letters be installed. The signs were not only more attractive and could be easily read, but they gave a more business-like appearance to the corporate headquarters, he thought. In addition, it was good for his ego as well as for those of the other top executives to see their names and titles displayed where they could be seen by employees, visitors, and customers.

The main entrance to the corporate headquarters, which was controlled by a receptionist, was about 200 yards away from the executive parking lot. The vice president did not use this entrance to enter the building because there was a private unlocked door adjacent to the parking lot that was reserved for the use of the executives utilizing that lot. The door at one time had been locked and each executive had been issued a key. However, the president of the company and several of the other top executives had misplaced their keys on a number of occasions. As a result, the locked door became too troublesome for these executives and so it became common practice to leave the door unlocked during the day to allow them to come and go without being inconvenienced. No one else used this door because of a sign on it that announced: "RESTRICTED ACCESS—AUTHORIZED PERSONNEL ONLY."

As the vice president hurried to his office, he passed a number of employees— some of whom were wearing badges. All spoke to him and called him by name although he was not wearing a badge. At one time all top executives wore badges, but over the years it had become common practice for none of them to wear the troublesome items. Also, badges were worn for identification purposes and everyone that counted in the corporation knew the top executives.

He remembered as he neared his office that the night before he had heard on a television news program that an FBI official had announced that terrorists were expected to become more active in the area in the near future and that the focus was high-technology companies. His company was mentioned specifically as a target. He reminded himself that he intended to call a meeting immediately upon his arrival in the office to discuss this problem. All persons in supervisory positions responsible for security in the company would be included: the guard captain, who was in direct charge of the security program; his immediate supervisor, a young staff assistant to the personnel director; the personnel director; and the vice president of industrial relations, who was responsible for the overall company security program.

The executive vice president planned to direct this group to develop a plan to include actions the company should take for the proper protection of top executives against the potential terrorist threat. He reflected as he entered his office that security had never been a problem in the company in the past. He, as well as the other top executives, had never given much attention to security and he was hopeful that the situation would not change so that the efforts of the top people in the organization could continue to concentrate on really important corporate problems. Probably, he thought, some additional guards would be needed to ensure security, but he hoped not too many would be required because a hiring freeze had recently been instituted.

What does this short scenario indicate about the ability of the vice president's company to cope with a terrorist attack—or any other type of security threat? Any experienced security executive oriented to corporate management problems would conclude that this company is vulnerable to a broad range of security risks, including terrorism, and that the meeting being planned by the executive vice president will probably not result in any worthwhile additional protection.

Quickly analyzing the thought process of the vice president allows us to understand this determination of vulnerability to a broad range of security-related threats. First, the executive vice president and the other key officers clearly do not regard security as an important function in the organization: They have relegated it to a minor role in the management structure. The reflections of the executive vice president show that security meant only a guard function to him; his concept of corrective action was "additional guards would probably be needed to improve security." The fact that a guard captain is in charge of the security function further proves that the company protection program is focused entirely on the guard operation. A guard operation without other supporting security functions, as noted later in the chapter cannot offer adequate, cost-effective protection to an enterprise and its personnel.

The placement of the security function in the organizational structure is another indication that it is not regarded as an important management responsibility. With the vice president of industrial relations in charge of the overall protection program, this could be the correct reporting level. However, the organization configuration below that level clearly demonstrates that the security function receives little if any top management understanding or support. The guard captain reports to a young assistant, who probably has little knowledge of security management.

Other indications in this short scenario further illustrate a general lack of understanding of the importance of security in the organization, which could leave the corporation as well as its personnel vulnerable, not only to a terrorist attack, but to many other threats. For example, the new signs identifying the parking places of all the top executives would be of enormous value to terrorists or others desiring to harm any of the executives: The signs act like beacons to identify top management personnel as well as the automobiles they drive. Authorities advise that identifying personnel in this way makes the job of an attacker much easier. The unlocked entrance to the corporate headquarters for the convenience of the top executives is another major gap in the security of the facility that could make it easy for a terrorist or other unauthorized individuals to gain access. And finally, the fact that the top executives do not wear identification badges is another serious gap in security procedures. They should set an example for others in the enterprise. By not wearing badges, they are announcing that this procedure is not important, with the result that ordinary workers can also be expected not to wear them.

After this review, it seems clear that, in this corporation, the convenience of the top executives takes precedence over everything else. Many basic security requirements are neglected. Their convenience should not be ignored, of course, but nor should it displace precautions necessary for their safety and protection.

We have already predicted that the actions being taken by the executive vice president—having a meeting at which he will direct that a plan for the protection of executives be developed—will not result in improved security: Those who will attend apparently do not have the knowledge or experience to cope effectively with the protection problems in the enterprise. Further, the organization has many other security problems that have not been recognized and that will not be neutralized by a security program focusing on the guard operation.

What, then, is a solution to the protection problems in this organization? One would be for the executive vice president to call in an experienced security consultant familiar with modern management techniques and the latest security techniques and equipment. A consultant qualified to cope with the protection problems in this enterprise would immediately recognize the shortcomings in the security program as presently operated and could be expected to recommend a complete, integrated protection program. An integrated security program is one that is designed to utilize a broad range of security techniques and controls, all interrelated and designed to neutralize potential damage-causing risks (see the following outline).

I. People Problems
   A. Theft of Assets
      1. Pilferage
      2. Fraud
      3. Records manipulation
      4. Forgery
      5. Embezzlement
      6. Industrial espionage
      7. Shoplifting
      8. Robbery and hijacking

    B.   Personnel Problems
        1. Gambling
        2. Loan sharking
        3. Disaffection
        4. Disturbed persons
        5. Disgruntled employees
        6. Absenteeism
        7. Misrepresentation
        8. Antisocial behavior
    C.   Malicious Destruction
        1. Incendiary fire
        2. Labor violence
        3. Vandalism
        4. Bomb and bomb threats
        5. Civil disturbance
        6. Terrorism
        7. Sabotage
    D.   Conflicts of Interest
        1. Employees with their own businesses
        2. Employees working for competitors
        3. Kickback situations
II.   Nonpeople Problems
    A.   Industrial Emergency
        1. Explosion
        2. Structure collapse
        3. Major accident
        4. Fire
        5. Radiation incident
        6. Hazardous material incident
    B.   Environmentally Caused Emergencies
        1. Tornado
        2. Flood
        3. Hurricane
        4. Earthquake
III. War or Nuclear Attack

THE SYSTEMS APPROACH

The basic objective of such a protection program is to avoid risks and to prevent loss-causing incidents from occurring. Such a protection program has been commonly referred to as the *systems approach* and the term *system* will be used during the remainder of this discussion to mean a complete, integrated protection program. According to Webster's dictionary, a system is "an assemblage of objects united by some form of regular interaction or interdependence." When applied to security, a systems approach involves three general steps that are carried out in order, as follows: (1) an analysis of vulnerabilities, (2) the adoption and implementation of effective security countermeasures, and (3) a test of the resulting operating system to ensure that it is working properly. It is an orderly, rational, and cost-effective method to use in the development of a program for the protection of assets and personnel in any enterprise.

Vulnerability Analysis

The first essential step in the systems approach—an analysis of hazards faced by an organization—is often not done, and an enterprise will adopt countermeasures without knowing clearly what the risks are or what is at risk. Losses occur for three basic reasons: (a) vulnerabilities are not recognized, (b) countermeasures adopted are ineffective, and (c) vulnerabilities change.

The effectiveness of a protection program depends, not only on the appropriateness of the countermeasures adopted, but also on the relevance of the countermeasures to the defined vulnerabilities. For example, the addition of more guards as a countermeasure will probably not improve security in the enterprise described at the beginning of the chapter unless all the vulnerabilities noted are also considered. A vulnerability analysis, then, should highlight the risks threatening the enterprise, the deficiencies in an existing protection program, the probability of the risks identified becoming actual events, and the impact or effect of such risks on the organization. Simply stated, problem definition is the first step in the design of any protection program, which is then followed by the adoption of countermeasures. Every enterprise, regardless of type, size, or location, constantly faces a wide variety of damage- or loss-causing risks that can be identified in a vulnerability analysis.

The recognition of security risks is not a common sense task that can be accomplished by individuals without specialized knowledge and experience in the protection field. A proper analysis can ordinarily only be done by an experienced security professional able to understand all of the exposures that threaten an organization. Knowledge of cost-effective countermeasures that are available to neutralize the defined exposures are also required. There was an apparent lack of such skills in the executive vice president's company: for this reason, one suggested solution to the problems faced by that organization was to retain a consultant who would perform all of the tasks required to adopt the systems approach in the design of a protection program for that enterprise.

However, a word of caution about the selection of security consultants should be offered for those not acquainted with the security field. There are some organizations selling hardware or services that will offer to conduct a security survey at little or no cost. Such an offer may appear to be a bargain when compared with the cost of a qualified, objective security consultant who is not interested in marketing products or services. But such a survey may not be a bargain in the end because the former company's objective may be only to sell the products or services being offered. Also, those offering to conduct the survey will often not have the broad knowledge necessary to conduct a vulnerability analysis that meets the criteria described earlier. Their knowledge and experience may be limited to the products or services they offer for sale.

As we are specifically concerned here with the issue of terrorism, no attempt is made to discuss all the requirements for the adoption of a program to neutralize *all* threats—only those that relate to terrorism. Remember that the hypothetical executive vice president was only concerned about the protection of the top executives of the organization and was going to direct that a protection program be focused on that threat. The protection of the top management personnel in any organization against a terrorist attack is, of course, an important consideration in any security plan: Terrorists in the past have often attacked top management personnel. However, there are other risks that must be included in a vulnerability analysis when the threat of terrorism is being considered. The following are the general exposures that should be considered in connection with a possible terrorist attack: (a) kidnapping; (b) hostage taking; (c) assassination; (d) hijacking; (e) bombing and bomb hoaxes; (f) attack on and seizure of facilities; (g) sabotage; and (h) activities to finance terrorist operations, such as theft—robbery and burglary—and extortion.

The activities of terrorists in the past also indicate that they carefully prepare for an attack, that they become familiar with the most vulnerable areas in an organization, and that they know where the most damage can be done. For example, an attack on an organization's computer center with explosives could seriously cripple the enterprise or perhaps even put it out of business. Utilities, likewise, are particularly vulnerable. An attack on transformer banks supplying power to an organization could interrupt the organization's activities for a considerable period of time until replacements could be obtained. As a result, a vulnerability analysis should identify all areas critical for the continued operation of the enterprise as needing particular attention.

Countermeasures

After the completion of a vulnerability analysis, the next step in the systems approach is the selection of appropriate countermeasures to neutralize the risks defined. Countermeasures can be placed into three general categories, as follows: (a) software, (b) hardware, and (c) people. The selection of appropriate countermeasures is important, not only from the standpoint of the neutralization of risks, but from the standpoint of cost effectiveness. Two cost-effective results can be expected if the systems approach is used in the selection of countermeasures. They are (a) better protection, with a resulting reduction in the cost of losses; and (b) reduction in the cost of the protective measures adopted.

When countermeasures are being selected, redundancy or "back up" protection should also be considered in the system planning so that the failure of one countermeasure will not result in a sensitive area or complete facility becoming vulnerable. For example, the failure of an individual to lock a door leading to a sensitive area, when it is not occupied, should not leave the area completely vulnerable to penetration. Instead, provisions for the area to be inspected periodically, either by security personnel or supervisory personnel responsible for the area, should reveal that the area is vulnerable because of the unlocked door. In addition, an alarm system might be installed and arrangements made to have it activated as soon as the area was not occupied so that any penetration through the unlocked door would result in an alarm being sounded.

Leverage is also a factor that should be considered in the selection of countermeasures. Leverage is the selection of countermeasures that will require the least investment and that will quickly and reliably neutralize a risk or number of risks. The installation of an alarm system in an area could represent leverage because other more expensive countermeasures might, as a result, be eliminated—such as frequent guard patrols or expensive barrier construction.

Another protection concept that needs to be considered in connection with the selection of countermeasures, which relates to both redundancy and leverage, is the establishment of lines of defense to delay an attacker. This idea has also been referred to as the *maze concept*. As an attacker advances into a target area, a series of countermeasures are encountered to cause delay, with the result that the situation can be controlled by the security organization or the penetration be discouraged. Also, compartments containing sensitive material that might be of value to an intruder can be identified and special countermeasures installed to protect those particular areas. A vault containing highly sensitive data and negotiables is an example of such a compartment. Special controls over such an area by personnel working in the area or near it could be established during working hours. During nonworking hours, the material in the vault could be protected by an alarm system, good vault construction, and periodic inspections by patrolling guards.

Software

As used in this discussion, *software* means any item, written or verbal, that is used to implement and operate a security program. Some examples of software include policies, practices, plans to cope with emergency situations including terrorist attacks, procedures, the configuration of the security organization, standards of conduct, and training programs for both security personnel and other employees of the enterprise. Basic to any protection program are policies and procedures: Through these items the security program is defined and the requirements to be followed by everyone in the enterprise specified.

Our earlier comments on the hypothetical company noted that the top management of the organization apparently did not regard security as an important management function and had not given it any particular attention. This is a fundamental problem; the attitude must be changed immediately because, without top management support and interest, a protection program cannot be expected to be successful. Such a change should be announced throughout the organization in a policy statement stressing the need for and the importance of security. The new policy could then be implemented through the issuance of procedures.

A security organization, and especially a guard force, cannot be expected to perform all of the tasks required to provide adequate protection in any organization: All employees and supervisors in the enterprise must assist. A security organization can provide all of the tools required; but in the final analysis, everyone in the organization must become aware of the need for security. The security procedures established should define and delegate to supervisors and all employees the responsibility they must each assume for the protection of the organization and personnel.

The personnel in this hypothetical organization should not be surprised by a change in attitude toward security on the part of top management; it can be assumed that they listened to the same news as the executive vice president and that they are well aware of the terrorist threat. In fact, they could be expected to welcome better security in the enterprise for their own protection and the security of their jobs. If any doubt lingers about whether employees know about a potential terrorist threat, a program of education stressing the threat and the need for improved security in the organization could be designed for presentation to all personnel. Such indoctrination material could be presented in the company newspaper, at staff meetings, in bulletins, and with other communication techniques.

In addition to a change in attitude toward security, the security habits of the top management personnel should also be revised. The lack of compliance with good security practices because of inconvenience—such as not wearing badges and having a private unlocked entrance to the facility—should be corrected immediately. An announcement throughout the management hierarchy should make clear that everyone in the organization will be expected to comply with all security procedures being established. Top management personnel should, by example, show that they are serious about compliance with new security procedures. Also, disciplinary actions for noncompliance should be set up in the procedures.

Attention should also be given to the organization of security in the enterprise. As the security program at the present time is organized around the guard function with emphasis on that activity, action should be taken to revise the organization structure to focus on system implementation and management. Security supervisory personnel familiar with security system implementation and management should be included in the new organizational structure.

The reporting level of the security organization in the corporate organization configuration should also be changed so that security begins to be regarded as an essential management function. The reporting level of the top protection executive should be to a senior officer not more than three steps below the chief operating executive.

One element in the procedural development that should not be overlooked is the appropriate arrangement for the screening of applicants. The screening process should require sufficient background checks to ensure that those being hired are of good character, are trustworthy, and meet hiring standards adopted by the enterprise. Unless this is done, unstable individuals or even terrorists could be brought into the organization, with the result that the entire enterprise and the employees could become vulnerable. The most elaborate security policies, procedures, and controls can be of little or no value if the applicant-screening process is not effective in eliminating such potential risks.

Also, training for the security organization should be included in the security system planning. The security organization members should, at all levels, be completely familiar with the objectives of the protection program and be thoroughly trained through the use of written procedures as well as verbal instruction with reference to their responsibilities and conduct.

Development of plans to cope with emergencies was listed as a software countermeasure requiring attention in the development of a security system. Included here should be advanced planning designed to facilitate the handling of all the various type of terrorists attacks that can be anticipated. The objective of such planning should be to develop solutions to predictable and routine problems in advance of an attack situation. Careful consideration during the planning stage of items of this type will result in speeding decisions and actions during an attack: those responsible for decision making during such a period will be able to concentrate on major problems and unpredictable or unusual circumstances that may develop; they will not be bothered with problems that have been solved in advance.

A number of organizations have provided for the formation of a *crisis response team* in their plans to cope with terrorist threats. The authority of such a group, as well as the limits placed on their actions, is normally defined in the plan. Training sessions may also be conducted for the members of the team so that they will become completely familiar with the organization's plan to cope with the attacks of terrorists and so that all team members become familiar with the responsibilities they will be expected to assume in an attack situation.

Hardware

The effective use of the second countermeasure specified in the systems approach—hardware—can result in the improvement of protection while at the same time providing for impressive cost savings through the reduction of security personnel. Hardware includes such items as fencing, barriers of all types, lights, locks, doors, gates, safes, vaults, or other special construction and electronic controls. Such items are particularly useful in establishing lines of defense and security compartments, mentioned earlier as being important in the planning of a security system. However, like all other countermeasures, hardware controls cannot be depended on to provide adequate protection by themselves; they should be interrelated with all other controls in a security system.

Electronic controls are valuable hardware items because they are reliable if properly selected and installed, and they are cost effective. A broad range of detectors are manufactured and marketed by a number of reliable companies. In general, they are used to signal exceptions in a protection system and to detect abnormal conditions. The capabilities of electronic detectors can be compared to the senses of a human, but they are usually more reliable. When properly integrated into a protection system, they are alert 24 hours a day, 7 days a week, while a human may not be alert at all times because of fatigue, emotional problems, or any number of other factors. Also, because of the cost factor, humans can only be scheduled periodically to check on items or areas requiring inspections.

Advances in technology and equipment in recent years have made available many techniques and electronic hardware for use in security systems that had not been developed a few short years ago. Computer and data processing technology, for example, is now available for use. By using such relatively inexpensive items as minicomputers, microprocessors, word processors, and modern communications methods many protection tasks can be effectively automated. The result is machine-like tasks that were previously performed by humans can now be done more reliably by machines. Also, significant cost reductions are realized when such technology is used to replace people in a security system. For example, security personnel that previously were required at access points to control personnel entering and leaving a facility or area can now be replaced through the automation of access points by computer technology, equipment, and coded identification cards.

In such a system, a minicomputer or microprocessor installed at a central point can be used as a processor of access information. Each individual would be issued an identification card coded for that individual—no other person would have an identification card with that code. The central processor would be programmed to allow the individual with that coded card to have access in accordance with the instructions programmed in the processor. To gain access, the individual would place the coded card in a card reader at the access point and the central processor, after identifying the card as valid, would unlock the access point and allow the individual with the proper identification card to enter. This type of control system can be further sophisticated to any extent desired. A personal identification number, commonly identified as a PIN, for instance, could be added to the process; and an individual with an identification card could also be required to enter the PIN identified with that card on a keyboard at the card reader location. The central processor would identify both the identification card and the PIN as valid before allowing access.

One of the most widely accepted electronic techniques for security control in recent years is the use of closed circuit television. This cost-effective technique extends the capability of security personnel. For example, a guard at a central control point or at a post can control multiple personnel access points if the traffic through those entrances is not too heavy. Personnel that would normally be needed to control these entrances can then be eliminated.

People

Throughout the discussion of the systems approach, people, it has been stressed, should be eliminated from the system whenever possible through the use of software and hardware. That does not mean that people should be eliminated entirely from the system: They are necessary to respond to exceptions or violations in the system; to make checks, inspections, and audits of the system; and to supply intellect and judgment in the system operation. If the activities of security personnel are limited to such tasks, and the software and hardware items are utilized effectively in a security system, the result will usually be a cost-effective, highly efficient operation.

In our hypothetical organization, security protection depended almost entirely on the guard operation. This outdated concept of security management at one time was an acceptable management practice. Security programs of this type were usually patterned after the operation of law enforcement agencies, and the effectiveness of such programs relied to a great extent on the psychological impact made by the presence of guards on post and on patrol. An enforcement image was encouraged through the use of uniforms, badges, guns, and other tokens of authority designed to emphasize an authoritarian approach. Uniformed personnel were usually oriented to police-type duties, such as parking and traffic control, and reacted to problems after they had occurred. The prevention of losses and damage was not the objective of these guards, but should be the objective of any effective protection program. Also, leading management authorities now stress that workers are no longer motivated by an authoritarian or fear-producing approach.[1]

In the implementation of the systems approach, guards may be an essential element in the system design, but their limitations should be considered. Also, because of the present-day high cost of people, guards should only be used when judgment and intellect are required and other countermeasures cannot be effectively utilized. For example, in late 1982, it was estimated that the average cost of one guard in the United States was $12,000 a year. This average included both contract and in-house guards. If an organization maintains its own guard force, this cost would be a great deal more for each guard used.

A cost factor that is sometimes overlooked is the total cost of guards required to maintain a post or patrol route around the clock, seven days a week. If in-house guards are used, the number of guards required is usually estimated to be 4.5, not only to provide for a regular 40-hour work week but to also compensate for reliefs and absences due to such things as vacations and sickness. The use of guards, as readily seen, can be a significant item in a security budget: Other controls should be utilized in a system whenever possible. Also, costs generated by guards continue during the life of the facility, while other effective controls, such as hardware, usually require only a one-time cost.

Security personnel needed to operate a security system, in addition to guards, ordinarily include a variety of other types of personnel, such as office workers, investigators, inspectors, and supervisors at all levels in the organization. A security organization may have highly qualified management personnel as well as other employees to operate a security system. However, a protection organization can not "go it alone"; the interest, support, and assistance of all levels of management in the enterprise are essential.

For example, in the earlier discussion of software, it was mentioned that the issuance of a corporate policy dealing with security requirements was necessary. Such a policy statement, alone, is not enough. Top management must, in addition, maintain the same management level of interest in having an effective protection program as it maintains over other operating elements of the enterprise.

Periodic management reviews of the program; reports as needed of discrepancies, losses, and lack of compliance with established security procedures; along with reports of corrective actions taken should be required by top management. Also, supervisors at all levels in the organization should be required to ensure that security procedures are being followed in their areas of responsibility. And they should be required to report losses or threats of losses to the security organization so that such incidents can be investigated and recommendations for corrections made. All violations of security procedures should be referred to the appropriate level of line supervision for correction and disciplinary action if required.

If a crisis response team is to be formed, as was suggested earlier, the team members should be designated by top management. Team members should be required to become familiar with the corporate plan so that they can cope with a terrorist attack and their individual responsibilities. Alternates should also be designated, in case a team member is not available when the team is needed. Personnel that might be appointed to the team include a senior corporate executive to act as chair, the top security executive, a key representative from the financial area, a top-level public relations representative, and a key member from the legal staff. All of the functional areas mentioned would usually be involved in coping with a terrorist attack, but others from various operating areas in the enterprise might be required and should be included if needed.

Some enterprises have found that the formation of a security advisory committee to provide advice and assistance to the top security executive is of great value. The responsibilities of one such committee were defined as follows:

- Reviews the corporate security program periodically to determine if any changes are required or if any additional protective measures are needed and advises on any policy or procedural changes required.
- Reviews new programs or policies being suggested for implementation that might have a significant impact on the company or organization units within the company. Acts as a sounding board so that the effectiveness of what is being proposed can be appraised from the standpoint of employee reaction, as well as the workability in operating areas.
- Reviews any criticism or suggestions individual company members may receive from supervisors or employees in operating areas so that recommendations for corrective action can be considered by the committee.
- Performs such other reviews as may be required.

Membership on such an advisory committee should be composed of individuals who can effectively advise and assist; they should represent key areas in the enterprise. Also, they should have sufficient stature and creditability in the organization and have sufficient information about the operation of the enterprise that they are able to offer useful opinions about security actions.

Bodyguards might also be needed for protection, though they are usually not used unless the vulnerability analysis indicates a serious, immediate threat against an individual or individuals in the enterprise. If bodyguards are used, they should be properly trained and have had experience, if possible, in this type of protection. The designation of guards or others in the security organization who have not had proper training would normally be a mistake: Personnel of this type would usually not have the background or experience to properly handle their duties. Also, it has been said that intelligence rather than brawn should be a key qualification for bodyguards.

The System Test

A test of the operating system is the essential third step in the system approach and is required for two reasons. First, risks or hazards still existing will be identified, and system deficiencies will be revealed. Second, system changes required to accommodate facility or organization revisions will become apparent. Spot checks, inspections, audits, created errors and tests can be performed by the regular work force as part of normal work assignments, as well as by employees operating the protection system. Arrangements should be made to test the system frequently.

Regular employees can be asked to make suggestions for the improvement of the protection program. Usually they will respond positively. Employees' comments and suggestions will give some indication of how well the protection system is operating and what changes, if any, should be made. Procedures can be established requiring supervisors at all levels to assume the responsibility for ensuring that employees under their supervision are complying with system requirements. Supervisory personnel can also be prepared to perform other tasks, such as inspections of areas and periodic audits of invoices, negotiable instruments, and inventories and to report any discrepancies to the security executive responsible for the operation of the system.

Protection personnel such as guards are normally assigned inspection tasks as part of their regular duties. All members of the protection organization also can be required to be constantly alert to any deficiencies in the operation of the system.

In addition to inspections, a common technique for testing the system is to insert errors to determine whether they are noted and reported. Test exercises can also be designed and conducted to ascertain how the system reacts. For example, a controlled test might involve a report of a bomb in a facility to check the reaction of those responsible for handling bomb threats. Of course, such exercises must be carefully supervised and controlled by trained personnel. Also, if a crisis response team has been designated, the members of this team might meet periodically to work test exercises involving terrorist attacks. A scenario involving the kidnapping of the chairman of the board or other top officers of the enterprise might be presented to the team and each team member be required to indicate a choice of action. In this way, any lack of knowledge on the part of team members will be highlighted and any deficiencies in the organization's plan noted and corrected.

JUSTIFICATION OF COSTS

Although cost effectiveness has been stressed throughout the system approach discussion in this chapter, some readers might gain the impression that the revision of the security program for the fictitious company presented in the scenario might be very costly because of the electronic controls suggested and the recommended upgrading of the security organization. As a matter of fact, the revised program suggested might be less costly than the existing one, which is now focused on the guard operation. The cost of personnel is generally the greatest cost in any security program. As a result, if the number of guards can be reduced through the use of other countermeasures, as suggested earlier, then a part or all of the resulting savings could be used for electronic controls and higher-grade management personnel, while at the same time improving protection.

Modern electronic controls are, of course, costly. But there usually is a one-time cost for such items, while the cost for guards is an ongoing cost that must be provided for in each annual budget. As most protection programs that are designed around the guard operation are labor intensive, it is usually not too difficult to realize considerable savings in personnel through the adoption of other counter-measures. In fact, effecting a savings of 25 percent through the adoption of electronic controls alone would not be unusual.

Assuming then that our hypothetical enterprise is reasonably large—a Fortune 500 company—and that it is labor intensive in security, it would not be unusual for 100 guards to be employed in the protection organization of that enterprise. If a 25 percent reduction could be realized, as indicated above, then 25 guards could be eliminated. If the average cost of one guard was $12,000 annually, then this reduction would mean that a savings of $300,000 a year in costs would result. And if company-employed guards were involved, the reduction would be consider-ably more—probably at least an additional 25 percent. With this amount of cost reduction, a considerable amount of electronic control equipment could be justified.

Also, this has not taken into consideration still other cost reductions that should result through other hardware and software items being integrated into the system. As a result of the adoption of the systems approach and the cost trade-offs that are possible, the revised protection program could be much less costly than the guard-oriented, labor-intensive program that previously existed.

Insurance in some organizations might be regarded as a protection factor to compensate for losses that may be suffered. Insurance was not mentioned in the countermeasures section because it will not prevent losses; it is effective only after a damage-causing incident occurs. The basic objective of the systems ap-proach—stated earlier in this chapter—is to avoid risks and prevent loss-causing incidents from happening. Insurance does not meet this criteria. However, insurance should not be overlooked as a protection against hazards that cannot be avoided through the use of countermeasures.

This cost justification discussion has not considered the savings that could also result from a reduction in losses in the organization because of a more effective protection program. Such losses would probably be unknown in our hypothetical organization, but should be considered an extra benefit resulting from the adoption of an effective protection program.

The costs of any protection program always require justification, as is the case with other operating costs in any organization. A security program that has been designed and implemented using the systems approach should be able to withstand the most rigorous management cost scrutiny. Once having passed that scrutiny, the security program may be the best investment the organization has ever made.

25

Transportation Security

Anthony J. Scotti

Mr. Schleyer knew he was a target. He wrote a memo stating if he was kidnapped he did not want anyone to negotiate his release. On September 5, 1977, Schleyer's car was in front. A follow car with bodyguards was in the rear. As they approached the street where the ambush was to take place, a lookout waved to his accomplice (10 seconds). Schleyer's cars turned into the street. A van with three people in it was parked on the corner. A car drove toward them going the wrong way on a one-way street (20 seconds). It cut in front of them, at the same time a woman rolled a baby carriage in front of the car (30 seconds). Schleyer's car hit the approaching car. The bodyguard's car hit Schleyer's car. One terrorist leaped from the blocking car, opened the doors of Schleyer's car (the doors were unlocked), and killed the bodyguards (40 seconds). The three men from the van opened fire, killing all the bodyguards in the backup car. Total elapsed time: 100 seconds.

The morning of March 16, 1978. Two cars, both Fiat 130s. Moro was in the lead car, accompanied by a driver and a bodyguard. Following in a separate car were three bodyguards. As they approached an intersection with a stop sign, a small white car pulled up in front of them and the driver jammed on the brakes (10 seconds). Moro's car hit the small white car, which had just passed them, and the security car hit Moro's car. Two men jumped from the white car that had just been hit (15 seconds), looking as though they were about to view the damage to their car. When they approached Moro's car, they fired into the car, killing the driver and the bodyguard. Meanwhile, four men dressed in Alitalia Airline uniforms machine gunned the bodyguards in the following car (20 seconds). They took Moro and put him into a waiting car and drove away. Total elapsed time: 45 seconds.

Threats of terrorism and kidnapping pose serious problems involving all aspects of security management. Effective management dictates that available resources be used wisely and concentrated on security weak points. One does not need to be a student of terrorism to realize that assassinations or kidnappings take place where the protection to the victim is most difficult. These acts take place where the risks are relatively low for the terrorist and the possibility for success is relatively high. Although there is a considerable amount of technology developed that offers impregnable protection at the home and place of business, this protection is breached—twice a day—when traveling to and from the home. Over 85 percent of all kidnappings and assassinations occur while the victim is in transit.

During this period of time the risk to the attacker is minimal; the vulnerability of the victim is at its maximum. This chapter focuses on this most dangerous period of time. Transportation security became a serious problem when, in the late 1960s, guerrillas in Latin America and elsewhere shifted their offenses from the countryside to the city, where they could be assured of wide and efficient media coverage for their cause, however small the organization. Ambushes took place in city streets rather than in a remote jungle.

When we consider, for instance, that more than 90 percent of all our personal travel is by car, we can understand why many security experts point to transportation as the weak link in the security chain. Several studies have shown that most kidnappings have occurred while the victim was traveling by car.

Vehicles are easy to identify and observe. There are many components on a car that make it easy to distinguish one car from another (license plates, color, body, make). A car is one of the few places where a person can be alone or at least dependent on a fixed number of security personnel, making it possible for the terrorist group to accurately estimate defenses and adjust its manpower accordingly.

Ironically, when we are in a vehicle we feel safe; actually the opposite is true. Vehicles can be easily followed and practice runs of potential ambushes are possible. Automobiles appear to be solid and to offer a great amount of protection because of the steel and safety glass. Although there is some protection, it is minimal—a .22 long rifle can penetrate the car door of a standard American sedan.

Traveling by car near the home, in the morning, is the most dangerous area and time for the VIP because one of the necessary ingredients in a successful ambush is fixing a time and a location. This task becomes increasingly easier near the VIP's home because of the following factors:

1. Most VIPs believe in promptness—especially in the morning.
2. In the area of the home it is difficult, if not impossible, to change routes.
3. About 90 percent of morning travel is by car.
4. We feel secure and confident in a car.
5. Cars are easy to identify.

No wonder that 95 percent of all kidnappings occur near the home. Throughout the world businessmen are becoming targets of kidnappings. Businessmen are chosen because they are believed to be wealthy, powerful and influential, representative of something important, or particularly valuable to someone. Whether a businessman truly fits into one of these categories makes no difference. As long as the terrorist or criminal thinks he does—that's all that counts!

A number of steps can be taken to minimize the danger of transit by vehicle. They can be categorized as:

1. Countermeasures (e.g., procedures, awareness, route planning, countersurveillance).
2. The automobile (e.g., armoring cars, tire protection, communications).
3. Defensive and offensive driving.

Since the third of these essential elements can only be acquired from actual "hands on" instruction and practice, this chapter discusses only the first two: preventive measures to reduce the possibilities of attack and modifications to automobiles so that they both better protect their occupants and better withstand terrorist assault.

COUNTERMEASURES

Surprise is an essential element to any successful kidnapping. This one element is the key to all the others. In order for a successful ambush to occur, the victim must be totally unaware of what is about to happen. Therefore, it is logical that reducing the element of surprise is of the utmost importance. How can a potential victim protect against surprise? Planning and surprise are inseparable. Analysis of the tactics of surprise points to a definite pattern. This pattern indicates that a successful ambush takes time to develop and actually occurs in stages. This is not to say that every ambush happens in this manner; but it is logical to assume that to use the element of surprise effectively requires planning, and from this planning comes two steps:

1.   *Target selection.* In the preliminary stages, usually more than one target is selected. Terrorists are not interested in an individual personally—they are interested in what he represents. They will, through meticulous surveillance, gather information about his lifestyle. Once the information is gathered, they will focus on the individual who is the most vulnerable. The Moro kidnapping appears to be a classic illustration of target selection. There is enough evidence to suggest that the Red Brigades had originally selected Berlinguer, the Communist Party leader of Italy, but he was a much harder target and Moro much easier.

2.   *Surveillance.* The group may employ surveillance on more than one person. Surveillance will take weeks, maybe months. The victim's movements will be analyzed and patterns of habit established. In some cases photographs are taken. Surveillance will continue until the group can predict, with reasonable accuracy, where a person is and when he is going to be there. Therefore it is necessary to develop a before-the-fact awareness program that will eliminate the element of surprise.

Surveillance Awareness

Planning is the essence of surprise and surveillance is the essence of a successful ambush. Surveillance is needed to acquire the necessary information for a successful plan. Therefore, developing a surveillance awareness program around the driving time period is essential. Changing the time of departure plus the driving route is a necessity. But unfortunately, in many cases, especially in the morning, it is impossible to vary time schedules by any great amount. Changing routes is desirable but many times, due to the location of a home or office, it is impossible. In most locations a driver has a 50–50 choice—to go right or left. The pattern of abduction near the home is not coincidental: It is simply hard to change routes near the home, therefore making it easy for a terrorist group to fix a time and location, which in turn makes the terrorists' job much easier.

The best line of defense is unpredictability. It must be made difficult to pinpoint the location of a potential target, though many people are not ready to accept this major change of lifestyle. It is at this surveillance stage of abduction that an early warning system must be developed.

Early Warning System

An early warning system requires that a close watch be kept for abnormal activity near the home and office. It is important to point out that it does not require much effort to be security conscious. In fact, most people are security conscious and do not realize it. As an example, when someone leaves his home in the morning, he could probably write a couple of pages of notes concerning the activities around it, such as types of vehicles in the neighborhood, children going to school, even new faces. In fact, most people can tell whether they are late or early by what they see when they leave the house.

Careful questions can be raised by a businessman such as: Isn't that a strange car parked across the street? The phone company must be working early this morning because they have a van parked nearby. Or, as he drives down the street, he should notice unfamiliar people in the area, an unfamiliar car, or a vehicle that just does not belong in the neighborhood. Most businessmen who are potential kidnap victims live in affluent areas—which usually dictate the type of vehicle that will be present in the area.

What has happened? A mental picture of what should be there and what should not be there has been presented; and when an object or person comes into the picture that doesn't belong, a signal is received that causes a question to be raised—what is it or he doing here? The key to an effective surveillance awareness program is alertness. The philosophy should be adopted that once is happenstance, twice is coincidence, and three times is enemy action. The level of awareness must be raised to a point where

- Strange vehicles parked near the residence or place of employment are noticed and reported to the authorities.
- People standing, walking, or sitting in cars near the residence or place of employment are noticed.
- An individual can recognize that he is being followed. If he feels he is being followed, he can simply drive around the block and notice if the suspected vehicle is still there.

An important point is to keep track of any unusual sightings. A small tape recorder can be used to register any unusual activity. From the tape a log can be made describing any strange vehicles. It should include:

- Make
- Model
- Year
- Color
- License number
- General condition
- Number of people in vehicle

And, if possible, a description of its occupants, such as their sex, age, size, hair color or style, and ethnic background, should also be noted.

A reporting system is mandatory if chauffeurs are used and drivers are changed often: It creates a useful information bank that the new driver can draw on. In addition, if the driver is not sure he has seen the same thing twice, he can check back into the log to make certain. If the log indicates a definite pattern is developing, then this pattern should be brought to the attention of the local authorities. Any information discovered should be relayed to the driver as quickly as possible. The driver should not be made to feel he is paranoid; in fact, he should be told he is doing a good job. A good way of doing that is to get information discovered back to him as soon as possible. What follows can be the best advice you can give a driver. "If he feels something is wrong, it is better to suffer a little embarrassment in the event you are wrong, than suffer the consequences if you are right!"

Test Program

A surveillance awareness test program can be developed to check on the alertness of those involved. Some simple methods to use are:

- Rent a car or van and park it near the residence. Then measure how long it takes before the strange vehicle is noticed.
- Follow in a rent-a-car or another unfamiliar vehicle and again notice if the surveillance is detected.
- Plant strangers around the residence and measure that response time.

An ongoing test program is beneficial if the threat level is high enough.

Route Planning

Route planning should be premeditated—not haphazard. It is easy to develop a rather scientific method of route planning. Using a map, lay out a number of different routes. If possible, vary the routes near the home and office. Then assign each route a number, let's say seven routes have been selected. Using the seven routes, make a table to assign each route to a day, but leave out two routes.

	Monday	Tuesday	Wednesday	Thursday	Friday
Route #	1	7	5	6	2

On Monday route 1 is taken, Tuesday route 7, and so forth. Then you can develop a table of random routes by changing the sequence of numbers and assigning them to a day. Example:

	Monday	Tuesday	Wednesday	Thursday	Friday
Week 1	1	7	5	6	2
Week 2	3	4	7	1	5
Week 3	6	3	2	5	1
Week 4	2	1	4	7	3

On week six you can change the sequence of routes by starting off at week three and taking route 6 on Monday, route 3 on Tuesday, then on Wednesday move up to week two and take route 7, Thursday route 1 and Friday route 5. What has been done is a set of dates have been blocked off in the table. Example:

	Monday	Tuesday	Wednesday	Thursday	Friday
Week 1	1	7	5	6	2
Week 2	3	4	7	1	5
Week 3	6	3	2	5	1
Week 4	2	1	4	7	3
Week 5	5	3	6	2	4

You can work any number of combinations—or add more routes. Although working with seven numbers is not a complete random sequence, it is better than driving the same route constantly.

Knowledge of the Terrain

This simply means knowledge of the area. Most vehicle ambushes occur near the home; therefore if an ambush does occur, there is a good chance it will happen in a terrain the victim knows as well as the terrorists. Careful scrutiny of the area near the residence and the place of employment can establish areas designated as *danger zones*. A danger zone is a location where terrorists will find it easy to fix the time a person will be there. A danger zone can be an intersection near your home that cannot be avoided, it can be an exit from an airport after you have arrived on a scheduled flight, or an exit or entrance ramp to a highway. At the danger zone area safe havens should be established. A *safe haven* is defined as an area that will afford you some safety, an area that the attackers would be reluctant to follow you into. They include:

- Police stations
- Hospitals
- Fire stations
- Large shopping areas
- Military bases

It is important to know where the safe havens are and how to get there. In the event of an ambush, there is no time to stop and ask for directions. The shortest possible route to safe havens should be known. If the driver of the vehicle is not capable of computing the danger zone areas, a member of the security department should develop a danger zone log. This log can be reviewed by the driver on a periodic basis and can be updated if necessary.

Preparation for Ambushes

Now that the planning stages of an ambush have been discussed, let's talk about how the actual ambush develops and the two driving tactics—moving and stationary—used to accomplish it.

Moving Ambush

In a moving ambush a car pulls along the victim's car and fires into the vehicle. In many cases a second car is used to slow down the victim's vehicle in order to give the attackers an easier target. The International Association of Chiefs of Police developed a set of statistics from information provided by numerous attacks and from studies of the sites of the attacks. These statistics indicate the following driver errors:

- The attack was completely unexpected. (Driver wasn't alert.) The driver suddenly found himself "boxed in" and unable to take defensive or evasive action. (Driver was not alert, observant, or driving defensively.)
- When the attack was launched, the driver attempted to veer to the right, away from the attacking vehicle, and in doing so, trapped his vehicle against the curb line of parked cars. This action gave the attackers more maneuvering room and enabled them to more effectively bring their guns to bear on the target vehicle. (Driver not alert; driver reacted to induce panic caused by the attackers' actions instead of acting defensively or offensively.)
- In one case, the driver attached no significance to or saw no danger in a vehicle full of young men following him. He thought they were "just young smart alecks out for a joy ride." (Driver not alert or trained.) In all cases the failure appears to be in one major area, inattentiveness!

Stationary Ambush

The stationary ambush seems to be the most popular. Basically a stationary ambush can be described as an action carried out by the terrorists that will force the victim's vehicle to a stop. They will try to stop the car in an area in which they have computed firing angles, which more than likely are designed to disable the driver. In a stationary ambush it is essential that the driver reverse direction and drive out of the firing area. No matter what type of an ambush it is, the first few moments are critical. It is important that some action be taken by the victim.

Anatomy of an Ambush

The Moro incident referred to at the beginning of this chapter is a perfect example of the perfect ambush. It was so well planned and executed that one can only speculate whether the incident could have been avoided at all. But some issues are nevertheless noteworthy.

- *Predictability.* The terrorists knew exactly where Moro was going to be. They had a location and a time. Moro's security people gave him five possible routes to take. The terrorists predicted the time and location with incredible accuracy.
- *Surprise.* The guards were not alert. Speculation is that perhaps they were relaxed by the fact the car that cut in front of them had diplomatic plates. But, at the same time, it is doubtful they ever saw the plates.
- *Car.* The car was not armored. In a country where vehicle ambushes are the national pastime and everyone of importance is driving an armored car, it was foolhardy not to use one.

Similarly, the Schleyer assault also was well planned and executed. His abduction was facilitated by the same factors: predictable schedule, even though Schleyer knew he was a target; the follow-up car was caught completely off guard; and no armored car! These two incidents bring up an excellent point about follow-up cars and bodyguards. If an individual feels that the threat level requires a back-up car with bodyguards—then the vehicle should be a virtual gun-ship. The bodyguards in the car should be alert to possible dangers, and their weapons should be on their laps ready to be used. It is foolish to have a back-up car with armed men in the vehicle if the men take two minutes to react.

Using hindsight, one can speculate on how these events could have been prevented. The obvious elements are (a) unpredictability, (b) alertness, and use of an armored car.

ARMORED CARS

The subject of armored cars is confusing, though it appears that in most incidents an armored car gives a driver those few seconds that can make the difference. The first major obstacle concerning armored cars is determining if one is necessary. Answering this question is difficult. But if there has been an incident that has prompted thought about an armored car—then one is probably needed.

The next step is to determine the level of protection needed. Most car armorers talk in terms of specifications established by underwriter laboratories (UL). Underwriter Labs has established ratings for bulletproof material. These standards are established by testing material at a close firing range (15 feet or less), firing at 12-inch-square samples. Indicators are placed behind the samples to catch any fragments. The lower ratings (I, II, III) must resist four shots placed three inches apart in a triangle in the center of the material. At the highest level (IV), the material must be able to resist one shot from a high-powered rifle at the center of the sample. Materials are also tested for flying fragments (spalling) and how they will perform in extreme temperatures. The levels of protection follow.

> No Level I
> Level II—.357 magnum, carb. 9mm
> Level III—Same as above, 44 magnum, 12 gauge, 30 carb.
> Level IV—Same as above, 30.06 military ball

The level of armoring must be determined by the type of weapon you want to protect against. An example is the UL's highest rating, level IV, which is 30.06 24″ barrel soft grain, 2,400 ft/sec. A NATO weapon can be as high as 2,900 ft/sec.

Reading the UL's standardized system, it becomes obvious that in order to establish the degree of protection needed, one must know the type of weapons that may be used in an attack; the method of the attack; and whether the attackers will be firing close or from a distance. Studies indicate 30 percent of all kidnap teams used automatic weapons. Other studies show that attacks are close range. Combining this data we can conclude that the level of protection should be level IV or higher. It is in this stage of the purchase where the armorer can be of great assistance. He will know as much about the levels of protection needed for certain areas of the world as anyone.

Type of Vehicle

The type of vehicle must blend in with the existing cars in that particular country. Also, there should be ample room in the car for four people. The car selected should:

- Blend into the vehicle environment.
- Be a four-door, which will allow comfort and ease of entering.
- Have a power unit—an engine size and gear ratio that will allow reasonable acceleration.

For example, in Italy, a Lincoln Town Sedan would not be the choice—Fiat would be the likely consideration. The color of the car should blend in with the preferred colors in the country. In most countries big, black cars signify importance.

Vehicle Design

Armored vehicles can be designed to

- Absorb the attack, take repeated hits, return fire, and call for help.
- Absorb the initial fire and break the ambush.
- A combination of the above.

The first of these armored vehicle designs is commonly used for the threat of assassination. The cost of these cars is directly proportional to how long you want to absorb fire. Cars armored to maximum ballistic levels are very expensive, running as high as $100,000. For a car to absorb the initial burst and then drive out of the ambush requires characteristics: (a) enough armor to absorb the initial fire, and (b) a design that remains maneuverable.

Whether additional armoring is needed in the engine department depends on where the individual lives. If the car is used mostly in the city, then armoring the engine compartment is usually not necessary. In the event of an ambush and radiator damage, the car need only go a short distance to break the ambush. But if the car is used in the countryside and may have to travel great distances to break free from the ambush, then engine compartment armoring is desirable.

Fuel Tank Armoring

Wrapping a fuel tank in ballistic fiberglass, Kevlar, or ballistic nylon will provide bullet protection up to certain levels. If there is a penetration, there is a chance for explosion. Aside from ignition caused by a bullet or an explosive device, there is the very real danger of being rammed in the rear, which can cause an explosion. The aircraft industry has used foam-filled tanks to reduce the danger of explosion. Foam normally is not applicable for the vehicle field because of fuel displacement and the problem of degradation over a period of time. Aero Tec Labs has come out with an excellent crushable bladder tank with internal foam baffling, which appears to be superior to any other foam application in the security vehicle market.

Perhaps the finest protection available is the Explosive Anti-Explosion System. This metallic (aluminum alloy foil) enclosure displaces but 1 percent of the fuel and has been successfully tested by the Canadian and British military, using tracer rounds and plastic explosives. Currently, a ballistic "Universal Tank" is being developed, stuffed with Explosafe, which will be ideal for the security car industry.

Body Armoring

The doors, windows, and rear of the passenger seat must be armored to the maximum threat level. If grenades are a threat, the roof and floor must be armored, which increases the price of the vehicle. The engine compartment is naturally armored. Armoring the battery, engine compartment and radiator requires discussions with the armorer. There are two basic philosophies concerning armoring—lightweight or heavyweight. The heavyweight people feel that in the event of an all-out attack, the car will be forced to stop. The car should be heavily armored so it can absorb as much punishment as possible. Adherents of the lightweight philosophy claim that no matter how heavily the car is armored, it cannot hold up under prolonged attack. Therefore, a lightweight, maneuverable car with a trained driver has a better chance to break the ambush.

Lightweight versus heavyweight armor may become a bigger problem in the future. As our fuel problems get worse, cars get smaller and lighter. The term *lightweight armor* may have to be redefined. As of this time, the state-of-the-art service appears to be adding 700 to 1,000 pounds to the original weight of the car. The key is not the 700 to 1,000 pounds, but the original weight of the car.

For instance, a 1979 Lincoln Town Coupe weighs 4,843 pounds—by adding 800 pounds of armor you are increasing the weight by 16.5 percent. Change the car to a Ford Granada, which weighs 3,200 pounds, and add the same 800 pounds; the weight goes up by 25 percent—a dramatic difference and an important measurement.

In breaking an ambush, the acceleration and handling capability of the vehicle are very important, and the rate of acceleration will decrease the same percentage the amount of weight increases. In other words, if the increase in weight is 25 percent, the acceleration of the vehicle will decrease by 25 percent, assuming no modifications to the engine or gear box. Table 25.1 gives you an idea of the percentage increase between various car and armor weights.

Table 25.1   Vehicle to Armor Weight Ratios

Vehicle Weight (lbs)	Armor Weight (lbs)					
	600	700	800	900	1,000	1,100
3,000	20.0	23.3	26.6	30.0	33.3	36.6
3,500	17.1	20.0	22.8	25.7	28.6	31.4
4,000	15.0	17.5	20.0	22.5	25.0	27.5
4,500	13.3	15.5	17.7	20.0	22.2	24.4
5,000	12.0	14.0	14.0	18.0	20.0	22.0

The following considerations are necessary when installing the material:

- Retention of panels require the use of high-tensile captive bolts. The design prevents them from becoming projectiles.
- Ballistic seals ensure that missiles cannot penetrate the vehicle at unusual angles.
- Fabrication of certain materials can reduce the inherent ballistic properties. Care must be exercised in the welding techniques, overlap construction, and general format.

- Sealants used to prevent moisture from entering the layers of armor are sufficiently resistant to contain edge stress. Particular care is given to hinges and locks.

Communications

Along with mobility, a good communication system is vital for survival. The principal's vehicle and all security vehicles should be radio equipped. Select an excellent vehicle radio that is not rugged and can be easily serviced. The vehicle antenna locations depend on the environment. In many areas of the world it is common for an executive or an official sedan to have a protruding antenna; however, when possible, an executive low-profile vehicle should have a hidden antenna if reception and transmission are not affected.

A variety of antenna configurations are commercially available. Some can be hidden in the side view mirrors, others wrap around the interior of the roof, or fit into the commercial AM radio antenna. No matter what the unique configuration is, the prime consideration must be reception and transmission quality, which must not be downgraded for a low-profile appearance.

Purchase and installation of radio gear should be assigned to a qualified communications technician. Installation in the principal's vehicle should be mission designed. The microphone should be within easy reach of both the driver and the occupant of the right-hand seat. If the principal rides in the back seat, he too should have a microphone or at least an activations system or a panic alarm— the latter in instances in which the driver and bodyguard are incapacitated or so totally occupied they cannot utilize the communications system. If the threat level is determined to be high, a danger zone–reporting system should be considered. This is a system whereby the driver radios when he is going into a danger zone and then radios when he is leaving the danger zone.

In the event the attackers gain entry into the vehicle and the driver or passenger cannot use the radios, there should be a concealed microphone and microphone switch in the vehicle. This will allow people at the other end of the radio transmission to hear what's going on in the car without the attackers knowing.

Tire Protection

Unfortunately, some armored car manufacturers and buyers have downgraded the importance of tire protection. The fact is, vehicle mobility is the key to survival. If the tires are shot or blown off, the vehicle is going nowhere, no matter how expensive the radials. The car needs a device that will allow it to move at high speed for at least one or two miles out of the kill zone of an urban ambush.

Although there are a number of runflat devices on the market, the buyer must be careful in the selection of tire protection. With some devices present the possibility in a cornering condition of a pulling away from the metal to expose the wheel rim flange to the road surface, which can seriously interfere with steering and braking. Foam-filled tires and tires with rigid sidewalls are not the answer, especially in a soft-soil condition. Foam presents a weight problem in terms of unsprung weight, while rigid sidewalls present problems if sharp, high-speed evasive maneuvers are attempted.

The Hutchinson V.P. No Flat tire core is a form of tire protection that is fairly expensive, restricted to Michelin tires, and of good ballistic protection capabilities. The Patecell Safety Wheel (a fairly expensive plastic runflat device) claims a 50 mph speed for 50 miles after the tires have been shot out. This would be excellent for a rural ambush, but urban incidents call for 70 to 90 mph speeds over a short dash of a half mile or until out of line or site of fire. The Patecell should be able to accomplish that requirement.

A device that is in wide use in security vehicles throughout the world is the Lindley Saftiwheel. The original wheel has saved lives, including the life of one of the most prominent leaders of the twentieth century. Because the original wheel was difficult to install, a new Safti-Wheel will soon be in production, which eliminates installation difficulties, is superior all around, and is cost effective. Cost- and performance-wise, the new Safti-Wheel may well be the finest device on the market if it passes further ballistic and driving tests.

Goodyear has announced a new flat-proof radial whose walls are three times thicker than the normal tire; however, at the time of this writing no published ballistic tests are available. There is some debate as to the handling capabilities in severe vehicle movements at high speed, such as sudden sharp turns, especially in soft sand or mud, due to the rigid sidewalls. If the tire passes intensive ballistic testing and handles well, it will be a boon to the security field.

Others of note are a protection package offered by Dunlop and the Tyron Safety Band out of the United Kingdom, which is available for most makes of cars.

Accessories

Accessories can also be confusing. They vary from car to car and what is standard equipment on one car is an additional accessory on others. Accessories come in several categories:

- Essentials
- Basics
- Functional additions
- Power options

One way of breaking accessories down into these categories follows. There is room for dispute in many of these selections.

Essentials

Automatic transmission
Four doors
Power steering
Power brakes
Tilt steering wheel
Electric window defogger
Air conditioning

Basics

Heavy-Duty Battery. Better to handle the strain from the multitude of electrical equipment on cars and a necessity for anyone living in a cold climate.

Heavy-Duty Radiator. Increases the engine's cooling capacity. Heat is what destroys engines.

Heavy-Duty Suspension. Will help eliminate body roll but will give a slightly harsher ride. It will make for a better-handling vehicle.

Functional Additions

Remote side control mirrors
Intermediate wipers
Protective side molding
Power antenna
Gauge package
Auxiliary lighting
Extra insulation

Power Options

Six-way power seats
Power windows
Electric door locks
Power trunk (from the glove box)

Most people in the automotive industry feel that the following list of equipment should be placed into the basic categories listed above.

1.   *Trauma kit.* Doctors can develop a package designed for treating gunshot wounds, burns, and heart failure. Its basic purpose is to keep someone alive until

they can get to a hospital. The trauma kit should not be kept in the trunk; it should be inside the vehicle ready for use.

2. *Tool kit in the trunk.* In the event of a kidnapping, someone may get stuffed in the trunk. A simple tool kit can get him out. Or you can make a switch that opens the trunk from the inside.

3. *Mirrors.* Good rear and side view mirrors should be installed on the car. They should be installed in a manner so the driver does not have to move his head to look to the rear, and he should have good vision to the rear. Good mirrors are defined as mirrors that do not distort the actual distance of the object. Many mirrors make objects seem further away than they really are.

4. *Public address system.* The driver and occupants should be able to talk to someone outside the car without opening the doors. Also, the driver does not have to drive up to someone to talk to him; they can stay a safe distance away and communicate.

5. *Optics.* Be sure there is little or no distortion through the windshield. When purchasing a car the ambient temperature of the environment is important. If the window is not designed properly, it can distort the view badly. The old bullet-resistant glass is ineffective against high-powered weapons and repeated hits.

CONCLUSION

Surprise is essential to the success of any terrorist assault or abduction. It is obvious, however, that any such operation requires extensive previous reconnaissance and surveillance; and it is precisely at this stage that an attack can, and must, be thwarted. The potential kidnap victim must develop countersurveillance techniques and preventive measures that can reduce the possibilities of attack. Accordingly, while the victim must learn to recognize a developing ambush, he must also know how to react to and evade an abduction attempt. To this end, the potential victim must analyze beforehand the ingredients necessary for a successful ambush and develop an awareness program to protect against them.

These efforts include route planning, the designation of both danger zones and safe havens, and the realization that, once an assault begins, the vehicle he is traveling in must never stop. First priority is fleeing the attack scene as fast as possible. In this regard, a potential victim must be assured that his automobile is armored and thus strong enough to withstand a fusilade of machine-gun fire and capable of withstanding damage to the engine and tires. The final preventive element is skilled defensive and, when need be, offensive driving—something imparted by actual experience.

26

Personal Survival Courses: A Matter of Choice

James R. Jarrett

The subject of personal protective strategies is broad enough to write books, not merely chapters, about. There are currently a number of books on the matter available, so this chapter will discuss only some broad generalities of protective techniques with a detailed analysis of training requirements and courses. Protective measures are, for the most part, simple, common sense actions most people simply do not think about. The low-profile image is the most basic and quite effective. Low profile simply means not flaunting status. Status is recognized by such obvious criteria as location of residence, type of vehicle driven, clothing worn, personal possessions and lifestyle, such as entertainment activities, travel, social circles, and amount of publicity. Among those things not so often associated with vulnerability reduction are inclusion in social registers, reserved parking spaces, regularly reserved or frequented tables at restaurants, seasonal box seats at theatrical and sporting events, personalized license plates, memberships in exclusive clubs, and a well-ordered and regulated existence.

The basis for any deliberate act of violence directed against a specific individual is intelligence. Intelligence is simply information about an intended or potential target. Therefore, a necessary integral component of any protective program must be effective counterintelligence procedures. The object of counterintelligence is to deny information or to provide disinformation. In other words, information about a principal and his family should be available strictly on a need-to-know basis. This is not as an involved or secretive business as might be expected. It is mainly a matter of identifying who needs to know what and developing procedures for verifying requests for information.

A basic concept in formulating a security plan is to realize that most of us lead lives that have patterns. Those patterns begin and end at home. Hence, information about the residence should be closely monitored. The use of unpublished phone numbers, post office boxes, last names with initial identifiers are among the simple, passive measures that can be adopted. This does not mean the information is not obtainable. These measures merely provide inhibiting barriers, making attempts to acquire specific information more noticeable, thus providing a potential alert mechanism. The low-profile image extends to clothing, as designer fashions and personally tailored clothes are earmarks of status. This consideration is more important when attempting to counter target-of-opportunity criminal acts and has little to do with sophisticated acts of criminal or terrorist violence.

The selection of a vehicle is extremely important because, as generally recognized, the most vulnerable exposure time is during travel, especially by private vehicle. One can purchase fully armored vehicles or an easily accessible sports car. Without a doubt, the worst possible choice of a vehicle is a convertible. For most purposes, though, some general guidelines for selecting a vehicle include vehicles with good road clearance and internal climate control, such as heat and air conditioning. Whatever vehicle is chosen, doors should be kept locked and windows kept up at all times. Accessories should include inside hood releases and locking gas caps, as well as puncture- and blowout-resistant tires. Antitamper devices should also be considered as minimum equipment.

All of us live in a threatening environment. The degree of threat we may be under is the product of a number of factors. Our occupation, where we live and work, what we do and where we go all contribute to the potential hazards we face. We can reduce the risks we face by altering our lifestyles and adopting security strategies, while at the same time avoiding a condition that can be referred to as *security paralysis*. This phenomenon can occur in a paranoid, overprotective environment where fear creates a dysfunctional atmosphere. It is interesting to note that this dysfunction is one of the aims of terrorism.

The Passive/Soft Versus Active/Hard Alternatives

The success of personal survival is the product of two variables. The first is perceptual, and the second comprises conditioning or training. Let us examine the perceptual issue first. If the principal does not or refuses to recognize the fact that he is under threat, personal survival becomes a matter of luck. On the other hand, if the principal recognizes that he does exist in a potentially hostile environment, the first order of business is to ascertain how serious the threat is. The next step is to develop procedures for dealing with it. The philosophical makeup of the principal becomes of the utmost importance in dealing with threat perception. For instance, a personality that tends to be of a liberal political persuasion with a Lockean viewpoint of his fellow man is far less likely to view life as hazardous, and when such a personality does recognize the world as a dangerous place, the party is inclined to avoid the utilization of force in dealing with threat. Hence, a program for this type of personality is normally very passive and consists almost solely of avoidance and access denial, with hard option responses seldom considered. Rarely is such a viewpoint converted to aggressive security unless an unfortunate incident strikes the individual or someone close to him.

The antithesis to this viewpoint is the aggressive, Hobbesian personality. This kind of personality often enthusiastically seeks sophisticated force response training in addition to the passive/denial techniques. This type of individual is far more likely to view immediate security as a personal responsibility and is consequently far more active in acquiring alternative methods of assuring survival in the face of violence.

As indicated earlier, there is ample material on personal survival available for both passive/soft and active/hard alternatives. It is the contention of this author that there is no such thing as too much training; therefore, the following discussion focuses on the consideration of the hard option and the requisite training for the effective utilization of counterforce. By way of an introductory, cautionary note, the following recommendations are offered. First, in developing a hard option response, do-it-yourself programs should be avoided. The complexities of responding to violent confrontation are enormous and response methods should be taught by personnel well versed in the alternatives available and with the capability of creating an illusory environment designed to teach specific skills and evaluate student responses. Second, there are few, if any, absolutes either in perception techniques or tactics. Beware of dogmatic approaches. Training must be designed to accommodate a wide divergence in physiological and psychological profiles.

Force-Response Training Principles

With the above thoughts in mind, let us proceed to the consideration of force-response training principles. Awareness and alertness are the first principles. Jeff Cooper the founder of the Gunsight training facility, Arizona, designed a color scheme to assist in identifying the various levels of awareness; white, yellow, orange, red. Most people today live in the category identified as Condition White. This is exemplified by the person so involved in his own world that he is totally unaware of his surroundings. If you want a classic example, watch the other drivers on the highway and note how few of them will make eye contact with you.

In the lifestyle alterations required for successful survival preparation, the subject must enter into an awareness level known as Condition Yellow, which means knowing what is going on around you. For instance, be aware of strange vehicles parked on your street, watch your mirrors as you drive to detect surveillance, know where the exits are in an establishment, choose a table at a restaurant where attacks can only come from the front. This care is not paranoia; it is a common sense approach that will in fact enhance your life by causing you to see and hear more of what goes on around you. Condition Orange symbolizes a perception of threat when defensive tactics are being considered. The operative word is perceived, but the threat does not, in fact, have to materialize. Assume a strange noise is heard in the residence at night and the subject elects to investigate. The Condition Orange response would include taking a weapon during the investigation. If the threat turns out to be unfounded, the weapon can always be returned and its immediate availability has caused no harm. However, if a defensive attitude is not adopted and the threat materializes, the absence of adequate response alternatives ensures the probability of victimization.

Condition Red involves identifying a threat and reacting to neutralize it. The reaction can be anything from running away to engaging the threat with deadly force. Within each of these conditions—including an additional condition added by this author and denoted as Condition Blue, which is the traumatic postincident phase—there are an enormous number of tactical preventative and reactive measures that can be employed. The acquisition of defensive skills is accomplished only through professional, structured, and intensive training.

Preventative protective technology such as electronic intrusion denial and detection are a must. The protective services of a bodyguard should also be considered; however, it is imperative to realize that any protective resource, be it structural, vehicular, electronic, animal, or human, can be breached or compromised. Hence, the ultimate responsibility for the defense of life must fall on the intended target. Based on the perceived threat level the target may be subject to, the time and capital investment needed to learn appropriate threat response alternatives will vary. For the principal selecting hard-option training, the training will be similar, if not identical, to that of a professional protective service agent. The curriculum of such training is discussed later in this chapter.

The most critical issue associated with force-response techniques is the employment of arms. It is the opinion of this author that weapons are mandated. Firepower, quite simply, is the definitive solution. Therefore, firepower is a necessary option. The use of firearms is not always necessary, but having the option is quite often the only guarantor of effective resistance. Knowledgeable resistance is effective in over 90 percent of attempted assaults. Such odds are sufficient justification for the mere presence of arms, which is a tremendous deterrent. Rhetoric aside, few of Hacker's *Crusaders, Criminals, or Crazies* are willing to actually die in the furtherance of their goals. Also, the psychological security provided by weapon availability is of significant benefit. The decision to be armed is critical and influenced by a number of variables. Arms are not for everyone and the decision, regardless of the risk level, is highly personalized.

Domestically, the right to keep and bear arms, especially concealed, is shrinking rapidly. (The propriety of this sociopolitical trend is beyond the scope of this work.) If a decision is made to be armed, the first step is to acquire the necessary training to effectively utilize the weapon. Such training must be geared to the utilization potential of the client. In other words, for the principal acquiring the necessary skills to employ deadly force in response to an assault, National Rifle Association Hunter Safety or Marksmanship classes are totally inadequate, and, in fact, may be deadly to the user. Defensive combat shooting is a science quite divorced from the traditional skills of hunting and target marksmanship.

Three probable sources for training remain: local programs sponsored by the police, private individuals, and commercial combat shooting schools. Programs sponsored by the police are fine for the average citizen desiring to use a weapon in his home. The courses, due to their short duration, are primarily geared to safety and basic marksmanship. Their greatest values are in the publicity generated by their presentation, the accident risk reduction, and the psychological and emotional security attendant on completion. For the executive client, such courses are of little value. Instruction from friends or private individuals may be a blessing or an invitation to disaster. The qualifications to teach such a vital and sensitive subject are rare. A common misconception is that police or military personnel, active or retired, are sufficiently qualified. Unfortunately, this is *rarely* the case. Few police and fewer military personnel are proficient in precise and selective armed survival skills, and the ability to teach the subject is even less common.

This leaves the commercial combat shooting schools. A number of these training centers are springing up around the country. Many are run by Walter Mittys or others with little, if any, legitimate experience or professional credentials. Several schools are run by current or past competitive combat shooting champions. These schools generally teach excellent reaction shooting skills but are often, though not always, poor in tactics. They have the tendency to teach shooting methods that are successful in competition. In real life, a firefight does not involve points and gamesmanship. Some of the schools are geared toward the survivalist crowd with emphasis upon militaristic type training and integrated family or group operations. This slant can be a plus depending on the qualifications of the instructors. A deficiency noted in these schools is that most of the training is geared toward a rural environment. Today's reality indicates that urban operations are a more likely probability. While no endorsement is offered here of any particular school, a strong theoretical and applied science approach is suggested. Caution is indicated if a school stresses only the mechanics of confrontation management. Also beware of a mercenary approach: Legal and moral considerations on the use of deadly force should be an integral part of any program.

In assessing the qualifications of the instructors, the following criteria is recommended for consideration. Instructors should have ground *combat* military experience, civilian law enforcement experience, preferably, street experience in a major city, a college background, martial arts training, teaching experience, and be articulate and professional in approach. The teaching philosophy should be one that stresses confrontation avoidance and places a premium on graduated response alternatives with situation control rather than suspect annihilation as the preferred modus operandi. However, the techniques and attitude in the employment of deadly force should be firm and presented in a noncompromising format. The instructors, in addition to having the requisite armed and defensive skills, should be politically and socially astute and possess strong intellectual abilities.

A serious recurring question in any discussion of personal weapon acquisition is one of legality. As alluded to earlier, the right to carry arms is rapidly shrinking throughout the United States. In foreign countries, the situation is far more restrictive. The following observations are made for consideration only, not as an urging to violate the law. Using the United States as a starting point, the carrying of concealed weapons is prohibited nearly everywhere. However, in some locations, concealed weapons permits are available. As a first order of business, an attempt should be made to acquire a weapons permit. If a permit is not available from local authorities, a search of other in-state or extra-state locations may reveal a more sympathetic agency. Use the corporate or personal attorney to assist in this matter. Even if the attorney does not agree with this step, survival is the more important consideration and the attorney works for you. The existence of a permit, even if from another state, *may* be an aid in the event of discovery by a police officer. There is no guarantee a discovery of such a violation will not result in serious legal difficulties. The circumstances of the discovery, the attitude of the officer, and the attitude and behavior of the principal will all have a bearing on the outcome. If a permit is not available, an individual is faced with the decision whether to carry a firearm illegally or surrender the option to use armed resistance. An examination of the Federal Bureau of Investigation's Uniform Crime Report reveals the appalling probabilities of falling victim to a crime of violence. Add to this the increasing activity of terrorist groups and one can show even through the most optimistic and conservative estimates an unacceptable risk factor. Contrast these probabilities with the chances of being stopped and physically searched by a police officer.

By way of a subjective judgment, it is better to be alive and in violation of the law then dead and legal. An evaluation on this issue is perceptual: no attempt should be made to coerce such a perspective on an unwilling candidate. The police and legislators are fond of saying that the province of protection is the exclusive domain of the police. In application, police rarely protect anyone; rather they are a reactive force that arrives postincident, takes a report, and then attempts to apprehend the perpetrator. This reactive, legal response does nothing to alleviate or negate the suffering or death sustained by the victim. The morality of the right to adequately defend oneself or the lives of loved ones and associates supersedes the legalities imposed by well-intentioned but unrealistic legislation. Thus, when deciding whether to be armed, the risks from both the criminal/terrorist element and the members of the various components of the judicial establishment must be juxtaposed.

The subjective personal decision arrived at must also bear the concomitant acceptance of both the positive and negative ramifications any such decision will have. The difficulties encountered in carrying weapons outside of the United States is quantumly greater than within the domestic territorial borders. Unless travelling by private air or water craft, a person should not carry weapons. Any weapons that are carried in a foreign country should be kept there. The ideal system for weapons procurement and use is through liaison with the host country's police, military, or intelligence services.

The selection of weapons for personal defense is an area deserving of a treatise in and of itself. The decision should be based on the following criteria: the physiological and psychological makeup of the user, the degree of concealability desired, where the weapon will be employed (for instance, the weaponry chosen for defensive purposes on a yacht or aircraft would differ from that chosen to be worn at the office), the cost of the armament, the aesthetic appeal of the weapon, and the firepower deemed necessary. No attempt is made in this chapter to recommend a caliber of weapon or resolve the revolver versus semi-automatic pistol debate. Each weapon has distinct advantages as well as disadvantages, and the school of training chosen will usually influence a person's choice in these matters. Pursuant to the criteria above, the selection process will reflect the priorities assigned by the user.

Training is the key to survival. Depending on the threat level defined, that training must be of appropriate depth. The term *training,* like terrorism, is a buzz word surrounded with all kinds of mystique. Training is the product of two variables with a common denominator. The formula can be presented in the following format: Training = (Knowledge + Repetition) ÷ Discipline. The most difficult of the variables to acquire is the discipline necessary for the intensive repetition by which one acquires the reflex actions vital to successful performance under stress. It has been observed that during periods of high stress, an individual will perform in almost direct relationship to the depth of his training. Training does more to alleviate panic than any other simple consideration. In fact, panic has been described as the absence of training. If a positive decision to acquire training has been made, the level of training needed, content, and presentation methodology must be evaluated before a selection is made. In the current market, *caveat emptor* is truly warranted.

All of the four training programs presented here include force utilization alternatives. The simple, low profile, passive response measures were discussed earlier and can usually be handled satisfactorily by in-house security managers or through personal research. However, when considering the acquisition of more sophisticated training, outside, highly specialized resources need to be used. Such training is expensive both in time and money but is extremely valuable once acquired and priceless if ever needed.

LEVELS OF THREAT RESPONSE TRAINING

Threat Response Training: Level I

This is the simplest of the programs designed and instructed by the author. This course is of primary benefit to the average citizen or small business owner, especially the older or less physically active participant. The threat level protection is against common criminal targets of opportunity actions. It is of limited value against a sophisticated criminal or terrorist action, especially an act involving multiple suspects. The course content is as follows:

Recommended length: 12–15 hours

Subject Areas

Legal/moral aspects of deadly force
Protection technology (locks, alarms, barriers)
Selection of firearms and munitions
Firearms safety
Defensive shooting techniques

Weapons transportation and concealment
Psychology of confrontation
Threat perception and identification
Suspect control procedures
Protective strategies for home, work, and travel

Threat Response Training: Level II

This course is an expanded version of the Level I program. The training is most beneficial for the average citizen, small business owner, and low-profile executive not associated with high-visibility or sensitive organizations. The course is of marginal value against sophisticated criminal or terrorist actions but of significant benefit against the common criminal or less accomplished political or cause activist. The course composition is as follows:

Recommended length: 24 hours

Subject Areas

Legal/moral aspects of deadly force
Protection technology (locks, alarms, barriers)
Firearms safety
Weapons and munitions selection
Characteristics and familiarization of firearms
Defensive shooting techniques
Weapons transportation and concealment
Psychology of confrontation
Stress conditioning
Threat perception and identification
Suspect control methods
Graduated force response techniques
Use of expedient weaponry
Weapons retention

Threat Response Training: Level III

This is an executive protection course and is designed specifically for the principal, though it may include selected members of his staff and appropriate members of his family. For the high-visibility principal, adequate training is a necessity, which must be far more intensive and broader in scope. It is the belief of this author that the security training of the principal should be identical to that of a professional protective service agent. In fact, the ideal situation is for the principal and his agent(s) to attend training together. The protectee can attend a somewhat abbreviated form of the training, but such training should be accomplished with selected members of his personal perimeter staff and family when appropriate. This procedure assists in developing confidence in the abilities of the participants, identifies areas of difficulty, and establishes good working rapport amongst the parties.

Program Duration

The program consists of 50 hours of professional instruction taught over an intensive, 6–12 day period, depending on the capabilities and time restrictions of the student(s). Classroom lectures, visual aids, and actual hands-on training exercises comprise the method of instruction.

Program Objectives

Training the principal, and selected members of his staff and family, in the tactics, techniques, concepts, and principles of executive protection and counterterrorist functions is the program objective. The program stresses all essential aspects of protective techniques for executives, celebrities, VIPs, and dignitaries.

Cost

Basic tuition cost, per student, is $1,250. Additional expenses for ammunition, personal weapons and gear, and a physical training uniform (GI) must also be borne by the pupil.

Weapons

Firearms that will be acceptable for student use must be examined and certified safe and fully operable by the staff armorer. The calibers acceptable are: .38 Special, .38 Super Auto, 9mm parabellum, .357 Magnum, and .45 ACP. It is highly recommended that the weapons used during training be the same or identical to those arms to be employed as protective resources.

Training Syllabus

Subject I: Theory and Problem Analysis, 3 hours
     A.   Legal/moral aspects of deadly force
     B.   The threat: Overview of the problem of international terrorism/Terrorist profiles/Kidnap-extortion-assassination modus operandi
     C.   Tools of the trade—an introductory glance
       Weaponry/Electronic aids/Body armor

     D. Psychology and physiology of violence and confrontation
Subject II: Armed Skills and Tactics, 20 hours
     A. Firearms and their tactical employment
        1. The handgun (pistol and revolver)
        2. The 12 gage pump shotgun
Selection, safe handling and care of firearms/grip, sighting. The draw and "leather"/multiple targets/night shooting/use of cover/basic ballistics/mental conditioning for combat.
     B. Expedient weapons
        1. Edged weapons
        2. Stick
        3. Improvised implements (credit cards, hypodermic syringe, belt, wire, etc.)
Methods of attack versus anatomical weak points/strategy of use/mental attitude/grip and stance, etc.
Subject III: Unarmed Combat Technique and Disarming Procedures, 12 hours
     A. Attack and defense using one's personal weapons versus vital points and the principles of balance, leverage, concentration of force and momentum.
     B. Neutralization of an unarmed threat to the protectee.
        1. Countering the approach
        2. Control methods
        3. Restraint techniques
        4. Suspect searches
No attempt is made to teach classical martial arts. Only practical methods that can be mastered speedily and applied under pressure are covered.
Subject IV: Physical Conditioning and Readiness, 2 hours
     A. Getting fit
The need for physical fitness as a survival tool/Recommended programs for the individual pupil to employ
     B. Staying fit
The importance of physical fitness maintenance. Techniques of maintaining fitness levels anywhere and under adverse conditions.
Due to the limited training time students will not participate in any physical training, but will be taught everything that they will need to know about building and maintaining their readiness levels on their own.
Subject V: Protective Methods, Tactics, and Principles, 11 hours
     A. Intelligence
        1. Research and data maintenance regarding threats and risks
        2. Liaison with law enforcement and other official agencies and bureaus
     B. Individual and team operations
     C. Risk surveys, threat analysis and assessment, and situation awareness
     D. Protective strategies
        1. Walking
        2. At protectee's home
        3. Theaters

 4. Functions
 5. At work
 6. Restaurants
 7. Vehicular protection and security assessment
 8. Travel
 9. Tactical evasive driving techniques*

The emphasis of protective strategies is on confrontation avoidance. Therefore, threat perception and identification are stressed as pre-emptive measures.

E. First aid and CPR

Essential traumatic injury skills; emphasis is on stabilizing the victim and evacuation to medical care facilities under protection.

F. Use of security aids
 1. Dogs
 2. Alarms
 3. Electronic surveillance
 4. Physical facility hardening

Subject VI: Hostage Survival, 2 hours

An overview of hostage incidents and behavioral strategies for survival.

The Level III and Level IV Threat Response Training courses were developed in cooperation with Bradley Steiner for the Executive Protection Program of the Phoenix Firearms Training Center. A terrorist training course is a good predecessor to the Level IV training. This course should be a duplicate of the courses taught to international terrorists: The goal is to assist the principal or protective service agent in thinking like terrorists and recognizing potential terrorist acts. Such training should include weapons, explosives, sabotage, document falsification, surveillance, surreptitious entry methods, intelligence-gathering techniques, disguises, and political theory. This kind of multiphase training is ideal, though not always necessary. The cost for such programs is obviously extremely time- and capital-intensive.

Threat Response Training: Level IV

This program is the most inclusive state-of-the-art instruction available for the individual student. The course is designed to provide the most professional approach possible for the training and evaluation of the professional protective service agent.

Program Duration

The professional protective service agent training course consists of 185 hours of instruction. The instruction may be given over an intensive five-week period or a phase instructional mode may be used to accommodate the needs of the client. Instructional format includes lectures, practical participation exercises, firearms and

---

* By special arrangement.

lethal/nonlethal unarmed combat and control related training, skills, and activities. In addition, the student is expected to do whatever homework and study may be required between formal instructional periods to effectively assimilate all material in the course.

Program Objectives

To train the individual for employment as a protective services professional in the executive-public figure protection industry is the objective. The qualified trainee will learn the techniques, tactics, skills, and technical understanding of the craft of protection and its related technology, so that he may provide professional services to corporate leaders, VIPs, and celebrities as a fully qualified and professionally competent personal security specialist.

A further goal is to teach the protective services student the proper use of firearms and other weaponry, as well as of the proper discretionary use of lethal/nonlethal force during the performance of his duties. The psychological/diplomatic/ethical aspects of protective services work is stressed so that the program graduate may be fully confident in dealing with all situations likely to occur.

Cost

Basic tuition cost, per student, is $3,500. Additional expenses for ammunition, personal weapons and gear, and a physical training uniform (GI) must be borne by the pupil.

Weapons

Students must provide their own sidearms. Weapons used in training should be identical to those used on duty. Acceptable caliber weapons are the .38 Special, .38 Super Auto, .45 ACP, .357 Magnum, and 9mm caliber. Weapons must be in excellent working condition and will be subject to examination by the staff armorer.

Training Syllabus

Subject I: Macro-Theoretical Analysis, 8 hours
    A.   Legal/moral aspects of deadly force
    B.   Weapons laws (concealment and procurement)
    C.   Political doctrine
    D.   Crisis geography
    E.   Threat examination: Overview of the contemporary international terrorist threat/Terrorist profiles/Kidnap-extortion-assassination *modus operandi*
    F.   Terrorist weapons
    G.   Psychology and physiology of violence, stress, and confrontation

Subject II: First Aid and CPR, 20 hours
Includes make up of complete emergency medical kit, treatment of major trauma injuries, poisoning, etc. Emphasis is placed on evacuation and stabilization techniques.

Subject III: Unarmed Combat and Control, 30 hours
A.   Attack and defense using one's personal weapons versus vital points, and the principles of balance, leverage, concentration of force, and momentum.
B.   Neutralization of an unarmed threat to the protectee
    1.   Countering the approach
    2.   Control methods
    3.   Restraint techniques
    4.   Suspect searches
No attempt is made to teach classical martial arts. Only practical methods that can be mastered speedily and applied under pressure are covered.

Subject IV: Employment of Expedient Weapons, 10 hours
A.   Expedient weapons
    1.   Edged weapons
    2.   Stick
    3.   Improvised implements (credit cards, hypodermic syringe, belt, wire, etc.)
Methods of attack versus anatomical weak points/Strategy of use/Mental attitude/Grip and stance, etc.

Subject V: Weapons Training, 40 hours
A.   Firearms: Techniques and tactics
    1.   The handgun (pistol and revolver)
    2.   The shotgun
    3.   Assault rifles
    4.   Sniper rifles
    5.   Special weapons (chemical, blast, SMGs, etc.)
Selection, safety, and maintenance of firearms/Grip, sighting, draw and "leather"/Characteristics of munitions/Multiple targets/Limited visibility shooting/Tactical movement/Use of vehicles/Entry-exit techniques for vehicles, windows, doorways, halls, stairwells, etc./Specialized techniques for aircraft and marine craft.

Subject VI: Principles and Procedures of Protection, 30 hours
A.   Intelligence
    1.   Research and data maintenance regarding threats and risks
    2.   Liaison with law enforcement and other official agencies and bureaus
    3.   Personnel and organizational background investigation techniques
B.   Individual and team operations
C.   Risk surveys, threat analysis, and assessment and situation management
D.   Protective strategies
    1.   Walking
    2.   At protectee's home

 3. Theaters
 4. Functions
 5. At work
 6. Restaurants
 7. Vehicular protection and security assessment
 8. Travel
 9. Tactical evasive driving techniques*
 10. Transportation and concealment of weaponry

The emphasis of protective strategies is on confrontation management. Therefore, threat perception and identification are stressed as pre-emptive measures.

Subject VII: Bomb Threat Procedures, 4 hours

Since over 70 percent of all violent attacks include some type of explosive device (letter bombs, car bombs, boobytraps, and emplaced or projected charges) considerable emphasis will be placed on the proper procedures for handling bomb threats.

Subject VIII: Protection Technology and Resources, 10 hours

 A.   Electronic surveillance and countermeasures
 B.   Alarms and antitamper devices
 C.   Use of dogs (guard, explosives detection)
 D.   Physical facility hardening
 E.   Tracking devices
 F.   Communications; equipment and procedures
 G.   Protective fashions
 H.   Body armor
 I.   Vehicle selection and modification

Subject IX: Mental and Physical Conditioning, 25 hours

Techniques and exercises to aid in the handling of stress during confrontation where violence is imminent or active. The maintenance and development of physical standards will be presented to cultivate mind/body unity for maximum efficiency and survival potential.

Subject X: Hostage Survival, 8 hours

 A.   Case studies of hostage incidents
 B.   Alternative behavioral strategies for survival

Subject XI: Special Skills**

The special skills portion is designed to implement integrated training for assault or rescue forces. Training may include mission-specific climatic or environmental tactics and procedures, advanced infiltration and extraction techniques, utilization of specialized weaponry, electronics, vehicles, explosives, and other assignment-related equipment.

---

* By special arrangement.
** Optional: Designed for organizational force option capability.

PROTECTIVE SERVICE AGENT: LUXURY OR NECESSITY?

In determining the necessity of employing a "professional protective services agent," the risk factor is obviously the primary consideration. Risk assessment is a matter of probabilities. Threat probabilities are determined generally by four variables concerning the protectee: visibility, sensitivity, vulnerability, and threat-specific. A brief examination of each of these variables is offered here.

Visibility is determined by the public exposure, either physically or through media sources, of the principal. Persons in prominent political, social, or economic/industrial positions are subject to visibility exposure. Examples of these positions by category might include political (e.g., president, governors), social (e.g., celebrities, persons holding controversial political or social opinions, members of eccentric cult or religious organizations, journalists) and economic/industrial (e.g., ranking officers in major corporate, industrial, or financial institutions).

Sensitivity exposure could include persons involved in sensitive endeavors, such as specific types of scientific research, or military and police officials. Personnel in this category may be targeted due to their activities or symbolic value. Vulnerability is generally determined by the amount of physical public exposure and the geopolitical environment. For instance, an executive of a multinational corporation is far more vulnerable in Latin America than in London. The last category of probability evaluation is threat-specific. In this case, the intended target is warned, either directly or indirectly, of a deliberate potential for violence. The warning may be the result of threatening phone calls, letters, and popular demonstrations, or the threat potential may be identified through intelligence activities by the police, military, or private sector. The principal may be exposed to one or all of the risk probabilities. Consequently, a decision to employ human protective resources should be based on the threat assessment recommendations of the security staff, outside security consultants, and the desires of the principal and his family. The advice of the local police or security services should also be sought; however, this source must be evaluated very carefully and in many cases it may be prudent to exlude such liaisons entirely.

Assuming the decision to employ a professional protection agent(s) has been made, the selection process is critical. The following is a discussion of considerations in the selection of a suitable candidate for such a sensitive position.

Personality

The personality of the candidate must be compatible with that of the principal and/or the principal's family, depending on the intended use of the agent. The agent and the protectee must like each other and have respect and confidence in the other's abilities. The protecting agent should be emotionally and psychologically *suitable* to the position. Quite often, this does not necessarily mean emotionally and psychologically "stable" in the contemporary sense, as defined by the psychologists and sociologists who tend to view anyone capable of exercising violence, even in a defensive capacity, as sociopathic. Common sense and pragmatics must be used to evaluate personality capabilities/liabilities rather than idealistic academic standards. This is not to say a mental case should be in a position of protective responsibility. The candidate and the protectee should have common interests. For instance, there is little in common between a senior executive who enjoys the ballet, theater, and chess and a young jock whose leading interests are disco dancing and football.

Other personality and behavioral traits desirable in a protection professional are awareness and alertness, energetic but controlled decorum, a good sense of humor, self-confidence, a strong but resilient ego, and a decisive and aggressive personality with a tendency to question. A good protection specialist is unlike a typical military, police, or security guard personality in that he is not likely to follow orders blindly and will possess a prominent capacity to exercise initiative and independent judgment in the face of criticism.

Intelligence

The mental agility of the subject must be well above average. A college degree is not a necessity but a college background is desired, as it is an indicator of initiative and desire, especially if the academic pursuits occurred after military service or during employment. College attendance immediately after high school is often a matter of convenience and the intellectual benefits are questionable. The candidate should be articulate and possess intellectual poise and analytical abilities especially in political and social affairs. Written expression on abstract subjects is an excellent indicator of these abilities.

Physical Appearance

Youth is a distinct disadvantage. The minimum age recommended by this analyst is 27–30 years old with an undefined upper age limit dependent solely on ability and physical condition. The physical size of the agent should be approximate to that of the protectee. Unless the principal is an entertainment celebrity whose security requirements include getting through a mob of screaming fans, extreme size is of no advantage and is often likely to prove a disadvantage. Rosie Greer for all his size was useless to Bobby Kennedy. Large physical size is commonly associated with bodyguards, and the guard is simply identified and eliminated first. A medium, athletic physique with coordination and speed is most desirable.

The physical appearance of the agent is vital. The protection professional must be able to blend with the environment of the protection principal. Therefore, a McCloud personality in a cowboy hat would be out of place in Manhattan. Likewise, a suave, continental type might be inappropriate in Dallas, Texas. The agent and the protectee should blend well. If the principal is in the habit of wearing three-piece suits, the agent should look and feel comfortable in the same. Avoid the obvious or the extreme, such as size: If you put a gorilla in a suit, you have exactly that—a gorilla in a suit. The hulking, knuckle-cracker in dark glasses is to be avoided by the principal wishing to take countermeasures against the sophisticated terrorist/criminal threat at large today.

Skills

The prior experience and background of the protective agent candidate helps determine skill levels, or assist in determining the ability to learn the very specialized skills necessary for a professional protection specialist. Prior police, military, and security backgrounds are desirable. Ideally, the subject should have all three, while ground combat experience is a priceless asset. Retired law enforcement or military personnel are not automatically suitable. An outstanding choice would be a former secret service agent, but even he should undergo retraining to equip him for the specifics of the position. Small arms (especially handguns), tactical training, human relations, martial arts, first aid, and driving expertise are desirable skills. However, unless the subject has been through a professional course designed for principal designee protection, suitable retraining must be acquired.

Use and Management

The use and management of a professional protection specialist is a delicate task. A top-flight professional possessing the physical and intellectual skills needed will not function as a security guard. Boredom is the greatest evil he faces; hence, the subject should be used in a meaningful and creative capacity within the protectee's lifestyle. For instance, a corporate executive could use an agent as a personal aide or administrative officer. The agent should not necessarily be a chauffeur but may sit with the principal or drive a lead or chase car. The agent should be near to the principal at the office and have visual control of access. He should accompany the principal to functions either directly or indirectly, depending on the circumstances. Compatability becomes critical here, because if the principal is not comfortable with the agent, he will not use him and the protection potential is immediately defeated.

Management considerations should include adequate, mandatory, physical, and skill maintenance training on a daily or weekly basis. Outside sources should be used to maintain loyalty determinations by attempting to subvert the agent— an unpleasant but necessary undertaking. The protectee must remember that when employing a personal protection agent, he is being constantly exposed to a potential assassin. Of particular value in the management of human protective resources is the utilization of coed teams. Physical strength is not a primary requirement and women can shoot as well as men. A mixed sex couple is far less obvious than several hulking guards. The protectee can move with greater comfort and less visibility utilizing male/female protective teams.

Under management, pay is a very important consideration. In today's economy and in attempting to draw the caliber of person necessary to the position, a salary of $35,000 per annum to start, clothing, lodging, and meal expenses is not unreasonable. To avoid burnout and as an incentive, liberally spaced vacation time as well as attendance at various security schools should be available. In the selection process, the protectee must like the agent, as must members of the family if the agent is to be used in that capacity.

Throughout this chapter, dogmatic absolutism has been shunned. Due to the complexities involved in providing adequate security, simplistic, all encompassing solutions are not available. Personal survival is a personal business. The risks, gains, and costs must be evaluated and ultimately decided on by the principal. Nothing is foolproof. There is no guarantee that if one does nothing that such a person will automatically fall victim to random or scheduled violence. Likewise, substantial investments of time and capital in technology, resources, and training are no guarantee the principal will be safe from attack. It is noteworthy though to mention that successful preventive measures are incapable of being evaluated. Nobody knows if a threat were ever present and if so, why did the threat not act.

On the other hand, failure is always quantifiable. Security failure is measured in fear, blood, and human misery. This chapter has attempted to provide some guidelines, both general and specific, about alternatives to victimization. The qualitative decisions regarding the relative value of human life must be made. The recognition that the innocent have greater value in life than do those who for whatever reason would prey on them is intrinsic to the issue. Such qualitative decisions are reflections of good and evil in a time when such distinctions are sometimes nearly impossible to define. A decision pregnant with the nearly god-like power of forfeiting human life is one that must be made in the innermost recesses of the conscience. No one can make such a decision for anyone else: It is a matter between an individual and his spirit. This author asks the members of the free nations of the world to recognize their individual worth and to refuse to be trampled beneath the bloody boots of terrorism and criminal violence. But, as is proper in a free society, the individual must decide. In this sensitive and critical area, personal survival is truly a matter of choice.

V

The Person

27

The Hardest Question

Richard W. Kobetz

H. H. A. Cooper

Money cannot buy personal security.

—Eric Hoffer[1]

Many people relish the spice of a little danger in their everyday lives. The desire for a taste of what might bring one's personal safety into question is probably in inverse proportion to the inherent dangerousness of one's position in life: Those with hazardous occupations are usually more grateful to have survived their rigors than those enjoying a more tranquil, stable kind of life. Whatever the case, there are few normal people who really enjoy involvement in sudden, unsolicited life-threatening encounters. For most, such adventures occur to *other* people or are to be vicariously—and safely—enjoyed through the medium of one's favorite television series. Violence is something that happens to the other guy, poor fellow—or serve him right, according to your personal perspective on these matters.

In our time, a good many whose life is in suburbia, with a safe if somewhat dull and increasingly tedious commute to an equally safe office or factory complex, are beginning to question that premise.[2] Looking over their shoulders, some can now sense, with apprehension, a brooding, unseen presence that may tinge their own lives with tragedy. Of these, perhaps, a majority, with the eternal optimisim of those who have attained the good life, simply hope that if no one makes too much of a fuss, whatever it is will go away. But an increasing number, more prudent and schooled in the art of self-help, know it will not. And they are resolved to meet its challenge before it consumes them.

An eye-catching poster neatly proclaims, "These Times Demand More of an Executive." The advertisement is for a deservedly respected daily newspaper, but its underlying sentiment perfectly mirrors the increasing demands on executive life in our age.[3] The modern executive has to face personal hazards of which earlier captains of industry could afford to be largely contemptuous. True, there has in every age been some Frick struck down by a malcontent, but the vast majority of executives in the United States had little to fear from such exotic sources. Even those whose business took them abroad with some frequency could reflect that while Uncle Sam was not universally beloved, his citizens' rights were generally respected and the almighty dollar bought a measure of safety rather than the reverse. By degrees, that comfortable picture has altered.

The term *terrorism,* capable of meaning all things to all men, has an increasingly familiar ring about it. The meaning for many executives has suddenly crystalized in all too personal a sense. The ordinary executive, not necessarily the very rich, the very powerful, or the doyens of the Fortune 500, woke up to the realization that, by accident or design, he might be a target.[4] A real enemy was out there murdering, mutilating, kidnapping, skyjacking, not some nameless whatever whose presence was vague and whose doings were ill-defined. A new factor had to be built into executive existence. If executives were to get on with their business of making money for themselves and other people, they had better be looked after while they did it. And so, in the sixties and seventies the term *executive protection,* no new one for sure, began to be extended to a whole new class of persons who had never needed it before. And with this extension came a whole range of problems. The people in the middle, as is ever the case, were caught in the crunch.

The most serious problem, generated by the dimensions the threat was now assuming, was an economic one. The problem, though burdensome, was never one calculated to trouble the very, very rich. They have always been able to afford, at least for themselves, the level of personal protection their wealth and status demanded. Similarly the "poor"—and here we are speaking in comparative terms of those at the very bottom of a relatively narrow class—were largely unaffected; they simply did not attract the lightning to themselves and if it struck at all, they were plain unlucky. With some shrinkage of the classes, the overall position remains substantially the same today. But those in the middle, the great bulk of all executives, face a greatly increased risk of victimization. And the economic wherewithal to provide the heightened level of protection their case would now demand is, for the most part, not there. The problem they face is not likely to go away of its own accord; as matters stand, the threat posed to executives by terrorism, in all its manifestations, is only likely to increase.[5]

In these uncertain economic times it is not in the cards that substantial resources will be diverted to providing the protection executives need. Some hard questions, indeed, are posed by this matter of executive protection. They concern the allocation of scarce resources to a job that is expanding in scope and complexity. What options are available that might commend themselves to those executives having more than a passing interest in their own safety and survival?

If you were rich enough—or important enough—it has always been possible to leave the matter of your personal security to someone else. This might evocatively be called the *De Gaulle* solution. It may be recalled that the French president admonished his bodyguards that it was *his* job to be De Gaulle, *theirs* to take care of him so that he could do it well. For those who can afford it, this solution has much to commend it. It leaves the business of providing protective services in the hands of the experts, and allows the protected person to get on with doing the job at which he is best. Such a level of protection is still possible today for a few heads of state, our own president among them.

For the rest, these massive displays of personal protection are largely cosmetic; they are simply too expensive to undertake with the thoroughness that is required. As for the private sector, who can afford such a display? And might not the very ostentation itself draw down the consequences that it is supposed to prevent?

How many bodyguards are needed to provide an effective screen, three, five—seven?[6] And these are the public face of the security operation. Behind such an apparatus is a tight administration concerned with advance arrangements, scheduling, intelligence and the like. None of this has much relationship to reality. Hard-pressed security departments do what they can, but most magnates and chief executives echo the U.S. Marine Corps and try to get along with A Few Good Men (and the very occasional woman).

The question must be raised, then, whether, given the current economics that govern the provision of protective services, even the privileged few should have these amenities conferred upon them. A trusted and efficient bodyguard can be a great comfort, provided he is not expected to perform at the level of Superman. Ideally, the bodyguard should be loyal, very fit, well trained, adaptable, unobtrusive, and sensitive to the needs of the situation. If he looks, talks, dresses and acts like an ambitious young executive, so much the better.[7] Logically, how many of these can you expect to gather together under one roof? In most cases, it comes down to this: you can have superlative protection some of the time, but you must reconcile yourself to the mediocre most of the time. There is no guarantee that the assassin, kidnapper, or whoever will accommodate himself to the most favorable segments of your security schedule.

Is it not the case that, in most boardrooms, a large measure of denial operates in these matters? We have these guys on the payroll (and we all know what they cost): They must be doing the job. Most executives would prefer not to enquire too closely. And most security directors, if they are honest about these things, would probably admit to themselves that they would just as soon have it that way. So far, we have only touched on the situation as it pertains to the top brass. What about the fellows a few rungs lower down the ladder? Under truly crisis conditions, or on special assignments, they may merit the occasional bodyguard, with whose presence they no doubt feel very uncomfortable. For the rest, they are on their own. Realistically, the vast majority of U.S. executives, whatever the sensitivity of their work or status, are expected to look after themselves. Can it really be otherwise?

Americans generally are a pretty independent lot. Even those whose means permit their whims to be catered to by others, enjoy doing things for themselves now and then. Many busy, senior executives can cook a passable omelette, fix an ailing automobile, even type the odd confidential memorandum. Surely, then, it cannot be wholly beyond them to undertake responsibility for their own security in an age of heightened risk? There are many, indeed, who might feel happy and challenged at the prospect. The hardest questions are these two: How much of their time and resources should be devoted to these matters? And what assistance might they reasonably expect from those to whom their working energies are ordinarily pledged? No useful, general answer can be given to these questions. Everyone's security needs are different.

Those whose business entails a good deal of risk need to dedicate more to guarding against it than others for whom danger is, ordinarily, an out-of-the-way occurrence. A careful, detached examination of individual security needs is a prerequisite. A little professional help is more than a little useful here. Those closest to the problem tend to see it out of proportion. They are rarely able to appreciate it in all its dimensions. Look at it this way: Only you can really improve your golf, but a good professional can save you a lot of time and anguish by showing you what is wrong with your swing.

The individual executive's security needs can best be considered under four broad headings: the home, the working environment, social and recreational interests, and travelling among them all. Each of these areas calls for a different assessment, and, according to the appraisal, a particular allocation of resources. The only constant is the executive himself; he is a part of all four settings. However the cake is sliced, the executive is the key to it all. Security is first and foremost a state of mind. The executive's own attitude towards his security determines his personal commitment to it and, to a large degree, the priority it receives in his affairs.

If, for whatever reason, the executive puts a low priority on matters relating to his own personal security, scant attention is likely to be paid to it and few resources will be allocated to seeing that he goes safely about his business. It is probably true to say that this is the case for a majority of executives in the United States. Their consciousness is generally raised only when they, or someone with whom they can identify, have suffered a nasty problem. Security is not a matter that commands much attention until it is breached. The busy executive is usually his own worst enemy in these matters.

Now we come to a very hard question indeed. The executive himself may have very good—if deplorable—reasons for ignoring or overlooking his own security needs. He may be just too pressed to attend to them. He may, generally, feel no apprehension for his safety, being blissfully unaware of the danger with which he is threatened.[8] Or he may be reacting to a well-appreciated sense of danger with a massive dose of denial. But those who employ him must surely operate to higher standards in these matters. They cannot shrug off the dangers by pleading the press of business. Nor can they remain blissfully ignorant of the dangers to which the pursuit of their business commits their executives. Denial can find no safe haven in the boardroom. Those who employ the executives threatened by these modern dangers as part and parcel of their calling have a duty towards them in these matters. The questions that must concern us here are, What is the nature and scope of that duty? And how is it to be discharged? It is prudent and responsible for those on whom those obligations fall to give this anticipatory consideration to them.

Given that it is, for the most part, unrealistic to expect that business enterprises shall furnish all, or even any, of their executives with permanent bodyguards, it is pertinent to enquire what these executives are owed in honor of their personal security. The universal watchword should be: *To each according to his need.* The concern for the personal security of individual executives must find practical expression in a measurement of those needs. The executive is entitled to know the extent of any extraordinary dangers he faces as a consequence of his job and those who employ him should make themselves responsible for seeing that those dangers are competently and professionally assessed. This is a process in which the executive, himself, must assist; but he cannot be expected to shoulder the responsibility unaided.

Some large enterprises have the advantage of an efficient, well-equipped, and directed security department capable of making the diagnosis and prescribing the treatment. Others do not, for their security needs have not, hitherto, demanded the type of services necessary for proper executive protection. This is a very specialized business; It is neither fair nor sensible to expect those whose main task is loss prevention to undertake the very difficult, and quite different, job of executive protection. The busy executive is owed the services of a conscientious security department, not too arrogant, on occasion, to seek specialist advice and assistance on matters beyond the scope of its own experience and range of activities.[9] Not seeking such advice promptly, where needed, can be a cause of liability if matters go wrong.

Those who employ the executive can orient and counsel him and, ultimately, fasten upon him the sense of responsibility for taking proper care of himself. But their duty does not end there by any means. Having discerned the risk, they must take the executive into their confidence so that he, too, is apprised of the dangers and of what is being done to meet them. This duty may be discharged by something as general as a briefing or orientation seminar. But where some particular danger threatens, where the executive, for example, is known to be a target, he must not only be told that this is the case, but also be given the opportunity to avoid or protect himself from the consequences of that unwelcome distinction.

He is entitled, too, to know what policies and provisions will apply in his case. What will happen if, for example, he is kidnapped? Will those who employ him bargain for his release? What resources do they have—and what are they prepared to commit—for the purpose of securing his release? Do his employers carry insurance for such contingencies? What is his own role in whatever arrangements might obtain in this unpleasant eventuality? Those whose employment carries foreseeable dangers—and the special hazards of being an executive under the circumstances we are considering here are foreseeable—are entitled to have any special knowledge pertaining to the risks shared with them. And they are entitled, too, to know what is being done to make them safe.

If the executive is to undertake, effectively, the task of protecting himself, he must be taught how to do so. Those who employ him must see that he has the training to do the job of looking after himself. In a troubled world, this requires more than handing out a few pamphlets or giving brief admonitory seminars on how violence might affect the working life of the executive. For the executive— and his loved ones—if they are at risk at all, are under the shadow of that risk while at rest, at play, and on the move, as well as while at work. Training must cover all these, otherwise there will be chinks in the armor that render its wearing quite pointless. Such training, if it is to be worthwhile, must be comprehensive and thorough.

It is the job of professionals, specialists able to suggest personal solutions to the executive's needs. Few organizations have all these skills in-house. For the majority, it is necessary (and for the rest, it probably makes sound economic sense) to employ reliable, outside consultants. Does the executive need an alarm system at his residence(s) (needs assessment)? What kind is best suited to meet his needs (technical selection)? Then follows the process of installation and, if the system is to be efficient and effective for the purposes for which it was designed, the executive and his family must be taught how to live with it and to operate it correctly. It is easy to brush these matters aside as tiresome. They are; and because they are often treated in that way, many home security systems are purely cosmetic and self-defeating. This is not an area for hobbyists or do-it-yourselfers. Not, that is, if you are after sound security.

The traveling executive needs a very special, and specialized, kind of training. It is not enough to instruct him to be alert; he must be taught in detail what he must look out for, the danger signals, the spoor of those who might do him harm. A good defensive driving course is a must for those who spend time on the road. Few businesses want to go to the expense of providing their executives with armored cars, and all that goes with them, but it is surprising what can be done with an ordinary automobile by a well-trained driver. Such skills increase the margin of safety and in a very dangerous situation, such as an ambush, can make the difference between life and death.

Under some circumstances, it may be advisable to train the executive in the handling and use of weapons, especially handguns. Nothing, perhaps, is so danger-ous as an executive carrying a loaded weapon with which he is unfamiliar and even afraid to use. Training for executives must always look toward the worst case.[10] The executive must be taught how to survive—if the situation is one in which survival is a possibility—until those concerned with his safety can do some-thing for him. Typically this is the kidnapping situation. Some have the natural stuff of which survivors are made, for others the "right" qualities and techniques have to be developed. The trained executive, like the trained soldier, has the better chance of survival.

The true executive blind spot is, all too often, his loved ones. It is useless protecting the executive if those who would harm or pressure him can be "got at" without hinderance. Any program of executive training for the purposes we have been considering must include family and others close to the executive. What use is the most sophisticated, best-installed home alarm system, if the wife opens the door to the kidnapper believing him to be the television repairman? What does it matter if the executive can do "bootleg" turns like a stuntman out of the "Dukes of Hazzard" if his wife happens to be driving when kidnappers try to force the family car off the road? The executive himself might have been trained to hold up under a Gestapo interrogation, but how well will he resist when it is his son in the hands of the terrorists? Training for family and loved ones is different in nature and degree, but it has essentially the same objective—keeping the executive safe and his mind on the job.

The executive is a valuable investment, a precious national resource. Terrorist and extremist groups hit lists are a measure of that value in strategic and tactical terms. Commerce and industry can be quickly distorted and destroyed by striking decisively at the key human element. The business executive is the symbol par excellence of capitalism; he is what makes the system, in all its variety, work. Those who hate capitalism get a dual satisfaction from striking at the executive for the action is expressive and instrumental at one and the same time.

The executive has all the strengths and weaknesses of being human. Unlike other assets, he can, at least, take part in the processes designed for his protection. He should be encouraged and materially aided to do so. Such a policy is certainly sound and responsible business. As the case is stated here, it may well be the law.

NOTES

1.   *In Our Time* (New York: Harper & Row, 1976), p. 26.

2.   "No one is fully safe. Are we not all vulnerable and mortal?" Michael Maccoby, *The Gamesman* (New York: Simon and Schuster, 1976), p. 220.

3.   *The New York Times,* October 23, 1982.

4.   Or, of course, she, in increasing numbers as women begin to capture the positions their talent and industry can rightfully command.

5.   It is interesting, reviewing the abundant literature of the past decade, that no responsible authority has predicted a decline in terrorism, or suggested a shift away from business as a target.

6.   The Schleyer and Moro cases gave a sickening demonstration of how ineffective is the numbers game. The well-prepared, determined assailant making use of the inestimable advantages of surprise and initiative can penetrate virtually any screen.

7.   It has been sagely observed in another context that, "One can't successfully follow St. Paul's technique of being all things to all men without a change of suit." Graham Greene, *Our Man In Havana* (New York: Viking Press, 1958), p. 8.

8.   As it has been picturesquely put, ". . . like a fly meticulously cleaning its wing in the shade of a descending swatter . . ." Vincent Bugliosi and Ken Hurwitz, *The Shadow of Cain* (New York: W. W. Norton, 1981), p. 40.

9.   Lawrence Peter's admonition should be borne in mind here: "A manager having problems in a specific area of his business is probably the least qualified to evaluate the competence of an expert in that special area." *The Peter Prescription* (New York: William Morrow, 1972), p. 44.

10.   ". . . It is always the unexpected that paralyzes men." Emma Lalthen, *Going For The Gold* (New York: Simon and Schuster, 1981), p. 51.

28

Avoiding Capture and Surviving Captivity

Gerardo Capotorto

The possibility of being kidnapped must neither become an obsession nor cause fatalistic attitudes, which definitely work in the favor of potential kidnappers. At the other extreme, a no-security attitude, two of the most widely held notions should be countered:

- "The chains imposed by security prevent me from carrying out my work in the best manner." It is better to agree on security measures with experts and to keep in mind that once kidnapped, one cannot work at all.
- "If they want to kidnap me, they will do it anyway." Even if this statement is accurate, terrorist groups, usually not having many people available for a kidnapping, do not want to risk them by taking chances beyond those normally planned for. Often, the objective most easily realized is the one chosen; for this reason, a few preventive measures may persuade kidnappers to direct their efforts toward targets that are equally remunerative but less risky.

Protection against risk of attacks in general, or of kidnappings in particular, cannot be limited to a listing of norms of conduct. It must consist of the acquisition of behavior and of habits that make kidnapping more difficult. Criminal or terrorist organizations usually try to reduce their own risk to a minimum; if the programming of an attack on a particular victim raises questions that are not easily resolved, the kidnappers generally desist from the attack or continue observing until the doubt is cleared up.

Apart from these considerations, an official who is conscious of his value to his family and to his organization must rigorously and relentlessly observe security principles to reduce the probability of becoming a victim. This does not mean that he must live in a state of continual tension; rather, having acquired an active attitude toward security, he can act by a sort of acquired instinct and thereby lead an almost normal existence.

DAILY SECURITY SUGGESTIONS

Some security-enhancing suggestions concerning typical daily activities are listed below. These norms of conduct are also generally recommended by qualified police agencies.

At Home
- Each family member, including children, must be aware of the need to put cautionary measures into practice. Therefore, all family members and servants must feel committed to preventing criminal actions or to limiting their damage.
- Do not open the door to anyone who is not expected or who has not clearly identified himself. When the door is opened, make sure that others are not waiting around near the entrance. There are many ways to check, including use of a simple peephole or a parabolic mirror, a video-intercom, or television systems.
- Pay attention to strangers who spend time in the neighborhood for no apparent reason. Follow the movements of cars that repeatedly pass in the neighborhood; if possible, note their license numbers and characteristics and inform security officers.
- Instruct family members and service personnel not to answer strangers who ask about the activities or schedules of the head of the family.
- If a telephone caller asks for the head of the family when he is not at home, ask the caller to leave a message, that the person called is unable to come to the phone. Do not allow the caller to realize that he is gone, or to ascertain his actual whereabouts.
- Do not allow repairmen or men who check gas or electricity consumption into the house if they do not have an appointment.
- When the family is absent, service personnel must not let any stranger into the house.
- Be suspicious of telephone calls in which unknown callers say they dialed the wrong number.
- Friends or persons who telephone often should be asked to report if they receive a busy signal during hours in which the telephone is normally used. This could mean that the telephone is being tapped, and the situation should be reported to the police.
- Do not grant telephone requests to go to some place other than home or the office if you are not certain of the identity of the person calling.
- Make sure that whoever visits the home is really the person who is expected.
- If possible, accompany children to school, even over a short distance. Make an agreement with the teachers that the children can be taken from school before the end of classes only by parents or other very well-known persons.
- Do not personally open large envelopes or packages arriving in the mail if they have a suspicious look about them.
- Avoid telling strangers about plans for short trips or about absences of any family member from the house.

- In certain cases it is prudent not to list the telephone number in the directory, or to place it under the name of another family member with a different surname.
- If it is necessary to keep confidential documentation at home, make sure that it is adequately protected.
- Keep an updated list of emergency telephone numbers.
- Never leave the keys to the house or apartment outside, within the reach of anyone (under the doormat or in a vase of flowers, for example).
- Do not accept unexpected packages addressed to the person who is being protected. If the sender is known but if the package is not expected, call to make a check. In case of doubt, tell the police.
- Before leaving home, attentively observe nearby areas, unknown persons and cars, those who stay or work in the neighborhood, vehicles that are parked or are waiting (with motors running), particularly those that have passengers inside. Take note of the characteristics of vehicles, their license numbers, and any other distinguishing features. If necessary, inform your security service or the police of the presence of persons or vehicles that have no apparent reason for being in the area. A person may not feel able to carry out a thorough check of the world in which his home is located, but after a while, he will notice that he is able to pick out a series of situations previously not noticed; by continuing this activity in his own neighborhood, will become so familiar with it that the presence of unexpected persons or things will immediately attract his attention.
- Try not to leave home at the same hour every day. Also, notice whether anyone is waiting near the entrance door.
- It is advisable to have security systems installed in the home that can provide an effective barrier, as well as a security alarm system. Such systems not only prevent access by unwanted persons, they may also reduce the risks of fires.

In Transit
- Always leave the car locked, even in the garage. Put a lock on the gas tank. Pay attention to signs of a break-in on the garage doors, to car doors that are open or tampered with, to car hoods that are opened or tampered with, to scratches or traces that may have been made by tools, to suspicious dents, etc. Be alert to any tampering with your vehicle.
- Check the wheel nuts and the hollow of the spare tire. Make sure the exhaust pipe is free and not blocked by foreign objects. When in doubt, do not touch anything and do not start the car—call the police.
- If possible, avoid habitual routes; use alternative routes even if it lengthens your commuting time. Avoid regular schedules of departure and arrival; if you suspect that you are being followed, change the direction of the car suddenly. If your suspicion was founded, drive toward a secure place or toward the nearest police station.
- Pay attention to traffic jams, to accidents, and to other obstacles. Be wary

of requests to stop, even those made by police in uniform. If possible, avoid the scene of an accident. If forced to stop, remain inside the car, close the doors, and try to catch the attention of a police agent. If you have a radiotelephone, transmit the situation immediately.

- Pay attention to vehicles that follow your car and those that you notice repeatedly, even if they are three or four cars away.
- Make notes of suspicious occurrences, car licenses, persons, or things. Always leave the notes in the car, never in your pockets, and at the first opportunity, tell the police. If you notice that you are being followed, try to travel on crowded streets; stay away from traffic obstructions; avoid wedging or passing other cars. Always try to allow yourself a margin of space in which to maneuver. In situations of extreme danger, keep in mind that you can move a car that blocks the street by hitting it in the side about one-third of its length from the front. Obviously, if you travel in a compact car and a much heavier vehicle is blocking the street, the attempt will result only in damage to your car.
- While driving, maintain a good safety space between your car and vehicles in front of you, particularly vans and trucks. Avoid becoming boxed between two vehicles. Do not always stop at the same gas station. Do not leave home with less than half a tank of gas. Always have your car washed or repaired in the garage or auto shop that provides the highest guarantee of security.
- If possible, use a car with a chauffeur. Sometimes, a previously agreed upon simple sign of understanding will help you to avoid anomalous situations. Help your chauffeur in making observations; you will increase your margin of security.
- If you regularly take taxis, avoid taking the first in the line or the one that stops next to the sidewalk where you are waiting. Do not allow the driver of the taxi to stray from the established route without a good reason. If something makes you suspicious, leave the vehicle as quickly as possible, noting, if you can, the license number.
- Your car does not necessarily have to have antiprojectile glass; anti-break-in glass and reliable security locks have proved effective.
- Keep in mind that cars that use antiprojectile glass must be strong enough to withstand six projectiles of the weapons in use and that they must have protection devices and endurance equal to that of the glass.
- Do not leave your keys with parking lot attendants. Before leaving a parking lot, make sure that the exhaust pipe is unobstructed.
- Avoid bad neighborhoods and streets, especially in the evening hours. Try to drive in the center of the road, and if you stop at a stop sign, wait attentively. If you notice that a vehicle that precedes you is forcing you to slow down in order to make you follow it, at the first favorable opportunity, pass it, remembering that the other car could swerve to prevent you from making the maneuver.
- If you travel by air, reserve a place just before leaving—if possible, under a false name. At the airport, pick up the boarding pass only at the last moment

or have someone you trust get it. Ask for the credentials of the person who comes to meet you at the airport of arrival.

- If you travel by train, try not to be alone in a compartment. Get used to keeping an eye on the baggage of each occupant. Never leave your baggage unprotected, and be immediately wary of abandoned luggage.
- Try to reserve hotels at the last moment to avoid being predictable. Keep in mind that telephones can always be monitored by the hotel telephone operator even if you can dial directly outside. Take precautions when you are in the room, so that you will be aware if someone tries to enter. Get used to setting up some elementary traps to ascertain whether your baggage was searched during your absence. It is prudent to take a room far from the bar, the restaurant, or night-life locales. Avoid allowing your address to appear on bills and on invoices—always use your office address. Do not let others know your plans.
- Use hotel safety boxes for confidential company documents, as well as personal valuables, including papers.
- Be aware that apparently chance meetings in hotels or in other places might be prearranged.
- It is advisable to photocopy all personal documents to be left at the office.
- Do not take walks near your home or office and avoid isolated or country roads. Do not walk along the same street every day at the same time; it is preferable to change streets and schedules often. Keep in mind that attacks are more likely if it is possible to await the victim at a convenient point.
- Avoid picking up hitchhikers, and do not stop to observe accidents or confusing situations in traffic. Use utmost caution if strangers ask you for help.

In the Office

In addition to ordinary procedures for checking and directing persons who enter the headquarters of the company, further procedures and special precautions should be adopted. Some of these are outlined below.

- Avoid excessive personal or family publicity (e.g., publications of photographs, news of places habitually visited, etc.).
- Do not leave important documents unwatched.
- Always keep boxes, closets, or safes that contain confidential documentation closed.
- Ask the personnel of the secretarial office
  not to furnish, without good reason, information on comings and goings, travel plans, reasons for absences, etc.;
  not to furnish telephone numbers, personal addresses, etc., to third parties;
  not to leave unguarded documents that contain travel plans, meeting plans, etc.;
  to avoid discussions about work, travel plans, etc., in public;
  to use maximum precautions when the mail arrives to protect against letter-bombs.

• In examining any package, it is wise to note
excessive weight in relation to size;
the presence of adhesive tape or protruding or unexplained string;
any special or inexplicable odor;
reinforcements with cardboard or metal (such reinforcements could contain
spring percussion pins).

Avoid opening any suspicious package; leave the task to experts. Do not
immerse a suspicious package in water; keep it far from heat sources; isolate it
and call the security service.

These suggestions are not exhaustive, nor do they pretend to foresee every
dangerous possibility. They are only an invitation to pause and think about new
situations, finding the best solution for each one. Even in doing this, one will not
be absolutely safe; but without doubt, the risk of becoming involved in the subsequent
phase, the kidnapping, will be greatly reduced.

THE KIDNAPPING

The kidnapping phase is short: The victim is almost always caught by surprise,
and within a few seconds he must make a choice, often a decisive one for his
survival, about how to react to the situation. Because the purposes, motivations,
and personalities of the kidnappers, the circumstances and scenario of the crime,
and the personality and attitude of the victim can be so diverse, it is useless and
perhaps dangerous to attempt to codify a single line of conduct.

This phase is the same whether the kidnapping is for extortion or for political
reasons. The victim passes quickly from a state of liberty to one of physical coercion,
with few possibilities for modifying his position. The carrying out of this phase
also signifies that all previous defenses of the victim have been overcome or rendered
useless and that the situation is, for the time being, under the complete control
of the kidnappers.

However, on the basis of interviews with persons who have lived through
this dramatic experience, from examination of judicial reports, and from the results
of police investigations, it is possible to extract some general information about
safeguarding the life of the hostage. Also, if the victim has developed an active
attitude toward security and a pattern of cautious behavior prior to the kidnapping,
his reasoning process will be better prepared to cope with fast-moving events.

It is important to remember that this is the worst moment, in terms of nervous
tension, for the kidnappers; an unexpected reaction by the victim could have dire
consequences. If one has been caught by surprise, any attempt to fight back is
useless; resistance would have the effect of worsening the situation. The crime is
completed in a very brief time, during which period the victim is often quickly
rendered unconscious by sleep-inducing drugs.

If the victim of an attack thinks it is possible and would be effective to resist,
he has a chance of putting the kidnappers at a disadvantage. However, this situation

is very complex, and one can unconsciously react in an ill-advised way with grave risk for one's own safety. It is necessary to make an immediate and precise evaluation, and it is well to remember that the primary objective is to survive and reacquire one's freedom.

IMPRISONMENT OF THE VICTIM

With this phase begins one of the most complex, most devastating, most difficult experiences in all human experience. Instantly, the kidnap victim passes to a state of prostration. He becomes an unprotected and helpless hostage whose human dignity is under attack. The fear of the unknown, the absence of affection, the dramatic change of one's own condition, the disruption of well-developed habits, the strange food, the impossibility of satisfying in a decorous manner one's primary needs, the physical and psychological violence, and the inability to organize one's own life have a devastating effect on the kidnap hostage.

One must discipline oneself to react rapidly, even if not forcefully; to overcome the shock caused by the new conditions; to immediately regain one's dignity and subsequently let it be understood that one is not prepared to lose it. Some kidnappers will be influenced by this strength. The wrongs that one has been subjected to often generate unexpected force of spirit, which strengthens the body even in the most difficult conditions, prevents spiritual collapse, and helps one to analyze the situation realistically.

In this phase, the victim experiences detachment from the world; it becomes difficult to be aware of the time; visual and acoustic isolation may be total; freedom of movement may be so limited as to impair blood circulation; the humiliation of being chained like an animal is enormous. But one survives. It is difficult to comprehend the powers of adjustment our organism is endowed with, the physical force that is unleashed by desperation.

The victim of an extortion kidnapping recounted the following experience: He was held hostage for about four months, during which time he was constantly in isolation, without any direct contact even with the kidnappers. He was kept in a narrow underground cell that did not permit him to stand up and that was illuminated constantly by a weak electric light. He was held by the neck with a chain, which prevented him from approaching a trap door, the only exit from the underground hole.

The isolation, the abandonment, not knowing anything about the outcome of negotiations, not knowing what his relatives were doing to save him, and not knowing the attitude of his friends and colleagues produced such anguish in him that he sometimes thought of suicide. He experienced some psychological relief by fantasizing situations from which he always emerged the absolute and dominant victor; more and more often, this became his world, his refuge, but whenever he took stock of his actual state, deep frustration pervaded him, throwing him cruelly back into a condition totally opposite from his fantasy. The weak light of the bulb and the narrowness of the cell gave him the almost physical sensation of pressure from the walls; the poor air flow made him fear suffocation. He felt that he was on the verge of madness and desperately disciplined himself not to dream. He began to develop a rational process that would enable him to live his life realistically, filling the long hours with activities to which he dedicated himself decisively.

Because his narrow cell did not permit him to remain in a standing position, he sometimes noted the overwhelming need to feel the weight of his own body on his legs. To achieve this, he would touch the ceiling with his shoulders, keeping his head lowered. He invented exercises that would keep his muscles active, involving by degrees all the muscles of his body. He developed a combination of mental and physical exercise that permitted him to find out how many parts of his body have a decisive function in survival.

The methodological employment of his hours led him to measure his cell, to calculate its volume, to count the number of bricks of which it was composed. He calculated the length of the chain, giving a value to each link; he determined its volume and its weight; he devised a system for detaching it from the wall.

He began to construct a calendar, moving a stick on the fissures of the bricks that formed the walls. He tried to calculate precisely how long he had been a prisoner, but he knew he had only a vague idea; he asked his jailer when the jailer brought food, but he was not given an answer. He estimated that approximately 22 days had passed since the date of his kidnapping, and from that day he began to keep track. Not being able to calculate the hours, he estimated them on the basis of the frequency of his bodily needs and the time at which he was brought his food.

He mentally ran through all the periods of his life, seeking to recall and consider only events that actually happened in the past. He started reciting almost forgotten poetry, and he realized the power of human memory. A believer, but no longer practicing a formal religion, he developed a closer relationship with God, drawing from it a great interior calm.

Each day he tried to make a great new discovery in his narrow cell. Always rational in every aspect of his experience, he came to consider being abandoned with no chance of being rescued. He was fatalistically prepared for the idea of not surviving. However, he did not abandon the possibility of exploiting any favorable situation; he developed a plan to undertake whenever the kidnappers were not around for two days. His mental organization permitted him to live and kept him from vegetating.

When his kidnappers freed him and told him to leave the cell, his calendar showed that 157 days had passed; in reality, his imprisonment had lasted 128 days.

In other cases, imprisonment is much more agitated. The hostage is often forced to undergo an uninterrupted barrage of questions, threats, accusations, disparaging comments about one's fate and the possibility of a happy outcome, blackmail, and psychological traps. In extortion kidnappings, these questions, mixed with threats and sometimes with beatings, tend to be aimed at measuring the exact economic possibilities of the kidnapping. Almost always, the information the kidnappers have is very superficial—far from a precise estimation of the victim's assets and liabilities. Estimation is usually based on apparent facts, deduced from visible or publicized information and from outsiders' perceptions.

The hostage situation is one of extreme difficulty for the victim. He must be convincing and credible, and he must believe that the action undertaken by his family confirms his own statements. Many kidnap victims, after being freed, have commented on the mistake of not having made general agreements with one's own family about the conduct to maintain during a possible kidnapping.

The situation for those who are kidnapped for political reasons is very different. Besides being a hostage, the victim in a political situation is accused in a grotesque political trial where the ideological motivations make any attempt at defense useless. In this phase, it is best to avoid polemical attitudes, but it is also dangerous to immediately express willingness to cooperate. This is a subtle game in which one's right to human dignity must be affirmed, while at the same time, an understanding of the motives of the kidnappers must be evinced, to give the appearance of a vague form of collaboration.

During the interrogations, the kidnappers try to surprise the kidnap victim so that he will make unguarded statements; they will use any expedient, from the friendly attitude of one to the hard and brutal attitude of another. The hostage must think through the answers he gives, to evaluate their consequences and possible verification, keeping in mind that he should stick to already known facts, to which his captors cannot give distorted or subjective interpretations.

The length of the interrogations, the ideological motivations of the kidnappers, the exploitation of occurrences, the depression of the hostage, and his anguish and anxiety, which grow with the length of his imprisonment, can be ably exploited by jailers, who are assured of parallel interests. Both the hostage and the kidnappers want to see the demands met.

Only infrequently is the victim's sentence decided beforehand; but it is outside his direct control, although he can by his attitude modify it, sometimes for the better and sometimes for the worse. The hostage often believes that by not contradicting his jailers, he keeps the threat of death or of mistreatment more remote; for this reason, he instinctively tries to establish a human contact to safeguard his dignity and to keep from being considered a piece of merchandise of exchange.

These subtle games, these psychological constructions, can cause the hostage to begin to depend on his jailers, to identify himself with and eventually to develop a contact with them, and in extreme cases, to collaborate unconsciously or convert to their ideologies. In other cases, when the hostage begins to identify with his jailers, he can develop a negative attitude toward those who are negotiating with the kidnappers. If the kidnappers' requests are not promptly met, he feels betrayed and abandoned; his friends are seen as enemies, responsible for various imaginary wrongs.

Not infrequently, the kidnap victim is exposed to violence; sometimes he is subjected to real torture. In such cases, it seems advisable to resist as long as possible. While this may seem a sadistic sort of advice, it should be kept in mind that if one gives the impression that torture is the way to obtain confessions, the violence is likely to become even more frequent and less humane.

During imprisonment, kidnap victims tend to exaggerate the negative content of their own attitudes, fearing the critical judgment of the public. For the sake of emotional well-being, the hostage must keep in mind that his main responsibility is to survive.

It is impossible to establish a rigid and predetermined model of conduct for victims in hostage situations. But it is worth noting that many kidnap victims have reported that while exposed to physical and moral coercion, they had the clear feeling of possessing more moral strength and of being enormously better than their jailers.

THE FAMILY

In this phase, like the previous phases, it is not possible to impose fixed plans, because the elements in play are extremely numerous and diverse. Economic, environmental, affective, cultural, and religious factors, health conditions, and the age of the victim are all significant, and, according to the situation, any of them may have preeminence over the others.

The family faces the first impact of a kidnapping alone. If the kidnapping happens at home, family members are often anxious witnesses to the crime; if the kidnapping occurs outside home, the family usually learns of the situation via a telephone call. After sending a message for help to the security service or to the police, family members are well advised to stop and not do anything, to discipline themselves to manage their emotions, and to wait calmly. If the confusion and desperation in the family have reached a chaotic level, the person with the most authority must begin to command the attention and the expectations of the others.

Kidnap negotiations require specific preparation and professionalism. They should be entrusted to trained persons who can form a task force. This force, which should include an authoritative representative of the family, must be given a mandate to act and to proceed in the name of the family. The task force should manage every aspect of the case and should delegate one member and a substitute to negotiate directly with the kidnappers.

Simultaneously with the creation of the task force, the family should seek help in alleviating its anxieties from an expert who possesses professional experience and is also endowed with psychological introspection. If the person selected is reliable, his work will be irreplaceable and the consequent trust he inspires will be invaluable.

Difficult questions from the family about the terrorists' modus operandi must not be pushed aside, but they must not be answered in a crude or traumatizing way. These questions reflect deeply felt emotions. Often, an examination of the questions themselves will bring to light possibilities for achieving favorable outcomes.

The first days of a kidnapping are highly stressful because of the continuing presence of friends and relatives who wish to show their solidarity, because of the presence of police officers who must carry out their investigations, and because of the mass media seeking news that might interest the public. As a kidnapping is prolonged, family members experience progressive deterioration of psychological defenses, physical weakening, and diminishing of the force of spirit, which gradually lead to increasingly frequent phases of depression.

The activity of the expert assumes decisive importance; he must use any means to prevent depressive states, to prolong the vitality of the family's psychological defenses, because as time passes, greater strength of spirit becomes more and more necessary. This activity, of course, is not an end in itself; it must be developed in tandem with the task force, and it has the overriding purpose of bringing about a favorable outcome to the episode. Three distinct and overlapping aspects are involved: the interrogation of the victim, the reactions of the family, and the negotiations. The family and the task force are at a disadvantage in that they can only guess at the attitude of the victim and the effort and tactics he has followed to prove himself credible to the kidnappers. They must undertake a process of evaluation in reverse. Here, the contribution of family members is decisive, because they must provide insights into the personality of the hostage and how strenuously he may have worked to make himself credible.

Sometimes many written communications come from the hostage to the family or to friends; the form and content of these messages can reveal a great deal about the attitude of the hostage. For example, the distortion of facts known only to spouses may be a signal to disclaim an earlier extorted message or a hint that the victim wants more decisive interventions.

In other cases, the almost total absence of written messages eliminates the possibility of any evaluation and also causes the family members extreme anxiety; this may arouse critical attitudes that can lead to initiatives that backfire on the hostage or that make his release less likely. The psychological expert at the family's side must defend the family members and try to prevent any external disturbance from worsening the already existing difficulties.

This mass of stressful circumstances is aggravated by economic factors that emerge from ransom negotiations and that may concern the kidnappee's salary during imprisonment, insurance payments, expenses for specialized agencies in the kidnap negotiations, or the amount of interest on requested loans. The family of the victim must be reassured of everyone's commitment to do all possible until the prisoner is released. When the kidnappee's company is involved, cooperation and mutual support should be maintained.

Things get complicated, unfortunately, when governmental responsibilities arise and when kidnappings for political reasons are justified on ideological grounds with social implications. These are very delicate situations, since the interests of the state must be juxtaposed with consideration for the individual. One can hardly deny the family of a victim kidnapped for political reasons the right to disassociate itself from the "reason of state" and to propose its own initiatives to save the life of a loved one. The family must play an important and decisive role, and they must be given guidance and direction to facilitate this task.

Appeals to personalities in government, to international bodies, or to charismatic authorities may be necessary; the media, particularly the television networks, must be wisely exploited. It requires a huge effort, but the family must increasingly underscore its presence, constantly renewing its efforts to move public opinion, to deepen the interest of the kidnappers in the social content of its interviews, to utilize government proposals.

Finally, experience has proved that each family member should have a recent photograph of himself or herself and should keep in the home faithfully updated, the following information:

- Name
- Nickname
- Place and date of birth
- Address of principal residence, and telephone number
- Address of secondary dwelling places, and telephone numbers
- Precise physical description (e.g., height, weight, any prostheses)
- Prescription for eyeglasses, if used
- Identifying characteristics (e.g., birthmarks)
- Chronic illnesses
- Special medicines and instructions for their use
- Pharmacies regularly used
- Vehicles (types and licenses)
- School (type, class, address, names of teachers)
- Recent information on educational qualifications, specializations, hobbies, etc.
- Information about friends residing in diverse localities, including their telephone numbers

It is wise to compile notes in one's own hand, to provide a sample of handwriting, which is sometimes not easily found among the papers of a kidnap victim. The notes could be read into a tape recorder as well. These notes could serve as an excellent tool for interpreting messages.

Finally, one must remember that everything, even this period of anguish, comes to an end. Whatever the outcome, the kidnap victim's family must know that they did everything humanly possible to be reunited with their loved one.

29

Surviving Captivity I: A Hundred Days

Leon D. Richardson

The ordeal of Leon D. Richardson, the Australian businessman kidnapped by leftist guerrillas in Guatemala and held for a hundred days in an underground cell, was described in Chapter 19. Repeatedly interrogated, the target of deliberate psychological harassment to try to keep him off balance, Richardson recognized the games played by his captors and launched his own campaign of psychological warfare. This chapter presents his story in his own words. Since his kidnapping, Richardson has written and lectured extensively about the experiences of being a hostage. Portions of this chapter have appeared in Kevin Sinclair, *Kidnap: A Victim's Story,* Hong Kong: Ted Thomas Limited, 1982, and in various articles written by Mr. Richardson.

"THIS IS THE ONE"

I was in Mexico on business, on a work-regimented week of visits with my local distributor and my sales agent, and took the opportunity for a short side-trip to Guatemala City to meet two of my company's regional representatives. The first was the manager of our operations in Mexico and the northern part of Latin America, Carlos Henriques. A taciturn, reliable businessman, a former soldier in the Portuguese colonial army, Henriques was a man of few words and decisive actions. He had worked for me for four years. The other man was Rudolfo Obregon, youthful, handsome, a relative newcomer to the firm. He was employed as a management trainee and was in charge of the distribution of our products in his native Guatemala.

Business began early on February 10, 1981. I had been up with the sun before breakfasting at the El Conquistador Hotel in Guatemala City with Carlos and Rudolfo. By 7 A.M. we were on the road, making the rounds of factories and plants in the capital of Guatemala to find out what customers thought of our products.

We left the hotel and began the round of calls. We traveled in Obregon's car. Eager to begin work, we had started a little too early in the day. At the first two plants we visited we found the managers had not yet arrived. At the third factory, we were luckier. I did my customary market survey, asking how our products were being used and how we could be of further help to the client. Then my two associates and I walked out of the factory to Obregon's Volkswagen.

It was only a short walk to Rudolfo's car parked at the curb but I was destined never to reach it! I was between the two men. We were talking intently about the image of our products in Guatemala. As we came out of the factory, we found ourselves in the middle of a group of eight terrorists, five men and three women, wielding automatic rifles. They all wore camouflage fatigues. I just managed to get a glimpse of three armed women guards who blocked all possible avenues of escape.

The terrorists moved with frightening speed and precision. Henriques and Obregon were forced to drape themselves over the car, where weapons were held at their heads. Henriques, I saw, looked shell-shocked. I did not notice Obregon's reaction. The three women stood a few yards away, aiming their weapons at the startled pedestrians to keep them away from the kidnapping.

"This is the one," I heard one of the men say, and a pistol was jammed hard up against my skull. A second thrust an automatic rifle barrel into my chest. I put my hands on the roof of the car, hoping to indicate complete surrender. I expected to die immediately. I had read of the endless toll of political assassinations in the country.

They picked me up bodily (I'm no lightweight), and hurled me into a pickup truck. My attackers then piled into the rear of the truck to join me as the vehicle took off down the street. Some kneeled on my back to keep me still as others tied my hands and feet with nylon rope. My hands were tied so tightly behind my back that my wrists ran with blood and my hands were to be numb for a week.

As the truck rattled towards the outskirts of Guatemala City, I was blindfolded and covered with a sheet of plywood. The vehicle was driven out of the city (the hustle of city noises grew fainter) and over what seemed to be a bumpy track.

I have tried to remember how long the journey lasted. There was about a 20-minute ride through traffic, then the truck stopped. I heard the men changing the tires of the truck, presumably to throw any followers into confusion. Not one word was exchanged by my abductors. I began to picture them as well-trained, experienced operators.

The truck then took off again, this time bouncing for about 30 minutes along a gravel road. It stopped again and I was roughly dragged from the back of the truck and crammed into a very small vehicle. I was doubled up, forced to lie down on the floor. I was in great pain and growing fear as the small car continued up winding hilly roads to its unknown destination.

I am fairly sure that when the vehicle stopped and I was finally hauled out we were in a farming area. Unseen hands took the binding from my legs, but left my arms twisted and tightly tied behind my back. Hands took me by either arm and pushed me forward. I stumbled, still blindfolded, across a dirt yard, then into a house. Suddenly I was lifted into space. Hands maneuvered me into position and then I was slowly lowered. The rope was undone when my feet hit solid earth again and I was pushed forward. A loud metallic clang behind me signalled a gate or barrier being shut.

THE TOMB

The blindfold was removed and it took me a few minutes to adjust to my new surroundings. This dark, dingy cubicle—one wall of which was of metal bars—was to be my home for a long, long time.

I was joined at the bottom of the shaft by two guards. They pushed me forward a few feet, then shoved me backwards so that I sat down on a bed. They pulled off my blindfold and I found myself facing two ghostly figures. The poorly ventilated, tiny room was badly lit, but I could see that the guards wore masks over their heads with eyeholes cut in the dark material.

I asked the guards in Spanish why I was there. They told me I would know soon enough. They said somebody would be coming that night to explain the situation to me.

Many hours passed and I sat in the pitch darkness of my underground cell. Then, from what sounded like far above me, I heard a scraping sound. Later I was to identify this as the hatch being removed from the chute that led down to my "tomb." Then came a squeaking sound, growing gradually louder. This, I was to learn, was the sound of someone descending a fixed ladder, which led from the house above down to my cell. A flashlight beam came on and in its light I could see the barrel of an automatic rifle aimed at my chest.

Once again I thought I was about to die. But the two men who had descended the ladder had come to talk, not to kill. One of them was the chief negotiator for the terrorists. He drew out a heavy pistol from his belt and pointed it at my head. The other man, a guard, kept his rifle trained on my chest.

I sat on the bed in my cell. The two men stayed on the other side of a stout door of steel bars. The terrorists' spokesman held a piece of paper on which was a long list of questions. He confined his interrogation to what was written on the paper. He refused to answer most of the questions I asked him.

In all, I was to meet five people. Three seemed to be guards; the two others were obviously well-educated, and acted as both interrogators and (as I learned later) negotiators. One was a local man and the other, by her accent, a Canadian woman. This was no soft, motherly figure. She was cold as ice and was the only woman I can remember that I actually grew to both hate and fear intensely. She acted as interpreter. I never saw their faces. They always wore hoods and never called each other by name.

"DON'T DO ANYTHING SILLY"

The man whom I was later to recognize as the kidnappers' chief negotiator lowered his pistol and aimed it continually at my chest as he put the written questions to me. He spoke in Spanish. I was grateful that my years of traveling had given me a working knowledge of the language. With a little difficulty, I understood what the negotiator was saying. The questions were detailed and precise. He asked my religion. Had I ever been in military service? How many members were there in my family? The questioning went on for long periods and it quickly became apparent that the kidnappers knew quite a lot about my business and were only asking for confirmation of what they already knew. I felt that some of the questions were tricks especially designed to see if I was telling the truth. I made a point of telling the truth whenever it would not hurt me.

Later the gang's negotiator asked me to nominate a person who could be trusted to raise the ransom demand that was being made. I realized then that my life could very well depend on my choice. I did not hesitate to name Tom Dundon, my son-in-law and good friend. There is simply no one I trust more. Tom is a cool, level-headed person and a shrewd businessman. I felt he would look after my interests best.

After the long questioning, the negotiator said something that gave me confidence. "Don't do anything silly like trying to kill yourself," he said. The thought had not occurred to me. I was preoccupied with trying to stay alive. But the remark made my spirits soar. If they did not want me to kill myself, they obviously meant me to stay alive. At least until they collected a ransom. The negotiator made it plain to me that I had been kidnapped purely for money and that there was no direct political motive in my abduction.

I took immediate advantage of the knowledge that I was not to be killed. I told the negotiator that I had a heart condition and if they planned to keep me alive they had better get me some medicine. The negotiator expansively told me to write down a list of what I needed and gave me a pen and a piece of paper.

The next day, the negotiator returned with the medicines on the list, including digitalis. The kidnappers apparently knew something about medicine. Digitalis has its drawbacks. If too large a portion is taken it overworks the heart and can kill instead of cure. The guards refused to hand any of the five different medicines over to me. Instead, they gave me the medicine in small doses as I needed it. This concern for my health and the care taken to ensure I could not commit suicide by taking an overdose reinforced my optimism that, at least for the time being, my captors wanted to keep me alive.

A LONG WAR OF NERVES

The interview with the negotiator was the first round in a long war of nerves. The war started almost immediately. Many feet beneath the ground, in a dank, steaming tomb, the kidnappers deprived me of light. The enforced darkness was a horrible cruelty, one of the worst aspects of my imprisonment. Regaining some confidence since my abduction, I reacted with anger. Two guards brought me down a meal, but I told them I was going on a hunger strike and would refuse to eat until I had some light. I hurled the food to the floor and kicked it away.

The guards left. The lights stayed out. The confrontation lasted for six days. Then, with no warning and no explanation the guards gave me a fluorescent light and a small flashlight. The week without light was one of several psychological tortures used by the kidnappers to force me to cooperate in raising my own ransom.

I decided in the early stages of my ordeal that psychological dominance was the name of the game. I began to apply my own form of psychological pressure on the guards in the same way as the kidnappers were putting pressure on me. "I couldn't let them get me down." One tendency I battled was the so-called Stockholm syndrome. I recalled that during their confinement, some of the Stockholm captives had become so reliant on their captors that they sided with them and tried to protect them as the Swedish authorities ended the incident. I was not going to succumb to the Stockholm syndrome.

I believe that my captors had been trained in psychology. If I was depressed or pretended to be depressed, the guards would be extremely friendly. This friendliness was not out of concern or compassion. The guards themselves, the three hooded men who were my only visitors apart from two negotiators, are generally the lowest men on the terrorists' totem pole. They have to keep the hostage relatively healthy and alive so he or she will live long enough for the kidnappers to collect a ransom. Kidnappers also generally need a measure of cooperation from their victim. They have to get the answers for test questions given by his family to check that he is still alive. They have to take photographs of the victim for the same purpose, proving to the outside world that he is still alive. They have to persuade him to write to his family and friends asking them to pay a ransom.

My guards were friendly to help achieve these aims. I suspected they also wanted an easy time and probably felt that if they were friendly to me I would not try to attack them, attempt to escape, or cause them inconvenience in other ways.

I tried to counter this discreet pressure with determination. I deliberately kept a psychological distance between myself and the hooded guards. I devised a carrot-and-stick approach to throw them off balance. At times I would be very friendly and would help the guards with their English language studies. On another occasion, I translated the rules of backgammon for them. But at times I would deliberately and suddenly switch my mood, become arrogant, fake anger and rage, insult them, and throw my food at them. Once a doctor was brought to examine me and I hurled a bucket of urine over him.

The simulated rages were my way of fighting back, of letting my captors know that they did not have psychological domination over me. It also helped me keep my spirits up and kept my captors asking me for cooperation, which I did not want to give them. I noticed that my captors followed a pattern very similar to my own. If my spirits seemed down, the guards were friendly, concerned, helpful. If I seemed depressed they would try to do something to cheer me up, like prepare a very good meal for me or give me books. But when I appeared to be in good spirits the guards would attempt to upset me. I was convinced this was deliberate gamesmanship with the guards attempting to keep me off balance.

They used many trifling tricks and devices in this psychological contest. I could not see behind the bars of my cell because it was shrouded with a curtain. My guards would often open the hatch at the top of the chute, then stay hidden behind the curtain rattling plates, moving around and making noises, unseen to me. I knew the aim of this exercise was to upset me and I steeled myself, determined not to get annoyed by it. I was determined not to lose the war of wits.

AN OFFER TO A GUARD

The guerrillas never called each other by name. They took extreme precautions against letting me see them. They constantly wore the bizarre hoods that made them look like characters out of a children's horror story. The guards were always very careful when they went into my cell. One guard would stand outside the bars with an automatic rifle trained on me as another opened the locked grille door and entered to remove my slop bucket or to bring in food. On only one occasion did I manage to catch a glimpse of the faces of my guards. It was late one night and they thought I was asleep. They were in the chute beyond the bars. By the dim light, I could see they were both young Latin types with Clark Gable moustaches.

I was able to strike up some conversations with one of the guards on the occasions when the man came down the chute by himself to deliver my regular dose of medicine. We talked about exercises and I asked my captor if he "worked out." Yes, said the guard, at a nearby gymnasium. From the floor above him, I had heard what sounded like someone skipping rope and bouncing a ball.

The "friendly" guard seemed to come from a poor family background, not surprisingly as most Guatemalans fit into this category. He seemed more pliable and less disciplined than the other two regular guards. Gradually, over the weeks, we built up a rapport through the steel bars. Finally, picking my time carefully, I made him an offer. I would give the guard $100,000 and a well-paying job for life in Spain if he helped me escape. The man showed immediate interest. All he had to do, I said, was to take me to my hotel and then fly with me to Mexico City. I would then see that he got to Spain, safely out of the clutches of his comrades.

We solemnly promised each other that neither of us would report the conversation to the other gang members. The guard was greatly excited and discussed the proposition again the next day when he brought down the medicine. Then he began to grow cool on the idea. Finally, he refused to discuss it any further.

What happened? I believe the man's enthusiasm waned when he thought of the revenge the guerrillas would take on his family if the escape bid succeeded. Probably there was also doubt in his mind whether I would keep my promise. But during his period of enthusiasm about reaping a rich reward to help the prisoner escape, the guard let slip a few items of information that I noted in my mind. The most important point, said the guard, was that it would be absolutely impossible for me to escape without the help of the guard. The security system was too good. There were a total of 15 people guarding the house above the cell, and there were normally five on duty at any one time.

During one of our whispered conversations, the guard confessed to me that he liked his job. By Guatemalan standards, he was very well paid and had lots of free time in which he could play football and go to the gym.

The worst enemy the kidnap victim has, I now believe, is inactivity and morbid contemplation of his fate. I battled against a sense of doom. "I'm not dead yet," I told myself, and determined that I was not going to give up without a struggle. Sooner or later, I told myself, my captors would make a mistake. When they did, I was going to be ready to take advantage of their slip. There would come a day, I thought, when my guards would not bring their guns with them into the cell, or the door would be unlocked, or the barred entry to the cell would be left open for a second too long. There would come a chance for me to make a break for freedom.

FUNGUS ON THE WALLS

I had plenty of time to get acquainted with my cell. From the floor of the farmhouse above me, a square chute lined with concrete blocks went down 17 feet into the earth. It was down this chute that I had been lowered on the rope. At the bottom, a small room led off the chute, a room about 10 feet square. Part of the room was screened off by a series of stout steel bars, embedded in concrete at the floor and ceiling. The guards could come down the ladder attached to the side of the chute, stand on their side of the barrier, and pass in food or question me with no fear of being attacked. I was never able to check, because the bottom of the chute was screened off from sight by a curtain, but I got the impression my cell was only one of a complex of prison chambers in an underground complex.

The hole was spartan and austere. It had a floor of rough, hand-hewn wood. The ceiling, about 8 feet high, was made up of slabs of masonite. My bed consisted of four concrete blocks on top of which were some rough boards. The mattress was a thin, hard piece of sacking like a gymnasium mat. I had a small wooden table made out of hand-hewn wood. There was also a small, tubular steel folding chair, which was to come in very useful as an exercise facility. The only other adornment in the cell was a bucket that was used for a toilet.

There was little air in the confined space of the cell. The only ventilation was a four-inch plastic pipe that stopped at ceiling level. The humidity was terrible. Fungus grew out of the walls in the dank heat. Mushrooms sprouted in the corners of my cell. A rash in the genital area caused me discomfort and pain. It was not a pleasant place.

Above me, I could hear people moving about. The low murmur of voices and the blare of a radio penetrated down the chute. Four times a day, the ladder would creak in the chute and guards would come down to attend to my needs. There were always two of them—and they were always armed with automatic rifles and pistols. They would bring down my medicine and food. One would cover me with a rifle as the other removed the slop bucket from the cell.

Although I could not see them, I knew when the guards were coming because the steps on the ladder creaked loudly when they put their weight on them. They always took extreme care when opening the steel gate that gave them entry into the room. It was secured with two heavy chains and a large padlock.

Strange sounds filtered down through the chute and the meagre ventilation pipes set into the ceiling. I tried to put them together, rather like conducting a mental jigsaw puzzle with most of the parts missing. There was the sound of ceaseless construction work, which intrigued me. I considered the possibility that the guards were extending the premises so they could in the future accommodate extra guests.

It was impossible to estimate how many people were in the house at the top of the chute. Sometimes there seemed to be a large crowd. At other times, I would wait breathlessly for hours and never hear a sound. One of the first things that happened when I was taken prisoner was a presentation by my captors of a small transistor radio. With this to help me, I was able to keep reliable track of the time. I noticed that on Sundays, there seemed to be a regular string of visitors to the house above. Groups of people seemed to arrive for Sunday breakfast. They included at least two children because their high-pitched voices echoed down from above. It reminded me of my three grandchildren in Australia.

Other sounds reached me: roosters crowing and dogs fighting. This led me to believe I was in a rural area. I noticed that saucepans and kettles brought to the cell were blackened as though they had been heated on a fire of charcoal. This led me to conclude that the house above did not have electricity, reinforcing the idea that we were in the countryside.

A SECOND ESCAPE BID

Using my knowledge of metallurgy, I was able to spot a weak bar in my cell door. I worked it free and ventured forth. I carefully climbed the ladder one night, making sure the steps did not creak. At the top, I discovered the shaft was closed off with a heavy steel sheet. The steel trapdoor was laid on a square of concrete blocks, thus making it protrude above the level of the floor. The steel plate was hot. I think the stove was above the plate, camouflaging the entry to the chute. On the three occasions I made it to the top of the shaft, I found I could not move the steel trapdoor. It was cunningly locked or secured from the other side. I think it lifted up like a trapdoor or the lid of a trunk.

Some of the sounds did make sense. It sounded to me ominously as though I was not the only prisoner in the underground complex. I suspect there were other cells there, at least one more, although I never heard another voice that sounded like that of a victim. Just before I was given my food and water three times a day, there would be a lot of sliding of steel doors, clanging of pots and other sounds that could have been the noise made by the guards servicing another pit cell.

Over the weeks of imprisonment, I worked on the idea of escape. I had worked with metals all my life and, with one ear cocked for the sound of the hatch at the top of the chute being opened, I would twist and bend the metal bars. Finally, I had stressed the metal sufficiently for me to remove a section. I could take it out and put it back in without its removal being noticed by the guards.

In the small hours of the morning, I would wait until the noises upstairs disappeared. Then I would remove the bar, stealthily creep up the squeaky ladder in the chute, and listen to the silence above the hatch. Once I reached the guards' weapons.

There were three automatic rifles in the small compartment at the top of the chute. I tried to work out how to use them, but although I had some familiarity with firearms gained during World War II, I could not operate the complicated automatic rifles. Reluctantly, after a futile effort to open the hatch at the top of the shaft, I crept back down the ladder, crawled back into my cell and replaced the iron bar.

On another expedition to the top of the shaft, I was not so lucky. Something alerted the guards. The trapdoor was suddenly pulled open and I was trapped on the ladder. The guard cried out an alarm and, shouting with rage, pulled his heavy pistol from his belt and began to strike me with the butt. I clambered back down the ladder, the guards coming after me kicking and cursing. In the space at the bottom of the shaft, the guards continued to hit me with their weapons. But behind their rage, I sensed a feeling of constraint, as though the guards were trying to frighten me rather than hurt me. They were careful to hit me about the shoulders and other parts of my body that would not cause serious injuries.

But as they threw me back into my cell, one of the guards snarled at me in Spanish: "If you try that again I will shoot you in the head." I got the idea that he was not joking. The incident with the guards did not overly frighten me. By this time, I believed my captors were determined to keep me alive, at least until the ransom was paid. Once the money was handed over, however, I thought I might be shot out of hand.

After my first escape attempt up the chute, the icy woman negotiator made a special visit to the cell to warn that if I ever succeeded in reaching the ground floor of the house above my underground tomb, I would be killed. I knew she meant it. On another occasion, a guard found me half-way out of the cell through the bar I had managed to remove. The guard slowly lifted his automatic rifle and pointed it at my head. He flicked off the safety catch and once again told me: "If I ever catch you out of your cell again, I will shoot you in the head."

It seemed to be their favorite threat. I was also warned that if I made another escape bid, they would cut off my right hand. This threat, too, was made by the woman. Despite these threats, I would still advise the kidnap victim to think escape, escape, escape. As long as you do, you are fighting back and keeping your respect and sanity.

CALCULATING THE ODDS

I gave myself a 20 percent chance of survival when I was first captured. Every day, I would examine my condition, review the latest development, and evaluate the odds of living through the ordeal and seeing my wife and family once more. Sometimes the odds were 80 percent. At other times, they again dropped to 20 percent.

Throughout my ordeal I asked myself: "Why me?" Of all the millions of people in the world, why me? What had I done to deserve this? From my world, the world of wide-ranging business travel in which I was my own master, I now found myself in an environment in which I had no options, no choices, no control over my destiny. The transformation was violent.

The worst feature of it was the open-endedness of the situation. I had always thought that to go to prison would be a terrible fate. But the horror of being kidnapped is even worse. Kidnapping is one of the most cruel, the most prolonged torture that can be inflicted on a human being. But the inspiring feature of the experience is man's ultimate ability to survive it, the powers of adaptation of the human body.

During the first few hours of my confinement, the thought of death was close to the surface of my mind. I took the prospect rather philosophically. I had never faced death before, apart from a heart attack several years previously, and I was uncertain how I would react. I said to myself that I had had a good life and everyone had to die some time. I would have preferred another time and place, but if death was to come calling in a cellar in a Guatemalan leftist guerrilla cell, then I was ready to face it.

STAYING FIT

As the shock of my sudden abduction began to wear off, I realized that my eventual survival would depend on staying fit and healthy. I was determined to stay strong and physically able so I could take advantage of any opportunity of escape.

To keep fit, I devised a stringent daily regimen of exercise, a strict schedule that left me weary and exhausted but that swiftly got me into tip-top shape. I also kept myself mentally busy with abundant reading material supplied by my captors.

But it was the hard, driving physical exercises that took up most of my time. I set myself an exhausting pace: five hours and thirty minutes a day of muscle-building exercises aimed at increasing both my strength and my stamina. One of the few items of furniture in my underground tomb was a cheap but sturdy steel tubular chair. I didn't have much room, but I took that chair and I would lift it in different directions, push it out, raise it up, push it behind my back ten to fifteen thousand times a day. I would also jog on the spot two hours and thirty minutes a day. They had given me a deck of cards. I used them to count my exercises. If I was doing press-ups, for instance, I would do a hundred press-ups, then remove a card from the deck. When the deck was finished I knew I had done 5,200 press-ups.

I also made makeshift weights by filling my socks with sand, and lifted these with my feet to strengthen my thighs. I knew I had to keep myself in physical condition because I might have a chance to escape and I knew that such a chance might be a split second. The tiniest fraction of a second might make all the difference if they were shooting at me with an automatic rifle while I was running.

After my release when I reached Mexico City and had a medical check-up, I was found to be fit. I had lost 38 pounds while in captivity. The loss of weight was accompanied by a drop in my cholesterol count and my blood pressure had come down. I was tired but in good health.

CONFUCIUS AND BAD POETRY

Wanting also to stay fit mentally, I asked for writing paper and pens and, to my surprise, I got a steady and adequate supply. Throughout my life, I have been a compulsive writer. I put my mind to work and thought of some recent technical breakthroughs that could be publicized. After my daily physical exertions, I would sit down with paper and pen and compose detailed technical reports for various trade journals. By the time of my release, I had finished 40 lengthy articles, but I was not able to take them with me when I left the hole.

Another of my interests is gourmet food. During my captivity, when the food was less than gourmet, I thought eternally of my favorite foods. I would mentally relish such great dishes as zabaglione, oysters Rockefeller, Caesar's salad, and other dishes that I had enjoyed. I ended up writing a cookbook. After all, I thought, I might be held for as long as two weeks! I had no idea my ordeal was to stretch out for more than three months.

It was the first time in my adult life that I had had spare time to do some serious reading, so I asked for the great classics—the works of Montaigne, Marcus Aurelius, John Dewey, Epictetus, Socrates, Aristotle, Confucius, and other great thinkers and philosophers. To my astonishment, the negotiator was back the next day with the requested volumes. Some were in Spanish, others in English. I consumed them with pleasure. This supply of reading materials continued for most of my confinement. They supplied me with expensive hard-cover books, some with price tags of up to $14. They sometimes gave me copies of the Sunday *New York Times,* which cost $5, and I kept up with world finance with regular copies of *Business Week.* The kidnappers spent a lot of money on magazines and books, but, after all, it was ultimately my money they were spending.

The deck of cards given me by my kidnappers also came in handy. Somewhere, I had read that Napoleon during his long exile had invented a new solitaire game. I attempted to emulate the emperor of France. I also pitted my wits against the cards. I had read that professional gamblers in Las Vegas train their minds to recall every card that is dealt, thereby giving themselves an advantage over the house. I tried to copy the technique. For hours I practised memorizing cards as I played blackjack against myself.

I also composed poetry. It was awful and I never put any of it down on paper, but it helped to keep me sane. Another exercise I used to keep my mind occupied was to design a garden I planned to plant one day. I visualized the roses and the vegetables and how they would grow. I laid out in my mind the design of a house I wanted to build one day, planning the interior decorations and the rooms.

HARD-BOILED EGGS

They gave me a balanced diet. There was a 50 percent chance I would live through the next meal and a 50 percent chance that I would not. They knew I had had a heart attack and they wanted to keep me alive, so they cooperated when it came to diet.

I had spent a lot of time in Latin America. When I was asked what sort of food I required, I thought of the many hazards. In that part of the world vegetables are not very sanitary. The vegetable itself does not contain germs but it is likely to be washed in contaminated water that carries diseases. So you can get gastroenteritis and other problems from eating vegetables. I told them, I didn't want any vegetables.

I told my kidnappers I wanted hard-boiled eggs in the shell. This would provide a high-protein diet and if the cooked egg came in the shell it would eliminate any chance of infection or contamination. I also said I wanted canned sardines, canned tuna, and canned beef. I also got bananas and papayas.

With the five and a half hours of daily exercise, the high-protein, low-carbohydrate diet, plus no doubt, the mental stress, I came to grip with my hips. My trousers, when I left, had eight inches of slack in the waist.

A HIDEOUS FACE

During my captivity, I had made a calendar that allowed me to keep track of the time. One Saturday, when my guards climbed down the chute to bring me breakfast and medicine, I confronted them. I said to them that in three days I would have been held 100 days—14 weeks. That would be following Tuesday.

"I've had enough," I said. "I am not going to stay any longer. If you don't let me out or give me definite information as to when I will be out by next Tuesday, I will kill myself."

The guards told me that I could not do that, that I did not have anything to kill myself with. I told them I knew how to do it, that I could kill myself. They left hurriedly and about an hour later one of them came back and told me not to do anything, that the next day, Sunday, or at the latest on Monday, somebody would come and tell me when I would be released.

Results were not long in coming. On Monday, a guard appeared with a sealed white envelope. He opened it and handed me a letter on a piece of high-quality writing paper. It was neatly typed in perfect English with not one word misspelled. It told me that I would be released in two days. The next day, the letter said, I would be permitted to have a bath, to shave, to trim my nails. It was the best news I had had since my abduction. My heart soared.

On the Monday when I was told I would be released on Wednesday, I asked my guards, "Why not tomorrow?" No, they said, Wednesday! I had to be washed, shaved, and cleaned up. They didn't want me to be seen with them on the street or in a car appearing scruffy and bearded because that might indicate to some alert policeman that I was a kidnap victim.

The next morning, when it came time to enjoy my ablutions, I was in for a shock. The guards appeared, bearing with them a tub of cold water, a razor, scissors and a mirror. I had not seen myself for 100 days, and as I looked into the mirror I saw with disbelief a hideous face staring back at me.

I looked like a victim from a Nazi concentration camp. My face was gaunt. I had not bathed or washed since my abduction. My beard was long and untrimmed. My nails were more than an inch long. My clothing was filthy.

The guards pointed an automatic rifle and a pistol at me and told me to get undressed. I did so, luxuriated in the cold water bath and washed myself as well as I was able with the bar of soap they gave me. Then I clipped away the matted beard and shaved and trimmed my hair and nails. I left a moustache, which I had never worn in my life. I felt like a new man.

The guards then told me they were going to take my clothes. I protested volubly, to no avail. I was worried how I was going to be freed the following day if I had no clothes, but the guards told me they had a dry-cleaning machine upstairs and that I had to be neat and tidy when I was escorted to freedom. With some misgivings, I watched them leave with my clothes. But in a couple of hours they were back with my suit, completely clean and not looking as though it had been slept in for 100 nights.

RELEASE OR EXECUTION?

I was frightened, really frightened, only two times. I was highly frightened when I was captured. Then I relaxed when I saw they were not going to kill me until the ransom was paid. But when they told me I would be released I started getting very frightened because I thought, well, they are going to take me out, they do not want to mess up the cell, they are going to take me out in the country somewhere and kill me.

From the news broadcasts I had picked up when the guards let me use a radio, I was aware there was a tremendous murder rate in Guatemala, with 40 or more victims every day. The kidnappers could kill me with practically no risk to themselves because it is such a commonplace activity.

On the day I was to be freed, the guards came for me about 5 A.M., just as the faint sound of the roosters in the unseen farm came down the air tube into the hole. I had too much adrenalin pumping through my body to allow myself to sleep. One guard pointed a machine gun at me and the other held a pistol.

I stripped and the guards began a slow and methodical search. They went through every stitch of clothing, every seam. They were apparently looking for notes or anything that might identify them.

The guards put wads of cotton padding against my eyes and taped them in place. Then they made me put on a pair of dark glasses. To the casual onlooker, I would have looked like a man wearing ordinary sunglasses. They put a rope around me, slung it under my armpits, and pulled me to the top of the chute. I walked through the house at ground level and again got the impression it was a small farmhouse.

With a guard clutching each arm, I was escorted into a vehicle. It had a seat that folded back and I got the impression it was an ambulance. Soon afterwards, I was moved into another vehicle where I sat in the back seat between two men. Two other members of the gang were in the front. They drove for three hours. I think this was a ruse by my abductors to throw me off the track, to disorient me so I could not tell the police where I had been.

Then they drove through a very rough field. I could not see where we were, of course, but my heart was in my mouth and I thought to myself that this was it, that in this field they were going to stop and assassinate me and that would be the end of it. But eventually they got back onto a main road and took me to a place that is near the center of Guatemala City.

I had to keep my head pointing straight ahead so I could not look sideways and see the faces of the guards. They briefly took the dark glasses and the pads of cotton from my eyes and told me to look at the house right in front of me.

Then they said they were going to drive around the block and come back and park in the identical spot and I was to get out of the car and walk straight ahead without looking back at them into the house, which was owned by the president of the Guatemalan Red Cross.

The car went round the block and pulled to a stop. I got out and stood with my back to the car. A guard stripped off the pads and slowly I walked toward the house. I did not look back. The car moved off. I passed a guard at the front of the house, then a maid took me to the Red Cross official.

After 100 days of hell and uncertainty, I was free.

TEN BASIC RULES OF SURVIVAL

After reflecting on my experience, I prepared a list of basic rules for those who face the same threat.

1.   Avoid going to the high-risk countries such as Italy, El Salvador, and Guatemala, to name a few. Unless you have a dire need to be there, do not take the chance.

2.   Check your security precautions. Are you spending enough on your own security? Equip yourself with the latest security aids—a lot of technological wizardry is available. Improve main gate and office security. Use I.D. cards for employees. Have your chauffeur trained in evasive-driving techniques. Put in better locks, better alarm systems. If you are in the slightest doubt about your personal security, hire a professional firm to survey your premises, office, and home, and install sufficient safeguards. Once you have paid for the advice, follow it. Take out kidnap insurance.

3.   Assess the risks. See if the profile of a typical kidnap victim resembles your own. Study how victims were grabbed and why. Are there any similarities between previous victims and yourself? If so, act now to reduce your risk.

4.   Study kidnapping. It is, unfortunately, an increasingly common crime. You should know how to react if you, a family member, an associate, or a friend is kidnapped.

5.   Get ready to react positively. Should a kidnapping take place, make sure that the police are brought in. Kidnap gangs invariably warn against your taking such action but my advice is to involve the police from the very beginning. If the victim is a foreign national, the local consular representative should be notified.

6.   Prepare for dealing with a kidnapping. Choose a negotiator in advance. Decide now on what you can afford to pay as ransom. A company should make advance preparations in case a member of the staff is abducted. Keep on file such information as fingerprints, blood types, passport numbers, credit card numbers, and medical history. These are all helpful in identification. Establish secret codes . . . "I am okay" may mean something different from "I am fine" or "I am well."

7.   Define danger zones. Most foreigners are snatched between airport and hotel. Take precautions to prevent this. Buy airline tickets under company names. Issue false itineraries. Drive on busy roads, and lock all car doors. Better still, travel inconspicuously and use public transport.

8.   Antikidnap consultants are worth their weight in gold. Contact them or have their telephone numbers handy should they have to be called in. They do not usually advertise but can be found if the right questions are asked.

9.   Prepare to survive. Self-pity is the captive's greatest enemy. Do not let yourself break down or become demoralized. Get off the defensive and on the offensive. Fight back mentally. Play mental games. Plan escapes. Dream up mental tricks to keep your mind active. Write poetry in your mind. Exercise vigorously, not only to be ready in case the opportunity comes to escape, but to occupy your time. Above all, never give up hope. Remember, your chances are good of eventually being freed.

10.   Pay the ransom if there is no other way for the corporation to secure the release of the hostage. There is no evidence to suggest that refusal to pay ransom stops kidnappings. If there is no other way to be freed, paying the ransom is the only option. Human life is more important than money. Governments faced with terrorist demands for the release of prisoners or other political concessions ought to try to stick to a no-concessions policy. The amount of the ransom will to a great extent depend on the skill and determination of the negotiator appointed by the captive, but it will not be small. In your discussions with your family and business associates, make the topic of raising large amounts of money one of the precautionary measures you address.

30

Surviving Captivity II: The Hostage's Point of View*

William F. Niehous

When someone has survived 1,219 days as a hostage of political terrorists, yet returned to "civilization" relatively normal, a number of inescapable assumptions are made.

- The person must be something special to have been separated from his family, friends, business, and normal life for that period of time and not to have suffered long-term physical and mental effects.
- Although the person seems all right, it probably will take years before the person is ready for and capable of handling responsibility.
- The person now must be an expert in survival.

While some amount of self-analysis is not only inevitable but necessary for a hostage victim, speaking from my experience it is possible to state emphatically that all three of those inescapable assumptions are not true. I believe that any normal person could have survived as I did. Often we like to think we are special, and a feeling of self-worth is obviously important to survival. However, survival is one of man's basic instincts.

Survivors of hostage situations often have been compared with prisoners of war. While in some cases this may be true, such an assumption should not be made in all cases. I never was physically tortured or placed on starvation rations. I was mentally tortured, simply from the unknown—how were my wife and sons and what was being done on the outside on my behalf. But my conditions of imprisonment were not as severe as, for example, those of the Iranian hostages or Vietnam POWs.

I returned to work at Owens-Illinois within three months of my rescue. I had spent 40 months in the jungles "resting," and three months was time enough

---

* Editor's note: "How to Survive as a Hostage" first appeared in an excellent monograph edited by Ambassador Martin F. Herz, *Diplomats and Terrorists: What Works, What Doesn't,* published by the Institute for the Study of Diplomacy, Edmund A. Walsh School of Foreign Service, Georgetown University, 1982. It is reprinted here with the permission of the Institute.

for me to get reacquainted with my family and friends. Besides, I itched to return to the business world.

I hold a position of responsibility, and I believe my company treats me no differently because of my experience as a hostage. I do not want to be treated differently. I do expect to be rewarded for my accomplishments, as any business manager does. Finally, I in no way consider myself an expert. I did survive a very difficult experience with no adverse effects. What I did to survive worked for me, and although I believe my "keys to survival" may be applied in other situations, I do not intend to set them up as *the* way to survive. I neither look for nor am I willing to accept that kind of responsibility.

However, having established my personal views of the limitations of discussing hostage survival, permit me to present the five keys that I believe helped me to survive.

First, I tried to be human. In the beginning, I was scared. So were those holding me. I quickly realized that since they outnumbered me at least 12 to 1, and all of them were well armed, I had best not antagonize them. Although we disagreed sometimes, I never became abusive toward them. Instead, I did what I later learned was what true experts recommend. Try to get them to recognize you as a human being, as a person with a family, and not simply as an object.

Likewise, I did not try to escape. I was moved frequently during my captivity, always at night and blindfolded. I did not know where I was in the jungles of Venezuela, and had I escaped I would not have known what to do, as I was not trained in jungle survival. Furthermore, I had no idea which direction to go to seek help. Escape was thus not an alternative.

Second, I communicated. Fortunately, I could speak Spanish, since none of the 250 to 300 persons holding me for 40 months could speak English. We discussed the weather, politics, international sports—all sorts of subjects. I also tried to write letters to my family, although only one was delivered, and since I was given paper and a pencil I kept a running diary of my thoughts and feelings during much of my ordeal. It is surprising, when one has the time to think about it, how much time and effort can be devoted to composing just the right sentence. Life as a hostage is very boring, and writing helped pass the time.

Third, I set individual goals. I would live until a specific date, whether it was my son's graduation, or my wife's birthday, or Christmas. As the date came and went, with my release not imminent, I did become despondent; however, I then set another goal for life some time in the future. I kept telling myself that those holding me surely would release me by the date of my next goal.

Fourth, I ate and exercised. Hunger strikes amidst publicity may have certain applications, but they do not work in the jungle. I was given three meals a day, comparable to what my guards ate but certainly nothing like home cooking. We ate armadillo, a delicacy in Venezuela, and spaghetti topped with deviled ham, and lots of beans and rice. I lost weight while I was a hostage, but not because the food was not there. There was no electricity, so no refrigeration. When they killed a deer, we had deer meat for breakfast, lunch, and dinner until it was gone.

I also tried to exercise as best I could, spending additional time designing simple exercises that could be done based on my confining circumstances. I was chained to a tree or pole each night, and the 10- to 12-foot chain prohibited my doing very strenuous exercises. However, I felt it was important to try to keep my body, as well as my mind, in some kind of reasonable shape.

My fifth key, and the most difficult to pass on, was to have faith. I had faith in God, my family and friends, my company, and even my captors that someday I would be released alive. Faith and hope go hand in hand in such situations. I believe hope is rooted in faith, and so faith can be a powerful tool for the victim. It was in my case.

A noted psychologist heard of my keys to survival and turned them into the acronym FACES, which not only describes my keys to survival as a hostage but which could help anyone "survive" in this world today. F is for faith; A is for aspirations or goals; C is for communication; E is for eating and exercising; and S is for sensitivity, or being human.

I also admit that during my nine years of working in a foreign country as the head of a local subsidiary of a multinational corporation, I had never taken seriously the possibility that I might be kidnapped. Our company does not manufacture products sold directly to consumers, so we do not have a highly visible name in Mexico, Spain, or Venezuela. I never thought I would be a target.

I was not observant of those around me. I learned later that those who kidnapped me had "tailed" me frequently, and even had ridden up the elevator with me in our office building in Caracas. I did not have a window in the front door of our Caracas home. Although we had bars on all the windows, we naturally opened the front to visitors. In my home in Toledo, I now have a window in the door, and I use it.

I rarely varied my time of departure to work, or the route. I should have. I didn't listen when people tried to give me some basics on how to reduce the risks of being kidnapped. I should have. My wife and I did not have updated wills. We do now.

We now share in handling our family's financial arrangements. I had done this myself, and when I was not around it was difficult for her to decipher what I had done, or why.

My experience was perhaps unique. I survived 40 months as a kidnapped hostage and lived to tell about it. The experiences of my wife and children, spending that same time without a husband and father, present equally sobering conditions.

I knew where I was and that I was alive and being fed and cared for reasonably well under the circumstances. They, for long periods of time, did not know whether I was alive or dead. They had to continue to exist, to move from Venezuela to the United States, to purchase a home, to continue living their lives without me.

We are together again. Our story has a happy ending. I hope no one ever has to undergo what the Niehous family did. But from adversity can come strength that can make the family even better than before, a new respect for what freedom, and the lack of it, really mean, and a new responsibility to help others live through it, too.

31

Reentry

Brian M. Jenkins

It's not over when it's over. Much of the former hostages' anxieties and bitterness relate not to the period of their captivity, but to their experiences after release.

To begin with, the former hostage feels that he has gone through an experience that no one, save perhaps another former hostage, can understand. Being kidnapped is a harrowing, frightening experience. It is only natural that most hostages have had some problems coping with it. Some may have discovered that they did not perform as bravely as they expected they would. Rightly or wrongly, the hostage often feels he has done something for which he should feel guilty. In retrospect, he may feel that he was too frightened or too docile, or that he collaborated with his captors to a greater degree than was necessary to survive.

The former hostage may have found himself identifying with his captors during captivity and still may do so. We know now that many hostages develop positive attitudes toward their captors. Upon release, they part company amiably, wish each other well. Some former kidnap victims recall their "hosts" almost fondly, noting that "they were exceptionally polite—especially for terrorists." Some speak of them with admiration: "They were dedicated men." "Their sincerity should be respected." Some hostages develop something close to affection for their captors. A few fall in love.

Some former hostages justify the actions of their captors, refuse to testify against them, defend their logic—and it bothers them. One former hostage admitted that he found himself identifying with the terrorists even after they cold-bloodedly murdered another hostage; this deeply disturbed him. Another former hostage, whose finger was mutilated by his kidnappers to increase pressure on authorities to meet their demands, later explained, "Sure, they cut off the end of my finger, but from their point of view it wasn't atrocious. For them it was logical; the ransom hadn't been paid."[1]

Grateful for having been spared? Fearful of retribution? Uncommonly compassionate? Latently sympathetic toward the political aims of their captors? None of these phrases fully explains why hostages and captors may become temporary comrades. Some elements of brainwashing are inherent in the situation: fear, fatigue,

This chapter is based on extensive interviews with former hostages conducted by the author and colleagues at The Rand Corporation.

disorientation in space and time, sensory deprivation. The hostage may be isolated, blindfolded, or locked in a dark room, unable to hear more than muffled voices.

Political extremists may lecture hostages on their political goals, but they seldom make any serious attempt to indoctrinate, convert, or recruit them. More often, the hostages are informed that they are simply pawns, bargaining chips, against whom the captors bear no personal malice, but who, unfortunately, may have to be killed if the kidnappers' demands are not met.

These are hardly ideal conditions under which to forge even temporary friendships. How does one explain it? Some of the reasons are simple and obvious. Others reveal how the human mind deals with extreme threats.

The hostage instantly tries to establish his own identity, some human bond with his captors. He knows he must move out of the category of human item to be bartered and become a human being—an individual he hopes it will be harder to kill. He may ask his captors about their lives, how they became terrorists, what they want to achieve. Or he may tell them about himself.

"I talked as hard as I could," wrote one former hostage, "explaining that we didn't share political philosophies but I ought to hear their side of the story."

While the hostage probably does not share the political goals and certainly does not approve of the tactics of his captors—least of all their choice of victim—it is difficult to talk with anyone for hours or days without seeing at least something of their point of view. The hostage also quickly recognizes that his interests and those of his captors coincide. Both would like to see the demands met: The hostage's life depends on it.

But these obvious reasons alone do not account for the change of heart. Another process is taking place that the hostage may not be aware of. Its essential ingredient is the inescapable threat of death, with the outcome a mere matter of whim from the hostage's point of view. The captors may kill him whether their demands are met or not. It is entirely up to the captor, omnipotent, a virtual god, with absolute power over life and death, before whom the hostage is helpless, frightened, humiliated, virtually an infant. Under these circumstances, the hostage unconsciously begins to assimilate—and even imitate—the attitudes of his captors.

Psychologists have come to label this set of reactions the Stockholm syndrome. Generally, they advise potential hostages not to resist these natural feelings, for they work both ways. The kidnappers also begin to develop a certain friendship with their hostage. In a close vote on whether a hostage will be executed or a split-second decision whether to pull the trigger during an assault by police, that relationship could save the hostage's life.

The fact that seizing hostages has become so common, that the reactions of hostages have become the subject of scholarly research, newspaper articles, and television talk shows, does not prevent the former hostage from criticizing his own performance while in captivity or make him immune to criticism by others.

One observer, highly critical of the performance of hostages after their release, wrote in a popular magazine, "It is . . . fair to expect that after their danger is safely past, hostages might avail themselves of the single form of resistance still remaining, which is to refuse to accede in retrospect to the aims of those who have victimized them. . . . What is at issue here is not their [the hostages'] gratitude but its peculiar nature, a sympathy for their captor and his cause which approaches ideologized collaboration."[2] Such comments are unfortunately typical of the judgmental attitude many assume toward the former hostage, and that he comes to expect. Before the term *Stockholm syndrome* became popular, another term was used: the *Turncoat syndrome*.

Critical of his own performance in captivity, the hostage expects such criticism from others. He did not evade capture. He did not heroically escape. He may ask himself if he has, in fact, been brainwashed. He typically believes that others do not think well of him.

In nearly all of our discussions with former hostages, the question was asked, "How did I do?" This question reflects the victim's doubts about his performance as a hostage measured against some yardstick of self-esteem, motion-picture heros, or standards of behavior inferred from the attitudes and comments of others. Most of us, having been spared the experience of captivity, of helplessly facing death, can live with our illusions of how we would perform. But the hostage feels embarrassed both during and after the episode. He has caused his company, his government, his family, and his friends considerable trouble and perhaps considerable expense. The way his colleagues, friends, and relatives treat him after his release may add to his sense of embarrassment.

Some former hostages feel permanently stigmatized by their experience. It is a reaction also noted in young men who suffer heart attacks. The victim may write himself off, as he believes others will, as "damaged merchandise" whose career is through. Whether a kidnapping in fact has adverse effects on a person's career is hard to tell, but it is certainly seen that way by former hostages. Diplomats who have been kidnapped complain that being kidnapped has the same effect on one's career in the foreign service as being declared *persona non grata* in a diplomatic post. Diplomats are sometimes declared *persona non grata* for reasons of personal conduct, but in many cases they are "PNG'd" for carrying out the instructions of their own government, for example, by delivering a speech that some local official finds objectionable. They assert that, whatever the reason, having been declared PNG carries a stigma that follows a person through his career— and so does having been kidnapped.

The universe of diplomats who have been kidnapped is too small to permit confirmation of this perception. Many kidnap victims were senior diplomats who retired soon after the episode. Some reevaluated their life and careers during captivity and elected to leave the foreign service. Of those who remained, some had their careers disrupted by a sudden unanticipated change of posts due to the kidnapping; they had to take whatever job was available. Others found that departmental concerns about their physical or emotional health led to assignments designed to give them a break which, in terms of career progress, translated into being put on the shelf for a while. Still other former hostages understandably refused to serve again in the region where they had been kidnapped, or in another area of the world where kidnappings were a problem, where they and their families would again face all of the stringent security requirements, all of the anxieties. The resulting mid-career change of regions was disruptive to their careers. This was particularly true of diplomats serving in Latin America, who normally receive repeated assignments in the region.

Corporate executives who have been kidnapped have faced similar as well as some different problems. If not in top management positions, their corporate careers also were disrupted by the need for sudden transfer, the possibility of being shelved for a period, their unwillingness to serve again in a high-risk area. In addition, the fact that the corporation had been compelled to pay a large ransom for their safe return obligated them to the company, at least in their eyes, in a way that was not conducive to career advancement. They could not easily leave to accept a better offer elsewhere after the corporation had paid a million-dollar ransom. They could not easily demand a better position or a raise in pay. The degree to which these perceptions are translated into reality, how former hostages have in fact fared in the corporate world since their release, is not known.

This is part of a more generalized feeling among former hostages of discomfort at being indebted to their company or family, especially if a ransom is paid. Colleagues and relatives may unwittingly add to this feeling of indebtedness, saying without saying, "We paid a lot for you."

Most hostages feel a strong need to tell the whole story. Sometimes they are discouraged from doing so by well-meaning friends or relatives who are concerned that describing the whole episode will be painful or embarrassing for the former hostage, and perhaps for them too. In some cases, former hostages have withheld the whole story even from their closest intimates, not only because it might be painful but also because they anticipated judgment. It is interesting to note that in our interviews, former hostages frequently said that this was the first time they had told the whole story, and to a total stranger! Asked how they felt about it, most of them said that it was a relief.

The well-meaning intent of relatives and colleagues to protect the former hostage from reliving the episode may in fact reflect their own embarrassment and may accentuate the feelings of embarrassment he is already experiencing. In some cases, former hostages appear to have been treated much the same as rape victims. Both of them are told not to talk about it; the entire episode is to be swept away, kept in the closet. Both kinds of victims also tend to feel that *they* are on trial.

In a cruel way, they *are* on trial. Most victims of terrorist kidnappings were selected because they represented governments and were therefore good bargaining pieces, because they represented political or economic systems or specific policies opposed by the terrorists, or because they worked for large corporations or belonged to wealthy families that could be compelled to pay large ransoms. Their personal behavior had very little to do with their kidnapping, except for the fact that they were available to the kidnappers, or at least, they were more available than other potential victims. Yet, many of us harbor medieval notions that bad things happen only to people who somehow deserve them. Rape victims confront this attitude: If a woman did not wear attractive clothes, walk down dark streets at night, or otherwise "induce" her attacker, she would not have suffered this terrible experience.

So it is with the former hostage. If he had followed every recommendation in the security briefing, he would not have been kidnapped. The former hostage is always vulnerable on that score. Not one former hostage can claim to have followed every bit of security advice, but neither can people who have not been kidnapped.

The judgment of others, however, goes deeper than the implied lapse of security. At its core, it represents a reaction to fear, which is what terrorism is all about. We find it difficult to accept the idea that virtually any one of us could be selected, stalked, yanked off the street, and threatened with death by terrorists. "That cannot happen to me. If it happens to someone else who is just like me, there must be a reason, something I don't know about, something he did that made him a victim and not me. I am different." Our own fear persuades us to blame the victim for his misfortune.

Although it may be therapeutic for the former hostage to relate the whole story, the most inappropriate and damaging moment for him to do so is before the microphones and cameras of the news media immediately on his release. At that moment he is exhausted, a bundle of mixed emotions—grateful to be alive, still frightened, angry, confused, impatient. Moments before, he probably thought he was going to be killed as kidnappers blindfolded him and thrust him into a car, or as police rushed through the doors of his cell. He may still be emotionally attached to his former captors. He is not likely to know all of the details that led to his release. Lacking facts, his judgment impaired, he may blurt out statements that he will later regret. It is a disservice to the former hostage to expose him to this situation. Fortunately, this is a lesson that has been learned, and most hostages are insulated from the press for at least a few days after their release.

With time, the former hostage begins to build up certain defenses against the criticism he expects to receive. He may begin to reconstruct his memory of the episode; certain parts are left out; self-deprecating humor may be injected into the account to mark the painful parts; the humor has an edge; the listener is challenged. Sometimes the whole episode is reduced to minor importance. Some former hostages recount their kidnappings as if they had been tea parties, although their colleagues recall that at the time of their release they were too emotionally shaken to even speak.

Psychological problems experienced by former hostages vary considerably. They include insomnia, nightmares, tremors, impotence, loss of appetite, restlessness, difficulties in concentration, loss of motivation, fear of the dark, fear of crowds, fear of being left alone, a sense of detachment, and feelings of alienation. A few former hostages have suffered breakdowns. One former hostage's hands trembled severely whenever he recalled the incident. Others would not sleep at night or slept with guns at their side. The wife of one former hostage noted that her husband "gulped his food" after his return. Some became more emotionally detached, whereas others sought physical contact—embracing and kissing friends. Some former hostages recall that they suffered no noticeable difficulties on their return, but only later began to experience the same symptoms other former hostages spoke about. Most of the symptoms fade with time. Sleep problems may last a year or more. Fear may persist for years.

Indeed, many former hostages appear to retain a great fear of their former captors and all other terrorists. Even years later, thousands of miles away, some mentioned that they had to be careful of what they said. They attribute vast, world-wide power to underground groups. Incidents that recall their captivity—a stranger approaching them on the street, a newspaper account of another kidnapping, being momentarily unable to find a light switch in a darkened room—could set off strong sensations of fear, including vivid memories of the sights, sounds, and smells of captivity.

Some former hostages experience more profound and permanent changes. Many said that they were not quite the same person on return. The experience is cataclysmic. It may change the hostage's personality, his outlook on life, his lifestyle. Many hostages review their lives during captivity. Career goals that previously drove the corporate executive may become less important. Others have mentioned that they are less certain about their ability to predict and plan for the future.[3] One former hostage tended to be more impulsive in his decisions. Still another was considered by his colleagues to have become more unpredictable.

Puzzling to colleagues and superiors, these changes can also cause problems within the corporation. A case in point is that of Baron Edouard-Jean Empain, chairman of one of the largest companies in Europe. Kidnapped and held for 63 days, 20 pounds lighter, barely able to walk due to a muscular condition related to his captivity, Baron Empain temporarily stepped down from the chairmanship on his release. He dramatically altered his previously conservative lifestyle and became a playboy. Describing his new outlook on life, he said, "The thing I regretted during my captivity was not having taken sufficient advantage of life, not having seen enough places, known enough girls."[4] After seven months, the Baron settled down somewhat and announced that he wanted to resume his position as chairman, but his fling with flamboyance offended and concerned the deeply conservative family and board members, who worried that he might no longer be suitable for the job. Ultimately, the baron did regain control of the corporation.

Many former hostages blame subsequent physical ailments on their captivity or believe that captivity exacerbated previous health problems. Former hostages have suffered heart attacks or strokes; others have developed phlebitis or other problems associated with the circulatory and nervous systems. It is not certain whether these are in fact related to physical treatment and stress suffered during captivity, or whether they may be related to the stress brought on by the postrelease problems of readjustment, family tensions, and concerns about careers. Medical science has only recently come to trace numerous physical problems to emotional stress.

In addition to having health problems, former hostages have complained about being accident-prone. Studies have in fact showed that former POWs experience a higher-than-normal incidence of accidents, along with a higher incidence of alcoholism and suicide, compared with similar populations who have not been captives. Accidents, alcoholism, and suicide, of course, are related. Again, it is not clear whether these problems are the direct result of the experience of captivity or the result of the postrelease experience. If they are the result of captivity, then prompt treatment can mitigate the problems. If they are caused by postrelease experiences, then preventive measures are possible through education and counseling.

The former hostage remains a prisoner of our perceptions, his ordeal protracted by callous ignorance or unwarranted concern. If possible problems of readjustment are not recognized and handled competently and sympathetically, the former hostage suffers unnecessarily. On the other hand, to describe all the possible readjustment problems of the former hostage is to paint a portrait of a hypersensitive, guilt-ridden, psychological cripple who may at any moment suffer a coronary or drive his car over a cliff. Noting that "people are careful around us," some former hostages complain that friends and colleagues treat them "as if we were nuts or that we would go nuts."[5] Former hostages express similar resentment toward eager psychiatrists who insist that they *must* have serious problems and *must* require treatment.

The portrait presented here is an artificial one, because it is built of the complaints and concerns of many hostages. It resembles in its totality no single former hostage. Although most former hostages have experienced some of the problems described here, most have found that reentry difficulties were mild and disappeared in a few months, swept away by the joy of being alive.

The former hostage gets a great deal of attention. He is lionized by the press, pampered by his family, watched closely for symptoms of readjustment problems. Family members are often overlooked, but they suffer problems too. During the period of a loved one's captivity, they go through tremendous stress, maintaining their composure, sometimes kept in the dark by government and corporate officials, sometimes compelled to decide exactly how much money their father, or husband, or wife is worth—the final offer to be made by negotiators. They are prepared for the worst by friends and relatives, inwardly rejecting the possibility that the hostage may be killed.

Family members have experienced nervous breakdowns and miscarriages, have become dependent on alcohol or drugs. The release of a hostage permits an emotional release in the family, but the result is not always happy. Relatives have mentioned that their concern for the well-being of the homecoming hostage forced them to suppress their own pent-up feelings of anger and fear. The wife of one former hostage admitted that she treated her husband terribly on his return and months later felt very guilty about it. In interviews, family members also often ask, "How did I do?" These reactions suggest that government and corporate efforts to ease the reentry problems of the former hostage should also take into account the readjustment problems of his family.

Not all the effects of having been held hostage are negative. Some former hostages have channeled their recollections and feelings into constructive efforts, writing books, lecturing those who face the threat of kidnapping, helping the families of kidnap victims. Some hostages have undergone profound religious experiences in captivity and a subsequent deepening of religious faith. While captivity may imperil some relationships, exacerbating conflicts among couples trying to return to a prekidnapping normality that no longer exists because the experience has changed at least one, and probably both, partners; in other cases, separation and the threat of death and loss have deepened relationships. Friends and family note that many former hostages display an enviable zest for life, that they have become more patient, more tolerant, and more generous toward their fellow human beings.

NOTES

1. See, for example, "The Kidnapped Baron," *Newsweek,* October 16, 1978, p. 24.

2. Dorothy Rabinowitz, "The Hostage Mentality," *Commentary,* June 1977, pp. 70–72.

3. This point was noted by Robert G. Hillman in "The Psychology of Being Held Hostage," *American Journal of Psychiatry,* 138:9, September 1981, pp. 1193–97. See also Frank M. Ochberg, "The Victim of Terrorism: Psychiatric Considerations," *Terrorism,* vol. I, no. 2, 1978, pp. 147–168.

4. Don Holt, "Kidnapped Baron Regains Corporate Power," *Fortune,* November 6, 1978, pp. 6, 49.

5. Victoria Marina, "Siege Leaves Mark on 2 Hostages," *Los Angeles Times,* May 20, 1979.

Index